Organizational
Reality

Organizational Reality

Reports from the Firing Line

FOURTH EDITION, REVISED

Peter J. Frost
University of British Columbia

Vance F. Mitchell
Embry-Riddle Aeronautical University

Walter R. Nord
University of South Florida

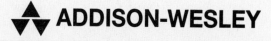 **ADDISON-WESLEY**

An imprint of Addison Wesley Longman, Inc.

Reading, Massachusetts • Menlo Park, California • New York • Harlow, England
Don Mills, Ontario • Sydney • Mexico City • Madrid • Amsterdam

Publishing Partner: Michael Roche
Project Coordination and Text Design: Interactive Composition Corporation
Cover Designer: Kay Petronio
Cover Photo: PhotoDisk, Inc.
Art Studio: Interactive Composition Corporation
Full-Service Production Manager: Eric Jorgensen
Manufacturing Manager: Hilda Koparanian
Electronic Page Makeup: Interactive Composition Corporation
Printer and Binder: RR Donnelley & Sons Company
Cover Printer: The Lehigh Press, Inc.

Library of Congress Cataloging-in-Publication Data
Organizational reality: reports from the firing line / [edited by]   Peter J. Frost,
    Vance Mitchell, Walter R. Nord. — 4th ed., rev.
        p.   cm.
    Includes bibliographical references.
    ISBN 0-673-98090-1 (pbk.)
    1. Organizational behavior.   I. Frost, Peter J.   II. Mitchell, Vance F.
III. Nord, Walter R.
HD58.7.074 1997
650—dc21   96-48068
                                                                                        CIP

ISBN 0-673-98090-1

12345678910—DOC-00999897

To Nola, Fran, and Ann

Contents

14 **INTERNATIONAL ORGANIZATIONAL LIFE** 443

15 **ENVIRONMENT** 491

Preface

The enthusiasm with which the previous editions of this book have been greeted by colleagues, students, and practicing managers far exceeded our initial expectations. The contrast between organizational life as presented in academic texts and the "reality" that emerges from the essentially nonacademic literature from which so many of our selections are drawn has provided a rich and flexible basis for teaching. The regularity with which students read well beyond assigned material and draw on their additional reading for class discussions attests to their reception of the book. Practitioners have also responded enthusiastically; managers frequently tell us that many of the readings describe "their" organization.

We do not believe the views presented in most academic textbooks are irrelevant. In fact, we believe that many of these normative views are both informative and potentially useful in solving organizational problems. However, it is ineffective to present them to students without complementary information about how organizations are experienced. This book attempts to fill that need for complementary information with a collection of articles, short stories, and plays about people in organizations.

The picture of organizations presented here is different from that portrayed in conventional textbooks because we draw on a wider variety of perspectives. We include ideas from organization behavior theorists, managers, service workers, blue-collar workers, poets, and short story writers. Moreover, we have intentionally placed more emphasis on the concerns of nonmanagerial employees than do conventional textbooks.

Since our objective is to convey human experiences, rather than to survey academic discourse about research and theory, this book, unlike the typical textbook, uses colloquial language and pays considerable attention to the emotional side of organizations. (We believe that emotions play a central role in organizational dynamics, a role that has not been appreciated fully by organizational theorists.) We predict, based on the experiences of ourselves and of others who have used our materials, that this book will arouse a broad set of feelings.

We pay careful attention to the sources of the articles included in this collection. Many of the selections come from what normally are considered mainstream business publications such as *Fortune,* the *Harvard Business Review,* and *The Wall Street Journal.* For example, the book includes "Environmentalism: The New Crusade" from *The Wall Street Journal* and "Managing Without Managers" from the *Harvard Business Review.* Other selections come from fictional works, academic texts and journals, and best-selling books. Still, a number of selections were written by critics of organizations and individuals who are discontented with many elements of modern life. Finally the book also includes selections from non-managerial journals such as *American Sociologist* and the *Journal of Occupational Mental Health.* We believe these selections, taken together, provide a useful picture of a number of aspects of modern organizations.

WHAT'S NEW

Many of the selections in this revised edition are new. The selections we have dropped were dated and have been replaced by more contemporary material. Other substitutions seemed to us more representative of the organizational reality we seek to present. A few selections that appeared in earlier editions have been "recalled" at the request of many colleagues. We have updated some readings by including recent reports on their progress (e.g., The Body Shop, The Disney Corporation).

We have added a chapter (Chapter 1) dealing with entrepreneurs—those whose scale of operation is small and those who work in large corporations or on a global basis. We have created this section in response to the widespread recognition of the need for entrepreneurial behavior in our society and to illustrate that entrepreneurs do exist in many places.

While previous editions have contained a number of selections dealing with ethics, we have elected to provide a separate section (Chapter 4) highlighting this important topic since so many instances of unethical business behavior have been noted in the media. Moreover, the reader will find numerous ethical questions that surface elsewhere throughout in the book.

Another new chapter (9) contains selections on secrecy in organizations. We have also included a number of provocative pieces on downsizing and its impact on people and organization in Chapter 10.

We have reorganized the book substantially to include sections on topics of contemporary importance. Perhaps the most important of these new chapters is that concerned with the environment (Chapter 15) and the urgency with which we need to address the ill health of our planet.

Increasing attention is being given to international business and management. Most traditional texts confine themselves to the economic and institutional aspects of international operations. The impact on individuals, however, more often than not is ignored. For this reason we have included a section (Chapter 12) devoted to considerations of personal alignments to works to life beyond that lived in organizations.

PEDAGOGY

The introduction to each chapter provides a rationale for our choices and a brief overview of the selections.

INSTRUCTOR'S MANUAL

We provide as a supplement to the book an Instructor's Manual, that provides suggestions for the use of each selection either as a mini-case, as the basis for a role play or an essay, or for class discussion. Frequently we include suggested questions for discussion. We also provide suggestions for using two or more selections together and for which course topics individual selections are appropriate.

ACKNOWLEDGMENTS

This book is the product of the efforts of many people. Once again, our contributions have been distributed equally throughout the book, and the ordering of names on the title page is simply a carry-over of the random selection procedures followed in preparing the first edition. Of course, no book is solely attributable to those whose names appear on the title page, and this book is no exception.

Sincere thanks to our colleagues at the University of British Columbia—Diana Cawood, Dianne Cyr, Carolyn Egri, Paul Frost, and Larry Schetzer; to Bob Berra of Washington University, Fiona Crofton of Simon Fraser University, and Bob Quinn of the University of Michigan for material they sent our way that, in one form or another, found its way into this revised edition and the fourth edition. Special thanks to Mark Maier of Chapman University for bringing to our attention "The Child and the Starfish," "The Cormorant," and poems by Natasha Josefowitz of the University of Massachusetts. We owe a debt of gratitude to the many university and professional students in our courses whose reaction to the previous editions guided this revision and served as a prod to our endeavor. We also thank the many astute and articulate students of organizations whose reports comprise this book.

We are grateful also for the valuable suggestions provided by William Haiel of George Washington University, Jay Knippen of the University of South Florida, Mark Maier of Chapman University, Mick McGill of Southern Methodist University, Glenn Pearce of Virginia Commonwealth University, B. Kay Snavely of Miami University, Peggy Snyder of the California State Polytechnic University, and Trody Somers of Towson State University who reviewed the preliminary manuscript.

Thanks to Caitlin McMorron Frost and Irene Khoo for technical and secretarial assistance.

A special thank you to Michael Roche, for his wise counsel on this project. He has been a continuing source of support and encouragement. Finally, our deep thanks to Jennifer S. Asplund, project editor, who shepherded this book through with grace, good humor, and skill.

Peter J. Frost
Vance F. Mitchell
Walter R. Nord

Introduction

Suppose that you are a visitor to Earth from the distant planet Utopia. One of your assignments is to bring back printed materials to Utopian scholars who are attempting to understand what Earthlings call "formal organizations." You have limited space, so you must choose very carefully. One option is to bring back one or two of the leading textbooks on organizational behavior. Another is to bring back articles, short stories, and plays about life in organizations. Which would you choose?

If you choose the textbooks, the scholars will most likely come to view organizations as systems that are managed in a rational manner in pursuit of certain stated goals. They will likely conclude that members of organizations are usually committed to achieving these objectives, oriented towards cooperation and concerned with each other's well-being. Another possibility, depending on the particular textbook you bring back, is that the scholars will conclude that organizations do not, in fact, operate rationally and cooperatively, but that, through the application of a certain set of procedures, techniques, and philosophies, any organization could be made to do so.

By contrast, if you happen to choose this book or almost any collection of materials from nonacademic sources, the scholars will derive quite different pictures. They may conclude that members at all levels of the organization frequently pursue their own interests at the expense of the common organizational goals. The scholars may conclude that individuals experience intense stress from task demands as well as intense, often bitter, conflict with members of their own work group and with members of other work groups and of other organizations. Organizational participants may be viewed as responding aggressively against these pressures and against whatever threatens their own interests. Furthermore, it is unlikely that the scholars will discern any set of principles, techniques, and philosophies that can convert organizations into rational, cooperative systems.

Most courses in organizational behavior, introductory business, and even management policy are based on textbooks and professional journals. Many students soon learn from job experience that the organizations described in their course work are not the same as organizations in the real world. These students may reject the organizational behavior field as soft, theoretical, or irrelevant and turn to accounting, finance, economics, information systems, or marketing for useful information about organizations. Other students accept text material while in school but never find ways to translate it into action when they become managers.

We do not believe the views presented in most academic textbooks are irrelevant. In fact, we believe that many of these normative views are both informative and potentially useful in solving organizational problems. However, it is ineffective to present them to students without complementary information about how organizations are experienced. This book attempts to fill that need for complementary information with a collection of articles, short stories, and plays (or whatever) about people in organizations.

The picture of organizations presented here is different from that portrayed in conventional textbooks because we draw on a wider variety of perspectives. We include ideas from organization-behavior theorists, managers, service workers, blue-collar workers, poets, and short story writers. Moreover, we have intentionally placed more emphasis on the concerns of nonmanagerial employees than do conventional textbooks.

Since our objective is to convey human experiences, rather than to survey academic discourse about research and theory, this book, unlike the typical textbook, uses colloquial language and pays considerable attention to the emotional side of organizations. (We believe that emotions play a central role in organizational dynamics, a role that has not been appreciated fully by organizational theorists.) We predict, based on the experiences of ourselves and of others who have used our materials, that this book will arouse a broad set of feelings.

Any claim that our perspective captures the true nature of organizational life better than others would be presumptuous and impossible to support. Nevertheless, we believe there is some justification for using "reality" in our title.

Basically we are talking about social reality. We believe that a considerable portion of what is taken to be reality in the social world is created by humans themselves, from how they think, talk, and feel about their experiences. In the language of leading scholars such as Berger, Luckman, and Weick, social reality is "socially constructed." Because there is a wide variety of human experiences, there are many different "social realities." We have sought to present a diverse set of thoughts, feelings, and perspectives. A more precise title for this book might be "Some Organizational Realities."

Philosophical issues aside, the reception that previous editions of this book have gotten from colleagues, their students, and our own students, including both workers and executives, leads us to believe that our approach complements traditional textbooks in exciting and informative ways. We hope that this updated collection will serve the same function.

Peter J. Frost
Vance F. Mitchell
Walter R. Nord

---

[1]See P. L. Berger, and T. Luckman (1967). *The Social Construction of Reality.* (Garden City, N.Y.: Doubleday, Anchor Books); K. Weick (1979). *The Social Psychology of Organizing*, 2nd ed. (Reading, Mass.: Addison-Wesley).

Organizational Reality

Chapter

1

Entrepreneurs

A number of doomsayers in recent years have decried the decline of entrepreneurship. Yet, we continue to find examples reported in the media of individuals who had an idea and made it grow into a flourishing and profitable undertaking. It seems that far from declining, entrepreneurship is alive and flourishing.

In this chapter, we include four illustrations of entrepreneurial success. In each of these selections, someone has had an idea and by following the entrepreneurial spark and working hard that idea has been transformed into a viable reality.

It takes something more than routine entrepreneurial spark to found a company, establish subsidiaries in four countries, and raise the capital required before you have a product to sell. "Global Start-Up" is the story of how a French electronics engineer with little business experience did just that in the face of seemingly insurmountable obstacles. What is more, the company's first two products have revolutionized the treatment of two serious and life-threatening common ailments. The products are now sold and used world-wide.

In 1990, Bo Burlingham described Anita Roddick's continuing struggle to keep The Body Shop responsive to challenges in "This Woman Has Changed Business Forever." Then The Body Shop was one of the most heralded and rapidly growing new organizations on the contemporary business scene. Helping such an organization to stay successful over the long term is an aspect of entrepreneuring that tends to test fully the capabilities and ingenuity of a founder. The question "Can The Body Shop Shape Up?" remains unanswered in the 1996 article by Ed Brown. Beginning in 1992 Anita's husband, Gordon, and other executives began spending increasing efforts on environmental projects to the neglect of the product line. Poor management and marketing decisions led to increasing problems. In 1994, the Roddicks concluded that the enterprise simply was too large for the informal approach they had followed since its founding. To what extent will Anita Roddick learn from past mistakes?

"Spotting a Golden Niche" relates a classic case of "a light going on in someone's head" and the follow-up that translated that "light" into a million dollar business that is still growing. The niche that was spotted was to sell the vacant advertising space in Yellow Pages telephone directories to national advertisers for inclusion in as many of the Yellow Page directories as possible. The story of how this idea was brought to reality is a fascinating account of entrepreneurship.

Truly, entrepreneurship can be found in many places, from the daring and insightful ideas of individuals to the continuing search for profitable innovations within large corporations.

Global Start-Up

Robert A. Mamis

Why Gérard Hascoët took his company international even before he had a product to sell.

Maybe it hadn't been done before, but founder-to-be Gérard Hascoët saw no reason why he shouldn't give it a shot: grab the world in one fell swoop with one fell chunk of seed capital. Set up however many subsidiaries he needed to capture the major markets, cover the rest of the map with a network of company-trained distributors and agents, and do it before the competition caught on. If he had a product he could sell in any country or culture without modification, wasn't it simply a matter of allocating resources?

Yes—provided he could find enough.

The daring business plan that Hascoët unfolded in 1985 established wholly owned subsidiaries in the United States, Italy, Japan, and West Germany virtually at the same time he launched Technomed International, the parent company, in his native France. The four subsidiaries would deal in the lion's share of the high-tech medical market; the leftovers, from the Urals to La Paz, would be attended by four regional managers out of the parent office. Hascoët was so committed to his one-world, one-market concept that in his design of it, even the support staff at Paris headquarters was to be a multinational mix, from the receptionist on up.

"The advantage of *starting* international," Hascoët stressed to acquaintances with enough money and patience to hear his schemes out, "is you establish an international spirit from the very beginning. Ours will not simply be a French company made over; it will be a world company." To be everywhere at once, however, would require some $5.5 million. And he was determined to get it all from individuals, rather than institutions, "because I want to have someone capable of signing a check without referring to a committee."

FIFTEEN REASONS WHY INVESTORS SHOULD HAVE DECLINED

1. There was no product.
2. No market studies had been performed for the proposed product.
3. One competitor was already in the field with an established product, and two others were about to enter.
4. No one had heard of Technomed International beyond Paris, yet its would-be founder projected sales of million-dollar machines to predictably skeptical doctors and hospitals around the world.
5. Before it could be sold in the United States—the world's largest market for medical products, at 40%—each device that Technomed might develop and manufacture would first have to earn approval from the Food and Drug Administration, a lengthy, costly, and possibly unsuccessful process.
6. For the next two largest markets, the product also would have to pass FDA-like scrutiny in Japan and meet rigorous manufacturing standards in West Germany.
7. Hascoët intended to subcontract most of the manufacturing; therefore, costs and schedules would be at the mercy of numerous suppliers in numerous countries with numerous inflation rates.
8. Currency fluctuations would play havoc with revenues.
9. Despite international patents, the machines could be reverse-engineered and duplicated in Taiwan, Singapore, Malaysia, Hong Kong, or even Japan.
10. Somebody else's technology might prove to be better in the end, somebody else's prices lower, somebody else's working capital more plentiful.
11. Attracting good people would be next to impossible; who would leave a good job to take a risk with an unproved chief executive officer?
12. There was no management besides Hascoët himself.
13. Hascoët was trained in electronic engineering, not business.
14. Hascoët saw no need for *anyone* in the company to be trained in business.
15. The French hadn't shown they were all that good at starting risky businesses, in any event.

ONE REASON WHY THEY DIDN'T

In 1985 Hascoët was unmistakably on a mission. At the age of 36, he had just resigned from a 12-year stint in the medical division of Thomson-CGR, a manufacturer and marketer that, Hascoët grew tired of complaining to deaf management ears, "was too much oriented to the French market." The field of diagnostic-imaging systems was expanding rapidly, yet his employer was hardly bothering to pursue it across the border. Not to be denied, Hascoët decided to join the management of an imaginative, farseeing, energetic company that would—his own.

"When you are not diversified with respect to product," he pleaded with the select group of investors he trusted would view it his way, "you have to be diversified with respect to geography. When one area is not generating sales, another will be. If you stick with one market and there is a recession, you're in big trouble. If you have world coverage, you avoid the fluctuation of markets."

Although the author of this worldwide enterprise had little business experience beyond haggling at the flea market, at least he recognized the folly of starting from scratch with insufficient funds. "Looking for money is not a productive activity when you're starting a business," explained Hascoët, who abhorred the thought of having to seek a loan after the seed capital was used up. "Banks don't anticipate the future; they understand only the past—the balance sheet. I have to have enough at the beginning so I won't waste my time thinking about it for at least a year."

"True, I need lots," he granted his audience, "but I promise I will not require more than what I've called for in this plan—$300,000 until the end of June, then $400,000, then a million, and so on." All agreed that Hascoët's aspirations demanded more money than French venturists were used to providing. So the venturists demanded more shares than French entrepreneurs were used to yielding. Six individuals put up most of the capital for 90% of the company; the principal threw in a few hundred thousand dollars of his own for the remaining 10%. Altogether, $5.5 million was pledged, to be disbursed as Hascoët met his business-plan schedules one by one. Technomed International was incorporated at the end of 1985 in a cramped office in downtown Paris. Hascoët has yet to go back to the backers for more capital. But he *has* moved Technomed into two sprawling floors of a new industrial complex on the outskirts of the city.

THE PRODUCT

It so happened that within France's active National Institute of Health and Medical Research (INSERM, something like our own National Institutes of Health), researchers had been pursuing a therapeutic technology that obviates the need for surgery by pulverizing kidney and gallstones from outside the patient's body. The intricate procedure, called lithotripsy (*litho* being Greek for stone, *tripsy* for who knows what), was just what the doctor ordered to get Hascoët off the mark. Devoted to pure research, the government-sponsored laboratory was seeking a commercial enterprise to develop its prototype into a marketable product. INSERM licensed Technomed to take over for a pittance in royalties. Hascoët called his machine-to-be the Sonolith and promised his investors he'd have one ready to sell within six months.

Why didn't Thomson or some other big company pick up the same emerging technology from the same labs for the same song and take the same chance on developing the same product? Because, Hascoët understood from his tour of duty in one, big companies don't think that way. "They don't like to subcontract an idea; they want to be the real father." Then they insist on spending huge amounts in R&D defending their portion of the market. But clinging to a market, Hascoët can now afford to scoff, "is like staring at your front wheel while you ride a bicycle; you observe that it is spinning properly, but you have no view of what lies ahead."

Selling the no-scalpel concept to highly skilled surgeons, whose highly billed dexterity was being replaced by computers, wasn't as tricky as Hascoët had initially feared. The winning appeal was that the machine makes everything easier and safer: you get the same professional fees, but all you have to do is push a button. Pretty soon, though, the surgeons will wise up: sure, who needs us if it can be done by technicians? And that argument is hard to counter. "In 10 years," Hascoët admits, "it *will* be all technicians. In 100 years, with our technology combined with biotechnology, there will be no surgery left."

THE SUBSIDIARIES

The United States constitutes the biggest market for Technomed's technologies, but due to rigid FDA regulations, there was no way to access it immediately. That's why Hascoët felt it was important to open several other markets while getting the FDA process under way. Until the FDA grants approval of a medical device, the manufacturer cannot sell the product to a test site at a profit (the tester is obliged to cough up the rest only after FDA approval). If Hascoët had entered the U.S. market exclusively, there would have been plenty of prestige, but pathetically little cash flow.

Lithotripsy is categorized by the FDA as a technology that is subject to the strictest degree of scrutiny. From the start of clinical trials to the receipt of permission to market the device typically takes at least two years. At first, Hascoët tried to squeeze by on a budget by hiring a specialty firm to steer the project through, but it soon became clear that internal control was needed to speed up the routine and gain on two competitors—Medstone International and Siemens—that had edged ahead in the U.S. market. Simply to meet FDA demands, Technomed has spent more than $2 million. Of the U.S. subsidiary's 37 employees, 6 have been exclusively involved in dealing with the FDA. Few companies Technomed's size fund their own regulatory affairs staff, but it has been worth every centime, Hascoët feels, merely to gain the time. And a corporate decision by anyone else to enter the U.S. marketplace, even with the technology now readily available, means the same tough two years before that company becomes a competitor.

In Italy, though, there was not even an hour's wait. While it contributes only about 7% of world sales, Italy has no health-hazard strictures whatsoever; buy a lithotripter, rent a storefront, and you're in business. Quick to snatch a first-place share there, Technomed created an Italian subsidiary because "the market had exploded in the past few years, and we wanted to be able to channel our sales most efficiently. You want Italians running an Italian business; French guys running an Italian business will not work."

CULTURAL VARIATIONS

Human body parts may be conveniently universal, but, Hascoët found, human market sectors irksomely aren't. Technomed's Japanese subsidiary, for example, cannot sell directly to the end user, as do its other three, because Japanese business protocol dictates that foreign companies deal through native intermediaries. So Technomed has a local distributor making the sales, while the subsidiary provides engineering and support. "In the States," observes Jérôme Lebon, vice-president of international sales, "once you staff your firm with Americans, there's no problem, even if the firm is a subsidiary of a European company. In Japan, however, it's a *big* problem. The perception of what is national is much stronger. The Japanese government and hospitals have to feel they are supported by Japanese people and Japanese firms, because they are far away from everything and feel we might withdraw someday."

In India, though, it's forbidden by law to deal with a distributor; only hospitals have import licenses. And in Germany a foreign product is not readily accepted from a distributorship; it does better if it comes from German speakers who directly represent the company. Even in Paris, Technomed faced conflict: when local customers sought local attention—rush delivery of machines, for example—Hascoët put them off. "I went the opposite way—speed up delivery time to *Japan*. It wasn't easy to explain that our priority had to be where our market was, not where our culture was."

Technomed's two French managers in Japan speak Japanese. "Most Japanese have difficulty with English," Lebon notes, "so knowing Japanese is important. Even though a foreigner can never hope to speak perfect Japanese and will be a foreigner for life, if he wants to have friendly commercial relationships, he'd better speak Japanese."

And if language isn't a barrier, subtle restrictions may be. Technomed has had a hard go of it selling machines in Germany, because stringent standards for electrical wiring—not for therapeutic efficacy—protect native competitors Dornier and Siemens. "Regulations like those discourage small companies like ours from doing business in some countries," Hudson admits. "It would cost thousands of dollars to pass the safety standards of Denmark and Sweden, for instance, and it's not worth the manpower and expense." Nonetheless, this June, Hascoët threw some manpower and expense into setting up his own department of international regulatory affairs, specifically to control the technical aspects of every product in every country where it is or might be sold.

WHAT, ME WORRY?

Slight and wiry, Gérard Hascoët has the coiled-spring air of a person who doesn't tolerate mistakes gladly, especially if made by himself. In any fast-growing company, however, lurks the possibility that the seemingly healthy entity actually is expanding faster than its structure and is in danger of collapsing from within. Technomed's variation on that theme seems safely to have passed. When recruitment lagged, the work force already in place became so overloaded that departments neglected to trade information not only internally, but with subsidiaries, distributors, even customers. Hascoët now has systematized intracompany communications, adapting a quality-circle approach he picked up overseas. Thus do engineers learn business.

France may be strong in basic research and garlic, but the country itself constitutes a scant 5% of the world market for high-tech medicine. Hascoët's (and his financiers') challenge in 1985, therefore, was not whether to do an instantaneous global rollout, but how. Was there, in fact, a market for lithotripters? What if the machines were too expensive, too clumsy, too unprofitable? What if there was no follow-up demand to enhance a therapy-product line? "Gut feelings were my only market study," Hascoët confesses, the logic being that if you ask consultants to do a market study for you and they are *capable of doing it*, you have arrived in that market too late.

Hence, the hurry out of the starting gate. "If I do not have the machine ready to treat patients by the end of June 1986," Hascoët had promised his investors, "you can take the rest of the money and run." The venture team barely had a chance to warm up. Less than six months passed between the day he bought Technomed's first screwdriver to the time the complex production model was plugged in at a hospital in Lyon. Close on the heels of Dornier, Technomed became the second commercial enterprise ever to treat a human with the new technique. And Technomed's was half the price. Credit Hascoët's past with his ability to cost out the product accurately, or there would likely be no Sonolith today.

But whereas in 1986 there was only one competitor in the field of noninvasive therapy, Technomed now faces several worldwide, with Siemens, the big bully, among them. As the market for the machines reveals itself globally, more giants, such as G.E. and Toshiba, undoubtedly will contend. Does Technomed care? "We *welcome* coming up against major players," senior vice-president for marketing and strategy Jean-Lue Boulnois rationalizes. "That's how you gain a market edge cheaply." It's costly for a small company to be first in a market; being slightly behind lets you position your product with features that distinguish it from the competitor's.

As of June 1, 1989, more than 100 Sonoliths had been shipped to 28 different countries, a second therapeutic system had begun selling successfully, and a promising third was in prototype. Technomed International S.A., the parent company, was scheduled to go public this fall on the Bourse in Paris. Should what its founder predicts actually come to pass—sales of $200 million by 1992—the stock will probably do *très bien, merci.*

Hascoët is here to tell us it will. "If after three years you think you can take a rest," he reflects in the language of global business—which he also is learning fast—"you make a big mistake."

This Woman Has Changed Business Forever

Bo Burlingham

How Anita Roddick has customers and employees clamoring for her brand of business.

Here it is, the start of another bloody *brilliant* decade, and Anita Roddick is worried. So what if *Vogue* has just anointed her a queen of the beauty industry? So what if her chain of eco-conscious cosmetics stores is the toast of England, counting the likes of Princess Diana and Sting among its boosters? So what if her company's shares continue to trade at a frigging 50 times earnings on London's stock exchange? *So bloody what?* These matters are of no interest to Roddick as she charges through the headquarters of The Body Shop International, the company she founded in a storefront 14 years ago.

What's worrying her at the moment is language. You know, *words*. Language is primary, she says, and it makes her nervous to find a whole new vocabulary creeping into her company. For the first time, people are talking about such things as three-year plans, net income, and average sale, and she doesn't like it, not one bit.

Language isn't all she's upset about, either. She's also feeling real annoyance, she says, at this obsession with meetings. "We're getting to a point where we can't fart without calling a meeting. And if I'm bored by them, and I run the bloody thing, Christ knows what other people must be thinking."

Then there's the problem of people spilling coffee on the new carpeting at headquarters, another thing that's been bugging her lately. Not that coffee stains rank high on her list of global concerns. But that's beside the point. "It's a symbol, a metaphor for a whole way of thinking. That lack of housekeeping, that lack of care. We talk about being lean and green. We deny that we have a fat-cat mentality, but I can see it creeping in. The paper that's wasted. The lights left on after a meeting. What it comes down to is arrogance. We think we're so brilliant, we're so successful that anything we do is all right, and that attitude really pisses me off."

If success is at the root of Roddick's worries, she has cause for concern. The Body Shop is already a legend in the United Kingdom, where the tale is told of a 33-year-old housewife with two young daughters, a husband yearning for adventure, and an idea for a store that would feature natural lotions and potions for the body. With a £4,000 ($6,400) bank loan, she and her husband proceeded to get the shop up and running, whereupon he took off for South America. By the time he returned 10 months later, the business had gone from one shop to two, and there was no turning back.

Nor did the pace slacken thereafter. For over a decade sales and profits continued to grow on average some 50% a year. By the end of fiscal year 1990, pretax profits had climbed to an estimated $23 million on sales of $141 million—despite the onset of a withering recession in British retailing. And here's the beauty part: in all likelihood, The Body Shop's *real* growth lies ahead.

That's because the company has barely begun to tap its potential overseas. Although it operates successfully in 37 countries, about 75% of its profits still come from its U.K. stores. The balance is shifting, however. For 13 years, The Body Shop has been acquiring experience abroad. Now, a number of the foreign operations are approaching the critical mass a retail chain needs to explode in a market. Meanwhile, after years of preparation, the company is beginning to make its big push in the United States, with Japan set to follow. And there's still room for expansion in such established markets as Canada, Germany, and the United Kingdom.

Even a professional skeptic, moreover, has trouble finding weaknesses that might keep The Body Shop from realizing these opportunities. "We're talking about a company that is capable of sustaining a growth rate of 40% to 50% per annum, not just this year or next year, but for 5 or 10 years," says John D.K. Richards, director of retail research at County NatWest Securities Ltd., one of England's leading securities firms.

What's even more extraordinary than The Body Shop's growth record, however, is the effect the company has on the people who come in contact with it. Indeed, it arouses feelings of enthusiasm, commitment, and loyalty more common to a political movement than a corporation. Customers light up when asked about the company and start pitching its products like missionaries selling Bibles. Franchisees, employees, and managers talk about the difficulty they would have going back to work in an "ordinary" company. Here in the United States, some 2,500 people had written in for franchises—before The Body Shop even got its U.S. operation off the ground. It's a kind of magnetism that even affects investment analysts. "I've never seen anything quite like it," says Richards. "The nearest comparison would be something like Flower Power in the 1960s."

The analogy is apt, particularly in the United Kingdom, where The Body Shop is almost as well known for its passionate environmentalism as for its cosmetics. The association goes back a long way. From the start Roddick has incorporated her environmental beliefs into the business—offering only biodegradable products, for example, and providing refillable containers. Today the company even has an Environmental Projects department that monitors its own internal compliance with its stated principles. Beyond that, it has used its shops as the base for a series of highly visible campaigns to save the whales, stop the burning of the rain forest, and so on.

Such activism has, if anything, enhanced The Body Shop's mystique. Once viewed as an intriguing but irrelevant remnant of the 1960s, it has increasingly come to define the mainstream. From the billboards in the London Underground to the advertising on commercial television, British companies now tout their ecological virtues. Far from a curiosity, The Body Shop is the symbol of this new business consciousness.

But environmentalism does not explain the attraction of The Body Shop, not even when coupled with a personality as dynamic as that of Anita Roddick or a manager as capable as her husband, Body Shop chairman Gordon Roddick. On the contrary, people tend to be suspicious of companies that profess devotion to social causes, and with ample reason. When altruism and business lie down together, neither one gets a good night's sleep. Indeed, it's generally expected that neither one will be alive in the morning.

What The Body Shop elicits, however, is the opposite of suspicion. Rather, it is the kind of intense commitment—Anita calls it "electricity and passion"—that companies spend fortunes trying to create, and that may yet make The Body Shop a $1-billion company by 1995. Less clear is how it actually pulls off this bit of alchemy, and Anita is not providing many clues as she races around her headquarters in Littlehampton, England, talking about language and meetings and the fat-cat mentality.

So where does that electricity come from? We are talking, after all, about a chain of stores that sells shampoo and skin lotion. Its success raises questions, not just about technique or strategy, but about some of the most fundamental aspects of business. What do customers really want from a product, and what do they want from the company that makes it? Are they motivated by forces that traditional marketing efforts ignore, and that traditional test-marketing techniques can't pick up? So, too, with employees. What do they want out of work, and what are they looking for in the organizations that provide it? Are they also motivated by forces conventional management techniques simply miss?

Those are perhaps the most important questions confronting business today. What The Body Shop's experience suggests is that it may be time to come up with some new answers.

INFORMATION, PLEASE

Appealing to the Hyped-out Customer

A sense of electricity and passion is not, in fact, the first thing that hits you when you walk into a Body Shop. It's the smell. A wave of exotic aromas greets you at the door and draws you in. The shop itself is bright and airy, very orderly, but with a whimsical touch. Along the walls are neat rows of products with names like Rhassoul Mud Shampoo, White Grape Skin Tonic, and Peppermint Foot Lotion. What's odd is the packaging. It is almost defiantly plain. Indeed, one whole side of the shop is covered with rows of shampoos and lotions in identical plastic bottles with black caps and green labels.

What's odder still is that no one seems to want to sell you this stuff. The salespeople are pleasant enough and quite knowledgeable about the products, but if you want advice, you have to ask for it. Nor will you find any photographs of beautiful models or promises about the miraculous benefits of using this or that cosmetic.

There is, on the other hand, plenty of information. Containers have clear, factual explanations of what's inside and what it's good for. On the shelves are notecards with stories about the products or their ingredients. There are stacks of pamphlets with such titles as "Animal Testing and Cosmetics" and "What Is Natural?" In a corner is a huge reference book called *The Product Information Manual,* providing background on everything The Body Shop sells. In some shops there's even a television set playing a video at low volume about, say, the company's manufacturing operation or one of its causes.

All of this is, of course, deliberate. In an industry built around selling fantasy, The Body Shop prides itself on selling "well-being." As a matter of stated principle, it pledges "to sell cosmetics with the minimum of hype and packaging" and "to promote health rather than glamour, reality rather than the dubious promise of instant rejuvenation." As for the shops, they are designed to be self-service, though not in the usual sense. Salespeople are expected to be able to answer any questions they might get, but they are trained *not* to be forceful with customers. In a similar spirit, the company refrains from advertising its products. Anita says she'd be embarrassed to spend a lot of money on ads for deodorant and skin lotion.

These policies reflect more than Anita's personal feelings and beliefs, however. They form the basis of the company's marketing strategy. That strategy begins with the premise that standard marketing techniques are increasingly ineffective. Consumers are hyped out. They have been overmarketed. The din of advertising and promotion has grown so loud they can no longer tell one pitch from another. Meanwhile, they are becoming more cynical about the whole process. They have heard too many half-truths, or untruths, from companies trying to move product. It doesn't matter if your particular company has wonderful products and is absolutely truthful in its marketing. Consumers have reached the point where they mistrust whatever they hear from anyone with something to sell.

All of which poses an enormous marketing challenge. How does a company cut through that cynicism and establish credibility with customers?

That's where the information comes in. The Body Shop establishes credibility with its customers by educating them. It tells them everything there is to know about its products: where they come from, how they're made, what's in them, how they're tested, and what they can be used for. It does all this, moreover, with a light touch, using anecdotes, humor, videos, and bright graphics. Few customers suspect they're in a classroom, but that doesn't keep them from learning.

Suppose, for example, that a customer is concerned about safety, as well she might be in buying a product that is applied to the skin. In this case, safety is intimately connected to product development. Most major cosmetics companies develop their products in laboratories. They must then test each product's safety by conducting extensive experiments on animals. The Body Shop, on the other hand, develops its products from ingredients that either are natural or have been used by humans for decades, if not centuries. Through brochures in the shops, it explains to customers in great detail not only what it does, but what it doesn't do—including animal testing. It reinforces the point by marking each container "Not Tested on Animals." It thus turns a basic consumer issue— safety—into a powerful tool for differentiating its products.

Similarly, The Body Shop uses information about ingredients to differentiate its products. The label on the Rhassoul Mud Shampoo, for example, notes that it is made from "a traditional Moroccan Mud from the Atlas Mountains . . . which has astringent and toning properties." To find such ingredients, Anita travels to the ends of the earth. Several times a year she visits remote areas of Third World countries, where she observes local customs and talks with native people about their methods of skin and hair care. The ideas she gets are incorporated into Body Shop products. Not coincidentally, her trips also produce the information that is used to educate customers in the shops.

All of this information has a cumulative effect. Customers get the message that they can find out anything they care to know about the way the company does business. They can also learn about other cultures, about environmental issues, about social problems—the teaching just won't quit.

"I've just taken what every good teacher knows," says Anita, who is herself a former teacher. "You try to make your classroom an enthralling place. When I taught history, I would put brilliant graphics all around the room and play music of the period we were studying. Kids could just get up, walk around, and make notes from the presentation. It took me months to get it right, but it was stunning. Now, I'm doing the same thing. There is education in the shops. There are anecdotes right on the products, and anecdotes adhere. So I've really gone back to what I know how to do well."

As a marketing strategy, moreover, the approach is extremely effective. It cuts through the cynicism of consumers. It clearly differentiates the company from its major competitors. And it creates significant problems for would-be copycats, who can't easily duplicate the level of information that The Body Shop offers. In short, it provides all of the classic marketing benefits that conventional techniques are increasingly incapable of delivering.

More to the point, it does all that by *humanizing* the company. Customers feel that they are buying from a company whose values and business practices they *know*. The effect is to create a loyalty that goes beyond branding. Customers actively promote the company and its products to their friends, and this word of mouth fuels growth. Meanwhile, The Body Shop has yet to spend a dime (or a shilling) on advertising. Indeed, it does not even have a marketing department—in an industry that is as marketing intensive as any on the face of the earth.

So what happens to the money that would ordinarily be spent on marketing? As it turns out, a large chunk of it is used to do for employees exactly what the company does for its customers.

THE BOREDOM FACTOR

Motivating the Hyped-out Employee

The Body Shop approaches its employees with pretty much the same assumptions that it has about its customers. The operating premise is that people who work for corporations are hyped out. Companies have come up with all kinds of clever techniques for inspiring a work force: compensation and benefit plans, motivational seminars, training programs, you name it. They don't work, or at least they aren't as effective as they once were. As cynical as consumers have become, employees are even more so. It doesn't matter how much you insist that you are committed to their welfare. It doesn't even matter if you believe it. Employees simply don't buy the argument that companies are in business to make their lives better.

And, of course, they're right. Granted, a company may do other things along the way to making a profit—create jobs, for example, or make quality products—but when you come right down to it, business is about making money. The more the better. And employees know it. You can argue that this is just reality, and if employees don't like it, well, that's too damn bad. But it's hard to deny how tough it can be to get anyone very excited about generating profits for someone else.

Many companies attack the problem with equity participation or incentive programs. The Body Shop does all that, too. But such techniques almost always have a catch-22. They work by focusing employees' attention on the very thing that causes the difficulty to begin with: the goal of corporate profitability. It's not that employees don't want their company to be profitable. It's that they don't really care very much. In fact, most of them probably feel pretty much as Anita does. "The idea of business, I'd agree, is not to lose money," she says. "But to focus all the time on profits, profits, profits—I have to say I think it's deeply boring."

Therein lies the crux of the problem. To vast numbers of employees, profits are boring, even if they get a piece of the action. What's more, everything else a company does becomes boring insofar as its real purpose is to maximize profits.

So how does The Body Shop get around this one? It takes more or less the same approach that it uses with customers. It attacks cynicism with information, creating an elaborate system that deluges its employees with newsletters, videos, brochures, posters, training programs, and so on. In this case, however, The Body Shop focuses on teaching its employees that while profits may be boring, business doesn't have to be.

Consider employee training. The Body Shop's training center is its school for employees, located in London. The admissions policy is somewhat unusual in that anyone in the company, including franchisees and their employees, can attend for free. What's more unusual, however, is the school's curriculum. For all the emphasis The Body Shop places on the training, there is virtually no attention paid to making money, or even to selling. The courses for shop personnel, for example, are almost entirely devoted to instruction in the nature and uses of the products. That means everything from Herbal Hair and Problem Skin to Aromatherapy II (Advanced). It's as if McDonald's were to offer free classes in Grades of Beef and Nutrition Counseling to every kid who flips burgers throughout the chain.

The courses obviously help to improve the general level of customer service in the stores, but they are designed with the *employees* squarely in mind. "[Other cosmetics companies] train for a sale," Anita says. "We train for knowledge." And, indeed, the courses have the desired effect. They are so popular with employees that the school can't keep up with the demand.

Anita brings the same attitude to every aspect of The Body Shop's educational system, even to something as basic as the company newsletter. Aside from the format, it has almost nothing in common with other examples of the genre. For one thing, it reads like an underground newspaper. More space is devoted to the company's campaigns to save the rain forest and ban ozone-depleting chemicals than, say, the opening of a new branch or the dropping of an old product. Even the latter, moreover, are handled with humor and flair. The design is dramatic, the graphics arresting. Sprinkled throughout are quotes, bits of poetry, environmental facts, and anthropological anecdotes.

Once again, the difference is Anita. She may be the only chief executive of a $100-million business who actually invests time and energy in the company newsletter. Her brother is part of the team that puts it out, operating from a Macintosh outside her office. She herself suggests articles, checks copy, chooses illustrations, and changes design. The point is not lost on people in The Body Shop. This is not some throwaway. This is a direct line of communication from the leader to the rest of the organization, and she is telling people about all the things that make the business interesting and exciting for her.

Anita, for her part, is almost obsessive about finding new ways to get across what she calls "that real sense of excitement." To her, an empty space is an opportunity to create an atmosphere, deliver a message, make a point. Wherever you go in the company, the walls are hung with photographs, blown-up quotes, charts, and illustrations. Waiting rooms and cafeterias are lined with informational displays. The sides of the warehouse and the corridors of the factories blossom with words and images and dazzling displays of Third World art.

She uses her trips abroad the same way. When she gets back, she will burst into a managers' meeting and regale the participants with tales of her adventures. She will tap into the company grapevine, planting "rumors" (as she puts it) with the "gossips." "I mean that in a positive sense," she says. "It's actually a good way to get the word out." Meanwhile, she will work on her next video and next slide show, through which she will deliver the news to the organization worldwide.

The effect on the company is electric, though not necessarily because the news itself is so riveting. What's riveting is Anita. She is, quite consciously, creating a role model. She wants each and every employee to feel the same excitement she feels. You can learn in business, she is telling them, you can grow, you can be somebody. But to do that, you have to care. "I want them to understand that this is no dress rehearsal," she says. "You've got one life, so just lead it. And try to be remarkable."

And it works. The message gets through, and it gets through for one reason alone: Anita believes it. She is not the least bit cynical about business. Shrewd? Yes. Calculating? In a sense. Manipulative? Often. But cynicism is simply not in her repertoire. She is passionate in her belief that education matters, customer service matters, even newsletters matter—they all matter. There is no hidden agenda here. Anita really doesn't regard these as tools for boosting sales and enhancing profits. She is saying that, to have a successful company, these things have to matter *in their own right*.

More to the point, she has been able to imbue her organization with the same attitude, and the effects are apparent in the shops. Employees understand why it's important to keep a shop clean, to display products well, to treat customers courteously—in short, to take care of all the little details a retailer must get right to be successful. The point is not that these details affect sales or profits, but that they affect customers, and customer service matters for its own sake. Once again, the company is humanized, to the benefit of everyone involved.

A BANNER OF VALUES

Creating a Global Community

On a cold night in January, a ragtag group of environmentalists gathers outside the Brazilian embassy in London. There are about 20 of them, the usual suspects, from such organizations as Friends of the Earth and Survival International. They have come to draw attention to the plight of the Yanomami Indians, a Stone Age tribe that is being wiped out by diseases brought to its remote Brazilian habitat by miners looking for gold. At the moment, however, there is not much attention to be drawn. Aside from an occasional passing taxi, the only people around are the protesters. Among them is Anita Roddick, founder and managing director of The Body Shop International.

She is there, moreover, in her official capacity. Recently her company has engaged in a worldwide campaign that has drawn much attention to the plight of all the inhabitants of the Amazon rain forest. The Body Shop and its franchisees have contributed

hundreds of thousands of dollars to their defense. It has mobilized employees for petition drives and fund-raising campaigns, carried out through the stores and on company
time. It has produced window displays, posters, T-shirts, brochures, and videotapes to
educate people about the issues. It has brought 250 employees to London for a major
demonstration at this very embassy—not on a dark night, but in broad daylight, with a
television crew broadcasting the event live, via satellite, to Brazil. It has even printed appeals on the side of its delivery trucks, reading: "The Indians are the custodians of the
rainforest. The rainforests are the lungs of the world. If they die, we all die. The Body
Shop says immediate urgent action is needed."

In the United States such corporate activism would be considered bizarre, if not
dangerously radical. In the United Kingdom it draws attention, but it no longer generates much surprise. That's mainly because The Body Shop has been acting this way for
years. Long before it launched its rain-forest offensive, after all, it waged similar campaigns against everything from the killing of whales to the repression of political dissidents. Almost as well known, and accepted, are its efforts to help communities in developing countries by setting them up as suppliers under a program it calls Trade Not Aid.
Then there's the soap factory it has built in a poverty-stricken section of Glasgow, Scot-
land, with the explicit (and well-publicized) purpose of providing jobs for people who,
in some cases, have been unemployed for upward of 10 years. Not to mention the community project that every shop is required to have and that every shop employee is expected to work in for at least one hour a week—a paid hour, that is, on company time.

Indeed, there is almost no end to the list of such Body Shop activities, most of
which have been widely reported in the British press. This inevitably raises a question in
the minds of many people, one Anita almost always hears when she appears before business groups. "They want to know, 'Isn't it all public relations? Aren't you just using these
campaigns and activities to create more sales and profits?' "

She bristles at the question. "Look," she says, "if I put our poster for Colourings [a
line of makeup] in the shop windows, that creates sales and profits. A poster to stop the
burning of the rain forest doesn't. It creates a banner of values, it links us to the community, but it will not increase sales. What increases sales is an article in boring *Glamour*
magazine saying Princess Diana uses Body Shop products. Then we'll get 7,000 bloody
phone calls asking for our catalog. You can measure the effect."

It's a provocative argument, but it's a little misleading. Most of the activities are, in
fact, intended to generate publicity for The Body Shop, and the company milks them for
all they're worth. Even Anita would admit, moreover, that—over the long term—they
do tend to increase sales and, yes, profits. What's most interesting, however, is the way
that happens. Indeed, this may be the single most striking aspect of The Body Shop's entire approach to business.

The first thing you have to understand is that the primary audience for these activities is not the public: it is her own work force. The campaigns, which play a major role
in her educational program, are anything but random attempts to promote goodwill.
They are part of a carefully researched, designed, and executed business strategy. She regularly turns down causes that don't meet her criteria, and she won't launch any campaign
until she feels confident of all the facts on the issues involved. She takes these matters far
too seriously to adopt a cause that might come back to haunt the company, or to carry
it out in less than a thoroughly professional manner.

More to the point, she wants causes that will generate real excitement and enthusiasm in the shops. "You educate people by their passions, especially young people," she says. "You find ways to grab their imagination. You want them to feel that they're doing something important, that they're not a lone voice, that they are the most powerful, potent people on the planet.

"I'd never get that kind of motivation if we were just selling shampoo and body lotion. I'd never get that sort of staying late, talking at McDonald's after work, bonding to customers. It's a way for people to bond to the company. They're doing what I'm doing. They're learning. Three years ago I didn't know anything about the rain forest. Five years ago I didn't know anything about the ozone layer. It's a process of learning to be a global citizen. And what it produces is a sense of passion you simply won't find in a Bloomingdale's department store."

The key word here is *bond*. For Anita is not just educating and motivating employees. She is not just selling cosmetics to customers. She is not just selecting franchisees, or establishing trade links with people in the Third World, or setting up factories to hire the unemployed. She is creating a community, a global community. The common bond, moreover, is not merely a mutual desire to save the Amazon rain forest. Rather, it is a belief that business should do more than make money, create decent jobs, or sell good products. The members of this community believe that companies should actually help solve major social problems—not by contributing a percentage of their profits to charity, but by using all their resources to come up with real answers. Business is, after all, just another form of human enterprise, as Anita argues. So why should we expect and accept *less* from it than we do from ourselves and our neighbors?

There are many people, of course, who would quiver at the prospect of companies becoming social activists. Some would contend that business ought to stick to its collective knitting and do what it does reasonably well. Others would note that, for many companies, knitting well is difficult enough without taking on society's problems in addition to their own. Still others would prefer to leave such matters to nonprofit organizations or to government, which is presumably more accountable for its actions.

But Anita doesn't buy any of those arguments. She believes that there is only one thing stopping business from solving many of the most pressing problems in the world, and it has to do with the way most of us think companies must be managed. That is precisely what she wants to change.

TRADING

Preserving the Start-up Spirit

Anita Roddick is reminiscing in her Littlehampton office. On the wall next to her are photographs of the original Body Shop in Brighton. The company no longer owns the store, she explains, but she is doing everything she can to get it back. "Then we'll put it back exactly the way it was in 1976. It's a real good reminder of the initiative and creativity that counts when you have no money."

Back then, Anita needed all the creativity and initiative she could muster, what with two children at home and her husband in South America pursuing his lifelong dream of riding from Buenos Aires to New York City on horseback. Before he had left, Gordon had run the numbers and told her she had to make £300 a week in order to stay in business. "I said, 'What happens, Gordon, if I don't?' He said, 'Give it six months and then pack it up and meet me with the kids in Peru.' "

So Anita had done all the things people do when they start a business they know nothing about, with no resources to fall back on. She worked around the clock, improvising as she went along. "We had only about 15 or 20 products," she says. "So we had the idea of offering five sizes of containers, which made it look like a bit more. And we had all handwritten labels with explanations of the products. We thought we had to explain them because they looked so bizarre. I mean, there were little black things in some of them. We had to say these were not worms. We were offering honesty of information that we didn't even know was honesty. We thought it was the only way to sell the products."

She goes on, talking about all the crazy things she did in the early days. Leaving a trail of strawberry essence on the street in hopes of luring customers with the smell. Planting a newspaper article about the morticians next door who were trying to shut her down because they thought a store called The Body Shop was bad for their business. Starting a refill service as an ecological way to reduce the need for new containers, which she couldn't afford.

It is obvious, as she talks, that she enjoys the memories. And yet, there is no trace of sentimentality in her reminiscences. She is not yearning for the good old days. Rather, she is remembering her own naïveté, and she is reminding herself how well she did *because* she was naïve. Her innocence, she is saying, led her to do the right thing.

"There was a grace we had when we started—the grace that you didn't have to bullshit and tell lies. We didn't know you could. We thought we had to be accountable. How do you establish accountability in a cosmetics business? We looked at the big companies. They put labels on the products. We thought what was printed on the label had to be truthful. I mean, we were really that naïve."

Anyone who has been involved in a successful start-up understands what she is talking about. There is terror, there is excitement. There is a sense of living by your wits, relying on your instincts, knowing that your dumb mistakes could sink you, hoping that they don't. And there is something else: a kind of simplicity, a clarity of purpose. You have a product, or a service, and everything depends on your ability to get customers to buy it. This is what Anita calls trading. "You set up a business without any understanding of business vocabulary. If you throw away all those words, you have trading going on. That's all it is. Here's a product. Here's the environment. Here's the buyer. Here's the seller."

Business on that level is exciting and rewarding. It is also very human. It is a simple activity centered on direct relationships between people. "I actually see it as ennobling," says Anita. "It's been going on for centuries. It's just buying and selling, with an added bit for me, which is the magical area where people come together—that is, the shop. It's trading. It's making your product so glorious that people don't mind buying it from you at a profit. Their reaction is, 'I love that. Can I buy that?' You want them to find what you are doing so wonderful that they are happy to pay your profit."

But businesses seldom remain on that level, not successful ones at any rate. They grow. They hire employees. They acquire assets and make commitments. Life gets complicated. Management structures are created. Responsibilities are delegated. Control becomes an issue. Reporting systems are developed. Financial discipline is introduced. And along with it comes a new language—the language of budgets and profits, of return on investment and shareholder value. In the process, business ceases to be just trading and becomes, in Anita's words, "the science of making money."

Professional management is the common term for this way of running a company. In the world of business, it is generally considered to be a good thing, not to mention an inevitable and necessary consequence of growth. Without it, we are told, a company can never reach its full potential. Sooner or later, it will be over-whelmed by chaos and die. The only way to avoid that fate—short of selling out or staying small—is to develop sophisticated, financially based management systems, to "cross the threshold" and become a full-fledged, major-league corporation.

But business is charged a steep price for this kind of "success." The bill is paid in the currency of cynicism—the cynicism of customers, of employees, of the community, even of other businesspeople. If companies are in business mainly to make money, you can't fully trust whatever else they do or say. They may create jobs, they may pay taxes and contribute to charity, they may provide an array of goods and services, but all that is incidental to their real purpose: to generate profits for shareholders.

Indeed, cynicism is so much a part of the way we view business that we don't even notice it until it is missing. No matter whether people hate business or love it, they share the same cynical assumptions about it. Then there's Anita Roddick.

Anita simply does not believe that companies need ever cross that threshold and start making decisions by the numbers. She finds it hard to understand why anyone would want to. "That whole goddamn sense of fun is lost, the whole sense of play, of derring-do, of 'Oh, God, we screwed that one up.' I see business as a renaissance concept, where the human spirit comes into play. How do you ennoble the spirit when you are selling moisture cream? It's everything we do before, during, and after we manufacture. It starts with how we look for ingredients. It's the initiative and the care and the excitement. It comes from education and breaking rules. And let me tell you, the spirit soars—God, does it soar—when you are making products that are life serving, that make people feel better and are done in an honorable way. I can even feel great about a moisture cream because of that."

Therein lies the most important lesson The Body Shop has to offer. Business does not have to be drudgery. It doesn't have to be the science of making money. It is something that people—employees, customers, suppliers, franchisees—can genuinely feel great about, but only on one condition: the company must never let itself become anything other than a human enterprise.

Oddly enough, that lesson is not a new one, as Anita often points out. There was a time when the world was filled with companies driven by a vision of improving the human condition. Many were started by Quakers and other people with deeply religious convictions. The managers who ran them were absolutely clear about their responsibilities to customers, to employees, to society as a whole. Some of these companies are still around today.

Along the way, however, something has been lost. "Businesses have forgotten that they are just buyers and sellers," says Anita. "We must never forget that. The whole value of this business lies in keeping it on the level where we know what we're trading. That's why I will never dilute the image of the shop. In our shops, we sell skin and hair care. Period. We know what the customer wants, and we fill those needs."

And that's really the point. It is trading, after all, that makes everything else possible, and yet that is precisely what she fears a traditional style of management would undermine. By establishing financial performance as the goal, it would throw the company off target. It would introduce powerful distractions. It would weaken The Body Shop's focus on the one thing that allowed it to succeed in the first place: its relationship with its customers.

In a sense, everything Anita does is designed to preserve that focus on trading. "What's imperative is the creation of a style that becomes a culture. It may be forced, it may be designed. But that real sense of change, that anarchy—I tell Gordon we need a department of surprises. Whatever we do, we have to preserve that sense of being different. Otherwise, the time will come when everyone who works for us will say The Body Shop is just like every other company. It's big. It's monolithic. It's difficult. This is going to be such a huge company in a few years. We just have to make sure we don't wind up like an ordinary company."

To be sure, her success will depend on many people, not least her husband Gordon, who oversees the operational side of the business. It is a role he has played ever since he returned from his adventure in South America, teaching himself what he needed to learn as he went along. To him, as well as Anita, belongs the credit of demonstrating that a company can be both passionately idealistic and exceptionally well managed. He himself, however, has no doubt where his inspiration comes from. "Creatively, this is Anita's company entirely," he says. "She says what she wants, and we make all her dreams come true."

Meanwhile, the pressures to conform keep growing. They come from shareholders, who want to maximize their earnings. They come from franchisees, who push the company to expand faster than its resources will allow. They even come from some employees and managers, who might be willing to sacrifice a little derring-do for the stability and security they think financial planning would allow. But mostly they come from the world in which The Body Shop operates—a world that doesn't care much about a company's social responsibility or its empowerment of employees if the benefits don't eventually show up on the bottom line.

But Anita has a vision. "I believe quite passionately that there is a better way," she says. "I think you can rewrite the book on business. I think you can trade ethically; be committed to social responsibility, global responsibility; empower your employees without being afraid of them. I think you can really rewrite the book. That is the vision, and the vision is absolutely clear."

And so she fights all the pressures. She fights them with language. She fights them with values. She fights them with education. And she fights them with her vision. "It's creating a new business paradigm," she says. "It's showing that business can have a human face, and God help us if we don't try. It's showing that empowering employees is the key to keeping them, and that you empower them by creating a better educational system. It's showing that you forsake your values at the cost of forsaking your work force. It's paying attention to the aesthetics of business. It's all that. It's trying in every way you can. You may not get there, but goddammit, you try to make the journey an honorable one."

After all, it matters. It all matters. For its own sake.

Can The Body Shop Shape Up?

Ed Brown

Anita Roddick is instantly recognizable behind the wheel of a diesel-powered Volkswagen Golf as she roars up to her Littlehampton headquarters, a building resembling a vast Chinese pagoda amid the rolling pastures of Sussex, England. The car is all green, naturally. With her hair flying and the sleeves of her work shirt rolled crisply like an army sergeant major's, the founder of The Body Shop International, Britain's most successful global retailer, pauses just long enough to admire her latest pet project: an enormous electronic sign that blares STEER CLEAR OF SHELL—BOYCOTT NOW at a Shell service station sitting forlornly across the road.

The question of the oil giant's responsibility for human-rights abuse in Nigeria is a current preoccupation of the perpetually crusading Roddick, but on a damp winter morning she is scowling at some equally disquieting news from her board of directors. Pre-Christmas sales figures from the U.S. were dismal, as they were for many retailers, and the mood at the home office is solemn. "It doesn't take a rocket scientist to see it hasn't been an easy ride for us over there," Roddick says glumly.

Weak U.S. sales are just one of the problems that have thrown the cosmetics concern into what its yuppio clientele would instantly recognize as a midlife crisis. Competition is increasing from a host of imitators such as Bath & Body Works, which has the marketing muscle of The Limited behind it. For the fiscal year ended in February 1995, The Body Shop's profits rose 13%, to $53 million, on sales of $349 million. But that's a lackluster growth rate compared with what the company has averaged in the past. And despite booming sales in Asia, in the critical U.S. market it actually lost money. Beyond balance-sheet woes, the company that likes to insist it puts principles before profits has been buffeted for two years by allegations, which Roddick angrily denies, that it has misled the public about everything from its stand against animal testing to the ingredients of elderflower eye gel.

All the bad news has tarnished The Body Shop's image as one of Britain's most glamorous growth stocks. Its share price has dropped 65%, from a high of $6.55 in 1992 to around $2.29 today.

No one disputes that enviro-activism was a brilliant way to launch a business. Roddick's soaps and lotions, made primarily of wholesome, natural ingredients attracted hordes of customers, New Age or otherwise. "You pay so much for a face cream, but you get a feel-good factor as well," says Andrew Campbell, director of Ashridge Strategic Management Centre in London.

But now that the 53-year-old Roddick has become a major player—since 1976 The Body Shop has risen from a single store in Brighton, England, to a multinational with 1,366 stores in 46 countries—the question becomes: Does she have what it takes to play hardball against giant retailers like The Limited?

Skeptics note that, until recently, Roddick and her husband, Gordon, the co-founder and chairman, were actively exploring ways to take the company private and turn it over to a nonprofit foundation that could use profits to finance good works rather than to pay dividends. The company says it shelved this idea when it became clear that the cost of financing the share buy-back would sap Body Shop's aggressive global expansion plans.

Still, investors remain wary—and given The Body Shop's history, that's understandable. While competitors like The Limited moved into selling soap in a big way in the 1990s, Roddick continued to devote more and more time to getting up on a soapbox. She had started by helping the environmental group Greenpeace launch a save-the-whales campaign in 1985, but quickly widened her horizons to include Amnesty International, the rain-forest activists Survival International, and the Friends of the Earth. "How can you ennoble the spirit," Roddick once remarked self-deprecatingly, "which you are selling something as inconsequential as a face cream?"

In the early 1990s, Gordon and other company executives also began spending an increasing amount of time launching environmental projects rather than revamping the company's aging product line. The head of finance was detailed to help set up a windmill farm in Wales, designed to ecologically replace the electricity used by the home office.

In the midst of this swirl of good works, critics on the left suddenly started attacking their erstwhile corporate ally—setting off the kind of media frenzy usually reserved for royals caught with their knickers down. A 1992 television documentary charged that The Body Shop made false claims about its stand against animal testing. (The Roddicks sued for libel and won more than $400,000 in damages.) In 1994 an American journalist, Jon Entine, writing in one of Roddick's favorite magazines, *Business Ethics*, broadened the charge of hypocrisy to include The Body Shop's environmental standards, charitable contributions, and efforts to buy materials from the Third World. Though Roddick dismissed the allegations as "recycled rubbish"—and an independent research group later concluded that Entine's charges were "broadly unfair"—she and Gordon were devastated by the negative press.

Amid all the uproar, the real news was that The Body Shop's business was losing its momentum. Robert Gluckman, a retailing expert who had been recruited as the company's international general manager, left in a nasty public dispute in 1992 complaining about The Body Shop's unstructured environment and lack of a strategic plan. In the U.S., meanwhile, the company was hiring and shedding managers with such velocity that it appeared to many like the quintessential British amateur. "They were clueless about what they wanted," says Janet Swaysland, who lasted less than a year as The Body Shop's vice president for communications.

About two years ago the Roddicks quietly concluded they had no choice but to launch a major makeover. The biggest change was their decision to step back from running day-to-day operations. Instead, they installed board member Stuart Rose as managing director. Rose promptly began restructuring the company, changing the top management team by bringing in other professional managers, installing tighter inventory and control systems, and streamlining processes.

Roddick herself seems more ambivalent about the new course, railing at the administrative bureaucracy she has been forced to adopt. "We've gone through a period of squashing one hell of a lot of the entrepreneurial spirit," she told FORTUNE. "We're having to grow up, we have to get methods and processes in, and the result of that is a hierarchy that comes in, and I think it's antiproductive." Roddick complains that it now can take a year or more to get a new product onto store shelves vs. the four or five months previously.

What Roddick does seem to have going for her is a willingness to learn from her mistakes. For years what made The Body Shop successful was that it didn't charge franchise fees or royalties, preferring to let the franchisers pocket them. Most of the company's earnings came from wholesaling the merchandise it makes, much like Italy's Benetton, which wholesales clothes to its stores.

That Roddick neglected to follow her own system for success in the U.S., where The Body Shop owns 113 of 272 stores, is one of the key reasons for the company's stumble there, analysts say. Rather than perfecting sales in its existing shops, the company charged into the top malls in the U.S. over the past two years, in hopes of gaining a foothold against the fast-expanding Bath & Body Works. It's not working. The U.S. operation lost $3.7 million in the first six months of fiscal 1996 on sales of $46 million. Same-store sales fell by 8%.

Bath & Body Works, by contrast, which has opened 412 stores in the past five years, is making a profit. Leslie H. Wexner, The Limited's chairman, says his rival's background as a manufacturer (and foreigner) worked against her in the U.S. "They're not retailers," he says. "We have an advantage—we know the territory." "It was just awesome to watch how fast they got into the market," Roddick admits.

Having been burned in retailing, Roddick now seems to have learned her lesson. As The Body Shop expands, it is sticking to its more profitable franchising strategy, the approach that made it successful in the first place. Today all but 12 of its 841 shops outside the U.S. and Britain are franchises.

So far, the Asian market has produced particularly explosive growth, with sales advancing by 39% in the first half of the 1996 fiscal year, to $18.2 million, and untapped areas like South Korea and the Philippines are just now coming onstream. In mature markets like Britain, The Body Shop's biggest, with 44% of its revenues, the company has launched new marketing strategies to revitalize sales. Since the country is nearly saturated with stores, the company has begun a program of direct-mail and in-home sales. In the U.S., for the first time it's taking out ads in print and on radio, and is fighting against The Limited with gift-with-purchase promotions and 2-for-1 offers.

The Body Shop is also revamping its product line while trying to maintain its green ideals. The results have been mixed: A nonaerosol hair mousse flopped, but a new line of cosmetics called Colourings is doing well.

It's going to take years to tell whether the new marketing and sales strategies can turn around the company's fortunes and to know to what extent Roddick will let her professional managers run the business at the expense of her beloved environmentalism. In the meantime, the fact that there's hardly a financial analyst who has much positive to say about the company prospects suggests that for now, investors should probably stick to buying The Body Shop's soap—but not its shares.

Spotting a Golden Niche

Pat Annesley

Sometimes the most brilliant ideas are the ones staring us right in the face.

Somebody takes a simple idea that has been staring us all in the face for years, and turns it into a money-making machine. That's my kind of success story.

There's something especially heartening about a couple of guys from Vancouver—*not* part of the local high-rollers scene—who have managed to break into a major U.S. industry. The industry is the Yellow Pages, conservatively worth about $8-billion a year in sales. What Yellow Spots Inc. of Vancouver has done is carve out a piece of those smashing revenues. Just a piece, mind you, but when you figure that if all the Yellow Pages filler space in the United States was sold it would be worth $140-million a year, the prospects are mouthwatering.

The concept is so simple, it's hard to believe it hasn't been tried before. The timing is perfect. And the whole thing is almost certain to make multi-millionaires of the two guys who started it, Arnie Nelson and David Horton. Both guys in their fifties who were getting a little discouraged at the way things were going for them just a few years ago.

They were fraternity brothers, back in their UBC days. Arnie went into broadcast sales, and for a while he was doing very well. David went into the money-lending business with a banking consortium and got hooked on small companies and doing deals. He went out on his own. And he did very well too, for a while. Then the recession came along in 1982 and Arnie lost his job, and David wasn't doing as many deals.

By June of 1985 Arnie had been unemployed for almost two and a half years. He was doing this little project or that little project, trying to put food on the table. He never did qualify for unemployment insurance. David was doing a little better because he still had an office and his usual assortment of irons in the fire. But even he was reduced to trotting out his MBA credentials and doing some consulting work.

On that momentous June morning three and a half years ago, Arnie was sitting in the kitchen of his rented condo in Richmond, looking up something in the Yellow Pages. His eye was caught by an ad for the Yellow Pages. Automatically his salesman's mind registered the genre: filler ad. Otherwise known as unsold space. Wasted space, from an adman's point of view. The Yellow Pages are full of them.

But the page Arnie happened to be looking at had five of them. *Five* unsold spaces? On one page? It really was, Arnie says now, "like a light going on."

That afternoon he was in the main library at Robson and Burrard, going through the U.S. Yellow Page directories. Counting, figuring, trying not to get too excited. Somebody had to have thought of the advertising potential in all that space, he thought.

Nevertheless, he had that feeling. He was onto something. He went to David. What if we could tie up all that space somehow and sell it to the big national companies looking for reinforcement advertising?

David was skeptical. But, like all doers of deals, David believes in listening to any deal that walks in the door, no matter how far-fetched it seems.

"I can supply you with an office and a phone," he said, "but no money."

It was the week before Arnie's fifty-first birthday.

Arnie's first thought was to try to interest Expo 86 in placing some spots in the directories of one of the major U.S. publishers. The timing was off, as it turned out. But the people at U.S. West Direct, a telephone company serving 13 states from Arizona to Washington, were interested in the concept. And there was at least "a glimmer" of interest in the media department at Baker Lovick, Expo's advertising agency. Next, Arnie called a couple of major Canadian advertisers, just to feel out their response to the concept. They liked it.

By January of 1986 he was ready to make his first approach to a major U.S. directory publisher, a subsidiary of Southwestern Bell. Arnie picked Southwestern because an article in *Business Week* singled them out as the most aggressive of the publishing subsidiaries of the seven "Baby Bell" telephone companies. In the intervening months he had continued to take on any selling project that would give him walking-around money. But at the same time he kept plugging away at his Yellow Pages research, along the way discovering the probable reason why nobody had yet tried to tie up unsold Yellow Pages space and turn it into a national advertising medium.

Only two years earlier a U.S. circuit judge named Harold Green had taken a look at AT&T's virtual monopoly in the telephone company business, and decreed that the territory had to be broken up. The result was the formation of the seven companies known as the Baby Bells—any two of which, incidentally, are expected to equal the old AT&T in size by 1990.

Among them the seven companies cover more than 90 per cent of the U.S. market, with a lot of small independents sharing the remainder of the pie. The Baby Bells were big business, growing fast, and so were their respective subsidiaries that were in the business of publishing directories. The subsidiaries were free to invade one another's territory and did.

Arnie went after Southwestern Bell, the apparent scrapper in the bunch.

He called. They called back, asking for more information. It was time to put something on paper. It had to go out on the old Smokebreaker stationery, and it was pretty slim at that. But eventually Southwestern Bell said: "Let's meet." Arnie flew to St. Louis.

"I came back elated," he says. "Not only did they seem to want to take the next step, but they gave me names of people to contact at Bell South and NYNEX." Within a couple of months he was on his way to Atlanta to talk to the Bell South people. Their reaction was equally favourable.

"So, now we had three companies that had not said no, and some good leads on the others."

It was get serious time. Time to raise some money, put together a decent business plan, get Arnie a bit of a draw so he could keep at it. These things were David's meat. In February, 1987, they picked up a VSE shell called Stray Horse Resources, re-named it Oriole Communications and launched the operating company—Yellow Spots Inc. The seed capital came from Primary Ventures, a local venture capital firm, and after they went public there was a series of private placements. Arnie and David and Primary Ventures (principals Malcolm Burke and David Yue) are still the principal shareholders.

By the time Arnie and David flew to New York to keep their appointment with NYNEX, they had their act together. It was the fall of 1987. Earlier that year David had run into a former classmate at a University of Western Ontario reunion, a man called Bob Beauregard, who was a top advertising man in the U.S. with J. Walter Thompson and temporarily between contracts. Beauregard got involved with Yellow Spots. There was a three-day brainstorming session in Vancouver, and a lot of things started to come together. Make it into a medium, said Beauregard, develop a rate card and see if you can get Gabe Samuels on a consulting contract. Samuels was a market research whiz fresh from the top job with J. Walter Thompson in San Francisco. Like David had been, he was a skeptic, but he agreed to a short-term contract to explore the possibilities. Between them Beauregard and Samuels were able to open a lot of doors in the ad agency business.

"All of a sudden," says Arnie, still relishing the wonder of it all, "we could talk to anybody we wanted to in New York."

The NYNEX appointment was with Bernie Bloomfield, vice-president of marketing for the company's Yellow Pages subsidiary. And he went for it. Yellow Spots signed its first publishers contract with NYNEX in April, 1988.

Asked if he was immediately taken by the concept, Bloomfield says, "I was immediately taken by David and Arnie, and that had a lot to do with my willingness to listen to them."

The concept, says Bloomfield, was not new. "It had been kicked around and argued for years." But it meant a big commitment, of both time and resources. Nor is Bloomfield sure Judge Green—who is still playing out his role as regulator of the telephone industry—would have allowed the subsidiaries of the Baby Bells to act in concert and put a national media plan together.

"But what I was impressed with was their commitment, my evaluation of their ability to stay with it, the willingness to commit the necessary resources and the determination to do it on a national basis. What they brought was a willingness to sell the concept, and that's the only way the product will be successful. I'm not sure about the regulations. However, no company has done it and it's because none of us has a national sales force."

The NYNEX contract came through in the spring of 1988. It was *the* catalyst for the company, says Arnie. Yellow Spots Inc. opened a New York office that June—on Madison Avenue, where else?—with Gabe Samuels on board full time as managing director. Samuels had long since ceased to be a skeptic. Gabe and Arnie are the New York team.

"You just can't imagine," says Arnie, "the kind of gratification I'm getting now. To be able to talk to senior executives of companies like Sears and Levi and Mastercard, and have them excited about the idea. . . and it's really just since August, 1988, that we now have a business."

For Gabe Samuels, the excitement came after looking at the market research on Yellow Pages. As an old J. Walter Thompson pro, he thought he knew all the advertising media inside and out, but until now ad agencies have not tended to get involved in anything as pedestrian as the Yellow Pages. Advertisers themselves don't tend to regard Yellow Pages ads as advertising. It's a cost of doing business.

But the Yellow Pages industry had done some solid research, and Samuels found himself looking at an advertising medium—potentially a new one and a national one—that reaches almost one fifth of the adult population of the U.S. on a daily basis, on a weekly basis more than half. The demographics were good—high income, high education, the heaviest users in the all-important 18 to 49 age group, with a slight emphasis on the male user. On average people refer to the Yellow Pages three and one half times per week. It's all pretty impressive stuff.

Yellow Spots comes at a time when the Yellow Pages industry is looking for new dollars, going after the national advertiser. It's also a time when the big national advertisers are becoming distinctly disenchanted with national network television. Recent research indicates that as many as 35 to 40 per cent of the viewers of the high-rated television programs never see a commercial—they routinely click out the ads with their handy-dandy remote control gadgets.

Not only that, but as Arnie points out, exclusivity can never be guaranteed on network television, no matter how big the buy. Fuji can buy the Olympics on NBC, but there's nothing to stop Kodak from taking the local station spot that's going to run on the same show.

"Exclusivity," says Arnie, "is the foundation of our business."

Yellow Spots will come out in the first directories—those published by NYNEX, Southwestern Bell and Pacific Bell—in March, 1989. Actually Southwestern doesn't have any big directories coming out that month, so the initial buy will be substantially NYNEX and Pac Bell.

By March, 1989, according to Arnie and David, Yellow Spots will really get going. That's the target date for getting in hand the research data on the results of the charter buy. They're convinced it's going to be an enormous success, given the demographics of Yellow Pages users plus the creative approach to small spaces. "Now we have approximately 40 percent of all the Baby Bells," said David Horton. "We'll end up dealing with 700 directories when we have all seven."

Somewhere along the line Yellow Spots acquired its own ad agency, the New York-based Ahern & Heussner. A&H has worked up some truly sparkling prototype ads for potential advertisers like Levi, Metropolitan Life, Mastercard and others. In effect, they've shown agencies how to use the space effectively, keeping in mind the reinforcement principle. Metropolitan Life uses Peanuts cartoons in its advertising—presto! A series of episodes running through the book. Levi likes the bum and the pocket—they get lots of them, up close and eyecatching. Humour. Educational stuff. Household tips. You name it. The company that promotes itself as "big ideas for small spaces" has a tailored-to-fit game plan for everybody. And as they say in their presentation, "there's no place like 100 million homes."

Yellow Spots' initial circulation when they go fully national—and it's when, say Arnie and David, not if—will be more than 123 million. Gabe Samuels has long ago worked out the cost per thousand and worked up comparisons with, say, a full page black and white buy in the top 25 national magazines.

No contest, says Samuels.

"We would be very disappointed," says David the money man, "if we didn't do $6.5-million gross this year. Based on the profit-sharing deal with the directory publishers, that's $2.6-million net. And that's only the beginning.

"Wait until the research comes out," say David and Arnie virtually in unison. "Wait until we have five directory companies signed. With only three advertisers, that's $20-million in sales."

I like it, I like it.

Chapter
2
Making It

"$\mathbf{M}$ aking it" has always been a long-standing concern. Whereas in earlier times it seems that hard work was associated with making it (i.e., succeeding), more recently the notion of making it has taken on a somewhat different connotation. As Daniel Rogers observed in his excellent book, *The History of the Work Ethic*, the notion that hard work leads to success appears increasingly to be more of a myth than a fact. As organizations have become larger and more impersonal, it appears that more than hard work and competence are required to make it. While competence and diligence are still relevant, it often appears that the appearance of competence is less strongly correlated with actual performance than managers frequently assume. So many *things* combine to determine the results of one's efforts that attributions of success or failure to individual persons, while still made, seem tenuous. Moreover, given the fact that these attributions are often difficult to support with documentation, appearances (and the manipulation of appearances) often play an important role in determining an individual's success. Under these conditions, success is a judgment call.

The contrast between this view of making it and the more traditional view is well illustrated by a story told by Karl Weick. It seems that three umpires were discussing their job of calling balls and strikes. One umpire said, "I calls them as they is." A second umpire said, "I calls them as I sees them."[1] The third umpire observed, "They ain't nothin' till I calls them." According to this view, "making it" is seen as having strong elements of subjectivity, arbitrariness, and even invention of facts.

Furthermore, our revised view of making it suggests that many of the elements contributing to a person being judged as successful involve social, political, and personal attributes that may have little to do with the technical aspects of work but in actuality contribute a great deal to a person's ability to get things done. Finally, as the readings in this chapter

---

[1] The Social Psychology of Organizing, 2 ed., Reading, MA : Addison-Wesley, 1979.

suggest, making it for many people has a more basic component than being successful: Making it often means merely surviving in the environment in which they find themselves!

Our first selection in this chapter, a poem by Samuel Foss called "The Calf Path," depicts humorously how people sometimes unwittingly fall into routines and ways of doing things that can prevent them from creating their own paths in life. The other selections in this chapter deal with how people make it in organizations. Kevin Dahill, from the book *Life and Death—The Story of a Hospital*, relates the work history and concerns associated with the job of a man who entered an organization at a very low level and as his career developed, progressed to a highly responsible position. Robert Schrank's "Furniture Factory," from his autobiographical *Ten Thousand Working Days*, is the story of his first job as a boy of fifteen and the lessons he learned from the older workers about survival in the work environment of 1932. Hugh Prather offers sound advice concerning the relationship between one's job and oneself in "Your Job Reveals Nothing About You," a selection from his book *How to Live in the World . . . and Still Be Happy*. Doug Tindal argues in "Take Charge" that the first week on a new job can make you or break you. He offers a number of suggestions concerning the perils managers face on assuming a new job and some hints on how to deal with them. More and more women are creating their own jobs in retail trade, business services, and health and social services. "Female Entrepreneurs Outdo Men in Job Creation" relates the record in Canada, where in recent years women have far surpassed men in creating their own jobs.

Another aspect of the importance of appearances and connections is brought out in Claudia H. Deutsch's "To Get Ahead, Consider a Coach." The closing anonymous poem, "The Man in the Glass," reminds us of the importance of maintaining personal integrity on our organizational journeys.

The Calf Path

Samuel Foss

One day thru the primeval wood
A calf walked home, as good calves should;
But made a trail, all bent askew,
A crooked trail, as all calves do.

Since then 300 years have fled,
And I infer the calf is dead.
But still, he left behind his trail
And thereby hangs my mortal tale.

The trail was taken up next day
By a lone dog, that passed that way.
And then a wise bell weathered sheep
Pursued the trail, o'er vale and steep
And drew the flocks behind him too
As good bell weathers always do.
And from that day, o'er hill and glade
Thru those old woods, a path was made.

And many men wound in and out,
And dodged, and turned, and bent about,
And uttered words of righteous wrath
Because 'twas such a crooked path.
But still they followed, do not laugh
The first migrations of that calf.
And thru the winding woods they stalked
Because he wobbled when he walked.

This forest path became a lane
That bent, and turned, and turned again.
This crooked lane became a road
Where many a poor horse with his load
Toiled on beneath the burning sun
And traveled some three miles in one.
And thus a century and a half
They trod the footsteps of that calf.

The years passed on in swiftness fleet,
The road became a village street.
And this, before men were aware,
A city's crowded thoroughfare.
And soon the central street was this
Of a renowned metropolis.
And men, two centuries and a half
Trod the footsteps of that calf.

Each day a 100 thousand route
Followed the zig-zag calf about,
And o'er his crooked journey went
The traffic of a continent.
A 100 thousand men were led
By one calf, near three centuries dead.
They followed still his crooked way
And lost 100 years per day.
For this such reverence is lent
To well established precedent.

A moral lesson this might teach
Were I ordained, and called to preach.
For men are prone to go it blind
Along the calf paths of the mind,
And work away from sun to sun
To do what other men have done.
They follow in the beaten track,
And out, and in, and forth, and back,
And still their devious course pursue
To keep the paths that others do.

They keep the paths a sacred groove
Along which all their lives they move.
But how the wise old wood gods laugh
Who saw that first primeval calf.
Ah, many things this tale might teach,
But I am not ordained to preach.

Kevin Dahill
Director of Activation

Ina Yalof

The picture window in his office is less than fifty feet from the framework of the new hospital. It is noon and the construction workers outside are just breaking for lunch. Five men, in plaid shirts, jeans, and hard hats, sit on the steel beams eight stories up, legs dangling, eating sandwiches.

His is one of the Horatio Alger stories of the hospital. A young boy starts his career working as a part-time messenger and now, sixteen years later, he's a hospital administrator.

This hospital played a big part in my growing up. I lived in this neighborhood, and if I got hurt playing stick ball or whatever in the street, my mother brought me here to the clinic. Everyone in my family has worked here at some point in their lives. My mother was first. A little over twenty years ago she took a part-time job in the evenings in the record room. At that time, the evening shift in medical records was made up of housewives from the neighborhood. It was the famous "seven-to-eleven shift"; seven in the evening to eleven at night. These women all became very close friends. A social network developed from it.

My father, who was a Teamster official at the time, took early retirement at age sixty. So for something to do, he latched onto a job here in the cashier's office. After what he had been through—major contracts with the Teamsters and getting involved with milk strikes in New York—he thought this job was a joke. He'd walk in here in the mornings and he'd work behind the window and cash checks and set payments on bills. He'd stroll home for lunch and watch a couple of soap operas and then stroll back and do his afternoon's worth of work. He always used to tell us, "A second grader could do this job. It's so easy." But he loved it. The only reason he retired from here was because at that time, if you were sixty-five, you were out. There was no question about it.

By then I had started college and worked here as a part-time messenger. My sister worked in patient accounts, and on down the line. I have three other siblings and every one has worked here in some capacity or another. So this place has played a large part in my life. And I'm sad but in some ways I'm happy to say both my parents passed away here.

My first full-time job was in 1969. I worked evenings at the information desk. Then I became evening supervisor of admitting, and then I was the night manager of the hospital for five years. It's a strange life, working nights, but it's interesting. There are

"Kevin Dahill" from *Life and Death, Story of a Hospital*, by Ina Yalof, 1988, pp. 303–306. Reprinted by permission of Ballentine Books.

people who have done it here throughout their entire career, but it's a very strange life. Your sleeping habits, your eating habits, are totally different than the normal routine that everyone else has. People look at you strangely when you pour yourself a Scotch on the rocks before you go to sleep at nine-thirty in the morning. Or you have a hamburger and French fries at six in the morning. Things like that. In my case, as a night manager, it was even more peculiar, because we would break up the week. I would do three nights a week from midnight till eight A.M., have two days off, and do two evenings of four to twelve. The police department always complains because they go week to week and they swing shifts. They do a week of midnights and a week of four to twelves. We broke it up right in the middle of the week. So your first day off was spent mainly sleeping, just to catch up.

It was sort of like a jet lag and I began to relate to childhood friends of mine who had fathers who were cops and firemen. When you went to their houses after school, you had to be real quiet. You always got the feeling there was something wrong with someone who slept all day.

But I liked nights. And as I look back on it, I even liked the environment. It's amazing what an *esprit de corps* there is on nights—the graveyard shift, as they call it—among everyone who is on it. The doctors need the porters much more at night than they do during the daytime and they can relate to them better. There are centralized locations where everyone goes for coffee and Danish, as opposed to different places where the doctors and nurses eat during the day. At night you're all the same. There's much more of a family-type atmosphere.

Toward the end of that period, the hospital created a department of patient relations and I was put in as the director. From there, I was promoted again to the new position of director of Government and Community Affairs. Then, towards the end of '86, I got a call from Joe Corcoran, the chief operating officer. He said, "Look, we've got these buildings going up and ultimately we're going to be moving the old hospital into the new one and we need a person to be in charge of the move, and we want you to do it."

So as of January first this year, I've been the Director of Activation. It's a huge undertaking, moving a whole hospital, and it requires a large staff to look after things. Equipment has to be tested and monitored, people have to be trained to work the new equipment. There are big things and small. The furniture has to be in before the staff moves in. We even have to plan for things like wastebaskets.

It's a job just getting people to pack, asking them to make major decisions like whether or not to throw out documents from 1958. I'm thinking of staging a contest as part of the major move, for the department that discards the most hard-copy records, because I think people just hold on to things in order to hold on to them. We would have some sort of a special prize—a trip or something like that.

We're probably going to move in floor by floor, mainly because we're going to get the building turned over to us by the construction people floor by floor. When they turn it over, they're turning it over in bare-bones fashion. We've got to get the equipment operating and make sure it works and that our staff knows how to work it. We've got to clean up the place so that the state can come in and review it and make sure it meets code requirements and so on. That process takes a lot of time.

Moving the patients will be no problem. Even patients with respirators and IVs. On a given day we're going to decide this is "orthopedics' day." So we'll move all the ortho staff and their patients to the new unit. If somebody is in traction, then they'll stay in the old hospital until they can be safely moved. We'll decide in advance which patients are going to be moved that day. We'll have a schedule on that morning. We'll know that John Smith, who is now in 401, bed 3, in the old Presbyterian, is moving to Garden North, 812, bed 2. I envision a cadre of transporters and volunteers. There'll literally be a parade of patients coming across the bridges over Fort Washington Avenue. It's not difficult, when you think about it. It's like moving a patient from one room to another; it's just a longer trip.

In terms of what keeps me awake at night when I consider the move, the transfer of patients is not it. Sure, we may lose a patient temporarily, a patient may end up in the wrong room for a little while. I mean, it's realistic to expect that *somebody* will have made a wrong turn *somewhere.* But that's not what worries me. I'm concerned about the human dynamics of the staff moving to the new building. The way I see it, our entire organization has to change. Take orthopedics again. We're bringing what are now four different inpatient orthopedics units together onto one floor. We have four head nurses moving into one unit. So now who supervises the floor? Will they get along? What happens to seniority? Now maybe I'm barking up the wrong tree, but I think that these are going to be issues we'll have to contend with. I think that kind of thing is going to transcend the overall activation effort. But I also think if we do this right, we can make it a positive experience. Theoretically this should be an exciting adventure.

A lot of my outward calm is strictly for show. I'm convinced that if I, above all people, show any signs of nervousness or apprehension, then we've blown it. I've got to instill confidence in people; not just in me, but in the process. There are times, though, when I just go somewhere and scream to myself or I whack a golf ball in an effort to work it out.

A lot of people say you shouldn't stay in any organization too long, and for years I disagreed with that. I've been very lucky in this hospital. The opportunities that I've had here have been wonderful. There's been no reason to leave. But now . . . now I think maybe I should give that some thought. I think most people resist change, and it's possible that after I get them moved, they're not all going to like me a whole lot. So after the new hospital is open, maybe I'd be better off like the Lone Ranger. Maybe I should just get on my white horse and ride off into the sunset.

Furniture Factory

Robert Schrank

It was 1932 and we were in the depths of the depression. If you were lucky enough to find a job, it was usually through a friend, and that was how I got my first full-time job in a Brooklyn factory that made frames for upholstered furniture. I was fifteen years old and lived in the Bronx, traveling on the subway for an hour and fifteen minutes each way, every day, six days a week for twelve dollars. I considered myself to be the luckiest boy in the world to get that job. When Mr. Miller the owner of the Miller Parlor Frame Company, interviewed me and agreed to hire me, he made it quite clear that he was doing a favor for a mutual friend and did not really care much about giving me a job.

Like most small factory offices, Mr. Miller's was cluttered with catalogs, samples of materials, some small tools, a rolltop desk with a large blotter pad worn through the corners. The whole place was in a sawdust fog with a persistent cover of dust over everything. Mr. Miller was a short fat man who chewed cigars and sort of drooled as he talked to me. He sat on the edge of his big oak swivel chair. I had a feeling he might slip off anytime. He never looked at me as we spoke. He made it clear that he was annoyed at people asking favors, saying that he did not like people who were "always trying to get something out of me."

The sour smell of the oak sawdust comes back to fill my nose as I recall the furniture factory. It is a smell I always welcomed until I had to live in it eight hours a day. There were days, especially when it was damp or raining, when the wood smell was so strong you could not eat your lunch. Next to the smell I remember getting to the factory and back as being an awful drag. But the New York subway that I rode to and from work for many years had two marked positive effects on me. First, I felt part of a general condition that nobody seemed to like. I was part of a group and we were all in the same fix, busting our asses to get to work in the morning and home at night. While I felt unhappy, it was made easier through the traditional "misery loves company," and there was plenty of that. And second, if I had a lucky day, there was the chance of seeing or being pressed up against some sweet-smelling, young, pretty thing who would get me all excited. Sometimes I tried a pickup, but it usually did not work because the situation was too public. With each person rigidly contained, it was surprising if anyone tried to move out of his shell. Everyone in the train would be staring to see what would develop. Almost nothing did.

To be at the furniture factory in Brooklyn by 8 A.M., I would leave my house in the Bronx by 6:30 A.M. While it was always a bad trip it became less so in the long spring days of the year as contrasted with December, when I most hated getting up in the dark. It was very important to be very quiet as I would feel my way around our old frame house, so as not to wake people up who had another thirty or forty minutes to sleep. I would sleepily make a sandwich for lunch, preferably from a leftover or just bologna, grab a cup of coffee—always with one eye on the clock—and run for the station. Luckily, we lived at the end of a subway line, and in the morning I was usually able to get a corner seat in the train. The corner seat was good for sleeping because I could rest against the train wall and not have the embarrassment of falling asleep on the person sitting next to me. It meant being able to sleep the hour-long trip to Brooklyn, and it was critical to set my "inner clock" so it would wake me up at Morgan Avenue station in Brooklyn. If it failed or was a little late, which sometimes happened, panic would ensue, as I usually would wake up just as the train was pulling out of Morgan Avenue. I would make a quick, unsuccessful dash for the door, and people would try to help by grabbing at the door. Then I would burn with anger for being late and maybe losing the job. When I would end up past my stop, I would have to make a fast decision to either spend another nickel and go back or go on to a double station where I could race down the steps to the other side of the tracks and catch a train going the other way without paying an additional fare.

The trip home from work on the New York subway in the evening rush hour is an experience most difficult to describe. The train, packed full of people, hurtles into a station. The doors slide open. There is always an illusion that someone may be getting out. That never seems to happen while a mass of people begin to push their way in. All strangers, we are not packed like sardines in a can, as is often suggested; the packing of sardines is an orderly process. The rush hour subway is more like a garbage compacter that just squeezes trash and rubbish into a dense mass and then hurtles it at very high speeds through a small underground tube. Unlike the morning, at night when I was exhausted from the day's work I never was able to get a seat, and that meant standing on my dog-tired feet for more than an hour and trying not to lean on the person next to me, an almost impossible thing to do. . . .

As I walked from the subway in the morning I could smell the furniture factory a block away. It was a powerful smell; as I said, I loved that oak at first. It was a perfume from the woods: a combination of skunk, mushrooms, and honeysuckle blended to a musk, a sweet contrast to the steel-and-oil stink of the subway. Yet, by the end of a day's work, the factory, its smells, its noise, its tedium all became so terribly tiresome and exhausting that leaving every day was an act of liberation.

The factory was a five-story loft building about half a city block long. The making of furniture frames began on the bottom floor where the rough cuts were made from huge pieces of lumber. As the cut wood moved along from floor to floor, it was formed, shaped, carved, dowled, sanded, and finally assembled on the top floor into completed frames. The machines in the plant included table saws, band saws, planers, carving machines, routers, drills, hydraulic presses, all run by 125 machine operators who were almost all European immigrants. My job was to keep the operators supplied with material, moving the finished stuff to the assembly floor, a sort of human conveyor. When I wasn't moving pieces around, I was supposed to clean up, which meant bagging sawdust into burlap bags. Sometimes the foreman would come and say, "Hey, kid, how would you like to run the dowling machine?" At first I thought that was a real break, a chance to get on a machine and become an operator. I told him enthusiastically, "Yeah, that would be great." I would sit in front of this little machine, pick up a predrilled piece, hold it to the machine, which would push two glued dowels into the holes. I soon found that I preferred moving parts around the plant and cleaning up to sitting at that machine all day, picking up a piece of wood from one pile, locating the holes at the dowel feeder that pushed in two preglued dowels, then dropping it on the other side. The machine had a sort of gallump, gallump rhythm that made me sleepy and started me watching the clock, the worst thing you can do in a factory. It would begin to get to me, and I would just sit and stare at the machine, the clock, the machine, the clock.

Those first few weeks in that factory were an agony of never-ending time. The damn clock just never moved, and over and over again I became convinced that it had stopped. Gradually, life in the furniture factory boiled down to waiting for the four work breaks: coffee, lunch hour, coffee, and quitting time. When the machines stopped, it was only in their sudden silence that I became aware of their deafening whine. It was almost impossible to hear each other talk while they were running, and all we were able to do was to scream essential information at one another.

The breaks were the best times of the day, for I could become intoxicated listening to the older men talk of rough, tough things in the big world out there. Being accepted was a slow process, and I was just happy to be allowed to listen. When I had been there for a couple of weeks, Mike the Polack said, "Hey, kid, meet in the shit house for talk." I was making it all right.

The coffee- and lunch-break talks centered around the family, sports, politics, and sex, in about that order. The immigrants from Middle Europe, and especially the Jews, were the most political. Most of them seemed to believe that politicians were crooks and that's how it is. The Jews talked the least about sex and the Italians the most. Luigi would endlessly bait Max (who would soon be my friend), saying that what he needed most was "a good woman who make you forget all dat political shit." There were a whole variety of newspapers published in New York at that time and one way workers had of figuring out each other's politics, interests, and habits was by the papers they read.

Max Teitelbaum would say to me, "See Louie over there. You can tell he's just a dummy, he reads that *Daily Mirror*. It fills his head with garbage so he can't tink about vot is *really* happening in the world." Arguing strongly in the defense of Franklin Roosevelt, probably too strongly, Mike the Polack told me with his finger waving close to my nose, "Listen, kid, vot I tink and vot I do is my business, and nobody, no politician or union or smart-ass kid like you is gonna butt into dat. You got it? Don't forget it!"

As people began to trust me, I was slowly making friends. Their trust was expressed in small ways, like when Luigi called me over to his workbench, held up a picture of Jean Harlow for me to look at as he shook his big head of black hair, all the time contemplating the picture together with me, and said, "Now, whaddya tink, boy?". . . Then he said, "OK, kid, you gotta work hard and learn something. See all those poor bastards out there outa work. Watch out or you could be one of dem." Luigi was a wood-carver who made the models for the multiple-spindle carving machine and was probably the only real craftsman in the place.

One day as I distributed work in process to the operators and picked up their finished stuff, I received one of my first lessons in the fundamentals of working that I would relearn again and again in almost every job I have had: How to work less hard in order to make the task easier.

Max Teitelbaum, a band saw operator just a few years out of Krakow, Poland, a slightly built man with sort of Mickey Mouse ears, twinkling eyes, and a wry smile, would upbraid me repeatedly with such passing comments as, "You are a dummy," or "You're not stupid, so what's da matter vit you?" Finally one day he stopped his machine, turned to me, and said, "Look, come over here. I vant to talk vit you. Vy you are using your back instead your head? Max Teitelbaum's first rule is: Don't carry nuttin' you could put a veel under. It's a good ting you wasn't helpin' mit der pyramids—you vould get crushed under the stones."

I said, "But Max, if the hand truck is on the third floor and I'm on the fifth, I can't go all the way down there just for that."

"You see," he said, "you are a dummy. Vy you can't go down dere? Huh, vy not? You tell me!"

"Well," I said, "it would take a lot of time—"

He cut me off. "You see, you are vorrying about da wrong tings, like da boss. Is he vorrying about you? Like da Tzar vorried about Max Teitelbaum. Listen, kid, you vorry about you because no von else vill. Understand? You vill get nuttin' for vorking harder den more vork. Now ven you even don't understand someting, you come and ask Max. OK?" Max became my friend, adviser, and critic.

By the end of my first weeks in the factory I began to feel as if I was crushed under stones. My body helped me to understand what Max was saying. I would come home from work on Saturday afternoon and go to bed expecting to go out later that night with a girl friend. For some weeks when I lay down on Saturday I did not try, nor was I able, to move my body from bed until some time on Sunday. The whole thing just throbbed with fatigue: arms, shoulders, legs, and back were in fierce competition for which hurt the most. I began to learn what Max meant by "Always put a veel under it and don't do more than you have to."

My third or fourth week at the factory found me earnestly launched in my quest for holding the job but doing less work—or working less hard. This was immediately recognized and hailed by the men with "Now you're gettin' smart, kid. Stop bustin' your ass and only do what you have to do. You don't get any more money for bustin' your hump and you might put some other poor bastard outa job." Remember this was the depression. Most workers, while aware of the preciousness of their jobs, felt that doing more work than necessary could be putting someone else, even yourself, out of a job. "Only do what you have to" became a rule not only to save your own neck but to make sure you were not depriving some other soul like yourself from getting a job.

In the next few weeks, I was to be taught a second important lesson about working. One day while picking up sawdust, I began to "find" pieces in the sawdust or behind a woodpile or under a machine. The first few times, with great delight, I would announce to the operator, "Hey, look what I found!" I should have figured something was wrong by the lack of similar enthusiasm from the operator. Sam was a generally quiet Midwesterner who never seemed to raise his voice much, but now when I showed him my finished-work discovery behind his milling machine he shouted, "Who the fuck asked you to be a detective? Keep your silly ass out from behind my machine; I'll tell you what to pick up. So don't go being a big brown-nosing hero around here."

Wow, I sure never expected that. Confused, troubled, almost in tears, not knowing what to do or where to go, I went to the toilet to hide my hurt and just sat down on an open bowl and thought what the hell am I doing in this goddamned place anyway? I lit a cigarette and began pacing up and down in front of the three stalls, puffing away at my

Camel. I thought, What the hell should I do? This job is terrible, the men are pissed off at me. I hate the place, why don't I just quit? Well, it's a job and you get paid, I said to myself, so take it easy.

While I'm pacing and puffing, Sam comes in, saying, "Lissen, kid, don't get sore. I was just trying to set you straight. Let me tell you what it's all about. The guys around, that is the machine operators, agree on how much we are gonna turn out, and that's what the boss gets, no more, no less. Now sometimes any one of us might just fall behind a little, so we always keep some finished stuff hidden away just in case." The more he talked, the more I really began to feel like the enemy. I tried to apologize, but he just went on. "Look, kid, the boss always wants more and he doesn't give a shit if we die giving it to him, so we [it was that "we" that seemed to retrieve my soul back into the community; my tears just went away] agree on how much we're going to give him—no more, no less. You see, kid, if you keep running around, moving the stuff too fast, the boss will get wise about what's going on." Sam put his arm on my shoulder. (My God! I was one of them! I love Sam and the place. I am in!) "So look," he says, "your job is to figure out how to move and work no faster than we turn the stuff out. Get it? OK? You'll get it." I said, "Yes, of course, I understand everything." I was being initiated into the secrets of a work tribe, and I loved it.

I was beginning to learn the second work lesson that would be taught me many times over in a variety of different jobs: Don't do more work than is absolutely necessary. Years later I would read about how people in the Hawthorne works of Western Electric would "bank work" and use it when they fell behind or just wanted to take it easy. I have seen a lot of work banking, especially in machine shops. In some way I have felt that banking work was the workers' response to the stopwatches of industrial engineers. It is an interesting sort of game of hide the work now, take it out later. In another plant, would you believe we banked propellor shafts for Liberty ships!

I learned most of the rules, written and unwritten, about the furniture factory, but I never got to like the job. After I had been there six or seven months, the Furniture Workers Union began an organizing drive. I hated the furniture factory, the noise, the dust, and the travel, so I, too, quickly signed a union card. I was just as quickly out on my ass. It was a good way to go, since my radical friends considered me a hero of sorts, having been victimized for the cause. The first time I ever considered suicide in my life was in that furniture factory as I would stare at the clock and think to myself, "If I have to spend my life in this hellhole, I would rather end it." Well, of course, I didn't; and as I look back, it was not the worst place I worked, but I was young and unwilling to relinquish childhood.

Your Job Reveals Nothing About You

Hugh Prather

I don't recall how old I was when I discovered that if I answered "architect" instead of "fireman" to the question "What do you want to be when you grow up?" I got a much more satisfying reaction from adults. I still remember vague feelings of guilt about not knowing what an architect did, but at the time that did not seem to matter. Today's five- or six-year-old is likely to answer "I haven't decided between palmistry and astrophysics," although there are some kids who can be quite firm about "doing charts."

All of this is probably very harmless because children seem to enjoy this little game as much as adults do. But just a few years later the same question can become terrifying if teenagers feel pressured to set out on the impossible task of trying to second-guess what high school specialty or college major will best prepare them for the future course of their life. Most parents ought to know that the young person's distress over this is not without foundation since so few of us have ended up doing what our education supposedly prepared us for, yet some of us still persist in requiring teenagers to exercise this rather silly form of precognition. It is of course fine to choose a major, but no one should have to kid himself about its implications.

Thinking that appearances are everything, the ego naturally concludes that "you are what you do." During our middle span of life the seemingly affable question "What do you do?" really means "Are you somebody?" and most of us think far too much about how to word our answer should some stranger at a party ask us this question, even though if we just took a moment to look at our feelings we would see that we really don't care what a stranger thinks of us. It is only our ego that attempts to judge, and being quite blind, all it can see is other egos. This common social line of attack and counterattack has so very little to do with what people are at their core that you would think it would be self-evident that a person's means of earning a living reveals only the most superficial and insignificant information about what he or she is, and yet the issue of career has become a source of great unhappiness.

It is now generally assumed that anyone is capable of doing anything. "Why then," our society asks, "have you settled for work that is mediocre?" We should somehow be more creative, more humanitarian, more productive, more something. So tangled up with our job are our feelings of self-worth that businesses, if they want their fair share of good employees, must periodically spend time rewriting job titles to make the same work sound more impressive. We have actually gotten to the point of disliking people for not doing more than they do, and we ourselves cannot sidestep the disgust, however mild, we think we have managed to reserve only for others. Surely it does not have to be proved that all of this is quite insane. And yet, if you wish to be happy, you must free yourself completely from this point of view. *You are not what you do; you are how you do it.*

You will not think better of yourself by engaging in a selection of those activities currently considered to be impressive. Nor will you recognize your worth by avoiding them. You will know that you are good when you consistently bring goodness to all you do. If the job is to straighten and clean for a small family, your work is no less holy than, for instance, that of a personnel manager who hires and fires hundreds of employees for a large corporation. We have such silly ideas of what is important work! For example, what more far-reaching activity could there be than devoting oneself to helping a child be happy and unafraid and to develop into a gentle, kind adult? How many people will this one child touch within a lifetime? Is seeing to this little person's happiness really less significant than composing music, throwing pots, being socially active or "living up to one's earning potential"?

YOUR CAREER FORMS BEHIND YOU

Most people have never stopped to ask themselves exactly what it is they are seeking in place of a good life *now.* There simply is no such thing as a career. People talk about pursuing a career as if all the turns were already mapped out and their destination set there waiting for them as solid and immovable as the town civic center. Except for the straight line of automatic promotions within organizations such as the armed services, a few large corporations, and some branches of civil service, none of us advances to our goal with a predictable precision, and even within the fields where this appears to happen a closer examination shows a nest of entangling exceptions, including the employee's health and will to endure, exigencies of location, family demands, government allocations, and the goodwill of superiors. It is not realistic to think in terms of "arriving at the top of your profession." There is no perfectly defined profession and no true top.

Our trail through life can be seen only in retrospect. It *does* all add up, but not in advance of the steps taken. If each small step is guided by the present instead of by a hodgepodge of fears about the future, we can discern a lovely wake flowing from the actions we have taken, including even our mistakes. There is a beauty, a just-rightness, within the course of every life, but so often the individual is blinded to it by constant worry and second-guessing.

The only thing you can know for sure is whether you feel at ease in the present about a step that is possible to take today. No one can adequately define all the consequences, see all the people this step will affect, and accurately determine whether the ramifications will be fair to everyone eventually touched by them. You merely delude yourself if you think your vision is that free of distortion. Why then attempt to resolve interminable future implications when it is simply not possible to do so? Instead of the fantasy of a glowing future, why not settle for the very real possibility of a satisfying present?

NOTHING HAS TO BE DECIDED IN ADVANCE

When we attempt to translate a fantasy into a worldly event, the result is a different order of reality. Like most people, I have run through many such fantasies in my life. My mental pictures of what it would be like to become a sculptor, ranch hand, secondary schoolteacher, real estate broker, guidance counselor, construction worker, psychologist, circuit lecturer, and a few other false starts were so unlike the reality of the work I ended up engaged in that it is really very funny to me now that I thought I could imagine in advance what my life would be like within these various fields.

A fantasy does not give firsthand experience. That is why no matter how informed we think we are, we do not know beforehand what will make us happy. Nor is there any reason to know since it is the degree to which we have developed our capacity to enjoy the present that determines our happiness and not our job classification. This does not mean that very little care need be taken in choosing one's way of making a living, for of course care should be taken. It means only that our freedom from conflict over whether today to ask for an interview, enroll in a class, question someone within a certain line of work, or buy a book or two on a particular field is a more reliable basis for making a decision than our fantasy of an entire future course of action that will entail hundreds of separate choices. Our desire to anticipate every move we will make for broad periods of time is nothing more than our present wish to struggle, and it is simply not necessary to indulge this form of false humility. All we ever need do is take the obvious steps before us today and let our sense of direction clarify as we proceed.

There is also a strong tendency within all of us to get ourselves into a difficult situation and then think we must see it through to the bitter end. Trusting in fantasies instead of our present perception of how things are going is a major contributor to this pattern. To decide beforehand what kind of job we deserve can cause as much unhappiness as deciding what kind of child we have a right to, as many parents unconsciously do. In their mind is a constantly escalating standard of acceptable manners, the proper height, an adequate IQ, sufficient social skills, a pleasing appearance, and so forth. Inevitably the child fails in some respect and feels their disapproval. Disapproval is irrelevant to appreciating children and working with them toward their, rather than our own, feelings of well-being. And just as with a child, a job must be looked at, taken as it is, and given time.

Relax into your destiny. Giving something time is quite different from forcing yourself to see it through to the bitter end. Let each workday come to you. Watch it approach without suspicion. Expect happiness from yourself, but expect nothing from the job. Approached in this way, happiness is a possibility in any situation. Take each task as it comes and do not constantly peer over it to the next task. Don't rush to complete it, or rush toward some hour on the clock. We need not stay on guard in order to see that a job is not working out, but we do have to let down our guard to enjoy what we have predefined as "work." We may not be able to change the task, but we are always free to change our definition of our function within it.

FINDING A JOB

Our discussion so far may seem insensitive to the many people who sincerely want to work but cannot find employment. This is obviously an extremely complex and difficult question, and the factors within these cases can vary so dramatically that any generalizations I make here would be unfair in light of at least some people's plight. So of course there are countless exceptions, and yet I believe a few things can be said that apply to some of those who find themselves in this predicament.

Many people—far more than consciously realize it—make themselves walk a very narrow path in finding work. For instance, there are entire categories of jobs they will not consider because of a certain self-image they believe must be maintained. Other occupations go unexplored because of their conviction that society, the economy, the present controlling minority, big business, or some other generalized enemy should not be forcing this kind of choice and they must stand alone against this outrage, even if it means their family's well-being. "I won't work for a company that . . . " "I won't live in a place where . . . " "I won't take orders from a boss who . . . " and yet it does not have to be that way. Clearly we should never do what is morally intolerable, but so often this is not the real issue. We think we must be right at all costs.

Another hampering bias is directed, curiously, at ourselves. *Most people tend to look down on what they do best.* This is merely further evidence of our aversion to what is easy and simple. Our areas of greatest strength are usually the ones to be given the harshest scrutiny, and of course if you look for fault anywhere long enough you are sure to find it. Instead of doing what we know how to do (which often is also the work we can do most peacefully), we assume that the higher pursuit is to enter a new field altogether, especially one that fits the current definition of "meaningful" work. Seldom is it sufficient to simply earn a living. Better to have an erratic income and be able to give the impression that we are sacrificing ourselves to set the world straight.

Unfortunately our friends are sometimes the ones most likely to distract us from our own quiet knowing. As a general rule you will be less confused and consequently miss fewer opportunities if you will decide for yourself whether a job fits your present needs and not even open yourself up to conflict by discussing decisions you are in the middle of. Strengthen your mind by reminding yourself that *you* are in the best position to know what you should be doing. And after you have started a job save yourself the pangs of doubt by talking as little as possible about the inevitable problems that accompany a transition of this sort. Few people can resist an opportunity to sow confusion. So do not give them one. Do not be afraid to stay close to your heart, to keep your own counsel. *Do not be afraid to know.*

Another cause of defeat, although far less conscious, is the unexamined premise that the job choice one is making is permanent. Out there awaits some eternal and just-right niche, and the only real problem is locating it. And yet, *there is no right job.*

"This is right" implies "this is permanent." It shouldn't, but it does. Who could believe he had finally found the right job or, worse, was "guided" or "led" to it and still feel perfectly free to quit at the end of the first day? Given this approach, it should not be surprising that most people's major concern is to avoid making a mistake. If you believe in the existence of a right job, you will also look on all other job as "wrong," at least for you.

Do you see the position this puts you in? Since there is a job that is best for you, most of the work that comes to your attention is a potential mistake and your life is now like walking through a mine field. Should you already have a job, you cannot help harboring the suspicion that you chose wrongly. We think we can somehow believe in the preexistence of a right course of action in one area of our life and yet not believe in it in every other area, and because this is impossible most people also suspect that they married the wrong person (which means, of course, they have the wrong children), bought or rented the wrong place to live in (so the neighbors aren't what they should be), and probably ate the wrong cereal for breakfast this morning. I don't think any of us has managed to escape this outlook entirely.

No more absolute and awful tyranny reigns than our own fear of being wrong. We have a simple choice. We can try to avoid all mistakes or we can relax. In seeking a job it is good to drop the notion that the universe has hidden away some haloed position just for you. Now at least you will not be haunted by the vague feeling that somehow you are not going about this job-finding business in the correct way. There are a thousand correct ways because there are a thousand peaceful ways.

Do not remain in fear. Very often if someone attempting to avoid the wrong job will accept just any job, a more pleasing position will appear shortly thereafter. There is no magic to this. The elimination of fear is the beginning of vision, and to give ourselves a broad range of options permits us to see opportunities we were blind to before. It is not uncommon for an individual who is unable to find a paying job to take volunteer work or to just begin helping someone for free and suddenly have a salaried position, or sometimes several at once, become available, much like the classic example of the couple who cannot bear children, decide to adopt, and instantly become fertile.

Once again, this phenomenon is not the mystery it first seems. So often the cause of our problem, whatever it may be, is fear, and the willingness to act in a simple, direct way will begin lessening it. The precise external results are not predictable—an adoption does not automatically render a couple fertile, and volunteer work does not consistently manifest a paying job. Nevertheless, openness to starting and continuing the small steps involved in walking around a problem will eventually result in leaving the problem behind. Overt manifestations of willingness reduce inner conflict, and an unconflicted mind can step over any hindrance.

Take Charge

Doug Tindal

The first week on a new job can make you—or break you.

It may not seem fair, but your first week in the new, executive job is going to make you or break you. Your first days will establish you as a strong performer who'll lead the company on to higher sales and wider profit margins than ever before. Or they'll mark you as a dud. Naturally, you won't head into the office on day one wearing your plaid sports jacket. You'll wear one of your navy blue suits—the one with the fine pinstripe would be a good choice—and, naturally, you'll wear the vest. So at least you'll look right, which certainly is a step in the right direction—but only a very, very small step, because there are so many pitfalls in a new job, so many envious skeptics waiting for you to slip, that your first days are downright perilous, to say the least.

What if you put your car in the president's parking spot? What if you get stuck in an elevator (sure, it could happen to anyone, but when it's your first day on the job . . .)? And what if Gladys from accounting is stuck in there with you? These are unlikely dangers, of course, but most of the perils of a new job are entirely real. And though they may be much more subtle, they're also much more serious.

Fortunately, there are things you can do and steps you can take (carefully) that will start you off on the right foot, as they say. There are correct moves to make—and a great many wrong ones to avoid—as you seek out the levers of power. And the key point to bear in mind, according to the experts, is that you should let the specifics of the job wait for a bit. Your first concern should be first impressions, and obviously this goes far beyond the appropriate suit or picking the right place to park.

You have to impress a lot of people. You have to impress upon your boss, and others at his level, that you're sharp and aggressive and on the move; you have to convince your peers that you're a team player, a trustworthy colleague. And the very first move, the experts say, is to make a good impression on your staff, to win their respect and trust—especially when it comes to the bright young fellow who may be all set to torpedo you because he wanted your job. The way you handle this situation will color the way the rest of the staff receives you. If you fire him, for example, you make risk a palace revolt—and lose his experience. If you let things slide, hoping that he'll soon grow to love you, you're probably deluding yourself.

Peter Frost is a consultant and professor of organizational behavior at the University of British Columbia, and he says it's probably a good idea to assume that someone in the

Reprinted by permission of Doug Tindal.

company has a grudge against you, even if you have no direct evidence. "It's very rare, in my experience, that a senior position is awarded without there being an internal candidate, and normally this individual feels a bit bruised when he doesn't get the job."

So what should you do? Dave Urquhart is a partner in the management consulting firm of Urquhart & Preger, Inc., in Toronto, and he recommends a very neat solution: "Chances are your subordinate was passed over because senior management figured he wasn't quite ready. So you go to him and offer to groom him—when you're ready to move on, you point out, he'll know everything he needs to know to step right into your shoes. This way, you convert a potential enemy into a valuable ally; and, you clear the way for yourself to advance, because generally, you can't move up in a company until you've prepared someone to take your place."

Urquhart says, incidentally, that when you get to the final stage of the hiring process, just before you take the job, it's quite legitimate to ask if there's an internal candidate, and if so, who. In other words, know your enemy.

There's another thing you should establish at this early stage: who will be your secretary? You may have the option of keeping the same secretary your predecessor had, and the obvious advantage of this is that she'll know all the ropes. The disadvantage is that some of them won't be *your* ropes; and if your predecessor is still with the company, your secretary may have conflicting loyalties.

So you might be better off to hire someone new. Either way, you should realize that your secretary can be much, much more than someone to answer phones and type correspondence; she (or he) can be your link to the great secretarial intelligence grid, and her perceptions of other people can be a big help.

Whenever you start a new job, you face a great many important questions that can be answered only over a period of time. You have to find out, for example, how much of your success depends on meeting performance standards such as sales targets or production quotas, and how much depends on pleasing the boss in subjective ways. If your boss is the kind of guy who likes to be at his desk by 7:45 A.M., then chances are he likes to see other people at their desks by 7:45. If you don't come in until 8:30, this may affect the way your boss perceives the quality of your work—no matter how good it is.

Frank Musten, an industrial psychologist who practices in both Ottawa and Toronto, points out that each company has its own set of norms: Should you work through the noon hour or should you take a two-hour lunch? Do you have to go to company parties? Does your spouse have to go, too? Should you join your staff in the lunchroom occasionally, to be friendly—or would they consider it an intrusion? Well, Musten says, try it: carry your bowl of tomato soup over to join the staff one day and see what happens. Nobody is likely to tell you to shove off, but if you're not welcome, you'll know it—for one thing, the conversation will dry right up.

But you don't necessarily have to obey all the norms. "If you try to become totally a company man, you'll be useless to both the company and to yourself," Musten says. "So you should decide which norms you can live with."

Frost adds that when you move into a company at a senior level, usually you're expected to stir things up a bit and make some changes: "In other words, there's a degree to which you have to make the company fit you, not the other way around."

Laird Mealiea is an associate professor of organizational development at Dalhousie University in Halifax, and he points out that your new company can provide a great deal of formal information about your job. "You should make an effort to get hold of all the company's policies and procedures manuals, job descriptions, personnel files—anything that describes your position and your relationship to others. These aren't gospel, of course; you have to weigh them against the information you pick up informally and find a balance."

Urquhart suggests a number of ways to pick up informal information: "You should take the initiative to go around and meet other managers throughout the firm," he says. "Try to get to know them a bit—not just what they do, but what they value."

"It helps you to build some bridges to these guys, so they'll be more receptive to co-operating with you when you need them and it gives you a line on what kinds of people get promoted in the company. It also gives you a chance to look for potential allies, people you can use to test your thoughts about the organization."

Urquhart suggests you should find out about any key people who've recently left the company: "Call them up, tell them you'd like to take them to lunch and pick their brains about where the company is at, who the key players are, all that stuff."

Finally, he suggests you meet with your predecessor and ask him about your new subordinates: which ones are top performers, which are marginal. Naturally, you won't necessarily be guided by his perceptions, but it's valuable to hear what he thinks; and it will probably tell you something about the way he ran the department.

Pamela Ennis, an industrial psychologist who has her own company, Pamela Ennis & Associates, Industrial Psychologists, says you should also speak with subordinates: "Find out about how independent they were under your predecessor, what controls there are on their actions, how they feel about their jobs, what kind of formal communications there are in the department—you want to do something like a miniature organizational survey."

Ennis has some interesting ideas about the world of power politics and the ways it can affect your first few days on the job. "Power politics is the informal world of management," she says. "It doesn't appear on any management chart and it's not studied in any of the texts, but unless you know how to play, any success you have will be short-lived. The first thing you have to understand about power is that it's not the same thing as authority. When you go into a job on day one, you have a certain amount of authority which comes to you automatically as a result of your position, but your power is almost nil—power is the ability to influence other people and this is something you must earn."

Ennis adds that the ways to power will vary from one company to the next because the sort of thing that influences the key people in one company may cut no ice at all somewhere else. In a company that's heavily dependent on information, you might have to learn to sweet-talk the computer—if you can figure out how to get a particularly lucid kind of monthly report from the maze of data stored in its memory, you may wind up with more clout than the president. In another company, one with a heavy marketing orientation, for instance, you may have to learn how to hustle and promote yourself.

Sometimes this means you'll have to learn a whole new language. Frost says you should be alert to casual conversation and notice if people tend to talk in the language of, say, finance. If your company is planning to expand its factory, do people say the expansion will cost $3.5 million, or do they say it will trim first quarter earnings by 17 cents a share? Naturally, you should copy the corporate style on things like this. "Also," he says, "try to pick out the corporate buzzwords. Do you hear people talking about LRC (linear responsibility charting) or MBO (management by objectives)? These things may be part of what makes your company tick."

In most companies, Frost says, there's a particular story that the old hands always tell the newcomers, and you should listen for it because it can reveal a lot about the way your new colleagues see themselves: "In one company I heard of from a colleague, there's a story about a nine-day fortnight. Years ago, the company had a serious drop in sales and they had to cut back. So everyone, from the president to the janitors, took off one day without pay every two weeks. They worked nine days, instead of 10, each fortnight, and they kept this up for several months until sales picked up."

New employees of this company soon hear about "the nine-day fortnight" and, if they're alert, they realize that it's a story about how these people pulled together, toughed it out through the lean times, and went on to win. So this company may place an unusually high value on cooperation and teamwork.

"In another company, the key people like to pretend that they don't take their jobs very seriously and that they never really work hard, so they're always talking about how they take four-hour lunches. In fact, they do often take four-hour lunches, but they never talk about what happens after the lunch—they go back to the office and work until midnight." Obviously, if you want to get anywhere in this company, you should take care to project an easy-going kind of image and make it look as though you're having a good time.

Arnold Minors is an in-house consultant specializing in organizational development for Imperial Oil Ltd., in Toronto, and he points out that most companies also have corporate myths. "The corporate myth is usually in the form of a prohibition," he says. "There's something—it could be anything—which, according to everybody else in the company, you *must not do*." For example: never make a presentation to the boss without using a flip chart. If you question this prohibition, Minors says, you'll probably find that it's not written down anywhere, that no one in living memory has tried to do it, and that, quite obviously, no one knows what will happen if you try. So the prohibition is a myth and the odds are that if you go ahead and do the thing—illustrate your presentation with an overhead projector instead of a flip chart, for instance—you may be able to pick up a reputation as a bold innovator.

Minors has just joined Imperial, and he says he spent nearly all his time during his first few days getting around to meet key people. This isn't always as easy as it sounds because, as Ennis points out, the real power points in your company may be far removed from the top positions on the organizational chart. You need to find out who actually gets things done, not who holds the title: The reason your secretary is sitting there with no typewriter could be that you sent the requisition to the head of supply services, when everybody knows nothing happens unless you send the requisition directly to Betty in the stockroom.

In your company, there are probably a couple dozen behind-the-scenes people just like Betty. These are the real movers and shakers, and it's so critically important for you to learn how to spot them that, with help from the experts—Frost, Urquhart, Mealiea, Musten, Ennis and Minors—we've put together a check list to help you:

- Whose names come up most often in conversation?
- Who do people turn to when they need information or advice?

- Who sits on the greatest number of key committees (the committees that allocate resources, money, staff, equipment, computer time and so on)?
- Who draws up the agenda for policy meetings?
- Who seems to give the most direction to these meetings (not necessarily who talks the most)?
- Who seems to have the easiest access to the president?
- Whose offices have the best view?
- Who has first call on staff time?
- When the president sends out a policy memo, who gets it?
- Whose departments got the largest budget increases last year?

The people whose names turn up most frequently on this list are the people with clout and, naturally, you should try to develop especially good relationships with them: as the experts point out, power rubs off. You can answer most of these questions by simple observation, and Laird Mealiea, the Dalhousie professor, says you should be able to complete all these observations within the first several weeks, depending on the size and complexity of both the job and the organization. But some questions, such as "Who gives the most direction to policy meetings?", require some judgment. You should check your judgments on these questions with other people and, in fact, Urquhart suggests you should try to find a mentor to help you.

Basically, he says, you should try to find someone in a senior position in the company who is willing to take you under his wing and point you in the right direction. Ideally, your boss should perform this role, but often he can't—especially at first: "Your boss has to watch you closely for the first few months to decide whether you can handle the job," Urquhart explains, "so it's often difficult for him to give you as much support as you may need. Because of this, at least one company I know of has began to appoint a senior executive to act as a mentor for each new manager."

So you find a mentor, and you learn about all the power points and the company's language, and you hear its particular story and discover what its values are, is there anything else you ought to do? Says Mealiea: "Once you've gathered all this information, so that you know the environment, you can begin to become successful at the job. You can shove your concerns about politics more into the background and get on with doing the job."

Minors, the Imperial Oil consultant, offers a good example. On his first day on the job, Minors wore a navy blue, pinstriped suit, with vest. Minors was known as a fairly stylish dresser on his previous job, but he says he doesn't stand out at all now because everybody at Imperial seems to dress well. "I haven't seen polyester since I got here."

The surprising thing is that Minors thinks this may be a problem. "As a consultant in organizational development, my job is to help people adapt to change in the organization," he explains, "and to do this I think I have to be seen as a bit of an individual, someone who is able to question the corporate norms. So," he says, "I may be forced to buy a pair of jeans."

Female Entrepreneurs Outdo Men in Job Creation

Canadian Press

OTTAWA—From 1976 to 1994, women created their own jobs nearly 50 percent more often than men.

But their incomes from self-employment stood at just a little more than half of those earned by men in 1993, Statistics Canada said Tuesday.

By 1994, about 600,000 Canadian women were self-employed, a three-fold increase from 197,000 in 1976, the federal agency says in an article in Perspectives on Labor and Income.

The number of self-employed men during that period doubled to 1.2 million.

"Although men still dominate the self-employment sphere of the labor market, women are playing an ever-increasing role, particularly in industries such as retail trade, business services, and health and social services," said Gary Cohen, author of the article.

Much job growth recently has been attributed to the growth and evolution of small business, adds Cohen. The shift to a service economy is in part responsible for the expansion of self-employment.

"But it can also be linked to the business opportunities that become available as a result of downsizing and restructuring of large corporate enterprises, coupled with the adoption of policies promoting contracting out and privatization by government."

About 84 percent of working Canadians are paid employees, with a small proportion who are unpaid family workers in small businesses like mom-and-pop stores. The 15 percent who are self-employed own a business, a farm or a professional practice.

Average annual earnings of self-employed women were $18,400 in 1993, compared with $33,400 for self-employed men.

Cohen said the lower incomes could relate to a number of factors. Part-time work was more common among women entrepreneurs than among either paid female workers or male entrepreneurs.

Also, while 21 percent of women entrepreneurs worked 50 or more hours a week, the comparable figure for men was 44 percent.

Self-employed workers were much more likely to be married than paid workers, Cohen says. About 72 percent of self-employed women were married in 1994, compared with 79 percent for male entrepreneurs.

"It seems likely that the safety net provided by an employed spouse might facilitate or encourage risk-taking for some entrepreneurs," Cohen said.

COMPARISONS

Women: Number of self-employed women in 1994: 598,000, up from 197,000 in 1976.

Men: Number of self-employed men: 1.2 million, up from 600,000 in 1976.

Full time: Proportion of self-employed women working full time: Two-thirds. Proportion of self-employed men working full time: 90 per cent.

Earnings: Average annual earnings for self-employed women in 1993: $18,400.

To Get Ahead, Consider a Coach

Claudia H. Deutsch

A few years ago Alix Kane, then a self-described "lowly peon" in the Guardian Life Insurance Company of America's human resources department, was charged with helping to set up a training program. She and her boss asked Roger Flax, a behavior coach, to hold seminars on behavioral change.

While he was there, he gave Ms. Kane a bit of private coaching. For several days they engaged in role-playing. As a video camera whirred away, Ms. Kane pretended that Mr. Flax was a subordinate, a boss, even the audience for a presentation. Then came the moment of truth: They watched the tapes. "I thought of myself as assertive, but I came across as aggressive," Ms. Kane recalled. "I realized I was putting people off."

Mr. Flax, who runs Motivational Systems Inc., of West Orange, N.J., helped her modify that behavior. "He gave me an accurate picture of my strengths and weaknesses, and an ability to adjust my behavior," said Ms. Kane, who now is a senior human resources consultant at the Guardian. "I have no question that it is one reason I got ahead."

Ms. Kane is one of a growing number of mid- and high-level executives who have turned to coaches to fix personality or communications problems hindering their careers. In some cases they hired the coaches secretly, at their own expense. Far more often, bosses pay to help technically skilled subordinates develop interpersonal skills.

Many executives who work with coaches have already attended seminars in public speaking, assertiveness training or other behavior-changing areas, and found they were not enough. "Training programs and seminars are generic," said Allan L. Weisberg, vice president of human resources at Johnson & Johnson Hospital Services, who has taken coaching in communications techniques. "Coaching is customized assistance for specific problems, and that's more important."

Indeed, private coaching is on the upswing, and for good reason. During the 1980's, companies eliminated management layers, which means many executives need every tool available to compete for a dwindling number of senior jobs. Companies are also stressing teamwork, which gives people with good interpersonal skills an edge.

"For high-level people, lack of skill is not usually what gets in their way," said Bernard M. Kessler, a divisional president at Beam-Pines Inc., a New York-based human resources consulting firm. "Their styles are just inappropriate for team playing."

Not surprisingly, behavior coaching is a fundamental part of outplacement services. "We coach job hunters on how to speak to the person interviewing them in his or her style, and on how to gauge the cultural language of the organization they are applying to," said James C. Cabrera, president of the outplacement specialists Drake Beam Morin.

But increasingly, coaching is catching on with people who are employed, but just not moving ahead as fast as they—or their bosses—think they should.

One 38-year-old management consultant recently hired a coach to help him win the attention of his firm's partners. In 10 meetings, complete with videotaped role-playing sessions, he and the coach worked on making him appear more self confident.

It worked—he recently negotiated a hefty raise and bonus. "Before I asked for it, she and I role-played it, practically scripted the conversation, put the body language together with the content," he said. "I asked for the money with a level of self-confidence that communicated that I deserved it."

The consultant, who requested anonymity, hired the coach himself, at a fee he would not disclose. Far more typically, companies will pay, often as much as $10,000 per employee.

Nancy Hutchens, a New York behavior consultant, was recently called in by a large company to work with a talented 31-year-old financial executive. She had the woman fill out psychological questionnaires, and talked to her peers, subordinates and managers. "She was such a bad people manager that they were afraid to promote her," Ms. Hutchens said. "She thought she was acting 'professional,' but others saw her as aloof."

Ms. Hutchens drew up behavior-changing steps—asking peers to lunch, discussing hobbies with subordinates. Eventually, the behavior became automatic. "Her boss says there's been a real transformation," Ms. Hutchens said. And, yes, she got the promotion.

The Man in the Glass

Anonymous

When you have reached your goal
In the World of Sports,
And you have worked the Big game,
That day,
Just go to the mirror,
And look at yourself,
And see what the man has to say.
For it isn't your family or friends or coaches
Whose judgment upon you must pass;
The fellow whose verdict,
Counts in your life,
Is the one staring at you from the glass.
You may fool all the world down the avenue of years,
And get pats on your back as you pass,
But, your only reward will be remorse and regret,
If you have cheated the man in the glass.

Chapter

3

Leadership

What makes a person an effective leader? How does the leadership process work? Do leaders really make a difference to organizational outcomes and to the lives and fortunes of people in the organization? Nobody seems to have definitive answers to these questions. Indeed, many behavioral scientists, after observing or being part of the innumerable studies, debates, and theoretical formulations focused on leadership, have thrown up their hands and turned to other concepts such as organizational structure, technology, and so on in an effort to understand and to explain organizational life. Yet the fascination and indeed preoccupation with leadership remains for researchers and practitioners alike. The search for effective leaders goes on. Training courses abound that promise the development of improved leadership ability, and research money is still allocated to its study. Owners of unsuccessful organizations, such as losing sports teams, regularly blame the managers and replace them with "better leaders." People continue to attach their hopes as well as their frustrations to those chosen as leaders.

We do not have answers to the questions we are posing here. We do feel, however, that one approach to a better understanding of what leadership comprises is to examine what some students of leadership have said recently, based on their research on leaders in the field, and to take a close look at some leaders in action in their organizations. Leaders described here and in other chapters of this book appear to be dynamic, purposive, and durable individuals. Frequently leaders are manipulative, creating and interpreting realities and moving people into those realities to accomplish their goals. They often are admired and respected by their followers, but sometimes they are feared and hated by these same followers. Successful leaders typically are good listeners; sometimes they listen in order to work with those who tell them things, sometimes to take advantage of them, but always because they are relentless in their pursuit of information upon which to base their future ideas and actions.

We suspect that most people will have encountered, worked for, competed with or even acted as individuals having some or all of the leadership characteristics described in the selections in this chapter. In "What Makes a Good Leader?" Gary Wills provides a very insightful analysis of the importance of the followers and of shared goals to the successful experiences of leaders. He also provides a fascinating account of Franklin Roosevelt as a leader who was responsive to his followers and who was an accomplished manager of meaning. Linked to this notion on leaders as managers of meaning are the ideas expressed in the review by Warren Bennis of *Leading Minds*. We have included his review, "The Leader as Story Teller," in part because of the ideas and images he draws from this rich book, but also because of eloquence and value of his own depiction, in this review, of effective leadership. Bennis draws attention to the need for effective leaders to be "deep listeners" who come to understand the needs of their followers and who are then able to articulate them very well, drawing people together to pursue common goals. Christopher Knowlton's "Imagineer Eisner on Creative Leadership," as the title implies, emphasizes another characteristic, the importance of creativity in leaders. In a follow-up piece by Jeffrey Sonnenfeld, written almost six years after the Knowlton article ("For Prince Eisner, New Battles to Fight"), the emphasis is on transcending the very success that earlier creativity can bring for leaders and their organizations.

The last two selections in this chapter are both directed toward managing in a rapidly changing environment, an environment that it likely to exhibit increasingly the characteristics described and advocated in these selections. "Managing in the '90s: The Androgynous Manager," calls for a blend of traditional masculine and feminine roles and values, more expressive rather than instrumental behavior. The authors, Alice G. Sargent and Ronald J. Stupak, see this blend and the resulting managerial style as necessary both to accommodate the increasing presence of women in management and to deal with the increasing complexities of managing effectively. In "The Postheroic Leader" David L. Bradford and Allan R. Cohen emphasize the importance of a coaching style of management. This style, which is calculated to develop the capabilities of subordinates and engender teamwork, stands in contrast with the top-down management of the past.

What Makes a Good Leader?

Garry Wills

I had just turned seventeen, did not know Los Angeles, had never even driven in a big city. I had certainly never backed a trailer up to a loading dock. But my father gave me a map, marked a warehouse's location, and told me to deliver a refrigerator there. I would have to get someone to help me unload it when I arrived. It was very clever of him. I knew what he was doing. But I complied anyway.

I had a chip on my shoulder, since my father left my mother to marry a (much younger) Hollywood model. While I was in California for a high school contest, he asked me to work at his nascent business for the rest of the summer. But for that offer I would not have stayed. He knew that the way to recruit a resisting son-employee was to give me independence—not only in things like deliveries but in sales and the purchasing of household equipment. If I failed, that might break down my resistance. If I didn't, pride in the work might renew a bond that had been broken. Paradoxically, by giving me independence he got me to do his will. That is the way leadership works—reciprocally engaging two wills, one leading (often in disguised ways), the other following (often while resisting). Leadership is always a struggle, often a feud.

Why, after all, should one person do another person's will? The answer that used to be given is simple: the leader is a superior person, to whom inferiors should submit. But modern democracies are as unsympathetic to this scheme as I was to the authority of my father. Patriarchal society, it is true, was rooted in a radical inequality between leaders and followers. Even ancient Athens, the first Western democracy, submitted to "the best man," according to Thucydides.

> *[Pericles], a man clearly above corruption, was enabled, by the respect others had for him and his own wise policy, to hold the multitude in a voluntary restraint. He led them, not they him; and since he did not win his power on compromising terms, he could say not only what pleased others but what displeased them, relying on their respect.*

Some still subscribe to that notion of leadership. How often have we heard that we lack great leaders now—the clearly virtuous kind, men like George Washington and Abraham Lincoln? The implication is that we could become great again with a great man to guide us. We would not mind submitting to anyone *that* good. (Of others we continue to be wary.)

I shall be arguing here that the Periclean type of leadership occurs rarely in history, if at all. Scholars have questioned Thucydides' description of Pericles' position—Athenians seemed quicker than most to ostracize leaders who thought themselves above the people. Why *should* people immolate their own needs and desires to conform to the vision of some superior being? That has happened in some theocratic societies, but then people were obeying God in his representative, and it was their belief in God's will that constrained them.

The Atlantic Monthly.

In a democracy, supposedly, the leader does not pronounce God's will *to* the people but carries out what is decided *by* the people. Some might object that in that case the leader is mainly a follower—he or she does what the community says when it speaks through elections, through polls, through constituent pressure. Because they are willing to compromise their principles, such leaders, unlike the Pericles of Thucydides, cannot displease their followers. They are bribed, if not with money then with acceptance, or office, or ego satisfaction.

We seem stuck, then, between two unacceptable alternatives—the leader who dictates to others and the one who truckles to them. If leaders dictate, by what authority do they take away people's right to direct their own lives? If they truckle, who needs or respects such weathervanes?

Most of the how-to manuals on leadership assume one or the other of these models—or, inconsistently, both. The superior-person model says the leader must become worthy of being followed—more disciplined than others, more committed, better organized. This sends aspiring leaders to the mirror, to strike firm-jawed poses and to cultivate self-confidence and a refusal to hedge.

Or the leader is taught to be ingratiating. This is the salesmanship, or Dale Carnegie, approach—how to win friends and influence people. It treats followers as customers who "buy" the leader's views after these have been consumer-tested and tailored for maximum acceptance.

The followers are, in this literature, a hazy and not very estimable lot—people to be dominated or served, mesmerized or flattered. We have thousands of books on leadership, none on followership. I have heard college presidents tell their student bodies that schools are meant to train leaders. I have never heard anyone profess to train followers. The ideal seems to be a world in which everyone is a leader—but who would be left for them to be leading?

Talk of the nobility of leaders, the need for them, and our reliance on them raises the clear suspicion that followers are *not* so noble. In that view leaders rise only by sinking others to subordinate roles. Leaders have a vision. Followers respond to it. Leaders organize a plan. Followers get sorted out to fit the plan. Leaders have willpower. Followers let that will replace their own.

We have long lists of the leader's requisites—determination, focus, a clear goal, a sense of priorities, and so on. We easily forget the first and all-encompassing need—followers. Without them, the best ideas, the strongest will, the most wonderful smile, have no effect. When Shakespeare's Welsh seer, Owen Glendower, boasts, "I can call spirits from the vasty deep," Hotspur deflates him with the commonsense answer, "Why, so can I, or so can any man. But will they come when you do call for them?" It is not the noblest call that gets answered but the answerable call.

LEADING BY LISTENING

Abraham Lincoln did not have the highest vision of human equality in his day. Many abolitionists went further than he did in recognizing the moral claims of slaves to freedom and recognition of their human dignity. Lincoln had limited political goals, and he was willing to compromise even those. He knew that no one who espoused full equality for blacks could be elected in or from Illinois—so he unequivocally renounced that position:

> *I am not nor ever have been in favor of bringing about in any way the social and political equality of the white and black races. . . . I am not nor ever have been in favor of making voters or jurors of negroes, nor of qualifying them to hold office, nor of intermarrying with white people; and I will say in addition to this that there is a physical difference between the white and black races which I believe will forever forbid the two races living together on terms of social and political equality. And in as much as they cannot so live, while they do remain together there must be the position of superior and inferior, and I as much as any other man am in favor of having the superior position assigned to the white race.*

But for that pledge Lincoln had no hope of winning office. The followers were setting the terms of acceptance for their leader. He could not issue calls they were unprepared to hear. (He *could* do it, of course—as Owen Glendower can shout summonses down into the deep. But it would be a waste of time.)

This Lincoln has disappointed people who think followers should submit to a leader's superior vision—those who want the leader to be active and the followers passive. Lincoln's leadership was a matter of mutually determinative activity, on the part of the leader and the followers. Followers have a say in what they are being led to. A leader who neglects that fact soon finds himself without followers. To sound a certain trumpet does not mean just trumpeting one's own certitudes. It means sounding a specific call to specific people capable of response.

Does this remove or reduce the heroic note in Lincoln's leadership—as if he were only *allowed* to lead, by followers who could refuse to respond? Well, what is the alternative—people who cannot refuse to follow? If that were the case, the leader would be marshaling automatons, not voluntary respondents.

It is odd that resentment should be felt toward the demands of followers when the limiting power of circumstance is so readily accepted. Even the most ardent hero-worshippers of Winston Churchill admit that he needed an occasion for the exercise of his skills. But for the Second World War we would never have known how he could rally English spirit. Yet followers conform more closely to a leader than a leader does to external circumstances. The leader can have both the skill for his or her role and the occasion for its use and still lack followers who will respond to the initiative or the moment.

So much for the idea that a leader's skills can be applied to all occasions, that they can be taught outside a historical context or learned as a "secret" of the control of every situation. A leader whose qualities do not match those of potential followers is simply irrelevant: the world is not playing his or her game. My favorite example of this is the leadership of Syrian holy men in the fifth century A.D. Those men, who made policy for whole communities, were revered for their self-ravaging austerity. The man who had starved himself most spectacularly was thought the best equipped to advise pious consultants. So delegations went to consult Simeon the "Stylite" ("pillar-man"), perched in his midair hermitage. Leadership was conditioned entirely by the attitudes of contemporary followership. Who would now write a manual called *The Leadership Secrets of Simeon Stylites*, telling people to starve and whip and torture themselves into command positions?

Closer to our time, Thomas Jefferson thought that the French Revolution had been less successful than the American one, not because the French lacked leaders but because they lacked discerning followers. A corrupt people is not responsive to virtuous leadership. The French spirit had been sapped, he claimed, by superstition (Catholicism) and despotism (monarchy). Napoleon, to retain the people's allegiance, had to revert to both, calling on the Pope to crown him Emperor.

It may seem that the Lincoln example has moved us too far from the Periclean "best man" toward the Dale Carnegie accommodator. If the leader is just an expediter of what other people want, a resource for their use, the people are not being *led* but *serviced*.

But Lincoln had no clear expression of popular will to implement. He had to elicit the program he wanted to serve, and that always involves affecting the views one is consulting. Even pollsters, seeking to understand what is on people's minds, affect the outcome by their mode of questioning. In Lincoln's constituency were some abolitionists, many defenders of slavery, and many more who wanted to avoid facing the issue of slavery. Unlike the abolitionists, who were leaders of a small elite putting pressure on the government from outside, Lincoln had to forge a combination of voters who would join him in at least minimal disapproval of slavery. He had to convince some people that it was in their own interest not to let the problem fester—he told them that they could not afford to take Stephen Douglas's hands-off attitude.

Many voters resisted Lincoln—as I did my father in the summer of 1951. Lincoln deferred to some of their prejudices—left them independent in that sense—in order to win agreement on a policy of at least some hope for ultimate manumission. He argued in terms of his listeners' own views. They celebrated the Declaration of Independence, with its claim that all men are created equal. How could they stay true to their political identity, based on the Declaration if they did not at some level oppose slavery? By keeping this option open for gradual approximation, Lincoln was able at a later period to take more-direct action. He temporized not to evade the problem but to prevent its evasion. G. K. Chesterton's *What I Saw in America* perfectly captured the delicacy of his operation:

> He loved to repeat that slavery intolerable while he tolerated it, and to prove that something ought to be done while it was impossible to do it. . . . But for all the this inconsistent consistency beat the politicians at their own game, and this abstracted logic proved most practical of all. For, when the chance did come to do something, there was no doubt about the thing to be done. The thunderbolt fell from the clear heights of heaven.

In order to know just how far he could go at any moment, Lincoln had to understand the mixture of motives in his fellow citizens, the counterbalancing intensities with which they held different positions, and in what directions those positions were changing moment by moment. The leader needs to understand followers far more than they need to understand him. This is the time-consuming aspect of leadership. It explains why great thinkers and artists are rarely leaders of others, as opposed to influences on them. The scientist absorbed in the solution to a problem does not have the energy or patience to understand the needs of a number of other people who might be marshaled to deal with the problem. That is something the popularizer of the great man's thought usually does. More important, the pure scientist does not tailor his view of (say) the atom to whatever audience he hopes to influence, as Lincoln trimmed and hedged on slavery in order to make people take small steps toward facing the problem.

My father was a natural leader who acted in small arenas. Even as a child, I thought it childish of him to want to get his way all the time. I did not notice then that he got his way by entering into the minds of others and finding something there that would respond to his attentions—as, on a vastly different scale, Lincoln found a grudging acceptance of the Declaration's pledge on which to build his strategy of emancipation. My father's tactics were different with me, with my sister, with the golfing friends I observed him with while caddying. There is something selfless in the very selfishness of leaders—they must see things as the followers see them in order to recruit those followers.

If the followers get marshaled toward action by a leader, the leader need not be loved or admired, though that can help. I had no great admiration for my father when I found myself responding to his initiatives. Conversely, one can admire or love people who are not, by virtue of that love, leaders.

AN INDISPENSABLE ELEMENT: A SHARED GOAL

Imagine a meeting called to consider a course of action—let us say, to mount a protest against an employer whose hiring and promotion practices discriminate against women. A speaker rises who is stunningly eloquent. Listener A knows and admires the speaker, would go anywhere to hear her speak, hopes to emulate her eloquence in his own way; but he does not care about the issue, and the speech does not bring him any closer to caring. Listener B, on the contrary, has never met the speaker, does not particularly like her, is disposed to resent the employer but had no hope of finding allies to resist him, and is now heartened to act in conjunction with others responding to the speaker. Who is the follower here? If, as seems certain, it is Listener B, then admiration, imitation, and affection are not necessary to followership. Agreement on a *goal* is necessary.

So far I have been discussing just two things—leaders and followers. That is better, at least, than discussions dealing with only one thing—leaders. But the discussions cannot get far without the goal. This is not something added on to the other two. It is the reason for the existence of the other two. It is also the equalizer between leader and followers. The followers do not submit to the person of the leader. They join him or her in pursuit of the goal. My father and I were working together for the success of his new business. Of course, he had separate motives for wanting me there, and I had motives for not wanting to be there; by definition, we could not share those motives. It was the thing we could share that created the possibility of leadership.

It is time for a definition: the leader is one who mobilizes others toward a goal shared by leader and followers. In that brief definition all three elements are present, and indispensable. Most literature on leadership is unitarian. But life is trinitarian. One-legged and two-legged chairs do not, of themselves, stand. Leaders, followers, and goals make up the three equally necessary supports for leadership.

The goal must be shared, no matter how many other motives are present that are not shared. Go back to the meeting that called for a protest against employer discrimination. The speaker may have had many ancillary motives for speaking—to show off her rhetorical style, to impress a sexual partner in the audience, to launch a larger political career. Her listeners would surely have many motives—some to improve their prospects with the employer or their standing among fellow workers. But the followers become followers only insofar as they agree with the speaker on a plan of action against the employer.

This plan is cast in terms of justice, though it is easy to think that this is only a rationale for the various motives, some shared, some not. Each is in this to get something different. David Hume, the eighteenth-century philosopher, said that people obey others for their own advantage; this writhing of various wormlike urges for advantage is far from the picture of idealistic leaders and docile followers.

Yet Hume, perceptive as he was, knew that people follow most reliably when they are convinced that what they are doing is right. He knew the utility of that belief. If, at the meeting to discuss discrimination, only those who would benefit directly from the protest were to join the speaker, that would limit the followership from the outset. And that small number would always be fraying away. The boss could buy off dissent by special favors to a few of the activists, or threats to the weakhearted. Once a given person got what she wanted, she would have no future motive for supporting her sisters. Private advantage shifts constantly and is a poor basis for public action. That is why Lincoln based his policy on the moral claim of the Declaration of Independence. Some thought that he did not go far enough, others that he went too far; but the moral ground of the Declaration was both broad and narrow enough to accommodate many positions while remaining fixed itself.

Lincoln had to persuade voters. He could not force them. Where coercion exists, leadership becomes unnecessary or impossible to the extent of coercion's existence. Loose use of the word "lead" can mislead. We talk of a policeman leading his prisoner to jail. But the policeman is not a leader in our sense—he is a captor. Though he is mobilizing another toward a goal, it is not a goal they share. The prisoner's goal is to get as far away from the prison as possible.

A slave master buying labor can "lead" slaves to his plantation, but that does not make him their leader. He is their owner. If I had worked for my father only because I needed the money and could get it nowhere else, I would not have been a follower, just an employee. Coercion is not leadership any more than mesmerism is. Followers cannot be automatons. The totalitarian jailer who drugs a prisoner into confession of a crime has not led him to some shared view of reality.

Nor does a leader just vaguely affect others. He or she takes others toward the object of their joint quest. That object defines the kind of leadership at issue. Different types of leaders should be distinguished more by their goals than by the personality of the leader (the most common practice). The crisis of mere subsistence on a life raft calls for one type of leader, democratic stability for another, revolutionary activity for still a third. Lincoln's compromise and flexibility were appropriate for *his* kind of leadership.

A GREAT LEADER IN OUR CENTURY: FDR

We like to believe that in some golden age there were leaders of such recognized integrity that the American people simply accepted their determinations, issued from on high. But even George Washington, in the deferential eighteenth century, was solicitous enough of public opinion to be called cowardly by some of his critics.

Only one twentieth-century president is consistently rated among the top three or four chief executives of our history—Franklin Delano Roosevelt. He has been taken as a model of leadership by many authors, notably Richard Neustadt, who wrote, in *Presidential Power*, the most influential modern book on that subject,

No President in this century has had a sharper sense of personal power, a sense of what it is and where it comes from; none has had more hunger for it, few have had more use for it, and only one or two could match his faith in his own competence to use it. Perception and desire and self-confidence, combined, produced their own reward. No modern President has been more nearly the master in the White House.

The emphasis is all on the leader's internal qualities—mainly his confidence, ambition, and determination: "Roosevelt had a love affair with power": "Roosevelt's methods were the product of his insights, his incentives, and his confidence." Neustadt describing Roosevelt sounds like Thucydides describing Pericles—here, at last, is a ruler who can, by sheer mastery, impose his views on the multitude.

But another school of historians—including the eminent Richard Hofstadter—has described Roosevelt as one who veered with shifting popular responses. "He was content in large measure to follow public opinion," Hofstadter wrote in *The American Political Tradition*, because he was "a public instrument of the most delicate receptivity." Roosevelt proved that "flexibility was both his strength and his weakness." The result was great energy employed in "harum-scarum" ways: "Hoover had lacked motion: Roosevelt lacked direction."

Some more-recent treatments of Roosevelt, notably Kenneth Davis's multivolume biography, have been more hostile than Hofstadter was in describing Roosevelt's subservience to public opinion. And, in fact, FDR's record seems hard to reconcile with the Neustadt picture of firm control. In New York politics Roosevelt first opposed and then cooperated with the Tammany political machine. He supported and then opposed Al Smith; promoted and then abandoned the League of Nations—"the first Democratic candidate [for president] who explicitly repudiated the League," Hofstadter writes. He fluttered back and forth on prohibition. As president he reversed himself on the balanced budget, on business consolidation, on farm subsidies, on labor protection, on aid to Europe. Friends as well as foes, from both the right and the left, noticed that the probusiness "First New Deal" of 1933 was profoundly at odds with the pro-labor "Second New Deal" of 1935—and many ascribed the change to Roosevelt's fear that the populist Huey Long was taking away some of his support on the left.

Which is it to be—the masterful Roosevelt of Neustadt or the scrambler after popular acceptance of Hofstadter? Can the two be reconciled? Not if we keep as our ideal the Periclean man, above the need for popular acceptance. If Roosevelt had power, it came precisely from his responsiveness to public opinion. And that came, indirectly, from the crushing blow that took from him, at the age of thirty-nine, all future use of his legs.

FORCED MATURATION

Students of Roosevelt are agreed that the polio attack of 1921 profoundly changed him. He might have become president without having had to surmount that obstacle, but it is unlikely that he would have been a great, or even a good, president. Before he was crippled, Roosevelt had been a genial glad-hander, an acceptable politician considered lightweight by the pros (men like Al Smith)—too anxious to please, clumsily ingratiating. Even in pictures from that time he seems a dithery Bertie Wooster in his straw boater. His caustic cousin, Alice Roosevelt Longworth, called him a sissy and a mama's boy. As the sole child of the frosty patrician Sara Delano Roosevelt, he had been sheltered from hardship, cushioned in privilege.

At the least, then, the struggle to walk again—always defeated but never quite given up—toughened Roosevelt. His legs withered away, but from the waist up the willowy youth became a barrel-chested man able to swing the useless parts of his body around to give an artful impression of overall strength. Some say that the suffering deepened his sympathy with others who were afflicted—and that was certainly true among his fellow "polios" (their favored term) at Warm Springs, the Georgia clinic Roosevelt established for his and others' use. He had a comradeship in that setting never experienced elsewhere: with its patients he shared his otherwise lonely fight to achieve mobility.

While granting all this, we should resist the sentimentalism that creeps into much of the discussion about Roosevelt's polio. Some talk as if polio sealed him with a redemptive mark of suffering. The Byronic hero is marked by deformity or defect in a way that drives him from the comforts of the prosaic world into the enforced solitude where genius creates an entirely new human vision, brilliant even if one-sided. The artist suffers, but he gains from his suffering, because it severs him from the herd.

Roosevelt's polio did not separate him from others but drove him out toward them—and not to crave sympathy. He would accept no pity. The shrewdest judges of polio's impact on Roosevelt are two authors who themselves suffered from polio— Geoffrey Ward and Hugh Gregory Gallagher. There is no sentimentality in these men's views of Roosevelt. They both see that what polio did was to make him preternaturally aware of others' perceptions of him. This increased his determination to control those perceptions. People were made uncomfortable by his discomfort. He needed to distract them, to direct their attention to subjects he preferred, to keep them amused, impressed, entertained. That meant he had to perfect a deceptive ease, a casual aplomb, in the midst of acute distress. He became a consummate actor.

For Roosevelt to "walk" in public, he had to balance on his locked braces and pretend to be using his legs while he was actually shifting back and forth from his cane to the man (often one of his sons) whose arm he gripped on the other side. The strain always left his suit soaked with sweat, the hand on the cane shaking violently from the effort, the son's arm bruised where his fingers had dug in. And all the while he would be smiling, keeping up pleasant banter, pretending to enjoy himself.

The danger was always there. His sticklike legs in their metal binding could snap easily if he fell. It was almost impossible for one person to raise him, with his heavy braces locking the legs in an unbending position. When he fell in the lobby of his office building, his chauffeur could not pull him up off the slippery floor, and Roosevelt had to recruit two other men in the lobby for help. The surprised men were the recipients of a flow of jokes and chatter that made it seem like Roosevelt was treating the episode as a particularly funny game. When they got him propped up again, Ward writes, "still smiling and laughing, but with his knuckles white on the handles of his crutches and his legs alarmingly splayed for balance, he said 'Let's go!' and started for the elevators once more." Roosevelt rarely fell in public, partly because he gave up the attempt at public "walking" as the years went by. But each time he did fall, it was a searing crisis to those few who understood how truly helpless he became.

The iron control of his own reactions, necessary for handling such a crisis, was something Roosevelt had achieved by the time he ran for president. While he was sitting in an open car in Miami in 1933, a would-be assassin, standing within twelve yards of the president, fired at him five times. Roosevelt stared at the man, unflinching, while Mayor Anton Cermak, of Chicago, who had been standing next to the car, fell, mortally wounded. The Secret Service tried to move the car away, but Roosevelt stopped it and had Cermak put into the seat with him. He then ordered the car to the hospital and tried to revive the dying Cermak on the way. FDR's calm command of the situation came from more than a decade of sitting in judgment on the passing scene, ready to make the proper moves to keep people from panicking at the sight of his helplessness. Franklin Roosevelt had always wanted to imitate his admired cousin Theodore and had usually failed—at Harvard, as a warrior, as a writer. But that day he displayed the same sangfroid Teddy had when an assailant wounded him during the 1912 campaign; TR gave his scheduled speech anyway, though blood was oozing from his shirt.

In less dramatic daily ordeals FDR kept control of others' reactions when he was lifted in or out of cars, carried up stairs, or straightened up again when he had tilted over in a seat without arms. He did this by telling jokes, or locking their eyes to his, or teasing others, making them think of their own vulnerability—as one polio has called it, "walking on your tongue."

When he had no one to carry him upstairs, he sat on the bottom step, reached backward to the higher step, and pulled up his body with his powerful arms, engaging in distracting talk as if he were not doing anything extraordinary. Someone had to be with him always. He was uneasy when no one could respond to a sudden threat—an accident or the need for help to the bathroom. He was especially worried at the thought of a fire in his house or on his boat. Despite this extreme dependence on those around him—he was carried to and from bed, lifted into and out of his bath, clothed by others—Roosevelt kept up a tiring regime of public activity, during which he looked only slightly inconvenienced. This "splendid deception," as Gallagher calls it, involved careful stage-management of all his appearances, ruthless suppression of any camera in his vicinity until he had settled into the pose he wanted to strike, and carefully constructed ramps, bathrooms, and rails wherever he was going to appear.

When he could not get out, he drew others in around him, maintaining a crowded schedule of interviews, entertainments, meetings with members of Congress, with the press, with celebrities. His press conferences were frequent, two a week or more, well staged to seem informal. The reporters clustered around Roosevelt's desk, so he did not have to move. They could not quote him directly, but that made the banter on both sides freer and more revealing. Roosevelt probed and learned from them while showing his dexterity in avoiding their attempts to learn anything he was not ready to say. His aides marveled at the bits of information he had managed to acquire. He liked to keep some mystery about his sources: it was another way of demonstrating that he was in touch.

To avoid podiums, where he might fall, Roosevelt invented the "fireside chat." Again, he could sit at his desk while the world came to him. For people used to seeing political oratory on newsreels or hearing speeches broadcast from auditorium, where the acoustics and the size of the audience made for slow and pompous delivery, Roosevelt's seated-in-the-same-room-with-you style gave a shock of intimacy. Cousin Theodore had been a tub-thumper. Woodrow Wilson was mellifluous but exalted. Herbert Hoover was pinched and pedantic. People felt that Roosevelt, unlike his predecessors, was confiding in them and consulting them. The man who seemed immobilized had ghosted himself into their front rooms.

INVALUABLE HISTRIONICS

Some might think it an insult to call a president an actor. It was certainly intended that way when Ronald Reagan was dismissed as "just an actor." But all politicians need some of an actor's abilities. They must feign welcome to unwanted constituents' attentions, cooperate with despised party allies, wax indignant at politically chosen targets. This is the work not of inferior politicians but of the masters. The three presidents normally at the top of historians' lists—Washington, Lincoln, and Roosevelt—all had strong histrionic instincts. Roosevelt could not go to the theater—or to church, for that matter—because of his logistical problems; but Washington and Lincoln were both avid theatergoers. Washington's favorite literature was Joseph Addison's play *Cato*. Lincoln's was *Macbeth*. Lincoln read aloud the speeches of Shakespeare to anyone who would listen to him.

Washington was a master of the telling theatrical gesture. Even his Christmas Eve assault on Trenton was more a *côup de theâtre* than a strategically meaningful step. His various resignations of office were choreographed. When he could not count on a response from his audience, he hesitated to act. Lincoln knew the impact of his haunting features and loved to pose for photographers. A great storyteller, he could milk a line for laughs as surely as Roosevelt did in his Fala speech—the one that feigned shock that enemies would think his Scottish terrier a wastrel.

An actor is not, as such, a leader. The appreciation of an audience is not motion toward some goal shared with the actor. Fans are not followers. But a popular leader must use some tricks from the actor's stock. Above all, a good leader must know what is appealing to followers and what risks losing that appeal. Roosevelt had that sensitivity to others' reactions, developed to an almost morbid degree, because of his awareness of their attention to his physical condition. He had to know, to a centimeter, the line that divides pity from compassion, condescension from cooperation, mere sympathy from real support. The French philosopher Denis Diderot said that the best actor sits inside his own performance as a cool spectator of the effects he is creating in an audience. Such actors will sense if an audience thinks they are playing a scene too broad and will rein in the effects. The actor is working at several levels of awareness—fiery in the character's emotions, icy in the adjustment of those emotions to the intended effects on onlookers. Feigned tears must be used to elicit real tears.

Roosevelt's manipulation of others' reactions to his own body perfectly prepared him to be an actor in Diderot's sense. He could change pity into admiration. He could keep intruders into his privacy off guard by a teasing challenge that made them look to their own defenses, too flustered to advert to his problem. He could put people at their ease or deliberately cause discomfort. He controlled people by the use of nicknames (a familiarity not to be reciprocated).

As president, Roosevelt ministered to a sick nation. Economic cures were being proposed on all sides, and Roosevelt was ready to try any of them, often in bewildering succession. He was criticized as an ignoramus because he hesitated between competing promises of cure. But he knew that the soul needed healing first, and the brand of confidence he had instilled in the patients at Warm Springs was the most measurable gift Roosevelt gave to the nation during the Depression. He understood the importance of psychology—that people have to have the courage to keep seeking a cure, no matter what the cure is. America had lost its will to recover, and Roosevelt was certain that regaining it was the first order of business.

In 1932–1933 a long interregnum between the election and a March inauguration was still constitutionally mandated. Poor Herbert Hoover had to lead the country as a lame duck for a third of a year. He tried to recruit Roosevelt's support for measures that FDR was in fact considering and would finally himself take—bank regulation, manipulation of farm prices, monetary control. But Roosevelt would not be drawn into these plans, sound as they might have been. He realized that the nation needed a clean break, a slap in the face, a sense that the past was being repudiated. It took cool nerves to watch the country slide farther into trouble, knowing he would have to pick up the pieces. But Roosevelt was confident to the point of foolhardiness in all his ways, and that was the thing called for in this desperate situation. When he took office, he closed the banks, imposed regulations far-reaching enough to be called (in time) unconstitutional, and filled the nation with a bustle of make-work, fake work, and real work. The patient was resuscitated, up off the bed, moving about. The perception of control and of direction returned to a nation that had felt itself drifting in a windless sea.

From then on Roosevelt would make many deals with the devil in order to keep his hold on those who might respond to his call. Since Congress was controlled by southern chairmen of the indispensable committees, he paid a price for their support—sabotaging anti-lynching planks in the Democratic platforms, putting off civil-rights action except in the public-works programs. The right wing yelled at him the loudest, but the left may have been more deeply disappointed. Social Security was a boon to the worker, but in a regressive form, making the poor pay disproportionally to get what the government was also giving (as a payoff) to the better-off. When Franco took over Spain in a right-wing coup, Roosevelt gave the legitimate government little help, for fear of losing the Catholic component in his Democratic coalition. When dictators came to power in Europe, Roosevelt placated isolationists, not to win their support but to neutralize them for a while. First things first. The audience had to be worked with many strings, and the strings must be kept from tangling.

Those who wanted ideological consistency, or even policy coherence, were rightly exasperated with Roosevelt. He switched economic plans as often as he changed treatments for his polio, and often with as little improvement. Some of his early "brain trust" advisers went off in disgust at his unwillingness to stick by their advice when the polls turned adverse.

The Depression was not really overcome by the New Deal. Its effects were ameliorated, its burdens shifted, its ravages cloaked over, and that kept people going until the world itself was changed drastically by war. The President could not do everything. But Roosevelt stiffened people's spines to face hardship, even when the hardship did not go away. He knew a good deal about spines. When he wheeled himself up to a war casualty who had had to cut himself free of wreckage by amputating his own legs, Roosevelt said, "I understand you are something of a surgeon. I'm not a bad orthopedist, myself." Legs spoke to legs. The public did not know the extent of Roosevelt's impairment; but it knew enough to feel that if he could go on as he did, gaily despite loss, so might they.

So, to go back to the alternative posed by Neustadt and Hofstadter, which is it to be? The dominating figure or the accommodating one? I am not sure that choice would have made sense to the patients at Warm Springs. They were certainly dominated by Roosevelt; but they seem to have felt his domination as their own liberation. He did not prevail by ignoring their demands. If anything, he anticipated those demands and tailored whatever he said or did to acknowledge and respect and further them. The demands were not all consistent, or sensible, or even constructive in the long run. But Roosevelt was quick to respond to them, ruling none out as beneath his notice or contrary to his program. He prevailed by service to them.

Which does not mean, by a long shot, that he was humble. Mother Teresa never had a potential rival in him. He wanted his own way. But he knew that the way to get it was not to impose it. And by the time he got his way, it turned out to be the way of many followers as well. He could win only by letting them win. Great leadership is not a zero-sum game. What is given to the leader is not taken from the follower. Both get by giving. That is the mystery of great popular leaders like Washington, Lincoln, and Roosevelt.

The final mystery is that this physically impaired man made his physical characteristics so comforting to a nation facing hardship and war. People drew strength from the very cock of his head, the angle of his cigarette holder, the trademark grin that was a semaphore of hope.

ANTI-TYPE: ADLAI STEVENSON

In 1952 liberals who grew up admiring Franklin Roosevelt thought that they had found his rightful successor in Adlai Stevenson. They hoped that he would go to Washington from the governor's mansion in Springfield as Roosevelt had gone from the governor's mansion in Albany. Stevenson was from families as socially prominent in Illinois as the Delanos and the Roosevelts were in New York. Roosevelt had grown up with the example of his cousin Theodore always vivid in his mind. Stevenson's grandfather was a model just as inspiring to him—Adlai E. Stevenson, for whom he was named, had been Grover Cleveland's vice president. Stevenson's father served in Washington with Secretary of the Navy Josephus Daniels, to whom FDR was undersecretary.

The similarities between Roosevelt and Stevenson are eerie—though not all of them were known during Stevenson's lifetime. Both men were raised by domineering mothers who followed their pampered sons to college. Sara Delano Roosevelt moved to Boston during the winters when Franklin was a junior and senior at Harvard. Helen Davis Stevenson rented a house in Princeton, near where Adlai was going to classes. Both Roosevelt and Stevenson were poor students who had trouble getting through law school—Roosevelt never did get his degree at Columbia, and Stevenson flunked out of Harvard Law.

Both men wed socially proper wives from whom they were estranged by the time they had national careers—the Roosevelts ceased having conjugal relations after Eleanor discovered Franklin's love affair with Lucy Mercer, and the Stevensons were divorced.

Each man depended on the ministrations of a devout female acolyte—Missy Le Hand was Roosevelt's indispensable social secretary–nurse–companion as he made his come-back from polio, and Dorothy Fosdick, of the State Department, helped assemble Stevenson's foreign-policy brain trust for the 1952 presidential campaign.

Though neither was much of a reader or writer, Roosevelt and Stevenson enjoyed the company of people who were and delivered the speeches they wrote with great style. Nei-ther was an ideologue, but both were progressive enough to be praised and damned as left-liberals. They were moderate reformers in their terms as governor, though both had been elected with the help of strong state machines—Tammany in New York and Jacob Arvey's Chicago organization in Illinois. (Arvey ordered Stevenson to run for governor after Stevenson had decided to run for senator.)

The liberals of 1952 were *almost* right—they almost got another Roosevelt. Stevenson was Roosevelt without the polio—and that made all the difference. He re-mained the dilettante and ladies' man all his life. Roosevelt was a mama's boy who was forced to grow up. Stevenson had noble ideals—as had the young Roosevelt, for that matter. But Stevenson felt that the way to implement them was to present himself as a thoughtful idealist and wait for the world to flock to him. He considered it beneath him, or wrong, to scramble out among the people and ask what *they* wanted. Roosevelt grasped voters to him. Stevenson shied from them. Some thought him too pure to de-sire power, though he showed ambition when it mattered. Arthur Schlesinger Jr., who wrote speeches for Stevenson and worked for him in the 1952 and 1956 campaigns, thought that Stevenson might feel guilty about wielding power because he had acci-dentally killed a playmate when he wielded the power of a gun in his boyhood.

Stevenson believed in the Periclean ideal of leadership—that a man should be above the pressures of the multitude, telling people uncomfortable truths. His admiring brain trust found this charming at first, but concluded that he overdid it. As Schlesinger said, "It was a brilliant device to establish Stevenson's identity. As a permanent device, it was an error." Stevenson kept some distance from the crowd by making "inside" comments that played to the intellectuals. This, too, got on the nerves of his entourage. Carl McGowan, the head of Stevenson's staff, had these rueful memories: "His wit was not as great as it was popularly assumed to be, but it was not as damaging as was believed, either. He always had a risky sense of humor—some of it was not funny at all."

Liberal intellectuals stayed true to Stevenson in the 1950s, despite misgivings, be-cause they were horrified by what they took to be the anti-intellectual alternative of Dwight D. Eisenhower. It was literally inconceivable to these people that a rational electorate would prefer Ike to Adlai—which shows how far out of touch they were with the American people and just how far Stevenson was from Roosevelt. Louis Howe, Roosevelt's great admirer-manager, would have had no trouble understanding Ike's appeal.

Not only did Stevenson think voters should come to him instead of he to them, but once in office he thought the power of the office would be self-enacting. He did not realize that it is only what one *makes of* the office that creates real followers. In-stalled as the U.S. ambassador to the United Nations, he clung to that position, with the perks he relished (parties every night, a delightful "harem" of adoring ladies), though his liberal friends repeatedly urged him to resign rather than keep on defending American actions in Cuba, Latin America, and Indochina.

When Stevenson found that he had presented false information to the world in the aftermath of his government's invasion of Cuba (at the Bay of Pigs), he was indignant that his own president had lied to him. He went to the New York apartment of his friend Alistair Cooke, the British journalist, and poured out his trouble over a drink. Cooke tried to comfort him with the thought that men who resigned from intolerable situations have made their contribution to history. Stevenson was shocked at the mere suggestion he would resign. That would be burning his boats, Cooke says he replied. Even then Stevenson did not grasp his real position with John F. Kennedy, who treated him like a patsy because he considered him one.

Later, when the left broke from Lyndon Johnson's foreign policy, Stevenson doggedly defended it. The journalist Murray Kempton, writing in the name of former Stevenson supporters, sent a private letter to Adlai begging him to resign. The government was telling lies. "The need now is for commoners, for men out of office. . . . I know that I am asking you to do one more messy and exhausting thing; but could you come out here and lead us?" But Stevenson was having too much fun on the embassy party rounds. His doctor warned him that his sybaritic life was a form of suicide. Friends were telling him the same thing. He died after a diplomats lunch in London, at age sixty-five.

Roosevelt, too, drove himself to an early death (sixty-three), but that was in his grueling fourth term as president during the Second World War. His talents had been put to maximum use because he could find common ground with those he sought to lead. He succeeded not by being a Pericles, as Thucydides presents Pericles, but by being what some of Pericles' defenders called a "demagogue." The word means, etymologically, "people-leader."

The Leader as Storyteller

Warren Bennis

Writing on leadership has become a growth industry in recent years, with writers churning out thousands of articles and hundreds of books on the subject over the last two decades. Of the handful that seem likely to endure, two that immediately come to mind are James MacGregor Burns's still resonant *Leadership* (Harper & Row, 1978) and James O'Toole's *Leading Change: Overcoming the Ideology of Comfort and the Tyranny of Custom* (Jossey-Bass, 1995). These two have now been joined by a third, Howard Gardner's superb new book, *Leading Minds*.

"The Leader as Storyteller" by Warren Bennis, *Harvard Business Review*, January–February, 1996, pp. 154–160. Reprinted by permission.

Subtitled *An Anatomy of Leadership*, Gardner's book is extraordinarily ambitious. It attempts to do nothing less than create a cognitive framework for all that has been learned about leadership. Like Gardner's earlier *Frames of Mind* (BasicBooks, 1983), *The Mind's New Science* (BasicBooks 1986), and *Creating Minds* (BasicBooks, 1993), his new book is the product of his research into creativity and influence, undertaken at Harvard University's Graduate School of Education.

Because Gardner is a good teacher who knows that the most effective lessons are often couched in good stories, he does not just present his theory of leadership in a text full of the italicized terms and simplistic charts that have become as obligatory as page numbers in recent leadership books. Instead, he fleshes out his theoretical notions in lively minibiographies of 11 twentieth-century leaders, beginning with Margaret Mead and ending with Mahatma Gandhi. In the context Gardner creates, these condensed lives have the force of letters from some of the great leaders of the recent past—letters that tell us, if only in a fragmentary way, what these men and women learned about the conduct of public life during their remarkable careers. The brief biographies are a delight and an education, full of useful hints and signposts, if not answers.

Before analyzing Gardner's achievement in some detail, let me say why his book is so important. Around the globe, humanity currently faces three extraordinary threats: the threat of annihilation as a result of nuclear accident or war, the threat of a worldwide plague or ecological catastrophe, and a deepening leadership crisis in most of our institutions. Unlike the possibility of plague or nuclear holocaust, the leadership crisis will probably not become the basis for a best-seller or a blockbuster movie, but in many ways it is the most urgent and dangerous of the threats we face today, if only because it is insufficiently recognized and little understood.

The signs of a leadership crisis are alarming and pervasive. Witness the change in leadership at some of our most respected corporations—General Motors, IBM, and American Express. Gardner acknowledges the deterioration of leadership in our corporations when he compares the leadership capabilities of two of GM's former leaders, Alfred P. Sloan, Jr., and Roger Smith.

In politics, it is the same. No head of a developed, democratic nation has more than a tentative hold on his or her constituency. President Bill Clinton has an approval rating that threatens to dip below 40% and faces opposition from Congress unmatched in recent history. In Great Britain, John Major's Conservative government teeters. Italy and Japan must manage with interregnum governments. A recent survey taken in Canada shows that its Progressive Conservative Party, in office for a decade, has the support of only 3% of the population. The same poll indicates that twice as many respondents—6%—believe Elvis is still alive.

The leadership crisis appears to be spreading. In the United States, senators are resigning, some without encouragement of scandal. The mood of the populace is unsettled, angry, sometimes foul, and, in a few horrifying recent cases, even murderous. And those who ostensibly lead agree only that things are terrible and getting worse. Among the general population, cynicism is rampant. I don't recall such a widespread loss of faith in our major institutions even during the tumultuous 1960s. Indeed, I can't remember a time when so many of our leaders themselves were so vocally disenchanted with government, including their own political parties, as they are today. Vice President Al Gore recently told an apocryphal story that perfectly captures the tenor of the times. A government pollster, clipboard in hand, asks people whether they are more satisfied with government today. Five percent say they are more satisfied, 10% say less, and 85% refuse to answer because they think the question is part of a government plot.

It was with this crisis very much in mind, with "Where Have All the Leaders Gone?" playing in my head, that I read Gardner's book. And although *Leading Minds* offers no magic formula, no quick cure, it does provide a framework for thinking about leadership in clear, unemotional terms that is the necessary first step toward resolving the leadership crisis that faces us.

One of Gardner's central ideas is that effective leaders—the Hitlers as well as the Roosevelts—tell or embody stories that speak to other people. By leaders, Gardner does not mean only CEOs or heads of state. In his view, leaders are all those "persons who, by word and/or personal example, markedly influence the behaviors, thoughts, and/or feelings of a significant number of their fellow human beings." (Gardner prefers the term *audience* to *followers* for those who are influenced.) He describes a continuum of leadership that starts with indirect leadership, exerted through scholarly work or other symbolic communication, and progresses to direct leadership of the sort exercised by world leaders through speeches and other means.

Gardner also charts leadership in terms of its widening impact: from influence exercised within relatively narrow domains, such as academic specialties, to influence exercised over larger communities, such as the influence Pope John XXIII exerted over the Roman Catholic Church. In addition, he describes a hierarchy of leadership based on creativity, with smaller-scale leaders such as educator Robert Maynard Hutchins at the bottom and visionaries such as Gandhi at the top.

The four factors Gardner lists as essential for effective leadership are a tie to a community or audience, a rhythm of life that includes isolation and immersion, a relationship between the stories leaders tell and the traits they embody, and arrival at power through the choice of the people rather than through brute force. Readers may or may not agree with the theoretical framework that Gardner modestly describes as not a model of leadership but merely the ingredients for a model. Whether they agree or not, however, they will find his stories of actual leaders full of insights into the myriad ways leadership expresses itself. Gardner is never so committed to his cognitive theory that he limits his observations to what fits neatly within his paradigm. With remarkable economy, he gives us more, not less; he provides not only the abstract and theoretical but also the concrete and historical.

Gardner's attempt to analyze leadership systematically is courageous, given the vulnerability of any overarching explanation to critical assault. But the magic of the book is this juxtaposition of the theoretical with the telling particulars. It is useful to learn that J. Robert Oppenheimer, head of the Manhattan Project and later a controversial spokesman for the responsible use of nuclear energy, began as an indirect leader within the relatively limited universe of theoretical physics. More interesting, however, is the idiosyncratic nature of Oppenheimer's leadership, vividly revealed in Gardner's account of Oppenheimer's career.

Gardner knows that the right anecdote can be worth a thousand theories, and he is best when he shows instead of tells. For example, rather than write at length on how Oppenheimer's leadership sometimes failed because of his arrogance, Gardner gives a single indelible example: Oppenheimer's icy dismissal of publisher Philip Graham for having failed to read some text in the original Sanskrit. In the same chapter, Gardner provides a glimpse of moral leadership when he recounts how President Lyndon Johnson (not one of Gardner's 11) ended Oppenheimer's unofficial banishment from public life by presenting him with the Enrico Fermi Award. Oppenheimer showed his profound understanding of the significance of Johnson's action when he said, "I think it is just possible, Mr. President, that it has taken some charity and some courage for you to make this award today. That would seem to me a good augury for all of our futures."

Again and again, Gardner gives us opportunities to think deeply about leadership by defining terms in which to do so and by describing and ordering the many forms that leadership takes. If this schematic approach sometimes gets a bit tedious, we know that in a page or two we will come to another illuminating moment, another small take-home lesson. This is the primary return on our investment of time. A secondary pleasure of the book is that it has us jotting notes to ourselves to find out more about leaders whom we might otherwise have overlooked, such as Angelo Giuseppe Roncalli, the future Pope John XXIII, who paused on his journey to the papacy to save Jews in the Balkans during World War II. Gardner's creativity, recognized with a MacArthur "genius" award, transforms what could have been a tedious slog through weighty subject matter into an intellectual thrill ride.

One of the great strengths of Gardner's book is that it avoids the false dichotomies that mar so much of the contemporary literature about leadership. However well intentioned, those who write about leadership have tended to become embroiled in one or more of the now familiar controversies on the subject. Three debates in particular have preoccupied those concerned with leaders and leadership.

The first of these debates is whether leaders are larger-than-life figures—heroes who can change the weather, as Winston Churchill said his ancestor John Churchill could— or whether they are simply vivid embodiments of forces greater than themselves. I think of this as a debate between Tolstoy and Carlyle. In Tolstoy's *War and Peace,* Napoleon and his Russian counterparts have very little to do with the ultimate outcome of the great battles with which they are identified. To use a metaphor that might have left Tolstoy tugging his beard in confusion, the leader in Tolstoy's view is just another surfer riding the waves of the zeitgeist, albeit the surfer with the biggest board. Carlyle, on the other hand, argues that every institution is the lengthened shadow of a great man. Had he been a Southern Californian, he might have written that great leaders don't just ride waves, they make them.

Instead of embracing either of these polarized views of leadership, Gardner is able to transcend them, even to reconcile them. Gardner never succumbs to the either/or thinking that is the province of what he describes as the five-year-old mind—five being the age Gardner chooses as representing the unschooled mind of the general public. In writing about General George C. Marshall, for instance, Gardner describes both the behavior of a hero—Marshall as a young officer who dares to confront General Pershing at their first meeting—and the career trajectory of a leader who sought to repair the economies of former enemies. If Gardner occasionally tips the scale in favor of Carlyle's view of leadership, who can blame him? After all, this is a book that recognizes the importance of stories in human affairs, and what stories are more compelling than those about heroes?

Gardner also rises above the persistent controversy over whether leaders are born or made. This debate is sufficiently widespread to have inspired a cartoon in which a nervous teenager presents a report card blackened with Fs to his CEO father and asks,

"What do you think, Pop, genes or the environment?" Gardner acknowledges the controversy, which has occasioned raised voices in a thousand faculty clubs, but instead of choosing sides, he presents useful data from both as part of the matrix of what we know about leaders. He reports that leaders do seem to have certain experiences in common. A remarkable number of the prominent figures of our time, including President Clinton, suffered the early loss of a father. And leaders seem to have certain traits in common as well. As my own study of dozens of contemporary leaders has revealed, whether in the arts, the political arena, or the corporation, leaders are almost always risk takers. (They also tend to be curious, energetic, and gifted with an acute sense of humor.)

Gardner not only can examine the controversy over nature versus nurture equitably, he also can consider it without obsessing about it. His ability to juggle contradictory notions is a sign of his maturity. To argue over whether leaders are born or made is an indulgent diversion from the urgent matter of how best to develop the leadership ability that so many have and that we so desperately need. A Nobel Prize awaits the person who resolves the question of whether leaders are born or made. But until some unanticipated breakthrough occurs or compelling new data emerge, the argument leads nowhere. The need for leadership in every arena of public life has become so acute that we don't have the luxury of dwelling on the unresolvable.

The third of the false dichotomies that Gardner so artfully avoids is the perceived conflict between expedient and idealistic leadership. The literature on leadership uses several different terms to describe those leaders who seize the moment without regard for the impact of their actions on the quality of other people's lives. *Machiavellian* is the harshest of these terms. The gentler ones typically crop up in discussions of contingency theory and "situationalism." But Gardner wisely avoids labels, choosing instead to show us that leaders are often both pragmatists and idealists. He correctly characterizes Hutchins, for example, as a "pragmatically tinged idealist," and talks of Sloan's desire to serve the nation while making money for General Motors.

In four decades of studying leaders, I have repeatedly found them to be what I call pragmatic dreamers—men and women whose ability to get things done is often grounded in a vision that includes altruism. Thus when Steve Jobs was recruiting John Sculley, then head of PepsiCo, for Apple Computer, Jobs knew to appeal not just to Sculley's ambition but also to his desire to leave a legacy that would go beyond boosting profit margins. Jobs is said to have asked the man who was to become Apple's next president and CEO how many more years of his life he wanted to spend making flavored water.

Scholars tackle two kinds of subjects. Some, like dry-fly fishing and the iconography of sixteenth-century French poetry, can be plumbed to their depths. Others, like leadership, are so vast and complex that they can only be explored. The latter subjects are inevitably the more important ones. You may question a few of Gardner's specific choices. For example, you may wonder if his work would have been more applicable to corporate life if he had chosen to focus almost exclusively on public leadership and its large-scale issues. But any such quibbles are only that, given the remarkable achievement of the book.

In the patterns of leadership that Gardner traces, several elements recur that have not been emphasized enough in earlier work on the subject. Travel, for instance, was even more important than formal education in shaping many of Gardner's leaders, including Roncalli and Gandhi. Gardner points out that nonauthoritarian leaders are more likely than authoritarian leaders to have traveled extensively abroad. Many leaders went on almost mythic interior journeys involving testing and rebirth. Gardner shows how Eleanor Roosevelt, who had to deal with both her husband's polio and his love for another woman, responded by reinventing herself as an increasingly independent advocate for the causes that were most important to her, notably women's rights and civil rights.

It is important, though, that we do not become too Carlylean in our view of leadership. Leadership is never exerted in a vacuum. It is always a transaction between the leader, his or her followers, and the goal or dream. A resonance exists between leaders and followers that makes them allies in support of a common cause. The leader's role in this process has been much analyzed. My studies show, for instance, that leaders are highly focused, that they are able to inspire trust, and that they are purveyors of hope. But followers are more essential to leadership than any of those individual attributes. As Garry Wills writes in *Certain Trumpets: The Call of Leaders* (Simon & Schuster, 1994), "The leader most needs followers. When those are lacking, the best ideas, the strongest will, the most wonderful smile have no effect."

Leaders are capable of deep listening: Gandhi demonstrated that when he traveled throughout India learning the heart of his people. But what distinguishes leaders from, say, psychotherapists or counselors is that they find a voice that allows them to articulate the common dream. Uncommon eloquence marks virtually every one of Gardner's leaders, but I have yet to see public speaking listed on a résumé. We seem to regard the ability to galvanize an audience as something almost tawdry, even dangerous. Yet it was the eloquence of Martin Luther King, Jr., grounded in the cadences of thousands of his father's sermons, that gave him the voice of a national, even international leader. That fact should be kept in mind by anyone trying to draw up a curriculum for future leaders.

Effective leaders put words to the formless longings and deeply felt needs of others. They create communities out of words. In *Leading Minds*, Gardner shows that he himself is just such a leader, able to articulate and clarify what many of us have been thinking on the subject for a long time.

Imagineer Eisner on Creative Leadership

Christopher Knowlton

With childlike enthusiasm, Michael Eisner outlines a pet project over a bowl of frozen yogurt in the Walt Disney Studios commissary. He intends to combine a retail store selling Disney doodads with a restaurant serving healthy, low-cholesterol food. The cuisine, he gushes, will be "fun, exciting, entertaining, and wonderful!" Then he admits that the concept doesn't tie in with Disney's other businesses and that most of his associates don't see much virtue in the plan. In a resigned voice he adds, "I've been driving everybody crazy."

Eisner is a CEO who is more hands-on than Mother Teresa. His chief duty at Disney is to lead creatively, to be a thinker, inventor, and cheerleader for new ideas—in founder Walt's own words, to be an Imagineer. Says Eisner: "Every CEO has to spend an enormous amount of time shuffling papers. The question is, how much of your time can you leave free to think about ideas? To me the pursuit of ideas is the only thing that matters. You can always find capable people to do almost everything else."

He uses a number of tactics to encourage, even induce, creativity in others. To come up with the layout for Euro Disneyland he called a meeting of a dozen of the world's most respected architects and had them brainstorm in a wildly creative session that became so heated, two of the architects began shoving each other and almost came to blows. "I'll use meetings, company anniversaries, anything to create some kind of catalyst to get us all going," says Eisner. He believes he must give his people free rein if he hopes to foster an entrepreneurial spirit within such a financially disciplined corporation.

As shepherd of the Disney flock, Eisner tries to promote a family-like camaraderie among his top managers. In late September he asked each division head to perform a skit for the anniversary dinner celebrating the team's first five years at the company. The skits peppered Eisner and President Frank Wells with barbed jokes about their management styles and big paychecks. At the end of this roast, instead of giving tit for tat, Eisner, Wells, Roy Disney, and their wives danced out onto the stage and performed a raucous kick line while booming out their spoof of "We Are the World."

Befitting a former English major at Denison University in Ohio who once had a passion for writing plays, Eisner thinks in terms of story lines. He applies that thinking to all the company's activities, whether he is building a $200 million hotel or a $10 million theme park attraction. "We ask, 'What is the story we want to tell when people walk into one of our new buildings? What are they going to feel? What is going to happen next?

And how will it end?'" He is using movie storyboards to create a chronology and schedule for the construction of his Colorado vacation home.

The ideas that grab him—and often he can't remember if they are his own or embellishments of someone else's—are those that surprise him and tease his imagination. He disdains ideas that seem too familiar. On the other hand, for an idea to succeed at Disney it can't be so avant-garde that it ceases to be commercial. The *Making of Me* attraction in Epcot Center's new Wonders of Life pavilion, which features footage of the birth of a baby, had its genesis in Eisner's own emotionally charged experiences at the delivery of his three sons. His tastes are mainstream and all-American, combined with a gut instinct for what new flavor might be popular next.

Appropriately for the chief of America's leading peddler of wholesome entertainment, Eisner sees his family as his inspiration. He follows the tastes, interests, and activities of his children with the vigilance of a police-beat reporter. His wife, Jane, often screens his ideas. Says he: "98.5% of my ideas revolve around things that we are both involved in. With the stuff that is really on the edge, I will ask her if I'm crazy. Of course she usually thinks I am."

For Prince Eisner, New Battles to Fight

Jeffrey A. Sonnenfeld

In Walt Disney's classic film "Pinocchio," Jiminy Cricket warbles, "When you wish upon a star, your dreams come true." But then what happens?

It looks like Michael D. Eisner, the man who helped awaken Disney from its Sleeping Beauty–like slumber a decade ago, is about to find out. The merger plan he has forged with Capital Cities/ABC gives Disney a communications pre-eminence bar none. But it also puts the heroic savior prince and his troops at the mercy of forces that could turn the creative Magic Kingdom into a contentious managerial empire.

The demons involve public perceptions and private myths, but they can be tamed:

- **The Peril of Public Tributes.** Everyone on Sunset Boulevard, Wall Street and the Infobahn seems enraptured by the strategic wisdom of the Capital Cities deal. But American society, including some envious Hollywood friends, can be notoriously

"For Prince Eisner, New Battles to Fight" by Jeffery A. Sonnenfeld, *The New York Times,* August 6, 1995. Reprinted by permission.

fickle, and we can expect this spotlight to pass in our normal cycle of myth-making and hero-debunking. As the widely admired chairman of Home Depot, Bernard Marcus, has warned his counterparts: "Beware of the dangerous vanity of believing your own press."

- **Bigger Is Not Always Better.** Industry analysts and admiring communications giants applaud the scope and reach of this powerful vertical integration of communication. Still, we see stunning vertical integration now in pharmaceuticals, but it is the scrappy little biotech firms that produce the break-throughs each week. And troubles at an advertising behemoth like Saatchi & Saatchi only remind us that economies of scale can be elusive in creative industries.

  Paradoxically, the Disney-ABC deal was facilitated by brilliant, well-regarded financiers—Warren E. Buffett, Herbert A. Allen, Sid Bass—rather than big investment banks. A rare example? Maybe, but in forging the deal they announced only a day after the Disney merger, Westinghouse and CBS also depended on personal over institutional savvy.

- **No Marriage Is Perfect.** Yes, there is tremendous synergy between Disney as a premier content producer and Capital Cities/ABC as an excellent multimedia distributor. But in any new relationship there are stages of discovery: expectations are clarified, work patterns refined, conflicts resolved. Despite the wonderful "coming full circle" quality of Mr. Eisner's career, anchored by a meteoric rise at ABC, the two cultures are very different.

  Once a cauldron of egos, ABC was transformed after Thomas S. Murphy, Daniel B. Burke and their fellow leaders from Capital Cities Broadcasting took over in 1985. Although critics had feared then—as they do now with Westinghouse's deal for CBS—that the new folks would stifle the network, management won people over with a style that replaced a celebrity-driven system with a culture of harmony and teamwork.

  This is not the Disney culture. The turnaround of Disney has relied more on bold, autocratic visions and the continued infusion of outside stars like Mr. Eisner and his first team of Frank G. Wells, Gary L. Wilson, Jeffrey Katzenberg and Richard H. Frank or the new top team of prominent external recruits like Stephen F. Bollenbach from Host Marriott and Joe Roth from Fox. Turnaround challenges and ready industry naysayers have fueled Mr. Eisner's need to be tough.

  Yet Mr. Eisner has proved that he is capable of managing disparate cultures. The Disney he inherited was dominated by a theme park–bred system where people proudly worked up the hierarchy, starting as ride operators. Mr. Eisner wisely kept that loyal culture intact. At the studios, though, he just as wisely revived a baseball-team culture of recruiting mobile, star talent.

- **The Myth of Invincibility.** The most precarious moments in a top leader's career don't follow a setback. Resilience, wrote the anthropologist Joseph Campbell, is key to the greatness of heroic character.

Indeed, associates suggest that Mr. Eisner is even stronger today having transcended the monumental trials suffered in the last two years: the helicopter death of Mr. Wells, Disney's beloved president; the stormy departures of Mr. Katzenberg and Mr. Frank; the disappointing debut of Euro Disney; failed plans for the Disney's America park near Washington, and his own emergency quadruple-bypass operation.

Instead, it is success that can undo a hero, who, heady after those first triumphs, begins to assume his own mythic persona. Then, an autocratic insularity can set in that threatens previous achievements.

When Mr. Eisner stepped in, Disney had less than $1.5 billion in yearly revenue, at most three films in production and a risk-averse culture whose executives fought turf battles before retreating early to the golf course. Working his magic, Mr. Eisner built a $10 billion multimedia programmer. Now with the Capital Cities/ABC deal and turnarounds on other fronts, notably Euro Disney, Mr. Eisner has proved his critics wrong. But any tendencies toward autocratic brilliance may be reinforced by this triumphant history.

Mr. Eisner can make a formidable team if he can tolerate the honest differences among, and criticisms from, respected thinkers like ABC's Robert A. Iger and Disney stars like Sanford M. Litvack, John F. Cooke and Dennis F. Hightower, as well as Mr. Roth and Mr. Bollenbach.

In the 1960's song "Celluloid Heroes," Ray Davies of the Kinks intones in words that still ring true today: "And those who are successful, be always on your guard; success walks hand in hand with failure, along Hollywood Boulevard."

Managing in the '90s: The Androgynous Manager

Alice G. Sargent and Ronald J. Stupak

We are witnessing a set of critical value shifts in American culture. The major shift affecting corporate America is from the vertical values (rugged individualism, autonomy, and independence) to the horizontal values (interdependence, mutuality, networking, and coalition building).

It is a transformation from a predominantly masculine value system to an androgynous one (*andro* is Greek for male; *gyne* is Greek for female). The new value set calls for each person to have a blend of values—competence and compassion, action and introspection. It is the style required for effective leadership in organizational America in the years ahead.

Such a blend mixes together two sets of values:

- The so-called masculine characteristics that managers will need to continue to exhibit—dominance, independence, a direct achievement style, a reverence for rational, analytical problem solving, a valuing of verbal behavior, and a competitive strategic approach;
- The so-called feminine characteristics—concern for relationships, a valuing of expressive behavior, attention to nonverbal behavior, the ability to accommodate and mediate, and a vicarious achievement style (enjoying the development of others).

For contemporary role models of androgynous leadership and management, we can look to Bill Cosby, Alan Alda, Frank Furillo of "Hill Street Blues," Corazon Aquino, Marian Wright Edelman of the Children's Defense Fund, and Barbara Jordan. In a recent *Business Week* survey, Colonel Potter from television's "M.A.S.H." was selected as the manager for whom most people would prefer to work, above Lee Iacocca.

In a sense, the 1960s and 1970s were about women; the late 1980s are about men. Books about men are proliferating. At least 25 universities have begun offering courses in men's studies. Men are beginning to re-examine the male experience and the costs paid for the overuse of competition, the absence of close male friendships in adulthood, and the Lone Ranger style. Furthermore, the definition of masculinity as macho warrior, wimp, or anything not considered feminine is under intense scrutiny.

The nature of management is changing as well. Today's managers spend 50 to 90 percent of their time interacting with people—70 percent of that in groups—and 50 percent operating outside the chain of command. An androgynous blend of competencies is critical for managerial effectiveness and organizational and corporate leadership.

MANAGEMENT REALITIES

How did things get the way they are? What accounts for the shift? Let's examine the context.

Transactional Realities at the Executive Level

Frank Sherwood, a major influence in the field of public administration, says that as one progresses up the managerial ladder, horizontal skills begin to replace vertical skills as the basis for effective leadership. In other words, as a person moves up the hierarchy, with accompanying increases in formal responsibilities, problems become broader and more complex as constraints become more similar. At the highest levels of an organization, horizontal administration rather than vertical administration becomes the key to power.

That point is critical, because the vertical skills of command and control are replaced by skills that emphasize making transactions across organizational borders, brokering coalitions, and building consensus. Negotiation, bargaining, and mediation start to become more important than directing, demanding, and doing. The need to master transactional competencies determines the status, character, and effectiveness of executives in the corporate arena.

Harold Leavitt in *Beyond the Analytical Manager* and James McGregor Burns in *Leadership* say that transactional leadership skills and human-relations skills are the ones needed to master organizational realities in the American democratic, incremental context. David McClelland says the evidence points overwhelmingly to the conclusion that women are more concerned than men with both sides of interdependent relationships.

As the "female" concern for interdependence becomes an essential perspective for effectiveness at the highest levels of management, the androgynous blend needs to become an operational reality at the highest levels of organizations.

The Service Economy and the Servant Leadership Style

As we evolve from an industrial economy to one that is 60 percent service-oriented, leadership requires both masculine and feminine dimensions of power. Surely unilateral power must be blended with synergistic power. Personal dominance may be effective in small groups, but leaders who guide large groups and massive corporations in the service economy must become effective in the more subtle and socialized forms of power and influence.

In today's marketplace, where increasing numbers of followers, employees, and clients want to have a voice in the management of their organizations, a socialized leadership style must replace the autocratic, directive style of the 1930s, 1940s, and 1950s. "Servant leadership," based on a firm belief in people, generates the empowerment required to move the massive organizations of corporate America onto the new strategic stage of multinational and international competition and interdependence.

The depth and breadth of the reaction to poor service has demanded that organizations demonstrate the sensitivity and feelings necessary to get closer to customers and clients. Feedback is "the critical dimension" for those committed to an androgynous style.

Organizational Families

In *The 100 Best Companies to Work for in America*, Robert Levering, Milton Moskowitz, and Michael Katz say that the number-one factor on their list of 12 themes for successful companies is that the excellent ones "make people feel part of a team . . . or a family."

High-performing organizations demand that good managers have both the head and the heart to be effective leaders. The powerful managers who are memorable are often gracious people as well. The positive, not the negative, face of power predominates at Dana Corporation, Walt Disney, Procter and Gamble, and Hewlett Packard. Surely that suggests that the traditional masculine way of explaining the influence of a manager on his or her followers has not been entirely correct. A good manager does not use sheer, overwhelming dominance to force subordinates to submit and follow. Instead, the nurturing style of expressing power, along with the "sharing" perspective of empowerment, seems to "flame the families" toward productivity in high-performing organizations.

To paraphrase James O'Toole's *Vanguard Management,* workers can no longer be treated as bastard step-children in the corporate clan, but must be viewed as legitimate stockholders empowered to participate actively in the "family enterprise."

The 21st Century's Paradigm for Productive Performance

Generative power as opposed to imperial power (which is ruthless) appears to be essential to long-term organizational excellence. Generative power, which implies the coming together of two independent beings, has become the paradigm of productive performance in the corporate world as we shatter the traditional boundaries between black and white, men and women, public and private, and national and international.

New frameworks must be created in the multinational, multicultural corporate environment. McClelland makes it clear that men attain "generativity" more easily if they abandon some of their traditional assertiveness; women, if they abandon some of their traditional dependency. The androgynous model is relevant for leadership effectiveness in the re-created world of production, performance, and service.

Women and the Workforce

The workforce is changing. In 1984 white males became a minority in the workforce, 49.3 percent. The United States has become a two-career economy, but our social policies have not caught up with those of other two-career economies—such as Norway and Sweden—in terms of day care and parental leave. Simply stated, women are a national resource.

When the members change dramatically, it becomes critical that organizations get ahead of the power curve to create leadership styles, skills, and perspectives that allow them to leverage the workforce in the most efficient and effective manner. An androgynous blend may be one of the answers.

Soft Is Hard: "Excellence" Revisited

Tom Peters and Robert Waterman in *In Search of Excellence* forever redefined management. Peters and Waterman insist that emotions, feelings, and relationships need to be as important in the content of MBA programs as logic and quantifiable objects. They conclude that Western society needs to counteract the detrimental, rational, "masculine" one-sidedness pinpointed in their analysis of business organizations:

"We don't argue for drastically tilting the balance toward either pathfinding or implementation. Rationality is important. . . . But if America is to regain its competitive position in the world, or even hold what it has, we have to stop overdoing things on the rational side."

Peters and Waterman understand the practical need for the implementation of feeling attitudes; in their words, "the exclusively analytic approach run wild leads to an abstract, heartless philosophy."

Old-guard definitions of management harped on productivity, obedience, and control. Peters' new definition is management as concern for people—employees inside the organization and customers and consumers outside—as well as a clear concern for quality, not merely quantity. Daniel Yankelovich undergirds that new definition when he says we have shifted from control to quality as the central principle of management. Managers who focus on quality need involvement, motivation, locality, commitment, and pride from workers. That implies organizations based on trust and caring—and on a leadership blend of male and female characteristics.

The androgynous leadership blend poses a relevant style for the macro and micro relationships necessary to manage organizations in the multigender, multinational, and multisocial environments in the years ahead.

A MODEL FOR MANAGERIAL EFFECTIVENESS

The significant questions for corporations today:

- Do organizations need the values and skills that women bring—caring, cooperation, conflict resolution, good communications, and an expression of a fuller range of feelings?
- Can "female" characteristics and behaviors become a greater part of the acceptable managerial style without jettisoning the best of "male" qualities?

Surely the answer to both questions has to be yes. Progressive corporations in the United States and abroad have flattened hierarchies, encouraged employee participation, and paid more attention to employees' feelings and personal needs. They recognize that workers will perform better when they feel a sense of ownership in their jobs and organizations. Workers also do better work when they believe that the organization values their personal well-being; they see the evidence in such issues as satisfying jobs, health, and family life.

A so-called feminine approach focuses on collaboration, caring, and socialized power. The more traditional, "masculine" approach focuses on analyzing problems, exercising unilateral power, negotiating, competing, and getting credit for one's impact. The androgynous manager integrates and incorporates and employs both sets of behaviors. He or she is both dominant and flexible, and combines independence and power with nurturing and intimacy (see the figure on page 82).

When workers operate under a social contract rather than an exploitation contract, managers need skills to deal with the whole person. They need both instrumental and expressive behaviors, competence and compassion, and support and direction.

Androgynous behavior can enhance a range of managerial functions, including the following:

- Conducting performance appraisals;
- Building, developing, and maintaining team effectiveness;
- Assisting in the career development of employees;
- Using a variety of decision-making styles;
- Dealing with conflict;
- Responding to new ideas;
- Dealing with stress.

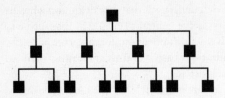

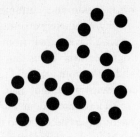

Traditional manager	New-style manager
Do as I say, not as I do	Models good interpersonal relationships
Rational	Rational and intuitive
Eliminates complexity; has all the answers	Comfortable with uncertainty and complexity
Compartmentalized experimentation permitted only in an R&D setting	Experiments; organization embraces errors
Standard operating procedures highly bureaucratic	Fairness; core set of values; deals with individuals
Chain of command	Networks
Conformity	Diversity

For example, the performance of a work team depends on trust, collaboration, communication, and interdependence among team members. It also depends on competence in the technical aspects of the task. The manager cannot just tell the team members to be trustful, collaborative, and communicative. Example works much better than precept; the manager needs to model the behaviors sought in the team members. Also, how team members feel about each other is as important as how they interact with the task at hand. The androgynous manager deals with feelings and task accomplishment, with support and direction, and with productivity and morale.

Instrumental Versus Expressive Behaviors

At the core of the androgynous blend of behaviors are instrumental and expressive behaviors. The former deals with data, results, ideas, and tasks—in effect, it is role behavior. The latter deals with self-disclosure, spontaneity, authenticity, and feelings.

Such behaviors become clear to us in our relationships with family and friends. Instrumental discussions begin with such questions as "Have you paid the insurance?" "Where should we go for dinner Saturday night?" and "Who is taking the car to the mechanic?" Examples of expressive behavior include "How did it go at the office today?" and "How do you feel about your work?"

If a couple engages in too much instrumental behavior, the relationship becomes stale and routine. Communication lacks spontaneity and self-disclosure, the kinds of expressive behavior that build closeness.

Supervisor/subordinate relationships also grow dull and rigid when they become instrumental, focusing only on such questions as "Is that job finished?" and "When do you plan to take your vacation this year?" More expressive behavior is called for. Examples include "How is that project going?" and "Where would you like to be in your career five years from now?"

On the job, the absence of expressive behavior produces ineffective, stilted performance-appraisal sessions. Staff meetings become frustrating; the remarks people make informally ten minutes after the meeting are much more meaningful than opinions expressed during the meeting.

TRAINING FOR ANDROGYNY

Today, managers do not have the luxury of autocracy. Management is defined as getting things done through people—between supervisor and manager, between manager and subordinate, and between manager and peer.

Given the way managers spend their time, organizational leadership becomes an influence-peddling, coalition-visioning, and power-negotiating process. Successful management styles tend to emphasize more collaboration and less competition, and different decision-making styles in different situations. Contingency decision making and situational leadership styles are becoming more widespread; however, we really have not moved to participative management. Instead, we see a blend of the benevolent autocratic style and the consultative style.

To take a giant step toward dealing with these facts and issues, we need a three-step approach to transforming management for the future:

- We must design valid models of managerial effectiveness at the first-line, middle-management, and executive levels—models based on the androgynous paradigm.
- We must define systematic methods for performance-appraisal systems that reinforce and reward the models.
- We must develop educational and training programs to "grow" managers based on the models.

How do we train androgynous managers? Certainly not in the business schools and public-administration programs of today. Sixty-thousand MBAs are graduated every year in the United States—many of them are our future managers—but most degree programs require only nine hours of management education. As Sterling Livingston, the 72-year-old president of the Washington, D.C.,-based Sterling Training Institute, has said, "Business schools teach how to problem-solve not problem-find; how to work more with money than with people."

The inability of our business schools to teach people management and team-building skills may be the reason for the recent wave of executive disenchantment with business-school graduates, along with the return to the belief that a liberal-arts degree is better preparation for general management. Management is indeed a second career for many engineers, doctors, scientists, lawyers, and the like. They need to be educated for that career with the same commitment and intensity that went into their first career choices.

Business-school curricula and management-development programs should include work in both the theory and practice of each of the seven androgynous manager competencies:

- technical competence;
- problem-solving competence (analytical skills, left- and right-brain thinking);
- self-awareness competence (awareness of the impact of one's behavior on others—introspection);
- interpersonal competence;
- team leadership and membership effectiveness;
- entrepreneurial competence;
- leadership.

The need is for practitioner/managers capable of modeling those behaviors.

The American Management Association is trying to begin a master's degree program in management, while some business schools are trying to broaden their course offerings. For example, Harvard is taking a step in the right direction by offering a class to its second-year MBA students and their spouses called "The Executive Family." Barrie Greiff, author of *Tradeoffs in Executive and Family Life,* teaches the course. It is designed to help future leaders of U.S. businesses balance the demands of a job with the demands of a family.

A life outside the office is beginning to be recognized as an important element for managers—an element that cannot be denied or ignored. (Remember, no one on his or her deathbed ever said, "I wish I had spent more time at the office.") But much more needs to be done to teach managers how to be androgynous in the office.

A MORE POSITIVE ROLE FOR CORPORATIONS

Outside of business schools, societal trends are moving people toward androgyny: women's liberation, two-career households, couples in their late 30s starting families and becoming more home-centered, and the focus on male role expectations. The movement is slowly percolating into the workplace. But organizations need to take a more positive role in promoting the androgynous management approach.

In a *Playboy* magazine report on contemporary men's values, the priorities were as follows: health, family life, love, friends, sex, respect for others, religion, peace of mind, work, education, and money. It is clear that attitudes and behavior are not connected. Work comes ninth, according to the men who filled out the survey, but for many, it remains number one in their lives. Some men are becoming conscious of other priorities and other management models. But from consciousness to behavior change is an important step. Organizations can help by rewarding managers who display androgynous competencies, for skill not only with tasks, but also with people.

Management in the 1980s and 1990s is about people, our most precious resource. To build supportive and effective workplace climates in which people can be creative and do work of high quality, we need a blend of both masculine and feminine behaviors. Then we will have a new managerial style that combines concern for people with concern for quality. We will have a style that values interdependent as well as independent ways of doing business. We will have a style that increases options for all managers to move beyond the constraints of stereotypical sex-role expectations.

The political, social, and economic environment is crying out for those who can lead, manage, and create with dignity, sensitivity, and integrity on the local, national, and international levels. It is essential that we in the United States re-invent the corporation. And, it is a fundamental requirement that we re-invent the "American Dream" based on rational, feeling, and integrated leadership styles grounded in the androgynous paradigm.

The Postheroic Leader

David L. Bradford and Allan R. Cohen

The enormous popularity of books on how to achieve excellence in organizations points to the unprecedented hunger that business people feel for a way to recapture the momentum of quality and innovation that was once the hallmark of U.S. business.

As valuable as these books might be, they focus almost exclusively on the total organization and speak to the chief executive officer, who makes large-scale decisions, even though the implementation of these plans falls to managers in the next levels down. The head of data processing, for example, cannot alter the organization's culture, create lifetime employment practices or invent a new corporate strategy.

Thus there lies a great gap between what is known about what organizations ought to be like and what individual managers need to do to achieve excellence. Yet it is the middle and upper-middle managers who hold the key to high performance. If they can produce, their leadership has a cascading effect on several levels of important subordinates.

Bradford and Cohen have developed an explicit leadership model to bridge the gap in attaining organizational excellence, one that suggests ways for managers to behave and influence every day. It asserts that the model of leadership used by most managers—that of the "heroic" leader who can know all, do all, solve every problem—is severely outdated and inadequate in eliciting the best performance in complex, contemporary organizations.

What do Bradford and Cohen offer in place of the John Wayne-style managerial hero? The postheroic leader: the Manager-as-Developer.

How can managers act in ways that will achieve excellence rather than block it? How can leaders act so that heroic overresponsibility doesn't prevent full use of subordinates' abilities, doesn't dampen their commitment to high performance and doesn't cause them to avoid taking initiative when problems arise?

The answer is not for the manager to renounce responsibility and abandon all control. Although some subordinates respond well to being left alone, there are too many important managerial tasks to guarantee that a no-boss-is-the-best-boss approach will work.

It is also futile to seek a magical midpoint between the extremes of too much and too little leader responsibility and control. Rather, an entirely new definition of leadership is required if a department is to be led into new and unanticipated areas.

This new definition is a fundamental reorientation away from the heroic model. Shared responsibility and control take the place of the individual hero carrying the burdens alone. For those who have staggered around trying to do it all—and have ended up forcing more burden onto their own shoulders by causing the very problems with subordinates that they wanted to avoid—the postheroic view of managing is a profound shift.

At the same time, no part of the new model is all that unfamiliar to any contemporary manager. Everyone knows about tapping subordinate talents, exciting them about the mission and building effective teams, just as astronomers in the time of Copernicus knew about the earth, sun and stars whirling in the heavens. Yet the "simple" reversal of putting the sun, rather than the earth, at the center of relationships caused a revolution in philosophy as well as science.

To achieve excellence in earthly organizations, a manager must first believe in the concept and then act in the creation of a team of key subordinates who are jointly responsible with the manager for the department's success. *At the same time that the manager works to develop management responsibility in subordinates, he or she must help develop the subordinates' abilities to share management of the unit's performance.* Only when all directly reporting subordinates are committed to joint responsibility for overall excellence—when pieces of the task are no longer conditionally delegated, but become parts of decisions—will control cease to be the sole province of the boss.

At the same time, only when subordinates become skilled in the managerial tasks required for total departmental success can the sharing of responsibility lead to excellence. Since neither willingness to accept overall responsibility nor ability to do so are automatic and instant, we have called this model the Manager-as-Developer. Skills have to be learned, common goals accepted, expectations changed and norms modified. Over time a team can be built.

This management model was created by examining leaders who achieve excellence and the images they seem to hold of managing. Rather than depending on heroic rides to the rescue—with the answers and the total responsibility—they have sought the far greater power and potential for excellence available in the commitment and abilities of their whole group. These managers have in mind a developmental, collaborative, galvanizing, but subordinate-centered image.

Unfortunately, a good, easily recognized image of this kind of leader does not exist. Flashes of description occasionally appear when leaders refer to times when "we were all in it together and we knew we could conquer the world." Certain inspirational moments display the quality of shared responsibility; the leader does not command yet is willingly joined in a pursuit where all are at risk.

Perhaps the image is most like a very demanding but supportive and inspirational coach, who works hard to bring the team along, insists on high standards and rigorous effort, but passes on all the knowledge that will help the athletes grow. This coach often works alongside the team, but delegates increasing responsibility for the game plan and especially for on-the-spot adjustments. From the sidelines the coach takes great pleasure in the centrality and achievements of the athletes.

But this coaching analogy imperfectly transfers to managing: The manager is a more involved participant in the action than a coach can ever be. Nevertheless, leaders who achieve excellence are less likely to be guided by images of the central, overresponsible and overcontrolling hero—an image that ultimately dilutes the effectiveness of technicians and conductors when they have expert subordinates doing complex and interdependent work in changing circumstances.

This new model calls for no less effort, energy, investment or imagination than does the Lone Ranger style. Since active engagement is necessary to undertake and sustain increased subordinate learning and overall responsibility, we think of the developer as postheroic rather than nonheroic. Indeed, for some managers who are used to rushing in with the answers, it takes heroic efforts not to be so heroic. Developer-managers learn to have impact without exerting total control, to be helpful without having all the answers, to get involved without demanding centrality, to be powerful without needing to dominate and to act responsible without squeezing others out.

THE CENTRAL ORIENTATION

What does it take to fulfill this tall order in management? First and foremost is a change in orientation. A whole new array of options open up when the leader's orientation becomes: "How can each problem be solved in a way that further develops my subordinates' commitment and capabilities?"

This new orientation may lead the manager to throw some problems back to subordinates ("I think you have a good handle on the difficulty, so why don't you do a first cut and come back in two days"). The manager may ask questions that help subordinates focus on the key issues, while at other times the leader can best aid development by exploring the situation jointly with a subordinate. There may also be times when it is most "developmental" for the manager to provide the answer. Whichever alternative is chosen, the underlying developmental orientation of the leader remains consistent.

What these responses have in common is achieving the dual goal of getting the job done while engaging subordinates in a way that helps them stretch. This orientation does not sacrifice task accomplishment for development (or vice versa). The leader is not saying, "I will develop today and put off solving the problem until tomorrow." Both goals are kept firmly in the forefront.

This postheroic orientation also requires that subordinate development not be restricted to off-site training functions. It occurs on the job—in real time with real issues. Fuller use is made of the already existing abilities of the subordinate while potential ones are developed.

Let's look closely at how a Manager-as-Developer would use this orientation to deal with a problem. Bob Young is faced with a problem: Increasingly, customers have been complaining about defective gaskets, a crucial component in the company's key product.[1] Concerned about this dangerous situation, Bob has called a special meeting of the operations committee. The four subordinate members of the committee have strong feelings—positive and negative—about one another and about Bob Young that make them reluctant to talk openly about the actual source of the problem: a change in supplies and inspection procedures.

This is just the sort of issue that is likely to elicit the heroic response; the organization is under severe time pressure to solve a crucial problem that subordinates are colluding to bury. Bob opened the meeting with his four subordinates as follows:

"As you know, we are having major problems meeting our deliveries on time. Furthermore, customers are reporting that quality is not up to standard. I have heard this from several of our very important customers, and I am quite bothered, as I am sure you are. You know that we are in a highly competitive market and they can go elsewhere. We have always prided ourselves on our ability to produce gaskets that have no defects, that our customers can use without worry. Our financial future is in jeopardy unless we quickly find out what is going wrong and correct it. You are the people who best know the situation; you know what causes it, and you know what the best solution looks like. Therefore, I want us in this meeting to work together and come up with the best answer."

This introduction signaled the importance of the problem, reminded subordinates of the company's identification with quality and gave an initial indication of how Bob wanted this situation to be tackled.

Yet subordinates know that words are cheap. What did Bob really mean? Was he out to find someone to blame? Did he really have an idea of how the problem should be solved and merely used a pseudoparticipative style to get them to buy into his solution?

In addition, Bob Young's statement indicated a change in the rules of the game. In trying to develop a management team with members who feel responsible for the operations of the plan and not just for individual areas, Bob Young was demanding that members change their ways of operating. No matter what objections they might have had to Bob's previous style, the subordinates had learned to live with (and around) it. Thus, they tested the waters very carefully before they jumped in and accepted at face value his statement about their enlarged responsibility.

First, they tried to revert to the previous way of operating by throwing the responsibility back to him.

"I don't know, Bob. You know the operations inside and out. What do you think the best solution is?"

Bob replied,

---

[1]Adapted from Bowen, D. D. Young Manufacturing in D. T. Hall et al., *Experiences in Management and Organizational Behavior,* New York: Wiley, 1982.

"This is the kind of issue we need to tackle together, because then we'll be sure not only of getting this problem solved, but we'll be able to prevent similar dilemmas in the future."

This exchange was followed by long silence; subordinates hoped they could outlast Bob and force him to take over. When it was clear that he wouldn't move in, there was another attempt to resurrect the old way of operating, in which information that might appear detrimental to any one of the four subordinates was kept from Bob while they worked out their problems on the side. The head of production, Don Blue, glanced over to the quality control manager, Roy Gray, and turned back to Bob:

"Bob, you are busy getting us major contracts. We don't have to take up valuable meeting time on this issue. Roy Gray and I will meet and come up with the solution, and I'll let you know tomorrow."

This suggestion gives the appearance of subordinates assuming responsibility, but it was actually an attempt to hide any dirty linen from Bob Young. Also, the response did nothing to build the operations committee into a mature team that could handle the major operating problems.

As a Developer, Bob Young recognized the presence of two problems: a technical one—quality products were not being delivered on time—and a managerial one—for some reason the operations group had been unable over the past several weeks to resolve the task problem. The defective gaskets problem wasn't news to any of them. Thus, Bob realized that if he delegated responsibility for solving the technical problem to two of his subordinates (or if Bob, being heroic, came up with an answer himself), he wouldn't solve the team/managerial problem even if a good technical solution was produced.

Rather than wading in to solve the problem personally, Bob decided that he had to hold his subordinates' feet to the fire while they solved the problem. He had to be sure they knew he expected them to work jointly on the solution. Bob thus responded to Don Blue's suggestion by saying:

"Don, I'm sure you and Roy could come up with something, but I also want all of us to improve our collective ability to solve problems. To do that we need to work on it together, since everyone's involved."

After a long silence Bob turned to Fran, the most junior member of the group, and asked for possible causes of the problem. Bob wanted to be certain that Don's seniority and dominant style would not keep Fran from contributing. After Fran made a few comments suggesting that the old-timers' resistance to new methods was an issue, the others leaped in to start blaming one another. A hail of "you didn'ts" and "you should haves" filled the room. Bob showed no signs of being upset about this arguing, and after several minutes, when the accusations had died down, he said,

"Let's see if we can keep our eyes on what happened and how to fix it. Pointing fingers only makes everyone defensive, which doesn't help quality control. What advantages did the old system have, and what were the goals in changing the system? Once we have these answers, we can determine the kind of changes we should make in purchasing practice so we get the advantages without the problems."

After Bob redirected the discussion into a problem-solving mode, the members collectively dug in to get at the basic issues. They acknowledged that they should stop playing at

"It's not my fault," and instead they set up a series of procedures for solving the immediate consequences of the procurement change. They also agreed that a more thorough discussion of inventory policy was needed and set a time the next day to work out the specifics.

Bob Young worked hard to increase the team's willingness to share the responsibility for managing the plant. He recognized that one general statement would not be sufficient. He wanted the team to own not only the problem, but the solution as well.

Instead of trying to get them to disclose the information that would give him determination of the solution or manipulating them to come up with his solution, he worked at how to get the problem solved while increasing the team's commitment and capacity to solve such problems. He kept standards high by using their tradition of quality as the measure against which they could all judge what was being proposed. And by sticking to his determination to increase shared responsibility, he helped develop the team's ability to work together on future problems.

Chapter

4

Ethics

"What should I do?" The question is one of the most persistent and important ones that managers and other employees face in their day-to-day lives in organizations. Sometimes, the practical answer is clear: Simply follow the rule book or draw on established practice in the company. More often, in the modern corporation, there is a great deal of ambiguity about the way to proceed. This may be so because the individual or the organization have not faced the situation before. The situation can be novel in any of a number of different ways. Ambiguity can occur because the interactions involved are cross-cultural, so that very different interpretations of right and wrong can exist. The decision might be biased by the potential for large corporate or personal gain or loss. The pressure then exists to maximize opportunity or minimize loss, perhaps at the expense of some other individual group, or corporation. What happens if we add the pressure of a high degree of stress to the situation—the stress of time constraints, of emotional intensity, of physical debilitation? Then the answer to the question "What should I do?"—even if given and acted on quickly—is likely to yield behavior and results that are intentionally or inadvertently unethical.

There are no simple rules for managing ethically. In many cases what is ethical must be felt as well as reasoned and the individual doing this will draw on his or her individual values and beliefs as well as the ethical context of the organization and the society in which that individual lives. What are these individual and organizational codes of ethics? The articles in this chapter reflect on this question and on the dilemmas we have raised here briefly. The selection, "The Test," is an account of a personal ethical dilemma. Did the man in the story *pass* the test? In "The Parable of the Sadhu," Bowen H. McCoy describes making and living with a decision that affects the life of another human being. In a poignant and dramatic story, he touches on all the critical aspects of the question "What should I do?" It is perhaps useful to walk in his shoes as the story unfolds and to ask oneself certain questions: "What would I do if I were faced with this same choice?" "How will I know if my actions are right or wrong?"

The next two selections are from the New York Times' recent series on "The Downsizing of America." "Justifying the Ax" relates some of the rationalizations corporate executives adopt to defend their actions to themselves and others. However, in "Guilt of the Firing Squads," executives unveil the pain and self-loathing they really experience as a consequence of their refusal to count the human costs of their actions.

In spite of the massive downsizing and pay cuts experienced by the employees of large corporations, executive compensation rose sharply in 1995 as reported in "Top Brass in U.S. Bucks Belt-Tightening Trend with Hefty Pay Hikes."

Making decisions one considers to be ethical may not bring with it much appreciation from other organizational members, as any whistleblower can probably attest to. Withholding liquor from a pregnant customer, in accordance with an ethical principle, cost some employees their jobs (in "Mother-to-be and Daiquiri Lead to Firings").

In "Moral Mazes: Bureaucracy and Managerial Work," Robert Jackall explores ways in which bureaucracy shapes the morality practiced in management. He compares and contrasts the original Protestant ethic with a more recent phenomenon that he calls the bureaucratic ethic.

Terminated employees have not been slow to attempt retaliation. Improper or unjustified firings have cost several corporations millions after botched firings. Not surprisingly, entrepreneurs offer seminars entitled "Teaching Managers Finer Points of Firing," many of which have long been basics in human resource management. Just how the firing process has operated in many firms is exemplified in "One Day You're Family; the Next Day You're Fired." The author's reactions touched off two responses; one of which—"In Downsizing, Do Unto Others . . . "—ably addresses the ethical questions associated with firing a long-time employee.

We end this introduction with a note to the reader. Ethics in business is an important and pervasive issue for everyone who is pursuing a professional career. Many of the readings in this book have an ethical dimension. In particular, chapters on secrecy, hazards, and the environment contain material that addresses the ethical question in organizational life.

The Test

S. I. Kishor

Six minutes to six, said the clock over the information booth in New York's Grand Central Station. The tall young Army officer lifted his sunburned face and narrowed his eyes to note the exact time. His heart was pounding with a beat that choked him. In six minutes he would see the woman who had filled such a special place in his life for the past 18 months, the woman he had never seen yet whose words had sustained him unfailingly.

Lt. Blandford remembered one day in particular, the worst of the fighting, when his plane had been caught in the midst of a pack of enemy planes.

In one of those letters, he had confessed to her that often he felt fear, and only a few days before this battle, he had received her answer: "Of course you fear . . . all brave men do." Next time you doubt yourself, I want you to hear my voice reciting to you: 'Yea, though I walk through the valley of Death, I shall fear no evil, for thou art with me.' . . . He had remembered that and it renewed his strength.

He was going to hear her voice now. Four minutes to six.

A girl passed closer to him, and Lt. Blandford started. She was wearing a flower, but it was not the little red rose they had agreed upon. Besides, this girl was only about eighteen, and Hollis Maynel had told him she was 30. "What of it?" he had answered, "I'm 32." He was 29. His mind went back to that book he had read in the training camp. "Of Human Bondage" it was; and throughout the book were notes in a woman's handwriting. He had never believed that a woman could see into a man's heart so tenderly, so understandingly. Her name was on the bookplate: Hollis Maynel. He got a hold of a New York City telephone book and found her address. He had written, she had answered. The next day he had been shipped out, but they had gone on writing. For thirteen months she had faithfully replied. When his letters did not arrive, she wrote anyway, and now he believed he loved her, and she loved him.

But she had refused all his pleas to send him her photograph. She had explained: "If your feeling for me had no reality, what I look like won't matter. Suppose I am beautiful. I'd always be haunted that you had been taking a chance on just that, and that kind of love would disgust me. Suppose that I'm plain (and you must admit that this is more likely), then I'd always fear that you were only going on writing because you were lonely and had no one else. No, don't ask for my picture. When you come to New York, you shall see me and then you shall make your own decision."

One minute to six . . . he flipped the pages of the book he held. Then Lt. Blandford's heart leapt.

A young woman was coming toward him. Her figure was long and slim; her blond hair lay back in curls from delicate ears. Her eyes were blue as flowers, her lips and chin had a gentle firmness. In her pale-green suit, she was like springtime come alive.

He started toward her, forgetting to notice that she was wearing no rose, and as he moved, a small, provocative smile curved her lips. "Going my way, soldier?" she murmured.

He made one step closer to her. Then he saw Hollis Maynel. She was standing almost directly behind the girl, a woman well past 40, her graying hair tucked under a worn hat. She was more than plump. Her thick-ankled feet were thrust into low-heeled shoes. But she wore a red rose on her rumpled coat. The girl in the green suit was walking quickly away.

Blandford felt as though he were being split in two, so keen was his desire to follow the girl, yet so deep was his longing for the woman whose spirit had truly companioned and upheld his own, and there she stood. He could see her pale face was gentle and sensible; her gray eyes had a warm twinkle.

Lt. Blandford did not hesitate. His fingers gripped the worn copy of "Of Human Bondage," which was to identify him to her. This would not be love, but it would be something special, a friendship for which he had been and must be ever grateful . . .

He squared his shoulders, saluted, and held the book out toward the woman, although even while he spoke he felt the bitterness of his disappointment.

"I'm Lt. Blandford, and you're Miss Maynel. I'm so glad you could meet me. May— may I take you to dinner?"

The woman's face broadened in a tolerant smile. "I don't know what this is all about, son," she answered. "That young lady in the green suit, she begged me to wear this rose on my coat. And she said that if you asked me to go out with you, I should tell you she's waiting for you in that restaurant across the street. She said it was some kind of test."

The Parable of the Sadhu

Bowen H. McCoy

Last year, as the first participant in the new six-month sabbatical program that Morgan Stanley has adopted, I enjoyed a rare opportunity to collect my thoughts as well as do some traveling. I spent the first three months in Nepal, walking 600 miles through 200 villages in the Himalayas and climbing some 120,000 vertical feet. On the trip my sole Western companion was an anthropologist who shed light on the cultural patterns of the villages we passed through.

During the Nepal hike, something occurred that has had a powerful impact on my thinking about corporate ethics. Although some might argue that the experience has no relevance to business, it was a situation in which a basic ethical dilemma suddenly intruded into the lives of a group of individuals. How the group responded I think holds a lesson for all organizations no matter how defined.

THE SADHU

The Nepal experience was more rugged and adventuresome than I had anticipated. Most commercial treks last two or three weeks and cover a quarter of the distance we traveled.

My friend Stephen, the anthropologist, and I were halfway through the 60-day Himalayan part of the trip when we reached the high point, an 18,000-foot pass over a

Reprinted by permission of *Harvard Business Review.* "The Parable of the Sadhu" by Bowen H. McCoy, September/October 1983, pp. 103–108. Copyright © 1983 by the President and Fellows of Harvard College; all right reserved.

crest that we'd have to traverse to reach to the village of Muklinath, an ancient holy place for pilgrims.

Six years earlier I had suffered pulmonary edema, an acute form of altitude sickness, at 16,500 feet in the vicinity of Everest base camp, so we were understandably concerned about what would happen at 18,000 feet. Moreover, the Himalayas were having their wettest spring in 20 years; hip-deep powder and ice had already driven us off one ridge. If we failed to cross the pass, I feared that the last half of our "once in a lifetime" trip would be ruined.

The night before we would try the pass, we camped at a hut at 14,500 feet. In the photos taken at that camp, my face appears wan. The last village we'd passed through was a sturdy two-day walk below us, and I was tired.

During the late afternoon, four back-packers from New Zealand joined us, and we spent most of the night awake, anticipating the climb. Below we could see the fires of two other parties, which turned out to be two Swiss couples and a Japanese hiking club.

To get over the steep part of the climb before the sun melted the steps cut in the ice, we departed at 3:30 A.M. The New Zealanders left first, followed by Stephen and myself, our porters and Sherpas, and then the Swiss. The Japanese lingered in their camp. The sky was clear, and we were confident that no spring storm would erupt that day to close the pass.

At 15,500 feet, it looked to me as if Stephen was shuffling and staggering a bit, which are symptoms of altitude sickness. (The initial stage of altitude sickness brings a headache and nausea. As the condition worsens, a climber may encounter difficult breathing, disorientation, aphasia, and paralysis.) I felt strong, my adrenaline was flowing, but I was very concerned about my ultimate ability to get across. A couple of our porters were also suffering from the height, and Pasang, our Sherpa sirdar (leader,) was worried.

Just after daybreak, while we rested at 15,500 feet, one of the New Zealanders, who had gone ahead, came staggering down toward us with a body slung across his shoulders. He dumped the almost naked, barefoot body of an Indian holy man—a sadhu—at my feet. He had found the pilgrim lying on the ice, shivering and suffering from hypothermia. I cradled the sadhu's head and laid him out on the rocks. The New Zealander was angry. He wanted to get across the pass before the bright sun melted the snow. He said, "Look, I've done what I can. You have porters and Sherpa guides. You care for him. We're going on!" He turned and went back up the mountain to join his friends.

I took a carotid pulse and found that the sadhu was still alive. We figured he had probably visited the holy shrines at Muklinath and was on his way home. It was fruitless to question why he had chosen this desperately high route instead of the safe, heavily traveled caravan route through the Kali Gandaki gorge. Or why he was almost naked and with no shoes, or how long he had been lying in the pass. The answers weren't going to solve our problem.

Stephen and the four Swiss began stripping off outer clothing and opening their packs. The sadhu was soon clothed from head to foot. He was not able to walk, but he was very much alive. I looked down the mountain and spotted below the Japanese climbers marching up with a horse.

Without a great deal of thought, I told Stephen and Pasang that I was concerned about withstanding the heights to come and wanted to get over the pass. I took off after several of our porters who had gone ahead.

On the steep part of the ascent where, if the ice steps had given way, I would have slid down about 3,000 feet, I felt vertigo. I stopped for a breather, allowing the Swiss, to catch up with me. I inquired about the sadhu and Stephen. They said that the sadhu was fine and that Stephen was just behind. I set off again for the summit.

Stephen arrived at the summit an hour after I did. Still exhilarated by victory, I ran down the snow slope to congratulate him. He was suffering from altitude sickness, walking 15 steps, then stopping, walking 15 steps, then stopping. Pasang accompanied him all the way up. When I reached them, Stephen glared at me and said: "How do you feel about contributing to the death of a fellow man?"

I did not fully comprehend what he meant.

"Is the sadhu dead?" I inquired.

"No," replied Stephen, "but he surely will be!"

After I had gone, and the Swiss had departed not long after, Stephen had remained with the sadhu. When the Japanese had arrived, Stephen had asked to use their horse to transport the sadhu down to the hut. They had refused. He had then asked Pasang to have a group of our porters carry the sadhu. Pasang had resisted the idea, saying that the porters would have to exert all their energy to get themselves over the pass. He had thought they could not carry a man down 1,000 feet to the hut, reclimb the slope, and get across safely before the snow melted. Pasang had pressed Stephen not to delay any longer.

The Sherpas had carried the sadhu down to a rock in the sun at about 15,000 feet and had pointed out the hut another 500 feet below. The Japanese had given him food and drink. When they had last seen him he was listlessly throwing rocks at the Japanese party's dog, which had frightened him.

We do not know if the sadhu lived or died.

For many of the following days and evenings Stephen and I discussed and debated our behavior toward the sadhu. Stephen is a committed Quaker with deep moral vision. He said, "I feel that what happened with the sadhu is a good example of the breakdown between the individual ethic and the corporate ethic. No one person was willing to assume ultimate responsibility for the sadhu. Each was willing to do his bit just so long as it was not too inconvenient. When it got to be a bother, everyone just passed the buck to someone else and took off. Jesus was relevant to a more individualistic stage of society, but how do we interpret his teaching today in a world filled with large, impersonal organizations and groups?"

I defended the larger group, saying, "Look, we all cared. We all stopped and gave aid and comfort. Everyone did his bit. The New Zealander carried him down below the snow line. I took his pulse and suggested we treat him for hypothermia. You and the Swiss gave him clothing and got him warmed up. The Japanese gave him food and water. The Sherpas carried him down to the sun and pointed out the easy trail toward the hut. He was well enough to throw rocks at a dog. What more could we do?"

"You have just described the typical affluent Westerner's response to a problem. Throwing money—in this case food and sweaters—at it, but not solving the fundamentals!" Stephen retorted.

"What would satisfy you?" I said, "Here we are, a group of New Zealanders, Swiss, Americans, and Japanese who have never met before and who are at the apex of one of the most powerful experiences of our lives. Some years the pass is so bad no one gets over it. What right does an almost naked pilgrim who chooses the wrong trail have to disrupt our lives? Even the Sherpas had no interest in risking the trip to help him beyond a certain point."

Stephen calmly rebutted, "I wonder what the Sherpas would have done if the sadhu had been a well-dressed Nepali, or what the Japanese would have done if the sadhu had been a well-dressed Asian, or what you would have done, Buzz, if the sadhu had been a well-dressed Western woman?"

"Where, in your opinion," I asked instead, "is the limit of our responsibility in a situation like this? We had our own well-being to worry about. Our Sherpa guides were unwilling to jeopardize us or the porters for the sadhu. No one else on the mountain was willing to commit himself beyond certain self-imposed limits."

Stephen said, "As individual Christians or people with a Western ethical tradition, we can fulfill our obligations in such a situation only if (1) the sadhu dies in our care, (2) the sadhu demonstrates to us that he could undertake the two-day walk down to the village or (3) we carry the sadhu for two days down to the village and convince someone there to care for him."

"Leaving the sadhu in the sun with food and clothing, while he demonstrated hand-eye coordination by throwing a rock at a dog, comes close to fulfilling items one and two," I answered. "And it wouldn't have made sense to take him to the village where the people appeared to be far less caring than the Sherpas, so the third condition is impractical. Are you really saying that, no matter what the implications, we should, at the drop of a hat, have changed our entire plan?"

THE INDIVIDUAL VS. THE GROUP ETHIC

Despite my arguments, I felt and continue to feel guilt about the sadhu. I had literally walked through a classic moral dilemma without fully thinking through the consequences. My excuses for my actions include a high adrenaline flow, a superordinate goal, and a once-in-a-lifetime opportunity—factors in the usual corporate situation, especially when one is under stress.

Real moral dilemmas are ambiguous, and many of us hike right through them, unaware that they exist. When, usually after the fact, someone makes an issue of them, we tend to resent his or her bringing it up. Often, when the full import of what we have done (or not done) falls on us, we dig into a defensive position from which it is very difficult to emerge. In rare circumstances we may contemplate what we have done from inside a prison.

Had we mountaineers been free of physical and mental stress caused by the effort and the high altitude, we might have treated the sadhu differently. Yet, isn't stress the real test of personal and corporate values? The instant decisions executives make under pressure reveal the most about personal and corporate character.

Among the many questions that occur to me when pondering my experience are: What are the practical limits of moral imagination and vision? Is there a collective or institutional ethic beyond the ethics of the individual? At what level of effort or commitment can one discharge one's ethical responsibilities?

Not every ethical dilemma has a right solution. Reasonable people often disagree; otherwise there would be no dilemma. In a business context, however, it is essential that managers agree on a process for dealing with dilemmas.

The sadhu experience offers an interesting parallel to business situations. An immediate response was mandatory. Failure to act was a decision in itself. Up on the mountain we could not resign and submit our résumés to a headhunter. In contrast to philosophy, business involves action and implementation—getting things done. Managers must come up with answers to problems based on what they see and what they allow to influence their decision-making processes. On the mountain, none of us but Stephen realized the true dimensions of the situation we were facing.

One of our problems was that as a group we had no process for developing a consensus. We had no sense of purpose or plan. The difficulties of dealing with the sadhu were so complex that no one person could handle it. Because it did not have a set of preconditions that could guide its action to an acceptable resolution, the group reacted instinctively as individuals. The cross-cultural nature of the group added a further layer of complexity. We had no leader with whom we could all identify and in whose purpose we believed. Only Stephen was willing to take charge, but he could not gain adequate support to care for the sadhu.

Some organizations do have a value system that transcends the personal values of the managers. Such values, which go beyond profitability, are usually revealed when the organization is under stress. People throughout the organization generally accept its values, which, because they are not presented as a rigid list of commandments, may be somewhat ambiguous. The stories people tell, rather than printed materials, transmit these conceptions of what is proper behavior.

For 20 years I have been exposed at senior levels to a variety of corporations and organizations. It is amazing how quickly an outsider can sense the tone and style of an organization and the degree of tolerated openness and freedom to challenge management.

Organizations that do not have a heritage of mutually accepted, shared values tend to become unhinged during stress, with each individual bailing out for himself. In the great takeover battles we have witnessed during past years, companies that had strong cultures drew the wagons around them and fought it out, while other companies saw executives supported by their golden parachutes, bail out of the struggles.

Because corporations and their members are interdependent, for the corporation to be strong the members need to share a preconceived notion of what is correct behavior, a "business ethic," and think of it as a positive force, not a constraint.

As an investment banker I am continually warned by well-meaning lawyers, clients, and associates to be wary of conflicts of interest. Yet if I were to run away from every difficult situation, I wouldn't be an effective investment banker. I have to feel my way through conflicts. An effective manager can't run from risk either; he or she has to confront and deal with risk. To feel "safe" in doing this, managers need the guidelines of an agreed-on process and set of values within the organization.

After my three months in Nepal, I spent three months as an executive-in-residence at both Stanford Business School and the Center for Ethics and Social Policy at the Graduate Theological Union at Berkeley. These six months away from my job gave me time to assimilate 20 years of business experience. My thoughts turned often to the meaning of the leadership role in any large organization. Students at the seminary thought of themselves as antibusiness. But when I questioned them they agreed that they distrusted all large organizations, including the church. They perceived all large organizations as impersonal and opposed to individual values and needs. Yet we all know of organizations where peoples' values and beliefs are respected and their expressions encouraged. What makes the difference? Can we identify the difference and, as a result, manage more effectively?

The word "ethics" turns off many and confuses more. Yet the notions of shared values and an agreed-on process for dealing with adversity and change—what many people mean when they talk about corporate culture—seem to be at the heart of the ethical issue. People who are in touch with their own core beliefs and the beliefs of others and are sustained by them can be more comfortable living on the cutting edge. At times, taking a tough line or a decisive stand in a muddle of ambiguity is the only ethical thing to do. If a manager is indecisive and spends time trying to figure out the "good" thing to do, the enterprise may be lost.

Business ethics, then, has to do with the authenticity and integrity of the enterprise. To be ethical is to follow the business as well as the cultural goals of the corporation, its owners, its employees, and its customers. Those who cannot serve the corporate visions are not authentic business people and, therefore, are not ethical in the business sense.

At this stage of my own business experience I have a strong interest in organizational behavior. Sociologists are keenly studying what they call corporate stories, legends, and heroes as a way organizations have of transmitting the value system. Corporations such as Arco have even hired consultants to perform an audit of their corporate culture. In a company, the leader is the person who understands, interprets, and manages the corporate value system. Effective managers are then action-oriented people who resolve conflict, are tolerant of ambiguity, stress, and change, and have a strong sense of purpose for themselves and their organizations.

If all this is true, I wonder about the role of the professional manager who moves from company to company. How can he or she quickly absorb the values and culture of different organizations? Or is there, indeed, an art of management that is totally transportable? Assuming such fungible managers do exist, is it proper for them to manipulate the values of others?

I see the current interest in corporate culture and corporate value systems as a positive response to Stephen's pessimism about the decline of the role of the individual in large organizations. Individuals who operate from a thoughtful set of personal values provide the foundation for a corporate culture. A corporate tradition that encourages freedom of inquiry, supports personal values, and reinforces a focused sense of direction can fulfill the need for individuality along with the prosperity and success of the group. Without such corporate support, the individual is lost.

That is the lesson of the sadhu. In a complex corporate situation, the individual requires and deserves the support of the group. If people cannot find such support from their organization, they don't know how to act. If such support is forthcoming, a person has a stake in the success of the group, and can add much to the process of establishing and maintaining a corporate culture. It is management's challenge to be sensitive to individual needs, to shape them, and to direct and focus them for the benefit of the group as a whole.

For each of us the sadhu lives. Should we stop what we are doing and comfort him; or should we keep trudging up toward the high pass? Should I pause to help the derelict

I pass on the street each night as I walk by the Yale Club en route to Grand Central Station? Am I his brother? What is the nature of our responsibility if we consider ourselves to be ethical persons? Perhaps it is to change the values of the group so that it can, with all its resources, take the other road.

The Downsizing of America: On the Battlefields of Business, Millions of Casualties — Part I

Louis Uchitelle and N.R. Kleinfeld

JUSTIFYING THE AX

Most chief executives and some economists view this interlude as an unavoidable and even healthy period during which efficiency is created out of inefficiency.

They herald the downsizings, messy as they are, as necessary to compete in a global economy. The argument is that some workers must be sacrificed to salvage the organization.

Sears, Roebuck and Company felt its very existence threatened in a world of too many stores and too many ways for people to buy what Sears sold for less. Cost cutting, in the form of 50,000 eliminated jobs in the 1990's, was part of the response. "I felt lousy about it," Arthur C. Martinez, Sears's chairman, said.

"But I was trying to balance that with the other 300,000 employees left, and balance it with the thousands of workers in our supplier community, and with 125,000 retirees who look to Sears for their pensions, and with the needs of our shareholders."

At the Newport News, Va., shipyard of Tenneco Inc., a diversified manufacturer, 11,000 of 29,000 workers have been shed since 1990, largely because of technological efficiencies like automated welding. It's also true that the Pentagon is buying fewer ships. Dana G. Mead, Tenneco's chairman, boasts that Newport News is now as efficient as any shipyard in the world. Four workers operating robots can cut all the ribs of a tanker, a task that had required 21 and took longer.

"The Downsizing of America—On the Battlefields of Business, Millions of Casualties" by Louis Uchitelle and N.R. Kleinfeld, *The New York Times*, March 3, 1996. Reprinted by permission.

"We put in automation to get more competitive," Mr. Mead said, adding that the change won important tanker and submarine contracts. "Then how many workers you build back depends on the rate the commercial business grows, and what the Navy decides to build."

Robert E. Allen, the AT&T chairman who has recently been turned into something of a symbol of corporate avarice for authorizing the elimination of 40,000 jobs, said that intensifying competition left him without choices. He said that with the Baby Bells free to invade AT&T's long-distance stronghold, AT&T's bloated staff of middle managers is no longer affordable.

"The easy thing would be to rest on our laurels and say we are doing pretty well, let's just ride it out," he said. "The initiative we took is to get ahead of the game a little bit."

Also intrinsic to the new message is that the lion's share of raises and bonuses must be channeled to those judged most talented and diligent. This new standard of "pay for performance" has made a growing divide among incomes a hallmark of the layoff era. In essence, a new notion of growth and job creation has emerged in which, rather than an expanding economy benefiting all, only the stellar performers—or those providentially in the right careers—come out ahead.

At the same time, some layoffs seem rooted in economic fashion. An unforgiving Wall Street has given its signals of approval—rising stock prices—to companies that take the meat-axe to their costs. The day Sears announced it was discarding 50,000 jobs, its stock climbed nearly 4 percent. The day Xerox said it would prune 10,000 jobs, its stock surged 7 percent. And thus business has been thrust into a cycle where it is keener about pleasing investors than workers.

How this all plays out is a matter of debate. Some contend that through these adjustments American companies will recapture their past dominance in world markets, and once again be in a position to deliver higher income to most workers. Others predict that creating such fungible workforces will leave businesses with dispirited and disloyal employees who will be less productive. And many economists and chief executives think the job shuffling may be a permanent fixture, always with us, as if the nation had caught a chronic, rasping cough.

GUILT OF THE FIRING SQUADS

It was time, no question. On a cool, pale afternoon, Charles Allen stepped across Fifth Avenue and entered St. Patrick's Cathedral to attend noon Mass. He knows the rite by heart. He goes every day.

Daily Mass is an old habit with new meaning for him. Things are on his mind. One signpost of the downsizing era is the multitude of executives who decided who would go. As a $90,000-a-year banking executive, Mr. Allen had to fire his share of workers. Many, to his mind, were not competent and got their just outcomes. One, however, will not vacate his mind.

As an officer in charge of operations of the Standard Chartered Bank, Mr. Allen had to dispose of one of the three currency traders in the Toronto branch. The consensus choice happened to be a woman who was indisputably the top performer, but had the weakest political bonds. "I knew that she was the best in the department," he said. "But she had not networked. And I had to inform her that she was terminated. And she looked at me with tears in her eyes and said, 'But Charlie, you know better.' I will never forget what she said and how she looked that day."

Each afternoon at Mass, he looks to put the past and the present in perspective. "It is a mark on my character," he said. "I feel a lesser person."

There is a sullen irony to Mr. Allen's story. He lost his own job last May and now wanders with the dispossessed.

As senior managers find themselves making almost pro forma decisions to detonate the careers of thousands of workers, a new management issue has engulfed them: how to prettify a message to their employees and to themselves that is inherently harsh.

Some executives are essentially resorting to camouflage to cope. Top managers at the Stanley Works have shucked their suits and ties and adopted sweaters and slacks, one reason being that they don't want to advertise their roles in these days of downsizing. Layoffs have reached 2,000 people.

Rationalization of a larger good plays a crucial part in enabling senior executives to accept what they do.

R. Alan Hunter, the husky president of Stanley, sat in the company cafeteria recently, in a dark sweater and turtleneck. "Is it better to have 100 people in a world-class plant or 120 in a plant that is not world class and might not survive?" he said. "You have to consider what is best for the shareholders and the organization."

He nodded at the commonly heard lament that businesses are firing their own customers. But he said this did not enter into his thinking because he didn't know where to insert it in the equation. "We know that if Americans have less money to spend, that is not going to help us," he said. "But that is so broad and huge an issue, it is difficult to bring into the decisions."

Studies and anecdotal evidence suggest that employer commitment to diversity has eroded in this wobbly environment. Many women, minorities and older workers express anxiety that they are more vulnerable. The most pronounced effect appears to be on minorities. Employment and earnings of blacks relative to whites have unquestionably declined since the 1970s, according to Labor Department data.

Mr. Hunter of the Stanley Works has it hardest when he returns home. He said he never tells his two children about laying off workers. His wife asks, however, and that is when phrases catch in his throat. "She'll say, 'Why are you doing it?'" he said. "I can answer that more easily to a Stanley employee than to my wife."

He tells her of the need to be more competitive, and she nods. Yes, when she goes shopping, she says, she certainly likes bargains.

Top Brass in U.S. Bucks Belt-Tightening Trend with Hefty Pay Hikes

Associated Press

NEW YORK—Pay for executives of many of the largest U.S. companies rose dramatically in 1995, despite widespread layoffs and restructuring to reduce costs, a published report said.

While earnings of most workers stagnated, chief executives at 76 of the biggest 150 U.S. companies enjoyed a 15 percent hike in median salary and cash bonuses, to more than $2 million, the *New York Times* reported Friday.

It's the fastest rate since the mid-1980s, when pay for performance became the norm for rewarding executives. Since 1988, median compensation packages have risen by 11 percent or less, the paper said, citing a survey conducted by executive pay expert Graef Crystal.

Adding the value of other compensation executives receive, namely stock options, the median increase was up by 31 percent in 1995, to nearly US$5 million, the paper said.

Since many of the companies saw a dramatic slowdown in profit growth last year, the survey suggests executive pay has become more closely tied to stock prices than company profits.

The deceleration came as the economy's "soft landing" took hold and the furious downsizing and cost-cutting of the last several years produced fewer and smaller gains.

Thousands of workers were laid off last year from many of the largest corporations.

Executive pay has climbed at an average rate of nine percent since 1990, while employee wages have never risen by more than four percent a year in the same period, the paper said.

The survey is considered preliminary because many companies have yet to file statements.

The 76 companies used in the survey come from the largest U.S. companies, as measured by the value of their outstanding stock.

The Weekend Sun, Saturday, March 30, 1996.

Mother-to-Be and Daiquiri Lead to Firings

Two cocktail servers were reluctant to serve alcohol to a pregnant woman. They were fired.

SEATTLE—Two cocktail servers tried to talk a pregnant woman out of having a straw-berry daiquiri and ended up losing their jobs.

Danita Fitch, 21, and G. R. Heryford, 22, were fired from a Red Robin restaurant in suburban Tukwila when they tried to stop a patron Heryford described as "very preg-nant" from having the drink on March 13.

A strawberry daiquiri contains two ounces of rum, and drinking alcohol during pregnancy has been linked to birth defects.

Jim Roths, Red Robin's director of operations, said Heryford and Fitch were fired because they did not treat the customer with "respect and dignity."

Heryford said he first asked the woman for age identification.

"I was hoping she didn't have it," he said. "Then I could legally refuse her service."

The woman produced ID showing her to be about 30, so he went to assistant manager Mike Buckley who ordered him to serve her.

Heryford told the *Seattle Times* he served the drink, but asked the woman twice if she wanted it without alcohol.

"She stood up and said, 'The baby's past due; it's had its chance,'" he said.

When Heryford told Fitch what happened, she peeled from a rum bottle the gov-ernment warning against alcohol consumption by pregnant women, placed it on the table and told the woman, "This is in case you don't know."

The woman complained and Buckley fired Fitch on the spot. Heryford was fired the next day.

Heryford said Buckley told them their job was not to lecture customers or offer opinions on prenatal care. But Heryford said he worried the woman "could have walked out of here and had a baby born with alcohol in its blood. Would we be responsible?"

"We were just trying to use our best judgment," he said.

Doug Honig, Seattle public education director for the American Civil Liberties Union, said the ACLU supports the right of an employee to express opinions, if they don't interfere with business.

"Let's say you serve high-cholesterol food," Honig said. "Do you have the right to warn customers that food could lead to heart disease?"

Reprinted by permission of the *St. Petersberg Times*.

Honig said the employer's right to do business outweighs an employee's right to interfere, no matter how good the intentions.

Under a federal law that took effect in November 1989, alcoholic beverages must carry warnings about birth defects and other health hazards related to drinking.

Fitch and Heryford say they hope to urge the state Liquor Control Board to set a policy on serving alcohol to pregnant women.

Drinking during pregnancy can cause fetal alcohol syndrome, which is the main recognized cause of congenital defects, including mental retardation.

Thousands of babies are born each year in the United States with fetal alcohol syndrome. The risk is particularly high for women who have more than two drinks a day and for women who drink in the first trimester of pregnancy.

Studies indicate even moderate drinking in the first month or two of pregnancy—often before women realize they are pregnant—can impair the child's intellectual ability upon reaching school age.

Said James West, head of the Alcohol and Brain Research Laboratory at the University of Iowa College of Medicine: "If the data we have on alcohol and birth defects, if even a fraction of that were available for some other substance, it would be banned."

Moral Mazes: Bureaucracy and Managerial Work

Robert Jackall

With moral choices tied to personal fates, how does bureaucracy shape managerial morality?

Corporate leaders often tell their charges that hard work will lead to success. Indeed, this theory of reward being commensurate with effort has been an enduring belief in our society, one central to our self-image as a people where the "main chance" is available to anyone of ability who has the gumption and the persistence to seize it. Hard work, it is also frequently asserted, builds character. This notion carries less conviction because

Reprinted by permission of *Harvard Business Review.* "Moral Mazes: Bureaucracy and Managerial Work" by Robert Jackall, September/October 1983, pp. 118–130. Copyright © 1983 by the President and Fellows of Harvard College; all rights reserved.

businessmen, and our society as a whole, have little patience with those who make a habit of finishing out of the money. In the end, it is success that matters, that legitimates striving, and that makes work worthwhile.

What if, however, men and women in the big corporation no longer see success as necessarily connected to hard work? What becomes of the social morality of the corporation—I mean the everyday rules in use that people play by—when there is thought to be no "objective" standard of excellence to explain how and why winners are separated from also-rans, how and why some people succeed and others fail?

This is the puzzle that confronted me while doing a great many extensive interviews with managers and executives in several large corporations, particularly in a large chemical company and a large textile firm. I went into these corporations to study how bureaucracy—the prevailing organizational form of our society and economy—shapes moral consciousness. I came to see that managers' rules for success are at the heart of what may be called the bureaucratic ethic.

This article suggests no changes and offers no programs for reform. It is, rather, simply an interpretive sociological analysis of the moral dimensions of managers' work. Some readers may find the essay sharp-edged, others familiar. For both groups, it is important to note at the outset that my materials are managers' own descriptions of their experiences.[1] As it happens, my own research in a variety of other settings suggests that managers' experiences are by no means unique; indeed they have a deep resonance with those of other occupational groups.

WHAT HAPPENED TO THE PROTESTANT ETHIC?

To grasp managers' experiences and the more general implications they contain, one must see them against the background of the great historical transformations, both social and cultural, that produced managers as an occupational group. Since the concern here is with the moral significance of work in business, it is important to begin with an understanding of the original Protestant Ethic, the world view of the rising bourgeois class that spearheaded the emergence of capitalism.

The Protestant Ethic was a set of beliefs that counseled "secular asceticism"—the methodical, rational subjection of human impulse and desire to God's will through "restless, continuous, systematic work in a worldly calling."[2] This ethic of ceaseless work and ceaseless renunciation of the fruits of one's toil provided both the economic and the moral foundations for modern capitalism.

On one hand, secular asceticism was a ready-made prescription for building economic capital; on the other, it became for the upward-moving bourgeois class—self-made industrialists, farmers, and enterprising artisans—the ideology that justified

---

[1] There is a long sociological tradition of work on managers and I am, of course, indebted to that literature. I am particularly indebted to the work, both joint and separate, of Joseph Bensman and Arthur J. Vidich, two of the keenest observers of the new middle class. See especially their *The New American Society: The Revolution of the Middle Class* (Chicago: Quadrangle Books, 1971).

[2] See Max Weber, *The Protestant Ethic and the Spirit of Capitalism,* translated by Talcott Parsons (New York: Charles Scribner's Sons. 1958), p. 172.

their attention to this world, their accumulation of wealth, and indeed the social inequities that inevitably followed such accumulation. This bourgeois ethic, with its imperatives for self-reliance, hard work, frugality, and rational planning, and its clear definition of success and failure, came to dominate a whole historical epoch in the West.

But the ethic came under assault from two directions. First, the very accumulation of wealth that the old Protestant Ethic made possible gradually stripped away the religious basis of the ethic, especially among the rising middle class that benefited from it. There were, of course, periodic reassertions of the religious context of the ethic, as in the case of John D. Rockefeller and his turn toward Baptism. But on the whole, by the late 1800s the religious roots of the ethic survived principally among independent farmers and proprietors of small businesses in rural areas and towns across America.

In the mainstream of an emerging urban America, the ethic had become secularized into the "work ethic," "rugged individualism," and especially the "success ethic." By the beginning of this century, among most of the economically successful, frugality had become an aberration, conspicuous consumption the norm. And with the shaping of the mass consumer society later in this century, the sanctification of consumption became widespread, indeed crucial to the maintenance of the economic order.

Affluence and the emergence of the consumer society were responsible, however, for the demise of only aspects of the old ethic—namely, the imperatives for saving and investment. The core of the ethic, even in its later, secularized form—self-reliance, unremitting devotion to work, and a morality that postulated just rewards for work well done—was undermined by the complete transformation of the organizational form of work itself. The hallmarks of the emerging modern production and distribution systems were administrative hierarchies, standardized work procedures, regularized timetables, uniform policies, and centralized control—in a word, the bureaucratization of the economy.

This bureaucratization was heralded at first by a very small class of salaried managers, who were later joined by legions of clerks and still later by technicians and professionals of every stripe. In this century, the process spilled over from the private to the public sector and government bureaucracies came to rival those of industry. This great transformation produced the decline of the old middle class of entrepreneurs, free professionals, independent farmers, and small independent businessmen—the traditional carriers of the old Protestant Ethic—and the ascendance of a new middle class of salaried employees whose chief common characteristic was and is their dependence on the big organization.

Any understanding of what happened to the original Protestant Ethic and to the old morality and social character it embodied—and therefore any understanding of the moral significance of work today—is inextricably tied to an analysis of bureaucracy. More specifically, it is, in my view, tied to an analysis of the work and occupational cultures of managerial groups within bureaucracies. Managers are the quintessential bureaucratic work group; they not only fashion bureaucratic rules, but they are also bound by them. Typically, they are not just *in* the organization; they are *of* the organization. As such, managers represent the prototype of the white-collar salaried employee. By analyzing the kind of ethic bureaucracy produces in managers, one can begin to understand how bureaucracy shapes morality in our society as a whole.

PYRAMIDAL POLITICS

American businesses typically both centralize and decentralize authority. Power is concentrated at the top in the person of the chief executive officer and is simultaneously decentralized; that is, responsibility for decisions and profits is pushed as far down the organizational line as possible. For example, the chemical company that I studied—and its structure is typical of other organizations I examined—is one of several operating companies of a large and growing conglomerate. Like the other operating companies, the chemical concern has its own president, executive vice presidents, vice presidents, other executive officers, business area managers, entire staff divisions, and operating plants. Each company is, in effect, a self-sufficient organization, though they are all coordinated by the corporation, and each president reports directly to the corporate CEO.

Now, the key interlocking mechanism of this structure is its reporting system. Each manager gathers up the profit targets or other objectives of his or her subordinates, and with these formulates his commitments to his boss; this boss takes these commitments, and those of his other subordinates, and in turn makes a commitment to *his* boss. (Note: henceforth only "he" or "his" will be used to allow for easier reading.) At the top of the line, the president of each company makes his commitment to the CEO of the corporation, based on the stated objectives given to him by his vice presidents. There is always pressure from the top to set higher goals.

This management-by-objectives system, as it is usually called, creates a chain of commitments from the CEO down to the lowliest product manager. In practice, it also shapes a patrimonial authority arrangement which is crucial to defining both the immediate experiences and the long-run career chances of individual managers. In this world, a subordinate owes fealty principally to his immediate boss. A subordinate must not overcommit his boss; he must keep the boss from making mistakes, particularly public ones; he must not circumvent the boss. On a social level, even though an easy, breezy informality is the prevalent style of American business, the subordinate must extend to the boss a certain ritual deference: for instance, he must follow the boss's lead in conversation, he must not speak out of turn at meetings, and must laugh at the boss's jokes while not making jokes of his own.

In short, the subordinate must not exhibit any behavior which symbolizes parity. In return, he can hope to be elevated when and if the boss is elevated, although other important criteria also intervene here. He can also expect protection for mistakes made up to a point. However, that point is never exactly defined and always depends on the complicated politics of each situation.

Who Gets Credit?

It is characteristic of this authority system that details are pushed down and credit is pushed up. Superiors do not like to give detailed instructions to subordinates. The official reason for this is to maximize subordinates' autonomy; the underlying reason seems to be to get rid of tedious details and to protect the privilege of authority to declare that a mistake has been made.

It is not at all uncommon for very bald and extremely general edicts to emerge from on high. For example, "Sell the plant in St. Louis. Let me know when you've struck a deal." This pushing down of details has important consequences:

1. Because they are unfamiliar with entangling details, corporate higher echelons tend to expect highly successful results without complications. This is central to top executives' well-known aversion to bad news and to the resulting tendency to "kill the messenger" who bears that news.

2. The pushing down of detail creates great pressure on middle managers not only to transmit good news but to protect their corporations, their bosses, and themselves in the process. They become the "point men" of a given strategy and the potential "fall guys" when things go wrong.

Credit flows up in this structure and usually is appropriated by the highest ranking officer involved in a decision. This person redistributes credit as he chooses, bound essentially by a sensitivity to public perceptions of his fairness. At the middle level, credit for a particular success is always a type of refracted social honor; one cannot claim credit even if it is earned. Credit has to be given, and acceptance of the gift implicitly involves a reaffirmation and strengthening of fealty. A superior may share some credit with subordinates in order to deepen fealty relationships and induce greater future efforts on his behalf. Of course, a different system is involved in the allocation of blame, a point I shall discuss later.

Fealty to the 'King'

Because of the interlocking character of the commitment system, a CEO carries enormous influence in his corporation. If, for a moment, one thinks of the presidents of individual operating companies as barons, then the CEO of the parent company is the king. His word is law; even the CEO's wishes and whims are taken as commands by close subordinates on the corporate staff, who zealously turn them into policies and directives.

A typical example occurred in the textile company last year when the CEO, new at the time, expressed mild concern about the rising operating costs of the company's fleet of rented cars. The following day, a stringent system for monitoring mileage replaced the previous casual practice.

Great efforts are made to please the CEO. For example, when the CEO of the large conglomerate that includes the chemical company visits a plant, the most important order of business for local management is a fresh paint job, even when, as in several cases last year, the cost of the paint alone exceeds $100,000. I am told that similar anecdotes from other organizations have been in circulation since 1910; this suggests a certain historical continuity of behavior toward top bosses.

The second order of business for the plant management is to produce a complete book describing the plant and its operations, replete with photographs and illustrations, for presentation to the CEO; such a book costs about $10,000 for the single copy. By any standards of budgetary stringency, such expenditures are irrational. But by the social standards of the corporation, they make perfect sense. It is far more important to please the king today than to worry about the future economic state of one's fief, since if one does not please the king, there may not be a fief to worry about or indeed any vassals to do the worrying.

By the same token, all of this leads to an intense interest in everything the CEO does and says. In both the chemical and the textile companies, the most common topic of conversation among managers up and down the line is speculation about their respective CEO's plans, intentions, strategies, actions, styles, and public images.

Such speculation is more than idle gossip. Because he stands at the apex of the corporation's bureaucratic and patrimonial structures and locks the intricate system of commitments between bosses and subordinates into place, it is the CEO who ultimately decides whether those commitments have been satisfactorily met. Moreover, the CEO and his trusted associates determine the fate of whole business areas of a corporation.

Shake-ups and Contingency

One must appreciate the simultaneously monocratic and patrimonial character of business bureaucracies in order to grasp what we might call their contingency. One has only to read the *Wall Street Journal* or the *New York Times* to realize that, despite their carefully constructed "eternal" public image, corporations are quite unstable organizations. Mergers, buy-outs, divestitures, and especially "organizational restructuring" are commonplace aspects of business life. I shall discuss only organizational shake-ups here.

Usually, shake-ups occur because of the appointment of a new CEO and/or division president, or because of some failure that is adjusted to demand retribution; sometimes these occurrences work together. The first action of most new CEOs is some form of organizational change. On the one hand, this prevents the inheritance of blame for past mistakes; on the other, it projects an image of bare-knuckled aggressiveness much appreciated on Wall Street. Perhaps most important, a shake-up rearranges the fealty structure of the corporation, placing in power those barons whose style and public image mesh closely with that of the new CEO.

A shake-up has reverberations throughout an organization. Shortly after the new CEO of the conglomerate was named, he reorganized the whole business and selected new presidents to head each of the five newly formed companies of the corporation. He mandated that the presidents carry out a thorough reorganization of their separate companies complete with extensive "census reduction"—that is, firing as many people as possible.

The new president of the chemical company, one of these five, had risen from a small but important specialty chemicals division in the former company. Upon promotion to president, he reached back into his former division, indeed back to his own past work in a particular product line, and systematically elevated many of his former colleagues, friends, and allies. Powerful managers in other divisions, particularly in a rival process chemicals division, were: (1) forced to take big demotions in the new power structure; (2) put on "special assignment"—the corporate euphemism for Siberia (the saying is: "No one ever comes back from special assignment"); (3) fired; or (4) given "early retirement," a graceful way of doing the same thing.

Up and down the chemical company, former associates of the president now hold virtually every important position. Managers in the company view all of this as an inevitable fact of life. In their view, the whole reorganization could easily have gone in a completely different direction had another CEO been named or had the one selected picked a different president for the chemical company, or had the president come from a different work group in the old organization. Similarly, there is the abiding feeling that another significant change in top management could trigger yet another sweeping reorganization.

Fealty is the mortar of the corporate hierarchy, but the removal of one well-placed stone loosens the mortar throughout the pyramid and can cause things to fall apart. And no one is ever quite sure, until after the fact, just how the pyramid will be put back together.

SUCCESS AND FAILURE

It is within this complicated and ambiguous authority structure, always subject to upheaval, that success and failure are meted out to those in the middle and upper middle managerial ranks. Managers rarely spoke to me of objective criteria for achieving success because once certain crucial points in one's career are passed, success and failure seem to have little to do with one's accomplishments. Rather, success is socially defined and distributed. Corporations do demand, of course, a basic competence and sometimes specified training and experience; hiring patterns usually ensure these. A weeding-out process takes place, however, among the lower ranks of managers during the first several years of their experience. By the time a manager reaches a certain numbered grade in the ordered hierarchy—in the chemical company this is Grade 13 out of 25, defining the top 8½% of management in the company—managerial competence as such is taken for granted and assumed not to differ greatly from one manager to the next. The focus then switches to social factors, which are determined by authority and political alignments—the fealty structure—and by the ethos and style of the corporation.

Moving to the Top

In the chemical and textile companies as well as the other concerns I studied, five criteria seem to control a person's ability to rise in middle and upper middle management. In ascending order they are:

1. **Appearance and dress.** This criterion is so familiar that I shall mention it only briefly. Managers have to look the part, and it is sufficient to say that corporations are filled with attractive, well-groomed, and conventionally well-dressed men and women.

2. **Self-control.** Managers stress the need to exercise iron self-control and to have the ability to mask all emotion and intention behind bland, smiling, and agreeable public faces. They believe it is a fatal weakness to lose control of oneself, in any way, in a public forum. Similarly, to betray valuable secret knowledge (for instance, a confidential reorganization plan) or intentions through some relaxation of self-control—for example, an indiscreet comment or lack of adroitness in turning aside a query—can not only jeopardize a manager's immediate position but can undermine others' trust in him.

3. Perception as a team player. While being a team player has many meanings, one of the most important is to appear to be interchangeable with other managers near one's level. Corporations discourage narrow specialization more strongly as one goes higher. They also discourage the expression of moral or political qualms. One might object, for example, to working with chemicals used in nuclear power, and most corporations today would honor that objection. The public statement of such objections, however, would end any realistic aspirations for higher posts because one's usefulness to the organization depends on versatility. As one manager in the chemical company commented: "Well, we'd go along with his request but we'd always wonder about the guy. And in the back of our minds, we'd be thinking that he'll soon object to working in the soda ash division because he doesn't like glass."

Another important meaning of team play is putting in long hours at the office. This requires a certain amount of sheer physical energy, even though a great deal of this time is spent not in actual work but in social rituals—like reading and discussing newspaper articles, taking coffee breaks, or having informal conversations. These rituals, readily observable in every corporation that I studied, forge the social bonds that make real managerial work—that is, group work of various sorts—possible. One must participate in the rituals to be considered effective in the work.

4. Style. Managers emphasize the importance of "being fast on your feet"; always being well organized; giving slick presentations complete with color slides; giving the appearance of knowledge even in its absence; and possessing a subtle, almost indefinable sophistication, marked especially by an urbane, witty, graceful, engaging, and friendly demeanor.

I want to pause for a moment to note that some observers have interpreted such conformity, team playing, affability, and urbanity as evidence of the decline of the individualism of the old Protestant Ethic.[3] To the extent that commentators take the public images that managers project at face value, I think they miss the main point. Managers up and down the corporate ladder adopt the public faces that they wear quite consciously; they are, in fact, the masks behind which the real struggles and moral issues of the corporation can be found.

Karl Mannheim's conception of self-rationalization or self-streamlining is useful in understanding what is one of the central social psychological processes of organizational life.[4] In a world where appearances—in the broadest sense—mean everything, the wise and ambitious person learns to cultivate assiduously the proper, prescribed modes of appearing. He dispassionately takes stock of himself, treating himself as an object. He analyzes his strengths and weaknesses, and decides what he needs to change in order to survive and flourish in his organization. And then he systematically undertakes a program to reconstruct his image. Self-rationalization curiously parallels the methodical subjection of

[3] See William H. Whyte, *The Organization Man* (New York: Simon & Schuster, 1956), and David Riesman, in collaboration with Reuel Denney and Nathan Glazer, *The Lonely Crowd: A Study of the Changing American Character* (New Haven: Yale University Press, 1950).

[4] Karl Mannheim, *Man and Society in an Age of Reconstruction* [London: Paul (Kegan), Trench, Trubner Ltd. 1940], p. 55.

self to God's will that the old Protestant Ethic counseled; the difference, of course, is that one acquires not moral virtues but a masterful ability to manipulate personae.

5. Patron power. To advance, a manager must have a patron, also called a mentor, a sponsor, a rabbi, or a godfather. Without a powerful patron in the higher echelons of management, one's prospects are poor in most corporations. The patron might be the manager's immediate boss or someone several levels higher in the chain of command. In either case the manager is still bound by the immediate, formal authority and fealty patterns of his position; the new— although more ambiguous—fealty relationships with the patron are added.

A patron provides his "client" with opportunities to get visibility, to showcase his abilities, to make connections with those of high status. A patron cues his client to crucial political developments in the corporation, helps arrange lateral moves if the client's upward progress is thwarted by a particular job or a particular boss, applauds his presentations or suggestions at meetings, and promotes the client during an organizational shakeup. One must of course, be lucky in one's patron. If the patron gets caught in a political crossfire, the arrows are likely to find his clients as well.

Social Definitions of Performance

Surely, one might argue, there must be more to success in the corporation than style, personality, team play, chameleonic adaptability, and fortunate connections. What about the bottom line—profits, performance?

Unquestionably, "hitting your numbers"—that is, meeting the profit commitments already discussed—is important, but only within the social context I have described. There are several rules here. First, no one in a line position—that is, with responsibility for profit and loss—who regularly "misses his numbers" will survive, let alone rise. Second, a person who always hits his numbers but who lacks some or all of the required social skills will not rise. Third, a person who sometimes misses his numbers but who has all the desirable social traits will rise.

Performance is thus always subject to a myriad of interpretations. Profits matter, but it is much more important in the long run to be perceived as "promotable" by belonging to central political networks. Patrons protect those already selected as rising stars from the negative judgments of others; and only the foolhardy point out even egregious errors of those in power or those destined for it.

Failure is also socially defined. The most damaging failure is, as one middle manager in the chemical company puts it, "when your boss or someone who has the power to determine your fate says: 'You failed.'" Such a godlike pronouncement means, of course, out-and-out personal ruin; one must, at any cost, arrange matters to prevent such an occurrence.

As it happens, things rarely come to such a dramatic point even in the midst of an organizational crisis. The same judgment may be made but it is usually called "nonpromotability." The difference is that those who are publicly labeled as failures normally have no choice but to leave the organization; those adjudged nonpromotable can remain, provided they are willing to accept being shelved or, more colorfully, "mushroomed"—that is, kept in a dark place, fed manure, and left to do nothing but grow fat. Usually, seniors do not tell juniors they are nonpromotable (though the verdict may be common knowledge among senior peer groups). Rather, subordinates are expected to get the message after they have been repeatedly overlooked for promotions. In fact, middle managers interpret staying in the same job for more than two or three years as evidence of a negative judgment. This leads to a mobility panic at the middle levels which, in turn, has crucial consequences for pinpointing responsibility in the organization.

Capriciousness of Success

Finally, managers think that there is a tremendous amount of plain luck involved in advancement. It is striking how often managers who pride themselves on being hardheaded rationalists explain their own career patterns and those of others in terms of luck. Various uncertainties shape this perception. One is the sense of organizational contingency. One change at the top can create profound unheaval throughout the entire corporate structure, producing startling reversals of fortune, good or bad, depending on one's connections. Another is the uncertainty of the markets that often makes managerial planning simply elaborate guesswork, causing real economic outcome to depend on factors totally beyond organizational and personal control.

It is interesting to note in this context that a line manager's credibility suffers just as much from missing his numbers on the up side (that is, achieving profits higher than predicted) as from missing them on the down side. Both outcomes undercut the ideology of managerial planning and control, perhaps the only bulwark managers have against market irrationality.

Even managers in staff positions, often quite removed from the market, face uncertainty. Occupational safety specialists, for instance, know that bad publicity from one serious accident in the workplace can jeopardize years of work and scores of safety awards. As one high-ranking executive in the chemical company says, "In the corporate world, 1,000 'Attaboys!' are wiped away by one 'Oh, shit!'"

Because of such uncertainties, managers in all the companies I studied speak continually of the great importance of being in the right place at the right time and of the catastrophe of being in the wrong place at the wrong time. My interview materials are filled with stories of people who were transferred immediately before a big shake-up and, as a result, found themselves riding the crest of a wave to power; of people in a promising business area who were terminated because top management suddenly decided that the area no longer fit the corporate image desired; of others caught in an unpredictable and fatal political battle among their patrons; of a product manager whose plant accidentally produced an odd color batch of chemicals, who sold them as a premium version of the old product, and who is now thought to be a marketing genius.

The point is that managers have a sharply defined sense of the *capriciousness* of organizational life. Luck seems to be as good an explanation as any of why, after a certain point, some people succeed and other fail. The upshot is that many managers decide that they can do little to influence external events in their favor. One can, however, shamelessly streamline oneself, learn to wear all the right masks, and get to know all the right people. And then sit tight and wait for things to happen.

'GUT DECISIONS'

Authority and advancement patterns come together in the decision-making process. The core of the managerial mystique is decision-making prowess, and the real test of such prowess is what managers call "gut decisions," that is, important decisions involving big money, public exposure, or significant effects on the organization. At all but the highest levels of the chemical and textile companies, the rules for making gut decisions are, in the words of one upper middle manager: "(1) Avoid making any decisions if at all possible; and (2) if a decision has to be made, involve as many people as you can so that, if things go south, you're able to point in as many directions as possible."

Consider the case of a large coking plant of the chemical company. Coke making requires a gigantic battery to cook the coke slowly and evenly for long periods; the battery is the most important piece of capital equipment in a coking plant. In 1975, the plant's battery showed signs of weakening and certain managers at corporate headquarters had to decide whether to invest $6 million to restore the battery to top form. Clearly, because of the amount of money involved, this was a gut decision.

No decision was made. The CEO had sent the word out to defer all unnecessary capital expenditures to give the corporation cash reserves for other investments. So the managers allocated small amounts of money to patch the battery up until 1979, when it collapsed entirely. This brought the company into a breach of contract with a steel producer and into violation of various Environmental Protection Agency pollution regulations. The total bill, including lawsuits and now federally mandated repairs to the battery, exceeded $100 million. I have heard figures as high as $150 million, but because of "creative accounting," no one is sure of the exact amount.

This simple but very typical example gets to the heart of how decision making is intertwined with a company's authority structure and advancement patterns. As the chemical company managers see it, the decisions facing them in 1975 and 1979 were crucially different. Had they acted decisively in 1975—in hindsight, the only rational course—they would have salvaged the battery and saved their corporation millions of dollars in the long run.

In the short run, however, since even seemingly rational decisions are subject to widely varying interpretations, particularly decisions which run counter to a CEO's stated objectives, they would have been taking a serious risk in restoring the battery. What is more, their political networks might have unraveled, leaving them vulnerable to attack. They chose short-term safety over long-term gain because they felt they were judged, both by higher authority and by their peers, on their short-term performances. Managers feel that if they do not survive the short run, the long run hardly matters. Even correct decisions can shorten promising careers.

By contrast, in 1979 the decision was simple and posed little risk. The corporation had to meet its legal obligations; also it had to either repair the battery the way the EPA demanded or shut down the plant and lose several hundred million dollars. Since there were no real choices, everyone could agree on a course of action because everyone could appeal to inevitability. Diffusion of responsibility, in this case by procrastinating until total crisis, is intrinsic to organizational life because the real issue in most gut decisions is: Who is going to get blamed if things go wrong?

'Blame Time'

There is no more feared hour in the corporate world than"blame time." Blame is quite different from responsibility. There is a cartoon of Richard Nixon declaring: "I accept all of the responsibility, but none of the blame." To blame someone is to injure him verbally in public; in large organizations, where one's image is crucial, this poses the most serious sort of threat. For managers, blame—like failure—has nothing to do with the merits of a case; it is a matter of social definition. As a general rule, it is those who are or who become politically vulnerable or expendable who get "set up" and become blamable. The most feared situation of all is to end up inadvertently in the wrong place at the wrong time and get blamed.

Yet this is exactly what often happens in a structure that systematically diffuses responsibility. It is because managers fear blame time that they diffuse responsibility; however, such diffusion inevitably means that someone, somewhere is going to become a scapegoat when things go wrong. Big corporations encourage this process by their complete lack of any tracking system. Whoever is currently in charge of an area is responsible—that is, potentially blamable— for whatever goes wrong in the area, even if he has inherited others' mistakes. An example from the chemical company illustrates this process.

When the CEO of the large conglomerate took office, he wanted to rid his capital accounts of all serious financial drags. The corporation had been operating a storage depot for natural gas which it bought, stored, and then resold. Some years before the energy crisis, the company had entered into a long-term contract to supply gas to a buyer—call him Jones. At the time, this was sound deal because it provided a steady market for a stably priced commodity.

When gas prices soared, the corporation was still bound to deliver gas to Jones at 20¢ per unit instead of the going market price of $2. The CEO ordered one of his subordinates to get rid of this albatross as expeditiously as possible. This was done by selling the operation to another party—call him Brown—with the agreement that Brown would continue to meet the contractual obligations to Jones. In return for Brown's assumption of these costly contracts, the corporation agreed to buy gas from Brown at grossly inflated prices to meet some of its own energy needs.

In effect, the CEO transferred the drag on his capital accounts to the company's operating expenses. This enabled him to project an aggressive, asset-reducing image to Wall Street. Several levels down the ladder, however, a new vice president for a particular business found himself saddled with exorbitant operating costs when, during a reorganization, those plants purchasing gas from Brown at inflated prices came under his purview. The high costs helped to undercut the vice president's division earnings and thus to erode his position in the hierarchy. The origin of the situation did not matter. All that counted was that the vice president's division was steadily losing big money. In the end, he resigned to "pursue new opportunities."

One might ask why top management does not institute codes or systems for tracking responsibility. This example provides the clue. An explicit system of accountability for subordinates would probably have to apply to top executives as well and would restrict their freedom. Bureaucracy expands the freedom of those on top by giving them the power to restrict the freedom of those beneath.

On the Fast Track

Managers see what happened to the vice president as completely capricious, but completely understandable. They take for granted the absence of any tracking of responsibility. If anything, they blame the vice president for not recognizing soon enough the dangers of the situation into which he was being drawn and for not preparing a defense—even perhaps finding a substitute scapegoat. At the same time, they realize that this sort of thing could easily happen to them. They see few defenses against being caught in the wrong place at the wrong time except constant wariness, the diffusion of responsibility, and perhaps being shrewd enough to declare the ineptitude of one's predecessor on first taking a job.

What about avoiding the consequences of their own errors? Here they enjoy more control. They can "outrun" their mistakes so that when blame time arrives, the burden will fall on someone else. The ideal situation, of course, is to be in a position to fire one's successors for one's own previous mistakes.

Some managers, in fact, argue that outrunning mistakes is the real key to managerial success. One way to do this is by manipulating the numbers. Both the chemical and the textile companies place a great premium on a division's or a subsidiary's return on assets. A good way for business managers to increase their ROA is to reduce their assets while maintaining sales. Usually they will do everything they can to hold down expenditures in order to decrease the asset base, particularly at the end of the fiscal year. The most common way of doing this is by deferring capital expenditures, from maintenance to innovative investments, as long as possible. Done for a short time, this is called "starving" a plant; done over a longer period, it is called "milking" a plant.

Some managers become very adept at milking businesses and showing a consistent record of high returns. They move from one job to another in a company, always upward, rarely staying more than two years in any post. They may leave behind them deteriorating plants and unsafe working conditions, but they know that if they move quickly enough, the blame will fall on others. In this sense, bureaucracies may be thought of as vast systems of organized irresponsibility.

FLEXIBILITY AND DEXTERITY WITH SYMBOLS

The intense competition among managers takes place not only behind the agreeable public faces I have described but within an extraordinarily indirect and ambiguous linguistic framework. Except at blame time, managers do not publicly criticize or disagree with one another or with company policy. The sanction against such criticism or disagreement is so strong that it constitutes, in managers' view, a suppression of professional debate. The sanction seems to be rooted principally in their acute sense of organizational contingency; the person one criticizes or argues with today could be one's boss tomorrow.

This leads to the use of an elaborate linguistic code marked by emotional neutrality, especially in group settings. The code communicates the meaning one might wish to convey to other managers, but since it is devoid of any significant emotional sentiment, it can be reinterpreted should social relationships or attitudes change. Here, for example, are some typical phrases describing performance appraisals followed by their probable intended meanings:

Stock phrase	Probable intended meaning
Exceptionally well qualified	Has committed no major blunders to date
Tactful in dealing with superiors	Knows when to keep his mouth shut
Quick thinking	Offers plausible excuses for errors
Meticulous attention to detail	A nitpicker
Slightly below average	Stupid
Unusually loyal	Wanted by no one else

For the most part, such neutered language is not used with the intent to deceive; rather, its purpose is to communicate certain meanings within specific contexts with the implicit understanding that, should the context change, a new, more appropriate meaning can be attached to the language already used. In effect, the corporation is a setting where people are not held to their word because it is generally understood that their word is always provisional.

The higher one goes in the corporate world, the more this seems to be the case; in fact, advancement beyond the upper middle level depends greatly on one's ability to manipulate a variety of symbols without becoming tied to or identified with any of them. For example, an amazing variety of organizational improvement programs marks practically every corporation. I am referring here to the myriad ideas generated by corporate staff, business consultants, academics, and a host of others to improve corporate structure; sharpen decision making; raise morale; create a more humanistic workplace; adopt Theory X, Theory Y, or, more recently, Theory Z of management; and so on. These programs become important when they are pushed from the top.

The watchword in the large conglomerate at the moment is productivity and, since this is a pet project of the CEO himself, it is said that no one goes into his presence without wearing a blue *Productivity!* button and talking about "quality circles" and "feedback sessions." The president of another company pushes a series of managerial seminars that endlessly repeats the basic functions of management: (1) planning, (2) organizing, (3) motivating, and (4) controlling. Aspiring young managers attend these sessions and with a seemingly dutiful eagerness learn to repeat the formulas under the watchful eyes of senior officials.

Privately, managers characterize such programs as the "CEO's incantations over the assembled multitude," as "elaborate rituals with no practical effect," or as "waving a magic wand to make things wonderful again." Publicly, of course, managers on the way up adopt the programs with great enthusiasm, participate in or run them very effectively, and then quietly drop them when the time is right.

Playing the Game

Such flexibility, as it is called, can be confusing even to those in the inner circles. I was told the following by a highly placed staff member whose work requires him to interact daily with the top figures of his company:

"I get faked out all the time and I'm part of the system. I come from a very differ-ent culture. Where I come from, if you give someone your *word,* no one ever questions it. It's the old hard-work-will-lead-to-success ideology. Small community, Protestant, agrarian, small business, merchant-type values. I'm disadvantaged in a system like this."

He goes on to characterize the system more fully and what it takes to succeed within it:

"It's the ability to play this system that determines whether you will rise. . . . And part of the adeptness [required] is determined by how much it bothers people. One thing you have to be able to do is to play the game, but you can't be disturbed by the game. What's the game? It's bringing troops home from Vietnam and declaring peace with honor. It's saying one thing and meaning another.

"It's characterizing the reality of a situation with *any* description that is necessary to make that situation more palatable to some group that matters. It means that you have to come up with a culturally accepted verbalization to explain why you are *not* doing what you are doing. . . . [Or] you say that we had to do what we did because it was in-evitable; or because the guys at the [regulatory] agencies were dumb; [you] say we won when we really lost; [you] say we saved money when we squandered it; [you] say some-thing's safe when it's potentially or actually dangerous. . . . Everyone knows it's bullshit, but it's *accepted.* This is the game."

In addition, then, to the other characteristics that I have described, it seems that a prerequisite for big success in the corporation is a certain adeptness at inconsistency. This premium on inconsistency is particularly evident in the many areas of public con-troversy that face top-ranking managers. Two things come together to produce this situ-ation. The first is managers' sense of beleaguerment from a wide array of adversaries who, it is thought, want to disrupt or impede management's attempts to further the eco-nomic interests of their companies. In every company that I studied, managers see them-selves and their traditional prerogatives as being under siege, and they respond with a set of caricatures of their perceived principal adversaries.

For example, government regulators are brash, young, unkempt hippies in blue jeans who know nothing about the businesses for which they make rules; environmen-tal activists—the bird and bunny people—are softheaded idealists who want everybody to live in tents, burn candles, ride horses, and eat berries; workers' compensation lawyers are out-and-out crooks who prey on corporations to appropriate exorbitant fees from unwary clients; labor activists are radical troublemakers who want to disrupt har-monious industrial communities; and the news media consist of rabble-rousers who propagate sensational antibusiness stories to sell papers or advertising time on shows like "60 Minutes."

Second, within this context of perceived harassment, managers must address a mul-tiplicity of audiences, some of whom are considered adversaries. These audiences are the internal corporate hierarchy with its intricate and shifting power and status cliques, key regulators, key local and federal legislators, special publics that vary according to the issues, and the public at large, whose goodwill and favorable opinion are considered essential for a company's free operation.

Managerial adeptness at inconsistency becomes evident in the widely discrepant perspectives, reasons for action, and presentations of fact that explain, excuse, or justify corporate behavior to these diverse audiences.

Adeptness at Inconsistency

The cotton dust issue in the textile industry provides a fine illustration of what I mean. Prolonged exposure to cotton dust produces in many textile workers a chronic and eventually disabling pulmonary disease called byssinosis or, colloquially, brown lung. In the early 1970s, the Occupational Safety and Health Administration proposed a ruling to cut workers' exposure to cotton dust sharply by requiring textile companies to invest large amounts of money in cleaning up their plants. The industry fought the regulation fiercely but a final OSHA ruling was made in 1978 requiring full compliance by 1984.

The industry took the case to court. Despite an attempt by Reagan appointees in OSHA to have the case removed from judicial consideration and remanded to the agency they controlled for further cost/benefit analysis, the Supreme Court ruled in 1981 that the 1978 OSHA ruling was fully within the agency's mandate, namely, to protect workers' health and safety as the primary benefit exceeding all cost considerations.

During these proceedings, the textile company was engaged on a variety of fronts and was pursuing a number of actions. For instance, it intensively lobbied regulators and legislators and it prepared court materials for the industry's defense, arguing that the proposed standard would crush the industry and that the problem, if it existed, should be met by increasing workers' use of respirators.

The company also aimed a public relations barrage at special-interest groups as well as at the general public. It argued that there is probably no such thing as byssinosis; workers suffering from pulmonary problems are all heavy smokers and the real culprit is the government-subsidized tobacco industry. How can cotton cause brown lung when cotton is white? Further, if there is a problem, only some workers are afflicted, and therefore the solution is more careful screening of the work force to detect susceptible people and prevent them from ever reaching the workplace. Finally, the company claimed that if the regulation were imposed, most of the textile industry would move overseas where regulations are less harsh.[5]

In the meantime, the company was actually addressing the problem but in a characteristically indirect way. It invested $20 million in a few plants where it knew such an investment would make money; this investment automated the early stages of handling cotton, traditionally a very slow procedure, and greatly increased productivity. The investment had the side benefit of reducing cotton dust levels to the new standard in precisely those areas of the work process where the dust problem is greatest. Publicly, of course, the company claims that the money was spent entirely to eliminate dust, evidence of its corporate good citizenship. (Privately, executives admit that, without the productive return, they would not have spent the money and they have not done so in several other plants.)

Indeed, the productive return is the only rationale that carries weight within the corporate hierarchy. Executives also admit, somewhat ruefully and only when their office doors are closed, that OSHA's regulation on cotton dust has been the main factor in forcing technological innovation in a centuries-old and somewhat stagnant industry.

---

[5] On February 9, 1982, the Occupational Safety and Health Administration issued a notice that it was once again reviewing its 1978 standard on cotton dust for "cost-effectiveness." See *Federal Register,* vol. 47, p. 5906. As of this writing (May 1983), this review has still not been officially completed.

Such adeptness at inconsistency, without moral uneasiness, is essential for executive success. It means being able to say, as a very high-ranking official of the textile company said to me without batting an eye, that the industry has never caused the slightest problem in any worker's breathing capacity. It means, in the chemical company, propagating an elaborate hazard/benefit calculus for appraisal of dangerous chemicals while internally conceptualizing "hazards" as business risks. It means publicly extolling the carefulness of testing procedures on toxic chemicals while privately ridiculing animal tests as inapplicable to humans.

It means lobbying intensively in the present to shape government regulations to one's immediate advantage and, ten years later, in the event of a catastrophe, arguing that the company acted strictly in accordance with the standards of the time. It means claiming that the real problem of our society is its unwillingness to take risks, while in the thickets of one's bureaucracy avoiding risks at every turn; it means as well making every effort to socialize the risks of industrial activity while privatizing the benefits.

THE BUREAUCRATIC ETHIC

The bureaucratic ethic contrasts sharply with the original Protestant Ethic. The Protestant Ethic was the ideology of a self-confident and independent propertied social class. It was an ideology that extolled the virtues of accumulating wealth in a society organized around property and that accepted the stewardship responsibilities entailed by property. It was an ideology where a person's word was his bond and where the integrity of the handshake was seen as crucial to the maintenance of good business relationships. Perhaps most important, it was connected to a predictable economy of salvation—that is, hard work will lead to success, which is a sign of one's election by God—a notion also containing its own theodicy to explain the misery of those who do not make it in this world.

Bureaucracy, however, breaks apart substance from appearances, action from responsibility, and language from meaning. Most important, it breaks apart the older connection between the meaning of work and salvation. In the bureaucratic world, one's success, one's sign of election, no longer depends on one's own efforts and on an inscrutable God but on the capriciousness of one's superiors and the market; and one achieves economic salvation to the extent that one pleases and submits to one's employer and meets the exigencies of an impersonal market.

In this way, because moral choices are inextricably tied to personal fates, bureaucracy erodes internal and even external standards of morality, not only in matters of individual success and failure but also in all the issues that managers face in their daily work. Bureaucracy makes its own internal rules and social context the principal moral gauges for action. Men and women in bureaucracies turn to each other for moral cues for behavior and come to fashion specific situational moralities for specific significant people in their worlds.

As it happens, the guidance they receive from each other is profoundly ambiguous because what matters in the bureaucratic world is not what a person is but how closely his many personae mesh with the organizational ideal; not his willingness to stand by his actions but his agility in avoiding blame; not what he believes or says but how well he has mastered the ideologies that serve his corporation; not what he stands for but whom he stands with in the labyrinths of his organization.

In short, bureaucracy structures for managers an intricate series of moral mazes. Even the inviting paths out of the puzzle often turn out to be invitations to jeopardy.

Seminars Teach Managers Finer Points of Firing

Andrea Gerlin

Staff Reporter of The Wall Street Journal

On cue, 70 managers in a hotel conference room turn to each other and say, "You're fired."

Then—to the chagrin of their instructor—they laugh.

"Is that what we do—bring people in, fire them and laugh at them?" scolds Dale Mask, a firing instructor for Padgett-Thompson, a division of the nonprofit American Management Association.

Firing lessons may be the hottest trend in management seminars. The nation's top career-seminar companies, including National Seminars Inc. and Career Track Seminars, are teaching managers how to sack workers. Attendance is robust. Two years after Padgett-Thompson started its firing seminar, the number of its sessions has grown to more than 150 a year, each drawing about 70 managers paying $145 each.

The popularity is partly attributable to more firings. The U.S. Bureau of Labor Statistics says that 10.1 million American workers were "displaced," or lost their jobs, between 1989 and 1992, 35% more than in the previous four-year period.

But a larger factor is employee retaliation. The number of discharge-related complaints filed with the U.S. Equal Employment Opportunity Commission has shot up 33% since 1990. And jilted ex-employees of firms such as Procter & Gamble Co. and All-state Insurance Co. have made headlines in recent years by winning multimillion-dollar jury awards after botched firings.

As a result, firing seminars devote limited attention to minimizing trauma for terminated workers and lots to minimizing employers' legal exposure. When Mr. Mask cautions managers in his seminar not to laugh at fired workers, for instance, he isn't worried about their feelings. He's worried about litigation.

"Seminars Teach Managers Finer Points of Firing" by Andrea Gerlin, *The Wall Street Journal,* April 26, 1995, p. B1. Reprinted by permission.

"We have a firefight on this hiring-firing front," he says, reciting an alphabet soup of legislation and agencies—the ADA, FMLA, ADEA, EEOC—with which employers can get into trouble over firing.

Yet can experts really teach managers how to fire without consequence?

No one claims to have found a foolproof way of avoiding litigation, or even costly verdicts. But instructors say they can improve a manager's chances of staying out of court, or winning in it, if worse comes to worst. In any case, they say that fear of litigation should never prevent managers from getting rid of unwanted workers. "There's no law that will keep you from doing what you need to do," asserts Mr. Mask.

The title of the Padgett-Thompson seminar is "How to Legally Fire Employees with Attitude Problems." Padgett-Thompson says participants will learn how to "legally, safely and confidently" rid their work forces of "foot draggers, whiners, jabbermouths, sharks and snoops," not to mention the "worker whose personality grates on everyone's nerves."

The 70 managers attending a recent seminar in Boston come from large companies and small, as well as from government agencies. Some were sent by employers, and others came of their own volition. A few are preparing for specific termination. Some, such as Scott Lefton, have had bad firing experiences they hope not to repeat. Mr. Lefton, operations manager at Fishman Transducers Inc. in Wilmington, Mass., once had a worker on the verge of being fired begin boasting of a large gun collection.

Although Padgett-Thompson employs several instructors, this session is led by the 51-year-old Mr. Mask, a termination enthusiast in a pinstripe suit. A former manager and small-business owner who now teaches seminars full time, he recalls axing "dozens" of employees during his 25-year career. He has also been forced to defend firings that employees legally challenged, but he declines to discuss those cases.

To the disappointment of anyone who took the title literally, Mr. Mask quickly concedes that attitude doesn't necessarily constitute grounds for termination. Rather, he says managers should closely monitor the performance of employees with poor attitudes. "A bad attitude will manifest itself in what they do," he says.

For managers who came to the seminar hoping to learn a quick and easy way to fire, monitoring performance and documenting lapses can sound like a long process. And Mr. Mask concedes that his seminar's marketing material can create unrealistic expectations. "A lot of people come to this seminar saying I'll be here Friday and I'll fire 'em Monday," he says. "Then they realize they have to go through this whole process."

A 22-point checklist distributed at the seminar suggests looking at each case as a jury or arbitrator would. Facts should be documented as incidents occur, and communication with the employee should be direct and timely. Evaluations should be objective and without secondhand information, suspicion or emotion. No firing should come as a surprise to the worker, who should have a fixed but reasonable period of time to reverse course, typically several months. Termination should be approved by management and discussed with legal counsel.

Timing is critical. Mr. Mask recommends midweek mornings as optimal to give the worker time to recover. Forget impersonal pink slips in pay envelopes, he adds. The session should be handled personally, not delegated to a subordinate. And except for the presence of a management-level witness, it should always be private. "Simply announce a decision has been made," Mr. Mask says. "Never apologize, agree or argue."

This should take no more than 10 to 15 minutes, followed by a prescheduled-appointment with a personnel representative. Afterward, the instructor advises implementing safeguards to prevent retaliation and to discourage defamation suits, giving accurate information about the firing only to people who need it.

During the seminar, Mr. Mask fields some questions from the battlefront. A chief executive asks how to deal with a rumor-mongering middle manager several layers down in her social-service agency. When she counsels the manager about her behavior, the manager repeats it to others "with a negative twist." Mr. Mask advises her to confront the manager, then to start documenting and securing witnesses for any further episodes.

Some observers worry that these seminars will only deepen a fear of firing that already pervades the workplace. Robert Brodie of outplacement firm Drake Beam Morin's office in Boca Raton, Fla., says of the Padgett-Thompson seminar, "Just the title frightens me."

Employees, of course, would be frightened to learn that the boss just attended a how-to-fire seminar. For that reason, Christina Shaw, human-resources director of Nantucket Cottage Hospital in Nantucket, Mass., doesn't intend to hang on her office wall the firing certificate she received after completing the seminar. "I'll put it in my personnel folder," she says.

One Day You're Family; The Next Day You're Fired

Wilfred Popoff

What amazed me most about my firing was the way civility was sacrificed in the process. Civility is something I've cherished all my life, a legacy of my upbringing, and until the other day I felt it had governed my relationship with my employer over 30-odd years.

It was a family-owned company and I had worked diligently for three generations of owners, without a trace of rancour touching our relationship; in fact, I always believed there was an abundance of mutual respect and trust. Come to think of it, I didn't even ask them for a job: They approached me. Those really were the good old days.

So I can only attribute my sudden firing, within several months of possible retirement, a dignified retirement I had seen so many others receive, to a total abandonment

"One Day You're Family; The Next Day You're Fired" by Wilfred Popoff, *The Globe and Mail,* March 14, 1996. Reprinted by permission.

of common civility, a phenomenon more and more prevalent today. You see, I was fired not because of anything I did or didn't do, but because of the need to cut costs in the quest for fantastic profits. Scores of others went with me. And how the affair was stage-managed tells more than one wishes to know about the uncivil environment surrounding contemporary capitalism.

On Friday afternoon all employees, about 300 in all, received a terse letter from the boss commanding attendance at a meeting in a hotel the following morning. The arrangement was reminiscent of military occupations portrayed in countless movies: The vanquished are summoned to the market square where officers of the occupying army register all people and direct them to various camps. In our case the officers were employees of a consulting firm, also strangers, who directed employees to various rooms, separating survivors from those marked for elimination. Of course, I was in the second group, although none of us knew what fate awaited us. Eventually the boss entered, gripped the lectern and read a brief statement: We all were finished, the decision was final.

Not only were we finished, our place of work a few blocks away had been locked up, incapacitating our entry cards, and was under guard. We could never go back, except to retrieve our personal belongings, and this under the watchful eye of a senior supervisor and one of the newly retained guards. I felt like a criminal. In my time I had managed large portions of this company, had represented it the world over and, until the previous day, had authority to spend its money. Now I couldn't be trusted not to snitch a pencil or note pad.

As I said, I was several months from early retirement. I'll be 55 later this year. Over many years I had been witness to numerous retirements. Almost weekly someone was around collecting for so-and-so who was retiring. There would be a party, presents, the obligatory card inscribed with witticisms and, of course, funny speeches. And, yes, there would be thanks from the current proprietor. It was all part of the civility that affected our lives.

My father used to say as he was preparing to go to a funeral: "If you don't go to funerals, you can't expect people to come to yours." As a boy I was puzzled. The dead won't come back for your funeral! He was talking about the *quid pro quo* that attends civility; it also stalks that great democratic institution known as capitalism.

After spending most of my adult life saying good things about my company and the family that owned it, I feel let down. And after devoting my life to defending capitalism, even when it was not a popular thing to do, I find myself part of a growing group of observers who are beginning to question its morality and wisdom. Actually these doubts have plagued me for several months now, so my firing wasn't the inspiration.

The current phenomenon known as downsizing is threatening to hurt capitalism by depriving it of the very thing it needs most: a market, This, however, speaks to the stupidity of capitalism today, not its abandonment of civility. But perhaps there is a connection.

In Downsizing, Do Unto Others . . .

Bob Evans

First we read of Wilfred Popoffs bewilderment and sense of betrayal over his firing by the Saskatoon Star-Phoenix (One Day You're Family; The Next Day You're Fired—March 14) and in particular of his distress over the churlish and insensitive way in which it was done.

Five days later, Cheryl Tibbetts responded with a well-crafted distillation of the finest in 19th-century management philosophy (A Sheep In Capitalist's Clothing—March, 19), unimproved by the slightest understanding of the psychological and social realities of work, or the longer-term deleterious effects upon the whole economy that proceed from actions that rupture the already tattered employer-employee relationship.

I have been involved in the curious business called outplacement for over 20 years. It might be a conceit to say that I have seen it all but I do not think that I have missed too much. An outplacement consultant's job is to advise organizations on how to plan and execute a downsizing or an individual dismissal in a way that minimizes the social, psychological and economic damage that attends these almost always unpleasant activities. As well, it is my job to counsel, train and support the dismissed employees so as to expedite their efforts to find new employment.

Mr. Popoff's reactions to his firing was about as normal as you are likely to find. As he pointed out, he went in a moment from trusted employee to convicted felon, from respected senior member of a team of men and women putting out a newspaper to one more body on the discard pile. He was hurt, he was deeply offended, he was bewildered by the turn of events and as a result he was questioning everything in an effort to make sense of his situation.

Did he turn his back on capitalism? It is more likely that he never turned toward it with anything approaching Ms. Tibbetts's ideological zeal. Capitalism for him and for most of us is an abstraction accepted with long personal lists of exceptions—a wishy-washy liberalism that, far from being a weakness, is the strength that defines this country and makes us the envy of the world.

I doubt that capitalism is the sort of "ism" that informed and guided his life. Certainly, it did not rank with civility in his hierarchy of values, nor with his good sense of community and fair play.

Mr. Popoff was fired and he reacted as you and I would have—as an ordinary human being who collided with an ugly reality.

"In Downsizing, Do Unto Others . . ." by Bob Evans, *The Globe and Mail.*

I have a problem with Ms. Tibbetts's nasty and narrow little take on that reality. To begin with, her assumption (or presumption) that business is purely an economic game flies in the face of our collective experience. It may be an economic game for the capitalists (in her definition). For the rest of us, businesses are where we earn our daily bread. Work is also where we find community—that sense of belonging and contributing and being somebody that our great-grandparents had and enjoyed and that has been lost as our society has changed; become urban, dispersed, mechanistic and individualistic.

Society changed, but our need for community did not. We want our business organizations to be our communities. In good times, they have done so—more or less. In bad times, they have let us down.

Ms. Tibbetts believes that this is irrelevant and that "our ideologies are a function of our current circumstances," as she put it. Ideologies are what we fall back upon when things become incomprehensible, and in that sense she is right. But ideologies are subordinate to basic human values. Ideologies change or die, values proceed. Ask Wilfred Popoff.

In 20 years of advising on the process of prying people loose from their work, community and self-definition, I have observed many things. Here are a few insights born of the experience of my "vocationally challenged" clients and the organizations that did the challenging.

Most employees do not buy in to the "corporate vision." They do not get excited about selling more Dino Puffs or capturing another 3 percent market share. The rhetoric that amuses the financial analysts does not always amuse the troops. What employees do buy into is honesty and consistency, even if the message is uniformly bleak. They often enjoy the work that they do and most of them do it well. And they treasure most the companionship, community and sense of belonging that their work provides.

Most downsizings do not achieve their started purposes; in fact, they often produce results quite different from the ones intended. Terminations that are perceived by others in the work force as ill-conceived or unfair or that are conducted harshly and disrespectfully can destroy morale and commitment, cause the best and brightest to put their resumes on the street, turn the lot of middle management into a living hell and hamstring the organization's ability to recruit good people. In time, that ill will can show up on the bottom line—in red.

The most important single task in a termination or downsizing is the protection and preservation of the dignity of the persons being fired. I realize that Ms. Tibbetts cannot factor this into her economic equation and I am sorry to hear that the outplacement types who orchestrated Mr. Popoff's departure seem to have the same problem. The problem is one of attitude. Let me explain it this way, using Mr. Popoff as an example. For 30 years he worked willingly and well for his company. We can safely assume that he was and is an honest, responsible, ethical and non-violent man. By what stretch of lunatic logic does senior management and the outplacement firm determine that at the moment of his firing and thereafter he is likely to take leave of the values and beliefs that have informed and guided his behavior for 54 years and become malevolent, dishonest and untrustworthy? Why would anyone assume that he cannot be permitted into his office for fear he might trash the computer or pee in the potted plants?

Firing does not turn people into ogres. In my experience, it usually has the opposite effect, causing them to fall back on their core values and stand tall on the moral high ground. In all of my years as an outplacement consultant, the worst behavior I witnessed during a firing took the form of a loud and colorful cascade of obscenities.

If you assume that people are going to behave badly at the time of dismissal and thereafter, you are then inclined to take "protective measures" such as delivering the news off-site, having gaggles of security guards and outplacement consultants doing crowd control, shaking people down for their passcards and keys, denying unsupervised access to the workplace, escorting people to the parking lot and so on.

A number of years ago, a smart psychologist named McGregor managed to sum up a good part of his life's work in one brilliant aphorism. He said, speaking to managers and executives, that "people will behave about the way you expect them to."

To Cheryl Tibbetts and her ilk, to the consultants who managed the downsizing at the StarPhoenix, to the senior managers there and to anyone now planning a termination or downsizing: Please check your assumptions and manage your expectations accordingly. It is the least we can do in the interest of maintaining the civility and mutual respect that have been our hallmarks as Canadians.

Chapter
5
Being Different

What is judged to be different is a function of contrast between it and what is familiar. Although the substantive dimensions along which contrasts are made change constantly, the experiences of individuals who are viewed by themselves and by others to be different on some *key* dimension may be quite similar to each other regardless of the substantive nature of the contrast. In other words, although what constitutes a meaningful difference is likely to change over time, the qualitative experiences of individuals who are perceived to be different (e.g., feelings of ostracism) may be quite similar. Of course, over time, as social systems such as organizations have experiences with people who are "different" in some way from some prior norm, the organizations may learn to manage differences. In fact their responses to people who are different may become a bit routinized, thereby, to some degree changing how people who are different are treated. For example, once an organization has changed one of its traditional practices, such as policies concerning observance of religious holidays, to meet the needs of one group of nontraditional employees, the traditional practices can never be as absolute as they were before.

In short, being different in organizations (or any human group) is probably always associated with a certain degree of tension. However, the sources of difference and the ways that organizations respond to them are apt to be continually changing.

Some of the tensions and the dynamics of differences are captured in the selections in this chapter and related selections elsewhere in the book. In the selection "Two Women, Three Men on a Raft," first published in 1977, Robert Schrank tells of a personal experience revealing how men's traditional perceptions of women have produced dysfunctional outcomes. In a later reading in Chapter 8, where Schrank and some others reflect on this original piece some two decades after it was written we see how women's experiences in organizations may have changed over time.

Similarly, Betsy Morris's article "Executive Women Confront Midlife Crisis" shows how members of the first generation of women to enter the managerial ranks in greater numbers have encountered problems previously thought to be encountered mainly by men. On the other hand, in the next selection, "Glass Ceiling Closes at Business Schools," we sense that some of the traditional problems may still be around but come to see that what some might interpret as a gender-related problem could very easily have more directly personal cause. This selection should help sensitize us to the fact that by interpreting problems experienced by people who are different on some key attribute to that particular difference may dehumanize that person in much the same way as blatant exclusionary prejudicial practices do.

Prejudice still seems to be prevalent in the interactions faced by managers drawn from minority groups. Black managers, for example, appear to be second-guessed by others more often when they make decisions than are white bosses. Richard Lacayo describes this situation in "When the Boss Is Black." We still have a long way to go before we have eliminated the distortions that are associated with skin color and its impact on how an individual's organizational performance is perceived and judged.

This same observation may be made for distortions created when religion serves to disqualify certain individuals from full participation in organizational life. Drawing on memories of his own childhood experiences, Howard S. Schwartz reviews Abraham K. Korman's book *The Outsiders: Jews and Corporate America.* Schwartz describes the feelings and consequences of religious discrimination, which as he points out are not only hurtful to those who are subjected to it by "in groups," but also serve to insulate the "in group" and the organizations they run from valuable sources of vitality and innovation.

People sometimes use the rules of an organization to justify actions that serve their own interest, even when the logic of the application appears ridiculous, even absurd, to others. This is one of the messages in "Disabled Aussie Swimmer Sunk for Lack of an Arm."

In "Institutional Bigotry" Roger Wilkins raises yet another dimension along which people are different, namely sexual preference. While the policy of the Air Force in this instance may have been extreme, Leonard Matlovich's experience of being discriminated against because he was a homosexual is by no means uncommon. Matlovich died of AIDS some years after the incident described in that article. The moving follow-up to the initial story is described in "Gay Vietnam Hero Buried with Honors."

When all is said and done, there are really more differences than similarities among organizational populations these days. It has always been important to recognize and harness differences between and among organizational participants. As we move into the twenty-first century, being different will be the norm, the reality. The challenge will be to create organizations in which this difference is celebrated and harnessed rather than being isolated and suppressed. In his lyrics for "Watching the Wheels," John Lennon captures some of the feelings that accompany the need to retain one's individuality while living out one's life.

Two Women, Three Men on a Raft—Part I

Robert Schrank

One afternoon in June, I left the cloistered halls of the Ford Foundation and within 36 hours found myself standing on the banks of the Rogue River in Oregon with three other uncertain souls who had embarked on a week of "survival training" sponsored by Outward Bound. It was a cloudy, cold day, and as we pumped up our rubber raft and contemplated the Rogue, we also wondered about one another.

Before embarking on a Greyhound for the raft launching site, we had gathered the night before at the Medford Holiday Inn. That night, the Outward Bound staff had distributed individual camping gear and waterproof sleeping/storage bags to the 20 of us, almost all novices, and had given us a short briefing on the perils of going down the Rogue River on a raft.

As they explained the nature of the trip, the Outward Bound staffers reminded me of seasoned military men or safari leaders about to take a group of know-nothings into a world of lurking danger. Their talk was a kind of machismo jargon about swells, rattlers, safety lines, portages, and pitons. Because they had known and conquered the dangers, it seemed they could talk of such things with assurance. This kind of "man talk" called to a primitive ear in us novices, and we began to perceive the grave dangers out there as evils to be overcome. In our minds, we were planning to meet "Big Foot" the very next day, and we were secretly thrilled at the prospect.

If the Outward Bound staff briefing was designed to put us at ease, its effect, if anything, was the opposite. Hearing the detailed outline of what would be expected of us increased our anxiety. "You will work in teams as assigned to your raft," said Bill Boyd, the Northwest Outward Bound director, "and you will be responsible for running your raft, setting up camp each night, cooking every fourth meal for the whole gang, and taking care of all your own personal needs."

The staff divided the 20 of us into four groups, each of which would remain together for the week on the raft. How we were grouped was never explained to us, but of the five rafts on the river, our raft, No. 4, was the only one that ended up with two women and three men. One of the men was a member of the Outward Bound staff, a counselor and guide who was considerably younger than his four charges.

The four of us on Raft No. 4 were all in our middle fifties. Each of us had experienced some modicum of success in his or her life, and Outward Bound had invited each of us in the hope that after a week of living on the Rogue River we would go back from the trip as Outward Bound supporters and promoters.

"Two Women, Three Men on a Raft" by Robert Schrank, *Harvard Business Review*, May–June, 1994, pp. 68-76. Reprinted with permission.

ON THE RIVER

Like most of the other 19 people on the trip, at the outset I had little or no idea of what to expect. I had participated in a few human growth encounter workshops, so I was prepared for, although again surprised at, how willingly people seem to accept the authority of a completely unknown group leader. Most people seem able to participate in all kinds of strange and, in many instances, new behaviors with no knowledge regarding the possible outcomes. This group was no exception. All of us had some notion of Outward Bound, but we knew nothing about each other, or our raft leader John, or the Rogue River.

Even though their preembarkation talk was filled with the machismo jargon I mentioned, the staff did not describe what we might actually expect to happen, nor did they talk about the many other river trips they had been on. I suppose the staff leaders assumed that the best way for a group of people to learn about themselves and each other is to let the experience talk to them directly.

The two women assigned to Raft No. 4 were named Marlene and Helen. Marlene was a recently divorced mother of five kids from Washington, whom a number of us had observed in her pink bikini in the Holiday Inn pool when we had arrived. Most of us acknowledged that because of that build we would love to have her along. Marlene used to wear her red ski suit at night and talked a lot about the good times she'd spent on the ski slopes. A top-notch skier, she said she divorced her husband because she was tired of making believe he was a better skier than she was.

Helen, a big blonde woman with a fierce sense of humor and a divorced mother of two grown boys, was at the time of our trip the president of the Fund Center in Denver, a coordinating body for local foundations, as well as a political activist. She and I became each other's clowns, and one night at a campfire she leaned over and asked me, "Bobby, is this just another plaything of the bored rich, or can we really learn something out here in this God-forsaken wilderness?" I told her I wasn't sure but we ought to give it a chance, which we certainly did.

One of the two other men was Bill, a very successful lawyer from Darien, Connecticut. He was the only one of the four passengers who was still happily married, since I too was divorced. Bill was a busy executive, but he managed to find time for hiking, skiing, and fishing. While Outward Bound took care of all our food requirements and most of our medical needs, Raft No. 4 had its own supply officer in Bill. His backpack was organized like a Civil War surgeon's field kit. He had all his changes of clothing scheduled, and when it rained, his extra plastic rainjacket kept me dry since mine leaked like a sieve. Though he and Marlene were obviously attracted to each other from the start, it was clear from his "happy family" talk that nothing was going to change, and it didn't.

The other man was John Rhoades, our heavily mustached, vigorous leader, in his early thirties, who saw himself as a teacher, educator, and trainer. As a progressive educator, John was overdedicated to the notion that no one can learn from anyone else since learning is a singular, unique experience.

The men and women of Raft No. 4 were a warm, friendly, outgoing bunch, each of whom helped create a nice, supportive atmosphere.

When we arrived at the river, each was anxious to pitch in and do his or her part. The staff distributed the rafts, each of which had a small foot pump, and Bill and I, with instruction from John, proceeded to inflate ours. It was one of our first chores, and we did it with a machismo fervor that suggested either previous knowledge, or that it was man's work or both. Marlene and Helen carried food bags, buckets, and ropes. It was a cold day, a gray mist hung over the towering Oregon pines, and I had a feeling that at least some of us, given a choice, would have opted for going back to the Holiday Inn. There was a lot of forced joking and kidding, with which we attempted to overcome some of our anxieties—we were whistling in the dark.

John gave each of us a Mae West–type life preserver and instructed us on how to use it. He told us, "You are not to go on the raft without it." Now with all of us bulging out of our Mae Wests, a Richter scale applied to anxiety would have registered eight or a full-scale breakdown. Postponing the inevitable, we shivered, fussed, and helped each other get adjusted to our life jackets. The trip down the Rogue River was beginning to take on a serious quality.

The rafts we used were small, about 10 feet long and 4 feet wide. The passengers sit on the inflated outer tube with their feet on the inside. Everyone is very close together with little or no room to move around. Also, unlike a boat, a raft has no keel or rudder mechanism, which means that it tends to roll and bobble around on top of the water. Unless the occupants work as a team and use their paddles in close coordination, it is very difficult to control.

While we were still on shore, John perched himself in the helmsman position at the back of the raft and said, "OK, I am going to teach you how to navigate the Rogue. When I say 'right turn,' the two people on the left side of the raft are to paddle forward and the two on the right are to backpaddle. When I say 'left turn,' the two people on the right are to paddle forward and the two on the left are to backpaddle. When I say 'forward,' I want everyone digging that paddle in like his life depended on it, and when I say 'backpaddle,' everyone paddle backward. When I say 'hold,' all paddles out of the water. Now, have you all got it, or should we go over it again?" We pushed the raft out over the beach pebbles and paddled out into the Rogue, which at this point seemed like just a nice pond. John barked his commands to us, and the team did just fine in the quiet water.

John told us that we were Raft No. 4 of five rafts, and it was important to everyone's safety that each raft maintain its position so that we could make periodic personnel checks to make sure no one was missing. John gave the command "forward," and because No. 3 raft was already far ahead of us and out of sight, Marlene, Helen, Bill, and I paddled vigorously.

As we proceeded down the river, John announced, "Each of you will take turns at being the helmsman." After some comment by Helen, this term was quickly corrected to conform to the new nondiscriminatory linguistics, as well as for the EEOC, to "helmsperson." John said that this person would be in charge of the raft—steering from the stern and issuing the commands.

As John talked, my mind drifted. I was suddenly overwhelmed by the grandeur and beauty of this great wilderness river road we were traveling. In awe of the hugeness of the trees, I did not hear or respond to a command. John, a very earnest fellow, was somewhat annoyed at my daydreaming and upbraided me, saying, "Look, we all have to concentrate on our job or we will be in trouble." And then he explained the nature of the rapids ahead.

He told us how to recognize a rapid's tongue (entrance), how to avoid "sleepers" (hidden rocks), and then how to ride the "haystacks" (the choppy waves that form at the outlet of the rapids) as you come through the rapids. He said that the most important art we would learn would be how to chop our paddles into the waves as we rode the haystacks. Since a raft has no seat belts, or even seats for that matter, unless you chop down hard, the rough water can bounce you right out of it.

As we paddled through the still calm waters, trying to catch up with Raft No. 3, Helen began to complain that she was already getting tired. "I'm just not used to pushing a paddle, but I'm damn good at pushing a pencil," she said. I, too, was beginning to feel the strain of the paddle, but rather than admit it to anyone, I just laughed saying, "Why this is nothing, Helen. You should canoe the St. John in Maine. That would teach you." Bill chimed in with "Yeah, this is nothing compared to climbing Pike's Peak."

As we moved down the river, a faint distant roar broke the silence of the forest. And as we drew nearer to it, our excitement increased. One might have thought that rather than a four-foot rapids, Niagara Falls lay dead ahead. I was relieved when, some distance before the rapids, John told us to head for the bank where we would go ashore and study the rapids first. As a team we would then decide together what kind of course to take through them.

We had been on the river now for a few hours, and, as it would be many times during the trip, getting on dry land was a great relief. Life on a small rubber raft consists of sitting in ankle-deep cold water, anticipating a periodic refill over both the side of the raft and one's genitals. If there was not time to bail out, we would just sit in the cold water. And even if there were time, we would still be soaking wet and cold from the hips down. Though this was our first chance to escape the cold water treatment, we quickly learned to look forward to such opportunities. The physical discomfort we felt together on the raft was overcoming our sense of being strangers by the time we disembarked that first time, we were a band of fellow sufferers.

At that point on the river, the bank was very steep, so we had a tough climb up a high rock cliff to get a good look at the rapids. Just before the rapids, the river makes a sharp 90-degree bend creating an additional danger. The swiftly running river could pile the raft up on the bank or into a hidden rock. After considerable discussion, during which Bill and I tried to demonstrate to Helen and Marlene our previous if not superior knowledge of boating, we agreed on taking a left course into the tongue while at the same time trying to bear right to avoid being swept onto the bank.

Coming up and down the steep river bank, Bill helped Marlene over the rocks, holding her elbow. A ways behind them, Helen commented to me, "Honestly, Bob, Marlene isn't that helpless." As we climbed into the raft, Bill helped Marlene again, and I, smiling sheepishly, offered my arm to Helen. I said, holding the raft, "Well, if we go, we all go together, and may we all end up in the same hospital room." Sitting herself down, Helen asked, "Who will notify the next of kin since no one will be left?" After they were seated, Bill and I huddled and agreed that if anything went wrong; he would look after Marlene and I would look after Helen.

Once back on the river, with John at the helm, we paddled into the rapid's tongue, where the raft picked up speed. Staying to the left but maintaining our right orientation, before we knew what had happened, we were roaring through the tongue, roller coasting through the haystacks, screaming with excitement. Flushed with our first real achievement, the raft awash with ice-cold water, we patted each other on the back for our first great success. While bailing out the raft, we paid each other compliments and convinced ourselves that we could master the Rogue River.

But this was our first set of rapids, and while John assured us that we had done well, he also reminded us of the meaner rapids yet to come with such potent names as Mule Creek Canyon, Blossom Bar, Big Bend, Copper Canyon, and Grave Creek. My God, I thought, did we really have to go through all of those terrible places?

Life on the Rogue included many other things besides shooting rapids. We pitched tarpaulins every night, lugged supplies in and out of the raft, and became accustomed to the discomforts of having no running water and of being absolutely frozen after sitting in cold water for the whole day. Nothing cements a group together like collective misery, and the people of Raft No. 4 had a real concern for each other as mutually suffering human beings.

Each raft carried a watertight supply bag of sleeping bags and personal clothing. The bag was strapped to the front of the raft and had to be carried to and fro every morning and night. When we tied up at our first campsite, Marlene and Helen each took an end and started to carry the bag from the raft up the bank. Bill ran after them yelling, "Hey, hold it. That's too heavy for you," and grabbed the bag. Throwing it over his shoulder, he said, "You shouldn't try to do that heavy stuff." Marlene smiled at him and said, "Bill, anytime, be my guest." Helen, who seemed to be a little annoyed, commented sarcastically, "Well it's great to have these big, strong men around now, ain't it though?"

When we came off the raft at night, most everybody instantly undressed to put on dry clothes, caring not one fig for a leaf or modesty. But even though on the surface it looked as though the physical sex differences had disappeared, the emergency nature of things exerted a different pressure, forcing each of us to "do what you know best."

Bill and I, for example, would pitch the tarpaulins each night and haul water, while Marlene and Helen would make the beds, clean the ground, and arrange the sleeping bags. Our mutual concern was evident; it was a beautiful experience of caring for one's fellow sisters and brothers, and I loved it.

After pitching our plastic tarpaulins (which were not much bigger than queen-size beds) as protection against the rain, the four of us would wiggle into our sleeping bags for the night. The first night Helen said she thought we were "four wonderful people gone batty sleeping on the hard cold ground when we could all be in soft feather beds." We laughed and helped each other zip up, arranged sweaters as pillows, and made sure we were all protected. Raft No. 4 was a real team.

During the days, I was beginning to learn some basics about rafts and rapids. Once the raft starts down the river and enters a swiftly moving rapid, the helmsperson must give and the crew respond to commands in quick succession in order to avoid hidden rocks, suck holes, boulders, and other obstacles, which can either flip the raft over or pull it under, bouncing it back like a ball.

As we approached the second rapids, we again went ashore to "look over our approach." It was a bad situation since the rapids planed out over a very rocky riverbed. Helen suggested that we let John take the raft through while we watch. "Now Bob," she said, "do we really care about this damn river? I don't care if we can squeak through these rocks or not. Hit your head on them or something and you could really get hurt." Bill, John, and I cheered us on.

When I became helmsperson, I discovered how difficult it is to steer a raft. The helmsperson can have some effect on the direction of the raft, and because Bill and I had some boating experience, we were at least familiar with the idea of using the paddle as a rudder. Neither Helen nor Marlene seemed to understand how to use a paddle that way, nor did they have the experience.

When one of the two women on our raft—more so Marlene than Helen—was the helmsperson, she would chant, "I can't do it, I can't do it;" Each time they cried out, neither Bill nor I would answer right away, but we would eventually try to convince them that they could. Typically, Marlene would say, "I don't know right from left. One of you guys do it; you're so much better."

At Copper Canyon, we needed a "hard right" command. With Marlene at the helm, we got a "hard left" instead. Bill and I looked at each other in utter disgust.

He asked Marlene, "What's the matter, honey?"

She said, "I don't know right from left. You be the helmsperson."

He said, "Why don't we write on the back of your hands the words 'right' and 'left'?"

Bill was kidding, but the next thing I knew, they were doing it.

Helen was mad and said to me, "Is it really necessary to make a baby out of her?"

"No," I answered her, "of course not. But she really doesn't know right from left."

As Marlene would say, "I can't do it," Bill and I would say, "Of course you can do it. It's easy; you're doing just fine." All the time we were speaking, we were thinking, "Ye gods! When is she going to give up?" Each time either Marlene or Helen would be helmsperson, we'd have the same conversation, each time Bill's and my reassurances would be more and more halfhearted. Before long, we weren't responding at all.

As the days wore on, Bill and I proceeded subtly but surely to take charge. The teamwork was unraveling. When we approached a tongue, if either Marlene or Helen were helmsperson, Bill and I would look at each other, and with very slight headshakes and grimaces, we would indicate agreement that things were not going well at all.

Once we had established that things were not going well, we then felt free to take our own corrective measures, such as trying to steer the raft from our forward paddle positions, which turned out to be an almost impossible thing to do. Not only is running the raft from the front not at all helpful to the person at the helm, but also if the helmsperson is not aware of the counterforces, the raft can easily turn around like a carousel. The unaware helmsperson is then totally out of control. Each time that would happen, Marlene would say, "I just don't know what's wrong with me," and Helen would echo her, "I don't know what's wrong with me either." Bill's and my disgust would mount.

Eventually, John became fed up with the inability of the bunch on Raft No. 4 to work together, which was mainly a result, he said, of the two "captains" in the front. As a last resort, he ordered each one of us to give a single command that he or she would shout as needed. My command was "hold," Bill's command was "left," Marlene's was "right," and Helen's was "backpaddle." John's teaching objective for the group was to get the four of us working together, or else. Needless to say, "or else" prevailed.

On the fifth day, Marlene was helmsperson. Bill and I were in the bow, silently anxious. Even voluble Helen was silent as the raft approached a fast-moving chute. At that time, only a clear, concise, direct command and a rapid response would be of any use at all.

Instead of a "hard right" command, we had no command. Marlene froze, the raft slid up on a big boulder, and in an instant we flipped over like a flapjack on a griddle. The current was swift and swept the five of us away in different directions. As I splashed around in the cold water, cursing that "goddamned dumb Marlene," I spotted Bill nearby. The two of us began together to look for Marlene and Helen, whom we found each grappling with paddles and gear they'd grabbed as the raft had gone over. We assured each other that we were OK and expressed relief at finding each other.

Cold, wet, and shivering uncontrollably, we made our way out of the river. To warm us and to keep us moving, John chased us around the bank to get wood for a fire. He stuffed us with candies and other sweets to give us energy. As we stood around the fire, chilled and wet, unable to stop shaking, we talked about what had happened, and why.

There was mutiny in the air now, and a consensus emerged. The four of us were furious at John and blamed him for our predicament. John retreated, but finally we were agreed that we would not have any more of this kind of thing. Regardless of John's wishes, anyone who did not want to be helmsperson could simply pass. Marlene was certain that she wanted no part of being at the helm, and Helen, though less sure, was happy to say, "Yeah, I just want to stay dry. I'll let you guys take the helm."

After becoming somewhat dry, sober, and a bit remorseful, the crew of Raft No. 4 returned to the river to resume our run down the Rogue. We had lost our No. 4 position, the other raft having run past us. John was helmsperson. Helen and Marlene were settled into their backpaddle seats. Bill and I, miffed over our mishap, felt self-conscious and fell silent thinking of the joshing we'd receive from the other rafts.

We slowly overcame the tensions of our crisis, and as the trip came to an end, we were friends again; the fifth day was forgotten. As we climbed out of the raft for the last time, Marlene said, "Well, the next raft trip I take, it will be as a passenger and not as a crew member."

That last night on the Rogue, we celebrated with a big party. The women dressed up in improvised bangles and baubles. I was the maître d', and none of us thought much about what really had happened on Raft No. 4.

Executive Women Confront Midlife Crisis

Betsy Morris

Shoya Zichy's pale-yellow living room on the Upper East Side has become an unlikely refuge for some of the best and brightest career women in New York City. In the past year they have made the pilgrimage here, sometimes in groups, sometimes alone, to visit with Ms. Zichy—to sip her wine, take in her oil paintings, seek her counsel, or counsel each other. Here they can share their darkest secrets; they can be outrageously un-PC; they don't have to make any apologies.

They are serious career women. They are trailblazers. They think lateral moves are for losers. But increasingly they have become unhappy with their lives, and some of them have made big changes.

Adrienne Glasgow, who'd been manager of international finance at Borden and treasurer of Reeves International by age 35, has recently quit her job as chief financial and administrative officer of her family firm. "I wasn't fulfilled," she says. Now she is consulting.

In May, Claire Irving started her own white-collar-crime detective agency. She bailed out of the mergers and acquisitions business eight years ago ("It wasn't burnout, it was boredom") and took a step toward self-determination by joining an investigations firm. Running her own show, she finds, is even better: "I am now doing it for me."

Françoise Jeanpierre, an MBA and a Fulbright scholar, left a promising career in international banking to start a consulting business two years ago. "I was often moving through home," she says. "I needed to *be* home."

And Ruth-Ellen Simmonds, who'd established herself as a turnaround specialist, walked away from an offer to become vice president for marketing at GTE Information Services. "I only have a finite amount of time. I really don't want to do the corporate b.s. over and over and over again. It's a waste of time. It makes me crazy. I need more to life than that."

Such sentiments had puzzled Ms. Zichy, even though she herself had taken about as dramatic as possible a midlife U-turn seven years ago. She had been an international banker and a vice president of American Express Bank when she quit and moved to Rockport, Massachusetts, to devote her time to painting. She thought her own experience rather unusual until she returned to the business world as a consultant last winter. "Here were all these extremely talented women," she says—women with MBAs; women with a dozen or more years in; women with executive positions; a surprising number of them without children and all the attendant work-family problems. They should have been on top of the world; instead, many of them were miserable.

"I started asking myself, 'Why are so many of these brilliant women burning out?'" she says. And she started building a new business—a combination of personality testing and counseling—to try to help them. It has been a land-office business so far: She's counseled 200-plus clients since the beginning of the year, many of them members of the Financial Women's Association of New York.

It is clearly a time of reckoning for baby-boomer businesswomen—the first big generation of "skirts," as they are still called in some corporate circles, to hit the age of 40 in a business suit. In many cases, the soul-searching has little, directly, to do with frustration about the glass ceiling. In very few cases does it seem to stem, directly anyway, from so-called work-family struggles. It can be tangled up with those issues, and it is frequently misdiagnosed, but this widespread angst is really something else: Large numbers of women find themselves going through the kind of midlife crisis their fathers and grandfathers went through. "Suddenly women know what men have known all along: that work is hard; work takes a lot of time; work isn't always a day at the beach," says Sharon McGavin, once a senior vice president at Ogilvy & Mather and now chief development officer for the American Red Cross in Greater New York. As former Labor Secretary Lynn Martin puts it, "Women are more aware of what's on the gravestone, which is not 'I worked for IBM.' "

These midlife crises are ultimately not about retreat but about redefinition. In great numbers, women executives emerge from this period making decisive midcourse corrections. Many have simply wearied of the male-dominated game and seek to do business more on their own terms. They change not only their jobs but their ideas of success as well. Some abandon the corporate ladder for the entrepreneurial shoestring. Some take the skills they have learned in business and apply them to more altruistic callings. A much smaller number than people generally think retreat to hearth and home.

Deloitte & Touche got a big surprise, for instance, when it decided to explore the reasons for unusually high turnover among its own up-and-coming female employees. As is true in many companies, executives there assumed women were bailing out mostly for family reasons. What the firm found, however, was that more than 90% of the Deloitte refugees it surveyed were working elsewhere; only a handful were home with small children, and most of those planned to go back to work. The generation of women that blazed new trails into the corporate suites is, evidently, blazing its own trails out.

To get a better snapshot of the phenomenon, FORTUNE enlisted Yankelovich Partners to survey 300 career women, ages 35 to 49, about their thoughts and feelings as they enter midlife. About 94% of the women surveyed were managers or executives. Nearly half had salaries of more than $60,000. The extent of their angst was astonishing. All but 13% said they had made or were seriously considering making a major change in their lives. Almost a third said they frequently felt depressed. More than 40% said they felt trapped.

More than half the women surveyed had friends or colleagues who were getting a divorce or seeking therapy. A third said they had friends who were having an affair. While personal issues were certainly a factor—a majority said they felt they were getting old and less attractive—much of their dissatisfaction stemmed from work. About 45% said they had started their own business or changed jobs, or were seriously considering doing so. Nearly 40% said they had gone back to school or taken a sabbatical, or were seriously thinking about it. A majority said they didn't have enough of a personal life. A third said they were bored. Their restlessness seems to be particularly acute right around age 40, and starts to diminish around age 45.

In most cases, motherhood had little correlation with the frustrations; women with and without children felt similarly. Nor did the glass ceiling seem to be much of an issue. While half felt their workplaces too dominated by men, more than 70% expected to make major career advances in the next five years.

In sum, the usual suspects can't be blamed; something new is afoot here. "There is some kind of profound something going on—a reassessment, a rethinking, a big gulp, whatever," says Ann Clurman, a partner at Yankelovich. "It is not biological. It has to do with self-image and the workplace. And I find this astonishing."

Confronting the problem can be especially hard for career women because any exploration of it leads almost immediately into dangerous territory: sexism, feminism, family, class (can anyone but whining yuppies afford to worry about such matters, much less take time off or jump career tracks?). Many women shudder at the very term "midlife crisis," associated as it often is with the worst kind of self-absorbed male behavior.

Furthermore, discussions of midlife crisis carry an unavoidable undertone of betrayal for this generation of women, which poured hopefully into the work force in the 1970s. It was a group imbued with 1960s idealism and haunted by the specter of Ira Levin's *The Stepford Wives*—desperate to get out of the house. And business was like a big fraternity rush: Women, whether as novelty items or not, were actually being invited to join such traditionally male clubs as the FORTUNE 500 and Wall Street.

"There was so much hype, so much hoopla along the way," says Jeri Sedlar, who was editor-at-large of *Working Woman* magazine until her own midlife reassessment four years ago led her to form an executive search firm with her husband. "I think it was pushing us on." The ambient enthusiasm may have unrealistically raised expectations of the role work and career could play in the lives of women, especially as the climb got steeper, the pyramid grew narrower, and the thrill of the chase faded away.

It was psychoanalyst Elliott Jaques who popularized the term midlife crisis in 1965—and defined it as the point at which people stop growing up and start growing old. It generally happens in the mid-30s, he said, can last for some time, and is different for different people. Depression, often in milder forms, is actually a much more common symptom than a new Porsche. Dr. Laurence Steinberg, psychology professor at Temple University and co-author of a recent book about midlife crisis called *Crossing Paths,* estimates that about 50% of all women and 40% of all men will go through some "significant reassessment" of their lives at this point. About 15% of both groups will have a full-blown crisis.

And yes, for some men that will be quite spectacular, involving sports cars and mistresses. But one of the more startling things about men these days is that most apparently are suffering silently. Midlife crisis "isn't as in vogue for men this decade. They are in a struggle for career existence," says Jean Hollands, who runs a corporate-counseling and executive-coaching firm in Silicon Valley. Many men in this age group were raised to see themselves, as their fathers did, as the family's major breadwinner. And many, drawing on the experience of their fathers, expected to achieve far more than they have—if not in title and pay, then at least in terms of job security and stability. But many have been shaken by the corporate reengineering of the past decade, with all the attendant layoffs and insecurity. Executive women in this age group are in a different situation. Starting out with much lower expectations, many got further in their careers than they'd imagined. They took risks; often the risks paid off. Despite widespread frustrations about discrimination in the workplace, many still seem to feel optimistic that they have maneuvering room. They don't feel as fungible as their white male counterparts.

And their socialization was quite different. Although most are major, if not primary, breadwinners for themselves or their families, they are not as hung up about it. Even the most ambitious were raised to expect their lives to be multidimensional, to include some combination of family, community, and outside interests—the kind of package their fathers had in the workplace of the 1950s and 1960s.

Several therapists and counselors say that their male clients would like to make big changes and explore new careers but fear what others will think. Many tell counselors their wives won't allow it. Says Deborah Arron, a Seattle-based attorney-turned-author who now counsels lawyers on, among other things, how to leave the legal profession: "Women feel much more courageous in this area. Men feel much more tied to convention."

For female executives, there is no convention. Just as they made their own way into the corporate suites, they are now making their own way out—and confounding the companies that had been grooming them for years. So many women have started their own firms that as a group they now employ about three-quarters as many workers in the U.S. as the FORTUNE 500. So many are joining the ministry that in clerical circles they've been dubbed the "midlife-crisis crowd." Increasingly, they are seeking high-level jobs at non-profits, according to subscription rates at *CEO Job Opportunities Update,* a newsletter that lists such job openings.

They are also taking high-level jobs elsewhere in corporate America, says Mary Mattis, vice president for research and advisory services at Catalyst, a New York–based women's research group. As part of Catalyst's consulting for its corporate clients, Mattis does what she calls "alumnae" interviews with women to see where they go after they leave. Contrary to widespread assumptions, "in most cases, women aren't going home to have or take care of children," she says. Sometimes women say they are because "it's a socially acceptable answer. You don't burn bridges. You don't have to explain." But much of the time, she says, "it's just not true."

The midlife exodus has taken on a life of its own. While men talk to executive recruiters when they want to make a change, women talk to other women. And for all the good fight that outfits like Catalyst are waging on behalf of women inside corporate America, outside there's an informal grapevine, an underground railroad in which women are reinforcing one another's "Who needs it?" attitude and helping one another find a better fit.

The attitude is reinforced at midlife for many high-powered women by a number of things: a sense of power about what they've accomplished; a sense of freedom from having proved themselves over and over; and increasing restlessness at having to play the game by the old male rules. "The dialogue in the press is not the same as the dialogue among ourselves," says Jeanpierre, the consultant. "This is a far richer and more diverse issue than can be classified by glass ceiling or work-family. It is an array of creative choices by people who reinvent themselves."

For many executive women, a midlife crisis is an excruciatingly painful process, a whopper of an identity crisis—like a divorce—tangled up with all sorts of other baggage. You must conceal it from your boss. If the doubts turn out to be passing fancy—as they do for many women who weather them and then continue on the same path—indiscretion could hopelessly derail you forever. You can't share them with most colleagues. Some would take advantage; others would blast you for selling out. Sometimes, after having invested so much and accomplished so much, you can't even admit a crisis to yourself.

That was the case with Janet Tiebout Hanson, one of the first women roughriders on Wall Street. Fresh out of Columbia University business school in August 1977, Hanson couldn't wait to get started. A week after graduation, she was a bond saleswoman at Goldman Sachs. It was the Wild West, spontaneous combustion, a frat house, she recalls, and she was thrilled to be part of it. Her work was her life; the firm was her family. A jock who had played everything from golf to field hockey to paddle tennis, she thrived on the competition, and it didn't take her long to make it onto the fast track. In 1986 she got a big break: She was named co-manager of money-market sales in the New York office, becoming the first woman to be promoted to management in sales, the most macho side of the house. The move put her squarely on a partnership track.

Hanson's four-year marriage to one of her Goldman colleagues had dissolved two years before; her ex-husband now sat across from her. Although she put up a brave front, "it was too brutal for words," she recalls. While he got on with his life, she obsessed over her career, even though she was keenly aware that her long hours and lack of contact with anybody outside Goldman were boxing her in. "I was always a happy person," she recalls. "I came from a happy family; I wanted to have a happy family. That was never going to happen. I was working 100 hours a week. There was no halfway."

So the following year, flush with cash at age 34, she quit to become a triathlete. "It was a massive cover-up," she says. "I had no credible reason for leaving." The firm threw her a big going-away party and presented her with a string of Mikimoto pearls, and all the while she kept thinking to herself, "This is the dumbest thing I have ever done."

It took her five months to get over what she now figures was a major depression and also to discover that she was only a weekend athlete. She was rehired by Goldman Sachs as an outside consultant in a job that lasted about a year. In the following three years she was married, had two children, and started climbing the walls. Although she had desperately wanted a family, she couldn't stand staying at home. "For 11 years I had been like the Rambo of fixed income; then suddenly I was home. I should've gone from heroin at least to methadone," she says. She spent much of her time at home talking on the phone with her friends at Goldman—watching the game from the bleachers, she says, and crazy to get back in.

Many women in this generation stayed in the game, postponed starting families, and looked up from their desks in their 40s only to wonder what had happened. They had felt a certain amount of control over the broad shape of their lives. First they wanted careers; then someday, somewhere along the line, they would make time for a husband; and yes, after establishing themselves in the workplace, then there would be time to consider children.

But the climb up the career ladder turned out to be time-consuming, all-consuming; and it was politically incorrect to warn that time could run out. While it became common knowledge that this generation of women could have babies well into their 40s, there was little talk of how difficult it could get after the age of 35. The dawning of that realization—right about the time a career is losing its luster—can shake the foundations at midlife. When Korn/Ferry International and UCLA's Anderson Graduate School of Management surveyed executive women in a major study three years ago, it asked how many had children. Fully 37% of the 439 women who responded did not. That compared with 5% of the executive men polled in a similar survey three years earlier. For some career women, the decision to forgo children is a definite choice; for others, it is more of an oversight.

"Probably women in such vast numbers have never had to go through this," says a 43-year-old New York banker, who for three years has been sneaking off to her infertility doctor, telling co-workers she had back problems and hoping that nobody would find out. Once a young hotshot, she feels that her career has collided with the glass ceiling, and she is considering looking for work in social service or philanthropy. "Maybe among some of the women who have not had children there is a stronger need to give back and do the nurturing in some other way," she says.

Such was the case for Denise Kuhlman, a 37-year-old attorney who pointedly wanted to avoid the career path of her mother, a traditional housewife who raised six children in the small blue-collar town of Poynette, Wisconsin, about 25 miles north of Madison. Kuhlman, the youngest in the family, grew up with older sisters who scoffed at the notion of becoming a teacher or a nurse, and most certainly didn't think it necessary for any woman to snag a man. "There was such a deemphasis on family," she recalls, "I didn't think I needed it."

Many of the social activists she admired as a young woman were lawyers. So she got a law degree at the University of Michigan in 1989 and went to work for the big Seattle-based law firm Lane Powell Spears Lubersky. She worked hard and got glowing reviews despite enduring two tragedies early on: Both her mother and one of her sisters died unexpectedly after she'd been with the firm a year. As far as she knew she was up for partner; she guesses she would have made it in about two more years had she hung in there.

But she just wasn't happy. Her speciality had become bankruptcy; mostly she represented creditors. While she enjoyed the negotiations and dealmaking, the litigation and fighting left her cold. "It's a guy kind of thing. You're working by their rules," she says. There was a code of behavior, and she always felt she was bumping up against it. "The times I got the biggest pats on the back were the times I screamed the loudest," she recalls. She still remembers a meeting in which six lawyers argued for two hours over how to draft a form involving some obscure issue amounting to not much more than $7,000. They were staking out their territory, a colleague explained. "You had to play the game that way. If you didn't, it was perceived as weakness."

"It wasn't that their way is bad," she says. "It's just that it isn't my way." She realized how far she was drifting from her idealistic goals when she had to repossess an old man's house for one of her clients four years ago.

Beyond that, the deaths in her family had put her face to face with all that she had rebelled against. "I started looking at what my life was all about," she says. And she couldn't stop thinking of her sister's wake. The whole town had turned out. The doctor was crying because he felt so badly; the neighbors offered to pitch in and take care of her sister's two young children. "I started to think, 'Who would come to my funeral? Would I have one that was jam-packed like hers was, or would there be nobody?'"

At the same time, it was dawning on her that she might never have a family of her own. "I love kids. I always thought I would have six kids. I figured it was just going to happen," she says. "I didn't realize the career I'd chosen would take me over and not let me do this other thing."

Without really knowing what she was going to do, Kuhlman began saving her money two years ago. "I didn't buy clothing, I didn't buy anything I didn't need, I stopped going into stores because I couldn't buy anything," she says. Then one March day last year, she took a walk around Seattle's Green Lake with a friend. By the time they had circled the lake, her mind was made up. She stood in the parking lot, knowing she had made the decision to quit. "Then I came home and called everybody up and said, 'Talk me out of it.' " When she notified the partner in charge of the bankruptcy group the next day, he didn't believe her. She finished the trial she was working on and left the firm a year ago.

Now she has accepted the realization that she might not have a family. But she is determined to have the kind of career she set out to have in the beginning. Although she is now doing freelance law to support herself, "I have no intention of practicing law in the future. In my heart of hearts, I want to do things that are good for people," she says. She has applied to go back to graduate school to study psychology.

For some women, the thrill of the chase is enough to offset ennui. But for others the chase just gets ludicrous, especially when it leads up a male-style hierarchy they don't necessarily believe in, and further and further away from what they love best to do.

Sharon McGavin, the Red Cross executive, knew she was about to bag another promotion when she left Ogilvy & Mather as senior vice president in 1988. She knew she had a shot at the top. (Shelly Lazarus, one of the her colleagues at the time, is now in the top job.) But she also knew that continuing to churn out ad campaigns was not going to sustain her. There wasn't enough newness. With the relief organization, by contrast, "at the end of the day there is a feeling that this is all very, very worthwhile," she says. Among other things, "my children are really proud of me." Taking the new job meant a huge salary cut, but her husband is a corporate attorney, and they decided they could manage after "a lot of staring at the old budget."

Simmonds, the turnaround specialist who now does a lot of her consulting for nonprofits, says her values too forced her to make a major midlife course correction. After growing, fixing, and then selling businesses, first for American Can and then for GTE, she says she began asking herself, "Was I really put here on earth to make a lot of rich white men richer?"

After a stunning career in advertising, Denise Larson, who is 40, is now deliberately trying to stay downwardly mobile. She had leap-frogged her way up Madison Avenue, advancing to ever bigger and better jobs: first becoming vice president at Young & Rubicam; then on to J. Walter Thompson, which doubled her salary; then on to Grey Advertising, which in turn made her part of a glamorous strategic planning team.

Along the way, she worked on campaigns for Kodak and Hallmark, and the Snoopy campaign for Metropolitan Life Insurance. But after 17 years, the thrill was gone. She was spending four days away from home and her 2-year-old daughter. "It wasn't the job. It was me. I was changing. l thought, 'I'm 37. I don't want to be doing this when I'm 47.' " Eventually she would make more money and maybe get another promotion. But she didn't like her role models: "I saw women whose lives I didn't want to lead—every other day at the shrink. Not that there is anything wrong with shrinks, but it is not the way I wanted to be spending my hard-earned money."

Two years ago, she joined one of her old clients, Philip Morris's Entenmann's unit (currently being sold to CPC International), where she is now market research manager. She has made it clear she doesn't want a staff or, for the time being anyway, to move up the corporate ladder. That allows her time for a life (she can drop her children off at school in the morning, for instance) and also allows her to stick to the work she loves most—talking to consumers and developing strategies for various brands.

Larson, who has two daughters and a husband who owns a veterinary practice, took a pay cut of about 20%. She says it has been something of a strain, "but it was definitely the right thing to do as a family."

Because companies are so hierarchical, she is constantly reminded of the choices she's made. "People always want to know what grade level I am," she says. But she has made peace with that. "You can view what you do as either in the box or out of the box," she says. "We need a little redefinition of work and success, and what all that means. I'm competitive, but in a different way. I want to see the brands succeed."

One reason some women weary of the game is the haphazard way they've played it. They took random walks down their career paths, following the advice of mentors rather than playing to their own strengths; taking whatever came along without necessarily taking stock of themselves. Some have reached midlife only to find they've been on the wrong path.

It was easy to do. When an opportunity knocked in the 1970s, women answered. They didn't know whether it would knock again, and they were flattered by those who took them seriously enough to take an interest in their careers. Somebody—usually male and usually senior—would suggest a direction, then volunteer to make the introductions, and then, there you were. You had a card that said Assistant Treasurer, Chase Manhattan Bank, and you could hand it out at parties, and everybody would be terribly impressed.

Carole Wright Brogdon never really stopped to consider the prevailing winds in her career until she turned 40 three years ago. She had become an accountant not so much because she reveled in spreadsheets but because she wanted to prove something. Her two older brothers were accountants; both of them were successful. "I was the girl coming up in the family. I wanted to show I could do it too," she recalls. She majored in accounting, graduating magna cum laude from the University of West Florida in 1974, and following graduation took a job at a small CPA firm in her hometown, Fort Walton Beach, Florida.

And she might have been content to stay there had it not been for her college professors, who were men. "They pushed me to work for one of the big accounting firms," she recalls. She moved to Atlanta in 1977 and, with their introductions, joined Main Lafrentz (later part of KPMG Peat Marwick). After five years she struck out for herself, first heading up accounting for one of Main's large clients, then practicing on her own, landing six years ago as director of national accounting for the Arthritis Foundation. She threw herself into the job, moving to a high-rise across the street from foundation headquarters and often working killer weeks.

But in 1992 she hit the wall. She didn't have anything more to prove, and she says, "I just didn't want to do it anymore." She continued to work for the foundation as an outside consultant for about a year and began asking herself, "What am I going to do when I grow up?" At a dinner with friends one night, she hit on an idea. She had enjoyed renovating several of her homes; she might try her hand at homebuilding.

With some financial help from a new husband and using proceeds from the sale of her old house, she started a construction company in Richmond Hill, Georgia, outside Savannah. So far, she and a partner have sold seven of the nine houses they've built. All her houses have big porches; her nickname in local construction circles is "the Porch Lady." She mostly handles the business side, but she also gets to pick out colors and consult on designs, giving vent to a creative side that accounting had stifled. She gets to wear blue jeans and work boots. "This just doesn't compare" with her old career, she says. "It is so much better."

Alexandra Hendrickson, who is now 41, also found herself much happier once she was free to pursue what she really loved. She thought she had been on the right track. After all, she did what was fashionable for bright, ambitious women her age, getting an MBA from Wharton, working for Bankers Trust for more than five years, and then branching out into marketing at American Express. "I grew up in New York; all my family is from New York. I had a very clear idea of what life held for me there," she says.

But American Express catapulted her into midlife turmoil in January 1992 when it closed her department and eliminated her job as director of new-product development. Although she could have moved elsewhere within the company, she opted to take a severance package. She hadn't been "massively unhappy," she recalls, but she hadn't been "wildly enthusiastic" either. She decided she wanted to make major change in her life. "I wanted to have an adventure."

She toyed with starting a business. An opera buff, she thought about going into fund raising. A friend suggested she brush up on her German and go to Prague; the transition to capitalism there appealed to her interest in economics. So she flew to Frankfurt, when she spent several months studying German, and then headed off on a tour of Poland and Hungary in search of a job.

"It was terrifying," she recalls. "I got rental cars and just drove around." Nobody would take her seriously because she didn't have enough international experience. So in October 1992 she took a job as a reporter for the Budapest *Business Journal,* a little startup newspaper two of her friends were launching. It was there that she heard of an opening at the local U.S. Agency for International Development and landed a two-year job as senior privatization and banking project manager.

It has been a terrific adventure. Before, she recalls, all her energy went to figuring out how to get "one more American Express card into the hands of one more American Express member." At the agency, she occupied herself with privatization in Hungary, involving big economic and political questions that fascinate her. Her contract with the agency expired at the end of August, and she had decided to try to transfer her new expertise to a job in private industry. "What I'd like to do next is help manage a privatized or startup company to make it competitive with Western business," she says.

Zichy followed the opposite geographical path: Born in Budapest, she spent part of her childhood in Cairo and then landed in New York. But like Hendrickson, she ended up in a midlife crisis induced in part by events at American Express. At American Express Bank, she found herself immersed in a stifling corporate culture, embroiled in a lot of politics and infighting she couldn't abide. The experience left her, like many women at midlife, feeling that the male system didn't appreciate the female way: "Our fire is in different places. We have the fire, but it is not necessarily directed at power and control," she says.

She had started as a teacher, with a master's in education from Boston University and a job she loved at a high school in Greenwich, Connecticut. But some of her friends had gotten jobs paying real money in the brave new world of business, and she was jealous. "I wanted to see what it was all about," she recalls.

Her way in, through a family contact, was a job at *Institutional Investor* magazine. As she was interviewing the head of international private banking for Citibank, he offered her a job, and presto, she was an international banker. That turned out to be just the ticket for Zichy, who loves to travel. She attacked her first two international banking jobs in an adventuresome spirit, first scouring Thailand and the Philippines in search of customers for Citibank, and then jetting off to places like Abu Dhabi marketing U.S. commercial real estate investments for Merrill Lynch.

But eventually her career track carried her into management and a much more buttoned-down setting. The further she climbed up the corporate ladder and away from her customers, the more the job chafed. At American Express Bank, where she eventually became a vice president in 1988, she got some friendly advice to get rid of her red jacket, put on a blue suit, and tame down her curly blonde hair.

When the bank reorganized its international real estate division, moving Zichy's job to Joliet, Illinois, in 1988, she bailed out. She spent five years as an artist, working by day in oils, red chalks, and some pastels, and having her work critiqued at night. She read nothing but painting books and surfaced only to do occasional consulting projects to supplement her income. "The whole world of derivatives came and went," she says. "It was very strange."

She developed quite a following among her old Wall Street friends and contacts holding four shows and selling 85 paintings through the period. Some commissioned paintings of their families. One of her old Citibank clients from Hong Kong bought six paintings right off her living room wall. Even so—and even though she had no family to support—she was finding her life "financially very scary." And, she says, "I needed more stimulation. I wanted to be connected with the business world again. I missed it."

Missing it is what happens to a lot of women. After all the twists, turns, and spills of a midlife crisis, some executive women even come full circle. George Ann Stokes, who for years has been one of the highest-ranking women, first at US West and now at Coca-Cola Foods, spent the past five years nursing herself through a bruising midlife crisis in the California wine country. Her career had been cooking along at US West; she was the vice president associate general counsel and apparently in line to succeed her boss, who was enthusiastically supporting her. Every time he would call her in to discuss the issue, she would say "yes, yes, yes," but inside she was ambivalent.

There was "a certain dead-endedness" about the job, she recalls. In conversations with her therapist, "I was having a real inner struggle over the meaningfulness of my work—figuring out my own needs vs. what other people expected of me and how much I had let other people's expectations define my destiny," she says.

In 1990 she took herself out of the running by requesting a job in the field—general counsel of the company's marketing resources group, which published the Yellow Pages directories and developed new services. Although the new job was much more interesting to her, it was perceived as a big step down. She received phone calls from other women at the company asking how she could have let them down so.

To make matters worse, her marriage to a prominent Denver banker, Malcolm Harding, began to unravel, and she slid into a serious clinical depression. "Ours was not a bitter, angry divorce," she says, but rather "a very painful one for both sides." (The couple had no children.) At the end of 1992, during a departmental reorganization, she decided to leave the company.

Throughout this difficult period, Stokes would escape to the Sonoma County wine country, finding solace with friends. "It is enchanted there, I'm convinced of it," she says. And on a visit the following March, almost on a whim, she decided to look at property. One rainy afternoon, she walked into a little gray and white house surrounded by redwoods and red geraniums. The sun came out and streamed through its French doors. She decided on the spot to buy it and move. It is, she says, "a very soulful kind of place."

It was there, in Occidental, California, a year and a half ago, that she began to put her life back together. She read books and slept late and held soirees with friends and did something she'd always wanted to do: plant a garden. "I thought, 'I'm 55; now I can retire and live happily ever after,' " she recalls.

But after eight months or so, she began to fidget. She had spent time at a nearby Zen center trying to find solace through spirituality, but "I wasn't finding it. It just felt forced." Gardening, she found, was much harder than she thought. The herbs wouldn't grow; the deer ate the geraniums. "It was such a shock," she says, to find she didn't like it much. She hired a gardener. Eventually, she found herself browsing through the want ads, toying with the idea of becoming a wine-tasting hostess in one of the wineries.

What caught her eye instead was a job as a part-time attorney for the Council on Aging, a senior-service agency in nearby Santa Rosa. It seemed the perfect answer, since she had always been interested in helping the elderly. It turned out to be the most stressful job she'd ever had. "It was me and three paralegals and an ocean of people coming in with all manner of problems, and I was out straight," she says.

When a friend first called last November to tell her that Coca-Cola Foods was looking for a general counsel, she said: "No way. I'm happy." But in truth she was tempted. She agreed to go for the interviews and became more hooked with each one. "I felt I was on ground my experience had prepared me for," she recalls. She joined the company last April and is clearly relieved to be back in the game.

"I can't think of a time in my life when I've felt so centered. I know what's important to me. I know what I'm good at," she says. And although she can't let go of the little gray house in the redwoods, "I'm much less inclined to think when I retire I'm going to go grow herbs."

More typically, however, women don't reemerge in big business but in small business—often their own. Janet Hanson, the Goldman Sachs dropout, discovered you can't go home again. She returned to the firm for two years only to find that she'd been shunted off the fast track. After doing a yearlong consulting project for Citibank, she started her own investment advisory firm, Milestone Capital Management, which specializes in short-term asset management for institutional investors. She hired her second husband to be her No. 2.

When she quit Goldman Sachs the first time, she had been making enough money not only to support herself but also to put a brother and sister through graduate school and set aside substantial savings. But by the time she started Milestone, she had two children and her savings were dwindling; she and her husband agreed to forgo salaries for the first two years and live off the proceeds of the sale of a house in Naples, Florida.

Milestone is in a cheery office park in Yonkers, ten minutes from her house. It clearly reflects her sunny disposition and her management style. The one-window office goes to her two employees, who keep tabs on the markets. A window office—"That's the power thing," she says. "This isn't a big power thing. This is a collaborative effort."

The way Hanson figures it, she took Goldman Sachs with her. One of her key employees is a hire from Goldman. One of her directors is a former Goldman partner; three others were Goldman vice presidents. Milestone manages more than $400 million in assets, and Hanson is clearly happy. "The way I look at it, I cut my losses 100%. I have a great husband, two great kids, a great business. I saved myself from utter destruction and ruin." Today a client has come down from Hartford to check her out, but Hanson already has done a deal with his boss, who also happens to be a woman.

"It's that chick thing," Hanson says.

That is how some experts believe women will have the most influence in business in the future—by doing things their way. It's the legacy that many in this generation of businesswomen hope to leave for the next: that they do have options; that they can make changes; that they can conduct business on their own terms. "The message of the day," says McGavin, "is that change is possible. You don't have to get it right the first time." Midlife may not ever be a day at the beach, but at least future generations of ambitious women may not have to be so badly burned.

Glass Ceiling Closes in at Business Schools

The resignation of Elizabeth Bailey as dean of Carnegie Mellon University's business school, effective next month, leaves only four female deans at accredited business schools, and none at top-ranked schools. A few years ago, there were as many as eight women deans at the 272 accredited schools, says a spokesman at the American Assembly of Collegiate Schools of Business.

Dean Bailey, who declined to be interviewed, said through a spokeswoman that women's issues weren't involved in her resignation.

Others, however, say women's issues can't help but be involved. "Women business school deans are still an endangered species," says Lynda Phillips-Madson, an associate dean at Vanderbilt University's Owen School of Management. "Regardless of the individual circumstances, I do see it as a loss for women," she says, because the appointments are critical for visibility.

Eugene Rackley, a recruiter at Heidrick & Struggles Inc., says the dean scarcity isn't for want to trying. "Every search committee tries to go out of its way to generate as many names [of women] as possible," he says, adding that the pool of qualified candidates is "pretty small."

Nonsense, retorts Anne Jardim, co-dean of Simmons College's Graduate School of Management. "This is part of the still-bigger problem of the situation of women in society."

Other women cite school jitters. "Search committees just don't want to take a chance on women," says Laurie Larwood, business school dean at the State University of New York at Albany. "They see it as a risk."

When the Boss Is Black

Richard Lacayo

As a manager at the Xerox branch office in Syracuse, N.Y., Chester Howell supervises a staff of about 20, mainly repair technicians and clerical workers. All but two are white. Howell is black. A former copier-machine repairman who rose through an affirmative-action promotion plan, he ran into some resistance when he first assumed his higher job. There were fierce arguments with one of his white assistant managers. "He questioned every decision I made," says Howell. "He wanted to double-check everything."

But was that prejudice? "Heck, no," insists his old antagonist, Vincent Venditti. "If Chet wasn't a minority person, the relationship would have been the same. He wasn't the first black manager I worked for." Venditti says his run-ins with Howell were not the reason he transferred to a Xerox branch office in Manhattan. But he does believe "some black managers are too sensitive."

The battle cry of the civil rights movement was equality. But in the workplace, the bottom line is authority. As more blacks move up into higher-level jobs and more whites find themselves working for black superiors, the two opposing principles can often collide.

Considering that it represents a reversal of centuries of black subordination, the rise of the black manager has been accomplished with remarkably little upheaval. But not without some strain. African Americans who have risen through affirmative-action plans can face resentment from white underlings. Some white subordinates fret over whether black bosses will favor other blacks. And the stories are common among black managers of white employees who ceaselessly buck their authority or who go over their heads to complain to higher-placed whites.

As a vice president at Rockwell International in Anaheim, Calif., Earl S. Washington oversees a mostly white work force of 1,500. "I find myself under the magnifying glass every day, proving that I understand how to run this business," he says. "All bosses are second-guessed," explains Xerox vice president Gilbert H. Scott, who heads a staff of 800 in the Southwest and California, 75% of whom are white. "If you're a black boss, you're probably second-guessed more."

Collier W. St. Clair, a vice president for the Equitable Financial Services Co., was a district sales manager in North Carolina in the early 1970s. One of his responsibilities was hiring, but many white applicants balked when they saw that their boss would be black. "A lot of them didn't come back for a second interview," he says. "I finally started asking people if they would have any problem working with me."

Since promotion is usually based on performance, the refusal of some whites to do business with black executives can be a source of frustration. David Grigsby is a broker at Merrill Lynch in Manhattan. When he prospects for clients over the phone, he does not always mention that he's black. That led to a surprise for at least one investor, who showed up to meet his adviser in person. He was "visibly shaken," Grigsby recalls. Not long afterward, the client asked for another broker. "It didn't take an Einstein to figure out what that meant," says Grigsby. Then he shrugs. "You have to develop a thick skin. You can't bleed to death every time something like that happens."

The American Institute for Managing Diversity, a research organization affiliated with Morehouse College in Atlanta, offers training for companies trying to manage increasing cultural mixing in the workplace. Institute director R. Roosevelt Thomas Jr. says racism is not always the explanation when a black supervisor creates discontent among white workers: "Sometimes people are not skilled at managing people who are different from themselves." As an agency manager in Atlanta a few years after his North Carolina post, Equitable's St. Clair presided over a 90-member office with just a handful of white workers. He found himself helping them cope with their minority status. Having been the only black in meetings of 300 or more people, he knew what they were going through. "Sometimes you just get lonely for somebody to relate to," he says.

Many black managers say their biggest problem is learning not to bristle at every challenge to their authority. The armed forces pioneered the elevation of blacks to supervisory ranks after President Harry Truman ordered desegregation in 1948. In 1987 Brigadier General Fred Augustus Gorden became the first black officer to serve as commandant of cadets at West Point. While he was walking across the campus one day, a white cadet failed to give the requisite salute. Gorden paused. Still no salute. He could have severely disciplined the cadet, but he chose simply to talk with him instead. "I've learned to pick and choose my battles," he explains.

But sometimes patience wears thin. If faced with a white employee who could not accept working under a black superior, says Rockwell International's Washington, he would help the recalcitrant employee find new work—at another company. "I'm not going to tolerate it," he says, "because I'm the boss."

The Outsiders: Jews and Corporate America

Abraham K. Korman
Reviewed by Howard S. Schwartz

Having read Abraham Korman's new book, *The Outsiders: Jews and Corporate America,* I find myself with peculiarly mixed emotions. Korman claims that America's largest corporations are anti-Semitic in that they do not permit Jews to rise to executive positions. On the one hand, he marshals the available data, his own and that of others, with great finesse. I am inclined to accept his argument. On the other hand, I cannot find myself surprised. Again, I have to agree with him that there is something wrong with an anti-Semitic policy that bars Jews from high corporate levels, and I agree that Jews have as much right to be there as anyone else; but I'm inclined to paraphrase Groucho Marx in saying that I would not want to be a member of a club that would bar me because I am a Jew.

Korman argues that Jews are excluded from executive positions because they are seen as outsiders by gentiles who form the bulk of American society and occupy the executive ranks of its large corporations. These gentiles are comfortable with each other and uncomfortable with those who are outside their group, such as the Jews. Moreover, they find each other more understandable, more predictable and, hence, easier to work with than they find outsiders. Because the managerial role is inherently ambiguous and uncertain, it leads those who are hiring for it to reduce uncertainty as much as possible by hiring those with whom they will be able to empathize and those whose behavior they will be able to understand and predict. Hence, executive insiders will tend to hire other insiders for executive positions, and they will tend to shun outsiders.

But in making ease of interaction and, therefore, insider group membership into a dominant criterion for selection, Korman says, corporations have effectively insulated themselves from innovation and creativity. They have become centers of groupthink. If American corporations could acknowledge that they have selected executives on the basis of insider membership and if they could change their ways, it would be to their advantage, to the advantage of American society, and to the advantage of outsider groups such as the Jews and others. Let my people in.

Here, Korman's argument is clear and persuasive. His writing is both passionate and precise, and his analysis of the tension between insider and outsider is fine phenomenology. I believe it explains much of the phenomenon of corporate anti-

The Outsiders: Jews and Corporate America by Abraham K. Korman, reviewed by Howard S. Schwartz in *AMR,* April 1989, Vol. 14, No. 2 pp, 303–305. Reprinted by permission of Prof. Howard S. Schwartz.

Semitism, but I wonder whether his exclusive reliance on the insider/outsider dynamic has not lead him to miss an element that should be considered if the full significance of corporate anti-Semitism is to be understood. Jews have not been considered just another group of outsiders. Country after European country did not systematically assault, rob, expel, and murder the Jews because they were different and because their differences made the natives uncomfortable. As Korman points out, Russia did not permit the Jews to immigrate for over 200 years; therefore, how could their presence have irritated the Russians?

When I was a kid, my family had a summer home in a community in northern New Jersey. The community, which was predominately Jewish, was located outside of a town that was, as far as we could determine, entirely gentile. One night I was walking to my friend Paul's house when a car drew alongside me and somebody asked where "Mocky Street" was. Thinking he said "Mohican," I started to give him directions. Somebody in the car grabbed my shirt, pulled me toward the car window, and began bashing my face. Somebody else began shouting, "Let's get out of here! Let's get out of here!" and my assailant gave me one last bash before the car pulled away. The geometry of the situation had worked to prevent him from hurting me very much, but he had managed to knock my glasses off, and when I found them unbroken I was very relieved. I went on to Paul's house. He wasn't there, but his mother was. I told her the story. She didn't seem surprised. After the extermination camps, who could be surprised?

To grow up Jewish, at least in my time, was to grow up with the knowledge that one's possibilities were limited. One knew that one could not be a member of certain groups, hold certain occupations, even go to certain schools. On the other hand, one also knew that there were other parts of this vast world that were entirely open. It was perhaps the grandeur of the possibilities that were open to me that permitted me to accept these limitations and to effortlessly give up the possibilities that were closed. I could be a scientist. I could be a writer. Hell, I could even be a revolutionary. Being a corporate executive was never something that I considered as an open possibility.

As I grew older I came to realize that the sense of limitation is deeply a part of the Jewish heritage. The Jewish God created people in His image, but He had not made them to be other gods. And anyone who had the *chutzpa* to think himself the equal of God would get it in the neck. The Jewish God could be talked to, bargained with, even upbraided, within limits, but it was always clear that there was a difference between the immortal and the mortal, and people were always on the short end.

Later, I came to understand that it was this belief in limitation, the frailty of man, and the tenuousness of life that was in large measure responsible for some people rejecting the Jews. Often the world of these gentiles was a world full of manic optimism, the denial of death, and the pursuit of a blissful perfection that was only possible for, and appropriate for, God. No wonder they did not want these Jews around. From their dreams, the Jews keep waking them.

Corporations puff themselves up: They become the alpha and the omega, the be-all and end-all, gods. They are built around the idea that those who become most what the corporation is, those who rise to the top, manifest this godliness the most. That's the reason behind the upward scramble to which Korman wants the Jews admitted.

When the God of the Jews spoke to Moses from the burning bush, Moses asked Him to reveal His name. He said, as near as English permits a translation, "I am

Reality." Subsequently, He commanded the Jews not to take any other gods before Him. I submit that it is because the Jews have honored this commitment that the *Fortune* 500 have not embraced them. Perhaps these corporations will change. That would be very nice, but I'm not going to hold my breath.

Disabled Aussie Swimmer Sunk for Lack of an Arm

SYDNEY (UPI)—Australian swim officials have disqualified a one-armed swimmer because he failed to touch the end of the pool with two hands

Greg Hammond, 16, a member of Australia's Disabled Olympic team scheduled to compete in New York in June, was disqualified from second place in the open men's 100-metre breaststroke championship Sunday at Narooma, 285 kilometres south of Sydney.

The championship's referee, Pauline Gill, reluctantly disqualified Hammond following the protest of coach Paul Pike under a rule that states "the touch should be made with both hands at the same time."

The disqualification has caused an uproar. The Sydney Daily Mirror condemned the disqualification in its editorial Wednesday:

"The history of competitive swimming in this country is littered with more than enough controversial blunders caused by rules that are bad or interpretations that are even worse."

Pike, whose protest led to the disqualification, said Tuesday he had no regrets about his action. "Greg has to meet the letter of the law, which he didn't do."

Institutional Bigotry

Roger Wilkins

A Federal court in the District of Columbia recently ordered the Air Force to reinstate Leonard P. Matlovich, a former sergeant who was dismissed five years ago because he admitted that he was a homosexual. Though it is on a narrower and more technical ground than I would have liked, I am delighted by the judge's decision.

Leonard Matlovich was a superb airman. He was a decorated Vietnam veteran whose service ratings were always excellent. There was nothing in Sergeant Matlovich's behavior in the service to single him out from anybody else except that he did his job far better than most people in the Air Force did theirs. But his spirit bothered him. He wasn't being honest with the world about himself. Part of his identity as a human being was his homosexuality. But he was hiding it, pretending it didn't exist, pretending he was something other than what he was. He was behaving as if he was ashamed of what he was and that made him ashamed of himself.

So he did a courageous thing: He announced his homosexuality. And the Air Force promptly threw this distinguished airman out of the service. The Air Force had a regulation prohibiting the retention of homosexuals in the service unless "the most unusual circumstances exist." The judge said the Air Force had engaged in "perverse behavior" in being unable to explain its policy, and ordered Matlovich reinstated.

I met Matlovich and another homosexual airman back when they were both fighting their original expulsions from the Air Force. The other airman, Skip Keith, was a mechanic trained to work on C-5A engines. He loved his work and had been judged to be good at it, but when he felt he had enough of hiding part of himself from the world, he too was tossed out of the Air Force.

I am not surprised that the Air Force could not explain its position clearly. Shortly after I met Matlovich and Keith, I had lunch with a group of journalists and an Air Force lieutenant general. During the course of the lunch, I asked the general why the Air Force tossed homosexuals out on their ears. He practically choked on his food. The best I could get from him was that when he was flying he wanted a wing man he could rely on. He couldn't answer why gay airmen would be more unreliable than anybody else. He just got more incoherent.

The general was black. If I had closed my eyes and changed his words a little bit, I could have imagined that tirade coming from a white general in 1940 trying to explain why the Army couldn't be integrated. Institutional bigotry in any form stinks, and men like Len Matlovich and Skip Keith are heroes to have stood up to it.

Gay Vietnam Hero Buried with Honors

WASHINGTON (AP)—Leonard Matlovich, a Vietnam War hero whose 1975 discharge from the Air Force for his avowed homosexuality became a rallying point for gay rights activists, was buried here Saturday with full military honors.

Matlovich, 44, died June 22 in Los Angeles, from complications associated with AIDS, a fatal virus-borne disease whose chief victims have been homosexual men and intravenous drug abusers.

He was buried in Congressional Cemetery just 20 blocks from the U.S. Capitol in a ceremony that mixed the military pomp of a horse-drawn caisson and a traditional three-volley salute by seven riflemen with eulogies from gay rights activists.

"The Air Force finally did it right and on Leonard's terms today," said Frank Kameny, a Washington gay rights activist who was instrumental in counseling Matlovich on testing the military's ban on homosexuality.

"It's a pity that they didn't do it 13 years ago," Kameny said as an Air Force color guard departed the cemetery.

Matlovich, who was awarded a Purple Heart after stepping on a Viet Cong land mine and the Bronze Star for killing two Viet Cong soldiers attacking his post, first challenged the Air Force's rules on homosexuality in 1975.

At the time, he was a technical sergeant working as a drug and alcohol abuse counselor at Langley Air Force Base outside Washington with nearly 12 years of service.

"After some years of uncertainty I have arrived at the conclusion that my sexual preferences are homosexual as opposed to heterosexual," Matlovich said in a memorandum to his commanding officer. "I have also concluded that my sexual preference will in no way interfere with my Air Force duties."

Following a hearing, Matlovich was given a general discharge from the service. His challenge of the action in court put his face on the cover of Time magazine, and in 1980 the Air Force was ordered to reinstate him with back pay.

Months later, Matlovich and the Air Force reached an out-of-court settlement in which he was paid a total of $160,000 in back pay and other compensation and given an honorable discharge.

"When Leonard lived in the neighborhood, he would come over here and walk," Lee Jenny, the administrator of the cemetery where many members of the nation's first Congresses are buried, recalled Saturday.

Ms. Jenny helped design the tombstone that Matlovich wanted for his grave as a memorial to gay and lesbian Vietnam veterans.

Matlovich's tombstone includes in the top corners pink triangles that were used by Nazis during World War II to identify homosexuals in concentration camps and that have since been adopted as a symbol in the gay rights struggle.

Under the triangles is the inscription:

"A Gay Vietnam Veteran"

"When I was in the military they gave me a medal for killing two men and a discharge for loving one."

Watching the Wheels

John Lennon

People say I'm crazy,
doin' what I'm doin'.
Well they give me all kinds of warnings,
    to save me from ruin.
When I say that I'm OK, well they look at me kind of
    strange.
"Surely, you're not happy, now: You no longer play the
    game."

People say I'm lazy.
Dreaming my life away.
Well they give me all kinds of advice.
    Designed to enlighten me.
When I tell them that I'm doing fine watching
    shadows on the wall.
    "Don't you miss the big time, boy?
    You're no longer on the ball."

Chorus: I'm just sitting here
watching the wheels go round and round.
I really love to watch them roll.

No longer riding on the merry-go-round.
I just had to let it go . . .

People asking questions,
Lost in confusion.
Well, I tell them there's no problem:
Only solutions.
Well they shake their heads and look at me
    as if I've lost my mind.
I tell them there's no hurry,
    I'm just sitting here doing time.

Chorus

I just had to let it go. . . .
I just had to let it go.

Chapter

6

Images

Whether people in organizations are consciously aware of it or not, they are constantly exposed to subtle and complex influences that play a part in determining what they think, feel, and do. Many of these images are created intentionally by organizational members to bolster their positions and to maintain or enhance the power and control they have over others. Examples abound in the readings we have selected in this chapter.

Words and phrases both reflect and shape our values. They influence what we see and do, what we consider important. They also blind us to other realities. In "Language Masks Human Place in the Nature of Things," David Suzuki argues that the terms we use for the environment tell us how we view and understand nature. The forest industry uses the words "decadent" and "overmature" for primary forests. Trees are only useful when cut down and are "harvested" and "culled" to make them more "normal." Language such as this creates a strong frame for seeing forests as economic resources to be managed for human benefit. This may not be incorrect. It is, however, an incomplete, partial frame on reality. The role of language here, as elsewhere, tends to hide the fact that it is simply one view of the way things are. When profit is involved, there is a strong incentive for those seeking profit to invent and enforce language that presents their position as the legitimate or only view of what is going on. Language, particularly in times of war, is designed to hide some realities and to emphasize others. Describing war as a "conflict" hides its meaning as an arena of slaughter and carnage. So does replacing the word "bombing" with "coercive diplomacy." (In *Talking Power: The Politics of Language* Robin Lakoff documents some prevalent language games used by people and organizations.) Sometimes such jargon serves to separate the person from the event, sanitizing the violence and life and death consequences from the consciousness of soldiers and the public back home. Some commentators have likened the recent Mideast war between Iraq and the coalition of United Nations countries to a

Nintendo video war game—a comparison that distances action from emotion, and hides the violence inherent in the action.

The use of space is symbolic. The office layout can influence attitudes and behaviors, suggests Suzyn Ornstein in "The Hidden Influences of Office Design." If this is so, it ought to be possible to create work space that enhances the experiences people have on the job. It may also be feasible to improve performance through better office design. Ornstein's article focuses on the issues and practices that relate to these premises.

The notion that colors and color preferences create images and have an impact on how we are seen and on how we see others is the focus of "Color: A Guide to Human Response" by James Gray, Jr. While we have no information on the accuracy or validity of the predictions and prescriptions in the article, we think it is important for managers and social scientists to explore the thesis that color does play a role in the image of self as conveyed to others and as experienced by them. Readers might reflect on their own color preferences and think about the way such preferences might effect their interactions with other people at work and at home.

We return next to the initial theme of this section—that language, attitudes, and actions are closely intertwined—this time with the emphasis on sexist language. In "That's No Lady, That's My Wife," Janet Elliott describes some of the common areas of language that reinforce sex bias such as stereotyping, sexist job titles, phrases that exclude one sex ("As you look at your face each morning when you shave. . . "). She points out that use of sexist language may not be intentional, but its effect is no less degrading. (For an insightful and readable discussion of the role of language in shaping attitudes and behavior, we recommend the book *You Just Don't Understand: Women and Men in Conversation* by Deborah Tannen, New York: William Morrow, 1990.)

Some influences pervade an organization and are a part of its culture. Often these influences are so taken for granted that it becomes necessary to challenge or to contradict the culture quite dramatically to reveal its elements and interconnections. Lehan Harragan, in "Games Mother Never Taught You," argues that many of the everyday objects, arrangements, and routines we encounter in our organizational lives can have influence on us. She analyzes the symbolic meaning that can be attached to the way one is paid; the time one comes to work; where one eats; one's working location and so on. She includes in her discussion a provocative description of the immobilizing and discriminating effect on women of the clothes they wear to work.

The realities outlined in this chapter reflect a world more complex than it may seem on the surface. It is a combative world; a world in which it is wise to be wary. We think it is important for people to pay careful attention to the settings, languages, and trappings of their organizations. The precise nature of organization images and their character and impact are beginning to be carefully charted by behavioral scientists.

Language Masks Human Place in the Nature of Things

David Suzuki

As kids, we used to chant "Sticks and stones may break my bones but names can never hurt me."

Yet words can be as dangerous as sticks and stones.

We learn to "see" the world through the lenses of our value and belief systems and they in turn are expressed in language. The words we use reflect these cultural assumptions.

Feminists demanded a change in the use of words such as "chairman," "spokesman," "fireman," because the masculinity of the terms implied that women are not expected to occupy such positions. And by deliberately substituting "person" for "man," we are constantly reminded of the inequities built into our society.

Years ago, in a discussion on the environment with former federal cabinet member, Mitchell Sharp, I tried to explain why we have to abandon the belief that steady growth, especially in the economy, must be the primary goal of government and industry.

He exclaimed, "I understand what you're saying but you're talking about an end to progress."

"Progress" and "growth" have become synonymous. And since we aspire to constant progress in the future, then growth has become our goal and there will never be an end to it.

Nowhere is the use of language more revealing than in the military where jargon is full of male sexual symbolism. Weapons are phallic, both in shape and explosive potential, while military personnel speak of various tactics as "deep penetration," "thrust," and "orgasmic release." Common terms such as "pick-up zone," "counter penetration," "rapid pursuit" and "rear penetration" have sexual connotations.

As we readjust to the rapid political changes occurring globally, we ought to get rid of the sexual terms and create a new battle language based on the "war" to save the planet. We're engaged in a global "struggle," a "fight" for survival and we have to "mobilize" people.

The forest industry is replete with words that indicate how its activity is perceived. Primary forests are described as "decadent" or "overmature" as if trees are wasted if they are not cut down. Logging is seen as a practice analogous to farming, from the "harvesting of crops" to the creation of "plantations." Foresters "cull" trees, remove "pest" species and refer to the use of pesticides, herbicides and fertilizers as "silvicultural practice."

Old growth forests that haven't been logged are called "wild" while the second growth after logging becomes a "normal" forest.

"Language Masks Human Place in the Nature of Things" by David Suzuki, *Vancouver Sun,* June 23, 1990, p.B6. Reprinted by permission of the author.

The word "management" implies we know what we are doing and can duplicate or even improve on nature.

The sign at a shopping plaza I visited said "No animals allowed" and the crowd swarming the mall obviously didn't feel those words referred to them.

Yet we learn in high school biology courses that humans occupy a position in the web of life next to our nearest relatives, the chimps and gorillas. Like all other mammals, we are warm-blooded vertebrates who have hair and feed our young with milk.

We are undeniably animals as if there is a fundamental demarcation that separates us. The word "animal" itself is a pejorative when used to refer to people and carries with it a connotation of uncontrollability and malevolence.

College students in the '50s referred to someone who would be called a nerd today as a "turkey." College women back then referred to male creeps as "lizards." A person who is a "chicken" is a coward, a "snake" is not to be trusted, an "ox" is stupid while a "mule" is stubborn.

A "wolf" is a leering flirt, a "black sheep" is a family disappointment while someone who has been made a "monkey" of or is an "ape" is not very bright.

The use of animal names to represent undesirable human traits is a denigration which also seems to elevate us.

It is the distancing and separation of humankind from the natural world, the sense of superiority to other living beings, that enables us to perpetuate the mistaken notion that we are not subject to the same laws that govern the rest of life on earth. It also seems to legitimate our treatment of wilderness and wildlife—if we are superior beings, then we can dominate the inferior and even try to improve them.

It's not easy to recognize the messages implicit in our words because the assumptions and attitudes are so deeply embedded in our culture. After a speech in which I mentioned the way we put animals down, someone pointed out that I had accused rich countries of "hogging" too much of the planet's resources. Other animals don't deserve to be downgraded by a species whose name has come to symbolize shortsightedness, destruction and greed.

The Hidden Influences of Office Design

Suzyn Ornstein

A good deal of attention has been directed at the suggestion that office design—including the arrangement of offices, furnishings, and physical objects present in the work setting—influences job performance, job attitudes, and impressions. With almost 40 million people currently working in 9 billion square feet of office space in the United States,[1] even relatively small influences of office design on performance, attitudes, and impressions could have a large impact on productivity levels and employee attitudes. Many managers are unaware of the relationship between office design and various organizational behaviors, attitudes, and impressions. In this paper, I will (1) identify and describe the ways various elements of office design influence attitudes and behaviors, (2) identify and describe symbolic messages conveyed by office design, and (3) elaborate on actions managers can take that may result in more efficient and effective work environments.

INFLUENCE OF OFFICE DESIGN

There are various elements of office design that influence attitudes, behaviors and, through symbolic messages, impressions. These elements of office design have been divided into two broad categories: office layout and office decor. Office layout includes the configuration of office space (who is located next to whom and where people are located), the type of office arrangement (e.g., conventional or open-office), and the arrangement of furnishings and objects within individual offices and common spaces (such as reception areas). Office decor includes style and type of furniture, decorative objects, and physical elements of the environment such as noise, lighting, and temperature. The effects of both layout and decor on attitudes, behaviors, and impressions will be discussed in turn.

Influences of Office Design on Behavior and Attitudes

"When Paul Harris, a large retailer of women's ready-to-wear clothing in Indianapolis, remodeled their corporate offices, all the buyers were moved into an open-office arrangement. This configuration—with no walls and few noise absorbing partitions—magnified the noise of the ringing

---

"The Hidden Influences of Office Design" by Suzyn Ornstein, *Academy of Management Executive*, 1989, (3) 2, pp. 144–147. Reprinted by permission.
[1] M. Pinto, "Open Hunting Season on the Open Plan?" *Corporate Design and Realty*, May 1986, pp. 82–84.

telephones, talking, copying and typing equipment to such levels that the buyers were practically unable to think in their 'offices.' Decision making time dropped from a few minutes to a few days!"[2]

Office Layout   The above example illustrates the impact a poor choice of office configuration can have on employee productivity. In this case, Paul Harris subsequently removed $30,000 worth of newly purchased office components and redesigned their offices in a more conventional (i.e., individual offices) plan.

Organizational experiences have confirmed that the configuration of office space and, in particular, the choice of traditional or open-offices has a great impact on employee behavior—especially on communication. For example, when a group of product engineers were moved from traditional offices to open-offices, it was found that both the quantity and quality of their ideas increased. In this case, the open plan allowed the engineers easier access to their colleagues by placing them in physical proximity to one another. The ease of collaboration resulting from the redesign of office space allowed for improved communication, which led directly to increased productivity. Similarly, a change to an open-office layout in a manufacturing firm resulted in an improved information flow—less time was spent on the telephone, doing paperwork, and in meetings, while more time was spent in face-to-face conversations. Of course, in the Paul Harris case, an open-office office plan was ill-advised because the nature of work involved numerous phone calls and a generally hectic work pace. The open-office plan magnified all activity so that concentration and, as a result, productivity were greatly reduced. Taken together, these experiences imply that configuration of office space should be determined based on the nature of the work to be performed. For example, people who work together should be placed near one another. In addition, the choice of traditional or open-offices should be determined by the importance of privacy and the noise levels resulting from the type of work performed.

Another element of office layout—the arrangement of furnishings within individual work spaces and common areas—also has been found to have an influence on employee behavior. For example, at a Southwestern Bell unit of AT&T (prior to divestiture), a change in the arrangement of desks within an open-office plan resulted in an improvement in on-time order processing from 27% to 90%, all within a one-month period. Considering that the improvement came at a time of increased workload, supervisors determined that the change in desk placement resulted in a gain in productivity equivalent to 88 weeks of worker time per year saved—or the work of approximately 1.5 full-time employees.[3]

As the placement of desks influences behavior, it has also been found that seating arrangement affects communications. People seated in chairs placed face to face are more confrontational in their behavior than are people seated at right angles. Chairs placed directly next to one another often result in rather limited communications among those seated, while chairs placed back to back generally result in no communication. Chembank discovered the power of seating arrangements when it redecorated its corporate boardroom.

---

[2] More information about Paul Harris' change in office design can be found in "The Trouble with Open Offices," *Newsweek*, August 7, 1978, pp. 84–86.

[3] The specifics of this office arrangement are discussed in R.N. Ford's "Job Enrichment Lessons from AT&T," *Harvard Business Review*, January-February 1973, pp. 96–106.

The original arrangement (in which the top board members sat on a dais directly facing the rest of the board members) was changed to one in which all the board members sat around a U-shaped table, with the top members seated around the base of the U. This new arrangement produced much greater participation by a majority of the board members.

The Buffalo Organization for Social and Technological Innovation (BOSTI) found that office layout was directly related to worker satisfaction or, more precisely, lack of satisfaction with their jobs. BOSTI found that the majority of employees were dissatisfied with their workplace because it was arranged in a fashion that was counterproductive to accomplishing the tasks they were required to perform.[4] The amount of space per employee has also been found to affect job satisfaction; greater space was related to increased satisfaction with work.

Office Decor   Various elements of office decor also have been found to influence individual behavior and attitude; for instance, the presence of artwork affects performance under stressful circumstances. Specifically, when people were asked to prioritize strategic decisions under time pressure, they performed much better when artwork was present in the work setting than when it was not.

The BOSTI studies found that lighting, temperature, and noise were all related to employee satisfaction. We all know that too much or too little lighting, too high or low temperatures, and a high level of noise can result in decreased job satisfaction. BOSTI also calculated the costs of turnover and absenteeism resulting from this decreased satisfaction. They found that with improvements in lighting, temperature, and noise, organizations could save from $270 to $472 per year per manager, from $162 to $282 per year per professional/technical employee, and from $85 to $148 per year per clerical employee.

Influences of Office Design on Impressions

"In meeting with their architects to make design decisions, Westinghouse asked that its image as a 'successful, technically superior company' be interpreted for three groups. For its industrial peers, the building should reflect strength, professionalism, and integrity. For the Orlando community, it needed to have a powerful and elegant presence without being ostentatious. Finally, for the buildings' employees, it wanted an inspirational state-of-the-art work environment."[5]

In much the same way that office design influences attitudes and behaviors, it also influences impressions through the conveyance of symbolic messages; that is, different elements of office design connote messages and images that people then use in forming impressions about the company.

Office Layout   The element of layout that has the greatest impact on impressions is the arrangement of offices themselves—the configuration. Office configuration—who is located next to whom and where—serves a symbolic function by sending messages

---

[4] All information about the BOSTI studies may be found in M. Brill's *Using Office Design to Increase Productivity*, Vols. 1 and 2, Grand Rapids, MI: Westinghouse Furniture Systems, 1985.

[5] This quote appears in K. Gustafson, "Westinghouse Generates a New Corporate Culture," *Corporate Design and Realty*, November-December 1984, pp. 51–56. Many of the corporate examples are described in detail in the September 1985 and February 1986 issues of *Corporate Design and Realty.*

about who and what is valued in the organization. For example, arranging offices by rank so that the highest-level executives occupy the top floor(s) and/or the largest and most nicely appointed office space (e.g., corner offices with large windows) and lower-level employees occupy successively lower floors and smaller offices conveys the message that the organization places a high value on status. Similarly, a company that arranges its offices so that the most senior managers are located together and are given the nicest offices sends a message to employees and outsiders alike about the importance the firm places on seniority. The top executives at Home Box Office chose not to move into the top floor (the fifteenth) of their new building, but rather selected the eighth floor because of its greater proximity to both the marketing and programming departments. Union Carbide serves as another case in point. When the company recently moved into its new headquarters building, all managerial-level employees were assigned offices of equal size so that employees and outsiders alike would recognize the importance the company places on equality.

Not only is office configuration important in conveying information about an organization's values, but the physical layout of the offices themselves—be they conventional private offices, open-offices, or combinations of the two—also serves to reinforce the company's values. For example, R.P.M. Carlson, chairman of the board and president of the National Bank of Georgia, chose to implement an open-office plan in the bank's new headquarters because he believed this plan would best foster a culture based on consensus and open communication. Similarly, in Procter & Gamble's new office, only open-office plans were provided so that employees would clearly recognize the importance P&G places on teamwork.

Office Decor   Although office decor may not connote messages about organizational values as clearly as does office layout, elements of decor have been found to serve as symbols by influencing individuals' impressions about office holders and organizations alike. Objects commonly found in reception areas influence impressions. Flags, logos, seals, and pictures of organizational leaders convey an image of an organization that provides a great deal of structure and limited autonomy for its employees. Certificates, trophies, and plaques also are perceived as suggesting a high degree of organizational structure as well as the value and rewarding of good performance. Plants and flowers have consistently been found to influence impressions of an organization's warmth and friendliness.[6]

Artwork has also been associated with perceptions of organizations, with the content of the artwork playing a crucial role. One firm that displayed an oil painting of men on horseback was perceived by women as being a cold, hostile, and unfriendly place to work. In fact, this company was having difficulty recruiting women. Further investigation revealed that the reason why many of the women formed this negative impression was they believed the painting depicted a battle between cowboys and Indians! Thus, it is not enough for managers simply to add artwork to a reception area, office, or boardroom—the content of the artwork must also be taken into account.

---

[6] The meanings of these and other objects are discussed in S. Ornstein, "Organizational Symbols: A Study of Their Meaning and Influences on Perceived Psychological Climate," *Organization Behavior and Human Decision Processes*, October 1986, p. 207–229.

IMPROVING YOUR OFFICE DESIGN

Although there obviously are no simple rules to making the best decisions about office design, there are some general guidelines that can be followed so that more effective and efficient designs may be developed and employed. These guidelines are as follows:

1. When changes in office design are pending—either as a result of moving to a new building or refurbishing the present facility—managers should seek input from the employees affected by the change. Doing so has at least three tangible benefits. First, as the people "in the trenches," employees often have specific knowledge about how their jobs actually are performed. Based on this knowledge they can make suggestions about what arrangements and configurations of office space should be most beneficial to enhanced performance. Likewise, they can identify design changes that would be detrimental to performance so that these designs can be avoided. Second, employees who are given an opportunity to contribute their ideas to the design decision are likely to be more satisfied with their jobs and the ultimate design that is implemented than are employees who are not given such an opportunity. Third, by soliciting employees' participation, it is more likely that the move to the new facility or the refurbishing will go smoothly. This will result from employees' greater psychological acceptance of the move and their increased willingness to make the necessary physical adjustments (e.g., packing their offices for relocation, using new machinery, etc.).

2. To implement more effective changes in office design, managers should thoroughly analyze the work to be performed in the space under consideration. Included in this analysis should be an assessment of the nature of the work and the physical constraints of any machinery needed to complete/augment the work. It would be appropriate for managers to focus on needs for privacy; quiet; communication among individuals, groups, and departments; and special events requiring unusual office space needs. If it is determined that privacy and/or quiet working conditions are desirable, traditional offices with floor-to-ceiling walls and doors should be selected. These choices should then be arranged according to individual, group, or department—contingent on communication needs. Those with the greatest needs for communication should be placed nearest one another. If it is necessary, or simply desirable, that groups of more than five people meet together, it is important that space be provided to accommodate these meetings. In many offices, it is also prudent to plan for machinery. Machines that make a good deal of noise or emit heat or noxious odors should be placed in a private area blocked off by doors, walls, and/or noise-absorbing partitions. Manufacturers' instructions should be followed in setting up machinery (personal computers, in particular). This often requires changes in lighting, seating, and furnishings. Ignoring these adjustments to machinery will generally result in reduced rather than improved productivity.

3. Because configuration and arrangement of offices convey specific messages to employees and outsiders about the value placed on status, productivity, and communication, managers need to consider the values, goals, and behaviors they want to reinforce by their selection of office design. Status differences may

be reinforced by office placement (highest-status positions placed on highest floor in office building), size (larger offices indicate more status), appointments (more expensive and greater variety of furnishings indicate greater status), equipment (greater amounts and expense indicate greater status), and type (traditional offices indicate greater status than open-offices). Status differences can be minimized by similarly sized, placed, styled, and decorated offices.

It is also important for managers to recognize that the decor and arrangement of furnishings within individual offices serve to reinforce company values, norms, and goals. Offices that are haphazardly arranged and decorated send clear signals about the lack of importance placed on detail and planning. Offices containing Spartan furnishings and decorations suggest the value of frugality and sticking to essentials. The arrangement of seating, particularly in the offices of top management, sends information to people that they use in forming opinions about the value the company places on communication and the importance it places on authority and structure in relationships. Decorative objects such as plants, artwork, and floral arrangements generally connote images of warm and friendly office holders. If these office holders are top-level managers, often these impressions will spill over to the way in which people perceive the entire organization.

4. Managers need to consider the influence office design has on outsiders who have cause to visit the facility. The offices should be arranged to promote simple and complete customer interaction. If necessary, signs should be placed so that the customer can easily find the area in which they are to conduct business. If clients/customers spend time waiting to conduct their business, a comfortable reception area should be created. This should include comfortable seating as well as decorative objects such as plants, flowers, and artwork. The inclusion of magazines and a telephone conveys the message that the organization really cares about its clients/customers.

5. Managers should also consider how the office design may influence the impressions made by potential employees. Office design should accurately convey to potential employees the values, goals, and behaviors actually desired by the organization. To determine the messages connoted by office design, an audit of hirees' perceptions, based on office design, could be completed. This information about what messages are actually conveyed could then be compared with the desired messages and changes made accordingly.

Office layout and decor are powerful influences on employees, customer, and community attitudes, behaviors, and impressions. Managers concerned with maximizing productivity and clarity of communication should view office design as a valuable tool for the accomplishment of their goals.

Color: A Guide to Human Response

James Gray, Jr.

How does color affect the impression you make? Color preferences offer clues to personality and guide human response.

Most interesting and revealing research and theory come from color expert Faber Birren. In his book *Color and Human Response,* he looks at personal color preferences and describes how color relates to personality. The colors people select and wear consistently are a large part of their image. Look around your office. What colors do people wear? Who wears warm colors and who wears cool colors? Birren found that.

> There is a major division between extroverts, who like warm colors and introverts who like cool colors. As to general response to color, it is wholly normal for human beings to like any and all colors. Rejection, skepticism, or outright denial of emotional content in color probably indicates a disturbed, frustrated or unhappy mortal. Undue exuberance over color, however, may be a sign of mental confusion, a flighty soul, the person who flits from one fancy or diversion to another and has poor direction and self-poise.*

The following commentaries, adapted from Birren's book, show how color and human response are connected.

Red. There are different red types. The first comes honestly to the color, with outwardly directed interests. He or she is impulsive, possibly athletic, sexy, quick to speak the mind—whether right or wrong. The complementary red type is the meek and timid person who may choose the color because it signifies the brave qualities that are lacking. Look in this person for more hidden desires, for more sublimation of wishes than usual. Where there is dislike of red, which is fairly common, look for a person who has been frustrated, defeated in some way, bitter and angry because of unfulfilled longings.

Pink. One of Birren's studies showed that many people who liked pink were dilettantes. They lived in fairly wealthy neighborhoods and were well educated, indulged, and protected. Birren found them to be "red souls who, because of their careful guardianship, hadn't the courage to choose the color in its full intensity." A preference for pink may also signify memories of youth, gentility, or affection.

Orange. Orange is the social color, cheerful, luminous, and warm rather than hot like red. Orange personalities are friendly, have a ready smile and quick wit, and are fluent if not profound in speech. They are good natured and gregarious and do

---

"Color: A Guide to Human Response" by James Gray, Jr. from *The Winning Image,* Ed. 3, 1982, pp. 66–71. Reprinted by permission of the author.

*Faber Birren, *Color and Human Response* (New York: Van Nostrand Reinhold, 1978)

not like to be left alone. In several instances, the dislike of orange has turned out to indicate a person, once flighty, who has made a determined effort to give up superficial ways for more sober application and diligence.

Yellow. On the good side, yellow is often preferred by persons of above-average intelligence. It is, of course, associated with oriental philosophies. The yellow type likes innovation, originality, wisdom. This type tends to be introspective, discriminating, high minded, and serious about the world and the talented people in it.

Yellow in the Western world has symbolized cowardice, prejudice, persecution. Some may dislike the color for this reason.

Yellow-green. From the few cases Birren encountered, he concluded that the yellow-green type is perceptive and leads a rich inner life but resents being looked upon as a recluse. There is desire to win admiration for a fine mind and demeanor but difficulty meeting others because of innate timidity and self-consciousness.

Green. Green is perhaps the most American of colors. It is symbolic of nature, balance, normality. Those who prefer green almost invariably are socially well adjusted, civilized, conventional. Green is perhaps an expression of Freud's oral character. Because the green types are constantly on the go and savor the good things of life, they are often overweight. The person who dislikes the green type may resist social involvement, and lack the balance that green itself suggests.

Blue-green. Birren associated the type with narcissism, or self-love. Most people who prefer blue-green are sophisticated and discriminating, have excellent taste, are well dressed, charming, egocentric, sensitive, and refined. Where a rare dislike of blue-green is met, there is an ardent denunciation of conceit in others, the attitude: "I am as good as you are!" Or, "Who do you think you are!"

Blue. Blue is the color of conservatism, accomplishment, devotion, deliberation, introspection. It therefore goes with people who succeed through application, those who know how to earn money, make the right connections in life, and seldom do anything impulsive. They make able executives and golfers, and they usually dwell in neighborhoods where other lovers of blue are to be found. Blue types are cautious, steady, often admirable, and generally conscious of their virtues.

A dislike of blue signals revolt, guilt, a sense of failure, anger about the success of others, especially if they have not expended the effort of the hater of blue. Successful people are resented as having all the good breaks and the good luck.

Purple and violet. Those whose favorite color is purple are usually sensitive and have above-average taste. Lovers of purple carefully avoid the more sordid, vulgar aspects of life and have high ideals for themselves and for everyone else.

Those who dislike purple are enemies of pretense, vanity, and conceit and readily disparage cultural activities which to them are artificial.

Brown. Brown is a color of the earth, preferred by people who have homespun qualities. They are sturdy, reliable, shrewd, parsimonious; they look old when they are young and young when they are old. They are conservatives in the extreme.

In a distaste for brown, there may be impatience with what is seen as dull and boring.

White, gray, and black. Virtually no one ever singles out white as a first choice; it is bleak, emotionless, sterile. White, gray, and black all figure largely in the responses of disturbed human beings. On the other hand, white is the color of innocence, virtue, truth and cleanliness. White is the preferred color for weddings and for formal social events.

Black-and-white contrasts also signal upper-class status. The famous Ascot races and other social events use white and black as primary theme colors.

A preference for gray, however, usually represents a deliberate and cultivated choice. Gray's sobriety indicates an effort to keep on an even keel, to be reasonable, agreeable, useful in a restrained way. To dislike gray is less likely than to be indifferent to it. It may be that a dislike is weariness of an uneventful life, or a feeling of mediocrity.

As to black, usually only the mentally troubled are fascinated by it, though there are exceptions. Some few persons may take to the color for its sophistication, but in this preference they may be hiding their truer natures.

People who dislike black are legion. Black is death, the color of despair. Such persons often avoid the subjects of illness and death, do not acknowledge birthdays, and never admit their age.

SELECTING COLORS THAT ARE RIGHT FOR YOU

1. Respect corporate or professional standards. If top level executives most often appear in navy and gray flannel, take the hint. It's a conservative environment and you will do well to follow the standard. Gray and navy are perhaps most readily associated with conservatism; bright or new tones are more liberal and may be de rigueur for fashion and design careers.
2. Don't be afraid of color. Respect professional and corporate standards, but let your personality shine through. The gray flannel suit or blazer comes to life with a scarf in the breast pocket, but to be safe, wear complementary colors.
3. Keep the season and climate in mind. White is generally considered bad taste in winter. Black absorbs heat on a humid, muggy day, but is comfortable in an air-conditioned office.
4. Complement skin and hair tones. Light skin and blond hair combined with white is a fade-out. Red hair and a ruddy complexion over violet and orange shocks. Cosmetic counselors in respected department stores conduct free color evaluations.
5. Select several colors that both complement your skin and hair color, and express your personality and buy clothes primarily in these colors. In addition it's difficult to own too many white shirts or blouses.
6. Consider the occasion. Delivering a speech at an after-six dinner meeting calls for dark, authoritative colors. Training a group of new employees might demand an authoritative, but less-threatening, gray flannel suit.
7. In choosing accessories, match and coordinate colors. Briefcases, shoes, and pocketbooks should not blatantly contrast suit or dress colors.

The following guidelines tell how to use color to alleviate a problem with body shape and size. It's actually impossible to separate clothing and color guidelines, and you should consider both to create the most effective style.

The tall, muscular male or female. Choose softer, lighter shades in gray, beige or light blues. Avoid color contrasts and bright colors that draw attention. Choose subtle combinations of blue and gray.

The tall, thin male or female. Medium-dark tans and blues work well. Use subtle color contrasts to break a long, continuous look, a tan and cream combination for example. Stick with solid colors; avoid bright colors and patterns.

The small, or short male or female. Stick with dark hues in blue or gray. Match colors rather than contrast them. Matched colors, especially dark colors, add power and authority. For example, a dark gray suit with a diagonally striped tie in medium to dark gray and navy is an authoritative color combination. For women, a medium-gray dress with a complementary, darker-gray jacket or blazer works well.

The hefty male or female. Wear neutral, less attention-drawing colors, gray or tan hues. Wear lighter, cooler colors, even in winter. Avoid bright colors. Wear dark colors only on occasions that demand added authority.

'That's No Lady, That's My Wife'

Janet Elliott

"Who was that lady I saw you with last night?"

"That was no lady, that was my wife." So goes Henny Youngman's old joke. Well, Henny Youngman and the supporters of changes in sexist language have something in common. They both know that language transmits values and behavioral models.

When you deliver a speech, it's important that your language be free of sexist terminology which may send values that insult or exclude some members of your audience.

Sexism was first defined in a children's dictionary published in 1972 by American Heritage Publishing Company. It referred to sexism as "any arbitrary stereotyping of males and females on the basis of their gender." Unfortunately much of our standard English is inherently sexist and reinforces inequality.

AVOID STEREOTYPES

However, by giving careful thought to your word choices, you can present fair, accurate and equal treatment of both sexes. First, be careful of words that refer to a stereotyped behavior. You don't want your careless choice of words to imply an evaluation of the sexes you don't really intend.

" 'That's No Lady, That's My Wife' " by Janet Elliott, *The Toastmaster*, August 1986, p. 14. Reprinted by permission of Toastmasters International.

As that old joke of Henny Youngman's shows us, the word "lady" is associated with a certain behavior. "Lady" can be used as a parallel to "gentleman." Although it is perfectly correct to say "ladies and gentlemen," be careful not to use the term "lady," with all its behavioral connotations, when the more accurate word would be "woman."

But referring to someone as "lady" is complimentary, you say. Think again. Because the word "lady" has been overused, all sorts of connotations have developed. Do you mean bag lady, ol' lady, the fat lady or perhaps even lady of the evening?

Another stereotype practice which can be very insulting to members of your audience is referring to an adult female as a girl. For example, when talking about women sharing a midday meal don't refer to the event as "lunch with the girls."

A woman old enough to hold a position as a secretary should not be spoken about as "girl," as in "my girl typed the letter." Before using the words "lady" or "girl," determine if you would use "gentleman" or "boy" in a similar circumstance describing a male. If not, you should reword your statement.

Difficulties also arise from the habitual use of clichés or familiar expressions which evaluate and stereotype. For example, using the phrase "man and wife" implies differences in the activity of each. An evaluation of the roles is communicated. A use of more equal terms is "husband and wife."

Another way you may inadvertently communicate a stereotype is by describing a woman's physical attributes and a man's mental or professional attributes. If you make an introduction of Carl Smith as a great surgeon and his wife as a beautiful redhead, you have not treated each with the same dignity or seriousness.

You might say the Smiths are an attractive couple—Carl is a handsome blond and Linda is a beautiful redhead. Or you could say the Smiths are highly respected in their fields; Carl is a great surgeon and Linda is a successful lawyer.

Some adjectives, depending on whether the person you are describing is a man or woman, communicate bias. Ambitious men, but aggressive women; cautious men, but timid women are examples of adjectives that stereotype.

SEXIST JOB TITLES

A second area that can be troublesome in inadvertently presenting a sex bias in your speech is in how you state job titles. I recently attended a meeting in which nearly 80 percent of the audience was composed of young college women. The speaker was addressing the subject of career options for communications majors in business. Throughout his speech he used the term "businessman" when referring to a business executive in general. Many members of his audience were offended by the exclusion.

When a job is open to members of both sexes, describing it by a common gender term is more accurate and effective than using one job title for men and another for women. Why not use the term "reporter" rather than "newsman," "mail carrier" rather than "mailman," "member of congress" rather than "congressman" or "police officer" rather than "policeman"?

When speaking of an individual who holds a particular job or office, it offends no one to use the specific gender term, such as "newspaperman" or "congresswoman." But be careful of that term "lady" again. NBC newsman Frank Blair referred to a female head of a jury as forelady of the jury. It was specific but not entirely correct, unless he commonly speaks of a man as a jurygentleman.

You can insult members of your audience by trivializing some job titles, such as poet to poetess, director to directress or usher to usherette. The original word can be used to indicate either sex.

It is not necessary to specify gender in job titles such as woman lawyer or male nurse, unless a gender modifier is relevant; i.e., as in a course on women writers or when specifying a particular fact, such as the first female astronaut. When you specify the gender of a profession, you are implying by the label that an exception to the rule has been made.

EXCLUDING ONE SEX

The use of terminology which excludes one sex is a third area that alienates your audience. A speaker at a seminar for men and women insurance agents turned off a portion of his audience when he began by saying, "As you look at your face in the mirror each morning when you shave . . . " He did not choose his words carefully to avoid offending by exclusion all those in his audience who have never shaved their faces.

The pervasive use of "man" to represent humanity in general either excludes women when they should be included, or creates ambiguous situations; leaving the interpretation up to the individual listener.

Many publishers have developed guidelines for the use of nonsexist language in textbooks and journals. For instance, Scott, Foresman and Company suggest that, "When man invented the wheel . . . " can become, "When people invented the wheel . . . "

McGraw-Hill Book Company Publications states in their Guidelines for Equal Treatment of the Sexes, "In reference to humanity at large, language should operate to include women and girls. Terms that tend to exclude females should be avoided whenever possible."

The use of "man" to refer to both women and men is ambiguous. The best way to avoid the problem is to replace the word "man," used in the general sense, with such words as "human" or "person" or "American" or "Japanese."

Similarly, the use of masculine pronouns to refer to women and men creates the same problems. Because the English language lacks a truly generic third-person singular pronoun, avoiding ambiguity and exclusiveness is not always easy. Linguists have even attempted to coin a common gender pronoun.

In 1859 Charles Converse proposed the pronoun "thon" which he derived as a contraction of "that one." It was listed in *Funk and Wagnalls New Standard Dictionary* of 1913 with the example, "Each pupil must learn thon's lesson." It was last recognized in the 1959 edition of Webster's *Second International Dictionary*.

Other coinages have come and gone, which suggests a continuing need for an appropriate common gender pronoun.

SHARED VALUES

Language is not only a means of communication, it does indeed express values and shared assumptions about our society. Languages continually evolve to include new concepts and ideas. English is now beginning to reflect the increasing equality of women and men in our society.

Most often sexist language is not deliberate. It is usually a matter of habit or laziness. It is easier to use ready-made sexist expressions than to reword in a manner that avoids sexism.

As George Orwell said in his essay, "Politics and the English Language," "Ready-made phrases are the prefabricated strips of words and mixed metaphors that come crowding in when you do not want to take the trouble to think through what you are saying."

You are now sensitized. You have been made aware of a few of the ways our language can perpetuate sexist values. As a speaker you owe it to your audience to examine your words and choose them with greater care. Both sexes deserve equal treatment in life and in language. You can do your part in not denying your audience that right.

Games Mother Never Taught You

Betty Lehan Harragan

To awestruck sightseers in the land of the business hierarchy, the achitectural grandeur is overpowering and impressive. Stately edifices dominate landscaped vistas of suburbia and mighty skyscrapers silhouette the profiles of major cities. Flowering gardens, soaring plazas, ample parking, vaulted lobbies, air conditioning, musical elevators, carpeted lounges, spacious dining rooms, and hundreds upon hundreds of linear offices bathed relentlessly in fluorescent brilliance dutifully impress gaping tourists.

But all this structural munificence does not divert the expert gamester who looks beyond the steel and concrete public visor of the corporate persona to identify the heraldic markings painted on the battle armor. Like the shields carried by knights of legend, the modern corporate building reeks with symbolism. Far from being a mere architectural wonder, every pane of glass, slab of marble, and foot of carpet performs a dual function in identifying the tournament site. The buildings are impersonal monuments to the power and wealth contained therein. Space itself, in both the exterior and interior layout, is weighted with abstract significance. Just as a heraldic seal reveals a great deal about the one using it, so spatial divisions reveal important information about the modern-day knights.

Today's business building, especially the corporate headquarters, is a physical representation of the hierarchical pyramid. It is the tangible game board. A walk through a large office, from floor to floor, is like threading a course through the hierarchy. Trappings of rank, position, and power are spread around the place like icons in a cathedral. They identify the important players and signal their positions in the game. Neophytes must grasp the design of the game board and learn the initial placement of the pieces before making any irreversible move.

Very often businesswomen approach the game of corporate gamemanship as if it were a throw of the dice which pits their future against pure chance, or luck. The real game for women more nearly resembles chess, in which one of the sixteen playing pieces is a strong female (the Queen) and the object of the game is to "check" the adverse King. Chess is an intellectual military exercise based on a combative attack against equally matched opposing fighting units. The descriptive play language of chess is indistinguishable from that of war "games" or football or business—lines of attack, defensive systems, infiltration, onslaught, sacrifice, control (territory or foes), power, weakness, strength, strategy, tactics, maneuver, surrender, challenge, conquer, win. Each pawn, rook, knight, bishop, queen, and king in the chess set is endowed with specific agility to move only in certain directions and for stipulated distances. Each piece is made clearly identifiable so that players and observers can watch the game progress and know exactly what moves have been made. Unlike cards, chess is a public game spread out for all to see.

So is corporate politics a public game. In business the so-called status symbols serve to identify the playing pieces and reveal their positions on the board. The masculine pecking system, regardless of the all-male activity, is replete with emblems and shared identity signals, many of which speak louder than words and obviate the need for verbal communication. If you've ever wondered why your boss pays inordinate attention to "silly" objects or personal privileges, very likely these are crucial business status symbols. Few of the customs and practices of business life are meaningless. They only look that way to women who have not learned the fundamentals of the game.

HOW TO TELL THE PLAYERS APART

Status symbols are two-way communications. If you can interpret them, they tell you where a coworker stands in the ranking system, and they tell others where you stand. For that reason, women cannot afford to ignore these ubiquitous symbols because each tiny accumulation of visible status is an increase in power or advancement. Indeed, as the game plays out, a woman often needs her power emblems more than a title or salary increase to effectively use any authority she acquires. It is difficult if not impossible for a pawn to behave like a bishop or queen if she doesn't have the mitre or crown that differentiates the chess pieces.

Most of the common status differentials can be perceived at even the lowest levels. As employees move up the hierarchical ladder, the emblems are gradually emblazoned with additional symbols or sophisticated refinements of the basic seal. Here are some of the categories of rank insignia which help you tell the players apart and prevent you from being bluffed by someone at your own level who tries to "pull rank" on you without justification. Conversely, a familiarity with the status symbols protects you from being duped by management if you are offered an empty promotion or promise which carries no visible authority emblem.

How You Are Paid

Not how much, *how.* Cash in a brown envelope indicates the lowest rank. A check thus becomes a status symbol, a sign of progress. If the wage is figured on an hourly basis or a weekly basis (the nonexempt jobs which are subject to overtime beyond forty hours), it has a lower status than jobs which are exempt from overtime. I remember a junior writer who tried to lord it over her friends with a claim that she had been promoted to professional ranks. She lost all respect and admiration when it was discovered that she still filled out "the little green slips" which were required for weekly time sheets. She thought she was a "writer" because she was allowed to write; her shrewd coworkers knew she was still considered an hourly clerical worker by management because that's how she was paid. An annual salary paid out in the standard semimonthly equal installments is a symbol of the supervisory and professional ranks. Very high levels of management often have options to tailor payment methods to suit their own convenience. Many executives don't get a check at all; they have it sent directly to their banks and deposited to their personal accounts. Corporate officers almost all arrange to have big portions of their high salaries "deferred," that is, not paid to them until some later date or in some other form. It pays to keep an eye on how superiors receive and cash their salary checks. Incidentally, some executives send their secretaries to the bank with their checks; these secretaries are worth wooing if you're trying to collect salary data.

What Time You Report to Work

Flexibility in choosing one's own working hours is a clear mark of distinction. The lowest degree of status is reflected in punching a time clock or being "signed in" by an overseer, the sure tag of a manual or clerical job. The time-clock insignia also extends to lunch hours and coffee breaks which are strictly regimented to the prescribed minute. As one moves upward into supervisory and professional ranks, *it is taken for granted* that you have a degree of autonomy in fixing your work hours and lunch times or breaks. Women frequently don't seem to recognize that they have this status privilege, or else they are afraid to display it, and use it. I'm often jarred when I have lunch with an apparent "executive" woman who suddenly bolts her lunch and dashes away because she'll be "late" getting back to the office within an hour. This is the time-clock thinking, lowest-level clerical insignia. If her boss is what she's afraid of (as many have told me), she is being treated as a time-clock employee and allowing herself and her job to be thus degraded. No brownie points accrue to a game player who refuses to wear her status symbols. You establish privileges simply by taking advantage of work-hour freedom according to the local department pattern.

Freedom to determine your own working hours does not mean you work shorter hours or ignore the working timetable your boss adopts. Some women consider it wise to dovetail their hours with their boss's—so they are always in the office at the same time. Others work more independently and arrive at the hour most convenient to their personal schedule and vary lunch periods to suit personal or business commitments. One woman executive I know has remained at the same job level for twenty years although a more astute gamester with her options would have progressed several steps. Her problem is low-echelon thinking; she still acts like a time-clock secretary. Even though she travels on business regularly, she schedules her trips for one-day, eighteen-hour commutes and gets home after midnight to appear in the office before nine the next morning. Bedraggled and exhausted, she complains about her terrible schedule, but neither her subordinates nor her superiors have any sympathy; they've long since chalked her off as lacking management potential. Men who progressed from a duplicate position scheduled their trips over two or three days each time; they knew better than to ignore status symbols. If you're uncertain about your status entitlement in time flexibility, watch what male colleagues and bosses do. Then go out and do likewise! Don't, for heaven's sake, complain about men who proudly display their ranking privileges and wonder why your hard work isn't appreciated after you've thrown away your own equality symbol.

Where You Eat

Not only when but where one eats is a status distinction. The lowest indication is being restricted to the premises as are many plant and factory workers. Freedom to leave the work premises (whether you do or not) is a step upward. Voluntary on-site lunching in large corporations is usually stamped with clear status distinctions. Lower-echelon workers go to the general cafeteria; middle-management dines in the executive lunchroom; and top officers eat in the private dining room. Senior executives can always drop into the general cafeteria if they want, but it takes a symbolic ID card to get into the executive dining halls. Anyone who is eligible to eat in the executive dining room but eschews the privilege to continue lunching with friends in the general cafeteria is pretty sure to be knocked out of the game very soon. If, for example, you had a boss who did that, you'd know it was time to look for a transfer or new job because you're stuck with a deadhead. See how attention to visible status emblems can tip you off?

In some companies even eating at your desk can reveal status. Did you get the food yourself from the friendly mobile vendor? Did a secretary order it from a good delicatessen and have it delivered? Was a complete hot-plate sent from the executive dining room? Or did you bring a sandwich from home in a brown paper bag?

Are you beginning to think all this is silly, like who cares? That's just it; nobody cares—if you're a woman. All your male colleagues and coworkers will ignore your eating habits as long as it keeps you out of their favorite rendezvous. They've already decided you belong with the brown-baggers (low-paid secretaries and clerks who bring their lunch), so it won't surprise them one bit to see you ally yourself with lower-status lunch groups. As an ambitious woman you have to care. It will never do for you to exclude yourself from the semisocial lunch and cocktail gatherings where more business is conducted, more information exchanged, and more contacts made than during the regular working hours. If you can't worm your way into a suitable lunch group, go to a movie or go shopping for a couple of hours, but definitely exercise your status prerogative.

The Mail You Get

Mail sorters, if they were so minded, could diagram the organizational chart by noting the incoming mail for various individuals and the routing pattern on memos. One of the first status symbols is an in-box on your desk. The next improvement is denoted by an out-box. Increasing status is determined by the style of the containers, utilitarian metal being at the lower end and hand-woven straw, hand-painted wood, or other elaborate designs being better. Perhaps because this symbol is so widely distributed, some statusy types dispense with this common denominator and have incoming correspondence neatly piled on the center of an empty desk (they probably have little of significance to do and hope their status symbols will carry them through to retirement).

More important than the box is the incoming contents. Daily deliveries of the *Wall Street Journal* and *New York Times* or regular copies of *Business Week, Fortune, Barron's, Forbes, U.S. News and World Report,* or economic newsletters are distinctive emblems. Company-paid subscriptions are status symbols in general, but the more management-oriented the publication, the higher the status rating, *Harvard Business Review* outranking the Gizmo trade journal by far.

Outgoing mail also has status value if your name is imprinted on the corporate letterhead, either by itself or as one of the partners or officers of a firm.

Your Working Location

In a factory, the operator at the end of the assembly line has more prestige than one near the beginning because the product is more valuable in its finished state. The principle of increasing value of work follows through to the top of the hierarchy where the office of the chief executive is obviously the ultimate in status and power and the choicest in location. Proximity to the power generator exudes status, with the office adjacent to the CEO being the most prestigious but the entire floor sharing in shadings of top rank. In a suburban complex with several buildings, the one with the executive offices is the power generator and a poor location there is superior to choice space in any lesser building. In short, physical locale is a status symbol, so the location of your office is one of the most telling emblems in revealing your rank in the hierarchy and your favor with the boss. It's an important piece in the game.

HOW SPACE CONFERS STATUS

The "executive floor" is known to most employees by virtue of the fact that they have never set foot on it. This is the true inner sanctum, and the power emanations are so strong that minor employees are afraid to get near. I've seen adult men literally shake in their boots at the prospect of answering a call to the executive floor. For those who are physically located "in the boondocks," "over in the boneyard," or "out in the sticks," (i.e., distant buildings or branch offices), a move to the headquarters city or building signifies a boom in status long before anyone knows if the shift was accompanied by a change in title or a better salary. Geographic and internal physical office moves can track an executive's path through the hierarchical labyrinth more clearly than a title change. A company may have hundreds of vice-presidents or divisional managers but the really important ones are distinguished from titular peers by that prime emblem of status—the office location.

Within the physical boundaries of every corporate department or operation much the same pattern of office locale identifies the ranking of subordinates and superiors. Most department layouts are square or rectangular. The corner offices, which are larger, brighter, and most secluded, are choice spots and the highest ranking executives naturally choose them. The remainder of the outside walls are customarily divided into small offices so that each has a window or a portion of plate glass. These are known universally as the "window offices" and have much higher status value than nonwindowed offices. Size is also an emblematic factor, so a large window office is more valuable than a small window office, but a small window office is superior to a much larger "interior" office.

The internal space in a typical office floor layout can be left wide open and filled with rows upon rows of desks (generally populated with clerical women). Here employees work in the wide-open area with no privacy and where they can be easily observed by the supervisors. Another solution is to partition the vast internal space with one or more rows of "interior" offices, each of which has walls to the ceiling and doors; these are real private offices but have no windows. The third alternative, and a highly favored one, is to erect movable partitions which enclose the desks of individuals in the interior sector. These tin or plastic partitions are waist- or shoulder-high; they block the view of a person sitting at the enclosed desk but allow any passer-by to look over the top and see the occupant at work. These constructions are well known to all working women as cubicles. Status-wise, they are a step up from the wide-open clerical or secretarial pool pattern (often referred to as "paper factories"), but not as prestigious as a fully enclosed office which carries more symbolic value even if it must be shared with another. A "window" office is generally considered an "executive" or supervisory symbol.

SYMBOLIC MEANINGS OF WINDOWS AND WALLS

Since window offices can be roughly defined as officers' quarters, the position of rooms "weights" their relative values. Proximity to the corner offices carries the most weight, then comes view. An unobstructed view of the skyline or gardens is far more prestigious than a window on the ventilating shaft or one overlooking the parking lot or delivery entrance. An office located on the traffic lanes, one in the center arena of business activity, represents higher status than one hidden away in an isolated nook or placed near the non-status "public" areas, such as cloakrooms, bathrooms, lounges, elevators, or storerooms.

Offices in the middle of the outside walls, that is, those that are equidistant from either corner office, are least desirable because the occupant's connection to either corner power generator is weak, tenuous, and not immediately identifiable. Michael Korda, the best-selling folk etymologist of sophisticated male business mores, attributes this mid-center office weakness to a power dead spot. In his book *Power: How to Get It, How to Use It*, he asserts that power flows in an X-shaped pattern from each corner office to the one diagonally opposite. The center of the space (where the X-lines bisect) represents the point at which the authority of the corner person peters out. Under his theory, the center of the floor layout is equivalent to a power blackout area and outer offices parallel with the center of the room are thus located in power dead-spots.

I've seen office setups where enclaves of competing executives use the X theory to amass power. With their cronies and subordinates flanking them, they set up hostile camps in each of the corners. Newcomers or nonaligned workers invariably float to the nondescript center offices. In firms where several executives have equal rank, for instance partners in auditing, law, or brokerage firms, they can apportion the corner offices by a coin toss and the power flow runs as easily down the sides as across a diagonal. Even so, the central offices are less prestigious because ranking executives like to have their closest allies physically near them. Proximity to a superior is undoubtedly the best gauge of status within a team group. Watch carefully when offices get switched around. It means that status symbols are changing hands and the rank of the movers is being visibly altered although their titles and salaries are unchanged.

A lot of women may think this game of musical chairs with office locations is also silly and unnecessary. It may be, but the accretion of status symbols is very serious business to ambitious businessmen. They know that a display of status symbols means as much in the corporate hierarchy as a chest full of medals does to an ambitious officer in the military hierarchy. If women are to function equally in the action arena of business they must be able to decipher the code and demand the proper rank insignia for themselves as they progress haltingly up the corporate ladder. To disregard the value of preferred office location is tantamount to selecting a rhinestone ring over a diamond because the first one looked "prettier." Refusing to wear epaulets which identify your business rank because you don't appreciate the genuine value is a disastrous mistake.

DON'T GARBLE THE LOCALITY MESSAGE

Judging from my personal observations during the past five years that women have begun moving ahead in corporate jobs en masse, it seems safe to say that many have ignored the status code. Which is to say that they get a better title but they seldom get the visible emblems of rank. If you believe you are making progress on your job, count the number of times you have changed offices. A meaningful promotion almost mandates an office change; a token title and slight salary increase does not give you the necessary authority to handle the new job unless subordinates and outsiders see that you were issued the appropriate rank insignia.

By and large, women are oblivious to rank symbols because so few working women have *any* office privacy that a room of one's own is—in comparative *women's* terms—the ultimate achievement. As long as it's private and "workable," women are inclined to "accept" any office offered them and make the best of the disadvantages that inevitably appear. I know women who have sat in the same office for the past twenty years. I don't know any men in that category. In the industry circles I travel, men who are that immobile were fired or quit years ago.

If you had trouble . . . in diagramming your department's organization chart or evaluating your own advancement potential, try a different tack. Make a floor plan of the office layout and see who's sitting where. This floor plan will guide you in determining which of several people on the same job level are the more favored or powerful—they will have offices very near the top-ranked superior, or they will have established a power enclave of their own in one of the opposite corners. Then locate your own office in relation to these authority areas. You should get a pretty good idea of what your superiors think of you and your potential according to the office they assigned you. It may be more than adequate by your personal comfort standards, but if it doesn't translate into appropriate status according to the male heraldic seal, you are being symbolically downgraded or dead-ended.

ALWAYS COLLECT YOUR EARNED MEDALLIONS

Reluctance on management's part to dispense money in the form of raises is understandable because of manifest business concern but unwillingness to issue women their status insignia is propelled by pure male chauvinism. A female corporate politician must be alert to this subtle form of sex discrimination and take steps to alleviate it. Specifically, *ask* for and fight for your office emblem. Before making a final decision on a new job offer, ask to see the office that goes with the job. If you get a promotion, inquire immediately about the new office that you'll get. If you discover you have a lesser status office than your job indicates, ask for the next vacant office in the area you decide you belong in. Keep your eye on possible office vacancies and ask for a more desirable location before they put a newcomer (usually a man) in a higher status office than you have. Keep asking.

One woman I know who was an analyst in the research department of a large investment firm reacted instinctively and volubly when her company moved to elegant new offices in a beautiful skyscraper. She was the only woman in an all male group and the covey of expensive industrial designers, office planners, and management consultants had settled her in a noisy isolated corner next to the coat room and elevator banks and off-kilter from the rest of the section. "I didn't know anything about office sites," she told me, "but I felt like I'd been slapped in the face. My intuition told me there was something seriously wrong and I refused to take the office. A young guy who had just arrived was settled in an office I liked, so I demanded that one on the basis of seniority. I loved the job, but I refused to appear at the office until I got the right accommodations. They put up a terrible fight, until I was mentally prepared to quit over the issue." Her determination paid off and she got the office space she selected. Later that year, one of the firm's partners brought his wife in to meet her, saying proudly, "I'd like you to meet the only woman in our research department." My friend pointed out that there was now another woman in research but he brushed that aside, saying, "I forget about her. I consider you our only woman because you are the only one who fought for your office!"

By contrast, a lawyer I know got a very good job in the corporate counsel's office of a huge industrial corporation. She's the only woman on the executive floor and since her first day's pro forma expense-account lunch with a few of the senior attorneys she has been totally ostracized by her colleagues. That was easily accomplished because her office (with a spectacular view from the top floor of a Manhattan skyscraper) is on a corridor on the opposite side of the building from the legal department. For all intents and purposes, she is physically as well as psychologically isolated from the counsel's team! Asked why she accepted that office she exclaimed, "Oh, it's beautiful! Carpets six inches thick, anything I request in the way of furniture and equipment, and that astronomical view. They originally apologized for it, saying nothing better was available, but I told them this was perfect. How much better could you get?" But when visiting executives from divisional offices and subsidiaries regularly take her for a temporary secretary, it's partly because she has no rank insignia, no team identification.

WATCH OUT FOR FEMALE GHETTOES

The retailing industry and fashion merchandising are typical of businesses where women predominate at lower levels and have moved upward in restricted areas to executive levels (a handful are getting close to the top). These industries are nevertheless dominated by male status symbols, and clever corporate politicians must analyze the patterns and play the game by classic standards. Many women who have "made it" through the twisted paths of historic blatant discrimination have had no opportunity to learn the game rules in entirety. They are particularly blind to status emblems or, to be more precise, they were furnished garbled emblems intended to ghetto-ize them and they now have difficulty unscrambling the hodge-podge.

I will be watching the progress of an executive friend who just began playing the corporate game in the retailing field. Helena has been floating on a relatively high plateau in specialty fashion retailing for the past several years. She's spent her entire career—close to twenty years—working with women colleagues whom she likes and admires. But once she was alerted to the broad ramifications of the corporate politics game, she recognized that her advancement opportunities were nonexistent in the retail complex where she was employed. She found a new job with a national consulting firm, using her expertise in fashion retailing as the wedge to negotiate a 50-percent salary increase. In her new firm all the employees and executives are women except for the vice-president in charge of merchandising, who is a man.

"After doing the same job for years, this offers an exciting new opportunity," she told me. "The company is dynamic, the vice-president, my boss, sounds very progressive, and the other women executives are tops in their fields, stimulating people to work with. Everything about the job seemed perfect—until I evaluated the status symbols, especially office location. I drew diagrams of the layout to analyze where my office was situated. The picture prompted me to reopen negotiations although I had accepted the job. I realized I'd be stalemated again if I didn't insist on the right office locale. I got it changed before I started."

Helena's analysis was perceptive gaming. The male vice-president had the most prestigious corner office. She had been assigned a large office next to the corner in the diagonally opposite area. All the women in that area were fashion specialists, too. Each of the corners held clusters of women experienced in various retail specialties. Helena is cognizant of the categorizing which restricts women executives to food, fashion, home furnishings, fabrics, domestics, cosmetics, accessories or whatever gave them their start. "When men start in ties, they don't end up tie specialists—they branch out to merchandising executives. When women start in dresses, they don't end up dress specialists—they're catalogued as high fashion, budget, sports, evening, lounge, or boutique. They are constricted by experience, not broadened to becoming merchandising generalists." This was the pattern she saw duplicated in the office layout at her new firm—women segregated according to narrow specialties. Since her goal was to break out of overspecialization, she perceived correctly that an office located in the midst of fashion specialists would lock her into the very trap she was escaping.

"I didn't explain *why* I wanted the particular office I chose; after all I'll be working closely with the fashion group at the beginning. But my career plan demands some proximity to the vice-president and a door on the traffic lane to his office. I'll use it for visibility and getting to know the types of merchandising clients who visit the V-P. I intend to move toward merchandising management, and my first successful game move was getting myself dissociated from all the specialty enclaves."

Office location is invested with good and poor status insignia. Office positioning has a direct relationship to job advancement. Certain office locales have high status value precisely because ambitious, aggressive people fight for them in order to get close to the central action area. Once again, watch how progressing men move closer and closer to higher superiors with every promotion. Careers and office insignia move in tandem.

WHEN STATUS EMBLEMS AND STEREOTYPES COLLIDE, MOVE!

Not much is known yet about potential boomerang effects when classic male rank symbols are acquired by women. One danger area is already evident—the office adjacent to a male senior executive. Sex, sexism, and female stereotypes can rear up to cancel out all the job benefits and rank status that traditionally accrue to men who achieve this enviable geographic site, which frequently has the invisible logo "next in line for the top job." When a woman earns that status locale, the invisible logo shifts to "she's sleeping with her boss," or "she's a glorified secretary (who's sleeping with the guy)."

Over a lunch, a female officer of a subsidiary company of a financial corporation explained how her advancement was nearly jeopardized because she occupied the office adjacent to the president. "I'm not quite sure how I got assigned to the office since I was one of several vice-presidents who were eligible for it. Probably a misguided attempt to prove they didn't discriminate against women, a laugh considering I was the only woman executive in the entire firm at the time. Take it from me, token women are more to be pitied than censured; like the first child of nervous parents we suffer from the ignorance of our elders." At any rate, she occupied what male colleagues looked upon as the most enviable office in the company, but it slowly turned into nightmare alley for her. "I had an important and demanding job but I was interrupted constantly. Executives from our own company as well as all outside visitors marched straight into my office, left messages for me to relay to the president, explained their problems to me, or dropped in for idle chats if the president got an important private phone call during their appointment."

At first she tried directing the men to the private secretaries and assistants, but each day there were other strangers who made the same automatic assumption—that the woman closest to the top executive was naturally his private secretary or assistant. "I foresaw the end of the line in my career if I remained in that close proximity to the chief executive. I was becoming identified with him and his work, not my own operating responsibilities. My authority was rapidly eroding as I was stereotyped into an 'assistant' or 'helper' to the great man. I decided I *had* to get out of there and I'm absolutely positive I'd never be where I am today, a functioning administrator and top management, if I'd allowed the implied tie-up of superior male-subservient female to continue."

The educational aspect of her story was how she made her moves to solve the problem. She assayed all the male vice-presidents who were equally eligible for the office. From the group she picked the man she disliked the most and who returned the feeling with a vengeance. He was also the one most envious of her position and most blatant about his raw ambition and his disparagement of her qualifications. When she invited him to lunch with her, he was wary and hostile. "He almost choked to death on a piece of fish when I asked him if he'd like to trade offices. He couldn't believe anybody would be so stupid as to give up the ultimate status symbol, and it took a while to convince him I was serious. Once he saw that (swallowing my story that I really *liked* his office better for its afternoon sunshine!), he joined the conspiracy with me to get the trade approved without any flak." Between the two of them they arranged the transfer smoothly and she regained her independence as a line executive. Her male accomplice gained his most cherished desire. "He was in seventh heaven in that office and the superior rank symbol pushed him steadily ahead. My freedom from that office allowed me to grow and develop on my merits and demonstrated performance; we both benefited. Best of all, he turned from an enemy into an ally. He is one of my strongest supporters and advocates."

PORCELAIN INSIGNIA THAT WON'T FLUSH AWAY

Toilets seem to be the major obstacle to women's equality. If you don't think so, you haven't heard the nuttiest arguments against the Equal Rights Amendment (i.e., the ridiculous fear that public restrooms will be coed). Or you haven't been faced with employment problems which evolve from the superior status symbolism of urinals. The good news is that women aren't entirely alone trying to revamp this physical hallmark of sexual supremacy; management is a nervous wreck as working women demand equal facilities and senior executives in many institutions expend as much energy on the dilemma of bathrooms as they do on the next quarterly earnings' prediction. Porcelain status symbols are proving to be nonbiodegradable.

Some companies try to evade the entire subject. To this day, the J. Walter Thompson Company advertising agency refuses to recognize indelicate functions. Its dozens of bathrooms hide decorously behind plain unmarked doors and nary a discriminatory word such as "Men's" or "Women's" sullies its pristine halls or executive offices. Pity the new male client or supplier whose initial contact is a woman executive (if any); the prime executive-to-executive bond has evaporated into embarrassed agony.

Some companies treat the subject like a huge, salacious joke. They are apt to be institutions that have given urinals the most visible priority status. One of the country's largest utilities (hardly the only offender in this category) left no doubt where its sympathies lay by installing men's urinals in spacious rooms off the well-lit hallways. Women's facilities (patronized by vast majorities of the working population) were jammed into dingy, cramped quarters on the unused stairway landings. Female complaints were dismissed cavalierly even though several women had been frightened or molested by rapacious public freaks who crept up the abandoned stairwell. The enraged women got together and organized a pee-in in the men's bathrooms until their class status was upgraded and the bathrooms were switched.

Some companies are just plain scared as women edge closer and closer to a highly prized male status symbol—"the key to the executive bathroom." One of the few women who arrived at this eminence insisted on her executive token and demanded her status key. She promptly ordered the sign changed from "Men" to "Executives." Every so often she pretends to use her key (of course she's the first and only woman to collect this rank emblem) just to see what male executive comes bounding out of his office to "check if it's clear." Privately she admits to gleeful friends that she'd never really use it. "I'll never give up my privilege to use the ladies' room. For one thing, I hear all the juicy gossip that doesn't get on the grapevine, or I hear things before any of the men at my level. But most of all because I'm in a position to help other women. I can get to know women from several departments and keep an eye on the progress of those I admire. Already I've pulled one promising young woman into my department simply from meetings in the bathroom. I'm anticipating the day when the women's bathroom becomes just as powerful a focal point as the men's urinals when it comes to internal political manipulation."

The Queen in the chess set (in case you don't know) can move any number of clear spaces in *any* direction, backward, forward, sideways, or diagonally. A lot of visible status symbols can be collected with that maneuverability.

WOMEN'S APPAREL IS A BADGE OF SERVITUDE

Men's clothing is not unique in assigning attributes to its wearers; women's clothing is historically symbolic, too. As far as I know, no contemporary feminist has researched the subject (no nonfeminist would care), but women who are moving into the male world of work must begin to pay attention to the symbolism of clothing.

Why are men's and women's clothes so different? Why, as a woman, do you wear what you wear? What is your conscious or subconscious motivation each morning as you dress for work? Why not just wear your bathrobe?

The phenomenon of sex differential in wearing apparel intrigued Lawrence Langner, a prodigiously successful businessman who was also an erudite scholar, a popular playwright, and a perceptive social observer. His many-faceted talents led him to the theater where he founded the Theater Guild and the Shakespeare Festival at Stratford, Connecticut. The importance of costumes to theatrical productions and the social significance of costumes impelled him to study the meaning and psychology of clothing throughout history. In 1959 he published his remarkable psycho-history of clothing through the ages, *The Importance of Wearing Clothes* (New York: Hastings House). Several years before the current wave of feminism erupted, his studies led him to the following conclusion about the marked dissimilarity between men's and women's clothes:

> Contrary to established beliefs, the differentiation in clothing between men and women arose from the male's desire to assert superiority over the female and to hold her in his service. This he accomplished through the ages by means of special clothing which hampered or handicapped the female in her movements. Then men prohibited one sex from wearing the clothing of the other, in order to maintain this differentiation.

Langner traced his hypothesis as far back as Spanish Levant rock paintings, circa 10,000 B.C. and followed the evidence through subsequent ages, civilizations, and cultures. He found the primary purpose of women's dress throughout history was to prevent them from running away from their lords and masters. The ancient Chinese bound the feet of growing girls to hopelessly deform the adult woman's feet; African tribes weighted women's legs with up to fifty pounds of "beautifying" nonremovable brass coils or protruding metal disks; in Palestine women's ankles were connected with chains and tinkling bells; Moslems swathed women in heavy, opaque shrouds from head to toe; upper-class women in Venice and Spain had to be assisted by pages when they walked in their gorgeous gowns because of the fashionable chimpanies or stilts attached to their shoes—some as much as a yard high!

The only exception to foot crippling was found among nomadic tribes where women were forced to keep up with their men during the seasonal migrations. In these groups, the women were the beasts of burden, walking with the animals and loaded almost as heavily with household goods. They could walk but could not run far.

In Western societies the ubiquitous hobbling device for women has been skirts, usually accompanied by dysfunctional stilted shoes. Although skirt styles changed over time and in various societies, skirts of all kinds served to encumber women. Skirts that consisted of long robes reaching to or below the ankles hampered movement by entangling the legs in layers of heavy textiles. In more "modern" times straight fitted skirts effectively bound the knees or ankles together to impede free stride and enforce an awkward, staggering gait. Whatever the society, skirts for females were characterized by their impracticality, inefficiency, and uncomfortable designs. Not only walking but sitting, bending, stooping, and climbing were totally enjoined via "female" dress. Utility, comfort, ornamentation, or sexual attraction has nothing to do with why females wear skirts or other distinctively "female" articles of clothing. These garments were invented thousands of years ago by men to label females as dependents and to "keep them in their place." In consequence, "female" apparel carries a universal symbolism of servitude—the badge of subservience.

In contrast the exclusive male clothing in every society where women were constricted consisted of divided garments—trousers or knickerbockers—which permitted free, unrestricted movement while protecting the wearer's extremities. Men exerted superiority over women by laying exclusive claim to clothing which gives the greatest mobility, freedom for action, and self-protection.

At all times, from earliest societies, women were prohibited from wearing the clothing of males—and vice versa. The penalties for breaking the strict laws against transvestitism ("a morbid craving to dress in garments of the opposite sex") were (and are) severe. In Deuteronomy, the Old Testament thundered the "moral" imprecations which many women feel bound by even in the twentieth century. "A woman shall not wear that which pertaineth unto a man, neither shall a man put on a woman's garment."

Despite these savage laws and vicious punishments, women have periodically rebelled against their enforced clothing shackles, especially skirts. Early American feminists of the 1850s took up the issue of women's dress reform. Amelia Bloomer is the best known of the many who took to wearing short skirts or tunics over loose trousers gathered at the ankle. "Bloomers" became the derisive term for any divided skirt or knickerbocker dress. One optimistic feminist, Helen Marie Weber, told the Women's Rights Convention of 1850 in Worcester, Massachusetts that, "In ten years time male attire will be generally worn by women of most civilized countries." She was at least a hundred years off in her prediction; it has taken until the 1970s for women to dare to flout the age-old inventions of man to keep her inferior and immobile.

There are still corporations that issue edicts to keep women employees in their place by forbidding women to wear slacks or pants suits to work. Such a company policy is telling women employees that they are inferior beings whose only status in the corporate setup is to serve their male masters. The clothing symbolism says: "You have no mobility in this corporation." No woman who understands the significance of corporate status symbolism would be caught dead working for such a company. Displaying a blatant badge of servitude is no way to progress in the male corporate milieu, but that is exactly what "female" dress codes dictated by men set out to accomplish.

Chapter

7

The Compulsion to Perform

Much of the work of traditional organizational behaviorists has one common objective: to increase the performance of employees. Treatments of such topics as motivation, compensation, training, attitudes, leadership, and supervision, to name a few, commonly focus on how more input and hence more output can be induced (some might say squeezed) out of individual workers. More generally it appears that the institutions that socialize young people (that is, our schools, churches, and universities) are in important ways directed to the same outcomes—preparing people who are oriented to performing in modern organizations or who are at least willing to tolerate the discipline of the workplace. Given the number of people who are currently bemoaning the decline of the work ethic, it is tempting to conclude that these efforts are not succeeding.

On the other hand, we are more concerned that these efforts might be too successful. We fear that many individuals are so fully indoctrinated with work values and routines that psychologically they are not free to make reasonable choices about how much work to do, how hard to work, and how central a role to let work play in their lives. The title of this chapter—the compulsion to perform—stems from this concern. The virtues of performing work roles are so deeply ingrained in people and the costs of commitments to work and careers are so little considered that individuals appear to play work roles compulsively without considering how they might allocate their time and energies in a more fully satisfying manner. The readings in this chapter focus on this compulsion and on some of the costs people pay as a result of the irresistible impulse to perform.

"If I can just finish *this* project/assignment/chore, *then* I will be free to do what I really want to; I can be me; I can be more balanced, and more satisfied!" This may be one of the fundamental laments and myths of the modern world of work. It would seem that the flow and variety of work we face and even seek out is endless. Yet one common assumption we seem to make is that there is relief, freedom, serenity just over the horizon—as soon as the current overload has been overcome.

In his lyrics for the song "Satisfied," Richard Marx captures the tension many people feel between wanting to be authentic now and delaying gratification while working intensively at their jobs. According to Sally Solo, many CEO's seem to want the scales tipped toward working harder. They argue that North American managers have it easy, and increasing global competition will require much more intensive effort in the future, as we see in "Stop Whining and Get Back to Work."

The dilemma such leaders face, however, is that they want their managers to be more balanced in their lives while redoubling their efforts to perform. The assumption seems to be that, somehow, managers will work harder *and* smarter in the future and that they will develop breadth and depth of perspective along the way. Natasha Josefowitz, in her poem, "Can't Do It All," points out the futility of this strategy. On the other hand, it is important to realize how much of a sense of purpose and of enthusiasm people can gain from dedicating their lives to work. Ina Yalof describes this feeling of enjoyment and of making a difference in the workplace in "José 'Pepe' Mayorca," a story told by a chef about his daily activities in a hospital.

One of the important issues in understanding the compulsion to perform is how little freedom we have to stop the process when it operates. Compulsion has internal as well as external sources. In "The Cormorant," we see a metaphor for workers caught in the trap of their greed and in the grip of others who manipulate that need. In "Feeling as Clue," the issue of emotion in the workplace is raised. Author Arlie Russel Hochschild discusses the way emotions can be managed by others so that organizational work can be done. Being taught to control and direct emotions in situations in which one might be provoked might help both workers and the firm. It can also create conditions where sanctions are placed on people so that they lose touch with their own true feelings and are unable to express them in ways that are healthy for them. Losing touch with one's emotions is an important concern for the individuals affected and for the organizations in which they work. Over time, this condition can lead to loss of productivity and of personal health. As the article "Death by Work" makes clear, a compulsion to perform can threaten the very lives of those who are trapped in their addiction to work. The story of senior executive Brian Foley's near-death experience is sobering. It suggests a need for change in how we work and how we need organizations to change to support a shift to more healthy connections between effort and excellent performance.

People who are always busy seem to take themselves and their work very seriously. This typically accompanies a compulsion to perform. What such individuals might be missing in life is described rather delightfully in Benjamin Hoff's blend of Taoism and Winnie the Pooh's life published as *The Tao of Pooh*. The excerpt we have chosen is entitled Bisy Backson, which is Pooh language for "I'm busy. I'll be back soon." It captures the frenzy in the life of the overcommitted and compulsively driven workaholic.

The case for a less frantic approach to work, with accompanying positive results at work and play is made by Ann Marie Cunningham in "A Case for Inefficiency." Finally, as a mirror on the effects of compulsive performance, we have included Harry Chapin's haunting lyrics from "Cat's in the Cradle." His words suggest that how we live our work has consequences outside the workplace and that when work consumes us it can lead to irreversible regrets later in life.

Satisfied

Richard Marx

We work our bodies weary to stay alive
There must be more to livin' than nine to five

    Why should we wait for some better time
    There may not even be a tomorrow
    Ain't no sense in losing your mind
    I'm gonna make it worth the ride

Don't you know, I won't give up until
    I'm satisfied
Don't you know, why should I stop until
    I'm satisfied

Ignore the hesitation, that ties your hands
Use your imagination, and take a chance

    I won't let my moment of truth pass me by
    I've gotta make my move now or never
    And if they turn me loose on this town
    They're gonna have to hold me down

Don't you know, I won't give up until
    I'm satisfied
Don't you know, why should I stop until
    I'm satisfied Yeah

Oh, don't you know, ain't gonna stop until
    we're satisfied
Don't you know, we shouldn't stop until
    we're satisfied

Don't you know, ain't gonna stop until
    I'm satisfied
Don't you know, we won't give up until
    we're satisfied

"Satisfied" by Richard Marx from *Repeat Offender* (1989) side 1 cut 2. Reprinted by permission of EMI-USA, a division of Capitol Records.

Stop Whining and Get Back to Work

Sally Solo

You say you're toiling like a galley slave? America's top corporate chiefs think your work-week looks like a picnic compared to what's ahead in the age of global competition.

With U.S. managers working harder than ever, many have got to wonder whether relief is in sight. The answer from their bosses: Forget it. Far from easing up, CEOs overwhelmingly believe that large American companies will have to push executives *even harder* to keep up with global competition. That's the bad news. The good news is that the chiefs also understand that to get more from managers, their jobs must be made more rewarding, with more incentives and greater autonomy.

Q   Which of the following two statements comes closer to how you feel about the management of large U.S. companies?

A   Large U.S. companies will have to push their managers harder if we are to compete successfully with the Japanese and other global competitors..............77%
As a result of restructuring and getting leaner, large U.S. companies are pushing managers too hard..9%
Not sure..14%

Q   How many hours a week, on average, do you expect a high-level executive in your company to work? How many for a middle manager?

A

	High-level executive	Middle manager
40 hours or less	2%	8%
41–49 hours	1%	21%
50–59 hours	58%	53%
60–69 hours	29%	9%
Not sure	10%	9%
Average	54 hours	49 hours

These are among the findings of the latest *Fortune* 500 CEO Poll. Clark Martire & Bartolomeo, an independent opinion research firm, conducted the survey between January 16 and 25. Some 206 CEOs of *Fortune* 500 and Service 500 companies answered our queries.

"Stop Whining and Get Back to Work" by Sally Solo, *Fortune,* March 12, 1990, p. 49. Reprinted by permission of *Fortune* Magazine.

The CEOs don't doubt that their managers are already working harder than they used to. Almost two-thirds of those polled say their executive subordinates work longer hours today than ten years ago. They've had to, say the chiefs, because of restructuring and increased competition. Texaco CEO James Kinnear says heads of companies must "set objectives and monitor employee performance—and if that leads to longer hours, then so be it!"

How hard do you have to work for one of these bosses? Real hard. On average, they figure a high-level executive should work about 54 hours a week, and nearly a third of them think such an executive should work over 60 hours a week. Most of them think middle managers should work at least 50 hours a week. If that strikes you as too demanding, don't look for sympathy from these CEOs: They say they put in an average of 61 hours a week.

The chiefs don't foresee mass burnout among managers. Argues Kinnear: "It's self-correcting. People get tired and they go home." Nor does USX chief Charles A. Corry see any cause for alarm. "It always seems you operate in a crisis environment in business," he says. "The pace of management is quicker today, but the essence isn't different from what it was in the 1960s."

Q   Are executives in your company working longer hours than ten years ago, shorter hours, or about the same number of hours?

A   Longer hours 62%
Shorter hours 2%
About the same 35%
Not sure 1%

To be sure, a few CEOs believe that the pressure has become too intense and has to be lightened. Says David R. Carpenter, CEO of Transamerica Occidental Life Insurance: "We can't beat people into the ground anymore." San Francisco Federal Savings CEO Patrick Price adds, "We must recognize the signs when managers are being pushed too hard and help out with people, systems—whatever it takes."

Although the majority think managers are working harder than before and must work harder still, some also believe, a bit paradoxically, that an executive who spends all day and most of the evening at the office isn't necessarily a boon to the company. "I think it's absurd for business people to be divorced from the community," says John Bryan of Sara Lee. Bryan estimates that he spends 20% of his time on good works, such as serving on the board of the University of Chicago. He requires similar commitments from his executives, even giving them time off from work for community service. He believes the "political and other" skills they acquire can then be applied back at the office.

Winston Wallin, CEO of Medtronics, also encourages altruism in his executives, with a measure of corporate self-interest in mind. "People get so focused on their own business," he says. "Executives who work 80 hours a week are not likely to have the breadth of knowledge they ought to have. Managers are likely to be more creative if they have a little balance in their lives."

So how do you get executives to compete more ferociously than ever—while maintaining balanced lives, of course? There were 206 different ideas about what kind of carrot and stick a company should use as motivation. One, offered only half facetiously by Sara Lee chief Bryan: "Fear as a motivator is pretty powerful these days." Most answers fell into three broad categories: Offer more money, offer more autonomy, and offer a sense of mission.

Fully 83% of the CEOs surveyed say they already give more incentive-based compensation to their managers than they did ten years ago. Asked what they could do to get more out of those executives, a CEO was most likely to say, "Become more incentive-oriented." Corry of USX explains, "It's a stimulating device. You get the manager to believe he can influence his own compensation." USX offers bonuses that may run up to 85% of an executive's base salary. Several CEOs touted employee stock ownership plans as a good way to give workers a stake in the company's success. "Employees as shareholders are very attractive," adds Bryan. "They have a slightly longer-term outlook."

Q   On average, how many hours a week do you devote to your job?

A   Under 50 hours   2%
     50–59 hours 28%
     60–69 hours 45%
     70–79 hours 21%
     80 hours or more 4%
     Average ....61 hours

Q   Is the amount of incentive-based compensation in your managers' pay packages greater than it was ten years ago, less than it was, or about the same?

A   Greater 83%
     Less 2%
     About the same 12%
     Don't know 3%

Increasing the autonomy of managers serves two purposes in the age of the fat-free corporation. First, it means that whole layers of management, and the paperwork that goes with them, can be trimmed. Second, employees who feel trusted by the boss are freer and more willing to do what's best for the company. Says Hasbro CEO Alan G. Hassenfeld: "If you treat people well and they have responsibility and authority, they'll produce. People should be incentivized and excited about what they're doing, and they'll perform well." At PPG Industries "everyone is called a manager because each of us— engineer, truck driver, secretary, etc.—manages an asset or a function," says Chief Executive Vincent Sarni.

The same CEOs who advocate giving underlings a lot of leeway also emphasize the importance of giving them guidance and a reason to do what they do. "I call it the 'all singing the same song' theory," says U.S. Bancorp CEO Roger Breezley. Super Valu Stores CEO Michael Wright says, "People need to feel there's a purpose in their jobs. They need to know they're working for more than a pay-check." Super Valu Stores' purpose, Wright explains, is to help entrepreneurs—the store owners his company services—succeed.

The CEOs endorse another route to working better, one that's easier identified than followed: eliminating work that doesn't really need to be done. Complains Breezley of U.S. Bancorp: "We automate and automate and automate, and the paperwork still grows and grows. We are documented to death." Robert G. Sharp of Keystone Provident Life Insurance argues, "We should be putting people on the critical jobs that need to be either improved or eliminated. Managers should examine all functions on a must-have, not a nice-to-have, basis."

In Japan, when a worker dies from exhaustion, they call it *karoshi,* or "death from overwork." There may still be time to prevent the problem in the U.S. before things get bad enough to name it. But are CEOs interested in tackling the problem?

Q   How should large U.S. companies better manage their executives?

A   Become more incentive-oriented 27%
Encourage productivity, creativity, innovation, and risk taking 27%
Give them more autonomy and decentralize decision-making 21%
Get them to work smarter, not harder 20%
Recruit and train better-qualified people 13%
Develop a corporate culture or mission, plan for it, and communicate it..10%
Push managers to work harder 9%
Focus on the long term 8%
Encourage better communication 5%

Totals more than 100% due to multiple responses.

Can't Do It All

Natasha Josefowitz

If I do this
I won't get that done
If I do that
this will slip by
If I do both
neither will be perfect.

Not everything worth doing
is worth doing well.

From *Is This Where I Was Going?* by Natasha Josefowitz, 1983. New York: Warner Books. Reprinted by permission.

José "Pepe" Mayorca

Ina Yalof

It's a tiny, overcrowded office, just inside the doorway into the kitchen. The wall of windows overlooks a huge room brought to life by the flurry of busy people in white uniforms. Two chef's hats sit in the corner of the office. A bulletin board on the wall is papered with computer printouts, schedules, and menus. As we talk, people periodically stick their heads in the door to ask him questions. "Tomorrow's fish. What kind will we have?" "Did the new icemaker arrive?" "When does the vegetable truck come?"

He's a short, pleasant man. He comes from Peru. He's been head chef for eight years, the youngest chef the hospital ever had. He's forty-two. "I live with an uncle now. We spend our weekends on a busman's holiday, trying out restaurants all over town. What I found is, my food here is just as good as any good restaurant in New York. And that's the truth."

The kitchen opens officially at three in the morning when my breakfast cooks arrive. They do all the breakfasts for the patients *and* the cafeteria, which opens at six-thirty for breakfast. They do breakfast for two thousand people or more. I used to do that before I became chef. I used to come in at one in the morning. You had to start cracking eggs then. One case of eggs contains thirty dozen eggs, and I got so good at it, I could crack eight cases in less than an hour. That's, let me see … two thousand eight hundred eighty eggs, or forty-eight eggs a minute. We broke them into this huge vat and then we'd beat them, strain them, and cook them. We used big paddles to stir the scrambled eggs. I used to make cereal, too. Fifty gallons of oatmeal, which you boil in huge vats. The vats, which are electrically heated, have spigots at the top, which let water in, and drains at the bottom. You fill them with water, cook in them, drain the food when you've finished, wash them, without ever moving them from their spot. You couldn't move them anyway because they're at least four feet high. When we do bacon or sausage for breakfast, you're talking about cooking one hundred pounds of bacon and sixty pounds of sausages.

As head chef, I'm responsible for ordering all the food for both the patients and the cafeteria. Eight thousand meals a day—special diets, kosher meals, you name it. When I get in, the first thing I look at is the census of the patients and see how many are in the house—this hospital can have nearly thirteen hundred patients when it's full. So we calculate the patient menus, and see what's going to be served in the cafeteria, and then I order exactly what I need. Sometimes you go a little bit over, but never under. It would cause a lot of problems to be under.

The key to being a chef, no matter where you work, is to like your trade. To like what you're doing. And, I suppose of equal importance is to produce good food. But

"José 'Pepe' Mayorca the Chef" by Ina Yalof from *Life and Death, Story of a Hospital.* 1988, pp. 184–186. Reprinted by permission of the publisher.

there are many other things that either make or break it for you. A good chef knows how to motivate his people. If you don't motivate them, you don't get anywhere. I repeat this over and over: Work with your people. My job is supposed to be sitting in this office, managing my staff, and doing paper work. And I do that. But I also go out and work with my staff, usually every day. I work with them, talk to them, understand their problems. I don't just want to be called a chef and wear this tall white thing on my head.

My day is long, but varied and interesting. If I'm not cooking with my staff, I sit down with my butcher and see all the cuts of meat that we need, and the amounts we have to order. I have to discuss the groceries with my steward and storeroom manager. I have to deal with my pot washers regarding sanitation and things like that. The baker is independent. The only time he works with me is when we have a special party.

The chief dieticians propose the menus to the food service director. I get called when those menus are accepted, and then comes my part. I sit down with the new menus and I make all the calculations about how much I'm going to need. The meat is first. We have a meeting with the director and food production manager, the chief dietician, and my head butcher, and I decide how much I'm going to use, the kinds of cuts that I want to use. After I finish with the meats, I have to cover the vegetables. Say they have for lunch fillet of flounder. We produce five hundred seventy-six orders. In order to produce that amount—each portion is about six ounces of flounder—what I order is two hundred fifty pounds of fillet of flounder. The fish comes in ice and water, so you have to order more. Then you have eggplant Parmesan on the menu, too. We use about sixty pounds of eggplant cutlets. Brisket of beef? I order six hundred pounds for one meal. Mashed potatoes—I use about two hundred forty pounds of peeled potatoes.

Cooking is my life. I always make time to cook. I like Italian food, but *real* Italian food. And I like Oriental food. I've thought about opening my own restaurant. I think this is what every chef looks for. But first of all I would have to find the right place. The way that the rents are now, it's very hard. Also, you don't meet too many good cooks anymore. A lot of people get involved in the food business because of the salary and they have free meals, but not because they like it. I have a lot of friends who own restaurants. I visit them. We talk. I walk into the kitchen, and I tell you, it's not what I want.

Working in a hospital is different from working in another large institution. Here you feel you're helping people to recuperate from their illness, or whatever. A lot of people, when they hear you cook for a hospital say, "Oh, that doesn't mean anything. Anybody can cook for a hospital." But that's not true. Especially if you are a proud cook and you like what you're doing. I have a big responsibility here. I run the whole kitchen. If I don't produce, nobody eats.

The Cormorant . . .

R. G. Siu

The second piece of advice is: Observe the cormorant in the fishing fleet. You know how cormorants are used for fishing. The technique involves a man in a rowboat with about half a dozen or so cormorants, each with a ring around its neck. As the bird spots a fish, it dives into the water and unerringly comes up with it. Because of the ring, the larger fish are not swallowed but held in the throat. The fisherman picks up the bird and squeezes out the fish through the mouth. The bird then dives for another and the cycle repeats itself.

To come back to the second piece of advice from the neo-Taoist to the American worker. Observe the cormorant, he would say. Why is it that of all the different animals, the cormorant has been chosen to slave away day and night for the fisherman?

Were the bird not greedy for fish, or not efficient in catching it, or not readily trained, would society have created an industry to exploit the bird? Would the ingenious device of a ring around its neck, and the simple procedure of squeezing the bird's neck to force it to regurgitate the fish have been devised? Of course not.

Greed, talent, and capacity for learning are the basis of exploitation. The more you are able to moderate and/or hide them from society, the greater will be your chances of escaping the fate of the cormorant . . .

It is necessary to remember that the institutions of society are geared to make society prosper, not necessarily to minimize suffering on your part. It is for this reason, among others, that the schools tend to drum into your mind the high desirability of those characteristics that tend to make society prosper—namely, ambition, progress and success. These in turn are to be valued in terms of society's objectives.

All of them gradually but surely increase your greed and make a cormorant out of you.

Feeling As Clue

Arlie Rusel Hochschild

Men are estranged from one another as each secretly tries to make an instrument of the other, and in time a full circle is made; one makes an instrument of himself, and is estranged from It also.
                                                                            —C. Wright Mills

One day at Delta's Stewardess Training Center an instructor scanned the twenty-five faces readied for her annual Self-Awareness Class set up by the company in tandem with a refresher course in emergency procedures required by the Federal Aviation Administration. She began: "This is a class on thought processes, actions, and feelings. I believe in it. I have to believe in it, or I couldn't get up here in front of you and be enthusiastic." What she meant was this: "Being a sincere person, I couldn't say one thing to you and believe in another. Take the fact of my sincerity and enthusiasm as testimony to the value of the techniques of emotion management that I'm going to talk about."

Yet, as it became clear, it was precisely by such techniques of emotion management that sincerity itself was achieved. And so, through this hall of mirrors, students were introduced to a topic scarcely mentioned in Initial Training but central to Recurrent Training: stress and one of its main causes—anger at obnoxious passengers.

"What happens," the instructor asked the class, in the manner of a Southern Baptist minister inviting a response from the congregation, "when you become angry?" Answers: Your body becomes tense. Your heart races. You breathe more quickly and get less oxygen. Your adrenalin gets higher.

"What do you do when you get angry?" Answers: Cuss. Want to hit a passenger. Yell in a bucket. Cry. Eat. Smoke a cigarette. Talk to myself. Since all but the last two responses carry a risk of offending passengers and thus losing sales, the discussion was directed to ways that an obnoxious person could be reconceived in an honest but useful way. The passenger demanding constant attention could be conceived as a "victim of fear of flying." A drunk could be reconceived as "just like a child." It was explained why a worker angered by a passenger would do better to avoid seeking sympathy from co-workers.

"How," the instructor asked the class, "do you alleviate anger at an irate?" (An "irate," a noun born of experience, is an angry person.) Answering her own question, she went on:

I pretend something traumatic has happened in their lives. Once I had an irate that was complaining about me, cursing at me, threatening to get my name and report me to the company. I later found out his son had just died. Now when I meet an irate I think of that man. If you think

"Feeling As Clue" by Arlie Rusel Hochschild from *The Managed Heart: Commercialization of Human Feeling*, 1983, pp. 24–34. Berkeley, CA: University of California Press. Reprinted by permission of the publisher.

about the other *person and why they're so upset, you've taken attention off of yourself and your own frustration. And you won't feel so angry.*

If anger erupts despite these preventive tactics, then deep breathing, talking to yourself, reminding yourself that "you don't have to go home with him" were offered as ways to manage emotions. Using these, the worker becomes less prone to cuss, hit, cry, or smoke.

The instructor did not focus on what might have *caused* the worker's anger. When this did come up, the book was opened to the mildest of examples (such as a passenger saying, "Come here, girl!"). Rather, the focus was kept on the worker's response and on ways to prevent an angry response through "anger-desensitization."

After about ten minutes of this lecture one flight attendant in the next to last row began tapping her index finger rapidly on her closed notebook. Her eyes were turned away from the speaker, and she crossed and recrossed her legs abruptly. Then, her elbow on the table, she turned to two workers to her left and whispered aloud, "I'm just livid!"

Recurrent Training classes are required yearly. The fact that a few fellow workers had escaped coming to this one without penalty had come to light only in the last ten minutes of informal talk before class. Flight attendants are required to come to the class from whatever city they are in at the time. The company provides travel passes to training, but it is a well-known source of resentment that after training, workers are often bumped from home-bound flights in favor of paying passengers. "Last time," the livid one said, "it took me two days to get home from Recurrent, and all just for *this.*"

Addressing a rustling in the group and apparently no one in particular, the instructor said:

> Now a lot of flight attendants resent having to commute to Recurrent. It's a bother getting here and a heck of a bother getting back. And some people get angry with me because of that. And because that's not my fault and because I put work into my classes, I get angry back. But then I get tired of being angry. Do you ever get tired of being angry? Well, one time I had a flight attendant who sat in the back of my class and snickered the whole time I was teaching. But you know what I did? I thought to myself, "She has full lips, and I've always believed people with full lips are compassionate." When I thought that, I wasn't so angry.

By reminding the class that ease in using company passes, like the overall plan of Recurrent Training, was out of her hands, and by putting herself in the role of a flight attendant and her listeners in the role of an angry passenger, she hoped to show how she removed *her* anger. In fact, she also reduced the anger in the class; like the back-seat snickerer, the finger-drummer relented. The right to anger withered on the vine. There was an unfolding of legs and arms, a flowering of comments, the class relaxer came forth with a joke, and the instructor's enthusiasm rose again along the path readied for it.

FEELING AS SUSCEPTIBLE TO PREVENTIVE TACTICS

To consider just how a company or any other organization might benignly intervene in a work situation between the stimulus and the response, we had best start by rethinking what an emotion or a feeling is. Many theorists have seen emotion as a sealed biological event, something that external stimuli can bring on, as cold weather brings on a cold. Furthermore, once emotion—which the psychologist Paul Ekman calls a "biological response syndrome"—is operating, the individual passively undergoes it. Charles Darwin, William James, and the early Freud largely share this "organismic" conception. But it seems to me a limited view. For if we conceive of emotion as only this, what are we to make of the many ways in which flight attendants in Recurrent Training are taught to attend to stimuli and manage emotion, ways that can actually *change* feeling?

If we conceive of feeling not as a periodic abdication to biology but as something we *do* by attending to inner sensation in a given way, by defining situations in a given way, by managing in given ways, then it becomes plainer just how plastic and susceptible to reshaping techniques a feeling can be. The very act of managing emotion can be seen as part of what the emotion becomes. But this idea gets lost if we assume, as the organismic theorists do, that how we manage or express feeling is *extrinsic* to emotion. The organismic theorists want to explain how emotion is "motored by instinct," and so they by-pass the question of how we come to assess, label, and manage emotion. The emotion signals danger. But every emotion does signal the "me" I put into seeing "you." It signals the often unconscious perspective we apply when we go about seeing. Feeling signals that inner perspective. Thus, to suggest helpful techniques for changing feeling—in the service of avoiding stress on the worker and making life pleasanter for the passenger—is to intervene in the signal function of feeling.

This simple point is obscured whenever we apply the belief that emotion is dangerous in the first place because it distorts perception and leads people to act irrationally— which means that all ways of reducing emotion are automatically good. Of course, a person gripped by fear may make mistakes, may find reflection difficult, and may not (as we say) be able to think. But a person totally without emotion has no warning system, no guidelines to the self-relevance of a sight, a memory, or a fantasy. Like one who cannot feel and touches fire, an emotionless person suffers a sense of arbitrariness, which from the point of view of his or her self-interest is irrational. In fact, emotion is a potential avenue to "the reasonable view."* Furthermore, it can tell us about a way of seeing.†

Emotion locates the position of the viewer. It uncovers an often unconscious perspective, a comparison. "You look tall" may mean "From where I lie on the floor, you look tall." "I feel awe" may mean "compared with what I do or think I could do, he is awesome." Awe, love, anger, and envy tell of a self vis-à-vis a situation. When we reflect on feeling we reflect on this sense of "from where I am."

The word *objective,* according to the *Random House Dictionary,* means "free from personal feelings." Yet ironically, we need feeling in order to reflect on the external or "objective" world. Taking feelings into account as clues and then correcting for them may be our best shot at objectivity. Like hearing or seeing, feeling provides a useful set

---

*We may misinterpret an event, feel accordingly, and then draw false conclusions from what we feel. (We sometimes call this neurosis.) We can handle this by applying a secondary framework that corrects habits of feeling and inference, as when we say "I know I have a tendency to interpret certain gestures as rejections." But feeling is the essential clue that a certain viewpoint, even though it may need frequent adjustment, is alive and well.

† A black person may see the deprivations of the ghetto more accurately, more "rationally," through indignation and anger than through obedience or resigned "realism." He will focus clearly on the policeman's bloodied club, the landlord's Cadillac, the look of disapproval on the employment agent's white face. Outside of anger, these images become like boulders on a mountainside, minuscule parts of the landscape. Likewise, a chronically morose person who falls in love may suddenly see the world as happier people do.

of clues in figuring out what is real. A show of feeling by someone else is interesting to us precisely because it may reflect a buried perspective and may offer a clue as to how that person may act.

In public life, expressions of feeling often make news. For example, a TV sports newscaster noted: "Tennis has passed the stage of trying to survive as a commercial sport. We're beyond that now. The women's tennis teams, too. The women are really serious players. They get really mad if they hit a net ball. They get even madder than the guys, I'd say." He had seen a woman tennis player miss a shot (it was a net ball), redden in the face, stamp her foot, and spank the net with her racket. From this he inferred that the woman "really wants to win." Wanting to win, she is a "serious" player—a pro. Being a pro, she can be expected to see the tennis match as something on which her professional reputation and financial future depend. Further, from the way she broke an ordinary field of calm with a brief display of anger, the commentator inferred that she really meant it—she was "serious." He also inferred what she must have wanted and expected just before the net ball and what the newly grasped reality—a miss—must have felt like. He tried to pick out what part of *her* went into seeing the *ball*. A miss, if you really want to win, is maddening.

From the commentator's words and tone, TV viewers could infer *his* point of view. He assessed the woman's anger in relation to a prior expectation about how pros in general see, feel, and act and about how women in general act. Women tennis pros, he implied, do not laugh apologetically at a miss, as a nonprofessional woman player might. They feel, he said, in a way that is *appropriate to the role* of a professional player. In fact, as newcomers they overconform. "They get *even madder* than the guys." Thus the viewers can ferret out the sportscaster's mental set and the role of women in it.

In the same way that we infer other people's viewpoints from how they display feeling, we decide what we ourselves are really like by reflecting on how we feel about ordinary events. Consider, for example, this statement by a young man of nineteen:

> I had agreed to give a party with a young woman who was an old friend. As the time approached, it became apparent to me that, while I liked her, I didn't want the [social] identification with her that such an action [the jointly sponsored party] would bring...I tried explaining this to her without success, and at first I resolved to do the socially acceptable thing—go through with it. But the day before the party, I knew I simply couldn't do it, so I canceled out. My friend didn't understand and was placed in a very embarrassing position. ... I can't feel ashamed no matter how hard I try. All I felt then was relief, and this is still my dominant response....I acted selfishly, but fully consciously. I imagine that my friendship could not have meant that much.

The young man reached his conclusion by *reasoning back from his absence of guilt or shame,* from the feeling of relief he experienced. (He might also have concluded: "I've shown myself to be the sort of fellow who can feel square with himself in cases of unmet obligation. I can withstand the guilt. It's enough for me that I *tried* to feel shame.")

For the sportscaster and the young man, feeling was taken as a signal. To observer and actor alike it was a clue to an underlying truth, a truth that had to be dug out or inferred, a truth about the self vis-à-vis a situation. The sportscaster took the anger of the woman tennis player as a clue to how seriously she took the game of tennis. The young man who backed out on his friend took his sense of relief and absence of guilty feelings as a clue to the absence of seriousness in his "old friendship."

Feeling can be used to give a clue to the operating truth, but in private life as well as on the job, two complications can arise. The first one lies between the clue of feeling and the interpretation of it. We are capable of disguising what we feel, of pretending to feel what we do not—of doing surface acting. The box of clues is hidden, but it is not changed. The second complication emerges in a more fundamental relation between stimulus and response, between a net ball and feeling frustration, between letting someone down and feeling guilty, between being called names by an "irate" and getting angry back. Here the clues can be dissolved by deep acting, which from one point of view involves deceiving oneself as much as deceiving others. In surface acting we deceive others about what we really feel, but we do not deceive ourselves. Diplomats and actors do this best, and very small children do it worst (it is part of their charm).

In deep acting we make feigning easy by making it unnecessary. At Delta, the techniques of deep acting are joined to the principles of social engineering. Can a flight attendant suppress her anger at a passenger who insults her? Delta Airlines can teach her how—if she is qualified for the job by a demonstrably friendly disposition to start with. She may have lost for awhile the sense of what she *would have* felt had she not been trying so hard to feel something else. By taking over the levers of feeling production, by pretending deeply, she alters herself.

Deep acting has always had the edge over simple pretending in its power to convince, as any good Recurrent Training instructor knows. In jobs that require dealing with the public, employers are wise to want workers to be sincere, to go well beyond the smile that's "just painted on." Gregg Snazelle, who directed all the commercials for Toyota's fall 1980 campaign, teaches his advertising students in the first class "to always be honest." Behind the most effective display is the feeling that fits it, and that feeling can be managed.

As workers, the more seriously social engineering affects our behavior and our feelings, the more intensely we must address a new ambiguity about who is directing them (is this me or the company talking?). As customers, the greater our awareness of social engineering, the more effort we put into distinguishing between gestures of real personal feeling and gestures of company policy. We have a practical knowledge of the commercial takeover of the signal function of feeling. In a routine way, we make up for it; at either end, as worker or customer, we try to correct for the social engineering of feeling.* We mentally subtract feeling with commercial purpose to it from the total pattern of display that we sense to be sincerely felt. In interpreting a smile, we try to take out what social engineering put in, pocketing only what seems meant just for us. We say, "It's her job to be friendly," or "They have to believe in their product like that in order to sell it."

In the end, it seems, we make up an idea of our "real self," an inner jewel that remains our unique possession no matter whose billboard is on our back or whose smile is on our face. We push this "real self" further inside, making it more inaccessible. Subtracting credibility from the parts of our emotional machinery that are in commercial hands, we turn to what is left to find out who we "really are." And around the surface of our human character, where once we were naked, we don a cloak to protect us against the commercial elements.

---

*It is not only in the world of commerce that we automatically assume insincerity. Political reporters regularly state not only what an officeholder or candidate wants to seem to feel but also how well he or she succeeds in the effort to convey that feeling. Readers, it is assumed, demand at least this much unveiling.

Death by Work

Salem Alaton

By the time Selkirk Communications Ltd. started going through a leveraged buyout in October of 1988, Brian Foley was thinking about death. As vice-president in charge of $100 million worth of television operations, Foley, at 42, had already reached that point in an executive career where he was keeping a bottle of nitro-glycerin pills in his pocket. That's when Southam Inc. tendered its Selkirk shares; a prelude to a wrenching Maclean Hunter Ltd. takeover of the broadcasting firm.

The doctors hadn't decided what was wrong with Foley's heart, but anybody, starting with his three adolescent sons, could have noticed that his health had long been under an all-pervasive assault from one primary source: work, a full-bore, maximum-stress, unrelenting careerism that had Foley, according to his wife Monica, "chalking up more air miles than God."

When not flying to Selkirk television stations in Alberta and British Columbia or to clients across the United States or to federal licence hearings in Ottawa, Foley's days were spent speeding in a yellow Camaro from his Stouffville, Ontario, home to the Selkirk head office in downtown Toronto, and on to Hamilton, where Selkirk's flagship station, CHCH-TV, was ailing.

"I remember thinking I couldn't believe I was meant to die," says Foley, whose frequent bouts of indigestion each seemed to presage a heart attack. Here was a workaholic putting in 16-hour days who still hadn't found his calling. "It struck me that if I wasn't meant to die, I was meant to do something else. And I was already busy 16 hours a day."

Foley feels closer to answering his inner calling today. He consults on business and personal matters in his leadership role with The Executive Committee, a continent-wide organization for CEOs who want to commune and share troubleshooting expertise. The Foley family's half-acre property in fashionable Unionville, Ontario, is up for sale, a sign of the fiscal spill that marked Foley's departure from the executive suite five years ago. But son Adam, 16, says of Dad today, "he's calmer, definitely calmer," while Sean, 20, believes his father "will probably live about 10 years longer for having left [Selkirk]."

Nothing is very unusual about Foley's experience in corporate culture, which in his case encompassed a lot of drinking, smoking and overeating within the workaholism. Yet the issues of overload and burnout are still barely addressed at executive levels.

"Down on Bay Street, about half the executives have high levels of behaviors that can do them in later," observes Professor Ronald Burke, a specialist in occupational stress who's on York University's faculty of administrative studies.

Foley, who'd bring two heavy briefcases to every meeting, adopted his career pace from his father. A partner in McKim Advertising Ltd., Larry Foley returned to the family's

"Death by Work" by Salem Alaton, *The Financial Post Magazine*, November 1994, pp. 90–94. Reprinted by permission.

Montreal home each night in time for some warmed-over supper and a chance to sleep in front of the television. That, it was understood, was the nature of success, evidenced by a winning scorecard of earnings. Brian, the eldest of three, absorbed those precepts so deeply that when you ask about his early sense of drive, he concedes. "That part of my life I didn't think about at all. I just did it."

Playing football and starting a fraternity were enjoyable at Montreal's Loyola College (now part of Concordia University), but by third year, "I started to think it was too much fun. I better get serious."

Bell Canada brought Foley to Toronto, but after a year he moved on to an ad agency where he developed media campaigns. Television reps started talking to him about selling rather than buying air-time, and then Selkirk dangled the opportunity to double his earnings.

By this point, 1971, Foley had been married a year to college classmate and reluctant bride Mary Monica Gleeson, who presciently feared that marriage might stymie her own career ambitions (after much deferring of her goals, she is now sales and marketing director for Riso Canada Inc., a digital duplication firm).

"Monica said to me, 'Well, you sold me on marrying you, and if you can do that you can do anything,'" says Foley. "So I started to sell and I had the good fortune to sell through that wonderful halcyon period of high inflation and enormous increases. And at the same time we did some legitimate turnarounds with some very difficult properties Selkirk owned." (By the time of the $600-million Maclean Hunter takeover, the largest in Canadian broadcasting history, Selkirk wholly or partly owned television stations in three provinces; radio stations across the country, including Toronto's CFNY; cable systems in Florida and Ottawa; and several other broadcasting-related operations.)

By 1979 he was vice-president of sales for Selkirk's continent-wide television division. The family was buying a new home every Olympiad and raising horses.

But unhappy patterns were established as well, starting with never being at home, "not having a clue who my three children were or my wife. Jamming in a vacation was always a pain," recalls Foley. Even a brief night of sleep was too much, Foley getting up at 3 A.M. to down a meal, "my mind going like that," he says, making furious circles with his hands. Activities were done flat out or not at all, and even jogging became a competition.

"Like everything else in my life, it couldn't just be a comfortable jog," says Foley. "It had to be, 'I'm going to run 5-kilometre races, I'm going to run 10-kilometre races.' This obsessiveness just permeated everything I took on."

In those "hard-living days" of sales, entertaining out-of-town clients wanting a big time in Toronto could mean going to lunch at noon and not getting done until midnight. "You weren't talking about sipping white wine or drinking spritzers—it was scotch and martinis, going until you couldn't see." At one point, a doctor Foley consulted asked him to keep track of his intake for two weeks. When she reeled at the boozing, Foley protested it had just been a heavy stretch of client visits; but going back over his daytimer showed that the period had been "typical of about 40 of my 52 weeks."

Cigarette smoking was curbed only to be replaced by cigarillos and then cigars, which were soon occupying half a refrigerator in the Foley basement. "I would easily, in a day when I was doing a lot of entertaining, smoke 15 cigars," says Foley. Driving his pregnant wife to work, he would light the first Cuban of the morning in the car: "I have no idea why she stayed married to me."

Still looking to reduce the 230 pounds on his 5-foot-10 frame, Foley spent many corporate years at 250, gulping "industrial-strength Diovol and waking up in the middle of the night thinking you were going to choke."

That litany of ills, it would seem, contained ample evidence that Foley's life in the executive ranks needed adjustment. Indeed, a close friend whose own battle with alcoholism concluded in suicide a year ago, used to ask if Foley saw himself as an alcoholic. Yet even Monica, a highly focused and disciplined woman, admits, "when Brian went through great periods of stress, I just didn't recognize it. To me, he was always totally above that. He was always in charge, he was always together, he was always on top of things."

The response is classic. And for all the noise about health awareness today, not seeing and acting upon indicators of personal overload—particularly those that implicate physical or emotional fitness—is still implicitly part of the job description for senior managers. "The thing that distinguishes executives more than other groups is just accepting that there is something that they can't deal with," says Dr. Jack Santa-Barbara, CEO of Corporate Health Consultants Ltd., a nation-wide firm that provides employee assistance program services.

Moreover, while ulcers, headaches, heartburn, insomnia, angina and other symptoms may serve as stress warnings of worse to come, hard-charging executives "don't have to have [symptomatic] disorders in order to be at risk," cautions Dr. Rob Nolan, a consultant to the Ontario Heart and Stroke Foundation and coordinator of the Health Psychology Services division of Ottawa General Hospital.

Together with Ottawa General's head of cardiology, Dr. Andrew Wielgosz, psychologist Nolan conducts studies in cardiovascular-behavior medicine, which links high-pressure living to physiological heart damage. Stress responses make the rate and force of the heart's contractions increase or prompt the nervous system to stimulate the contraction of blood vessels. Either way, blood pressure experiences a rapid, if temporary, climb, potentially injuring artery walls and promoting the onset of atherosclerosis.

Thus, it's the repeated fight-or-flight rush of hormones fueling so much high-level decision-making that really exacts the toll, says Dr. Barbara Killinger, Toronto psychologist and author of *Workaholics: The Respectable Addicts.* "The body can't take the constant pumping of adrenaline associated with that. That's why these people die of heart attacks and strokes."

Even if oblivious to disease, don't people at least sense their lack of ease—that is, contentedness, fulfilment, joy? Not necessarily: just as Brian Foley long failed to take stock of his life, Dr. Edward Wasser, medical director of Medisys Health Group Inc., asks business leaders to rate their satisfaction with life and finds that "many say the question has never occurred to them." Medisys, a firm specializing in occupational health, conducts physician consultations that run for up to 75 minutes and incorporate the results of an extensive questionnaire that sketches a stress "map" of the patient.

"You've got someone working 80 hours a week, no exercise, diet sucks, and you ask, 'How's your communication with your wife?'" says Dr. Wasser. "They say, 'Pretty good.' What would she say? 'Terrible.' You ask, 'How are things going?' 'Pretty good.' And then you open up their stress map and they've got burnout."

Keeping the lid on in this way has long been conflated with masculine virtue. Recent years have featured much talk of how women executives are assuming the health-related perils men always faced in the boardroom. However, whether the difference relates to biology or conditioning, women are often quicker to note and acknowledge the impact of stress.

"There are a number of women who have left corporate life to start their own business, primarily to control their own lives," observes Susan Lilholt, vice-president, corporate partners, for the Canadian Association of Women Executives and Entrepreneurs.

Brian Foley was somewhere along the road to that decision himself by the time of the Maclean Hunter buyout. That year, sitting at government hearings at which Selkirk was applying for a new licence in Ottawa, Foley listened to citizen focus groups wonder why Canadians needed another television channel, and found himself thinking, "Well. . . right. What am I doing here?"

Foley had actually experienced such feelings of exhaustion in the early '80s. Then his answer was a two-year executive MBA program, adding all-night studies to his daily work. "Rather than decreasing activity, I said the way to do it is to really move into high gear with another 35 stressed-out executives," Foley says.

At first, his response to leaving Selkirk in July of 1989 was similar. Within weeks he accepted the presidency of Image Group Canada Ltd., a high-end postproduction house, but only on condition he be free to pursue other projects, since, Foley says wryly, "that wouldn't be a full-time job for a guy like me, running a $12-million company when I'd run a $100-million division and all that."

In a fitful search for ground beneath his feet, Foley also entered an "ill-conceived" partnership to produce videos, worked as executive producer on Variety Club telethons, chaired committees at the Banff Television Foundation and generally manifested such acute restlessness that his doctor suggested therapy.

Predictably, he responded in the negative. "I was feeling so lost with the world. I didn't have any control left and I think, now that I look back on it, I didn't have any self-esteem, because, of course, everything that I was to the world was what I did. I wasn't a vice-president any more and who the hell wanted to know somebody who wasn't a vice-president?"

Sure enough, many former work associates thought to be friends never called again. Monica, who had to work out her own resentment over the years of being "an accessory" to her husband's career, today believes that "he had to learn that his identity was not on a business card, it was not on the door of an office. The businessman had taken over the person, and when you take away that layer and you're confronted with, 'My God, who am I?' that's very traumatic."

Emblematic of the pretence Foley was clinging to during those turbulent days was an ostentatious navy-blue limo he had leased to do business in. One night, an airport driver bringing Monica home after a business trip loudly admired Foley's car in the driveway and exclaimed that his company would love to get the vehicle. The man was in luck; Foley had finally started doing a reality check, and soon after that night the limo was off the Foley driveway and in the employ of the cab company.

What Foley started to get in place of such false trappings were some answers to the Who-am-I question. He read a lot of books on personal development, explored men's issues, made it to that therapist's office and spent 18 months there. Instead of focusing more concern on his heart through angiograms and the like, he channeled his ruminations on mortality into volunteer work at a hospice that Monica had co-founded and returned to his Roman Catholic parish.

Perhaps best of all, when son Sean suggested his father join him in performing in a local production of *West Side Story,* Foley agreed. Foley showed so much flair that the director blended another part into it, and father and son made their stage debuts together.

At first reveling mainly in the applause, Foley fell in love with the creative process, doing workshops in everything from scene study to clowning. He admits to getting "immense pleasure" out of this pursuit, which is nowadays woven in and out of a relatively flexible consulting schedule. His activities as Foley Management Group Inc. have kept him narrowly into six figures, although well below previous peaks.

And even the consulting work has demanded key attitudinal changes. Being coached by business speaker and trainer Tom Stoyan at the start of his duties with The Executive Committee, Foley was told in straight terms that his listening skills were poor. Today, it seems, empathy is Foley's vocation, avocation and marital strategy. "At times," says Monica, "I still feel uncomfortable with him because I'm not used to someone being around and being caring, supportive."

The crux of the change was "my realization that I had to script my own life," Foley says. "I had really been living my father's life." Perhaps the clinching vision of mortality came in those last months at Selkirk, watching the faceless accounting teams striding through the halls, packing everything in boxes, "picking the carrion off the bones" of all those decades and lives, including his own, that had gone into building that firm. Powerless and unwanted, Foley could only watch until he couldn't bear to watch any more.

"I was a eunuch, really, as were the other operating guys," says Foley, still a bit heavy under the eyes, still freighted with more bulk than he needs, but all in all a profoundly remade man. "I asked them to live up to the deal on my contract and they did. And I woke up one morning with no place to go. Then the journey started."

Bisy Backson*

Benjamin Hoff

Rabbit hurried on by the edge of the Hundred Acre Wood, feeling more important every minute, and soon he came to the tree where Christopher Robin lived. He knocked at the door, and he called out once or twice, and then he walked back a little way and put his paw up to keep the sun out, and called to the top of the tree, and then he turned all round and shouted "Hallo!" and "I say!" "It's Rabbit!"—but nothing happened. Then he stopped and listened, and everything stopped and listened with him, and the Forest was very lone and still and peaceful in the sunshine, until suddenly a hundred miles above him a lark began to sing.

"Bother!" said Rabbit. "He's gone out."

He went back to the green front door, just to make sure, and he was turning away, feeling that his morning had got all spoilt, when he saw a piece of paper on the ground. And there was a pin in it, as if it had fallen off the door.

"Ha!" said Rabbit, feeling quite happy again. "Another notice!"

This is what it said:

> GON OUT
> BACKSON
> BISY
> BACKSON.
> C.R.

Rabbit didn't know what a Backson was—in spite of the fact that he is one—so he went to ask Owl. Owl didn't know, either. But we think *we* know, and we think a lot of other people do, too. Chuang-tse described one quite accurately:

> *There was a man who disliked seeing his footprints and his shadow. He decided to escape from them, and began to run. But as he ran along, more footprints appeared, while his shadow easily kept up with him. Thinking he was going too slowly, he ran faster and faster without stopping, until he finally collapsed from exhaustion and died.*
>
> *If he had stood still, there would have been no footprints. If he had rested in the shade, his shadow would have disappeared.*

You see them almost everywhere you go, it seems. On practically any sunny sort of day, you can see the Backsons stampeding through the park, making all kinds of loud Breathing Noises. Perhaps you are enjoying a picnic on the grass when you suddenly look up to find that one or two of them just ran over your lunch.

Generally, though, you are safe around trees and grass, as Backsons tend to avoid them. They prefer instead to struggle along on asphalt and concrete, in imitation of the short-lived transportation machines for which those hard surfaces were designed. Inhaling poisonous exhaust fumes from the vehicles that swerve to avoid hitting them, the Backsons blabber away to each other about how much better they feel now that they have gotten Outdoors. Natural living, they call it.

The Bisy Backson is almost desperately active. If you ask him what his Life Interests are, he will give you a list of Physical Activities, such as:

"Skydiving, tennis, jogging, racquet-ball, skiing, swimming, and water-skiing."

"Is that all?"

"Well, I (gasp, pant, wheeze) *think* so," says Backson.

"Have you ever tried chasing cars?"

"No, I—no, I never have."

"How about wrestling alligators?"

"No . . . I always wanted to, though."

"Roller-skating down a flight of stairs?"

"No, I never thought of it."

"But you said you were *active*."

At this point, the Backson replies, thoughtfully, "Say—do you think there's something . . . *wrong* with me? Maybe I'm losing my energy."

After a while, maybe.

The Athletic sort of Backson—one of the many common varieties—is concerned with physical fitness, he says. But for some reason, he sees it as something that has to be pounded in from the outside, rather than built up from the inside. Therefore, he confuses exercise with *work*. He works when he works, works when he exercises, and, more often than not, works when he plays. Work, work, work. All work and no play makes Backson a dull boy, Kept up for long enough, it makes him dead, too.

Where'd he go? That's how it is, you know—no rest for the Backson.

Let's put it this way: if you want to be healthy, relaxed, and contented, just watch what a Bisy Backson does and then do the opposite. There's one now, pacing back and forth, jingling the loose coins in his pocket, nervously glancing at his watch. He makes you feel tired just looking at him. The chronic Backson always seems to have to be *going* somewhere, at least on a superficial, physical level. He doesn't go out for a *walk*, though; he doesn't have time.

> *"Not conversing," said Eeyore. "Not first one and then the other. You said 'Hallo' and Flashed Past. I saw your tail in the distance as I was meditating my reply. I had thought of saying 'What?'—but, of course, it was then too late."*
>
> *"Well, I was in a hurry."*
>
> *"No Give and Take," Eeyore went on. "No Exchange of Thought: 'Hallo—What'—I mean, it gets you nowhere, particularly if the other person's tail is only just in sight for the second half of the conversation."*

The Bisy Backson is always On The Run, it seems, always:

GONE OUT
BACK SOON
BUSY
BACK SOON

or, more accurately:

BACK OUT
GONE SOON
BUSY
GONE SOON

The Bisy Backson is always going *somewhere*, somewhere he hasn't been. Anywhere but where he is.

> *"That's just it," said Rabbit, "Where?"*
>
> *"Perhaps he's looking for something."*
>
> *"What?" asked Rabbit.*
>
> *"That's just what I was going to say," said Pooh. And then he added, "Perhaps he's looking for a—for a—"*

For a Reward, perhaps. Our Bisy Backson religions, sciences, and business ethics have tried their hardest to convince us that there is a Great Reward waiting for us somewhere, and that what we have to do is spend our lives working like lunatics to catch up with it. Whether it's up in the sky, behind the next molecule, or in the executive suite, it's somehow always farther along than we are—just down the road, on the other side of the world, past the moon, beyond the stars. . . .

"Ouch!" said Pooh, landing on the floor.

"That's what happens when you go to sleep on the edge of the writing table," I said. "You fall off."

"Just as well," said Pooh.

"Why's that?" I asked.

"I was having an awful dream," he said.

"Oh?"

"Yes. I'd found a jar of honey . . . ," he said, rubbing his eyes.

"What's awful about that?" I asked.

"It kept moving," said Pooh. "They're not supposed to do that. They're supposed to sit still."

"Yes, I know."

"But whenever I reached for it, this jar of honey would sort of go someplace else."

"A nightmare," I said.

"Lots of people have dreams like that," I added reassuringly.

"Oh," said Pooh. "About Unreachable jars of honey?"

"About the same sort of thing," I said. "That's not unusual. The odd thing, though, is that some people live like that."

"Why?" asked Pooh.

"I don't know," I said. "I suppose because it gives them Something to Do."

"It doesn't sound like much fun to me," said Pooh.

No, it doesn't. A way of life that keeps saying, "Around the next corner, above the next step," works against the natural order of things and makes it so difficult to be happy and good that only a few get to where they would naturally have been in the first place— Happy and Good—and the rest give up and fall by the side of the road, cursing the world, which is not to blame but which is there to help show the way.

Those who think that the rewarding things in life are somewhere beyond the rainbow—

"Burn their toast a lot," said Pooh.

"I beg your pardon?"

"They burn their toast a lot," said Pooh.

"They—well, yes. And not only that—"

"Here comes Rabbit," said Pooh.

"Oh, there you are," said Rabbit.

"Here we are," said Pooh.

"Yes, here we are," I said.

"And there you are," said Pooh.

"Yes, here I am," said Rabbit impatiently. "To come to the point—Roo showed me his set of blocks. They're all carved and painted with letters on them."

"Oh?" I said.

"Just the sort of thing you'd expect to see, actually," said Rabbit, stroking his whiskers thoughtfully. "So by process of elimination," he said, "that means Eeyore has it."

"But Rabbit," I said. "You see—"

"Yes," said Rabbit. "I see Eeyore and find out what he knows about it—that's clearly the next step."

"There he goes," said Pooh.

Looking back a few years, we see that the first Bisy Backsons in this part of the world, the Puritans, practically worked themselves to death in the fields without getting much of anything in return for their tremendous efforts. They were actually starving until the wiser inhabitants of the land showed them a few things about working in harmony with the earth's rhythms. Now you plant; now you relax. Now you work the soil; now you leave it alone. The Puritans never really understood the second half, never really believed in it. And so, after two or three centuries of pushing, pushing, and pushing the once-fertile earth, and a few years of depleting its energy still further with synthetic stimulants, we have apples that taste like cardboard, oranges that taste like tennis balls, and pears that taste like sweetened Styrofoam, all products of soil that is not allowed to relax. We're not supposed to complain, but There It Is.

"Say, Pooh, why aren't you busy?" I said.

"Because it's a nice day," said Pooh.

"Yes, but—"

"Why ruin it?" he said.

"But you could be doing something Important," I said.

"I am," said Pooh.

"Oh? Doing what?"

"Listening," he said.

"Listening to what?"

"To the birds. And that squirrel over there."

"What are they saying?" I asked.

"That it's a nice day," said Pooh.

"But you know that already," I said.

"Yes, but it's always good to hear that somebody else thinks so, too," he replied.

"Well, you could be spending your time getting Educated by listening to the Radio, instead,"
I said.

"That thing?"

"Certainly. How else will you know what's going on in the world?" I said.

"By going outside," said Pooh.

"Er . . well . . . ." (Click.) "Now just listen to this, Pooh."

"Thirty thousand people were killed today when five jumbo airliners collided over downtown
Los Angeles. . .," the Radio announced.

"What does that tell you about the world?" asked Pooh.

"Hmm. You're right." (Click.)

"What are the birds saying now?" I asked.

"That it's a nice day," said Pooh.

It certainly is, even if the Backsons are too busy to enjoy it. But to conclude our explanation
of why so busy . . .

The hardheaded followers of the previously mentioned Party-Crashing Busy-body religion failed to appreciate the beauty of the endless forest and clear waters that appeared before them on this fresh green continent of the New World. Instead, they saw the paradise that was here and the people who lived in harmony with it as alien and threatening, something to attack and conquer—because it all stood in the way of the Great Reward. They didn't like singing very much, either. In fact—

"What?" said Pooh. "No singing?"

"Pooh, I'm trying to finish this. That's right, though. No singing. They didn't like it."

"Well, if they didn't like singing, then what was their attitude towards Bears?"

"I don't think they liked Bears, either."

"They didn't like Bears*?"*

"No. Not very much, anyway."

"No singing, no Bears. . . . Just what did *they like?"*

"I don't think they liked anything, *Pooh."*

"No wonder things are a little Confused around here," he said.

Anyway, from the Miserable Puritan came the Restless Pioneer, and from him, the Lonely Cowboy, always riding off into the sunset, looking for something just down the trail. From this rootless, dissatisfied ancestry has come the Bisy Backson, who, like his forefathers, has never really felt at home, at peace, with this Friendly Land. Rigid, combative fanatic that he is, the tightfisted Backson is just too hard on himself, too hard on others, and too hard on the world that heroically attempts to carry on in spite of what he is doing to it.

It's not surprising, therefore, that the Backson thinks of progress in terms of fighting and overcoming. One of his little idiosyncrasies, you might say. Of course, *real* progress involves growing and developing, which involves changing inside, but that's something the inflexible Backson is unwilling to do. The urge to grow and develop, present in all forms of life, becomes perverted in the Bisy Backson's mind into a constant struggle to change everything (the Bulldozer Backson) and everyone (the Bigoted Backson) else *but* himself, and interfere with things he has no business interfering with, including practically every form of life on earth. At least to a limited extent, his behavior has been held in check by wiser people around him. But, like parents of hyperactive children, the wise find that they can't be everywhere at once. Baby-sitting the Backsons wears you out.

"Here's Rabbit again," said Pooh. *"And Eeyore."*

 "Oh—Rabbit," I said.

 "And Eeyore*,"* said Eeyore.

 "I asked Eeyore—," said Rabbit.

 "That's me," said Eeyore. *"Eeyore."*

 "Yes, I remember," I said. *"I saw you just last year, out in the Swamp somewhere."*

 *"*Swamp*?"* said Eeyore indignantly. *"It's not a Swamp. It's a* Bog*."*

 "Swamp, Bog. . . ."

 "What's a Bog?" asked Pooh.

 "If your ankles get wet, that's a Bog," said Eeyore.

 "I see," said Pooh.

 "Whereas," continued Eeyore, *"if you sink in up to your neck, that's a Swamp."*

 "Swamp, indeed," he added bitterly. *"Ha!"*

 "Anyway, I asked Eeyore," said Rabbit, *"and he said he didn't have the slightest idea what I was talking about."*

 "It appears that I'm not alone in that," put in Eeyore. *"You don't have the slightest idea, either. Obviously."*

 "Just what is *the Uncarved Block?"* asked Rabbit.

 "It's me," said Pooh.

 "You?" said Eeyore. *"I came all the way over here—"*

 "From the Swamp," I added helpfully.

 "—from the Bog, to see Pooh*?"*

"Why not?" asked Pooh.

"Anything for Rabbit to keep busy over," said Eeyore sarcastically. "Anything at all, apparently."

Now, one thing that seems rather odd to us is that the Bisy Backson Society, which practically worships youthful energy, appearance, and attitudes, has developed no effective methods of retaining them, a lack testified to by an ever-increasing reliance on the unnatural False Front approach of cosmetics and plastic surgery. Instead, it has developed countless ways of breaking youthfulness down and destroying it. Those damaging activities that are not part of the search for the Great Reward seem to accumulate under the general heading of Saving Time.

For an example of the latter, let's take a classic monument to the Bisy Backson: the Hamburger Stand.

In China, there is the Teahouse. In France, there is the Sidewalk Café. Practically every civilized country in the world has some sort of equivalent—a place where people can go to eat, relax, and talk things over without worrying about what time it is, and without having to leave as soon as the food is eaten. In China, for example, the Teahouse is a real social institution. Throughout the day, families, neighbors, and friends drop in for tea and light food. They stay as long as they like. Discussions may last for hours. It would be a bit strange to call the Teahouse the nonexclusive neighborhood social club; such terms are too Western. But that can roughly describe part of the function, at least from our rather compartmentalized point of view. "You're important. Relax and enjoy yourself." That's the message of the Teahouse.

What's the message of the Hamburger Stand? Quite obviously, it's: "You don't count; hurry up."

Not only that, but as everyone knows by now, the horrible Hamburger Stand is an insult to the customer's health as well. Unfortunately, this is not the only example supported by the Saving Time mentality. We could also list the Supermarket, the Microwave Oven, the Nuclear Power Plant, the Poisonous Chemicals. . . .

Practically speaking, if timesaving devices really saved time, there would be more time available to us now than ever before in history. But, strangely enough, we seem to have less time than even a few years ago. It's really great fun to go someplace where there are no timesaving devices because, when you do, you find that you have *lots of time*. Elsewhere, you're too busy working to pay for machines to save you time so you won't have to work so hard.

The main problem with this great obsession for Saving Time is very simple: you can't *save* time. You can only spend it. But you can spend it wisely or foolishly. The Bisy Backson has practically no time at all, because he's too busy wasting it by trying to save it. And by trying to save every bit of it, he ends up wasting the whole thing.

Henry David Thoreau put it this way, in *Walden*:

> *Why should we live with such hurry and waste of life? We are determined to be starved before we are hungry. Men say that a stitch in time saves nine, and so they take a thousand stitches to-day to save nine tomorrow.*

For colorful contrast with the youth-destroying Bisy Backson Society, let's get back to Taoism for a moment. One of the most intriguing things about Taosim is that it not only contains respect for the old and wise, but also for the figure known as the Youthful Immortal. The Taoist tradition is filled with fascinating stories (fiction) and accounts (fact, embellished or otherwise) of those who, while still young, discovered the Secrets of

Life. However the discoveries were made, the result in each case was the same: a long life of youthful appearance, outlook, and energy.

For that matter, Taoist Immortals of all age levels have traditionally been known for their young attitudes, appearances, and energies. These were hardly accidental, but resulted from Taoist practices. For centuries in China, the general life expectancy was not much more than forty years, and hardworking farmers and dissipated aristocrats often died even younger than that. Yet countless Taoists lived into their eighties and nineties, and many lived considerably longer. The following is one of our favorite examples.

In 1933, newspapers around the world announced the death of a man named Li Chung Yun. As officially and irrefutably recorded by the Chinese government, and as verified by a thorough independent investigation, Li had been born in 1677. When over the age of two hundred, he had given a series of twenty-eight, three-hour-long talks on longevity at a Chinese university. Those who saw him at that time claimed that he looked like a man in his fifties, standing straight and tall, with strong teeth and a full head of hair. When he died, he was two hundred fifty-six years old.

When Li was a child, he left home to follow some wandering herbalists. In the mountains of China, he learned from them some of the secrets of the earth's medicine. In addition to using various rejuvenative herbs daily, he practiced Taoist exercises, believing that exercise which strains and tires the mind and body shortens life. His favorite way of traveling was what he called "walking lightly." Young men who went for walks with him when he was in his later years could not match his pace, which he maintained for miles. He advised those who wanted strong health to "sit like a turtle, walk like a pigeon, and sleep like a dog." When asked for his major secret, though, he would reply, "inner quiet."

Speaking of that sort of thing, let's return to *The House at Pooh Corner*. Christopher Robin has just asked Pooh a question:

"What do you like doing best in the world, Pooh?"

"Well," said Pooh, "what I like best—" and then he had to stop and think. Because although Eating Honey was a very good thing to do, there was a moment just before you began to eat it which was better than when you were, but he didn't know what it was called.

The honey doesn't taste so good once it is being eaten; the goal doesn't mean so much once it is reached; the reward is not so rewarding once it has been given. If we add up all the rewards in our lives, we won't have very much. But if we add up the spaces *between* the rewards, we'll come up with quite a bit. And if we add up the rewards *and* the spaces, then we'll have everything—every minute of the time that we spent. What if we could enjoy it?

The Christmas presents once opened are Not So Much Fun as they were while we were in the process of examining, lifting, shaking, thinking about, and opening them. Three hundred sixty-five days later, we try again and find that the same thing has happened. Each time the goal is reached, it becomes Not So Much Fun, and we're off to reach the next one, then the next one, then the next.

That doesn't mean that the goals we have don't count. They do, mostly because they cause us to go through the process, and it's the *process* that makes us wise, happy, or whatever. If we do things in the wrong sort of way, it makes us miserable, angry, confused, and things like that. The goal has to be right for us, and it has to be beneficial, in order to ensure a beneficial process. But aside from that, it's really the process that's important. *En-*

joyment of the process is the secret that erases the myths of the Great Reward and Saving Time. Perhaps this can help to explain the everyday significance of the word *Tao*, the Way.

What could we call that moment before we begin to eat the honey? Some would call it anticipation, but we think it's more than that. We would call it awareness. It's when we become happy and realize it, if only for an instant. By Enjoying the Process, we can stretch that awareness out so that it's no longer only a moment, but covers the whole thing. Then we can have a lot of fun. Just like Pooh.

> *And then he thought that being with Christopher Robin was a very good thing to do, and having Piglet near was a very friendly thing to have; and so, when he had thought it all out, he said, "What I like best in the whole world is Me and Piglet going to see You, and You saying 'What about a little something?' and Me saying, 'Well, I shouldn't mind a little something, should you, Piglet,' and it being a hummy sort of day outside, and birds singing."*

When we take the time to enjoy our surroundings and appreciate being alive, we find that we have no time to be Bisy Backsons anymore. But that's all right, because being Bisy Backsons is a tremendous waste of time. As the poet Lu Yu wrote:

The clouds above us join and separate,
The breeze in the courtyard leaves and returns.
Life is like that, so why not relax?
Who can stop us from celebrating?

A Case of Inefficiency

Ann Marie Cunningham

Bertrand Russel thought that four hours of work a day was plenty for anyone. William Faulkner regretted it was possible to do more: "One of the saddest things is that the only thing a man can do for eight hours a day is work. You can't eat eight hours a day, nor drink eight hours a day, nor make love eight hours a day—all you can do is work."

Most great hunches and major breakthroughs seem to have popped into people's heads when they weren't working—when they were staring into space, goofing off or even sleeping. Stanislaw Ulam, the Polish expatriate physicist who, with Edward Teller, hit on the design for the hydrogen bomb in 1951, was considered spectacularly lazy by his colleagues at Los Alamos. While everyone else worked around the clock to win the Cold War, he never appeared at the lab before ten and was gone by four. When other scientists went hiking in the New Mexican mountains, he remained at the foot of the trail and watched through binoculars.

James D. Watson, one of the three unravelers of the structure of DNA, was too lazy a doctoral candidate to take chemistry or physics. He was drawn to science by the partying at conventions, and went to Cambridge, England, where he hooked up with Francis Crick and Maurice Wilkins, to learn biochemistry. The three were well matched: Crick girl-watched incessantly and subscribed only to *Vogue*. At the height of the race with Linus Pauling to decode DNA, Wilkins disappeared regularly for fencing lessons. Watson spent afternoons on the tennis court, showing up at the lab "for only a few minutes of minor fiddling before dashing away to have sherry with the girls at Pop's." He pondered DNA at the movies, where he spent almost every evening.

Cat's in the Cradle

Harry Chapin

My child arrived just the other day;
he came to the world in the usual way.
But there were planes to catch and bills to pay;
he learned to walk while I was away.
And he was talkin' 'fore I knew it,
and as he grew he'd say,
"I'm gonna be like you, Dad,
you know I'm gonna be like you."

And the cat's in the cradle and the silver spoon,
little boy blue and the man in the moon.
"When you comin' home Dad?"
"I don't know when, but we'll get together then,
you know we'll have a good time then."

My son turned ten just the other day;
he said, "Thanks for the ball, Dad,
come on let's play.
Can you teach me to throw?"
I said, "Not today, I got a lot to do."

He said, "That's okay."
But his smile never dimmed, it said,

"I'm gonna be like him, yeah,
you know I'm gonna be like him."

Chorus

Well he came from college just the other day;
so much like a man I just had to say,
"Son, I'm proud of you, can you sit for a while?"
He shook his head and he said with a smile,
"What I'd really like, Dad,
is to borrow the car keys;
see you later, can I have them please?"

Chorus

I've long since retired,
my son's moved away;
I called him up just the other day.
I said, "I'd like to see you if you don't mind."
He said, "I'd love to Dad, if I could find the time.
You see, my new job's a hassle and the kids have the flu,
but it's sure nice talking to you, Dad,
it's been sure nice talkin' to you."
As I hung up the phone,
it occurred to me,
he'd grown up just like me;
my boy was just like me.

Chorus

Chapter
8

Controlling and Resisting

All organizations face a difficult dilemma. Often, the primary concern of individuals is to satisfy their own self-interests while the concern of organizations is to induce individuals to work toward some collective end. To resolve this dilemma, organizations often go to great lengths to control what individuals do. In response, individuals try to avoid such constraints. In short, controlling and resisting are two processes that permeate organizational life.

Early in this century, Frederick Taylor tried to convince all who would listen that workers and managers had compatible interests. Since that time, students of organizations have echoed this theme. The fact that people have been motivated to write and to read so much about the possibility of such commonality suggests another fact—the commonality is not all that obvious to many. While we, too, believe that a considerable amount of organizational conflict could be avoided, we also see considerable evidence of inherent conflict. Moreover, that inherent conflict divides not only labor and management but also managers and workers. Depending on where a person stands on a particular issue, the efforts of others to assert their own interests can be perceived and labeled in quite different ways. For example, an employee's refusal to follow a supervisor's directive to use a more economical production method can be viewed as insubordination, resistance, or evidence that the employee has an "authority problem." On the other hand, the same act could be construed as principled commitment to quality work, to professional norms, or to personal ethics.

Such labels themselves are part of the process through which individuals pursue their own interests—by seeking to control others and by resisting the efforts of others to control them. These efforts to win and to resist control are some of the most interesting facets of organization reality. The selections in this chapter capture a number of ways in which these struggles occur. It is important to recognize that people at all organizational levels attempt to control and to resist. Although some of these attempts are subtle and even humorous, their earnestness should not be overlooked.

While resisting is something that is often attributed to lower level participants, sometimes it appears to be a response of managers to requests and expressions of resistance by subordinates. In "The Art of Saying No: On the Management of Refusals in Organizations," Dafna Izraeli and Todd D. Jick capture a few of these instances in describing four types of managerial refusal ceremonies for saying no. Each ceremony has the purpose of controlling employees while maintaining their commitment to the organization and shaping their expectations and actions. However, as Izraeli and Jick point out, even if subordinates accept the verdict, the manipulations may have deleterious effects on employee morale, commitment, and motivation.

In "Intimidation Rituals: Reactions to Reform," Rory O'Day describes a spectrum of behavior that those with formal authority use to control others. It is especially instructive to note how efforts at control may escalate from subtle hints to severe punishments.

The next selection contains retrospective commentaries on Robert Shrank's "Two Women, Three Men on a Raft." It provides additional insights into the changing dynamics of power and resistance in relationships between men and women. Shrank's original article (see Chapter 5) revealed how men's unconscious concerns about their power in relation to women can have disastrous consequences. This update reinforces that point while calling attention to the bilateral nature of control resistance relations. While reading the original piece in its context of the 1970s we tended to see the root of the problem as exclusively in the assumptions made by men. However, the updated comments broaden our perspective by inviting us to consider that in the 1990s the problem may have changed not because men changed their assumptions about the power of women but because women have changed how they respond to resisting being treated as helpless. This helps us to see that to understand controlling we need to study resistance and/or its absence. Thus resistance is a core topic for the study of organizational reality. When we take resistance as worthy of study, we gain deeper appreciation of some everyday aspects of organizations such as the cartoons in offices.

Such insights are revealed in the next selection by Linda Forbes and Elizabeth Bell, "Organizational Survivors: Images of Women in the Office Folklore of Contemporary Organizations." The authors encourage us to realize that we can get more than just a laugh out of the cartoons around organizations. Among other things the cartoons reveal some of the assumptions and issues around which the twin processes of controlling and resisting take place.

Although it is common to describe these individuals as "resisting" rather than "controlling," a moment's reflection reveals that both words are referring to rather similar processes through which individuals act to advance and to protect their own interests. The remainder of this chapter focuses on some of these actions.

"Señor Payroll," a wonderful short story by William E. Barrett, shows how a group of Mexican-American stokers foiled sustained efforts of managers to exercise bureaucratic control. Another short story, "The Catbird Seat" by the renowned James Thurber, describes a sophisticated scheme devised to fight back against a manager. While reading both stories, it is useful to identify the ways that resisters defined situations and sources of power that these definitions allowed them to call on.

So far, we have focused on control and resistance up and down the organization hierarchy. The final selection is "The Ratebuster: The Case of the Saleswoman" by Melville Dalton. This classic study reveals how people at the same level pursue and protect their interests vis-à-vis each other.

We do not want to suggest that members of organizations are always at cross-purposes. However, as this chapter makes clear, organizations cannot be understood without considering the formal and informal means that people at all levels use to try to assert their own interests.

The Art of Saying No: On the Management of Refusals in Organizations

Dafna Izraeli and Todd D. Jick

INTRODUCTION

The study of organizational culture has recently been furthered by examination of the content, function, and underlying meanings of symbols, language, stories, ideologies, rituals and myths. It has been argued that these mechanisms of culture-building convey multiple meanings. On one level, technical or instrumental information may be conveyed while, at another, one can characterize the ceremonial nature of communication in terms of its expression of values, premises, and interests embodied in the definition of the situation. This ceremonial level primarily "says things," conveys a message, rather than "does things." Thus the construction and maintenance of these common understandings or shared meanings have become increasingly subject to political analysis as to their role in sustaining and legitimating authority, in securing or preserving a semblance of order, harmony, and consensus in organizations. Wilkins (1983) noted that stories commonly told in organizations are important indicators of the social prescriptions concerning how things are to be done, the consequences of compliance or deviance, and an overall guide to what kinds of people can do what. In more subtle ways, symbols of culture convey beliefs about the use and distribution of power and privilege as reflected in rituals and myths which legitimate those distributions.

What becomes interesting is how people come to believe, accept, and legitimate power and authority. Multiple elements of everyday life in the organization serve to transmit and reaffirm the existence and legitimacy of authority and of the ability of some people to define for others who they are and what it is they are doing.

Management does not have an absolute monopoly over the definitional process. The framing of organizational problems, the interpretive schemes, and the basic definition of reality are rarely uncontroversial. Anthropological studies of life on the shopfloor are rich in their documentation of the world of workers who operate with a different cultural tool kit and whose version of "what is going on here" is frequently very different from that of management.

In the face of such tensions and conflicts, management typically seeks to build and sustain consensus while reinforcing their control. How is this done? Tools of management include selective recruitment, training, promotion, role modeling, organizational and physical design, and direct communication of desired norms and values.

But, according to Smircich and Morgan (1982), effective leadership perhaps relies most on the management of meaning to the extent that the leader's definition of the situation serves as a basis for action by others, actions oriented to the achievement of desirable ends from the leader's viewpoint. Thus, the manager's role is portrayed as "framer of contexts, a maker and shaper of interpretive schemes (who) must deal with multiple realities." This management of context and meaning is a far less visible form of control than traditional supervision in that it achieves compliance on the basis of value premises. But it is a critical ingredient in the glue which holds an organization together. Ultimately, these invisible controls powerfully influence what people do and don't do, what people say and can't say, and what people have and can't have.

THE CASE OF REFUSAL CEREMONIES AND SCARCE RESOURCES

One arena in which these mechanisms are manifest is in the distribution of incentives in organizations. For those who manage the organization, mobilizing and sustaining the willing cooperation of participants is a core dilemma. Pfeffer (1981, xi–xii) similarly observed that "one of the major tasks of managers is to make organizational participants want and feel comfortable doing what they have to do." Managers are assisted in accomplishing this by the widely accepted ideology that their authority is legitimate as well as by controlling the distribution of incentives of resources of both a material and symbolic nature.

However, the task can be especially difficult because there are always some people in the organization receiving less than they expect or less than they deem themselves entitled. Thus, the organization seeks ways to "cool out" their frustration and disappointment so as to retain the commitment and willingness of employees to give energy and loyalty to the organization's desired goals and purposes. Members must be helped to see how things are different from what they perceived and to shift their behavior accordingly. Organizations thus attempt to influence members to want less, to delay their gratification, to set policies as to who should have what, etc.

Two environmental conditions increase the prevalence with which organizations must engage in such influence rituals: a shift from economically good times to times of relative economic scarcity and an expansion of perceived entitlement. Both conditions lead to a negative shift in the ratio of those to whom the organization says "yes" to those to whom it says "no".

Consider two contemporary examples: organizational retrenchment, in which given or expected resources are typically taken away, and quality circles, in which generated requests for incremental resources may be discouraged. In both cases, a culture must be "re-worked" and power and influence exercised. In the first case, an ethos of expansiveness must give way to an ethos of frugality, restraint, and sacrifice. In the second case, beliefs in opportunity and change—stimulated by the development of quality circles—whet the appetite and encourage participants to make demands on organizational resources. Yet, the organization inevitably finds itself setting limits, defining domains, and establishing controls over resource distribution. In both cases, "reality" is brought in line with management's new definition of "what this organization needs." The result is that persons who expected to receive some benefit and may even have been initially encouraged in their expectations, must be helped to accept the new reality.

The art of saying "no" then is a process of redefining the situation and of managing meaning. The situated activity in which this is done we call a "refusal ceremony." It is through such ceremonies that we will illustrate the process by which the dominant culture is reaffirmed.

Refusal ceremonies may be classified as a specific case of breaking bad news. They are usually defined as unpleasant events by all participants involved. They are part of the dirty work of a manager's job. The task of saying no is usually assigned to the immediate superior who is expected to absorb the stings and arrows of the subordinate's disappointment. Since refusing requests is a normal part of everyday life in organizations, the immediate superior has sufficient credibility for the task.

Our presentation focuses on the negative response of a superior to an initiative taken by a subordinate. We are describing one phase in a communication process, that in which the superior's response gives meaning to the action of the subordinate. The superior's response is the definition of reality in which the subordinate is invited to share.

SAMPLE AND DATA COLLECTION

The data for this study were collected from a convenience sample of 89 respondents, 67 or whom were enrolled in graduate business courses and 22 in an under-graduate business course. Most were part-time students who were also currently employed. All have had some previous work experience and the number of organizations virtually equalled the number of respondents. Overall, though, the sample reflects individuals at relatively early stages of their careers. The great majority may be classified as lower participants. The data were collected anonymously.

Respondents were asked to describe an incident in which their request for resources was denied by someone superior to them. The specific instructions were as follows:

You've asked for, or let it be known, you'd like something such as a budget increase, an additional secretary, larger office space, assignment of a new project, salary hike, etc. However, you found that it would not be granted.

Please describe: (a) the nature of the request; (b) what was said to you regarding the refusal; (c) how it was said, (e.g., verbally, in memo form, grapevine), and, (d) your reactions and feelings.

Please be as specific as possible about the chronology of events, the communications and/or dialogue between you and your supervisor(s), and the resolution.

Analysis of our data suggests four types of ceremonies are conducted to convey refusals: normative invocation, status denial, rites of attrition, and rites of benevolence.

I. NORMATIVE INVOCATION

The most prevalent ceremonial strategy to explain and legitimate a refusal is the appeal to higher order values, such as rationalism, and to their structural manifestations. Technical efficiency and functional rationality are aspects of organizational ideology which legitimate the division of labour and the system of authority. Decisions made on those grounds become legitimate and by implication, correct. "We can't afford to increase your budget this year," "It's against company policy," "It's the rule here," "The interests of the organization require that," are statements tendered as reasons for not granting a request.

Normative invocations are occasions for the superior to explicate "the organization's point of view" and in so doing, to reaffirm management's right to define what the prevailing point of view is in the situation. The following examples are taken from our data:

Subordinate 1: "It's not in the budget."

"Requested to hire an additional manager to cover afternoon shift operations. Was told could not afford to add to head count during decline in sales. Response: frustrated because I was convinced of the need and felt that the expense could be justified."

Subordinate 2: "It's against corporate policy."

"Requested a foreign car instead of the standard North American car (company vehicle). Was refused on grounds that corporate policy did not allow for exceptions of this nature. Response: Was only marginally disappointed—did not feel the request would be granted in any event."

Subordinate 3: "You haven't the seniority."

"On the part-time job requested more hours of work for the summer. The request was refused as management replied that the number of hours allotted was based on seniority and individuals who had been with the firm longer than myself were able to obtain more hours of work. Response: I felt that work performance is a more important criterion than seniority, however, since the company places more importance on seniority, I accepted the explanation with reluctance."

Subordinate 4: "In the interest of the company."

"Requested a transfer of work classification to be retrained in a different functional area of the organization. Was told 'no'—as you are effectively performing your current job to the satisfaction and best wishes of the organization. Response: Although I understood the organization's point of view and was happy they considered me a top performer, I was bothered that they did not consider my feelings regarding the present job."

Subordinate 5: "The needs of the organization."

"Requested a subordinate be transferred for his and the Company's benefit. Was told no, not now. Needs of my boss' organization too great at this time to release him, perhaps later. Response: Felt as if I had been out of line in making the request (which I wasn't) and felt hesitant about any future requests."

Subordinate 6: "We can't afford it."

"Requested a pay raise. Was told not possible due to budget constraints. Response: Did not believe my bureau chief, I knew there was money available for raises and that it was his discretion solely that determined that distribution."

In the above cases the refusal is rationalized in terms of the rules of behaviour generally followed. In no case was the right of the superior to make the decision, and impose it upon the subordinate, questioned. The wisdom of the decision was questioned, even the wisdom of the criterion used for making the decision was criticized. Subordinate and superior, however, share an understanding of how the organization works. That understanding includes the belief that each holds about his/her relative authority and power in the situation. The ceremonies of refusal are micro-events in which these beliefs are tested against the reality and then either validated and reinforced, or weakened and perhaps transformed.

There are a number of reasons why normative invocations are the most frequently used rhetoric for conveying refusals. First, as already noted, they have high legitimacy in the organizational culture. Furthermore, reference to rational considerations impersonalize the refusal and veil the power dimension in the interaction between subordinate and superior. They are, in addition, difficult to refuse, since lower participants are usually less knowledgeable about rules and budget allocations than are their superiors. However, even when the subordinate is fully aware that the explanation is dishonest, as in the case of subordinate 6, few are ready to challenge and announce that the king has no clothes.

II. STATUS DENIAL

Organizational cultures define what kind of people are entitled to what sort of treatment. People are sorted for entitlements according to their technical skills as well as many other less formalized criteria, such as class, race, sex, age, and personal connections. The subordinate who initiates a request is frequently making a claim to being a certain kind of person or to having a certain status which entitles him/her to make the request and expect that it be granted.

A status denial ceremony is an occasion when the rejection of the claim forms the basis for the refusal. The message conveyed is that "you are not what you present yourself to be." This strategy shifts the responsibility for the refusal from the organization to the individual. If effective, the subordinate will perceive the organization as acting equitably and him/herself as inadequate. When the inadequacy is defined as remediable, and the subordinate is led to believe that s/he may become what s/he has professed to be (provided s/he completes the project, gets more experience, etc.) then fervor of effort is likely to ensue.

Subordinate 7: "You will get what you deserve."

"A better rating on my annual evaluation was requested. I was told it would not be granted because I did not 'stand out in the crowd'. I had a verbal interview. I was very angry. I requested and obtained a second verbal interview. I requested a full explanation of the evaluation process

and criteria. I presented my case based on the criteria. At a third interview I was informed my rating had been improved as I had requested. I was informed that the improved rating was not due to my efforts but because my manager's superior thought I deserved the rating."

Another form of status denial is to insist that the subordinate has not met the time requirements for that which s/he requests, as in the following examples:

Subordinate 8: "You're not here long enough."

"I had requested an increase in salary from $160 to $200 per week. I had been employed a year and a half in what I considered an above average job. I was refused on the basis that no one got a raise until working two years."

Subordinate 9: "You're not old enough."

"I worked in a commercial bank. Asked to be promoted to commercial banking officer from division assistant. I was told that I was too young and not ready for the position (I was only 22 years old.)."

Merton (1982) referred to such time considerations as "socially expected durations"; namely, culturally prescribed and socially patterned expectations about the amount of time something will or should take. They are not the same as actual durations. The enactment of a socially expected duration as a justification for refusal may reflect the belief that during a specified time something will occur which is not likely to occur in less (or more) time. Time then becomes the measurable substitute for whatever process is supposed to occur.

Status denial may also take the form of discrediting the subordinate's presentation of self and accrediting him/her with a less attractive identity. The superior may select from a variety of labels (too aggressive, too impatient, uncooperative, poor team worker), any or all of which might serve to disqualify the subordinate for the very benefits being sought. Discrediting has high fear arousal potential and in that sense may belong to the category of intimidation ceremonies.

Intimidation rituals (O'Day, 1974)* aim to dissuade the subordinate from pursuing his/her claim to entitlement. The dominant emotion aroused is that of fear—of the consequences of not changing the course of action. Intimidation may be conveyed in many styles from that of direct overt threat to the light hearted manner in the following case:

Subordinate 10: "Things could get worse."

"I worked as a bricklayer this summer for a small, single owner company. The owner was my boss, he worked beside me and one other employee. I was earning $6/hr as was the other guy. After six months we both approached the owner and asked him if he could give us a 50¢/hr. raise. The owner refused stating in a half joking, half serious way that we were lucky to have a job in the first place."

In sum, status denial represents the harshest threat to the personal identity and future role of the individual. In demeaning, threatening, or exposing the status of the individual, this tactic reinforces the sanctity and impenetrability of organizational rules, values, and stature.

---

*O'Day (1974) describes the intimidation rituals (nullification, isolation, defamation and expulsion) performed in progression by middle level bureaucrats to control the reform initiatives of a subordinate.

III. ATTRITION

Rites of attrition are a form of "non-violent" resistance in which refusal is frequently implicit but not openly voiced. If successful, they produce motivational fatigue as the subordinate gets used to his/her condition and comes to accept it. Attrition takes two forms: avoidance and stalling.

Avoidance takes place when the subordinate's initiatives are disattended. Telephone messages are not responded to, letters are not answered. After one or two attempts, the subordinate may either get discouraged or get the message and withdraw from further initiatives.

Avoidance is more likely to take this form in large organizations where relations are relatively formalized and the person to whom the communication is directed is not the immediate superior or at least not personally known to the subordinate. These conditions make the use of informal modes of access to those in authority more difficult. Such inaccessibility may be specifically fostered for that purpose. Avoidance, however, may also occur in face to face encounters as in the following example related by a newly tenured associate professor:

"I wrote my Dean asking for an extended leave. He didn't reply. I met him several times after that at faculty meetings but each time he avoided raising the issue. I was forced to be the one to raise it. I began to feel like a nag. Last time he walked right by me as if I weren't there. I knew I better not raise the issue there."

Avoidance is most likely to deter only the more timid and those whose position in the organization is precarious. If the subordinate persists, the superior may be persuaded to shift to another ceremonial strategy.

"My hands are tied" or "It's not up to me" is another type of avoidance ritual in which the superior avoids dealing with the issue by pointing to other individuals, groups or organizations who may be, credibly, presented as constraining action on the part of the superior. Organizations that generate a large number of committees provide fertile ground for the use of this ritual. The superior may relate a dramatized description of the intricacies and complexities of the organization's decision making process to convince the subordinate that "It's not up to me." The superior may offer to "look into it" and thus shift from an avoidance to a stalling ceremony.

Stalling refers to tactics used to gain time, such as "I'll look into it," or "You look into it." As different from avoidance, stalling tactics convey the message that something is being done to remedy the situation. Stalling may also have an attritional effect but successful stalling rites sustain the subordinate's belief in the organization's good will toward him/her and the hope that at some time in the future the matter will be resolved to the subordinate's satisfaction, as in the following example:

Subordinate 11: "I'll get back to you."

"Requested an increase in salary. The initial response was positive with the supervisor (owner of Co.) agreeing with my request and saying he would get back to me. A few weeks passed with no response so I approached him. Again a few weeks passed and then I was told it would come in the form of a bonus and pay increase at the end of the year. It's been 6 months since my request and although they haven't said no, I haven't seen any increase or been informed of the amount."

In "I'll look into it" the manager presumably takes it upon him/herself to pursue the matter further after the subordinate leaves. This expression of intent and good will may be lent greater credibility by a jotting down of a note as an indication to the subordinate that the manager is resolved to do something, as if once recorded "I'll look into it" takes on an "as good as done" quality.

"You look into it" transfers responsibility for the next step to the subordinate. S/he is asked to do something which is presented as necessary before anything else can be done. This may require preparing a report explaining his/her position on the issue or collecting data which may be difficult to obtain:

Subordinate 12: "Bring me proof."
  "I requested additional office help (1 person) for duties the junior marketing assistant had in addition to her researching and analyzing functions; since when her work load backs up, so does mine. (I am the senior marketing research assistant.) The refusal was based on the overall all-corporate freeze, in addition to the lack of long term history regarding the amount of work that such an extra person would have—in other words, I couldn't prove that there would always be 40 hours of work per week for a secretary."

Successful stalling may be extended for a relatively long time until either the superior is replaced or circumstances change so as to make the initial request no longer relevant. The following incident reveals how the first supervisor was spared the refusal while her replacement shifts responsibility for solving the problem to the subordinate, an implicit discrediting ritual:

Subordinate 13: "Wait till things settle down."
  "I requested an exchange of offices, to be nearer my boss and co-workers. My boss and co-workers were clustered at the other end of the building. I wanted to be more involved in their work. My boss said to wait until 'things settled down,' then until the organizational development project was finished. I waited 12–18 months. My boss moved up to executive director, reporting to the Vice-President, and my new boss told me (2 weeks ago) that no change would be made; I was also told that it was up to me to overcome the obstacle of distance and to find ways to integrate myself into the activities of my co-workers."

Stalling ceremonies are successful when they convey a message of good will and get the manager off the hook, if only temporarily. The general cultural norm according to which it is not nice to refuse a request, makes it generally more difficult to say "no" than to say "yes". Thus, rites of attrition may reflect as much of the general culture as the local organizational values and norms.

IV. BENEVOLENCE

A refusal may take the form of a benevolence rite in which the organization affirms its concern for the subordinate as a human being. Examples of benevolence are "for your own good!!" (FYOG) and "See how fair we are." (SHFWA) In FYOG the meaning of the refusal is inverted and redefined as being in the real interest of the subordinate. In SHFWA the subordinate is offered a consolation prize.

In FYOG ceremonies the benevolence may be directed to the subordinate either as a member of the organization (the public career) or as a person and member of a family (the private career). In both, the presumption is that the superior's understanding of the subordinate's goals and the means for their achievement is greater than that of the subordinate. The primacy of the superior's concern for the subordinate's welfare is the dominant posture. In relation to the public career, typical statements are "the job is not right for you," "you think you'll like it but you won't," "a pay increase now will arouse a lot of hostility," etc. When the benevolence is strongly paternalistic scratching the surface reveals "intimidation." Statements like "If I raise this with the board, they'll think you're a trouble maker" or "I'm willing to do this for you but you will have to bear the responsibility."

"For your own good" as a private person is a tactic most likely to be used to mollify a married woman. It involves the debunking of the dominant ideology that links success with power and position and invokes an alternative value system that links success with happiness and family life: "For your own good, what do you need all that extra responsibility, it'll create tensions, at home" or "your husband might resent your having to work weekends." The manager's concern may extend beyond the woman to the welfare of her husband as in "how can we send you abroad, what will your husband do, make cocktail parties?"

"See how fair we are" is the implicit message when the subordinate is offered an alternative or consolation prize, one less costly to the organization. Consolation prizes include change in job title instead of a job, a trip to a conference, or half (quarter?) of whatever was asked for, whether time, money or some other resources. The prize may have greater symbolic than substantial value, as when the refusal is redefined as a compliment, another example of meaning inversal.

Subordinate 14: "You're too good for a better job."

"Perhaps one year ago I requested of my boss to be placed on a new project. I had been working on one project which was very large and important for a year and a half and I felt I was no longer learning what I should have been learning as a third year engineer. My boss himself explained to me that I was in a sort of catch-22 situation. In performing the responsibilities which had come to me I exhibited a consistency and reliability which caused upper management to feel confident in me handling my position. I had done so well at my job in terms of defining my role and my interrelationships with the other disciplines that I was irreplaceable. I was told that I would have to follow the project through to completion. My boss did help to bring some change into my job by getting me involved with the college recruitment effort. Although this extra responsibility only took one day every three weeks it gave me the diversification I desired. The way my boss posed the explanation was very flattering."

Being irreplaceable may also be a reflection of the lack of attractiveness of the tasks performed rather than of the special skills of the subordinate. In the case being irreplaceable would not be perceived as a consolidation.

"Cooling out" (Goffman, 1952) the subordinate is an important part of refusal ceremonies and may be done most painlessly by benevolent tactics. In Goffman's study the individual (mark) needs to be cooled out so that he does not "squawk," create a row, or be an embarrassment to the organization in some other way. Our concern has been with the refused member who needs to be "cooled out" and then "cooled in" to the culture so that his/her commitments are once again harnessed to the purpose of the organization (as defined by managers).

CULTURE-WORKING AND REFUSAL CEREMONIES: FINAL THOUGHTS

The lion and the calf shall lie down together but the calf won't get much sleep.
                                        Woody Allen, *Without Feathers*

Refusal ceremonies have been shown to be an important part of the acculturation process. On one level, they convey explicit guidelines and information about "the way things are done around here" and they contribute to socialization. The employee, "learns," for example, the policies, priorities, and goals from the superior's viewpoint—and the rules of the game in that particular organization.

The art of saying no can also be characterized as a form of culture-working activity in so far as these ceremonies serve to define realities, who people are (e.g., their status), and what influence people can exercise. In this sense, we have indicated how culture is intertwined with structure (i.e., power and control), how defining the terms of reality can be a prominent tool in a manager's "cultural tool kit." This is what Pfeffer (1981) referred to as the institutionalization of organizational culture whereby ". . . the distribution of power, the making of certain decisions, or the following of certain rules of operation . . . become defined as part of the organization's culture." (p. 299) Similarly, Smircich and Morgan (1982) characterized this type of process as "power-based reality construction."

In a sense, it appears as if the subordinates have been "brought into" the dominant culture—i.e., accepted the legitimacy of the distribution of power and authority as shared social fact. Subordinates implicitly agree to operate according to certain rules and, to some extent, concede their autonomy. Thus, refusal ceremonies reaffirm the purposes, values, norms, beliefs (i.e., culture) of the organization as defined by managers, and sustain institutional order. Moreover, Pfeffer (1981) argues that the distribution of power ". . . is perpetuated because people come to believe that this is how things always were, always will be, and, always should be." (p. 299)

However, the reaffirmation and perpetuation of culture also arouses resentment and tensions—which may indeed test the strength of the dominant culture. Many of the refused subordinates in our study reported feeling frustrated, angry, alienated, and resentful. While part of the message of the refusal ceremony may indeed be to underscore the relative unimportance or powerlessness of the subordinates, it creates (perhaps) unintended consequences as well. In some few cases, the employee actually resigned. In others, employees tried to resist the refusal—albeit within the ground rules of "evidence" defined by management. For many, the disgruntlement resulted in demoralization, discouragement, and even some questioning of the derivation of policies, and authority positions. Thus, it was not always clear that these people were indeed appeased and discouraged from pursuing benefits denied them by the organization and willing to do what they were expected to do. (In fact, there is literature on the management of extreme cases of protest (e.g., O'Day, 1974; Ewing, 1983).)

Although the perception of the ground rules may be shared and the distribution of power generally accepted, this is not to suggest that there is complete harmony, collaboration and consensus. Accepting the cultural ground rules is different from liking them, or feeling part of them. Although the subordinates typically complied with the refusal and rarely confronted their superiors with their dissatisfaction, they clearly had not bought all the values. That is, being "in" the culture and enacting behaviour within its terms is distinct from being "of" the culture, internalizing the dominant values and definitions of reality. The subordinate is typically not an equal partner in the determination of the culture and thus the dialectic tension: the more the culture is reaffirmed, the more the potential for resentment and opposition.

In order to maximize the reaffirmation of culture and minimize the opposition, the effective management of refusal ceremonies is often a prerequisite for advancement in a managerial career. Breaking or reconfirming bad news to subordinates provides situations in which the tension between the organization's interest and human variability is most exposed. Managers are expected to attend to preserving organizational legitimacy and disattend any ethical doubt that may cause them uneasiness much as medical students acquire a look of professional cool when handling an exposed gut. Refusal ceremonies may require actions for managers that seem insincere, dishonest, or unfriendly but as Goffman (1952) observed, "certain kinds of role success require certain kinds of moral failure."

The following account reported in Margolis (1979: 126–7) is by a scientist who failed the test and consequently was forced to "jump off the managerial mainline and settle for a technical sideline."

> You see, one can be very competent technically, but there are other skills. After two promotions I found that you just come up to a harsher level of reality than just doing your research.
> The first time you're told to go tell a lie to a bunch of people, you make speeches to your boss about fairness and everything. I did that and he looked at me and said, "Frank, this is not the Supreme Court, and don't you tell me about fair and not fair. This is it and this is the story."
> What happened was this. We were making some new rules about raises which were screwing some people. I had to say that you couldn't get more than one raise a year. Since I had been involved in giving some people three raises in one year, some of the people would have known that I couldn't honestly tell them that one raise was all you could get in a single year. At least I couldn't say that that was consistent with our past—the way things had always been done. So I was told to say that nobody was being hurt and that that was the way things had always been done. I said I couldn't and that we couldn't lie to our people since they'd know it and that would be like asking them to join your lie. You know, you say it and then you see who reacts and mostly people don't say anything because they don't want to get into trouble. Well, I wouldn't say it so my boss announced it. I was there though; I was listening and I didn't say anything.

The scientist in this narrative is sensitive not only to his own complicity in what he considers an unethical act, but also to the complicity of the subordinates who by their silence "join the lie" and consequently reaffirm the implicit theories which generate it. Garfinkel (1967) used the term "reflexivity" to describe the ways in which the very acceptance of the usage of a familiar term or rule, by being understood as intended, reinforces the term of rule's familiarity and further assures the actors of its reality and propriety.

Refusal ceremonies are rather routine occurrences in organizations which through their regularity and importance transmit and reaffirm the organizational culture. They are micropolitical events through which those who invoke facts and arguments, or rules of reason, not sanctioned by the culture—or contemplate the possibility of doing so—are typically brought in line and serve as examples for others. Nevertheless, it must also be suggested that further research on organizational culture should identify the conditions under which the very reaffirmation of culture hardens resistance and provokes redefinition of the underlying structure of power and control.

Intimidation Rituals: Reactions to Reform

Rory O'Day

The reaction of authority in social systems to the reform initiatives of a subordinate is viewed as a series of intimidation rituals. These rituals divide into two major phases, each involving two distinct steps. The first phase, *Indirect Intimidation,* includes the rituals of *nullification and isolation;* the second, *Direct Intimidation,* the rituals of defamation and expulsion. Why these rituals for protest-suppression in organizations are powerful tools in the hands of the middle manager is discussed. Attention is also given to various images projected by the organizational reformer and reasons for resistance to reform from within an organization.

This paper characterizes the reactions of superiors in social systems to a reform-minded subordinate as a series of intimidation rituals. Each successive "ritual of control" represents an escalation in the efforts of authority to discourage an individual (and those who may support him or her) from continuing to seek reform.

MIDDLE MANAGEMENT'S MECHANISM OF CONTROL

The rituals of intimidation satisfy the two primary concerns of authorities confronted by a subordinate who appears not only able to articulate the grievances of a significant number of other system members but also capable of proposing solutions to them. Their

Reprinted with permission from NTL Institute, "Intimidation Rituals: Reactions to Reform," by Rory O'Day, pp. 373–386, *Journal of Applied Behavioral Science,* Vol. 10, No. 3, copyright 1974.

first concern is, of course, to control the reformer so that he does not succeed in recruiting support. Their other concern is to exercise this control in ways that absolve them of any wrongdoing in the matter. The individual in question must be controlled in such a way that he neither continues to be an effective spokesman nor becomes a martyr. When superiors are confronted with a reform-minded subordinate, they want his silence or his absence, whichever is easier to achieve. The "authorities" must also preserve their carefully managed image of reasonableness, and would prefer that the reformer leave voluntarily rather than be removed officially.

For purposes of illustration, this presentation will describe intimidation rituals used by various organizations in the service of protest-suppression, for organizational authorities prefer to *intimidate* a reform-minded individual rather than commit organizational energy to the structural and personnel changes required to transform a "non-conforming enclave" into a legitimate subunit.[1] It is further suggested that an organization undergoes major changes that incorporate and accommodate a group of dissidents only when the intimidation rituals do not succeed in silencing the individuals who constitute the "leading edges" of the reform movement.

In the discussion that follows, I will be concerned primarily with the reformer who emerges from the lower hierarchy in an organization and challenges the *middle hierarchy*. A reformer threatens middle management in three distinctly different ways. The first threat is a function of the validity of his accusations about the inadequacy of specific actions of middle-level members and his suggestions for correcting them. If the reformer is correct, those in the middle will fear that those at the top will punish them when they discover the truth. The second threat comes from the moral challenge presented by such a reformer, for his demand for action will reveal the strength or weakness of middle management's commitment to the organization. And thirdly, the reformer's challenge may indicate to people at the top that middle management is unable to maintain order in its own jurisdiction. To protect their interests, middle-level bureaucrats therefore feel their only defense against reform-minded subordinates is intimidation.[2]

The rituals of intimidation involve two phases: *Indirect Intimidation,* which has two steps, *nullification* and *isolation;* and *Direct Intimidation,* which also comprises two steps, *defamation* and *expulsion.*

PHASE I: INDIRECT INTIMIDATION

Step 1: Nullification

When a reformer first approaches his immediate superiors, they will assure him that his accusations or suggestions are invalid—the result of misunderstandings and misperceptions on his part. His superiors, in this phase, hope that the reformer will be so awed by authority that he will simply take their word that his initiative is based on error. If, however, the reformer insists, his superiors will often agree to conduct an "investigation." The results of such an investigation will convince the reformer that his accusations are groundless and that his suggestions for enhancing organizational effectiveness or revising organizational goals have been duly noted by the appropriate authorities.

Bureaucratic justification for this response usually rests on the argument that this method copes with the system's "crackpots" and "hot-heads," discouraging them from disturbing the smooth, routine functioning of the organization with their crazy ideas and their personal feuds. But middle management also uses these rituals of nullification to handle a potentially explosive (for them and others in the organization) situation quickly and quietly, in order to prevent unfavorable publicity, maintain the organization's state of pluralistic ignorance, and prevent the development of a sympathetic and concerned audience for the reformer's ideas. The explicit message is: "You don't know what you're talking about, but thank you anyway for telling us. We'll certainly look into the matter for you." Members of the middle hierarchy then proceed to cover up whatever embarrassing (for them) truth exists in the reformer's arguments.

The protest-absorption power of the ritual of nullification derives from an element inherent in bureaucracies: the always-attractive opportunity to avoid personal responsibility for one's actions. Thus, if people attempt reform at all, they generally do not proceed beyond the first ritual, which is a process designed to quash the reformer and allow his superiors to reaffirm the collective wisdom of the organization, while clearing their consciences of wrongdoing. Nullification even gets the would-be reformer off the hook—and he may remain grateful to the organization for this added convenience. This shedding of personal responsibility allows the reformer and the authorities alike to compromise in the belief that although it might not be a perfect organizational world, it is nevertheless a self-correcting one.

Repeated exposure to the nullification ritual (the "beating your head against the wall" phenomenon) is expected to convince any sane organizational member that a reformist voice or presence is unwelcome. He is expected to take the hint and stop pestering his superiors with his misguided opinions. Gestures of generosity on the part of the middle hierarchy are not unusual if he decides to leave the organization—and such concern is usually expressed by offering to help the individual find employment opportunities elsewhere.

Step 2: Isolation

If the reformer persists in his efforts, middle management will separate him from his peers, subordinates, and superiors, thereby softening his impact on the organization and making it extremely difficult for him to mobilize any support for his position.

Middle managers argue that these procedures represent the exercise of their rights of office in the service of protecting the organization. But these attempts to isolate the reformer can also be seen as a show of force, as a way of reassuring their own superiors (if they are paying attention), their subordinates, and perhaps themselves that they can maintain order in their own jurisdiction.

Attempts at isolating the reformer include closing his communication links, restricting his freedom of movement, and reducing his allocation of organization resources. If these do not neutralize the reformer, he will be transferred to a less visible position in the organization. In these rituals, the bureaucratic message is: "If you insist on talking about things which you do not understand, then we will have to prevent you from bothering other people with your nonsense."

Systematic unresponsiveness to a reformer's criticism and suggestions is a particularly interesting form of isolation. This lack of response is meant to convince the reformer of the invalidity of his position; but if he presses his right to be heard, it may be used to create a feeling of such impotence that the reformer overreacts in order to elicit a response from his superiors. This overreaction may then be used to demonstrate the reformer's psychological imperfections.

When subjected to organizational isolation, most people come to see the error of their ways or the handwriting on the wall. When an individual learns that there is still time to mend his ways, he usually steps back in line and becomes a silent participant in the organization. When he realizes his career in the organization is at a standstill, he may decide to leave as gracefully as possible while he can still leave under his own steam. Middle managers closest to him then often offer him assistance in finding a new job, with the assurance that "*we* only want what is best for *you*."

Most forms of isolation are designed to persuade the reformer of the futility of trying to initiate change until such time as he is instructed by his superiors to concern himself with change. The reformer practically guarantees his defeat if he reacts to systematic organizational unresponsiveness by confronting his superiors in ways that violate policy or law. The temptation to confront administrative unresponsiveness in dramatic and often self-defeating ways stems in large part from the intense frustration induced by the reformer's belief that systematic unresponsiveness violates his basic rights of freedom of expression and carries with it the implication that he is personally ineffectual (Turner, 1973). Administrative unresponsiveness to what the reformer believes are crucial issues both for himself and for the organization may be sufficiently frustrating to compel him to act, however rashly, in order to clarify the situation. From the administration's point of view, this can be seen as "flushing the rebels out into the open," "giving them enough rope to hang themselves," or, more formally, deviance-heresy conversion (Harshbarger, 1973).

PHASE II: DIRECT INTIMIDATION

Step 3: Defamation

Should the reformer refuse to remain silent, and instead mobilizes support for his position, middle management will begin to impugn his character and his motives. "When legitimate techniques fail—the middle hierarchy might resort to illegitimate or non-legitimate ones" (Leeds, 1964, p. 126). Middle managers will often distort events or even fabricate instances of misconduct in order to intimidate not only the reformer but also those who would listen to or believe him.

Defamation attempts to cut the reformer off from a potentially sympathetic following by attributing his attempts at reform to questionable motives, underlying psychopathology, or gross incompetence. This three-pronged attack is meant to blackmail the reformer into submission and to transform a sympathetic following into a mistrustful crowd of onlookers or an angry mob that feels resentful at having been deceived by the reformer.

From the vantage point of the reformer, the Kafkaesque or Alice-in-Wonderland quality of the rituals of intimidation becomes particularly evident at this time. The reformer finds himself faced with charges which only he and his accusers know are either false or irrelevant in relation to the value of his reform initiatives. The reformer is in a double bind. His superiors will use their offices and positions of trust and responsibility to create the impression in the minds of others in the organization that their accusations of incompetence, self-interest, or psychopathology are true. If the reformer continues in the face of these accusations, he risks being viewed as power-hungry or irrational. If he allows himself to be intimidated by the threat of lies, he allows his superiors to win by default.

One tactic of the superior is to accuse the reformer of acting out his Oedipal conflicts. Such a personalization of a subordinate's reform efforts (especially a younger subordinate) permits his superior to present himself as a harassed "father" faced with a troubled "son," and blocks any examination of his conduct that might reveal provocation on his part. In this way the bureaucrat hopes to persuade others in the organization to respond to the reformer as a sick person in need of therapy or as a child in need of nurturing—a stance that allows him to take on the role of "good father" in relation to other subordinates and to the reformer, if and when the latter capitulates and admits his need for help and guidance.

Rituals of defamation are undertaken by superiors in order to focus attention away from themselves and onto the reformer. The superiors hope that by casting enough doubt on the motives, intentions, and personality of the reformer, enough people in the organization will think that "where there is smoke, there must be fire." The message of this ritual is: "Don't listen to him (his message) because you can't trust a person like him."

Like the rituals of nullification and isolation, the ritual of defamation is both an end in itself and a preliminary to the final ritual of expulsion. The superiors hope by threatening to destroy the reformer's reputation and his character, he will retreat into silence and passivity or leave the organization for greener pastures; if, however, the reformer continues his efforts, his superiors have laid the groundwork for his expulsion.

If the ritual of defamation is undertaken, its target is usually indeed a reformer and not simply a nonconformist or a deviant. His superiors would not need to engage in public tactics of intimidation if there were no substance to his challenge. It is precisely the validity of his reform initiatives that leads his superiors to attempt to destroy his credibility. If this destruction of the reformer's credibility with his peers, subordinates, and top management is effectively conducted, others in the organization will desert his cause and he can be dismissed easily as an undesirable member of the intact organizational team.

Step 4: Expulsion

When neither nullification, isolation, nor defamation can silence the reformer or force his "voluntary withdrawal" from the organization, the middle hierarchy seeks an official decision for his dismissal.

If successful, at least three aims may be achieved thereby. Obviously, by expelling the reformer, his superiors will cut him off from any actual or potential following and weaken any opposition to their authority. An official dismissal also serves as a warning to other budding reformers that middle management has the necessary power and authority to expel troublemakers. Finally, the act of expulsion—a verdict of unfitness—supports the contention that the reformer is an immoral or irrational person.

Of course, the middle hierarchy would prefer the reformer to withdraw voluntarily. Managers want to avoid the public and formal proceedings that often accompany an official request for dismissal of an employee, for the accuser (superior) can often then be scrutinized as carefully as the accused, if the accused person wishes to avail himself of the opportunity. The expulsion ritual involves the formal submission of evidence, the keeping of records, the establishment of independent investigative bodies, and the right of cross-examination, which all function to threaten the image of managers as reasonable, honest, and hardworking servants of the organization. Formal dismissal proceedings are also avoided by middle management because in some fundamental sense they imply that the organization has failed and that they, in particular, have shown themselves unable to maintain order.

THE RITUAL CYCLE ABSORBS AND DESTROYS

Indirect Intimidation attempts to absorb the accusations and suggestions of the reformer, first by depriving him of effectiveness or validity, then by treating him as if he were an "invisible person." The object here is to define the reformer as "harmless." It also attempts to absorb protest by psychologically and physically exhausting the reformer so that he comes to doubt his own experience of reality, his abilities to accomplish the task he sets for himself, and its significance. The authorities hope that the reformer will come to believe the task he has set for himself is humanly impossible and that his fatigue and confusion are the result of his inability to accept human nature for what it is. Short of this, they hope that the reformer will come to feel so inadequate that he will be grateful for continued employment by the organization, in any capacity. ("You're welcome to stay aboard as long as you don't rock the boat.")

Direct Intimidation attempts to destroy protest through destruction of the *character* of the reformer (defamation) or, if necessary, of his *position* in the organization (expulsion). Direct Intimidation represents middle management's active attempt to destroy the reformer as a source of legitimate grievances and suggestions and to terrorize, if necessary, other organizational members. Successful rituals of defamation create a "bad" person, enabling the "good" organization to close ranks once again and benefit from the curative properties of solidarity when he is cast out of the system. In this sense, the ritual destruction of the person (Garfinkel, 1956) necessarily precedes the destruction of his place in the organization.

In sum, Figure 1 portrays the specific cycles of intimidation rituals. Cycle 1 is most preferred by all organizations, while Cycle 4 is the least preferred. Cycle 2 is preferred to Cycle 3.

THE REFORMER IMAGE

Throughout this discussion, the individual subjected to the rituals of intimidation has been referred to as the *reformer,* a generic term for any organizational member who resorts to voice rather than to avoidance when faced with what *he* regards as a situation or organizational deterioration or imperfection. Voice is defined as

> . . . *any attempt at all to change, rather than escape from, an objectionable state of affairs,*
> *whether through individual or collective petition to the management directly in charge, through*
> *appeal to a higher authority with the intention of forcing a change in management, or through*

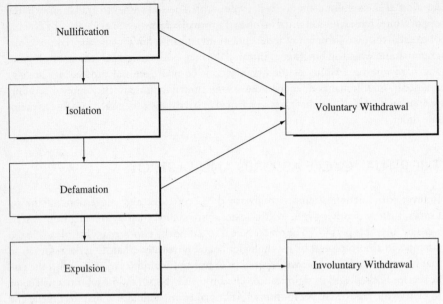

Figure 1.   Cycles of Intimidation Rituals

various types of actions and protests, including those that are meant to mobilize public opinion (Hirschman, 1970, p. 30).

Therefore, in the sense in which it is being used here, "reformer" includes the various meanings contained in such labels as "internal muckraker" or "pure whistle-blower" (Peters & Branch, 1972), "innovator in innovation-resisting organizations" (Shepard, 1969), "crusader for corporate responsibility" (Heilbroner, 1972), "nonconforming individual" (Etzioni, 1961; Leeds, 1964), and "heretic" (Harshbarger, 1973); but it is not intended to include the various meanings inherent in the term "organizational change agent."[3] Thus *"reformer"* refers to any member who acts, in any way and for any reason, to alter the structure and functioning of the organization, when he has *not* been formally delegated authority to institute change.

Why Intimidation Works

From this definition we can see that it is the organization which has the power to define the "reformer" as such, and attaches the stigma to many a well-meaning individual who does not see himself in a protest role. It is often the case that a potential reformer initially thinks of himself or herself only as a hard-working and loyal member of the organization who is simply trying to make things "better" and wishes to be "understood" by busy but well-meaning superiors. However, by the time authorities begin the rituals of defamation, the most naive individual usually realizes that, at least in the eyes of his superiors, he poses a threat to the established order (Herbert, 1972).

The inside reformer is vulnerable to all the intimidation rituals that his particular organization has at its disposal. The reformer outside an organization is usually vulnerable only to the rituals of nullification, isolation (in the form of systematic un-responsiveness), and defamation, unless the organization he is challenging is able to pressure the parent organization into doing the intimidating for it (McCarry, 1972).

Authorities in formal organizations are rarely directly challenged by subordinates. As in the Hans Christian Andersen tale, most individuals do not presume to stand in public judgment of their organizational superiors. Belief in the wisdom and power of the people at the top serves to keep most individuals silent about their grievances concerning the status quo and their ideas (if they have any) for enhancing organizational effectiveness or revising organizational goals. Subordinates do not generally demand, as part of their organizational contractual arrangements, the power to hold their superiors accountable for actions in direct and continuing ways. So intimidation rituals are held to be a last resort—reserved for organizational members who resist, for whatever reason, the usual mechanisms of social control (Millham, Bullock, & Cherrett, 1972).

In their discussion of the obstacles to whistle-blowing, Peters and Branch (1972) include the "loyal-member-of-the-team" trap, the feeling that "going public" is unseemly and embarrassing, and the fear of current and future job vulnerability. Thompson (1968) and Peters and Branch (1972) also refer to the subconscious accommodative device of the "effectiveness trap," an organizational argument that permits its members to avoid conflict on an immediate issue in order to ensure "effectiveness" on some more important issue, at some future time. The curator mentality and emotional detachment generated by the bureaucratic role; the tendency to resort to wishful thinking that organizational deterioration and the consequences of bad policy must soon stop simply because they cannot go on; and the fear that one disagrees with a particular exercise of power only because one is too weak to handle it further contribute to inaction on the part of most "loyal" organizational members (Thompson, 1968).

Reformer as Bad Guy

In point of fact, the protest-absorbing and protest-destroying power of intimidation rituals derives, in large measure, from their infrequent use by organizations. Conversely, if more members were willing to turn their various dissatisfactions into reformist activities, intimidation rituals would lose much of their power.

To understand the effectiveness of organizational intimidation one must examine the reasons why peers and subordinates usually fail to support the reformer, withdraw support, or even actively resist his efforts. Their passive or active resistional members who continue to harbor some doubt about the reformer's guilt, the fear of retaliation against "sympathizers" usually dampens their enthusiasm for the reformer's cause and suppresses all but ritualistic expressions of concern for his plight.

SEIZE THE DAY

It is not possible here to do more than raise the issue of whether one should attempt to change organizations from within or whether one should create alternative organizations. Large formal organizations are going to be with us for a long time to come

(Heilbroner, 1972), and their members are going to have to devise ways to make them more democratic, because there really is no place to run to anymore.

The serious reformer should be prepared to take advantage of organizational crises. He must learn how to recognize, expose, and make concrete those administratively designed arrangements that do not satisfactorily resolve critical problems. For it is in a time of crisis that an organization is open to solutions to the basic problem of survival. Organizational members will be eager to adopt new structures that promise to relieve the uncertainty and anxiety generated by a crisis (Shepard, 1969). If the organization has become weak internally, if it contains corruption and indolence at various levels, if the organization is beset by energy-consuming external pressures, and if the organizational elite lack the resources or the will to initiate changes essential for organizational survival, then the organization might well be ready for successful reform from within (Leeds, 1964). Such an organization might not be capable of successfully administering the intimidation rituals.

Internal organization reform is a difficult process. The cause of reform as well as constructive revolution cannot be served by deluding ourselves as to the ease of restructuring human society (Heilbroner, 1972; Schon, 1973). The reformer's life is not an easy one. But neither need he feel doomed from the start by the inevitability of the success of intimidation rituals mobilized against him.

NOTES

1. "Nonconforming enclave" refers to the existence of number of organizational members who, through collective effort, ". . . could potentially divert organization resources from their current commitments, undermine organizational effectiveness, or form a front capable of capturing control of the organization" (Leeds, 1964, p. 155).
2. In a related context, Etzioni (1961, p. 241) asserts, "Once deviant charisma has manifested itself, despite . . . elaborate preventive mechanisms, counter-processes are set into motion. These are of two kinds: those which attempt to eliminate the deviant charisma; and those which seek to limit its effect."
3. It is possible, however, that an organizational change agent might find himself undergoing the rituals of intimidation if he insists that effective action be taken on his proposals for change, particularly if such action would threaten certain organizational power arrangements.

REFERENCES

Bion, W. R. *Experiences in Groups.* New York: Basic Books, 1959.

Etzioni, A. *A Comparative Analysis of Complex Organizations.* New York: The Free Press, 1961.

Garfinkel, H. "Conditions of Successful Degradation Ceremonies," *American Journal of Sociology,* 1956, *61,* 420–424.

Harshbarger, D. "The Individual and the Social Order: Notes on the Management of Heresy and Deviance in Complex Organizations," *Human Relations,* 1973, *26,* 251–269.

Hartz, L., *The Liberal Tradition in America.* New York: Harcourt, Brace and World, 1955.

Heilbroner, R. L. *In the Name of Profit.* New York: Doubleday, 1972.

Herbert, A. *Soldier.* New York: Holt, Rinehart and Winston, 1972.

Hirschman, A. O. *Exit, Voice, and Loyalty.* Cambridge, Mass.: Harvard University Press, 1970.

Leeds, R. "The Absorption of Protest: a Working Paper," in W. W. Cooper, H. J. Leavitt, and M. W. Shelly, II (Eds.), *New Perspectives in Organization Research.* New York: Wiley, 1964.

McCarry, C. *Citizen Nader.* New York: Saturday Review Press, 1972.

Millham, S., Bullock, R., and Cherrett, P. "Social Control in Organizations," *The British Journal of Sociology,* 1972, *23,* 406–421.

Peters, C., and Branch, T. *Blowing the Whistle: Dissent in the Public Interest.* New York: Praeger, 1972.

Schon, D. S. *Beyond the Stable State.* New York: Norton, 1973.

Shepard, H. A. "Innovation-resisting and Innovation-producing Organizations," in W. G. Bennis, K. D. Benne, and R. Chin (Eds.), *The Planning of Change,* Rev. ed. New York: Holt, Rinehart and Winston, 1969, pp. 519–525.

Slater, P. E. "On Social Regression," *American Sociological Review,* 1963, *29,* 339–364.

Slater, P. E. *The Pursuit of Loneliness.* Boston: Beacon Press, 1970.

Thompson, J. C. "How Could Vietnam Happen? An Autopsy," *Atlantic Monthly,* April 1968, *221* (4), 47–53.

Turner, R. H. "Unresponsiveness as a Social Sanction," *Sociometry,* 1973, *36,* 1–19.

Walzer, M. "Corporate Responsibility and Civil Disobedience," *Dissent,* Sept.–Oct., 1969, pp. 395–406.

Wilcox, H. G. "The Cultural Trait of Hierarchy in Middle Class Children," *Public Administration Review,* 1968, *28,* 222–235.

Two Women, Three Men on a Raft—Part II

Retrospective Commentaries

Robert Schrank

Robert Schrank assesses the Rogue River raft trip . . .

DELIVERANCE

What really happened on the river? Why did the raft flip over? Not until I was back in the comfort of my office did I begin to understand, and the realization of the truth was as shocking as any of the splashes of cold water had been on the Rogue. It became clear to me that not only had I been unhappy with a woman as helmsperson, but also that Bill and I had subconsciously, by habit, proceeded to undermine the women. When one of the other two men was in charge, I was comfortable, supportive, and worked to help him be a better helmsperson. When a woman was at the helm, I seemed to direct my activity at getting her replaced rapidly by one of the men.

A most revealing part of the raft experience, however, was not so much the power relationship between the sexes, which I think I understood, but how Bill and I unconsciously or automatically responded to protect our power from female encroachment. When the trip started, I knew that I might have some difficulty accepting a woman at the helm, but I did not realize that the threat would be so great that I would actually desire to see her fail. On that trip I did something new: I actively tried to sabotage Marlene's and Helen's efforts to lead.

Bill and I were unconsciously building on each woman's doubts about herself with negative reinforcement of her leadership role. The effect of our male, sabotaging behavior was to increase Helen's and Marlene's doubts about themselves as leaders. For each of them, their lifelong conditioning that a woman ought to be a passive sweet thing came into play, and eventually both of them gave up the helm because men "do it better."

If the reader thinks males are just threatened in the outdoors, look what happens to us indoors. First, there is the machismo business, which is a cultural way of granting power to males. To the macho male, it is his role to take care of the woman, particularly in the face of imminent danger, and in the course of things, he should never yield any power. In most organizational settings, the male need to be in charge in the presence of females may be subtle, which may make it harder to identify than on a raft on a swift-flowing river. If all the male readers of this article would write down just one way to undermine the budding woman executive, there would be quite a list.

"Two Women, Three Men on a Raft" by Robert Schrank, *Harvard Business Review*, May–June, 1994, pp. 77–80.

Judging from firsthand experience and reports from other people, I believe that what happened on Raft No. 4, Inc., occurs in most organizations when women enter positions of leadership. An exception might be organizations that have been run by women from their inception. Because organizations are usually designed as pyramids, the moving-up process entails squeezing someone else out. The higher up the pyramid, the more the squeeze. As women enter the squeezing, men are doubly threatened; first, the number of pyramid squeeze players is increasing; second, because the new players are women, our masculinity is on the block. The resentment of men toward women managers is also exacerbated by the realities of a shrunken job market.

As more women become managers in organizations, there will have to be a shift in power. The men who hold that power in fierce competition with each other will not expand the competition by encouraging women to become part of the battle without considerable changes in their own consciousness. In a wilderness setting, all decisions, either one's own or the group's, have immediate consequences, such as being dumped out of the raft, as we saw. The rightness or wrongness of decisions in organizations is not so obvious since they may have no perceptible effects for days or even months. During this time lag, the male unconscious activity can occur to undermine the female.

Will women in administrative positions be supported, ignored, or subconsciously sabotaged by men who find their power threatened? As most experienced administrators know, a major problem in running an organization is directly related to the level of subordinate support. How should the organization go? Straight ahead, hold, turn left, or turn right? These decisions are judgments that may be tough, but the leader must make them; and unless they are supported by the subordinates, they might as well never have been made.

A command of "hard right" can be executed as hard-hard, half-hard, and soft-hard, the last one being equal to just a facade of cooperation. That situation is the most dangerous one for the leader who presumes that orders are being executed, while in fact the raft is foundering. I suspect that one of the reasons that a woman has trouble is because the lack of support she receives from one man gets reinforced by others; it is a collective activity. Things might have been different on Raft No. 4 had we been willing to confront each other. It might have spoiled the fun, but we all might have learned something.

At first, I thought there might not be much of an analogy between navigating a river and a big bureaucracy. Now I think there is. The requirements turn out to be different, and yet the same. The river is more easily understood: how it flows, its hydraulics, its sleepers, or its chutes, and women, like men, can learn these things. A big organization also has sleepers and chutes, but recognizing their existence is a far more political than intellectual task. Women trying to navigate most organizations may find them more complex than the Rogue, but they need to look for similar hazards. The sleepers and chutes will be vested groups of men, who, when their power is threatened, will pull any woman down for tinkering with their interests.

. . . and reassesses the trip 17 years later

After my trip down the Rogue River 17 years ago, I suspected that more had happened there than I realized at first. Only after an extended period of reflection, however, did my conscious mind grasp what my unconscious had known all along—that during the course of the trip I had effectively conspired with John and Bill to sabotage the performance of Helen and Marlene. In the article, I admitted as much.

Before the article appeared, I showed the manuscript to several people, all men. "Really now, Schrank," the response was, "you're not going to publish that foolishness, are you?" But I did, and then other men asked whether I really believed "that crap you wrote" or whether I hadn't made up "all that stuff about what we do to women." I thought their comments suggested that I had somehow betrayed a male tribal secret.

Women have undoubtedly made progress in the corporate workplace since the article first appeared, but certainly not as much as they had expected. We have new laws, rules, and policies relating to women in the workplace, but what we haven't changed much is the male behavior. Women have fallen short in their goals—of crashing through the glass ceiling, for instance—because I think we underestimate the potency of the male need to maintain their power.

Piglet in *Winnie the Pooh* referred to sensing something in an "underneath sort of way." That is hard to do. We can abide scrupulously by the laws, rules, and policies we create in order to assure women an equal opportunity in the corporate workplace and still not overcome the problems that afflicted—and eventually capsized—Raft No. 4.

John and Bill thought that what I wrote was all in my imagination, that it never really happened. "Didn't we try to help them?" they asked. Yes, we did. We told them what to do. We gave them their turns at the helm. We even wrote "left" and "right" on Marlene's hands to help her keep track. But in Piglet's underneath sort of way, we also did everything we could to keep them from succeeding. Why?

Why did our "underneath" behavior conflict so violently with our stated aims? I think it's because we never looked underneath.

When females threaten to move into positions of power, men are threatened twice: first, that they'll lose their authority over the women, and second, that they'll lose prestige and standing with the male, that is, the important, members of the tribe. When I grew up in the Bronx, no self-respecting boy would ever have sponsored a girl into our daily stickball game on the street. Now, as grown businessmen, we still hear that little boy's voice saying, "Hey, get lost. This ain't no girls' game."

We need the laws affirming women's rights. We need the rules and the regulations. But we can't mistake the proclamation of equal opportunity for the realization of it.

I think what we have to do, especially we men, is keep trying to get to our underneath side. Instincts and hormones are mysterious things, not easily understood—and not an excuse for anything. But they are a reason for certain behavior. We need to understand more about what motivates the behavior that lies underneath our surface actions and intentions. Not so that we can justify it, but so that we can change it.

FAITH WOHL *retired at the end of 1993 as a director of human resources at DuPont after a 20-year career at the company. She is now with the U.S. General Services Administration in Washington, D.C., where, as director of workplace initiatives, she oversees child care, elder care, and telecommuting for federal employees.*

The adventure on the Rogue River contains an old and a new lesson. As it describes the behavior of women and men in a work situation, it could have happened yesterday—or perhaps tomorrow—instead of nearly 20 years ago. That constancy is what makes the article a classic.

As a woman who has worked in the business world since the 1950s, I know that what Bob Schrank experienced on the river happens every day in a regular work setting. Sexual tensions and attractions still intrude; men still undermine women unconsciously and deliberately; women still diminish themselves through lack of confidence or experience; and men *and* women are still leery of seeing women in leadership roles. Schrank was right in his revelation—startling as it seemed in the 1970s—that even when you substitute Armanis for Mae Wests, the male-female conflict persists.

I remember reading the article when it first appeared and seeing it as a mirror that showed clearly what was happening all around me and my female colleagues. We all knew with the conviction of our own personal experience and disappointment that it was just these behaviors that would keep us women from climbing the corporate ladder. Men would act to preserve their positions of power, and they knew how to do that with behaviors both subtle and obvious.

Today I read the story quite differently. Now I see it as a tale about what happens when managers fail to create the environment in which a diverse team can achieve trust and mutual respect. The result was there in a throwaway line in the story—the raft lost its place in line. Translation: it lost competitive position. Perhaps in the smoother waters of the 1970s, when growth and success seemed infinitely possible, the raft could find another line and try again. Today the discipline of the marketplace would likely leave the raft on a rock, as it has left so many well-known enterprises recently.

So Schrank's revealing anecdote is really about what happens when management fails to address critical human resource issues in the "permanent white water" that one leading management consultant has defined as today's business climate.

Why did this happen on the raft, and what can we learn from it? It was clear that the men were interested only in being in charge. Oddly, they saw that in the role of helmsman (helmsperson, in clunky 1970s politically correct talk). Yet the helmsman wasn't really in charge. In fact, on that raft, no one was in charge except, perhaps, the river. As the men struggled to take over and colluded against the women so they could give their simplistic orders, they were living out the now-outdated command-and-control style of large bureaucratic organizations. Today's rapids demand something very different—highly responsive work teams whose members can act independently and collectively without being "led" by an order giver.

Read in the context of the 1990s, this classic reveals many points that should concern us. It shows us that diversity cannot be a "flavor-of-the-month" program. Business has talked the language of diversity for the last 20 years without really getting the message. In fact, diversity is a key business strategy that must be learned and practiced because it is linked to the success of the venture. It shows us that creating a team is a complex problem that entails more than simply assigning a group of people to a common task. Creating the environment in which a team can develop from a group of individuals demands thoughtful effort. And the story shows us that success will elude all ventures, whether boating or business, led by people who do not understand these lessons, especially when the current is as swift and the water is as roiled as it is in the business world today.

SHEILA WELLINGTON *is president of Catalyst, the independent not-for-profit organization that works with business and the professions to effect change for women through research, advisory services, and communication.*

While the Bill, Bob, and John of 1994 might still behave as corrosively as they did in 1977, a trip down the Rogue River today would reveal a much changed Marlene and Helen. They wouldn't for a minute sit back passively and let the men take over the helm because they are "so much better" at steering. In the last 17 years, women have learned a few things. One of them is that leading a business today has very little to do with white-water rafting and shooting the rapids.

The metaphor of Raft No. 4 is dated. The world of enterprise no longer revolves around the physical strength of the male hunter who slays the beast and drags it home (or the prowess of the river navigator, for that matter). Today's successful business "warrior" is marked by an awareness of the changing world and the leadership and team-building skills that bespeak brains, not brawn, metaphorical or otherwise.

The Marlenes and Helens of today are just as educated as the Bills and Bobs, if not more so. In 1991, women earned more bachelor's degrees (53.9%) and master's degrees (53.5%) than men (compared with 46.1% and 47% respectively in 1977). They also earned 43% of all law degrees (up from 22.4% in 1977) and more than one-third of all MBAs (compared with just one out of seven in 1977).

Furthermore, women have entered the ranks of corporate management. The percentage of executive, administrative, and managerial employees who are female has exploded from a mere 2.5% in 1977 to 42% in 1993. Although women have not attained the highest reaches of corporate management in large numbers, there is a critical mass in the pipeline. In 1977, 46 women were directors of America's leading corporations. Today there are 500 such women—not nearly enough, to be sure, but more than ten times as many as 15 years ago.

I won't rule out the possibility that one or more of the men on the raft might have changed, too, in 17 years. Many progressive companies today are led by men who have responded positively to the challenge of assimilating women into their workplaces. They're smart enough to seek the best talent in whatever shape, size, and color it comes. They know that if Marlene and Helen don't get their turn at the helm and the support they need to do the job, there's a good chance that at least one of them will leave to paddle her own canoe. (By the way, fellas, it just might turn out to be an ocean liner.) Such leaders have come to realize that we're all in the same raft and that whether or not we stay dry depends less on the brawn of the helmsperson than on the collective skill of the team and its members.

ELEANOR PETERSEN *was the first woman chair of the Illinois Fair Employment Practices Commission, a founder and officer of a federal savings and loan created to make mortgage loans to minorities, and founder and president of the Donors Forum of Chicago, a regional association of grant makers. She has been retired for eight years and lives in Chicago.*

I was "Helen" in Bob Schrank's raft, and when I read his article in this magazine 17 years ago, it made me angry. I was angry at Bob and the other two men for the games they'd played, and I was very angry—and chagrined—at my own failure to realize what was going on. It took the article to show me just how loaded the deck had been against us.

Now, 17 years later, I'm still angry. Not at Bob, whose insight into his own behavior was illuminating and, in fact, courageous, and no longer at myself, because I have worked hard to make things better for women and minorities. I am angry at U.S. society. I am impatient and discouraged at how little progress we have made in almost 20 years. I have come to believe that the power structures of our political, educational, and corporate institutions are deeply conservative and authoritarian, that the authorities they conserve are still overwhelmingly male and white, and that change is insultingly slow.

It takes time, we're told, to rise through the pipeline in any profession or organization. How much time? Women have been pushing hard against the glass ceiling on business promotions for at least 30 years, but 30 years is not enough. Blacks have been pressing for equal opportunity since the end of the Civil War, but five generations is not enough. The suffragist movement began its struggle for equal political rights more than a century ago, and we now have 7 women senators out of 100. Are we supposed to be proud of that achievement? Wouldn't shame be a more appropriate reaction? The pipeline argument is a sham and a disgrace.

For many years, I've worked with foundations. Over the last two decades, in order to get more money for women, we've made a huge, successful effort to get foundations to hire more women and an equal, much *less* successful effort to move them up to decision-making jobs and to seats on foundation boards. In that whole 20 years, foundation grants to women's and girls' organizations have risen from 3% of total foundation giving—to 4%. So now, at last, women have begun to set up their own foundations, run by women to raise money for women.

Women, especially young women, have to start doing the same kind of thing in business and politics, because the pace of "acceptable" change is too courteous, too ladylike, too accommodating. Many in my generation went along with that leisurely, unproductive rate of change, exactly the way Marlene and I went along in that raft. We let the men take care of us. We allowed ourselves to be comfortable and irresponsible. We were all victims, of course, men and women alike, because instead of learning new skills and new ways to work together, we all just repeated old roles in an old, authoritarian world.

Today I would no longer let that happen. I would make myself take the helm and the responsibility no matter how frightened I was. And I would make the men give it to me. You can't bring about change politely. You have to be tough. You have to be rude.

Before the civil rights movement, people said to blacks, "Don't try to move too fast." But after 100 years of waiting, they lost patience and so took change into their own hands. Women must do the same.

Organizational Survivors: Images of Women in the Office Folklore of Contemporary Organizations

Linda C. Forbes and Elizabeth Bell

In offices all across the U.S., employees are openly criticizing workplace practices. These critiques are scathing indictments of organizational values, hierarchies of power and privilege, and work-a-day stresses. Unlike the happy hour "gripe session," this organization-bashing goes on in plain sight, like an "I Spy" game, under the very noses of management. This brutal criticism, at the expense of the organization, is also expensive to the organization, appropriating company time, resources, and energies.

"Office folklore"—outrageous cartoons, parodies of company policy, and pithy one-liners—is wordprocessed, photocopied, faxed, and posted in millions of offices across the U.S.[1] The bulbous character clutching its sides in hysterical laughter, captioned "YOU WANT IT WHEN?!!," is a staple of office life.

This essay is an invitation to take a second and a critical look at the bulletin boards, doors, and walls of contemporary organizations. The creative and communally created

Figure 1.

YOU WANT IT WHEN?!

"Organizational Survivors: Images of Women in the Office Folklore of Contemporary Organizations" by Linda C. Forbes and Elizabeth Bell, March 1996.

messages of office folklore serve as humorous, but also serious, reminders of the gaps between organizational "realities" and organizational "ideals." The levels of hilarity and hostility drawn on the textual bodies of office folklore are surprising, as the images argue graphically and metaphorically against the rhythms, rationality, and discourse of bureaucracies.

THE WOMEN OF OFFICE FOLKLORE

For managers who undergo weeks of management training, often with questionable reward, the following item encapsulates a multitude of frustrations.For subordinates, the cartoon aptly captures managerial lack of commonsense and real world viewpoints. This cartoon is also an example of how organizational members can be "trained" to overlook the obvious in their offices: Office folklore blends into the background, like grey carpeting and "Please Post" memoranda, of everyday organizational life.

While the people depicted in "Welcome, Gentleman, to Advanced Management Training" are typically drawn as white, middle-aged, male managers, this essay looks at another "genre" of office folklore which often portrays unflattering images of women— posted by women. The pictures of women in these collections are not pretty ones. Unlike the once popular shopfloor pin-up girl, or the perfectly dressed and coiffed "working women" of contemporary advertising, images of women in office folklore are frequently loud, abrasive, and grotesque. For the woman who posts Figure 3 on the bulletin board behind her, it is a backdrop, a mirror, and a vent for her frustration. Most important, it responds to the vagaries of organizational life in a way that she cannot.

Figure 2.

"WELCOME, GENTLEMEN, TO ADVANCED MANAGEMENT TRAINING."

I try to take just
ONE DAY AT A TIME...

but lately several days
have attacked me at once

Figure 3.

Why are the images of men and women so different in these items? In an attempt to answer this question, we spent several months walking our own organization, collecting items of office folklore, and talking with the women of the support staff who participate in creating and disseminating office folklore. Notably, these are not "women *in* management," but women who are managed.[2]

As we chatted in their front-stage workspaces, usually about an item posted in front of us, women brought their collections out of file drawers and file folders, pouring over them with the attention and pride usually reserved for baby pictures. The comic self-portraits they post on bulletin boards and doors not only paint a powerful critique of organizational life as viewed from the bottom, but serve to question organizational operating assumptions. In the following textual analysis of the visual and verbal messages about organizational women, office folklore is vivid testimony to the personal costs of organizational survival.[3]

THE WOMEN OF OFFICE FOLKLORE AND ORGANIZATIONAL ASSUMPTIONS

The images in office folklore challenge a number of *assumptions* about organizations, their structure, purpose, and pace. These taken-for-granted assumptions about organizations are often unspoken commitments, rules internalized by company members, that

Figure 4.

guide and control organizational behaviors. The women drawn in office folklore, however, do not take these controlling practices "lying down."

Assumption #1: Organizations Are Ruled by the Time Clock

Bodies in organizations have traditionally been viewed as resources to be controlled and harnessed by the organization. The lower these bodies are within the company hierarchy, the more they are controlled: time clocks, breaks, bathroom privileges, and lunch hours are evidence of the ways in which bodies are tied to work stations and ruled by the "factory whistle" and alarm clock.[4]

The images of women in office folklore are not ruled by the time clock, but instead by the biological rhythms of PMS (Pre-Menstrual Syndrome). Even though there is no woman pictured in Figure 4, PMS is an exclusively female ailment. This painfully thin, regal, yet haughty cat challenges the viewer in three ways: pre-menstrual syndrome is a given, although it is largely misunderstood by both men and the medical community. Although the cat does not hold a gun, the image implies that looks can indeed kill. And "Any questions?" is more of a challenge than an invitation. This cartoon captures PMS as a time of irritability, instability, and intolerance—a time that pays no attention and gives no power to organizational time clocks.

Assumption #2: Organizations Are Places of Rationality

The rational, orderly, and well-structured organization has no room for emotionality, chaos, and violence[5]—except in the images of women posted on the walls and bulletin boards. Figure 5 recalls the Dirty Harry antics of Clint Eastwood, but places the gun in the hands of a comically demented office worker. Despite the efforts of the NRA (National Rifle Association)and the magazine *Women and Guns,* the image of a woman with a gun is still an incongruous one and a "safe" caricature in the office. The image of a man with a gun in the office, however, seems dangerously and frighteningly real. The irrational and violent in office folklore are counterpoints to the rationality and order of organizational structures—but all safely trapped in $8\frac{1}{2} \times 11''$ frames.

Assumption #3: Organizations Are Places of Work and Economic Activity

Ruled by the bottom line and market share, organizations are governed and driven by an economic rationality. Instead of profit and loss statements, however, office folklore paints a portrait of the physical and emotional costs for support staff personnel. The title, "Support Staff Burn-Out," and physical maladies paint this woman as an organizational veteran, an NCO long accustomed to life in the bureaucratic trenches. She has

Figure 5.

GO AHEAD, LAY SOMETHING
ELSE ON MY DESK!

paid the price for her company's market share and profitability, not with her work alone, but with her body. This woman is not the victim of economic rationality, but a survivor of it.

Assumption #4: Organizations Are Slow, Thoughtful, and Deliberate Agencies of Change

Change, whether systems, operations, or products, occurs at a snail's pace in organizations always tempered by thoughtful deliberation. One woman-centered item deliberately subverts this image of organizations: The streamlined image of a car is both quantified and technologized in the office "bitch." The speed at which she can be invoked

Figure 6.

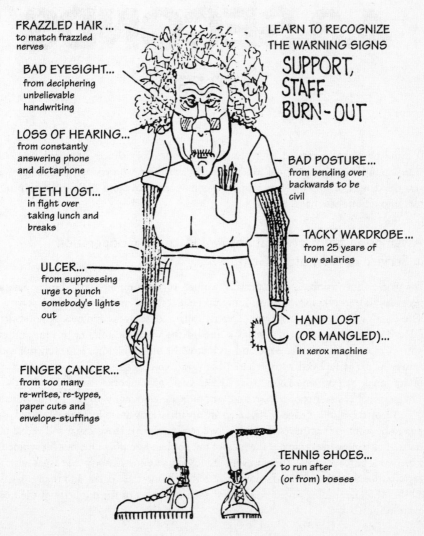

FRAZZLED HAIR ...
to match frazzled
nerves

BAD EYESIGHT...
from deciphering
unbelievable
handwriting

LOSS OF HEARING...
from constantly
answering phone
and dictaphone

TEETH LOST...
in fight over
taking lunch and
breaks

ULCER...
from suppressing
urge to punch
somebody's lights
out

FINGER CANCER...
from too many
re-writes, re-types,
paper cuts and
envelope-stuffings

LEARN TO RECOGNIZE
THE WARNING SIGNS
SUPPORT,
STAFF
BURN-OUT

BAD POSTURE...
from bending over
backwards to be
civil

TACKY WARDROBE...
from 25 years of
low salaries

HAND LOST
(OR MANGLED)...
in xerox machine

TENNIS SHOES...
to run after
(or from) bosses

—— WARNING ——

I CAN GO FROM

0 TO BITCH IN

4.3 SECONDS

(OR LESS)

Figure 7.

is mind-boggling compared to typical bureaucratic sluggishness, the "red tape" and "run-around" of organizational functioning. All of these women-centered images suggest the danger of the hysterical woman—one wrong move and the organization tumbles into emotional chaos.

Assumption #5: Organizations Are Places of Cooperation in Service of Corporate Goals

For women in organizations, especially women of the support staff, the cooperation necessary for accomplishing organizational goals often demands a kind of servitude. The "girl" who brings the coffee, screens calls and visitors, and sets appointments ("Have your girl call my girl") walks a fine line between the roles of servant and employee, mother and worker, wife and secretary.[6] In office folklore, however, the cooperative helper is replaced with irritated body and voice: Figure 8 is a far cry from the professional, helpful, and cooperative "Kelly Girl" of temporary agencies' advertising. The personal costs of cooperation and servitude are eloquently voiced in this portrait.

All of these folk images of women in organizations are photocopied, faxed, and posted by women themselves. They are vivid reminders that these visual and verbal portraits of clerical workers are not the men of the Fordian assembly line, but the women of paperwork bureaucracies. These images argue *eloquently, collectively, and safely* with the organizational tendency to reduce women to their work, their desks, and their job titles, all the while reminding organizations and their members of the duplicity of their own assumptions.

4. For further reading on control of the body in organizations, see Joan Acker, "Gendering Organizational Theory" in Albert J. Mills and Peta Tancred, *Gendering Organizational Analysis* (Newbury Park: Sage, 1992), 248–260.

5. For an implicit discussion of organizations as "bulwarks against chaos," see Barry A. Turner, "The Symbolic Understanding of Organizations," in Michael Reed and Michael Hughes, eds., *Rethinking Organizations* (London: Sage, 1992), 46–66.

6. For a treatment of the roles secretaries, receptionists, and gatekeepers assume, see Rosemary Pringle, *Secretaries Talk* (London: verso, 1988).

7. Donna Haraway, *Simians, Cyborgs, and Women: The Reinvention of Nature* (New York: Routledge, 1991), p 166.

8. Michel deCerteau argues for an acknowledgment of the creative and dynamic ways people negotiate through cultural structures. This negotiation is both strategic and tactical: strategies "produce, tabulate, and impose" the structural places of power, while "tactics use, manipulate, and divert those spaces." In *The Practice of Everyday Life,* trans. Steven Rendall (Berkeley: University of California Press, 1984), p 30.

9. William Bascom, "The Functions of Folklore," in Alan Dundes, ed., *The Study of Folklore* (Englewood Cliffs, N.J.: Prentice-Hall, 1965), 279–298.

10. For an extended analysis of office folklore as opportunities to resist the partitions of hierarchy, time, and space in organizational life, see Elizabeth Bell and Linda C. Forbes, "Office Folklore in the Academic Paperwork Empire: The Interstitial Space of Gendered (Con)Texts," *Text and Performance Quarterly* 14 (1994): 181–196.

"When I Woke Up This Morning
I Had One Nerve Left,
And Damned If You Ain't Got On It!"

Figure 8.

Señor Payroll

William E. Barrett

Larry and I were Junior Engineers in the gas plant, which means that we were clerks. Anything that could be classified as paperwork came to that flat double desk across which we faced each other. The Main Office downtown sent us a bewildering array of orders and rules that were to be put into effect.

Junior Engineers were beneath the notice of everyone except the Mexican-American laborers at the plant. To them we were the visible form of a distant, unknowable paymaster. We were Señor Payroll.

THE POLITICS OF OFFICE FOLKLORE

While organizational members may be laughing, joining together to create these portraits of work that illustrate the gap between organizational "realities" and organizational "ideals," the politics of office folklore are deadly serious. Single motherhood, two-income families, and middle-aged women caught between childcare and caring for elderly relatives are economic, and daily, realities. Combined with corporate downsizing, the shift to temporary and contract labor, and globalization, suddenly work is "feminized, whether performed by men or women":

> *To be feminized means to be made extremely vulnerable; able to be disassembled, reassembled, exploited as a reserve labour force; seen less as workers than as servers; subjected to time arrangements on and off the paid job that make a mockery of a limited work day; leading an existence that always borders on being obscene, out of place, and reducible to sex.*[7]

Office folklore is more than a humorous response to this feminization, it is the active creation of resourceful people who seek to make organizational life habitable.[8]

"Mary had to call in dead today. She's used
up all her sick days."

Figure 9.

All traditional folklore—whether tales, jokes, songs, or rituals—serves four purposes: to entertain, to educate, to validate culture, and to control individuals. Office folklore, however, is especially illustrative of folklore's basic paradox:

> *Even while [folklore] plays a vital role in transmitting and maintaining the institutions of a culture and enforcing the individual to conform to them, at the same time it provides socially approved outlets for the repressions which these same institutions impose on him [sic].*[9]

Office folklore is one "socially approved outlet" for critiquing the "repressions" of organizational life.

While it may be tempting to wander the office, diagnosing organizational diseases posted over the coffee machine and photocopier, neither the study of folklore nor organizational culture is a forensic medicine. The "symptoms" of organizational dis/ease might better be viewed as an art of organizational living. A step back from the "little pictures" on bulletin boards can reveal several "big pictures" of organizational landscapes. The very presence of office folklore can be framed and interpreted in the following ways:

- **Office folklore is evidence of creativity.** These resources do not belong to the organization, but to its members. Office folklore is a reminder that organizations purchase the talents and time of their members; and workers return the favor. Rather than succumbing to technology as dehumanizing and enslaving, these same technologies are borrowed from, and paid back to, the organization in $8\frac{1}{2} \times 11''$ expressions of organizational culture.
- **Office folklore is evidence of community.** This is an *esprit de corps* that goes beyond job titles and the organizational chart, crossing hierarchial lines, times, and spaces.[10] No corporate mandate could create or regulate this camaraderie.

- **Office folklore is evidence of ownership.** Employees help make the organization habitable and comfortable within the rigid walls of corporate structure. Office folklore is a kind of wallpaper, individually and communally recreated, on the crawlspaces of organizational life.
- **Office folklore is evidence of pleasure and play at work.** While organizational control and its resistance has been theorized in critiques of industrialization and capitalism, office folklore testifies to the ways that people play at their work and work at their play. The political division between work and play is just that—political.

These conclusions, however, can all be reversed. Office folklore can be argued as evidence of groupthink and sloganeering, of a bumper sticker mentality in a t-shirt world. Office folklore is insubordination, at best, and sabotage, at worst; it offers criticism without constructive ideas for change. Office folklore is deliberate pilfering and petty theft. It is a continual and costly drain of company resources and company time. Office folklore is inappropriate, bawdy, and distasteful—neither work nor play.

Both sets of conclusions paint a fundamentally different view of workers and managerial attitudes toward them. Like the various interpretations of "Welcome, Gentlemen, to Advanced Management Training," the "truth" of the organizational world, and its various constructions, lies somewhere in between. In between individual and organization, control and resistance, work and play, rigid rules and flexible tolerance is the crawlspace of office folklore.

NOTES

1. For a broad sampling of the many forms of office folklore and urban folklore, see the following collections: Alan Dundes and Carl R. Pagter, *Never Try to Teach a Pig to Sing: Still More Urban Folklore from the Paperwork Empire* (Detroit: Wayne State University Press, 1991); *Urban Folklore from the Paperwork Empire* (Austin: American Folklore Society, 1975); *When You're Up to Your Ass in Alligators: More Urban Folklore from the Paperwork Empire* (Detroit: Wayne State University Press, 1987); and the works of Nicholas Locke, who labels his collections "office graffiti": *You Want it When?!!: The Complete Office Graffiti* (London: Proteus, 1979) and *Office Grafitti 2* (London: Proteus, 1981).

2. In our initial fieldwork, we did not set out to talk only with women. But we soon discovered that most clerical and reception positions in our organization were filled by women. 1987 statistics from the U.S. Labor Department reveal that 99.1% of secretaries employed in the United States were women; 94.6% of typists were women. See Evelyn Nakano Glenn and Roslyn L. Feldberg, "Clerical Work: The Female Occupation," in Jo Freeman, ed., *Women: A Feminist Perspective* (Mountain View, Calif.: Mayfield, 1989), 287–311.

3. The "lessons" available in folktales are always open to interpretation. Much recent work in folktales, for example, concentrates on the gender-based lessons and how girls and boys are socialized differently in folktales. See, for example, Jack Zipes, *Don't Bet on the Prince* (New York: Routledge, 1987) and Ruth Bottigheimer, *Grimms' Bad Girls and Bold Boys: The Moral and Social Vision of the Tales* (New Haven: Yale University Press, 1977).

Those Mexican-Americans were great workmen: the aristocrats among them were the stokers, big men who worked Herculean eight-hour shifts in the fierce heat of the retorts. They scooped coal with huge shovels and hurled it with uncanny aim at tiny doors. The coal streamed out from the shovels like black water from a high pressure nozzle, and never missed the narrow opening. The stokers worked stripped to the waist, and there was pride and dignity in them. Few men could do such work, and they were the few.

The Company paid its men only twice a month, on the fifth and on the twentieth. To a Mexican-American, this was absurd. What man with money will make it last 15 days? If he hoarded money beyond the spending of three days, he was a miser—and when, Señor, did the blood of Spain flow in the veins of misers? Hence it was the custom for our stokers to appear every third or fourth day to draw the money due to them.

There was a certain elasticity in the Company rules, and Larry and I sent the necessary forms to the Main Office and received an "advance" against a man's paycheck. Then, one day, Downtown favored us with a memorandum:

"There have been too many abuses of the advance-against-wages privilege. Hereafter, no advance against wages will be made to any employee except in a case of genuine emergency."

We had no sooner posted the notice when in came stoker Juan Garcia. He asked for an advance. I pointed to the notice. He spelled it through slowly, then said, "What does this mean, this 'genuine emergency'?"

I explained to him patiently that the Company was kind and sympathetic, but that it was a great nuisance to have to pay wages every few days. If someone was ill or if money was urgently needed for some other good reason, then the Company would make an exception to the rule.

Juan Garcia turned his hat over and over slowly in his big hands. "I do not get my money?"

"Next payday, Juan. On the 20th."

He went out silently and I felt ashamed of myself. I looked across the desk at Larry. He avoided my eyes.

In the next hour two other stokers came in, looked at the notice, had it explained and walked solemnly out; then no more came. What we did not know was that Juan Garcia, Pete Mendoza and Francisco Gonzalez had spread the word and that every Mexican-American in the plant was explaining the order to every other Mexican-American. "To get the money now, the wife must be sick. There must be medicine for the baby."

The next morning Juan Garcia's wife was practically dying, Pete Mendoza's mother would hardly last the day, there was a veritable epidemic among children and, just for variety, there was one sick father. We always suspected that the old man was really sick; no Mexican-American would otherwise have thought of him. At any rate, nobody paid Larry and me to examine private lives; we made out our forms with an added line describing the "genuine emergency." Our people got paid.

That went on for a week. Then came a new order, curt and to the point: "Hereafter employees will be paid ONLY on the fifth and the 20th of the month. No exceptions will be made except in the cases of employees leaving the service of the Company."

The notice went up on the board and we explained its significance gravely. "No, Juan Garcia, we cannot advance your wages. It is too bad about your wife and your cousins and your aunts, but there is a new rule."

Juan Garcia went out and thought it over. He thought out loud with Mendoza and Gonzales and Ayala, then, in the morning, he was back. "I am quitting this company for different job. You pay me now?"

We argued that it was a good company and that it loved its employees like children, but in the end we paid off, because Juan Garcia quit. And so did Gonzales, Mendoza, Obregon, Ayala and Ortez, the best stokers, men who could not be replaced.

Larry and I looked at each other; we knew what was coming in about three days. One of our duties was to sit on the hiring line early each morning, engaging transient workers for the handy gangs. Any man was accepted who could walk up and ask for a job without falling down. Never before had we been called upon to hire such skilled virtuosos as stokers for handy gang work, but we were called upon to hire them now.

The day foreman was wringing his hands and asking the Almighty if he was personally supposed to shovel this condemned coal, while there in a stolid, patient line were skilled men—Garcia, Mendoza and others—waiting to be hired. We hired them, of course. There was nothing else to do.

Every day we had a line of resigning stokers, and another line of stokers seeking work. Our paperwork became very complicated. At the Main Office they were jumping up and down. The procession of forms showing Juan Garcia's resigning and being hired over and over again was too much for them. Sometimes Downtown had Garcia on the payroll twice at the same time when someone down there was slow in entering a resignation. Our phone rang early and often.

Tolerantly and patiently we explained: "There's nothing we can do if a man wants to quit, and if there are stokers available when the plant needs stokers, we hire them."

Out of chaos, Downtown issued another order. I read it and whistled. Larry looked at it and said, "It is going to be very quiet around here."

The order read: "Hereafter, no employee who resigns may be rehired within a period of 30 days."

Juan Garcia was due for another resignation, and when he came in we showed him the order and explained that standing in line the next day would do him no good if he resigned today. "Thirty days is a long time, Juan."

It was a grave matter and he took time to reflect on it. So did Gonzales, Mendoza, Ayala and Ortez. Ultimately, however, they were all back—and all resigned.

We did our best to dissuade them and we were sad about the parting. This time it was for keeps and they shook hands with us solemnly. It was very nice knowing us. Larry and I looked at each other when they were gone and we both knew that neither of us had been pulling for Downtown to win this duel. It was a blue day.

In the morning, however, they were all back in line. With the utmost gravity, Juan Garcia informed me that he was a stoker looking for a job.

"No dice, Juan" I said. "Come back in 30 days. I warned you."

His eyes looked straight into mine without a flicker. "There is some mistake, Señor," he said. "I am Manuel Hernandez. I work as the stoker in Pueblo, in Santa Fe, in many places."

I stared back at him, remembering the sick wife and the babies without medicine, the mother-in-law in the hospital, the many resignations and the rehirings. I knew that there was a gas plant in Pueblo, and that there wasn't any in Santa Fe; but who was I to argue with a man about his own name? A stoker is a stoker.

So I hired him. I hired Gonzalez, too, who swore that his name was Carrera, and Ayala, who had shamelessy become Smith.

Three days later, the resigning started.

Within a week our payroll read like a history of Latin America. Everyone was on it: Lopez and Obregon, Villa, Diaz, Batista, Gomez, and even San Martin and Bolivar. Finally Larry and I, growing weary of staring at familiar faces and writing unfamiliar names, went to the Superintendent and told him the whole story. He tried not to grin, and said, "Damned nonsense!"

The next day the orders were taken down. We called our most prominent stokers into the office and pointed to the board. No rules any more.

"The next time we hire you *hombres*," Larry said grimly, "come in under the names you like best, because that's the way you are going to stay on the books."

They looked at us and they looked at the board; then for the first time in the long duel, their teeth flashed white. *"Si, Señores,"* they said.

And so it was.

The Catbird Seat

James Thurber

Mr. Martin bought the pack of Camels on Monday night in the most crowded cigar store on Broadway. It was theater time and seven or eight men were buying cigarettes. The clerk didn't even glance at Mr. Martin, who put the pack in his overcoat pocket and went out. If any of the staff at F & S had seen him buy the cigarettes, they would have been astonished, for it was generally known that Mr. Martin did not smoke, and never had. No one saw him.

It was just a week to the day since Mr. Martin had decided to rub out Mrs. Ulgine Barrows. The term "rub out" pleased him because it suggested nothing more than the correction of an error—in this case an error of Mr. Fitweiler. Mr. Martin had spent each night of the past week working out his plan and examining it. As he walked home now he went over it again. For the hundredth time he resented the element of imprecision, the margin of guesswork that entered into the business. The project as he had worked it out was casual and bold, the risks were considerable. Something might go wrong anywhere along the line. And therein lay the cunning of his scheme. No one would ever see in it the cautious, painstaking hand of Erwin Martin, head of the filing department of F & S, of whom Mr. Fitweiler had once said, "Man is fallible but Martin isn't." No one would see his hand, that is, unless it were caught in the act.

Sitting in his apartment, drinking a glass of milk, Mr. Martin reviewed his case against Mrs. Ulgine Barrows, as he had every night for seven nights. He began at the beginning. Her quacking voice and braying laugh had first profaned the halls of F & S on March 7, 1941 (Mr. Martin had a head for dates). Old Roberts, the personnel chief, had introduced her as the newly appointed special adviser to the president of the firm, Mr. Fitweiler. The woman had appalled Mr. Martin instantly, but he hadn't shown it. He had given her his dry hand, a look of studious concentration, and a faint smile. "Well," she had said, looking at the papers on his desk, "are you lifting the ox-cart out of the ditch?" As Mr. Martin recalled that moment, over his milk, he squirmed slightly. He must keep his mind on her crimes as a special adviser, not on her pecca-dillos as a personality. This he found difficult to do, in spite of entering an objection and sustaining it. The faults of the woman as a woman kept chattering on in his mind like an unruly witness. She had, for almost two years now, baited him. In the halls, in the elevator, even in his own office, into which she romped now and then like a circus horse, she was constantly shouting these silly questions at him. "Are you lifting the ox-cart out of that ditch? Are you tearing up the pea patch? Are you hollering down the rain barrel? Are you scraping around the bottom of the pickle barrel? Are you sitting in the catbird seat?"

It was Joey Hart, one of Mr. Martin's two assistants, who had explained what the gibberish meant. "She must be a Dodger fan," he had said. "Red Barber announces the Dodger games over the radio and he uses those expressions—picked 'em up down South." Joey had gone on to explain one or two. "Tearing up the pea patch" meant going on a rampage; "sitting in the catbird seat" meant sitting pretty, like a batter with three balls and no strikes on him. Mr. Martin dismissed all this with an effort. It had been annoying, it had driven him near to distraction, but he was too solid a man to be moved to murder by anything so childish. It was fortunate, he reflected as he passed on to the important charges against Mrs. Barrows, that he had stood up under it so well. He had maintained always an outward appearance of polite tolerance. "Why, I even believe you like the woman," Miss Paird, his other assistant, had once said to him. He had simply smiled.

A gavel rapped in Mr. Martin's mind and the case proper was resumed. Mrs. Ulgine Barrows stood charged with willful, blatant, and persistent attempts to destroy the efficiency and system of F & S. It was competent, material, and relevant to review her advent and rise to power. Mr. Martin had got the story from Miss Paird, who seemed always able to find things out. According to her, Mrs. Barrows had met Mr. Fitweiler at a party, where she had rescued him from the embraces of a powerfully built drunken man who had mistaken the president of F & S for a famous retired Middle Western football coach. She had led him to a sofa and somehow worked upon him a monstrous magic. The aging gentleman had jumped to the conclusion there and then that this was a woman of singular attainments, equipped to bring out the best in him and in the firm. A week later he had introduced her into F & S as his special adviser. On that day confusion got its foot in the door. After Miss Tyson, Mr. Brundage, and Mr. Bartlett had been fired and Mr. Munson had taken his hat and stalked out, mailing in his resignation later, old Roberts had been emboldened to speak to Mr. Fitweiler. He mentioned that Mr. Munson's department had been a "little disrupted" and hadn't they perhaps better resume the old system there? Mr. Fitweiler had said certainly not. He had the greatest faith in Mrs. Barrows' ideas. "They require a little seasoning, a little seasoning, is all," he had added. Mr. Roberts had given it up. Mr. Martin reviewed in detail all the changes wrought by Mrs. Barrows. She had begun chipping at the cornices of the firm's edifice and now she was swinging at the foundation stones with a pickaxe.

Mr. Martin came now, in his summing up, to the afternoon of Monday, November 2, 1942—just one week ago. On that day, at 3 P.M., Mrs. Barrows had bounced into his office. "Boo!" she had yelled. "Are you scraping around the bottom of the pickle barrel?" Mr. Martin had looked at her from under his green eyeshade, saying nothing. She had begun to wander about the office, taking it in with her great, popping eyes. "Do you really need *all* these filing cabinets?" she had demanded suddenly. Mr. Martin's heart had jumped. "Each of these files," he had said, keeping his voice even, "plays an indispensable part in the system of F & S." She had brayed at him, "Well, don't tear up the pea patch!" and gone to the door. From there she had bawled, "But you sure have got a lot of fine scrap here!" Mr. Martin could no longer doubt that the finger was on his beloved department. Her pickaxe was on the upswing, poised for the first blow. It had not come yet; he had received no blue memo from the enchanted Mr. Fitweiler bearing nonsensical instructions deriving from the obscene woman. But there was no doubt in Mr. Martin's mind that one would be forthcoming. He must act quickly. Already a precious week had gone by. Mr. Martin stood up in his living room, still holding his milk glass. "Gentlemen of the jury," he said to himself, "I demand the death penalty for this horrible person."

The next day Mr. Martin followed his routine, as usual. He polished his glasses more often and once sharpened an already sharp pencil, but not even Miss Paird noticed. Only once did he catch sight of his victim; she swept past him in the hall with a patronizing "Hi!" At five-thirty he walked home, as usual, and had a glass of milk, as usual. He had never drunk anything stronger in his life—unless you could count ginger ale. The late Sam Schlosser, the S of F & S, had praised Mr. Martin at a staff meeting several years before for his temperate habits. "Our most efficient worker neither drinks nor smokes," he had said. "The results speak for themselves." Mr. Fitweiler had sat by, nodding approval.

Mr. Martin was still thinking about that red-letter day as he walked over to the Schrafft's on Fifth Avenue near Forty-sixth Street. He got there, as he always did, at eight o'clock. He finished his dinner and the financial page of the *Sun* at a quarter to nine, as he always did. It was his custom after dinner to take a walk. This time he walked down Fifth Avenue at a casual pace. His gloved hands felt moist and warm, his forehead cold. He transferred the Camels from his overcoat to a jacket pocket. He wondered, as he did so, if they did not represent an unnecessary note of strain. Mrs. Barrows smoked only Luckies. It was his idea to puff a few puffs on a Camel (after the rubbing-out), stub it out in the ashtray holding her lipstick-stained Luckies, and thus drag a small red herring across the trail. Perhaps it was not a good idea. It would take time. He might even choke, too loudly.

Mr. Martin had never seen the house on West Twelfth Street where Mrs. Barrows lived, but he had a clear enough picture of it. Fortunately, she had bragged to everybody about her ducky first-floor apartment in the perfectly darling three-story redbrick. There would be no doorman or other attendants; just the tenants of the second and third floors. As he walked along, Mr. Martin realized that he would get there before nine-thirty. He had considered walking north on Fifth Avenue from Schrafft's to a point from which it would take him until ten o'clock to reach the house. At that hour people were less likely to be coming in or going out. But the procedure would have made an awkward loop in the straight thread of his casualness, and he had abandoned it. It was impossible to figure when people would be entering or leaving the house, anyway. There was a great risk at any hour. If he ran into anybody, he would simply have to place the rubbing-out of Ulgine Barrows in the inactive file forever. The same thing would hold true if there were someone in her apartment. In that case he would just say that he had been passing by, recognized her charming house and thought to drop in.

It was eighteen minutes after nine when Mr. Martin turned into Twelfth Street. A man passed him, and a man and a woman talking. There was no one within fifty paces when he came to the house, halfway down the block. He was up the steps and in the small vestibule in no time, pressing the bell under the card that said "Mrs. Ulgine Barrows." When the clicking in the lock started, he jumped forward against the door. He got inside fast, closing the door behind him. A bulb in a lantern hung from the hall ceiling on a chain seemed to give a monstrously bright light. There was nobody on the stair, which went up ahead of him along the left wall. A door opened down the hall in the wall on the right. He went toward it swiftly, on tiptoe.

"Well, for God's sake, look who's here!" bawled Mrs. Barrows, and her braying laugh rang out like the report of a shotgun. He rushed past her like a football tackle, bumping her. "Hey, quit shoving!" she said, closing the door behind them. They were in her living room, which seemed to Mr. Martin to be lighted by a hundred lamps. "What's after you?" she said. "You're as jumpy as a goat." He found he was unable to speak. His heart was wheezing in his throat. "I—yes," he finally brought out. She was jabbering and laughing as she started to help him off with his coat. "No, no," he said. "I'll put it here." He took it off and put it on a chair near the door. "Your hat and gloves, too," she said. "You're in a lady's house." He put his hat on top of the coat. Mrs. Barrows seemed larger than he had thought. He kept his gloves on. "I was passing by," he said. "I recognized— is there anyone here?" She laughed louder than ever. "No," she said, "we're all alone. You're as white as a sheet, you funny man. Whatever *has* come over you? I'll mix you a toddy." She started toward a door across the room. "Scotch-and-soda be all right? But say, you don't drink, do you?" She turned and gave him her amused look. Mr. Martin pulled himself together. "Scotch-and-soda will be all right," he heard himself say. He could hear her laughing in the kitchen.

Mr. Martin looked quickly around the living room for the weapon. He had counted on finding one there. There were andirons and a poker and something in a corner that looked like an Indian club. None of them would do. It couldn't be that way. He began to pace around. He came to a desk. On it lay a metal paper knife with an ornate handle. Would it be sharp enough? He reached for it and knocked over a small brass jar. Stamps spilled out of it and it fell to the floor with a clatter. "Hey," Mrs. Barrows yelled from the kitchen, "are you tearing up the pea patch?" Mr. Martin gave a strange laugh. Picking up the knife, he tried its point against his left wrist. It was blunt. It wouldn't do.

When Mrs. Barrows reappeared, carrying two highballs, Mr. Martin, standing there with his gloves on, became acutely conscious of the fantasy he had wrought. Cigarettes in his pocket, a drink prepared for him—it was all too grossly improbable. It was more than that; it was impossible. Somewhere in the back of his mind a vague idea stirred, sprouted. "For heaven's sake, take off those gloves," said Mrs. Barrows. "I always wear them in the house," said Mr. Martin. The idea began to bloom, strange and wonderful. She put the glasses on a coffee table in front of a sofa and sat on the sofa. "Come over here, you odd little man," she said. Mr. Martin went over and sat beside her. It was difficult getting a cigarette out of the pack of Camels, but he managed it. She held a match for him, laughing. "Well," she said, handing him his drink, "this is perfectly marvelous. You with a drink and a cigarette."

Mr. Martin puffed, not too awkwardly, and took a gulp of the highball. "I drink and smoke all the time," he said. He clinked his glass against hers. "Here's nuts to that old windbag, Fitweiler," he said, and gulped again. The stuff tasted awful, but he made no grimace. "Really, Mr. Martin," she said, her voice and posture changing, "you are insulting our employer." Mrs. Barrows was now all special adviser to the president. "I am preparing a bomb," said Mr. Martin, "which will blow the old goat higher than hell." He had only had a little of the drink, which was not strong. It couldn't be that. "Do you take dope or something?" Mrs. Barrows asked coldly. "Heroin," said Mr. Martin. "I'll be coked to the gills when I bump that old buzzard off." "Mr. Martin!" she shouted, getting to her feet. "That will be all of that. You must go at once." Mr. Martin took another swallow of his drink. He tapped his cigarette out in the ashtray and put the pack of Camels on the coffee table. Then he got up. She stood glaring at him. He walked over and put on his hat and coat. "Not a word about this," he said, and laid an index finger against his lips. All Mrs. Barrows could bring out was "Really!" Mr. Martin put his hand on the doorknob. "I'm sitting in the catbird seat," he said. He stuck his tongue out at her and left. Nobody saw him go.

Mr. Martin got to his apartment, walking, well before eleven. No one saw him go in. He had two glasses of milk after brushing his teeth, and he felt elated. It wasn't tipsiness, because he hadn't been tipsy. Anyway, the walk had worn off all effects of the whisky. He got in bed and read a magazine for a while. He was asleep before midnight.

Mr. Martin got to the office at eight-thirty the next morning, as usual. At a quarter to nine, Ulgine Barrows, who had never before arrived at work before ten, swept into his office. "I'm reporting to Mr. Fitweiler now!" she shouted. "If he turns you over to the police, it's no more than you deserve!" Mr. Martin gave her a look of shocked surprise. "I beg your pardon?" he said. Mrs. Barrows snorted and bounced out of the room, leaving Miss Paird and Joey Hart staring after her. "What's the matter with that old devil now?" asked Miss Paird. "I have no idea," said Mr. Martin, resuming his work. The other two looked at him and then at each other. Miss Paird got up and went out. She walked slowly past the closed door of Mr. Fitweiler's office. Mrs. Barrows was yelling inside, but she was not braying. Miss Paird could not hear what the woman was saying. She went back to her desk.

Forty-five minutes later, Mrs. Barrows left the president's office and went into her own, shutting the door. It wasn't until half an hour later that Mr. Fitweiler sent for Mr. Martin. The head of the filing department, neat, quiet, attentive, stood in front of the old man's desk. Mr. Fitweiler was pale and nervous. He took his glasses off and twiddled them. He made a small, bruffing sound in his throat. "Martin," he said, "you have been with us more than twenty years." "Twenty-two, sir," said Mr. Martin. "In that time," pursued the president, "your work and your—uh—manner have been exemplary." "I trust so, sir," said Mr. Martin. "I have understood, Martin," said Mr. Fitweiler, "that you have never taken a drink or smoked." "That is correct, sir," said Mr. Martin. "Ah, yes." Mr. Fitweiler polished his glasses. "You may describe what you did after leaving the office yesterday, Martin," he said. Mr. Martin allowed less than a second for his bewildered pause. "Certainly sir," he said. "I walked home. Then I went to Schrafft's for dinner. Afterward I walked home again. I went to bed early, sir, and read a magazine for a while. I was asleep before eleven." "Ah, yes," said Mr. Fitweiler again. He was silent for a moment, searching for the proper words to say to the head of the filing department. "Mrs. Barrows," he said finally, "Mrs. Barrows has worked hard, Martin, very hard. It grieves me to report that she has suffered a severe breakdown. It has taken the form of a persecution complex accompanied by distressing hallucinations." "I am very sorry, sir," said Mr. Martin. "Mrs. Barrows is under the delusion," continued Mr. Fitweiler, "that you visited her last evening and behaved yourself in an—uh—unseemly manner." He raised his hand to silence Mr. Martin's little pained outcry. "It is the nature of these psychological diseases," Mr. Fitweiler said, "to fix upon the least likely and most innocent party as the—uh—source of persecution. These matters are not for the lay mind to grasp, Martin. I've just had my psychiatrist, Dr. Fitch, on the phone. He would not, of course, commit himself, but he made enough generalizations to substantiate my suspicions. I suggested to Mrs. Barrows when she had completed her—uh—story to me this morning, that she visit Dr. Fitch, for I suspected a condition at once. She flew, I regret to say, into a rage, and demanded—uh—requested that I call you on the carpet. You may not know, Martin, but Mrs. Barrows had planned a reorganization of your department—subject to my approval, of course, subject to my approval. This brought you, rather than anyone else, to her mind—but again that is a phenomenon for Dr. Fitch and not for us. So, Martin, I am afraid Mrs. Barrows' usefulness here is at an end." "I am dreadfully sorry, sir," said Mr. Martin.

It was at this point that the door to the office blew open with the suddenness of a gas-main explosion and Mrs. Barrows catapulted through it. "Is the little rat denying it?" she screamed. "He can't get away with that!" Mr. Martin got up and moved discreetly to a point beside Mr. Fitweiler's chair. "You drank and smoked at my apartment," she bawled at Mr. Martin, "and you know it! You called Mr. Fitweiler an old windbag and said you were going to blow him up when you got coked to the gills on your heroin!" She stopped yelling to catch her breath and a new glint came into her popping eyes. "If you weren't such a drab, ordinary little man," she said, "I'd think you'd planned it all.

Sticking your tongue out, saying you were sitting in the catbird seat, because you thought no one would believe me when I told it! My God, it's really too perfect!" She brayed loudly and hysterically, and the fury was on her again. She glared at Mr. Fitweiler. "Can't you see how he has tricked us, you old fool? Can't you see his little game?" But Mr. Fitweiler had been surreptitiously pressing all the buttons under the top of his desk and employees of F & S began pouring into the room. "Stockton," said Mr. Fitweiler, "you and Fishbein will take Mrs. Barrows to her home. Mrs. Powell, you will go with them." Stockton, who had played a little football in high school, blocked Mrs. Barrows as she made for Mr. Martin. It took him and Fishbein together to force her out of the door into the hall, crowded with stenographers and office boys. She was still screaming imprecations at Mr. Martin, tangled and contradictory imprecations. The hubbub finally died out down the corridor.

"I regret that this has happened," said Mr. Fitweiler. "I shall ask you to dismiss it from your mind, Martin." "Yes, sir," said Mr. Martin, anticipating his chief's "That will be all" by moving to the door. "I will dismiss it." He went out and shut the door, and his step was light and quick in the hall. When he entered his department he had slowed down to his customary gait, and he walked quietly across the room to the W20 file, wearing a look of studious concentration.

The Ratebuster: The Case of the Saleswoman*

Melville Dalton

THE SALESWOMEN

Of the six people in the boys' department only the head was male, and he made sales only occasionally. Two of the women were high sellers—Mrs. White and Mrs. Brown. Mrs. White was fifty-nine years old, large physically and somewhat taciturn. She had worked at Lassiters for fourteen years. Mrs. Brown was a small active person, thirty-two and had been with the store for eight years. Masters told me that when she started in the store she was much taken with Mrs. White and copied and improved upon Mrs. White's selling techniques. Then, too, Mrs. Brown had the insights that came from close personal experience in outfitting her son. Over a period of several months they developed a rivalry. For the last six years or so, according to Masters [Mike Masters, head of the boys' department], they were coldly polite to each other when it was necessary to speak. Masters regarded existence of this hostility as one of his major problems. His professed ideal was that the women should all be circulating among the customers, busy all the time and cordial to each other.

The other three salesgirls were Mrs. Bonomo, thirty-five, a quiet amenable person, in the department for four years; Mrs. Selby, forty-eight, an employee for five years, who took things as they came without being much disturbed—though judging from her behavior and remarks she made, she disliked Mrs. White much more than she did Mrs. Brown. Mrs. Dawson, at twenty-two, was the youngest member of the department. She had dubbed Mrs. Brown and Mrs. White "saleshogs." She had worked there less than two years. She liked Mrs. Brown despite the epithet she had given her. Mrs. Dawson had two years of college, the most schooling in the department.

The saleswomen received from $1.75 to $2.25 per hour, depending on how long they had been in the department. Records of sales (dollar-volume) for the department

*The names of the individuals in this case and the department store (Lassiters) are fictional. The incidents described took place in the boys' department of Lassiters. The saleswomen in the department were all on commission.

As Dalton observed in a portion of this article which was omitted here, it is common for members of work groups who are on a commission or other system of incentive payments to avoid showing each other up. In other words, there are informal standards about what members of the group perceive to be a reasonable amount of work. Individuals who produce significantly above this level are often called "ratebusters" or "grabbers" by social scientists. Members of the work group often apply less complimentary labels and even sanctions to individuals who violate the output norms. At Lassiters, ratebusters were called "saleshogs" by their peers—*Ed. note.*

were kept for the past year and varied from month to month. These records established the quota for the current year. Once this was equaled, the women started drawing commission pay at the rate of five percent. Commission was paid separately once a month.

Before describing the selling tactics of Mrs. Brown and Mrs. White, the ratebuster types, it is instructive to note the average daily sales established over a six month period[1] by the five saleswomen. Mrs. Brown with $227 average daily sales is over twice as much as Mrs. Dawson and Mrs. Selby, nearly twice as much as Mrs. Bonomo, and $74 more than the second ratebuster, Mrs. White. Masters assured me that Mrs. White had slowed up noticeably in her selling over the last two years, but in terms of dollar sales and her constant challenge to Mrs. Brown she should still be classified as a ratebuster, or a ratebuster in decline.

Lassiters had an employee credit union. Masters had access to the complete membership which was seventy-six. He gave me *rank only* of the five saleswomen based on the individual amounts deposited in the credit union. (He was so shocked when I requested the total savings of each of the saleswomen that I gladly accepted the partial data.) Mrs. White stood third in the store, and Mrs. Brown was fourth. Mrs. Selby ranked forty-ninth and Mrs. Bonomo was sixty-sixth. Mrs. Dawson was not a member. These data alone do not tell much, but they do indicate that Mrs. White and Mrs. Brown were among the top investors, and that commission was important in their behavior.

Saleswomen	Average Daily Dollar Sales
Mrs. Brown	227
Mrs. White	153
Mrs. Bonomo	119
Mrs. Selby	110
Mrs. Dawson	101

RATEBUSTER TACTICS

Mrs. Brown apparently had more personal relations with customers than anyone in the boys' department. She learned from Masters when specially-priced merchandise was coming in. She telephoned customers she knew well and made arrangements to lay away items of given size and style that were scheduled to go on sale. When she had filled these private orders there was little of the merchandise left for the general public when the official sale day arrived. These sales by telephone constituted about fifteen percent of her total sales. Relatively new customers who bought heavily a time or two she filed in her retentive memory and took steps to acquaint them with her special services.

Among her repeat buyers was a working woman with four sons who treated their clothing roughly. Every six weeks this woman came in to buy nearly complete outfits for the boys. This included shirts, underwear, socks and blue jeans, which amounted to what the sales force called a "big ticket" of about $120.

Mrs. Brown had another woman customer who did not believe in having the younger boys of her five sons wear the older boys' outgrown clothing. She did not come in much oftener than once a year to buy complete outfits, usually just before Easter, which could run to two hundred dollars or more. Mrs. Brown acted as though she had an exclusive right[2] to these customers, and several others that she knew who had only two sons. When Mrs. Brown expected these people, she would skip her lunch hour for fear she might miss them, or ask Masters to make the sale and ring it up on her cash drawer in case the woman came when she was out to lunch. He was glad to do this. When business was very good, whether she expected specific customers or not, she ignored the coffee breaks (ten minutes each morning and afternoon) and the lunch hour, leaving the selling floor only long enough to eat a sandwich in the dressing room.

She also had a practical monopoly on sales for boys on welfare. These boys had to be presented by an agent on the welfare organization the first time they did business with the store. Masters turned the welfare customer over to Mrs. Brown and forever afterwards[3] she made the sales. In some cases the welfare officer brought the boy, or boys, with their only clothes on their backs, to buy a complete outfit with extra socks, handkerchiefs and underwear. (Shoes were not sold in the boys' department.) In any case, Mrs. Brown took care of the sales then and afterwards.

Mrs. Brown's housekeeping area was just inside the entrance from the parking lot. She watched this approach closely. When she was not busy, or was talking to the other members of the department, she could break off instantly—even when she was telling a joke—and move toward the door. If she did not recognize the person she formed some judgment on him based on the affluence of his dress and his bearing. If the customer had a boy along, she judged whether he would be hard to fit. In her own words, she had a theory that "the kids who are tall and skinny or short and fat are hard to fit."[4] Thus she made quick appraisals of everybody who moved toward the department. If she approached a customer and learned that he was not as promising as he looked, she often brought the person to one of the other saleswomen and presented him with a statement of what he wanted as though—according to the women—she was giving them an assured sale. She made no revealing comment on the matter, but she seemed at the same time to be putting a restraint on her rivals.

Mrs. Brown's most galling behavior to the group was her practice of getting sale claims on as many prospective buyers as possible. She thus deprived the other saleswomen of a chance at the buyers. For instance, as she was serving one person, she would see another coming through the door—which she nearly always faced even when busiest. Quickly she would lay a number of items before the first person with the promise to be back in a moment, then hurry to capture the second customer. If the situation were right, she might get her claim on three or four buyers while two or more of the saleswomen were reduced to maintaining the show cases, and setting things in order so as not to appear idle. Mrs. Brown was able to do this because her own housekeeping and stocking area (assigned by Masters) lay between the entrance to the store and the other sections of the boys' department. Only Mrs. White would challenge her by intercepting a patron. The rivalry between them never came to a visible break. As noted earlier some of the other saleswomen resented Mrs. Brown's behavior and privately called her a "saleshog." She was not called that by Mrs. Bonomo and Mrs. Selby who thought—as they said—that Mrs. Brown in action was a "show in itself."

A standard device was used by Mrs. Brown, for ends not intended, with the understanding and collaboration of Masters. On very slack days she frequently left the store shortly after one or two o'clock to do "comparative shopping," that is, to compare the selling prices of items that Lassiters sold with the prices that other local stores charged for the same or similar items. Sometimes Mrs. Brown actually did this, but often she would attend a matinee, or go home to catch up with her housework, or just take a nap. (Her time card was punched out by Masters at the official quitting time.) In any case, to the favorable implications of "comparative shopping," the further obvious inference was made that her absence from the store allowed the other salesgirls to make more commission. (Actually, business was so slow on some days, because of weather, etc., that it was not possible for any of the saleswomen to earn bonus pay.)

Mrs. Brown's conduct may suggest total indifference to the group. But possibly because she was a female in our society, she was not as nonconformist as the grim ratebusters in industry. Some of these could work for years without exchange of words with people, only a few feet away, that they knew hated them. To a degree Mrs. Brown was concerned about her group. Every week or so she would buy a two pound box of choice chocolates from a candy store near Lassiters and bring it in to share with the group. She could have bought a less expensive grade of candy at Lassiters. Sharing of the candy was almost certainly calculated (she ate little of it herself) but it appeared spontaneous and was received without hesitation. The saleswomen could not direct an unqualified hostility toward her.

She had another uncommon practice which made her stand apart from all of Lassiters' employees. Despite her determined assault on the commission system she did not use her right to a discount on items that she might buy for herself or members of her family. She took her fifteen-year-old son to a local independent department store to buy his clothes. She vigorously declared that "I don't want anything that [Lassiters] has." She was emphatic to the group—and implicitly condemned them—that she did not want to participate in the common practice of getting legal price reductions in addition to the regular employee discount by buying items at the end of a season. For example, an assortment of women's purses would be delivered to the selling floor. This was the "beginning of the season" for that batch of purses. The saleswomen with friends in the purse department would look at the display and select ones that appealed to them. These were laid away until the "end of the season" when they could be bought at the sale price which was further reduced by the regular discount. Mrs. Brown would have nothing to do with such items. She clearly did not want it said that she was taking advantage of her job.

A likely interpretation is that she sensed she was rejected and widely criticized for her methods and high bonus pay. She feared that some envious salesperson would report any borderline activity on her part to top management. Her own explanation implied that her esthetic taste could not be satisfied by the merchandise at Lassiters. In effect she downgraded the status of the store. As part of this complex she also implied that she was morally somewhat above the group. Also she may have been posing to hide her possible guilt feelings about her treatment of the group.

Although the aim of this paper is not to deal with morale problems, it was glaringly clear that Masters damaged group feeling by routing welfare customers to Mrs. Brown, and by ringing up some of his sales on her cash drawer. His tacit approval of her behavior discouraged the other saleswomen from attempting to control her.

NOTES

1. Masters gave me these figures based on an average of 44 hours a week and including the back-to-school buying months of August and September 1969.
2. Probably she was encouraged by the customers to think that way; certainly some customers waited for her to be free to serve them.
3. The other saleswomen knew about this and resented it. Grateful to Masters for allowing me to observe and talk with the saleswomen, I naturally did not ask him why there was no sharing of such sales among his force. I inquired, but there was no voiced conception of a "day's work" among the saleswomen. This general practice of informal rewarding is not uncommon in industry where it is sometimes done even with the knowledge and cooperation of individual officers of the union. (Lassiters was not unionized.)
4. Alteration of coats and trousers was done free by the store's tailor. But measuring and marking and the extra trying on were time-consuming. In the extreme cases this was futile. In any case Mrs. Brown avoided customers with "odd size" boys unless she knew them to be liberal buyers and worth her time.

Chapter
9
Secrecy

There appears to be a curious inconsistency in the thinking of many students of organization. On the one hand, when they write about communication, they emphasize the importance of openness and sharing information widely. Their major concern seems to be with trying to help managers open up communication channels. This position seems to assume that managers and other organizational participants want to share information. On the other hand, many of these same students acknowledge that "information is power."

If information is power, or, as we believe an important source of power, then there will be times when people want to keep it to themselves. The selections in this chapter reveal that, in fact, secrecy is a major concern of people throughout organizations. Issues over secrecy are related to individual privacy, corporate technological advantage, and the competitive positions of nations as well as corporations.

In the selection "Politicians Should Never Forget Cardinal Telephone Rule," Ken MacQueen looks at privacy beyond the workplace. Although the episode described concerns government officials, it should warn all managers that their conversations are not as private as they often assume.

"At Apple, Proper Business Attire May Someday Include a Muzzle" reveals the importance of secrecy to modern organizations and how difficult it can be to maintain. Even people who have no intention of communicating company secrets can inadvertently do so with a casual remark over lunch.

In "CIA Leader Wants Agency Active in Industrial Spying," James McCartney looks at the secrecy issue in national policy and international competitiveness. Is it possible that the economic viability of the United States and other modern nations could depend on their willingness and ability to engage in industrial espionage? Should our government, through such units as the CIA, become involved?

Since these selections describe events of the last few years, they emphasize the role of relatively new technologies. Consequently, it may appear that concerns about privacy and secrecy in organizations are of recent origin. Few things could be further from the truth. While new technologies have added tools, spying on workers and attempting to obtain illicit information about competitors have been a part of organizational reality for a long time. In light of the role of new technologies, the attention currently focused on these issues should not be surprising. In our view, it is also noteworthy how little attention students of organizations have devoted to them until now.

Politicians Should Never Forget Cardinal Telephone Rule

Ken MacQueen

Former B.C. attorney-general Bud Smith lost his cabinet portfolio for violating a cardinal rule of modern politics: Don't say anything into a telephone that you wouldn't want to see on the front page of tomorrow's newspaper.

It is a rule Prime Minister Brian Mulroney and his cabinet follow religiously and one that Manitoba Premier Gary Filmon has learned, to his disgust.

Thanks to cellular and car telephones—which broadcast with radio waves rather than through telephone lines—eavesdropping is almost as popular now as during the days of the rural party line.

No one group has embraced this sad lapse in ethics more ardently than political junkies—as Smith learned too well.

He was angered and disgusted Wednesday when a New Democratic Party MLA released tape recordings of two embarrassing telephone calls Smith had made, apparently on his car telephone.

The calls—one to a senior bureaucrat, one to a reporter—recorded attempts by Smith to discredit a Victoria lawyer hired by the NDP to privately prosecute a former cabinet colleague of Smith's.

The incident has quickly degenerated into one of the ugliest slugging matches in recent B.C. political history—no small feat.

Politicians and the public seem at a loss to decide who committed the most disgusting deed.

Reprinted by permission of *Southam News*.

Was it Smith for apparently attempting to meddle in a private prosecution even though, as attorney-general, he has a legislated responsibility to be the impartial chief law officer of the Crown?

Or was it NDP justice critic Moe Sihota, who sifted through tapes of many of Smith's private telephone calls and released recordings of the two conversations.

"There are some serious questions about the ethics of that," Sihota admitted.

Sihota said he was given the recordings by a person not connected to the NDP. Suppressing knowledge of what Sihota calls Smith's "tampering with the administration of justice" would have been a greater wrong, he insists.

At any rate, Smith did find his conversations on the front page of Thursday's papers.

Indeed, by accident or design, the Vancouver Province ran the entire transcript of his conversation opposite a full-page advertisement for cellular telephones. "CELLULAR LEADERS STRIKE AGAIN," said the ad's headline.

Debate rages over whether acting on information gathered by monitoring cellular and other radio-telephone frequencies may violate privacy laws. It is illegal to tap telephone lines without court authorization. But cellular calls can be monitored by using commercially available radio scanners in much the way that hobbyists, most news organizations and some criminals can monitor police, fire and ambulance radio broadcasts.

"No question, it's an area that's been a problem for a while," said Sgt. Val King, head of the RCMP computer crime section in Ottawa.

"The problem is . . . is it a private communication if it's sent out over public airwaves? Is the scanning of that considered illegal? Those are some of the questions that are still to be answered by the courts."

But while monitoring the airwaves for cellular calls may fall into a legal grey zone, there is little doubt that it is common practice in the world of hardball business and politics.

Just last month, Filmon accused federal officials of eavesdropping on private cellular telephone conversations between members of his delegation during the Meech Lake constitutional discussions.

"There was a couple of instances in which calls we made by cellular to people for specific information were known by federal people within 20 minutes of the call," Manitoba's premier said.

The charge was flatly denied by the prime minister. In fact, Mulroney said he warned the premiers against using cellular telephones, noting that ministers in his cabinet have found that conversations on their car telephones have been monitored.

Indeed, the offices of many senior cabinet ministers are equipped with at least one secure telephone, designed to thwart either telephone taps or radio monitoring.

"That's generally known, that you shouldn't be saying too much into any phone, including your car phone . . . or even your regular office phone," said Tom Van Dusen, press secretary to Deputy Prime Minister Don Mazankowski.

Sunni Locatelli, a spokesman for the prime minister's office, said there is no cabinet directive, but "cabinet ministers are reminded that cellular telephones are not a secure means of communication."

The federal Liberal party, not wishing to air its backroom dealings, banned radio scanners from last month's leadership convention in Calgary.

In Victoria, the Social Credit government is rushing to limit further damage.

An electronic sweep of all areas of the legislature, from ministerial offices to the press gallery, has been ordered.

At Apple, Proper Business Attire May Someday Include a Muzzle

G. Pascal Zachary

John Sculley is in the throes of a nightmare. Clad in white pajamas, Apple Computer Inc.'s chief executive officer dreams that careless employees have leaked confidential information, causing his company's demise. "Apple Suffers Information Hemorrhage," a tabloid headline screams. Mobs of angry customers storm the company's offices, dubbed "the leaky palace." Apple was "too free, too open," a television newscaster intones.

Mr. Sculley never actually had this nightmare. Last December, he and others acted out the drama for an in-house video crew. Since then, Apple has shown the six-minute video to every new hire and hundreds of veteran workers as part of a big internal campaign aimed at educating employees on the perils of loose lips.

Apple has always had a problem keeping secrets. Gossip about its latest developments is valuable currency in the social milieu of Silicon Valley. It suggests you are hip, "an insider," says independent software developer Heidi Roizen. But recently leaks have become more frequent and more unsettling. Now Apple is determined to plug them.

In March, Apple hired a manager of information security who promptly launched a war against leaks. Among the weapons are buttons for the workforce of 13,000 ("I know a lot but I can keep a secret") and brochures on the importance of secrecy. "Information protection coordinators"—staffers who volunteer to help spread the word—patrol their work groups.

Apple also has plastered its office walls with posters on the dangers of spilling inside information. One shows Albert Eisenstat, Apple's senior vice president and former chief legal counsel, wearing sunglasses and a white British barrister's wig. He warns: "The law says that Apple can dismiss any employee who discloses confidential or proprietary information. . . . But we'd rather not. Honestly."

"At Apple, Proper Business Attire May Someday Include a Muzzle" by G. Pascal Zachary, *Wall Street Journal*, 1989, p. A1. Reprinted by permission of *Wall Street Journal* © 1989 Dow Jones & Company, Inc. All rights reserved worldwide.

Another features Delbert Yocam, president of Apple's Pacific division, gagged by a table napkin and holding aloft his utensils. The message: beware of gabbing about the company in restaurants. A third pictures Christopher and Sue Espinosa, two employees who are married. They caution that "there are some things that are so confidential they shouldn't be revealed even to your closest relatives, friends and significant others."

Apple's campaign may win awards for cuteness, but probably not for effectiveness. Some suspect the program may even be backfiring. "It almost seems as if the more Apple tries to do, the worse the leaks get," says Daniel Ruby, editor of MacWeek, a trade magazine devoted to news about Apple's Macintosh computer. Sensitive information has been leaked in at least three incidents since the campaign began. Apple refuses to discuss the incidents.

The most alarming leak involved a mysterious group of software pirates called the New Prometheus League. The group, which surfaced in early June, mailed floppy disks containing some of the Macintosh's secret software code to an undetermined number of people, including a computer-industry analyst on Wall Street.

The group, named after a Greek god who stole fire from the gods and gave it to man, said in a letter that accompanied the disks that it wanted to make it easier to make copies of the Macintosh. Apple has never licensed the computer's code to anyone and has successfully defended in court its copyrights, barring competitors from making compatible but less expensive versions of the machine. The disclosure apparently wasn't damaging, but it highlighted Apple's vulnerability. The New Prometheus League hasn't been heard from since that incident.

Apple has proven that it intends to do more than plead with employees to button up. Three months ago, Apple fired a software engineer who had disclosed plans for some future products on a computer bulletin board. David Ramsey, the engineer, claims he didn't think the information was confidential because Mr. Sculley had disclosed similar information to a trade journal late last year. "There's one set of rules for executives and another for everybody else," says Mr. Ramsey, who has since joined another electronics firm.

Stolen Thunder

In July, there was yet another leak. MacWeek managed to get its hands on the still-secret Macintosh IIci—two months before the new machine was to be introduced. MacWeek says its coup was courtesy of an outside firm that had been loaned the machine by Apple.

The magazine's editors pored over the computer, testing its capabilities and photographing its innards. A detailed account of the machine and a picture were splashed on the cover of the magazine's July 25th issue. Apple has assigned several former Federal Bureau of Investigation agents now on staff to try to identify the leaker.

The incident wasn't highly damaging to Apple. At the most, it robbed the company of some suspense in its introduction of the computer. But it illustrated the difficulties the company faces in trying to put a lid on inside information.

Silencing the Multitudes

At one time or another, some 11,000 outside developers are privy to various secrets about products in development. The firms, which make software or accessories for Apple computers, often get prototypes of new products months before they are announced publicly. Apple swears the developers to silence by requiring them to sign a pledge of secrecy. Prototypes are also "marked differently in very subtle ways, so if there's a picture or description in the press we can track down the source," says Kirk Loevner, director of Apple's developer group.

More recently, however, Apple has stepped up efforts to enforce secrecy among outside developers. Staff detectives drop in without warning more frequently to check for security violations. Apple has punished some developers in the past by denying them access to important technical data and the opportunity to get new products before they hit the market.

Apple's anti-leak campaign has sparked some concern within the company. Some workers think the effort conjures up a sense of working under an Orwellian Big Brother, ironically an image Apple used in a famous 1984 television commercial attacking rival International Business Machines Corp. "People are working scared," says one worker who asks not to be named. In particular, Mr. Ramsey's firing raises "a lot of fear about job security," the worker adds.

Jane Paradise, Apple's manager of corporate information security, says the company isn't spying on workers. "We're not a police state—far from it," she says. The drive to tighten security has a lot of support among workers, she insists. "Employees have been outraged by the leaks," she says. "Awareness is up. We're making progress."

She may be right. Employees seem to be embracing the campaign. After Mr. Ramsey was fired, for instance, he was treated as a pariah by former co-workers. "It was though I had some dread communicable disease," Mr. Ramsey recalls.

In any case, Apple's campaign isn't likely to put Mr. Sculley's nightmares entirely to rest. That's partly because of people like Charles Farnham. Mr. Farnham, a San Jose engineer and a passionate Apple fan, has made a hobby of collecting and doling Apple secrets out to other devotees.

"The universe is divided into three types of people," he says. "Those who sleep with the machine, those who use the machine and the business people. Guess which category I'm in?"

Selling a Scoop

Mr. Farnham recently rummaged through several of Apple's dumpsters while a cohort recorded the escapade on videotape for posterity. Mr. Farnham says his foraging turned up scores of technical reports and 20 discarded computer monitors. He combed the company's garbage, he says, to highlight the lax security.

On another occasion, Mr. Farnham persuaded an Apple employee to give him copies of the company's plans for a portable computer. Mr. Farnham sold a story about the plans to a computer weekly. Documents he found during another foray in the corporate garbage can went to a computer users group in Kansas City; the group gave them away as a door prize at a meeting in June.

Mr. Farnham says he is skeptical that Apple will succeed in protecting its secrets. "It all comes down to how many people like me are floating around," says Mr. Farnham. "If there's zero, they don't have a problem. If there are 100, Apple's in big trouble."

CIA Leader Wants Agency Active in Industrial Spying

James McCartney

The United States has become "a victim" of worldwide industrial espionage, according to CIA Director William Webster.

Because of this, the nation must vastly increase its intelligence capabilities in business and economics if it is to remain competitive in the post–Cold War world, Webster argued in an interview.

"It is certainly our role to detect and identify that type of activity and to assist our policy-makers in confronting it," said the CIA chief.

"High technology is no longer our private campground," Webster said, and the United States must learn what its competitors are doing if there is to be "a level playing field."

Webster's proposal to increase economic spying, destined to be controversial, would represent a major shift in emphasis for the CIA intelligence efforts, which for 40 years have concentrated on the military power struggle with the Soviet Union.

It was immediately questioned by Sen. Arlen Specter, R-Pa., a member of the Senate Intelligence committee, and was questioned by a former CIA chief.

"I do not think it is a healthy thing to start eavesdropping on our economic competitors," Specter said. "I don't think the American taxpayers expect us to do that unless it is defensive."

In a separate interview, former CIA Director William Colby warned that "there are limits" to what the CIA should do in economic intelligence because of the nation's free economy.

"What if we discover the Japanese have found a great new electronic gizmo?" Colby asked. "If you gave the information to General Electric, TRW would go up in smoke."

Webster discussed his economic spying proposal in detail in a wide-ranging interview in which he predictably argued for increased spending on intelligence activities despite abatement of tensions between the world superpowers.

The CIA, he said, faces pressing new challenges in combating terrorism and drug trafficking, monitoring arms control agreements and following power struggles in an increasingly unstable Third World.

Webster conceded, however, that over the next five years the CIA "will be sharing in some of the reductions that Defense is experiencing," a view increasingly shared among lawmakers on Capitol Hill.

Webster granted the rare interview in the wake of several sharp attacks on the CIA in recent weeks, in which questions have been raised about whether the agency is ready to adapt to a world without a Cold War.

A former National Security Council staff member, Roger Morris, described the agency as "a rusting relic of the Cold War . . . with often no apparent vision save conflict." A recent Newsweek story attacked the agency for what it described as a series of intelligence failures, including failure to foresee the collapse of communism in Eastern Europe.

The intelligence budget, now highly classified, is believed to amount to about $30 billion for 1991—an all-time high. The CIA has about 14,000 employees, worldwide, also a peak.

In the interview, Webster, a soft-spoken former appeals judge from St. Louis and former FBI director, also asserted that:

- Many countries in the Middle East are obtaining fast-flying, relatively long-range missiles capable of carrying both chemical and biological weapons, threatening a new era of instability.
- New arms control treaties, involving both strategic and conventional arms, will require extensive verification facilities.
- The Soviet military threat has not disappeared, even though it has receded, and will require continued monitoring for many years to come.
- Covert action by the CIA, its most controversial area of operations, will continue to be necessary to encourage democratic movements around the world.
- CIA agents on the ground, so-called "human intelligence," should be expanded to improve the quality of the agency's analysis.

Regarding his campaign for improved business intelligence, Webster said national security in the future is likely to depend far more heavily on economic factors than on military, as in the last 40 years.

At this point, he hastened to add, the CIA has not embarked on a specific program of direct business spying, declaring that "these are policy judgments for the future," but adding that "we have done major things to improve our capabilities."

Webster indicated that an internal debate on exactly how far the United States might go in spying is still under discussion in the intelligence community.

"I don't want to say, 'Don't worry fellows, we're not doing anything,' " he said, smiling. "We want to know what they are able to do and what they will be able to do in the future."

"We want to track their technical progress, but that is different than trying to steal their technology."

He singled out for special attention "new centers of economic strength—the European Community, a powerful reunified Germany and "an increasingly strong Japan."

Chapter
10
Rises and Falls

Conventional textbooks on management and organizational work concentrate for the most part on upward mobility and how to achieve it. Comparatively little recognition is given to the frequency with which hitherto successful managers "fall from grace." The economic disasters associated with recession have led to increased recognition of this aspect of organizational life in the popular press and business-oriented media. The selections in this chapter describe various types of "falls." We see some of the reasons for these falls, as well as their impact on the individuals concerned.

"The Downsizing of America: A National Heartache" summarizes the demographics of the downsizing corporate America has experienced in recent years and illustrates some of the human tragedies that have resulted.

David Kirkpatrick looks at the "rises" side in "Is Your Career on Track?" Kirkpatrick uses illustrations drawn from several large corporations to show that the trend for upward mobility in organizations is coming much more slowly. This change in organizational life has been noted elsewhere by Judith Garwood as "plateauing." One consequence that Kirkpatrick notes is that managers really get to know their jobs, which did not happen in the days when promotions came every few years. Lateral assignments, once greeted as a sign of failure, are increasingly coming to be viewed as a fresh challenge.

Failure to accurately assess the situation with which a rising star is confronted can damage the individual, as Sally Quinn discovered in her brief struggle with CBS in "We're Going to Make You a Star." In this case the struggle took on Kafkaesque proportions as neither side appeared to know which reality they were inhabiting. The emotional, psychological, and physical costs to individuals and, at times, the costs to organizations, may be very high if a system is either too loose or too programmed and depersonalized.

"Howyadoon? Fuller Brush Calling" by Cathryn Donohoe describes the experiences of a long-time Fuller Brush sales representative. We see the decline of what once was an American institution and the dedication of one employee to his vanishing craft as a door-to-door salesman. The selection that follows is from Arthur Miller's *Death of a Salesman*. A theme that has received far too little attention is examined here: obsolescence. This process is often more brutal than retirement because it has few of the humane, social institutions that make retirement a somewhat dignified process. Retirement is an expected event that organizations can handle through routine procedures such as gifts, parties, and speeches, thus submerging any sense of personal failure. However, there are few such procedures for handling an individual such as Willy Loman, whom the organization defines as obsolete.

In "Dancing with Headhunters: Scenes from the Downsized Life," the author describes his few ups and mostly downs during his lengthy search for another job after being fired.

The Downsizing of America: On the Battlefields of Business, Millions of Casualties—Part II

Louis Uchitelle and N.R. Kleinfield

A NATIONAL HEARTACHE

Drive along the asphalt river of Interstate 95 across the Rhode Island border and into the pristine confines of Connecticut. Stop at that first tourist information center with its sheaves of brochures promising lazy delights. What could anyone possibly guess of Steven A. Holthausen, the portly man behind the counter who dispenses the answers?

Certainly not that for two decades he was a $1,000-a-week loan officer. Not that he survived three bank mergers only to be told, upon returning from a family vacation, that he no longer had a job. Not that his wife kicked him out and his children shunned him. Not that he slid to the bottom step of the economic ladder, pumping gas at a station owned by a former bank customer, being a guinea pig in a drug test and driving a car for a salesman who had lost his license for drunkenness. Not that, at 51, he makes do on $1,000 a month as a tourist guide, a quarter of his earlier salary. And not that he is worried that his modest job is itself fragile and that he may have to work next as a clerk in a brother's liquor store.

That, however, is his condensed story, and its true grimness lies in the simple fact that it is no longer at all extraordinary in America. "I did not realize on that day I was fired how big a price I would have to pay," Mr. Holthausen said, in a near whisper.

"The Downsizing of America: On the Battlefields of Business, Millions of Casualties—Part II" by Louis Uchitelle and N.R. Kleinfield, *The New York Times*, March 3, 1996. Reprinted by permission.

More than 43 million jobs have been erased in the United States since 1979, according to a New York Times analysis of Labor Department numbers. Many of the losses come from the normal churning as stores fail and factories move. And far more jobs have been created than lost over that period. But increasingly the jobs that are disappearing are those of higher-paid, white-collar workers, many at large corporations, women as well as men, many at the peak of their careers. Like a clicking odometer on a speeding car, the number twirls higher nearly each day.

Peek into the living rooms of America and see how many are touched:

Nearly three-quarters of all households have had a close encounter with layoffs since 1980, according to a new poll by The New York Times. In one-third of all households, a family member has lost a job, and nearly 40 percent more know a relative, friend or neighbor who was laid off.

One in 10 adults—or about 19 million people, a number matching the adult population of New York and New Jersey combined—acknowledged that a lost job in their household had precipitated a major crisis in their lives, according to the *Times* poll.

While permanent layoffs have been symptomatic of most recessions, now they are occurring in the same large numbers even during an economic recovery that has lasted five years and even at companies that are doing well.

In a reversal from the early '80s, workers with at least some college education make up the majority of people whose jobs were eliminated, outnumbering those with no more than high school educations. And better-paid workers—those earning at least $50,000—account for twice the share of the lost jobs than they did in the 1980s.

Roughly 50 percent more people, about 3 million, are affected by layoffs each year than the 2 million victims of violent crimes. But while crime bromides get easily served up—more police, stiffer jail sentences—no one has come up with any broadly agreed upon antidotes to this problem. And until Patrick J. Buchanan made the issue part of the presidential campaign, it seldom surfaced in political debate.

Yet this is not a saga about rampant unemployment, like the Great Depression, but one about an emerging redefinition of employment. There has been a net increase of 27 million jobs in America since 1979, enough to easily absorb all the laid off workers plus the new people beginning careers, and the national unemployment rate is low.

The sting is in the nature of the replacement work. Whereas 25 years ago the vast majority of the people who were laid off found jobs that paid as well as their old ones, Labor Department numbers show that now only about 35 percent of laid-off full-time workers end up in equally remunerative or better-paid jobs. Compounding this frustration are stagnant wages and an increasingly unequal distribution of wealth. Adjusted for inflation, the median wage is nearly 3 percent below what it was in 1979. Average household income climbed 10 percent between 1979 and 1994, but 97 percent of the gain went to the richest 20 percent.

The result is the most acute job insecurity since the Depression. And this in turn has produced an unrelenting angst that is shattering people's notions of work and self and the very promise of tomorrow, even as the president proclaims in his State of the Union Message that the economy is "the healthiest it has been in three decades" and even as the stock market has rocketed to 81 new highs in the last year.

Driving much of the job loss are several familiar and intensifying stresses bearing down upon companies: stunning technological progress that lets machines replace hands and minds; efficient and wily competitors here and abroad; the ease of contracting out work, and the stern insistence of Wall Street on elevating profits even if it means casting off people. Cutting the payroll has appeal for the sick and the healthy—for gasping companies that resort to it as triage and to the soundly profitable that try it as preventative medicine against a complicated future.

The conundrum is that what companies do to make themselves secure is precisely what makes their workers feel insecure. And because workers are heavily represented among the 38 million Americans who own mutual funds, they unwittingly contribute to the very pressure from Wall Street that could take away their salaries even as it improves their investment income.

The job apprehension has intruded everywhere, diluting self-worth, splintering families, fragmenting communities, altering the chemistry of workplaces, roiling political agendas and rubbing salt on the very soul of the country. Dispossessed workers like Steven Holthausen are finding themselves on anguished journeys they never imagined, as if being forced to live the American dream of higher possibilities in reverse.

Many Americans have reacted by downsizing their expectations of material comforts and the sweetness of the future. In a nation where it used to be a given that children would do better than their parents, half of those polled by *The Times* thought it unlikely that today's youth would attain a higher standard of living than they have. What is striking is that this gloom may be even more emphatic among prosperous and well-educated Americans. A *Times* survey of the 1970 graduating class at Bucknell University, a college known as an educator of successful engineers and middle managers, found that nearly two-thirds doubted that today's children would live better. Whitecollar, middle-class Americans in mass numbers are coming to understand firsthand the chronic insecurity on which the working class and the poor are experts.

All of this is causing a pronounced withdrawal from community and civic life. Visit Dayton, Ohio, a city fabled for its civic cohesion, and see the detritus. When Vinne Russo left his job at National Cash Register and went to another city, the 85 boys of Pack 530 lost their Cubmaster, and they still don't have a new one. Many people are too tired, frustrated or busy for activities they used to enjoy, like church choir.

The effects billow beyond community participation. People find themselves sifting for convenient scapegoats on which to turn their anger, and are adopting harsher views toward those more needy than themselves.

Those who have not lost their jobs and their identities, and do not expect to, are also being traumatized. The witnesses, the people who stay employed but sit next to empty desks and wilting ferns, are grappling with the guilt that psychologists label survivor's syndrome. At Chemical Bank, a department of 15 was downsized to just one woman. She sobbed for two days over her vanished colleagues. Why them? Why not me?

The intact workers are scrambling to adjust. They are calculating the best angles to job security, including working harder and shrewder, and discounting the notion that a paycheck is an entitlement.

The majority of people polled by *The Times* said they would work more hours, take fewer vacation days or accept lesser benefits to keep their jobs.

Even the most apparent winners are being singed. A generation of corporate managers have terminated huge numbers of people, and these firing-squad veterans are fumbling for ways to shush their consciences.

Richard A. Baumbusch was a manager at CBS in 1985 when a colleague came to him for advice: Should he buy a house? Mr. Baumbusch knew the man's job was doomed, yet felt bound by his corporate duty to remain silent. The man bought the house, then lost his job. Ten years have passed, but Mr. Baumbusch cannot forget.

One factor making this period so traumatic is that since World War II people have expected that their lives and those of their children would steadily improve. "It's important to recall that throughout American history, discontent has always had less to do with material well-being than with expectations and anxiety," David Herbert Donald, a social historian at Harvard, said. "You read that 40,000 people are laid off at AT&T and a shiver goes down your back that says, 'That could be me,' even if the fear is exaggerated. What we are reacting against is the end of a predictable kind of life, just as the people who left the predictable rhythms of the farm in the 1880s felt such a loss of control once they were in the cities."

As the clangor from politicians over the jobs issue has begun to be heard, aspirants to public office may find an audience in that group of households in which a lost job produced a major crisis.

The Times poll revealed something of their signature. Only 29 percent, versus 49 percent of the entire population, say they are as well off as they imagined at this juncture of their lives. The vast majority feel the country is going in the wrong direction, and they are more pessimistic about the economy. They are more likely than the overall population to be divorced or separated.

They are better educated. Politically, they are more apt to label themselves liberal. They are more likely to favor national health insurance, and to say that curbing government programs like Medicare, Medicaid and welfare is a misguided idea. And more than 65 percent, compared with 45 percent in the whole population, want the government to do something about job losses.

Wherever one turns one encounters the scents and sounds of this sobering new climate. Ask Ann Landers. Last year, when she adopted a stone-hearted view in her column to a laid off worker, lecturing him that he had a "negative attitude," she was swamped by 6,000 venomous letters, one of the largest outpourings to any of her columns. "They were really giving me the dickens," Ms. Landers said. "This is the real world, girl. Now I am trying to be supportive."

People run into acquaintances and don't ask how their job is, but whether they still have it. Surf the Internet or flick on the comedy channels and take in the macabre jokes: Sales clerk: "What size are you?" Customer: "I'm not sure. I used to be a 42 Regular. But that was before I was downsized." Wife: "But why'd they fire you?" Husband: "They said something about the company making too much money. If the business tanks, they said they'd call me back."

Such graveyard humor is pervasive in Scott Adams's popular comic strip, Dilbert, about a 1990's computer engineer who quakes under a gruff and hectoring boss. In one strip, Dilbert competes with Zimbu, a monkey, for a job, and loses. In another, the boss informs Dilbert that he is about to become involved in all aspects of the company's production. "Dear Lord," Dilbert realizes. "You've fired all the secretaries." Raw material arrives daily in the form of E-mail from demoralized workers.

In an effort to somehow cauterize the emotional damage of the dismissals, managers have introduced a euphemistic layoff-speak. Employees are "downsized," "separated," "severed," "unassigned." They are told that their jobs "are not going forward." The word downsize didn't even enter the language until the early 1970s, when it was coined by the auto industry to refer to the shrinking of cars. Starting in 1982, it was applied to humans and entered in the college edition of the American Heritage Dictionary.

Meanwhile, the word layoff has taken a fresh meaning. In the past, it meant a sour but temporary interruption in one's job. Work was slow, so a factory shift would be laid off. But stay by the phone—until business picks up. Today, layoff means a permanent, irrevocable goodbye.

Is Your Career on Track?

David Kirkpatrick

Forget the old rules. Promotions are coming more slowly. Lateral moves are in. But if you're trying for the very top, you still need to stick close to the P&L.

Gauging your career progress has always been more art than science, but what on earth are you supposed to make of the signals you're getting now? You haven't been promoted in quite a while, but then neither have many of your peers—at least not *really* promoted, though some have been shuffled into completely new areas. Out in the job market there's that clomping herd of baby-boomers behind you, or around you, or ahead of you. And as you fight your way up the corporate slope, you start to wonder if it's worth the effort. Maybe you should think about quitting, about becoming an entrepreneur like some of your former colleagues.

If you're confused, take heart. You are not alone. Figuring out where your career stands has never been harder. Says David Rhodes, 38, of the consulting firm Towers Perrin: "The rules are changing, but we don't know what they are yet." Palo Alto consultant Paul Leinberger, 42, echoes the thought: "What it means to be on the fast track today is quite unclear." And yet, from all the confusion, from the tumult of restructuring, globalization, mommy tracks, empowerment, and work teams, new wisdom is emerging to enlighten today's aspiring executives on what's really happening with their careers.

The most striking change in the rules of career progress: You may go years between promotions and still be doing just fine. Many managers are sitting in jobs longer regardless of their age, talents, or skills. Explains Rhodes: "When companies flatten organizations, that limits the number of rungs on the ladder, which lengthens the time between promotions." Susan Doten, 31, is director of marketing in Quaker Oats' pet food division, and she has moved quickly through six jobs in nine years. But the managerial pyramid has flattened so markedly that, she says, "I will hang out at this level for a lot longer than I hung out at the lower levels. There are about 13 marketing directors in U.S. grocery products, then only four vice presidents of marketing at the next level." Consultant Rhodes predicts that by 2000 the typical large corporation will have half the management levels and one-third the managers that it has today.

Promotions are slowing for another reason. Many companies that once moved the best and brightest on a fast track to a new job every 12 to 18 months are wondering if that isn't *too* fast. Says Blair Sheppard, 37, director of the human resource management research center at Duke's Fuqua business school: "American firms after restructuring are much closer to meritocracies than they used to be." And that means they want people to stay in place longer so it's clearer whether they succeeded or failed. David Hogberg, 37, a pet food marketing manager at Quaker, encountered this phenomenon early. In 1982 he was working his way up the ladder in the company's manufacturing operations, getting promoted roughly every year. Then he became manager of manufacturing for Kibbles 'n Bits dog food, and his boss decided to keep him there three years. He looks back: "It seemed like an eternity, but this was a big job, with 70 people working for me. I trusted that in the long term it wouldn't be a career setback."

It wasn't, and he thinks no other path would have taught him what he learned: "I got to see the effects of changes I made and work through their implications. It helped me learn to approach every job as a long-term opportunity, to stand back and ask what changes we need to make in this whole picture, even if it has been done one way for the last 15 years."

If you can't move up right away, you can sometimes move across, and this may be a smart idea. As Doten of Quaker Oats Puts it, "I may eventually have to move to another area to grow myself." Growing yourself makes sense because the future corporate honcho will be a generalist—not a production or finance or marketing person, but a people person, more a leader than a master of any one discipline. Says recruiter Henry de Montebello, 44, of executive search firm Russell Reynolds Associates: "In the future everybody will have strategic alliances with everybody else, and the executives who thrive will be well-rounded. You can't be a specialist at senior levels anymore."

Anne Pol, 42, of Pitney Bowes buys that message. Five years ago, after a career spent mostly in human resources, she left a senior position in that function to run a plant that makes parts for mailing machines. She considered herself a candidate for the company's highest jobs but knew she needed solid operating experience to have a reasonable shot. Then she came back to the top personnel job and a position on Pitney Bowes's 11-person corporate management committee, but only on condition she could go back to operations later. This spring she returned to the heart of the company, as vice president for manufacturing operations in the mailing systems group. Her conclusion: "It's very obvious that lateral moves are necessary if you want to progress up the corporate ladder."

If assessing your accumulation of job titles is more complicated than it used to be, surely you can still get a quick read on your status by checking your salary—can't you? Not so fast. For the organization men of the Fifties and Sixties, the longstanding rule of thumb was that you were doing okay if you earned your age times $1,000. Today you can't go by such simple rules—even adjusted for inflation. For one thing, people prefer compensation in different forms than they used to. They are more likely to want a piece of the business, or profit sharing. "It's give me money or give me equity," says de Montebello. "People will take extraordinary risks in their careers for equity."

By contrast, the perks so cherished by organization men no longer carry as much weight. In typical boomer voice, a 30-year-old middle manager at a big Manhattan public relations firm says, "All those executive dining rooms and bathrooms generally just satisfy somebody's ego. I'd rather have cash in hand than spend it to take a limo from point A to point B."

In general, after accounting for inflation, rising managers today make about as much as or perhaps a bit more than they did two decades ago. But headhunter de Montebello states an opinion advanced frequently by human resources experts : "There's no formula for how much you should make. The test is, Where are your peers? If your classmates, the people you started with, are all group VPs and you're an assistant controller, there's a discrepancy. But then you may be a serious tennis player and having more fun."

Comparing your achievements with those of your peers is harder than it used to be because the number and nature of your cohorts may vary enormously, depending on your age. Managers of all vintages worry about the career impact of 78 million baby-boomers surging through the work force. But whether *you* have reason to worry depends on how old you are and with which group of baby-boomers you are competing.

Just because boomers all grew up listening to the Beatles and Rolling Stones, that doesn't mean they all sing the same song today, especially when it comes to career attitudes. After all, they were born over a 19-year period. Edith Weiner, 41, of the Manhattan trend analysis firm Weiner Edrich Brown, credibly argues that boomers should be divided into three subgroups.

The leading edge is the so-called Woodstock generation, who were roughly 18 to 23 in 1969 and are 39 to 44 today. This group pioneered emancipated styles of life in their youth, helped initiate the women's movement, and fought against—or in—the Vietnam war. When they entered the job market the economy was, aptly, booming. There were ample entry-level slots for them, and their attitude reflected a certain cockiness because they felt they had changed society. When it came time to buy a house, by today's standards it was easy to afford.

The second group, today about 33 to 38, didn't test social barriers nearly so hard. Yet they were affected enough by the freewheeling Sixties to have felt considerable confusion about career goals, and typically they didn't decide until relatively late what they wanted to do. They took their first stab at the job market during or after the recession of the mid-Seventies and began to feel a competitive squeeze for jobs and housing.

By the time the third wave of boomers, now 26 to 32, emerged from school, competition was so keen in both job and housing markets that economic success became the consuming goal in their lives. This is the tough group that helped define the word yuppie and that unashamedly sought megabucks at a tender age on Wall Street.

While no objective evidence demonstrates that these last are stealing promotions from older boomers, the first two groups are definitely hearing footsteps behind them. And they don't like it. A successful 43-year-old who runs two business units and manages 150 people at a major money center bank is leaving her job, partly, she says, because of the competitive pressure she feels from young MBAs. The woman, who started

22 years ago as a secretary to a branch manager, complains: "These 1980s graduates we call yuppies are incredibly aggressive. They will lick your shoes to get you to do something for them. And once you do they'll forget your name. These little twits are coming in and eating our lunch."

For all the pressure they feel, the early boomers still have a demographic advantage over the legions that trail them. Thanks to the birth dearth of the Depression and World War II, relatively few older managers stand in the way of boomer promotions to the high-level jobs that survive. In addition, many older executives are bailing out well before age 65, lured by entrepreneurship and fat retirement packages, or are being restructured out. Guess who will fill their positions? In some reviving industries the older generation of managers was so decimated by cutbacks in the Eighties that boomers face truly extraordinary opportunities. At companies like Bethlehem Steel, Caterpillar, and Navistar International, their careers could thrive.

Younger boomers who haven't yet received the promotions they feel they deserve may also benefit as their more successful comrades, who got the early promotions, move further up in the hierarchy. That's because of the birth dearth that followed the boom. Says Sylvester Schieber, 43, the optimistic director of research for the Wyatt consulting firm: "The people at the back end of the baby boom will be more likely to get these fill-in promotions. You only dead-end if you go to sleep at your desk." In short, the youngest and oldest boomers find a career advantage in being adjacent to a birth dearth. Those stuck in the middle, with masses of peers above and below them, face a tough slog the rest of their lives.

One of the most important changes in the career picture, affecting not just baby-boomers but all ages, is occurring not around today's managers but inside them. Personal fulfillment and the flexibility to do more of what one wants are becoming top-rank career goals. Says Pitney Bowes's Anne Pol: "The key issue for people today is getting satisfaction in your work and feeling that you are making a contribution." It's a feeling people have always sought. But earlier generations were more willing to suppress this desire in return for other rewards, primarily job security. For all their careerism, many baby-boomers, steeped in the heritage of the Sixties, are decidedly ambivalent about compromising personal goals in pursuit of a job somewhere up there in the corporate empyrean. Consultant Leinberger observes: "The baby-boom generation places creativity and self-expression at the center of their being. They view themselves as walking works of art." This ethos has extended to managers of all ages. As one navigates corporate America, one can almost hear the voices crying, "Don't fence me in!"

If independence, control, stimulation, and a feeling of satisfaction are what people increasingly crave, few profess to care about their title. Says Burke Stinson, 48, a public relations manager for AT&T: "Folks are less concerned about the trappings than if the job itself is rewarding, the company progressive, and the environment comfortable—does it nurture me as a guy or gal on the way up?"

Janet Cooper, 36, relishes her job as Quaker's assistant treasurer because she finds the changing capital markets exciting. "I could take another job and make more money," she says. "But it would be a trade-off for doing something less interesting each day." George Foyo, 43, a sales vice president for AT&T's national accounts who just returned from a four-year general management assignment in Spain, feels the same way: "I'm very strongly motivated by change and challenge. Compensation and title are less important."

This resistance to categorization also expresses itself in a sense, sometimes disquieting, of being endlessly in motion. "People today consider themselves to be in a constant state of change," says Edith Weiner. Are you married? Currently. Do you have children? Not yet. Consider the highly satisfied Peggy Clarkson, a cheery 38-year-old who, thick appointment book always at her elbow, manages a staff of six marketers for IBM in Norwalk, Connecticut. How does this 16-year Big Blue veteran and mother of two feel about her career? "Right now I'm very happy in my job," she says. "I love it. It allows me to balance career and home very well." Right now.

Managers are seeking deeper satisfaction just when many employers are less likely to give them the wider and more rewarding responsibilities that come with a promotion. Something's got to give, and it may take the form of managers bailing out, or of companies changing policies in an effort to keep them. Says a 32-year-old man who left IBM in 1988 after eight years to join a small software company: "In a big company you're always trying to avoid the brick wall. Now my status depends on how I perform. I don't care about my title. I'm looking for a challenge."

Smart companies trying to retain such people are finding ways to create more challenge and satisfaction for managers who otherwise might feel stuck. AT&T senior vice president of human resources Harold Burlingame says, "We are starting to have broader bands for people. Instead of getting a $10,000 raise and moving on, they can earn much more within a job as they grow in and grow their business." At IBM, where restructuring eliminated 6,200 of 34,000 management jobs in the U.S. between 1986 and 1989, those that remain have more autonomy, at least according to higher-ups. Says Dick Hallock, director of employee relations for IBM: "We're driving responsibility down so that within each job there's more room for growth and development. In some areas we use the slogan, Make it your business."

But companies aren't attacking the problem sufficiently. Indeed, employees often complain that when they learn more and broaden themselves, the company doesn't notice. Quaker human resources vice president Robert Montgomery, 43, says that "plateaued" managers are bailing out, and his company, like others, isn't yet doing enough to keep them.

Career-conscious women face a whole additional set of considerations. No independent career expert interviewed for this article denies that a glass ceiling curtails corporate advancement for women, and most volunteer it as one of the most important factors shaping the future of today's managers. Yet a substantial number of experts also believe that women's careers may thrive in the corporate environment of the future. Neil Yeager, 37, who recently wrote *Career Map: What You Want, Getting It, and Keeping It*, says, "Women know how to network in a less politicized way. They know how to nurture relationships and empower other people. They manage groups better than men. And they have a greater appreciation of motivations other than money." Those are just the qualities companies will need in the Nineties.

With the struggle up the ladder especially trying and confusing for today's managers, it's little wonder that many seem particularly interested in an ancient question: Just what, finally, is career success anyway? Judith Bardwick, 57, a La Jolla, California, consultant, insists that there are other ways to cope with nonpromotion than to feel that you've failed. "Don't sit in the corner and suck your thumb," counsels a stern Bardwick, who proffers similar advice in seminars to employees at companies like BellSouth, Kraft General Foods, and Pacific Gas & Electric. To address those feelings without quitting, she suggests, "take your ambition to another area of life. Get involved with your local school board, for example. Or go get the education to increase your flexibility on the job."

While corporate backwaters still exist—often in human resources, public relations, and legal, among others—even fast-trackers will occasionally find themselves spending a brief time in one. "Both line and staff jobs will be expected for the CEO of the future," says IBM's Hallock. International experience will surely be a plus as well, he says.

But staying close to profit and loss responsibility remains the most important talisman for those with their eyes on top management. Says author Yeager: "For getting to the top, the bottom line is still the bottom line." Seek such responsibility early, and try to ensure that the results you produce for the company can be measured in dollars and cents.

Beyond that, IBM's Hallock offers this advice: "Take the initiative in your own development. Learn new things. Read widely. Absorb as much as you can, whether or not it's related to your current job, so you can put it into context. You've got to understand the mission objectives of your employer and relate your own efforts to the company's overall goals."

We're Going to Make You a Star

Sally Quinn

The countdown: Dick Salant, president of CBS News, was beaming. Hughes Rudd was chuckling to himself and Sally Quinn was fending off questions about her sudden rise in TV news. The setting was a luncheon at "21" in New York and the guests included members of the press, who were given an opportunity to meet and chat with the CBS correspondents who will go on the air next Monday. Salant was saying he'd love to switch the time of the *CBS Morning News* show from 7 A.M. to 8 A.M. but he'd run into opposition from the fans of *Captain Kangaroo*. "I know because I raised all my children on *Captain Kangaroo*." If the new team is a success, Salant said naturally he'd take credit for the show, but if the show bombs he said he's going to find someone to point the finger at. Who dreamed up Rudd and Quinn? he was asked. "That was Lee Townsend." Townsend, the executive producer, however, modestly disclaimed credit. "It was a group effort," he told Eye, *Women's Wear Daily*, Tuesday, July 21, 1973 . . .

When Gordon and I first discussed the job I told him I had grave reservations about his choice. I reminded him that I was controversial, opinionated, flip, open and had no intention of changing. Was he sure this was what he wanted on television? Did they really want me to say what came to my mind during the ad libs, and would they not try to turn me into a bland, opinionless, dull-but-safe marshmal-low? And I wondered aloud whether, if we were supposed to be journalists, we could maintain any kind of objectivity and still express controversial opinions—or any opinions, for that matter.

"Paley wants controversy," Gordon had said. "And so does Salant. You can get away with much, much more at that hour than you ever could on the *Evening News*."

I had doubts and so did a lot of people I talked to, but I figured CBS knew what it wanted.

I also pointed out to Gordon that I had a rather unconventional life style. I had been living on weekends with Warren, I explained, and if I moved to New York I would move in with him. I would also be talking about him openly and freely in interviews. I saw nothing wrong with it, and I had no intention of hiding the fact.

I think Gordon gulped a little at that one, but he gamely said that was just fine, I could say anything I wanted to. After all, CBS was not hiring me because or in spite of my personal life.

On Friday morning, June 22nd, the first piece about me appeared in *The Washington Post*. The head ran "SHOWDOWN AT SUNRISE," and it carried pictures of me and Barbara opposite each other. I wasn't too crazy about that. It created an atmosphere of rivalry I would have preferred to avoid. But my editors laughingly pointed out that I was now a public personality and had no say in the matter. They also pointed out that it was clearly the right angle for the story. They were right.

TV critic John Carmody had written, "Although a number of her candid interviews had attracted CBS's attention, it was, ironically enough, her appearance on Miss Walters' *Not for Women Only* TV program that whetted the network's interest." He quoted Salant as saying that the format of the revamped show would "have no relationship to the *Today* Show" and would "retain the integrity of the basic news show." But also as predicting that "*Today* is ripe to be taken."

Stuart Shulberg, the producer of the *Today* Show, was quoted: "We welcome fresh competition. *Today* has led the morning field for so long that we could run the risk of growing too fat, smug, and sassy. This will speed up the pace, sharpen our competitive spirit, and provide the kind of honest competition we need and relish. May the best program win."

Barbara Walters was quoted: "The only thing I can say as a woman in broadcasting is that I welcome any new member to the fold. . . . I have respect and friendship for Sally. I know her very well. And I applaud both her and CBS for a very smart choice."

And Sally Quinn said: "Barbara is a great friend of mine and one of the most professional people I've ever known. As far as competing with each other, we covered the Shah's celebration in the desert of Iran together last year and stayed in the same dormitory. That's like being in combat together, and I imagine this will be a somewhat similar situation."

And we were off. . . .

Monday, rehearsals began. Thank God. Now they were going to roll it all out for us, lay it on, let us in on all the fabulous plans for the first week of shows. And it was about time. I had begun to have doubts, but I knew that they would disappear as soon as we got to the studio and saw what they had for us.

We were to arrive at 6 A.M. to start getting the feel of getting up early. We would watch the *Morning News*, then go into a simulation of what our anchor booth was going to look like (it wasn't nearly ready) and tape a news broadcast. We were to write it from the same wires and newspapers that John Hart had used earlier.

Lee Townsend was jittery. Townsend, the most even-tempered man I know, was also as irritated as I had ever seen him. He had been against the promo tour (though he didn't object violently enough) because he felt we could have better used our time rehearsing. His objections had been overridden by Blackrock, which—who? I never got the pronoun straight—had insisted that it was necessary. So Townsend was nervous and angry because we had been away and virtually co-opted by the PR department, and because it was then clear to him that we didn't have a super-duper razzle-dazzle show to put on the air in a week's time. And no real studio to rehearse in.

He had reason to be more than nervous, and we did exactly what we had done for the pilot except at greater length. We wrote a little news and a few lead-ins to film pieces, and Hughes wrote an essay. I couldn't think of anything that morning, and besides, I'm not an essayist. I'm a reporter and interviewer. Hughes would do essays, which he did marvelously, and I would do what I did best.

In front of the camera, they outfitted me with an ear-piece on a wire, called a Telex, which enables them to talk to you from the control room. They handed us mikes, rolled our copy onto the TelePromTers, and away we went. It was a disaster. There were two cameras and I didn't know which one to look at. The stage manager waved his hands around, but I hadn't a clue what he was trying to tell me. I was fumbling my words and couldn't read the prompters. They were shouting in my ear through the Telex to do this and do that, and three minutes here and twenty seconds there, and ad lib here. The ad libs were always by surprise, and I would fumble around trying to think of something clever to say about a film piece we had just seen. It might have been a bloody plane crash or a dairy farm. It BOMBED, and I was shell-shocked by the time it was over. Suddenly I *knew* this was the way it was going to be. There was nothing I could do about it. It was too late to get out of it.

I was even more upset when everyone came out of the control booth and said it was just fine and all it needed was a little smoothing out and we would be just great by the end of the week. No mention of any guests for interviews, no mention of any special film pieces that would lend themselves to interesting, informative ad libs and, most frightening of all, no mention of anything I should do to improve myself. I realized fully for the first time that I didn't know anything, and I panicked.

As we were filing down the stairs to the *Morning News* section, Jim Ganser, one of the producers, caught up with me. He was to be the only one at CBS who really tried to help me.

"Try to punch your words a little more," he sort of whispered out of the side of his mouth, as though he didn't want anyone to hear.

I fell on him. "What? How? What do you mean?" I said desperately. "Tell me, for God's sake. Tell me what I'm doing wrong."

And he told me. "You're wrong to expect anyone to give any help or guidance of any kind. You're a big star now, and people figure if you're a big star you must know what you're doing. Nobody's going to stick his neck out to help you."

I went to the ladies' room and threw up. But I had to hurry. Hughes and I were the "big stars" of a large press luncheon at the "21" Club, and we were late. . . .

We finally got into our own studio on Friday, and we rehearsed there Friday and Saturday. Nothing went right. Friday morning after John Hart's last show someone came into the Cronkites, where we were working, and said that the staff of the *Morning News* was having a farewell party for John and the old producer. I hadn't really seen John to talk to him. I like and respect him a great deal, but we had been so busy working the lobster shift (that's the night shift in newspapers) that we just hadn't had a chance to see each other.

"Oh, great, I'll go up and tell John goodbye," I said, jumping up from my chair.

"I wouldn't if I were you," someone said. "There's a great deal of hostility up there toward the new team. And the atmosphere upstairs is more like a wake than a party. I think you had better forget it."

That was the first I had heard of resentment or hostility on the home team front. It worried me because, except for Townsend, Hughes and me, the "team" was the same. There had been no staff changes. I had found that curious. If they had really wanted a whole new format, with more entertainment and a lighter mood, I thought that they would surely have tried to bring in some people who were more in the show-biz line. The *Morning News* staff was very good. But they were hard-news oriented, and Gordon had said the idea was to take on the *Today* Show.

That morning when I went in to get my makeup done for the rehearsals my hair was a mess. While I was upstairs, the woman who was doing my makeup said her friend Edith, the hairdresser for *Edge of Night,* was right down the hall and maybe she would roll my hair up on the hot rollers for me. She called Edith, and a round-faced woman in her late fifties, with reddish hair, big, wide innocent eyes, a very strong New York accent, and dyed-to-match pants, vest, blouse, and shoes, came rushing in. Edith said she would be delighted. She had the lightest, most soothing touch, and the whole time she did my hair she told me how great I looked and how terrific I was going to be on the air and that she was honored to do my hair. Then she asked who my official hairdresser was.

"Hairdresser? I don't have a hairdresser." Both women were stunned. "You have to have a hairdresser," they chimed. "Every woman on television has one. You can't just go on with your hair like this every morning."

Edith asked me if she could be my hairdresser and said she was sure that if I asked they would let me have one. I told Lee and Sandy Socolow about it and they both went blank. Nobody had given my hair a thought. They okayed it right away, but it indicates how little thought went into the planning for the first woman network anchor. Edith was a godsend. She not only took care of my hair, she took care of my ego.

After the rehearsal on Saturday, I was about to leave. No interviews were lined up for me for the following week. The big interview for Monday was with Patrick Buchanan, the President's speech writer, and that would be out of Washington. I had no idea what film pieces were going to be used. They weren't sure.

I was so depressed and scared that I didn't really care. I wanted to go somewhere and hide. As we were leaving (Sunday was a free day) Lee Townsend gave me a big smile and said, in a way I couldn't decide was joking or not, "Let me know if you have any good ideas tomorrow for the show."

Sunday was the worst day of my life. I thought about ways to disappear where no one would hear from me for years and would think I had been kidnapped by some freak. I considered the possibility of having plastic surgery so I would never be recognized as Sally Quinn. I fantasized about going on the broadcast and saying, "Good morning, I'm Sally Quinn and we are not prepared to do this show and I don't know what I'm doing up here." I thought seriously about calling Salant and Manning and telling them. I came close to quitting.

The water pipes broke in our apartment and I had to go to a friend's place on West End Avenue to wash my hair.

When I got out of the shower, I put on a large white robe that was hanging on the door. I came out of the bathroom draped in that robe and I said to Warren, who had been babysitting me all day, "I really feel like one of those ancient Aztec virgins who has been chosen to be sacrificed on top of the temple of the gods. All the other virgins are wildly jealous of her because she has this fabulous honor bestowed on her. What they don't know is that she doesn't want her heart cut out with a knife anytime by anyone. It hurts."

I went to bed at 5 P.M. It was bright and sunny outside, and I could hear the children playing on Riverside Drive and happy couples walking and chatting and laughing as they strolled in Riverside Park.

"I will never be happy again," I thought. "My life is over."

I never went to sleep. We had been coming in around 4 or 5 in the morning that week, but it wasn't proper preparation for coming in at 1:30. The alarm went off at 1:00 A.M. Warren was waiting to walk me to my limousine, which arrived promptly at 1:30 A.M. It was like being escorted in a golden carriage to the guillotine.

I didn't feel too hot. I figured it must be because I hadn't slept. I slipped into the gloamings of the enormous black car and we glided over to Hughes' apartment, the Apthorpe, a few blocks away on West End Avenue. He hadn't slept either. We didn't say a word. A few minutes later we arrived at the studio and went directly back to the *Morning News* area and into the Bullpen.

In front of each of us was a pile of news wire stories, the first edition of *The New York Times* and the *Daily News*. Bob Siller, the copy editor, was there and so was Dave Horowitz, one of the assistant producers. They would make up the "line-up." The line-up was a sheet on which the show was blocked out minute-by-minute. Taking all the film pieces and counting their time, they would, along with Hughes and me and Lee Townsend, decide what the top news stories were and allot a certain amount of time to each, from forty-five seconds to a minute, and then block out time for commercials (we had only network commercials for the first six weeks) and station breaks. They would leave about a minute and a half for Hughes' essay, and what was left—roughly five minutes—would be allotted for "ad libs."

While this was going on, Hughes and I read the papers and the wires to get an idea of what stories we wanted to use. When we had finished, about 3 or 3:30, Bob and Dave came back with the line-up designating which one of us would write which stories and which lead-ins to film pieces. If the film piece was ready, Hughes and I would try to take a look at it so that we could write a clearer lead-in; if not, there was generally some kind of script. Often the film piece wasn't ready. Horowitz and Siller, with our advice or without, would figure out which film piece seemed like the best topic for conversation and block in a certain amount of time for ad libs after those pieces. There was some freedom to move around, but not much. Everything we were to say we typed out on our enormous typewriters.

We had two writers who were to do the weather, sports and late-breaking news. Hughes was to read all the sports. We had tried to divide it, but I didn't understand sports and kept fumbling and breaking up in the middle of the report. Hughes hated it too, but it wasn't quite as ridiculous when he did it.

By the time Hughes and I would have read everything thoroughly, discussed camera angles with Bob Quinn, our director, who came in about 4, written all our news items, lead-ins and station and commercial breaks, had something to eat at our desks (it was called "lunch" and usually came from the CBS cafeteria, known appropriately and without affection as "the Bay of Pigs"), it would be about 6 A.M.—time for Edith and Rickey, the makeup person, to arrive and get us ready.

At around 3:30 I had started to break out in a cold sweat and I became weak and dizzy and slightly nauseated. I couldn't concentrate on what I was writing. Finally I went into Townsend's office and passed out. I tried to get up about 4 A.M. and write, but I stayed at my typewriter for about twenty minutes and then went back to Townsend's office and passed out again. I thought it was probably because I was tired and nervous, but by then my throat was so sore and I was coughing so badly that I could barely talk. I had shivers and had to be wrapped up in a blanket.

Everyone piled into Townsend's office and stared at me in horror. "Do you think you can do it?" Lee asked, terrified.

"I just don't know, Lee." I didn't.

I think at that point I was more scared not to go on than to go on.

"I'll try. I'll really try. But I can't talk. And I'm so dizzy. Is there any way I could get a vitamin B shot or something to give me quick energy?"

By then it was 5:30 in the morning and I was so sick I couldn't breathe. I kept trying to sit up and I would just fall right down. I couldn't tell whether the beads of perspiration on my head were from temperature or desperation. Finally Townsend said that they had to get me to a hospital. Somebody had a car and they carried me out to the front of the building, stuffed me in the car, and drove two blocks away to Roosevelt Hospital to the emergency room. A young doctor took me back to examine me and take my temperature. I had a temperature of 102 and he said he thought I might have pneumonia. I was coughing so badly that my body was racked. "You don't understand," I practically screamed. "I'm making my television debut in an hour."

"So I've heard," he smirked.

"Well, I can't possibly go on like this. Can't you give me a vitamin B shot or something? Anything."

He said that in my condition a vitamin B shot wouldn't do any good. The only thing he could do for me was to give me a throat spray that would stop me from coughing for a few hours. But he suggested that I get to a doctor immediately afterward for proper medication.

"Anything else I could give you now," he said, "would knock you out." Oh, how I wished . . .

He left the room and came back a few minutes later with the most enormous syringe I have ever seen, with a needle a mile long.

"Forget it," I said, backing away from him.

"Don't get hysterical," he said, laughing, "This is a throat spray. I'm not going to stick the needle in you."

He stuck the needle in my mouth and sprayed a gooey liquid, which coated the inside of my throat.

Lee grabbed me, back we went into the car, and we screeched off around the corner and back to CBS as though we were bank robbers getting away.

It was a little before 6:30. Edith and Rickey were frantic, and Hughes looked as though all his blood had drained out of him. Edith rolled my hair while Rickey sponged some makeup on me. I lay down while all this was going on. The hot rollers stayed in too long and I looked like Shirley Temple when my hair was combed out. There was nothing we could do about the frizz. At about ten minutes to seven they finished on me. I was still so weak and dizzy that I could barely move, and all I can remember is a large fuzz of Warren leaning over me asking me if I was all right, Townsend in a frenzy, and Hughes pulling himself together as he walked into my dressing room. "Hughes—" I tried to smile—"get me off this horse immediately." Hughes tried to smile, too, but he wasn't very convincing. "Don't worry," he growled, "you'll make it, kid."

I tried to say thank you, but the throat spray had a numbing effect, like Novocain, and I couldn't feel whether my tongue was touching the roof of my mouth or whether I was forming my words properly.

"You look beautiful, darling, just beautiful. You'll be wonderful, I know you will," Edith was murmuring.

I looked in the mirror. I was hideous. My hair was frizzy, the granny glasses looked wrong, and the only thing I owned that wasn't blue (I hadn't had time to shop that week) was a yellow battle jacket that made me look like a dyke.

"Well," I thought, "there's no way anybody is going to accuse me of being a sex bomb this morning."

Somebody shoved a pile of telegrams in my face and I tried to read. They were all amiable, from close friends and family, but it was upsetting me. "Oh, God," I thought, "if only they knew how terrible I'm going to be."

They were screaming for me to get into the studio and I ran in, got behind the desk, had my mike adjusted, and somebody handed me my Telex, which I stuck in my ear.

"One minute," yelled the floor manager.

My mouth was dry. No possibility of talking. I looked at Hughes. He was looking at me as though we were copilots and I had just been shot. He tried to smile. I tried to smile back.

"Thirty seconds," said the floor manager.

I looked straight outside the glass partition to the newsroom and saw everyone staring.

"Five seconds," the floor manager said.

For a fleeting moment I thought maybe I would wake up and find out this wasn't happening.

An arm went out to me and a finger pointed. I gazed at the TelePromTer.

"Good morning," I read, "I'm Sally Quinn. . . ."

I don't remember much else about that hour. I was propped up with several pillows because I was so weak and dizzy that I couldn't sit up by myself.

I coughed a lot. I remember a swirl of sweltering bright lights, moving cameras, different noises and shouts in my ear through the Telex—"Turn to Camera 2, thirty seconds to ad-lib, five seconds till commercial, ten seconds more of interview"—hand signals, desperate and self-delirious mumblings . . . and then it was over. And when it was over I felt completely numb. Nothing. . . .

When I walked back into my office there were three bouquets. One was from Charlotte Curtis, then editor of *The New York Times'* Family, Food, Fashions and Furnishings, now editor of the op-ed page of *The Times* and probably the woman I admire most in journalism. One from Vic Gold, former press secretary of former Vice President Spiro T. Agnew and now a columnist. And one from Connie Tremulis of "Flowers by Connie," Rockford, Illinois.

I still have their cards.

Everybody was talking at once and saying what a great show it had been and how did I ever get through it, and, boy, what a terrific start we had gotten off to, and how terrible the *Today* Show was outdoors in front of Rockefeller Center. I don't remember seeing Hughes. I remember Lee Townsend taking me by the hand and leading me outside to a taxi. I put my head back on the seat and stared out the window as we went whizzing up Central Park West. It was a beautiful day. I thought about all the people walking along the street and bicycling in the park and about how happy they looked. I thought how odd it was that my work day was over and it was only 8, and that that was going to be my life from now on. And how depressing it was. I did not think about the show. It had not happened. Nor did Lee mention it. . . .

During the first week, I had not seen or heard from Gordon. I debated whether or not to call him or leave a message, but then I figured if he wanted to see me he would have come back or sent a note. I will never understand why, after the first show, he didn't come screaming back to the *Morning News* and fire everybody, or put Hughes on with straight news, tell the world I had terminal pneumonia, and send me away to some hideaway studio in Connecticut with his trustiest producers and cameramen to work me over.

As far as I knew, nobody had seen or heard from Gordon. I waited each day for him to ask me into his office and explain gently that I needed some kind of training; that they were going to change the format, get a new set and a jazzy producer, set me up with taped interviews, get me out of reading the news, get me voice lessons, make me put on contact lenses, and demand that I grow my hair longer and cut out the ad libs.

Nothing.

The broadcast Monday was uneventful, including my first live television interview. It was—I still have a hard time believing this was the best person CBS could think of for my TV interview debut—the designer Emilio Pucci. I discovered that he was branching out from lingerie into sheets and men's wear.

Hughes did not participate. He wasn't all that anxious to, didn't particularly like to do interviews, and I'm sure he didn't have all that much to talk to Pucci about anyway, except the fact that they were both World War II pilots.

I called Gordon and left a message after the show. I was told he was out. Gordon soon became for me a Major Major Major figure from *Catch-22*. Hard to reach. . . .

My health all along had not been good. I still felt dizzy and nauseated in the early mornings, and I was constantly exhausted though there wasn't anything wrong with me as far as anyone could see.

There was, however, a major cosmetic problem.

For the first time since I was seventeen years old, I was developing acne. And it was getting bad. Rickey switched to an allergenic makeup, but it didn't help. The makeup and the bright lights must be doing it, I decided. I should have my face cleaned.

I remembered that a classmate of mine from Smith had a mother who ran an Institute of Cosmetology on East 62nd Street, which I occasionally read about in *Vogue* or

Harper's Bazaar. Her name was Vera Falvy, and she was a Hungarian with the most beautiful complexion I had ever seen.

Mme. Falvy examined my face carefully and asked about my eating habits, health, and life style. She knew I was on TV but had no idea of the hours or the pressure. She felt the breakout was caused by emotional tension. I would need regular treatment. We made another appointment and she gave me a special lotion which I was to use under, or preferably instead of, makeup.

Altogether I visited Madame six times, and the bills ran close to $300. She did her best, but the tensions kept building and my face got worse. My complexion has never been the same. I have scars on my face to show for those horrible months. . . .

That week I got a call from Barbara Howar. We chatted for a bit and Barbara, who had had her own TV shows, gave me a few pointers. She told me that I was coming along really well and shouldn't worry. Then she said, "Why don't you look at the right camera when the show is closing each day? Half the time the camera zooms out to the newsroom while you're looking straight ahead into the camera in the studio, and whenever the camera is in the studio you're looking across at the newsroom. You've got to keep your eye on the red light."

"Red light?"

"For God's sake," she screamed, "hasn't anyone told you about the red light?"

"No," I said. "What about it?"

"There's a light on the side of the camera," she said, "and when it goes on red it means that camera is on you and that's where you're supposed to look."

"Oh, no," I moaned. "No wonder. I saw that light flash on and off but I didn't know what it meant.". . .

Thanksgiving was the next day, and we never had holidays off. It was the tenth anniversary of Kennedy's assassination. When I looked at the line-up that morning, I saw that the only scheduled interview was one I had done several weeks earlier with a woman who had written a diabetic cookbook.

I couldn't believe it. Hughes complained to no avail. That seemed like the final straw. On the tenth anniversary of a president's death we were to do a mediocre (at best) taped interview with a diabetic-cookbook writer. There was no hope for any of us, or that broadcast.

Without staff meetings, there was still no coordination. Things hadn't gotten better. Usually, we didn't know who the guest was to be until we came on the program, and half the time it was someone neither of us was interested in or wanted to interview. We wrote lists of suggestions and notes, but nothing ever came of them. It is not that the people on the staff were incompetent, but just that there was zero direction, that morale was low, and that there was no coordination.

We had a rule about not accepting guests if they'd already been on the *Today* Show, and they had the same rule about our show. What that meant was that we hardly ever got any of the good people because the *Today* Show had a much larger audience and no publisher would allow his author on our show unless he couldn't get him or her on the *Today* Show.

I thought that was dumb. I thought we should take people who'd been on the other show, then try to do a better, or a different kind of interview. We were in a no-win situation.

Another problem I kept hearing about third-hand from my friends was that some of them had talked their publishers into letting them go on our program because they were friends, and then for some odd reason they were rejected. This happened to Art Buchwald and Teddy White. There would be some vague explanation; but usually there were about three people involved in setting up the interviews, and often they weren't there when I was, so I couldn't find out. It was a mini-example of the total method of functioning at CBS. It was exasperating and, in the end, useless to try to do anything about anything.

The broadcast was beginning to take on a slight death smell. I had to get out. . . .

I've often asked myself how CBS could have made so many mistakes, how they could have let me go on the air with no experience.

Part of my despair during that terrible time had stemmed from trying to fathom where I had gone wrong. The thing is, nobody really yet understands the medium. Television isn't even fifty years old. Shows go on and off every month, people are hired and fired ruthlessly, because nobody knows what will work and what won't. They don't know what terrible vibes a great-looking or -talking person may give out over the air or what good vibes a clod may transmit. So they don't want to make decisions—especially long-term ones. Therefore nobody does. It's what Sander Vanocur calls the "how-about?" school. Somebody said, "How-about-Sally-Quinn?" and there was a generalized mumble, and that was it. They hired me and nobody ever did anything about it again. Mainly because they didn't know what to do.

So much money is at stake—millions and millions of dollars in advertisements—that those who make mistakes cost their company a lot of money. If they do that too often they lose their jobs. On newspapers everything doesn't ride on one story or one series but on the long run. Everyone in television is basically motivated by fear.

And television news is run by the network. It is not really autonomous. Those in charge of entertainment have ultimate charge over the news programs. CBS News has a buffer between the management and the news division: Richard Salant. In fact, that is his primary function. He is a lawyer, not a newsman, and he is able to negotiate the vast differences of approach between the news side and Blackrock and to work out acceptable compromises. . . .

Thursday of the first week, Small asked me to come down to his office. Gordon was sitting there. I was surprised, to say the least. He hadn't told me he was coming down. He asked where I would be later in the day. He said he would call.

He called around 3:30 and asked if I could have a drink with him. I suggested he have a drink with Ben [Bradlee, *Washington Post*] and me, since they were old friends.

He hedged. Then he said he could get a hotel room and stay over if I wanted him to. We could have dinner. I suggested we all have dinner. He hesitated. I couldn't figure out what he wanted. "Well, Gordon," I said finally, "what do you want?"

He mumbled something about dinner for the two of us and how he could get a hotel room. I said I thought it would be more fun with the three of us. He blew up. . . .

"Gordon," I said quietly, "I'm going to quit CBS. I'll try to be out in about six weeks. But I've got to find a job first. Just get Small to let me stay in Washington until then. I can't—won't go back to the anchor job. But I don't want to just quit and have it look like I was a total loss. I want to have a great job to go to. Will you do that much for me? Just hold them off for a while?"

He looked relieved. "I'll do it," he promised.

We walked in silence to the Watergate Terrace Restaurant and made polite conversation through dinner. Nobody ate anything. I ordered gazpacho but I couldn't swallow it. As we were leaving I asked Gordon what I had been longing to ask him since we went on the air.

"Gordon, why did you do it? Why did you hire me and then throw me on the air like that with no training? Why did you do it to me?"

"What if I had told you we wanted to make you the anchor on the *Morning News* but that you'd have to have about three to six months' training on one of our local stations first. Would you have done it?"

"Of course not."

"That's why.". . .

The morning after I quit, Hughes signed me off: "Sally Quinn is leaving CBS News for *The New York Times*—not necessarily sadder, but certainly wiser. And we hope she's happier there than she was here. For one thing, the help over there don't have to get up as early as they do here."

I thought it was touching and funny in Hughes' own gruff way.

Later that morning Richard called to say that Don Hamilton, Director of Business Affairs, wanted that day to be my last day. I pointed out that I had two film pieces to finish and that I intended to work two more weeks, that I had two further weeks of vacation coming to me, and that therefore they could count me on the payroll for another month. I wasn't to start at *The Times* until March 18.

Richard said Hamilton wouldn't buy that. I told Richard that I would call Salant or Bill Paley if I had to, and give interviews about what a cheap crumby outfit CBS was if I heard another word on the subject. Just get me the four weeks' pay. I didn't care how he did it.

Richard understood that I meant it. A half hour later he called back and said, "It's all set."

It still made me chuckle, though, that such a huge corporation would be so unbelievably cheap, especially under the circumstances. But I don't know why I was surprised, after what I had been through.

Saturday, I got a letter from Dick Salant.

> *Dear Sally,*
>
> *In case you missed the AP story, I am attaching it. It quotes me absolutely correctly.*
>
> *I am terribly sorry that things did not work out as we all expected and hoped. The fault, I honestly believe, was ours—mine.*
>
> *In any event, best wishes for every sort of satisfaction and happiness. And if you can bear it, do drop in so I can say goodbye and good luck.*
>
> *All the best,*
>
> *Dick Salant*

The AP story was enclosed. It said: "CBS News President Richard Salant said Thursday that CBS would not hold her to her contract. Asked if he considered Miss Quinn's move a slap at CBS, Salant said, 'No, not at all. She doesn't owe us a thing. We owe her a lot. And we damn near ruined her by making a mistake and pushing her too far too fast."

On February 7 Gordon Manning was fired from his job as news director. He was given a job as "vice president and assistant to the president of CBS News."

Gordon had been news director for nine years. His ten years were up in June and he was to receive a pension. That's why he was given that job, to hold him over so he could get his pension. He was fifty-seven in June, 1974. Somehow Gordon managed to redeem himself, partly by landing Solzhenitsyn for Walter Cronkite to interview. He stayed on after June and became a producer for the public affairs division of CBS News.

Bill Small was given Gordon's job. Sandy Socolow was given the Washington bureau. The day the change was announced Small was in Gordon's office.

Reached there, he said he was completely surprised by the promotion. "I've only been at this desk for six hours," he said. "I'm just trying to find out where the men's room is and where they keep the key to the liquor cabinet."

On February 28 Lee Townsend was fired. They had no ready title for him to assume. He was later assigned to the investigative unit. The new *Morning News* producer was the Rome bureau manager, Joseph Dembo.

Howyadoon? Fuller Brush Calling

Cathryn Donohoe

Nothing stops the Fuller Brush man. Not snow, not rain, not heat—and certainly not the little lady at her kitchen door who tells him there's nothing she needs today.

"Invariably, the one that says that is the one that buys the most," David Schenerman explains.

Schenerman is 58. He has been a Fuller Brush man for 30 years. He is one of the last of the shoe-leather door-to-door salesmen, the kind who will walk any street, ring any bell, dodge any dog to conjure up a sale and close on it. He works, after all, on commission alone.

Every three weeks he wears out the heels on his support shoes, every two months the soles. He works when he's tired, when he's sick and when he's injured. When laryngitis steals his voice, he talks with his hands. One day when he couldn't speak he simply pointed to the products in his sample case and to his sales brochure. That, he says, was one of the best sales days he ever had.

"Howyadoon? Fuller Brush Calling," by Cathryn Donohoe, *Insight* Magazine, May 28, 1990, p. 42. Reprinted by permission of *Washington Times*.

And this morning, as he looks for a place to park and start his rounds in Steven-son—an upper-middle-income development of about 1,000 lawns north-west of Baltimore—he drives his white Chevy Nova with one hand. The left, held up to keep the blood from flowing toward it, wears oozing gauze around the ring finger, which was nearly lopped off below the nail in a camping accident two days before. For the pain he takes nothing. He needs a clear head to drive and to sell.

What he sells is an 84-year-old name. For years it was part of the American weave, one celebrated not just in hundreds of farmer's daughter jokes in the 1930s but in the movies and the glossy magazines as the epitome of door-to-door sales as well. To anyone over 40 these days—as most of the Schenerman customers are—the name can be an open sesame.

"Hi! Fuller Brush! Howyadoon? I got the mops on sale, and the brooms!"

Open sesame! He's in the kitchen. But that doesn't mean he'll make the sale.

"Here are the moth deodorant blocks for the closets. Keeps the closets smelling fresh. The moths are coming. And our sponge mops are on sale, and the feather dusters. And now, this is great: the over-the-door rack. We do a great job with that. For lingerie. It even handles heavy winter coats."

The lady of the house, a regular customer, resists by indirection: "I wish my kids would use them."

"This they will. It's real sturdy. Because it's steel, and it's vinyl-coated. Notice the way everything is beveled, so you don't have any sharp edges. You can put towels, lingerie, necklaces, heavy winter coats on there. And I got the good, super, mini carpet sweeper."

More indirection: "People don't use carpet sweepers like they used to."

"But this is great. This uses no electricity, works by friction. And by the way, you can adjust it to different heights for rugs or wood. And it picks up dog hairs and cat hairs better than a vacuum cleaner."

"I think I have everything," the lady says.

"Right. You got the mops and brooms last time. Scissors? Oh, and I got a good sale on the knives, the professional knives—"

"I have knives."

"—and a super sale on household shears. Ironing board cover?"

"I just bought one. Look, my husband told me I could not spend any more money this week. If I buy anything today, it's divorce, OK? So why don't you come by in a cou-ple of weeks, and maybe I can buy something then, OK?"

"Good enough. Catch you next month."

And he's out.

He sprints down the driveway, listing to starboard with his brochure, his sample case and a brown sack of gifts—white plastic funnels, mesh scrub squares, plastic rain bonnets and the traditional Fuller vegetable brushes—in his good hand.

He is an independent contractor, a man with his own business, working fulltime and exclusively for Fuller Brush. And in 12 years in this neighborhood he has built up a bevy of repeat customers whose buying patterns he reviews each morning before he leaves home. Sometimes they buy, sometimes they don't. When they don't, he knows they will buy next time.

"I'm not trying to convert anybody. It's not a pressure thing," he says. "I'm looking for people who are interested. If there's no interest, I'm gone."

He drives past 200 houses every day, checking driveways and garages for cars that tell him someone is behind the door. Once he parks, he will talk to 20 people—regulars as well as those he canvasses cold—and close, on the average, 10 sales.

That comes to $40,000 to $50,000 worth of Fuller products sold each year at a commission rate he refuses to reveal, though he says he will not quarrel with 35 percent to 50 percent. (Who knows? It might be higher.) It puts him among the company's top 100 salesmen.

"I do well," he says.

Not bad for a high school grad from Newark who pushed planes on the USS Coral Sea, then sold shoes and insurance when the Korean War ended. Schenerman and his wife, Toby, a high school teacher, have put three children through college, one as far as a doctorate and another to a master's.

The secret to all this, he says, is "the ABC of selling: Always Be Closing." That and the knowledge, picked up over 30 years, of how to negotiate the major obstacles.

First come the Dogs. "Even if they know you, you gotta be careful," he says, staring at a chain leash snaked across a front porch. In spite of it all, they got to him twice, and now he takes tetanus shots every five years.

Then comes the Door. "First of all, a good percentage of doorbells don't work. So you don't trust the doorbell. You knock too. If you don't get any answer, you get out fast. You don't make money talking to a door," he says.

"You go to the kitchen door if you can. You like to get them relaxed, and generally they're in the kitchen. If you go to the front door and they have to run in from the kitchen, they won't be relaxed."

The rest is ABC.

"Hi! Fuller Brush! Howyadoon?"

It's the kitchen door again and the lady of the house in a bathrobe.

"I don't have the pants hangers that you like on sale. But I got the deodorant moth protection for the closets. And this is great: the barbecue brush. It's a new item. You can scrape the grill with it. This is the last one. Take it. Take it."

"I'll give you a kiss," says the lady. "What happened to your hand?"

"I put it in the wrong place. Look, here's something you're gonna love. This is the best bathroom cleaner to ever hit the market. You squeeze a little bit of that on, and scrub, and it gets off all the stains in the bathroom. Lime, scale, rust, hardwater buildup. $6.98 for two. They're on an introductory special."

"I've got so much of that crap, it's unbelievable," says the lady of the house.

"I got the prelaundry. Takes out grass stains, grease stains, chocolate, mustard, catsup, perspiration. You buy two, you get the third one free on the sale. It's three times stronger than Spray 'n' Wash. Let me show you the can. Look, there's the can. It'll take out any stain. Grass stains, grease stains, chocolate, mustard, catsup, perspiration. We do a fantastic job with it."

"Naah."

"This is the new brush that gets your refrigerator coils clean."

"That's it. I want that."

"OK. A dozen? I'm kidding. You want one for your daughter? And I got a fantastic sale on scissors. And this is the new upholstery brush. That gets all the lint off the chairs and couches."

"It does?"

"Yeah. It's excellent. It gets lint off your chairs, your upholstery, your couches. It's the old-fashioned upholstery brush. We brought it back. See the way the tip is made? It picks everything up nicely. It has a wooden handle. And you know Fuller. It'll never wear out."

"I think that's a good idea."

"One will be enough? If you're going to get one for your daughter, you might as well get it on sale."

"She's getting a new sofa."

"There you go."

"It's going to be leather."

"Well, then she won't need it."

"So much of this junk I buy and I have," says the lady of the house. "Here, save your hand! You want me to write it up for you?"

Total this sale: $15.21.

When Schenerman takes time to reflect on his work, he talks first about selling, then about listening. To him, in some ways, they are one and the same.

"When you're selling, you always have to be selling. Get in, get the business and go," he says. "But sometimes you're like a bartender. People tell you things they probably wouldn't even tell their husbands. You let it go in one ear and out the other; you never repeat anything. You might not get a sale that day, but you gotta listen if they want to talk."

For more than 30 years he has been more than a bartender. He has rushed an injured boy to the hospital. He has played ambulance to five women in labor. One thing he has missed out on: "I've never been propositioned in 30 years. I don't know what's wrong with me."

In fact, he prefers to see husbands around. "When the woman's alone, she's afraid her husband will think she's spending too much. But when he's there, she'll say, 'Dear, can I buy this?' And he'll say, 'Sure, go ahead.' So I end up with a bigger sale."

To most people under 40, according to Fuller's own studies, the name that Dave Schenerman sells means either nothing or something their parents bought.

"Younger people will say, 'When I was a little kid, I remember the Fuller Brush man coming around,' " says Russ Imler, nine years with the company and a member of the board of directors of Fuller Industries in Great Bend, Kan.

Observers of the industry say the company's studies turned up even more. "There was absolutely no recognition of whether the company is still in business and, if so, how you bought one of their products," says George Hescock, an executive vice president of the Direct Selling Association, a Washington-based trade group.

Twenty-five years ago Fuller Brush had about 100,000 field representatives, by Imler's estimate. Today it has 13,000—80 percent of them women, most of them part-timers who sell by telephone to friends and neighbors, and none of them pledged exclusively to Fuller unless, like Dave Schenerman, they choose to be.

But even more, the Fuller story is the tale of a small company gobbled up by a corporate giant that, according to Imler, was geared toward retail and mail-order sales and "did not understand" the direct-sales tradition.

So when Sara Lee Corp. (which, as Continental Foods of Chicago, bought Fuller 22 years ago) last year offered to sell Fuller to Imler and a small investor group he heads, he jumped at the chance. It meant taking private again the business Alfred C. Fuller began in his sister's basement in Boston in 1906.

The brand-new, old-fashioned Fuller Brush is heading down a bumpy road. Under Sara Lee it had begun selling through mail-order catalogs and in discount stores. Company officials expect that to continue. Yet even as the deal became final last month, Imler resigned as Fuller Industries' president—in a conflict, according to one employee, over the new company's direction.

To Schenerman, one of the few old-timers left, it's just good news that the company is back. He disdained Sara Lee's focus on recruiting part-timers. "I'm a professional," he says, "and I don't consider the part-timers professionals. They just don't have the product knowledge I have."

"Hi! Fuller Brush! Howyadoon?"

The lady of the house, a gray-haired woman in a white T-shirt, hangs up the kitchen phone. "My friend says, 'Don't start an affair with the Fuller Brush man, because everybody tells jokes about it.' "

"Look, I got the new microwave oven cleaner and the microwave sponge. You get both of them for $3.99. And this is great: the new upholstery brush. Detergent OK? You should need another one. You want me to put you down for one? Good. These are the new skirt hangers. I got the 10-year light bulbs and a super sale on the knives. How about the degreaser and the steel sponges?"

"I have a self-cleaning oven," says the lady. "There isn't much I don't have."

"How about the can opener? Egg slicer? Jar opener? Those are great."

"Somebody said the jar opener was pretty good."

"OK, I've got two kinds. This one you mount under the cabinet and this one you hold in your hand. Both are good. It's just a matter of taste. This one you stick in the drawer. See, the inside ring is for small jars and the outside ring is for big jars. You put it on there, and it opens the jars instantaneously. $9.99. You want two? Or three? It's good for somebody who has trouble opening things. They make nice presents. How many do you want me to put down?"

"I don't know if I want any. Don't get excited."

"OK. You know me. I don't get excited. How about a window brush? You don't have to climb a ladder. Push broom? Ironing board cover? Let me look. You need an ironing board cover, hon, and the pad too. The whole set."

"I don't want the jar opener."

"They're really good. The only trouble is, once you try that jar opener, you'll want more for gifts. You'd order a whole bunch of them. They are just real helpers. They are really good."

"I know. I've heard people talking about them. How thick is it?"

"It's real easy to handle. They're nice. And they come in a box in case you want to use them as gifts. You know, if you have an aunt or somebody who has a hard time opening jars."

"I think I'll take that."

"One or two?"

"I want one for myself. It's for jars, right?"

"Yes. It'll open a jar. And you know what else I've got that you're gonna love? One of my favorites. The kitchen scissor."

"No. Finished."

"The toilet bowl swab?"

"Finished," says the lady of the house. "They used to say, 'If you don't go out, you won't spend any money.' Now it's not true."

Total for detergent, pad, cover, jar opener: $46.16.

Dave Schenerman finished his day at noon because of the throbbing pain in his left hand. By then he had racked up $249 in sales. This in spite of the women who assured him there was nothing they needed or wanted to buy.

But for the Fuller Brush man, this is the world as it was meant to be. "The more noes you get," Schenerman says, "the closer you are to a yes."

Death of a Salesman

Arthur Miller

From the right, Willy Loman, the Salesman, enters, carrying two large sample cases. The flute plays on. He hears but is not aware of it. He is past sixty years of age, dressed quietly. Even as he crosses the stage to the doorway of the house, his exhaustion is apparent. He unlocks the door, comes into the kitchen, and thankfully lets his burden down, feeling the soreness of his palms. A word-sigh escapes his lips—it might be "Oh, boy, oh, boy." He closes the door, then carries his case out into the living room, through the draped kitchen doorway.

Linda, his wife, has stirred in her bed at the right. She gets out and puts on a robe, listening. Most often jovial, she has developed an iron repression of her exceptions to Willy's behavior—she more than loves him, she admires him, as though his mercurial nature, his temper, his massive dreams and little cruelties, served her only as sharp reminders of the turbulent longings within him, longings which she shares but lacks the temperament to utter and follow to their end.

LINDA, *hearing Willy outside the bedroom, calls with some trepidation:* Willy!

WILLY: It's all right. I came back.

LINDA: Why? What happened? *Slight pause.* Did something happen, Willy?

WILLY: No, nothing happened.

LINDA: You didn't smash the car, did you?

WILLY: *with casual irritation:* I said nothing happened. Didn't you hear me?

LINDA: Don't you feel well?

WILLY: I'm tired to death. *The flute has faded away. He sits on the bed beside her, a little numb.* I couldn't make it. I just couldn't make it, Linda.

LINDA, *very carefully, delicately:* Where were you all day? You look terrible.

WILLY: I got as far as a little above Yonkers. I stopped for a cup of coffee. Maybe it was the coffee.

LINDA: What?

WILLY, *after a pause:* I suddenly couldn't drive any more. The car kept going off onto the shoulder, y'know?

LINDA, *helpfully:* Oh. Maybe it was the steering again. I don't think Angelo knows the Studebaker.

WILLY: No, it's me, it's me. Suddenly I realize I'm goin' sixty miles an hour and I don't remember the last five minutes. I'm—I can't seem to—keep my mind to it.

LINDA: Maybe it's your glasses. You never went for your new glasses.

WILLY: No, I see everything. I came back ten miles an hour. It took me nearly four hours from Yonkers.

LINDA, *resigned:* Well, you'll just have to take a rest, Willy, you can't continue this way.

WILLY: I just got back from Florida.

LINDA: But you didn't rest your mind. Your mind is overactive, and the mind is what counts, dear.

WILLY: I'll start out in the morning. Maybe I'll feel better in the morning. *She is taking off his shoes.* These goddam arch supports are killing me.

LINDA: Take an aspirin. Should I get you an aspirin? It'll soothe you.

WILLY, *with wonder:* I was driving along, you understand? And I was fine. I was even observing the scenery. You can imagine, me looking at scenery, on the road every week of my life. But it's so beautiful up there, Linda, the trees are so thick, and the sun is warm. I opened the windshield and just let the warm air bathe over me. And then all of a sudden I'm goin' off the road! I'm tellin' ya, I absolutely forgot I was driving. If I'd've gone the other way over the white line I might've killed somebody. So I went on again—and five minutes later I'm dreamin' again, and I nearly—*He presses two fingers against his eyes.* I have such thoughts, I have such strange thoughts.

LINDA: Willy, dear. Talk to them again. There's no reason why you can't work in New York.

WILLY: They don't need me in New York, I'm the New England man. I'm vital in New England.

LINDA: But you're sixty years old. They can't expect you to keep traveling every week.

WILLY: I'll have to send a wire to Portland. I'm supposed to see Brown and Morrison tomorrow morning at ten o'clock to show the line. Goddammit, I could sell them! *He starts putting on his jacket.*

LINDA, *taking the jacket from him:* Why don't you go down to the place tomorrow and tell Howard you've simply got to work in New York? You're too accommodating, dear.

WILLY: If old man Wagner was alive I'd a been in charge of New York now! That man was a prince; he was a masterful man. But that boy of his, that Howard, he don't appreciate. When I went north the first time, the Wagner Company didn't know where New England was!

LINDA: Why didn't you tell those things to Howard, dear?

WILLY, *encouraged:* I will, I definitely will. Is there any cheese?

LINDA: I'll make you a sandwich.

WILLY: No, go to sleep. I'll take some milk. I'll be up right away. . . .

[*Editor's note:* The scene shifts to Howard Wagner's office the following day.]

WILLY: Pst! Pst!

HOWARD: Hello, Willy, come in.

WILLY: Like to have a little talk with you, Howard.

HOWARD: Sorry to keep you waiting. I'll be with you in a minute.

WILLY: What's that, Howard?

HOWARD: Didn't you ever see one of these? Wire recorder.

WILLY: Oh. Can we talk a minute?

HOWARD: Records things. Just got delivery yesterday. Been driving me crazy, the most terrific machine I ever saw in my life. I was up all night with it.

WILLY: What do you do with it?

HOWARD: I bought it for dictation, but you can do anything with it. Listen to this. I had it home last night. Listen to what I picked up. The first one is my daughter. Get this. *He flicks the switch and "Roll out the Barrel" is heard being whistled.* Listen to that kid whistle.

WILLY: That is lifelike, isn't it?

HOWARD: Seven years old. Get that tone.

WILLY: Ts, ts. Like to ask a little favor if you . . .

The whistling breaks off, and the voice of Howard's daughter is heard.

HIS DAUGHTER: "Now you, Daddy."

HOWARD: She's crazy for me! *Again the same song is whistled.* That's me! Ha! *He winks.*

WILLY: You're very good!

The whistling breaks off again. The machine runs silent for a moment.

HOWARD: Sh! Get this now, this is my son.

HIS SON: "The capital of Alabama is Montgomery; the capital of Arizona is Phoenix; the capital of Arkansas is Little Rock; the capital of California is Sacramento . . . " *and on, and on.*

HOWARD, *holding up five fingers:* Five years old, Willy!

WILLY: He'll make an announcer some day!

HIS SON, *continuing:* "The capital . . ."

HOWARD: Get that—alphabetical order! *The machine breaks off suddenly.* Wait a minute. The maid kicked the plug out.

WILLY: It certainly is a—

HOWARD: Sh, for God's sake!

HIS SON: "It's nine o'clock, Bulova watch time. So I have to go to sleep."

WILLY: That really is—

HOWARD: Wait a minute! The next is my wife.

They wait.

HOWARD'S VOICE: "Go on, say something." *Pause.* "Well, you gonna talk?"

HIS WIFE: "I can't think of anything."

HOWARD'S VOICE: "Well, talk—it's turning."

HIS WIFE, *shyly beaten:* "Hello." *Silence.* "Oh, Howard, I can't talk into this . . ."

HOWARD, *snapping the machine off:* That was my wife.

WILLY: That is a wonderful machine. Can we—

HOWARD: I tell you, Willy, I'm gonna take my camera, and my bandsaw, and all my hobbies, and out they go. This is the most fascinating relaxation I ever found.

WILLY: I think I'll get one myself.

HOWARD: Sure, they're only a hundred and a half. You can't do without it. Supposing you wanna hear Jack Benny, see? But you can't be home at that hour. So you tell the maid to turn the radio on when Jack Benny comes on, and this automatically goes on with the radio . . .

WILLY: And when you come home you . . .

HOWARD: You can come home twelve o'clock, one o'clock, any time you like, and you get yourself a Coke and sit yourself down, throw the switch, and there's Jack Benny's program in the middle of the night!

WILLY: I'm definitely going to get one. Because lots of time I'm on the road, and I think to myself, what I must be missing on the radio!

HOWARD: Don't you have a radio in the car?

WILLY: Well, yeah, but who ever thinks of turning it on?

HOWARD: Say, aren't you supposed to be in Boston?

WILLY: That's what I want to talk to you about, Howard. You got a minute? *He draws a chair in from the wing.*

HOWARD: What happened? What're you doing here?

WILLY: Well . . .

HOWARD: You didn't crack up again, did you?

WILLY: Oh, no. No . . .

HOWARD: Geez, you had me worried there for a minute. What's the trouble?

WILLY: Well, tell you the truth, Howard. I've come to the decision that I'd rather not travel any more.

HOWARD: Not travel! Well, what'll you do?

WILLY: Remember, Christmas time, when you had the party here? You said you'd try to think of some spot for me here in town.

HOWARD: With us?

WILLY: Well, sure,

HOWARD: Oh, yeah, yeah. I remember. Well, I couldn't think of anything for you, Willy.

WILLY: I tell ya, Howard. The kids are all grown up, y'know. I don't need much any more. If I could take home—well, sixty-five dollars a week, I could swing it.

HOWARD: Yeah, but Willy, see I—

WILLY: I tell ya why, Howard. Speaking frankly and between the two of us, y'know—I'm just a little tired.

HOWARD: Oh, I could understand that, Willy. But you're a road man, Willy, and we do a road business. We've only got a half-dozen salesmen on the floor here.

WILLY: God knows, Howard, I never asked a favor of any man. But I was with the firm when your father used to carry you in here in his arms.

HOWARD: I know that, Willy, but—

WILLY: Your father came to me the day you were born and asked me what I thought of the name of Howard, may he rest in peace.

HOWARD: I appreciate that, Willy, but there just is no spot here for you. If I had a spot I'd slam you right in, but I just don't have a single solitary spot.

He looks for his lighter. Willy has picked it up and gives it to him. Pause.

WILLY, *with increasing anger:* Howard, all I need to set my table is fifty dollars a week.

HOWARD: But where am I going to put you, kid?

WILLY: Look, it isn't a question of whether I can sell merchandise, is it?

HOWARD: No, but it's a business, kid, and everybody's gotta pull his own weight.

WILLY, *desperately:* Just let me tell you a story, Howard—

HOWARD: 'Cause you gotta admit, business is business.

WILLY, *angrily:* Business is definitely business, but just listen for a minute. You don't understand this. When I was a boy—eighteen, nineteen—I was already on the road. And there was a question in my mind as to whether selling had a future for me. Because in those days I had a yearning to go to Alaska. See, there were three gold strikes in one month in Alaska, and I felt like going out. Just for the ride, you might say.

HOWARD, *barely interested:* Don't say.

WILLY: Oh, yeah, my father lived many years in Alaska. He was an adventurous man. We've got quite a little streak of self-reliance in our family. I thought I'd go out with my older brother and try to locate him, and maybe settle in the North with the old man. And I was almost decided to go, when I met a salesman in the Parker House. His name was Dave Singleman. And he was eighty-four years old, and he'd drummed merchandise in thirty-one states. And old Dave, he'd go up to his room, y'understand, put on his green velvet slippers—I'll never forget—and pick up his phone and call the buyers, and without ever leaving his room, at the age of eighty-four, he made his living. And when I saw that, I realized that selling was the greatest career a man could want. 'Cause what could be more satisfying than to be able to go, at the age of eighty-four, into twenty or thirty different cities, and pick up a phone, and be remembered and loved and helped by so many different people? Do you know? when he died—and by the way he died the death of a salesman, in his green velvet slippers in the smoker of the New York, New Haven and Hartford, going into Boston—

when he died, hundreds of salesmen and buyers were at his funeral. Things were sad on a lotta trains for months after that. *He
stands up. Howard has not looked at him.* In those days there was
personality in it, Howard. There was respect, and comradeship,
and gratitude in it. Today, it's all cut and dried, and there's no
chance for bringing friendship to bear—or personality. You see
what I mean? They don't know me any more.

HOWARD, *moving away, to the right:* That's just the thing, Willy.

WILLY: If I had forty dollars a week—that's all I'd need. Forty dollars,
Howard.

HOWARD: Kid, I can't take blood from a stone, I—

WILLY, *desperation is on him now:* Howard, the year Al Smith was nominated, your father came to me and—

HOWARD, *starting to go off:* I've got to see some people, kid.

WILLY, *stopping him:* I'm talking about your father! There were promises
made across this desk! You mustn't tell me you've got people to
see—I put thirty-four years into this firm, Howard, and now I
can't pay my insurance! You can't eat the orange and throw the peel
away—a man is not a piece of fruit! *After a pause:* Now pay attention. Your father—in 1928 I had a big year. I averaged a hundred
and seventy dollars a week in commissions.

HOWARD, *impatiently:* Now, Willy, you never averaged—

WILLY, *banging his hand on the desk:* I averaged a hundred and seventy
dollars a week in the year of 1928! And your father came to me—
or rather, I was in the office here—it was right over this desk—and
he put his hand on my shoulder—

HOWARD, *getting up:* You'll have to excuse me, Willy, I gotta see some
people. Pull yourself together. *Going out:* I'll be back in a little
while. *On Howard's exit, the light on his chair grows very bright and
strange.*

WILLY: Pull myself together! What the hell did I say to him! My God, I was
yelling at him! How could I! *Willy breaks off, staring at the light,
which occupies the chair, animating it. He approaches this chair,
standing across the desk from it.* Frank, Frank, don't you remember
what you told me that time? How you put your hand on my shoulder, and Frank . . . *He leans on the desk and as he speaks the dead
man's name he accidentally switches on the recorder, and instantly*

HOWARD'S SON: ". . . of New York is Albany. The capital of Ohio is Cincinnati,
the capital of Rhode Island is . . ." *The recitation continues.*

WILLY, *leaping away with fright, shouting:* Ha! Howard! Howard! Howard!

HOWARD, *rushing in:* What happened?

WILLY, *pointing at the machine, which continues nasally, childishly, with the
capital cities:* Shut it off! Shut it off!

HOWARD, *pulling the plug out:* Look, Willy. . . .

WILLY, *pressing his hands to his eyes:* I gotta get myself some coffee. I'll get
some coffee . . .

Willy starts to walk out. Howard stops him.

HOWARD, *rolling up the cord:* Willy, look . . .

WILLY: I'll go to Boston.

HOWARD: Willy, you can't go to Boston for us.

WILLY: Why can't I go?

HOWARD: I don't want you to represent us. I've been meaning to tell you for a long time now.

WILLY: Howard, are you firing me?

HOWARD: I think you need a good long rest, Willy.

WILLY: Howard—

HOWARD: And when you feel better, come back, and we'll see if we can work something out.

WILLY: But I gotta earn money, Howard. I'm in no position to—

HOWARD: Where are your sons? Why don't your sons give you a hand?

WILLY: They're working on a very big deal.

HOWARD: This is no time for false pride, Willy. You go to your sons and you tell them that you're tired. You've got two great boys, haven't you?

WILLY: Oh, no question, no question, but in the meantime . . .

HOWARD: Then that's that, heh?

WILLY: All right, I'll go to Boston tomorrow.

HOWARD: No, no.

WILLY: I can't throw myself on my sons. I'm not a cripple!

HOWARD: Look, kid, I'm busy this morning.

WILLY, *grasping Howard's arm:* Howard, you've got to let me go to Boston!

HOWARD, *hard, keeping himself under control:* I've got a line of people to see this morning. Sit down, take five minutes, and pull yourself together, and then go home, will ya? I need the office, Willy. *He starts to go, turns, remembering the recorder, starts to push off the table holding the recorder.* Oh, yeah. Whenever you can this week, stop by and drop off the samples. You'll feel better, Willy, and then come back and we'll talk. Pull yourself together, kid, there's people outside. . . .

REQUIEM

[*Editor's note:* Biff & Happy are Willy's sons. Charley is a neighbor.]

CHARLEY: It's getting dark, Linda.

Linda doesn't react. She stares at the grave.

BIFF: How about it, Mom? Better get some rest, heh? They'll be closing the gate soon.

Linda makes no move. Pause.

HAPPY, *deeply angered:* He had no right to do that. There was no necessity for it. We would've helped him.

CHARLEY, *grunting:* Hmmm.

BIFF: Come along, Mom.

LINDA: Why didn't anybody come?

CHARLEY: It was a very nice funeral.

LINDA: But where are all the people he knew? Maybe they blame him.

CHARLEY: Naa. It's a rough world, Linda. They wouldn't blame him.

LINDA: I can't understand it. At this time especially. First time in thirty-five years we were just about free and clear. He only needed a little salary. He was even finished with the dentist.

CHARLEY: No man only needs a little salary.

LINDA: I can't understand it.

BIFF: There were a lot of nice days. When he'd come home from a trip; or on Sundays, making the stoop; finishing the cellar; putting on the new porch; when he built the extra bathroom; and put up the garage. You know something, Charley, there's more of him in that front stoop than in all the sales he ever made.

CHARLEY: Yeah. He was a happy man with a batch of cement.

LINDA: He was so wonderful with his hands.

BIFF: He had the wrong dreams. All, all, wrong.

HAPPY, *almost ready to fight Biff:* Don't say that!

BIFF: He never knew who he was.

CHARLIE, *stopping Happy's movement and reply. To Biff:* Nobody dast blame this man. You don't understand: Willy was a salesman. And for a salesman, there is no rock bottom to the life. He don't put a bolt to a nut, he don't tell you the law or give you medicine. He's a man way out there in the blue, riding on a smile and a shoeshine. And when they start not smiling back—that's an earthquake. And then you got yourself a couple of spots on your hat, and you're finished. Nobody dast blame this man. A salesman is got to dream, boy. It comes with the territory.

BIFF: Charley, the man didn't know who he was.

HAPPY, *infuriated:* Don't say that!

BIFF: Why don't you come with me, Happy?

HAPPY: I'm not licked that easily. I'm staying right in this city, and I'm gonna beat this racket! *He looks at Biff, his chin set.* The Loman Brothers!

BIFF: I know who I am, kid.

HAPPY: All right, boy. I'm gonna show you and everybody else that Willy Loman did not die in vain. He had a good dream. It's the only dream you can have—to come out number one man. He fought it out here, and this is where I'm gonna win it for him.

BIFF, *with a hopeless glance at Happy, bends toward his mother:* Let's go, Mom.

LINDA: I'll be with you in a minute. Go on, Charley. *He hesitates.* I want to, just for a minute. I never had a chance to say good-by.

Charley moves away, followed by Happy. Biff remains a slight distance up and left of Linda. She sits there, summoning herself. The flute begins, not far away, playing behind her speech.

LINDA: Forgive me, dear. I can't cry. I don't know what it is, but I can't cry. I don't understand it. Why did you ever do that? Help me, Willy,

I can't cry. It seems to me that you're just on another trip. I keep expecting you. Willy, dear, I can't cry. Why did you do it? I search and search and I search, and I can't understand it, Willy. I made the last payment on the house today. Today, dear. And there'll be nobody home. *A sob rises in her throat.* We're free and clear. *Sobbing more fully, released:* We're free. *Biff comes slowly toward her.* We're free . . . We're free . . .

Biff lifts her to her feet and moves out up right with her in his arms. Linda sobs quietly. Bernard and Charley come together and follow them, followed by Happy. Only the music of the flute is left on the darkening stage as over the house the hard towers of the apartment buildings rise into sharp focus, and The Curtain Falls.

Dancing with Headhunters: Scenes from the Downsized Life

G. J. Meyer

I'm not getting any interviews.

I call and call and call, looking for leads. But when I turn one up and send in my résumé, nothing comes back. When I follow up the résumés with phone calls, secretaries get rid of me so smoothly that before I know what's happened I'm talking into a dead line.

This has been going on for weeks, and it's starting to scare me.

Then one afternoon the phone rings and it's a man I've been trying to reach, a headhunter named Roger Bullard in the Atlanta office of Russell Reynolds. He's looking for a P.R. vice president for Holiday Inns; he's seen my résumé and he has nice things to say about it.

Would I rather meet him in New York or Atlanta? He has offices in both places.

"Your choice," I say. "I'd vote for New York."

I wait while Bullard checks his calendar, "Monday in New York, then. Nine o'clock. Go ahead and make your reservations, and tomorrow call my secretary to confirm."

First thing the next morning I give Bullard's secretary my flight number, tell her I'll be arriving at my hotel on Sunday evening. She gives me the Russell Reynolds address and reminds me to be there at nine.

"Dancing with Headhunters: Scenes from the Downsized Life." by G. J. Meyer, *Harper's Magazine*, July, 1995, pp. 37–56. Reprinted with permission.

The offices, when I arrive, are like something out of the London home of a maharaja. All the walls are paneled the expensive way. Sheraton furniture, thick rugs, gleaming parquet floors. I'm gleaming, too: shoes, collar, cuffs. The crease in my trousers could draw blood, and I'm feeling good about the fact that despite my nervousness I managed seven good hours of sleep and an early jog in Central Park.

A mirror near the elevator indicates that I don't look like what I am: a guy out of work, thrown out of two corporations in the past three years, a little bitter, more than a little overeager.

I tell the receptionist that I'm there to see Mr. Bullard. With a slightly quizzical look she answers that he's not in yet, and I say I know I'm early. Moving delicately, not wanting to wrinkle the suit I've carried so carefully a thousand miles, I lower myself onto a leather sofa. Gingerly, keeping my fingertips clear of the ink, I open the *Wall Street Journal* on the coffee table in front of me and settle in to wait.

At nine the receptionist looks over at me, dials her phone, has a brief, inaudible conversation, hangs up, and looks at me again.

"You did say you have an appointment with Mr. Bullard?"

"Yes, I did. Nine o'clock."

"I'm sorry . . . but Mr. Bullard isn't scheduled to be in New York today."

When I call Atlanta, Bullard's secretary sounds almost as shocked as I feel. She can't understand how this could have happened. They were expecting me in New York *next* Monday. She thought that was understood.

In Edvard Munch's painting "The Scream," a solitary, empty-eyed figure stands in a roadway clutching its head, mouth open wide. I hope that's not what I look like as I walk the streets of Manhattan during the next several hours, seeing and hearing nothing, waiting for it to be time to return to La Guardia. But that's how I feel. Without making a sound, I scream all the way back to Wisconsin.

Today is Friday, the thirteenth of September, the ninety-eighth day of my unemployment. Ninety-nine days ago I was vice president for communications of the J. I. Case Company, a multinational manufacturing corporation with sales of more than $5 billion a year. Three years before that I was a vice president at McDonnell Douglas Corporation, a firm that needs no introduction.

And for more than three months now I have been a man with no particular need for an alarm clock, no place where I really need to go in the morning.

This afternoon, to kill a few hours and take my mind off a telephone that will not ring, I play nine holes of golf. For the first time this year it is difficult to find the ball. Pale leaves are beginning to clutter the fairways, making small white objects hard to see. On the day I was let go, the sixth of June, the Wisconsin summer was just beginning. I had expected that finding work would take a few months, during which I would be free to sleep late, to stay away from neckties for a while, to savor the sweetest part of the northern year.

Now it's fall that is just beginning, and I'm no closer to finding work than I was a season ago. I've had shots at jobs, but every shot has missed. I never got a second chance to meet with Roger Bullard. Holiday Inns, he told me, has put its search on hold.

I keep hearing politicians say that the recession is over. A nice thought. But what I see, wherever I look, is more and more good people with good credentials being let go for the first time in their lives and not being able to find work. I know an amazing number of capable, experienced, college-educated, unemployed people. Never in my life have I seen so many people lose their jobs. And I can't name one who has found a new job. Not one.

Ninety-eight days. Three months and a week. Not a long time according to the formula that says a job search is likely to last one month for every $10,000 of annual salary. By this formula, my wait has quite a way to go. The general rule for executive "separation packages" is this: the less you need, the more you get. If your annual compensation has been in six digits for years and the first digit isn't a one anymore, you can expect full pay and benefits for a year and a half, possibly even longer. Six-figure salaries starting with one are good for about a year, six months at a minimum. If your salary is well short of six figures and you have worries about the mortgage and tuition bills, watch out: you're down in dog-eat-dog territory, where they try to get you out the door with as little money as possible.

I have been among the immensely fortunate in this regard. At J. I. Case, after only two and a half years of work, I was promised up to a year with full pay and benefits while I looked for a new job. My wife, Pam, quit her own odious job before we knew mine was in danger and is now trying to get herself established in insurance sales. I hope she succeeds. Though my separation package is a wonderful cushion, it's also temporary, and I'm amazed at how much we've grown used to making and spending every month. Rivers of money flow in and just as quickly flow out: money to keep the kids in school, to keep the house and cars going, to keep all of it insured and the IRS satisfied. I don't like to think about how quickly all this could sink us.

The first thing I felt the first time I was fired was surprise—bone-rattling shock at finding myself, for the first time since the week I graduated from grade school, without a place in the world of work. My luck had been so good for so many years that I'd learned to think of it as something I had earned, something I was owed. The idea that it could turn bad so abruptly was, for a while, impossible to absorb. I walked the streets in an almost trancelike state, as if I were on the bottom of the sea, cut off from everything, not like other people anymore. I started to daydream about walking through my front door one afternoon and seeing dozens of people—old bosses, old colleagues, the very people who had done this to me—leap out from behind the furniture and yell "Surprise! Surprise!" In my daydream they're wearing party hats. They explain how the whole thing had been part of some experiment, and how sorry they were to have had to put me through it. Ah well, I say with a smile, all's well that ends well.

But each time I come home, they are not there.

My first job, at age thirteen, was mopping floors in a decrepit drugstore for fifty cents an hour. Twenty years later, I was moving between jobs of a kind my parents could hardly believe, with an income that passed the furthest limits of my imaginings; I've traveled the world, won semi-high honors, had my picture in the papers, floated above the fields of Normandy in a hot-air balloon.

And now, suddenly, I call it a good day if someone will take my phone call or answer my letter.

I know that not one percent of the human beings now alive in the United States of America, not one tenth of one percent of the current inhabitants of Earth, could possibly find me an object worthy of pity. I know too that this is as it should be: imagine feeling sorry for a man whose situation is so tragic that it causes him to play golf on

Fridays. Imagine feeling sorry for somebody who is still drawing full pay ninety-eight days after being fired and still has months of full pay ahead of him whether he gets out of bed or not.

And yet I feel sorry for myself constantly. And I want everybody I know to feel sorry for me.

I am ashamed of myself, of all my feelings: murderous rage, envy, fear, and, mostly, shame itself. On a simple level I'm ashamed of myself for being out of work, for getting my family into such a fix, for allowing myself to become an "executive" in the first place and then letting the whole thing go so wrong. I'm ashamed of myself for losing. When I hear the guy next door start his car in the morning and drive away, I'm ashamed to be in bed. I'm ashamed to rake leaves on weekday afternoons, because everybody in the neighborhood will know—as if they didn't already—that I don't have an office to go to anymore. The deeper shame has to do with my weakness in the face of what feels like the most painful crisis of my life but which is, in fact, a mere inconvenience compared with what millions of people face every day.

Yet I'm jealous of anybody who still has the kind of job I used to have, of almost anybody who has a job, period. My envy of the people who put me here and are still drawing their giant salaries and piling up their gigantic pension points is as murderous as my resentment.

I envy people who took fewer chances than I did and are now in the safe if charm-less harbors that I set sail from years ago: the post office, the Navy, reporting jobs at daily papers. I also envy people who took more chances than I did and broke free of salaries and corporations and bullshit. I spend a lot of time wondering where I might be today if I had taken more chances.

If envy caused cancer, I'd be dead by Sunday.

Calm down, I tell myself. Stop pacing. Find something sensible to do.

But I find that I can't do any such thing.

What will I be like by Christmas?

I think I can tell you how it will happen, if it's going to happen to you. The first thing they'll do, when they've made their preparations, is to get you out of your office and into a room with some geek from Human Resources.

If you're a vice president, your executioner will be a V. P. also—possibly a senior V. P. Directors are done by directors, managers by managers, et cetera, on down almost to the ranks of the blue-collar folks who even today do actual work for a living even in these United States of America.

From the moment you pass through his door, the H.R. geek will appear to be in visible pain. He wants you to understand that he, too, is a human being, a nice guy, and that his mother didn't raise him for this kind of thing.

(Is it flippant of me to call these people "geeks"? Originally the word referred to individuals who did revolting things for money at carnivals and fairs. I don't think I'm being flippant at all.)

"God," said McDonnell Douglas Corporation's senior vice president for Human Resources ten seconds before he fired me. "God, this is going to be hard." He twisted, literally writhed, in his chair. Then he swung back toward me and quickly got down to his work.

Once the geek has delivered his message and demonstrated the depths of his humanity, he'll get up out of his chair and come around from behind his desk. You'll be drawn up after him by some mysterious force resembling magnetism, and together the two of you will glide out the door and down the hall to some smaller office that you probably never noticed before, where somebody you've never seen is waiting to tell you not to worry, everything is going to be fine.

Sometimes other people are waiting in other little rooms nearby, but if you behave yourself you'll never know about them. There might be a company lawyer, for example. You won't see him unless you say something that indicates a less than perfect willingness to be agreeable. Somebody from security might be hidden in the wings, too.

The stranger awaiting you in the little office, the one telling you that everything is going to be all right, is the outplacement geek. He's been brought in, and will be paid handsomely, to "guide you through your transition."

The assigned outplacement geek will be the nicest of nice guys—one of the main reasons he was called to his profession in the first place. He'll give you a small, slightly rueful smile. He'll say that he understands what a shock this is but that he also knows something important: that it's very likely the start of a better life not just for you but for your whole family. If he was ever fired himself, he'll tell you about it, encouraging you to appreciate how beautifully that worked out in the end. Or he'll tell you about one or two of his past clients—how one of them is now King of Samoa and the other is expected to be nominated for the Nobel Prize next week. He'll ask whether everything will be okay at home, whether you expect to have trouble telling your spouse. When you say no, he'll give you his card and urge you to take things easy for a while, but then to come see him at his office.

"I know it can be hard to believe at a time like this," my first outplacement geek told me, "but it really is true that this could turn out to be the best thing that ever happened to you."

The outplacement geek wants to think of himself as a useful citizen, a kind of midwife, not as an accessory after the fact. Understandable, of course. Not many of our mothers had anything like this in mind for us when they brought us into the world. Not many of us want to do these things we do for pay.

A guy in Connecticut, a friend of a friend, tells me that Gerber Products has a search on. I wait until just after six and try to call the company's vice president for Human Resources, Curtis Mairs. Calling very early or very late in the day is a good tactic: the secretaries are usually off duty then. Today it works: Mairs picks up his own phone, and he doesn't hang up as I hurriedly introduce myself. I say I've heard he's looking for a P.R. exec. Not wanting to repeat what may have been my big mistake with Booz, Allen, I say I'd like the name of the recruiter handling the search.

"You might try Steven Seiden," he says. "In New York," and hangs up. There's a New York listing for Seiden Associates, Inc., in my *Directory of Executive Recruiters*. And it is indeed headed by a Steven Seiden. I spend much of the evening writing and rewriting a letter.

First thing the next morning I call Seiden's office and get his fax number. Then I drive to the EconoPrint shop and have my letter and résumé transmitted. Next I put both into a manila envelope, drive to the post office, and send them off by Priority Mail.

The next night Seiden calls. We talk for a long time. He goes through my résumé line by line, asking for details about everything.

"Well," he says finally, "all of it sounds pretty impressive. On the face of it. As far as it goes."

On the face of it? Does he think I'm pretending to be somebody I'm not?

He asks me to describe my appearance. When I do so, fumblingly, he asks how tall I am. How much I weigh. Whether I have a beard. A mustache. He asks me to send a photo of myself.

What?

We agree that I will also send him samples of my work.

Once again I sit up late composing a letter intended to make me seem brilliant and clever, motivated but not desperate. When I'm satisfied, I put it into an envelope with a fat stack of supporting evidence: corporate annual reports, articles and speeches, official descriptions of my last two jobs, charts of departments I've headed, a survey showing that business editors rated one of those departments among the best in the country after I'd been running it for seven years. Fat yellow envelope in hand, I'm at the post office when it opens in the morning.

Early the following week, Seiden calls to say he's received my envelope, has examined most of the contents, and finds it "very impressive—assuming it all checks out."

Does he think I've forged this stuff?

Days later I arrive home to find a message saying that Seiden wants me to call him.

"Listen," he says when I reach him, "I'm in a meeting and can't talk now. But I want you to know that I really am interested in you for the Gerber thing. I'll be back to you soon. This search is *not*"—the italics are in his voice—"going to go ahead without you. I'll be back to you soon—in hours, not days. You'll hear from me again in hours, not days."

Taking Seiden at his word, I begin to watch the clock. The day ends without another call. The next day ends the same way, and so does the week. Then it's weeks, not days. After a very long time I try to call him, don't get through, leave my name and number.

More than a week after that Pam and I arrive home one Sunday night and find a message on the machine. The voice of Steven Seiden says, in a bored way, that he's returning my call. He has left his home number but cautions me not to disturb him after ten-thirty New York time—precisely the time I hear the message. After a moment of agonizing I decide to wait.

The next morning I call, leave a message, get nothing back. In the evening I call him at home. His wife says in a cheery voice that he's gone out briefly but will call me back soon.

He doesn't. He never calls again. Eventually, many weeks later, an envelope arrives from his office. In it is a copy of the news release announcing that a new vice president of communications has been appointed at the Gerber Products Company.

The winner is from Chicago. I recognize his name. He's the guy who told me about the Gerber search in the first place.

Small world.

This doesn't need to turn out to be the best thing that ever happened to me. I'll be satisfied, I'll be grateful, if it turns out to be something less, than a disaster. If it ends with me in a new job that's more than barely tolerable, with my life not totally deranged and Pam and the kids not permanently hurt. If it ends that way I will, so help me, get down on my knees in gratitude.

What I keep thinking about, though, is not exciting new opportunities or the delights that are still to come.

What I think about is Bobby Joyce.*

Bobby Joyce lived in my neighborhood when I was a kid and was a year ahead of me in high school. He was a big, good-looking Irishman of the black-haired, white-skinned, Snow White type—cocky, arrogant, unfailingly sarcastic, athletically brilliant. When I picture him I always see him chewing gum, smiling a kiss-my-ass smile. He showed us how it was possible to be cool even in a cassock and surplice. I'm sure he didn't chew gum while serving Mass, but it isn't hard to picture him that way.

Thirty years out of high school, I found myself seated next to another old-timer from the neighborhood, Jimmy Monahan, at some sort of downtown business lunch. Jimmy had been a few years ahead of Bobby Joyce in school, which put him several years ahead of me. He'd always been the friendly sort, though, even to us little guys. When I ran into him he was the advertising manager for an insurance company. He had the creased face and tired, unjudging eyes of a decent man for whom life has not been a picnic. As the luncheon broke up and we were moving toward the door he somehow mentioned Bobby Joyce—how miserable it was, what had happened to him.

I couldn't let it go; I had to ask. Bobby had become an accountant, Jimmy said, and spent decades with the same company before losing his job. After a year of failing to find a new one, Bobby killed himself. He did it by jumping off the Union Avenue viaduct onto some old railroad tracks at the northern edge of the neighborhood where we'd all been schoolboys together.

I don't know what season it happened in. But in my mind's eye I see it as a raw winter's day, a black-and-white turned-up-collar day like some scene from *On the Waterfront.* It's hard to draw a connection between the spent man I see pulling himself up onto the viaduct's concrete railing and the beautiful boy I remember.

Bobby Joyce, uncrowned king of the kids, dead of a year without work.

If outplacement resembles anything, it's probably purgatory. You don't want to be there, you wouldn't be there if you'd been better or smarter or luckier, and the only point in being there is doing what you can to get out. And there's the sheer brutal shock of it, the difficulty of believing that you really are dead.

When you find yourself in outplacement it's because your former employers have paid to get you in. The price of admission is not trivial: a month and a half of your salary is the standard. What you get for this is working space with desk and phone, access to a pot of coffee, the use of a clerical staff and various office equipment and a pitiful excuse for a library. You share in the services of a receptionist who answers the phone by saying "executive offices" and takes any messages you're lucky enough to get. For what it's worth, you get the advice and the pep talks of your assigned counselor.

You can go to outplacement every day or every other day, once a week or once a month. It depends on how determined you are, or how futile the whole thing has started

---

A pseudonym.

to seem. If nothing else, outplacement can give you a reason to put on a white shirt and tie and get into your car in the morning. You are saved from never getting out of your pajamas, from slowly descending into a vegetative state.

The counselors will tell you that if you're serious about getting out of purgatory, you're going to have to telephone everybody you know—and a great many people you don't.

"*Mr. Johnson? Mr. Johnson, my name is Jerry Meyer. I'm the vice president of communications at the J. I. Case Company here in Wisconsin. Joe Smith at Consolidated Amalgamated gave me your name. About a week ago I sent you a letter that I hope has reached you by now. As my letter indicated, I've reached a point in my career where I'm interested in exploring some new options, and I'm wondering if you've heard of any searches it might be worthwhile for me to check out.*"

Dave, who used to be the head of security at J. I. Case and has become my best friend in outplacement, somehow got a copy of a directory of all the corporate security chiefs in America. Every day, hour after hour, he goes through it page by page, entry by entry, dialing and talking, dialing and talking, gradually accumulating leads like a prospector panning for gold. So far, his leads have not led to a single interview. The problem, I guess, is that he's well past fifty. But he never gives up, and although he makes a lot of sour jokes, he never complains. He never even slows down.

In outplacement, if you know what's good for you, you force yourself to be as much like Dave as you can. You listen attentively to the counselors as they tell miracle stories about people just like you who wrote and wrote and called and called and got absolutely nowhere until one day—wonder of wonders—the job of their dreams fell swooning into their arms. Above all, you force yourself to dig deeper and deeper into the directories and dredge up more and more names. There are hundreds of headhunter firms in the U.S. today, many thousands of individual headhunters. And one of the rules of outplacement, is that if you haven't sent your résumé to some particular headhunter within the past six months, it's time to do so again. If you send out a thousand résumés in June and are still out of work in December, do it again. There's enough work in this to keep anybody busy for a lifetime. As for whether it actually makes sense, is actually going to pay off . . . well, what else are you going to do?

So you pick up that phone and you force yourself to make those calls. But unless you're luckier than most or the job market gets a lot better, you'll discover that it's possible to send off five hundred résumés with five hundred customized cover letters and not get a single reply more substantial than a preprinted postcard saying thanks.

You'll learn that after a while it can become very hard to think of new people to call, harder still to call for the third or the fourth time. You'll find that gradually some of your fellow deceased aren't showing up very often anymore. Some will drift away completely, and you'll remember their dark jokes about becoming a security guard or moving north to where somebody's son-in-law knows about a job driving a delivery truck. You'll wonder what happened to them but won't really want to find out.

You'll see how every week a little more confidence has been drained from the eyes of the people who keep coming back, so that after a while they look as if they're afraid of life. You'll reflect that exactly the same change must be taking place in your own eyes. You'll want to stay home and never get out of your pajamas. But you won't dare.

Václav Havel writes that modern society is held together by fear—fear of loss, mostly; so we accumulate more and more things with which to assure ourselves that it isn't necessary to be afraid and that our compromises haven't been for nothing. It is fear, Havel believes, that drives us to accept corruption and dishonesty, to pretend we are what we aren't.

Ultimately, having given away almost everything that matters, we end up defining ourselves by our possessions. Gradually we become incapable of imagining goals higher or more meaningful than a fine house or a fine car. We abandon hope without even realizing we've done so.

I have friends who wear gold Rolexes and cashmere sports coats, but when you get to know them it turns out that, they regard their own lives as misbegotten messes of fear and greed and disappointment. It's no wonder that so many of them—people with summer houses and BMWs—turn out to be quietly desperate for retirement. I think they see retirement as their last chance to go back to being the people they were when they were starting out, back to being themselves. Too often, though, by the time they reach retirement they're so hollowed out they no longer remember who they once were. Their idea of fulfillment has come down to six days of golf a week.

Before entering the corporate world, I had many jobs in many fields: naval officer, newspaper reporter, public relations consultant. Looking back, none of these was better than the one in which I was a "blubberer," scraping sealskins for a fur company in Alaska. Physically, this was the hardest work I've ever done, bloody and greasy and foul. Five hours of it would exhaust the best of us. And it required living for months on a barren island where the sun literally never broke through the clouds, a place without stores, movies, television, beer, girls, or even a record player.

What was wonderful about the Alaska job I can see only in retrospect: it had no bullshit. No politics, no pretense of any kind. Our job was to finish all the skins on hand as quickly as we could without damaging them in the process. When skins came in we worked like brutes, pushing dull knives through resistant tissue until our hands bled. But when we were finished nobody expected us to hang around pretending to be working or pretending to be eager for more.

In my first ten or so years of adulthood, through graduate school and the Navy and Vietnam and my first adult, civilian jobs, I got accustomed to wearing a necktie and to *being* something rather than simply doing something for pay. But through it all I daydreamed about getting free. Until I was well into my thirties I almost always thought of my jobs as interruptions, intrusions into the parts of life in which I could come closest to being me.

But gradually, by thousands of steps each as insignificant as the twitch of a second hand, we get broken in. By infinitesimal stages we change from rebellious colts to seasoned, stolid wheelhorses. Somehow we come not merely to accept the harness but to need it. To be deeply uneasy, even deeply afraid, without it.

Considering how little I've enjoyed or been satisfied by many of the jobs I've had, it is increasingly strange to me that I now find it so painful to awaken every morning to the realization that I have no work to go to; that no one is expecting me anywhere. I think of this before I open my eyes, and the thought always comes as a sharp stab. Back when I was a colt, shying at the halter and kicking at the traces, I couldn't have imagined all this freedom hurting as much as it does.

At times I've said, in talking with friends, that maybe I'm never going to find another corporate job. I always say next, in what I hope is a cavalier tone, that if that's how things work out it won't really matter much. But until recently this was just bluster. I didn't mean it, didn't really believe that anything of the kind could happen. Now I believe. Now it looks not only possible but likely. And I do think it matters.

Several of the friends I value most have told me that they hope I never go back into a corporation. Write, they advise; teach. I invariably reply that I'll probably end up doing something like what they suggest. But before making a final decision, I add, I owe it to myself to look carefully at all the options. I need to look into the corporate possibilities too, I say, because that's the responsible thing to do.

After some experimentation I settle on the word "responsible" as particularly good in this context. It seems to suggest that although I am, of course, rich in options, and although, of course, I know the right thing for me would be a spot in academia or in the world of authors (someplace where I would be free not only to share my wisdom with the human race but to do so in sneakers and a sweatshirt), I also need to remember my obligations to wife and children and all that.

Declining to suggest these things would involve an admission that I have at present no options at all, that as a matter of hard fact I would grab the first really solid job opportunity that came along, regardless of whether it was back in the defense business or back in the agency business or at East Jesus Community College. But I don't seem to be capable of that kind of truthfulness. I can't admit how naked I feel and how helpless, can't admit that if anyone gave me one more shot at the fat-cat world I'd snatch at it like a hungry beggar snatching at a dollar bill.

I make a file for every job lead that comes my way. Each contains a thin stack of pages: ads clipped from newspapers, formal job descriptions when I can get them, brief handwritten records of phone conversations, copies of letters sent to headhunters, and their replies, if any. In the early weeks of my search, as the files accumulated, I lined them up in a row on a coffee table in the bedroom, overlapping them, so that the names formed a column.

Early on it was a pretty impressive display: Philip Morris, Digital Equipment Corp., Holiday Inn, Rhone-Poulenc, Ameritech, Gerber, Imcera Group, Union Carbide. Big, rich corporations. It seemed hard to believe then that at least one of these wouldn't lead to an offer of some kind.

Since then my little display has withered as completely as the leaves of summer. Gradually, as I've been told or have figured out for myself that I'm not in contention for this or that job, I've moved my files to a cardboard box in the basement. I call the box my department of dead letters.

Since then I've been answering ads that describe jobs for which I am—or so I honestly believe—ridiculously overqualified. My active-leads file now is, consequently, as fat as it's ever been. But with jobs I would have sneered at in June, July, or August.

SPRING

The first of the mallards and Canada geese have made their appearance in Wisconsin. I have fewer job prospects than I had last summer. A birthday has passed, so that I'm now one year older and have that much less value on the executive meat market. My professional credentials grow just a little staler with every passing month.

I could go to truck-driver school and learn to operate one of those huge tractor-trailer rigs. I could pull vast loads from coast to coast and back again. Maybe buy my own diesel eventually.

Or maybe my neighbor Jim would give me a job in the little air-filter factory he runs. He's constantly complaining about how impossible it is to find minimally competent and dependable people. I'm minimally competent. A year's take-home pay probably wouldn't cover a lot more than the taxes on my house, but it would be better than no job at all. And it could make me a local legend: the former briefcase carrier who spent the last twenty years of his life inserting tab A into slot B seventeen times a minute, forty hours a week.

For that matter, I could try standing behind the counter at McDonald's or Burger King or Kentucky Fried Chicken. I would wear a little paper hat and dread the thought of having to wait on somebody who knew me when.

In another daydream I simply stop looking for work, stop having my hair cut, stop going anywhere or doing anything that could possibly involve the unnecessary expenditure of fifty cents. I never buy a new piece of clothing, never again own a car, turn my yard into a vegetable garden and my kitchen into a canning factory. Slowly I evolve into the crazy old man of Racine, Wisconsin, as my house falls in around my ears. And when I'm truly old and the last of my money is gone, I use a real-looking toy pistol and enter upon a career of armed robbery. If I'm caught, no tragedy: I'll be put in a place where there's a warm, dry bed and free food every day.

Of all the companies on the list above my desk, the list that couldn't conceivably fail to generate a job offer, I am now down to a single possibility: The Principal Financial Group.

The Principal's headhunter, a New Yorker named Jim Wills, passed through Chicago and met with me over dinner. He said he was looking at scores of candidates and hoped to give the company a list of about half a dozen names representing a spectrum of different backgrounds and skills. In the next month he called to say that I had been promoted from his shortlist to the company's.

The month after that two of the company's executives flew out from Des Moines and spent four hours questioning me. They seemed to be decent sorts—Iowa-wholesome again, and Iowa-cautious. I didn't learn much from or about them in the course of our talk, and I didn't see how they could have learned much about me. I was grateful, though, that they didn't bring any psychologists.

A month later I'm scheduled for a two-day visit to Des Moines that will include a meeting with the CEO. The company sends me tickets that will put me on an early-morning flight from O'Hare. On the day before the start of my trip, I go for an especially long jog so that I'll be especially relaxed when it's time to sleep. Before ten that night I drink a cup of warm milk, get into bed, open the less-than-fascinating new biography of Woodrow Wilson that's been my bedtime reading for weeks now, and wait for the nodding-off to start as usual after a few pages.

Before the first nod, though, Pam comes running up the stairs. According to the television a freakish spring blizzard has struck to the south of us in Illinois. O'Hare is in chaos—flights canceled, people stranded by the hundreds. I leap out of bed. It takes me an hour of waiting on the phone to find out that the departure time for my flight has already been postponed indefinitely, with cancellation possible. In another half hour I have a new reservation on a flight out of Milwaukee and have managed to reach my designated contact at The Principal and tell him of the change. By the time I go back to bed every part of my nervous system is on red alert. I try to lose myself in Woodrow Wilson but can't think about anything except the blizzard and whether I'm going to be able to get out of Milwaukee in the morning and how in the hell I'm going to cope with a full day of interviews if I don't get to sleep soon.

I turn out the light, try to fall asleep, realize after a while that it isn't going to happen. Eventually, I creep to the bathroom and surreptitiously, embarrassedly, sneak one of the little (and now rather old) red-and-white sleeping pills that a doctor once prescribed for jet lag. This is the first sleeping pill of my life; I don't know how they work and don't want to ask because I don't want a debate. An hour later, still no closer to sleep and more desperate than ever, I take a second pill. Not long after that I am sound asleep. When the alarm goes off very early in the morning the skies over Wisconsin are clear. I reach the Milwaukee airport with time to spare, my flight takes off on schedule, and I arrive in Des Moines without difficulty.

There is a problem, though: the person who has arrived in Des Moines doesn't seem to be me. My mind, my perceptions, my whole system seem to be—I'm not even sure what word to use—refracted, perhaps. Everything has been thrown slightly but disorientingly off center. It's not that I feel bad really. I simply don't feel that I'm here somehow. I don't feel connected in the usual way to the things I'm experiencing. My experiences don't seem to be mine.

Hour after hour that day I'm led from office to office, from meeting to meeting, and none of it ever feels entirely real. I seem to be able to move and smile and answer and ask questions in a solidly normal way, but as each meeting ends, I have alarmingly little memory of what's just been said. It's the same that night, when an executive vice president takes me to dinner and wants to know all about the day's meetings and what I think about what I've seen. I have to struggle to find things to tell him.

That night I sleep well (without further chemical assistance, needless to say), but though I feel more like myself on Tuesday morning, part of me is still in some fourth or fifth dimension, some distant cosmos where two plus two makes three point eight or four point one.

The next day starts with a long meeting with the CEO. He, too, is curious about yesterday's meetings, and again I try to conceal the trouble I'm having remembering even the names of the people I met. The CEO seems a nice enough man. He also seems dry, narrow, dull. Is it the chemicals that make me think so?

I'm put in a car and taken on a tour of Des Moines. People have been telling me proudly how much the city has grown, how much is going on here. To me, today, despite all my genuinely good memories of the place, it seems the dreariest town of its size I've ever seen. The downtown, which supposedly has been booming for nearly twenty years, looks comatose. The suburbs are exactly how Gertrude Stein would have pictured the suburbs of Des Moines: a flat and barren expanse of mud and clapboard, clapboard and mud. No there there.

When everyone is finished with me, I have hours to kill before my flight. The weather has turned steamy warm, so I set out on a walk. I circle through the downtown area. It's as much a blank from the sidewalk as it had been from the car—nothing of interest, nothing happening, not a single shop I'd like to browse in.

Then, because there doesn't seem to be anything more to look at downtown and it's still too early for the airport, I set out for the neighborhood that years ago everyone regarded as the best in town. South of Grand, it's called; Pam and I and most of our friends thought of it as the place where the upper crust lived. If we were to move to Des Moines now, it's where we would look first for a house. Twenty minutes of fast walking get me there, and when I arrive I see it hasn't changed at all. It's what I remember. But somehow, without changing and without deterioration, it has diminished. It's exactly what I expected and at the same time it disappoints. What comes to mind as I walk the streets on this warm and humid afternoon with plants of every description starting to push up out of the ground, what I keep thinking of is—mildew.

MILDEW? This has to be the chemicals, still messing with my head.

I become aware of how urgently I'm hoping that everything went well—how desperately I want these people to like me, be impressed by me. In a similar situation in a different culture I would sacrifice a ram on the steps of The Principal's headquarters. I would prostrate myself in the spilt blood and pray for deliverance at the foot of what is said to be the tallest building between Chicago and the Coast.

Then, in the midst of all this fervent aspiration, a simple question pops up:

Why?

Why have I got my whole existence centered on this thing?

Because I need a job, obviously. Because if The Principal doesn't offer me a job I'm going to have to keep repeating this process until somebody does. Or until I'm no longer allowed to repeat the process, or have become incapable of doing so. Because I've lost control of my own life and don't know how to get it back except by seducing somebody into hiring me.

But it is clear to me, walking these streets, that I don't want to live here; that I have no real interest in The Principal Financial Group; that I haven't seen a single way in which working there could possibly be interesting, or absorbing, or fun; and that this time it's not the chemicals talking.

On the flight home I compose a letter telling Jim Wills that I no longer want to be considered for the job. By way of explanation I say that even after my two-day visit I still don't understand what the company is looking for, I say further that I can find no way of judging whether I would like the job or would do well in it, or whether, over the long term, management would be happy with me even if in my own opinion I was doing the job well.

That night I run the letter through my word processor and seal it in an envelope. But in the morning I can't mail it. It's exactly the letter I would send if I were safely in a job instead of being desperately in need of one. But how could I possibly explain to Pam, to my children, to my parents, to the world, that although, as far as I can tell, the interviews in Des Moines went well enough, I've decided to drop out? That although this is a strong and profitable company and its leaders are clearly at least somewhat serious about the possibility of offering me work, and although I don't have a single other live prospect, I've decided to call the discussions off. How could I defend such an act?

After all these months of doing everything possible to find a job and not getting a single offer, after seeing more and more people lose their jobs and have no more luck than I'm having, after growing more and more accustomed to seeing beggars on the streets of every city I visit, I cannot throw this chance away. Even though the job's attractions are mainly the escapes it offers—an escape from fear, from insecurity, from shame—turning my back on it would be pure bravado. And pure bravado, these days, carries a higher price than I can afford to pay.

I tell myself to grow up, that dramatic gestures are for children. That it's still far from clear that they're going to make me an offer. Until they decide, I can continue to look elsewhere. It's not inconceivable that something better will come along very soon. It is merely extremely improbable.

If I'm offered the job and take it and it turns out to be as boring as I expect, well, hell, I've had boring jobs before. That's why they call it work. When I start feeling bored I'll have no trouble remembering how lucky I am to have a job. I'm not good at slogging through day after day of tedium, pretending to care about things that don't interest me, but I've proven that I can do it.

Eventually Wills calls to tell me that among the candidates the company has examined, I'm the sole survivor. However, there is now an inside candidate they want to consider, and that's going to take time. A week later, Wills calls again. He's a little vague, but conveys the impression that I'm still the leading candidate, that the inside candidate has been tested and found wanting. But now another *outside* candidate has emerged. Nothing can happen until this new prospect has been seen and checked out. My mind blossoms with questions, the biggest of which is whether these people are going to keep digging up new candidates until they finally succeed in locating one who doesn't trouble them in the way I, apparently, do.

On a Friday afternoon, after another two or three weeks of silence, Wills calls yet again. The Principal's decision makers have told him they now have everything they need. They intend to make their decision during the week after next.

Ten working days at most. Even if the process runs true to form, I reason, and takes twice as long as predicted, we're still only talking about twenty working days. That's nothing compared with what's already behind me. It's now something like four months since I first had dinner with Wills. Ten months since I started looking for a job. Even twenty more days of only slightly embittered uncertainty are nothing, absolutely nothing, compared with that.

Late on Monday afternoon, at the end of the first day of the week when nothing can possibly happen, I tear a long, narrow strip from the edge of a sheet of yellow legal paper. I tape one end of this strip to the bottom edge of a picture frame across the room from my desk. It hangs there like a ribbon, like some award I've given myself for getting through a whole day of final-phase waiting. On Tuesday afternoon I do the same thing. And on Wednesday. When the week is finally over five shreds of paper hang from my picture frame like a row of military decorations, one for every twenty-four hours of agony endured. It pleases me to look at them. They represent the only kind of achievement that seems to be within my grasp these days.

The next five ribbons come harder.

Ten full months without a job. Human eggs fertilized the day I was fired are bawling babies now. The end of my separation-benefits package is coming into view. I have nothing to hope for but word from The Principal Financial Group.

SUMMER

Everything is green outside when Jim Wills calls to tell me that The Principal has reached its decision. More than six months after starting their search, four months after I was drawn into it, they've decided not to offer the job to anyone.

Chapter
11
Hazards

Some years ago when Maslow's hierarchy of needs was the core concept in classes on human behavior, it was commonly assumed that most American workers had their lower level needs such as safety fulfilled. While that assumption was probably wrong then, as people have become more aware of the hazards that workers encounter in their daily tasks and the health hazards from the accumulation of stress over their careers, that assumption is less likely to be made today. Still, conventional textbooks give very little attention to such risks. The selections in this chapter are intended to correct that unfortunate omission.

"Automation: Pain Replaces the Old Drudgery" describes the cumulative-trauma disorders workers in business and industry are experiencing as a result of new technology coupled with pressure to get the work out.

We have included several articles that highlight hazards that exist because of the products made by organizations and the processes used to create them. E. S. Evans reports the impact of one in "Ailing Ex-Workers Tell of Long Years amid Asbestos Dust." The Story of David Marsing in "Killer Results Without Killing Yourself" suggests some of the hazards of a high stress job and explores a strategy for getting beyond them. "Crisis in Bhopal" by Paul Shrivastava is the story of the Bhopal Chemical spill disaster.

The remaining selections deal with other hazards, some of which are the product of government efforts to protect employees from hazards. Well intentioned governments efforts can backfire as described by Bob Baker in "Overtime Takes Toll on American Workers," by Don Wycliff in "Blacks Debate the Costs of Affirmative Action," and in "The Right to Privacy: There's More Loophole than Law," by Michele Galen and Jeffrey Rothfeder.

In the next selection, "Danger in the comfort Zone" Judith Bardwick tells us that much of the security American workers felt in the past may be gone forever. Unfortunately, some of the hazards of work extend beyond the workplace. Finally, the impact on family life and particularly children is described by Brian O'Reilly in "Why Grade 'A' Execs Get an 'F' as Parents."

The exerpt from "Under the Influence," the unauthorized story of the Anheuser-Busch dynasty, is a chilling illustration of why some executives may not have the time to give to their children. The demands apparently placed on advertising agency executives by the CEO of Anheuser-Busch were extreme and failure to comply could mean instant firing. Working with this company appeared to be hazardous to one's health.

Automation: Pain Replaces the Old Drudgery

Peter T. Kilborn

For nine years, Paula Tydryszewski has operated a video display terminal in New Jersey's tax collection office. She types numbers and names from tax returns at woodpecker speeds into a keyboard that is tied to a big computer in the center of the room.

Ms. Tydryszewski and the 111 other full-time data entry clerks do white-collar work with blue-collar rhythms and discipline. They are tethered to their tasks by machines that let them do vastly more work than they could have done 15 or 20 years ago with paper and ledgers and typewriters.

Like Ms. Tydryszewski, an increasing number of workers around the country say they are suffering from ailments caused by the repetitive motion of their jobs. These potentially disabling ailments include cysts, inflammation of tendons, nerve damage that can lead to a loss of feeling in the fingers, and arm or shoulder pain.

Shift in Values a Factor

Occupational health specialists, labor unions and the Federal Government say tens of millions of workers, like the keyboard operators here, are at risk of these cumulative-trauma or repetitive-motion disorders. The Bureau of Labor Statistics said the disorders accounted for 48 percent of the 240,900 workplace illnesses in private business in 1988, up from 18 percent of 126,100 illnesses in 1981. The problem showed up first in factories and is now spreading through the growing office sector of the economy.

Experts attribute some growth in injuries reported to more awareness of a relationship between the ailments and work. Another factor is a shift in values: in the late 20th century, safeguarding the environment and protecting one's health are probably cherished as much as keeping the economy going and keeping one's job.

Experts say the actual numbers of injuries are proliferating because people are being pressed to work hard—in private industry to keep up with foreign competition, in government to hold down spending.

Automation has done away with heavy lifting by humans and replaced it with light lifting at rat-a-tat-tat speeds.

"We're really asking people to do more," said Don Chaffin, director of the University of Michigan's Center for Ergonomics, which studies ways to adapt working conditions to suit workers. "That has a cost."

Vern Putz-Anderson, who leads a group of professors at the university who are studying the disorders, said, "More than half the nation's workers now have jobs with the potential for cumulative-trauma disorders."

Among the jobs are those in the automobile and textile industries, and in meatpacking, where carcasses are turned into steaks and chops by a sort of assembly line in reverse.

With better workplace and equipment design, and with more breaks for relaxing, occupational health specialists say most problems can be avoided. But many employers have been slow to acknowledge a link between work and the disorders. And some workers, including Ms. Tydryszewski, are reluctant to report injuries, out of fear that employers will let them go or shift them to lower-paying jobs.

Nor can workers' problems be easily linked to cruel bosses. "New Jersey is fighting a budget deficit, and putting tax receipts into the bank promptly means the state can collect that much more interest before it pays its bills," said Barbara Jo Crea, assistant chief of the New Jersey Division of Taxation. "The mission of this branch is to deposit the money."

ONE WOMAN'S STORY: SCARS ON ARMS TELL OF PAIN

Ms. Tydryszewski's problems are showing up in her work. Her union, Local 1033 of the Communications Workers of America, points to two two-year-old incisions on her left wrist, one across the base to remove a ganglionic cyst, a formation of syrupy fluid on sheaths surrounding the tendons; the other incision running lengthwise, from the palm about two inches up the arm, to relieve a more serious condition known as carpal tunnel syndrome.

The cyst, a grape-sized lump, appeared first. "I kept pushing it back inside for two years," Ms. Tydryszewski said. "One morning it wouldn't stay down, so I went to the doctor. I had surgery and did exercises. Then I dropped a milk bottle. I had no feeling in three fingers. So I had surgery for that."

Now at the end of each day, Ms. Tydryszewski said, muscles near the back of her neck tighten into a knot, and her right arm has begun to hurt. But she said she would not complain; she is afraid of losing her $18,000-a-year job.

In early May, her supervisor sent her a memorandum. "My records indicate that you received a written warning for excessive errors on Nov. 8, 1989," it said in part. "As of today, you have not made any improvement in this area. On April 26, 1990, as documented by computer compiled statistics, you entered 189 documents with 264 errors."

Management repeatedly advises Ms. Tydryszewski to take more time, but taking more time means falling below its requirement that she make 8,000 keystrokes an hour. Working faster, on the other hand, could mean more visits with the surgeon.

WORKPLACE CHANGES: COMPUTERS SPREAD; SO DO PROBLEMS

In the past, most reported cumulative trauma disorders arose in heavier work, especially in meat and poultry-packing plants and in automobile assembly. The Federal Occupational Safety and Health Administration has won agreement from several leading meat-packers to correct working conditions that contribute to the disorders, and in February it cited a 2,000-employee General Motors parts plant in Trenton for 40 cases of workers who needed surgery to correct repetitive-motion injuries.

But the disorders are now showing up widely in computer work. Supermarket checkout clerks appear to be getting them as a result of the twisting motions they make in sweeping people's purchases over the little windows through which laser beams record the product and the price. And they are proliferating among millions of office workers, who also have other concerns stemming from the use of computers, including exposure to radiation.

Sixty-one percent of 645 Associated Press news employees who participated in a recent Newspaper Guild survey said they had neck and back pains, said the union's research director, David J. Eisen. And a study by the National Institute of Occupational Safety and Health and the University of Michigan said 38 percent of the reporters and editors at the Long Island-based newspaper Newsday had similar complaints arising mostly from the speed and the time that reporters spend using their terminals.

The Los Angeles Times surveyed 1,200 news employees and found more than 17 percent, mostly reporters, complaining of symptoms of various types of disorders. "Two or three have needed surgery, and six or seven have been diagnosed with carpal tunnel syndrome," said Michael G. Manfro, the newspaper's safety and environmental affairs manager. He said the company now provides better working equipment that requires less strain to operate, along with special glasses.

OSHA'S VIEW: LAWS MAY TAKE YEARS TO ENACT

Gerald F. Scannell, the head of the Occupational Safety and Health Administration, said that in view of the rising injuries, the agency would soon issue voluntary guidelines for meatpacking companies to use in preventing the disorders. Later, perhaps in August, he said it would issue guidelines for all other industries. The guidelines, he said, could be followed by regulations that would have the force of law, but that could take years. Until then, OSHA can go after employers over repetitive-motion injuries by charging them for unsafe working environments.

Mr. Scannell said he also supported a proposal of Senator Frank R. Lautenberg, Democrat of New Jersey, to triple, to $30,000, the amount OSHA can fine employers for each worker found to be working in violation of health and safety laws, but he said he opposed the Senator's proposal that OSHA raise the limit unilaterally every five years to keep pace with inflation.

Roger L. Stephens, OSHA's top specialist in the science of adapting the things people use to avoid pain or injury, said workers had always done awkward repetitive tasks, but infrequently enough or slowly enough that their tissues and tendons restored themselves. "Today," he said, "we see a lot of production demands."

Repetitive-motion ailments, like writer's cramp and tennis elbow, have plagued people for ages, but their connection to the workplace is fairly new. Among the most common are ganglionic cysts; tendinitis, an inflammation of the tendons; tenosynovitis, another form of tendon-sheath inflammation; peritendinitis, an inflammation of the area around the tendons; bursitis, an inflammation of a sac of fluid over bones that allow movement of the tendons, and carpal tunnel syndrome.

Carpal tunnel syndrome seems to arouse the most concern because of the involvement of the vital median nerve. The nerve runs down the arm and through a tunnel at the wrist, about an inch in diameter, into the hand, where it services most of the palm, the base of the thumb and the other fingers except the last. Ten tendons, enveloped in sheaths and running parallel with the nerve, protect the nerve and control the fingers. A ligament forms a belt across the tendons and binds the wrist bones, adding more protection.

Doctors say frequent and awkward maneuvers of the hand and wrist irritate the tendons over months and years. This can cause the tendons to inflame, and to squeeze and rub the median nerve, ultimately damaging it.

Proper posture can help prevent carpal tunnel syndrome. This means sitting in an upright "piano" position at the keyboard. Ideally, one's arms are parallel to the floor and there is some support for the wrists.

Symptoms of carpal tunnel syndrome are numb and tingling fingers, usually at night, and loss of feeling. Early on, it can be treated with rest, a job change, wrist splints that avert unnatural movements, and cortisone.

As symptoms worsen, the last—and usually effective—resort is cutting the ligament at the base of the wrist. As Dr. Putz-Anderson wrote in a book, "Cumulative Trauma Disorders," after recovery "it is important that the worker is not returned to the same job or task that precipitated" a disorder.

Even so, some of the victims of the disorders who work for the State of New Jersey return to their old jobs after they are cured.

AT THE KEYBOARD:
THE WORKER'S BODY DOES THE ADJUSTING

Trenton's tax collection office, similar to other data entry centers in the state government, uses two large rooms, one for smokers and one for non-smokers. The clerks sit at tables, each about a yard wide, with white formica tops. Chairs can be adjusted for height and to rock but nothing else. Some people bring in pillows.

On the tables in the data processing offices are 16-year-old terminals, about half the size of conventional desk-top computers. Neither the keyboards nor the screens can be tilted, turned, raised or lowered. Because they cannot adjust the equipment, the clerks adjust their bodies.

During the peak of the tax season, from February until June, the office hires about 200 temporary clerks at $7.53 an hour. In the most intensive six weeks, the temporary clerks get an incentive: 10 cents an hour more for every 500 keystrokes an hour above 8,000.

In a tacit acknowledgement of a connection between the injuries and computer work, the New Jersey Department of Health has issued guidelines for the safer use of video display terminals. Among other things, they urge installation of more adjustable chairs, work tables and computers.

Ms. Crea said she and the Division of Taxation supported such changes. But in view of budget problems, she said, new equipment "is not in the cards."

Some state clerks like the work. Robin Sabol, 32 years old, who works in a Labor Department data-entry office, said that her required keystroke rate was 10,000 an hour but that her actual rate was 18,000 to 21,000. "I like to push myself," she said. "Ten thousand is boring and monotonous." As for aches and pains, she said: "Sometimes it gets to you. But if you like the job, you're going to do your best."

But complaint and discomfort seem more the norm. In a survey of 118 clerks at the tax office completed two weeks ago by Local 1033, 81 percent said they had had hand or wrist pain, 47 percent experienced numbness or tingling in their fingers, and 82 percent had had arm or shoulder pain. In addition, 15 percent said a doctor had found them to have tendinitis, 8 percent said they had cysts on the hands or wrists and 7 percent— eight workers—had carpal tunnel syndrome.

Terri Croushore, who is 35 and sits near Ms. Tydryszewski, has not had maladies as acute as her colleague's in her four years on the job. But Ms. Croushore, who does 14,000 keystrokes an hour when the work is heavy, says she is beginning to get a burning sensation in her elbows, a tingling in her wrists and numbing in her fingers. She doesn't complain. "They would just tell me to slow down," she said.

FLOOD AWAITED: MANY MORE CLAIMS ARE EXPECTED

New Jersey officials say they accommodate injury cases when employees can bring persuasive evidence from doctors that an injury is job-related. The worker receives full pay and benefits without losing any of the 10-day-per-year sick leave. Ms. Tydryszewski, who was out for six months in 1988, said she had never heard of the policy, but even if she had she might have had a tough time proving her case.

Ms. Crea said she had had only two requests for sick-leave benefits related to cumulative trauma disorders, one involving carpal tunnel syndrome and the other tendinitis. The requests were denied, she said, because they were deemed "pre-existing conditions."

New Jersey officials, like many employers, say they have to be tough about granting benefits to people who allege work-related disorders, partly because of budgetary constraints, partly because the ailments are often hard to trace to any single cause.

For those reasons, and others like fear of demotion, disability claims for treatment of the disorders are low. Stover H. Snook, ergonomics director at the Liberty Mutual Insurance Company in Boston, said repetitive-motion injuries accounted for 1 percent of his company's claims and 1.5 percent of the cost of the claims.

"But it's a major health problem," he said. "In the past, workers would tolerate it just so they could get work. Now they're less tolerant of pain and discomfort. Any employer that has large numbers of employees doing these tasks has got to worry about the floodgates."

Ailing Ex-Workers Tell of Long Years amid Asbestos Dust

E. S. Evans

"When I walked up the steps into the courthouse," Bernard J. Schaefer told a federal jury. "I had to stop and rest before I could make it."

Schaefer, 80, of Florissant, had come to U.S. District Court in St. Louis to tell the jury that he was suffering from asbestosis and how he got the often disabling lung ailment. He had worked 32 years in an asbestos-products plant in St. Louis County.

He and four other longtime employees of the plant, their wives and the widows of two others are suing eight American, Canadian and British suppliers of raw asbestos fiber. They allege that they were not warned that breathing asbestos dust could cause lung ailments and cancer.

The multimillion-dollar suit here is one of about 20,000 that have been filed in courts across the country.

The civil trial resumed today in Judge William L. Hungate's courtroom. It began last week and was expected to last at least two more weeks.

Schaefer and other plaintiffs testified last week that they suffered from shortness of breath. They described the asbestos shingle-and-pipe plant where they worked as constantly clouded with asbestos dust. Dust collection machinery often failed, they said, and respirators were seldom used because workers had not been advised of the health hazards until the 1970s.

Coughing as he spoke, Schaefer said shortwindedness stopped him from continuing the odd-job work he did after retiring in 1966 from the Certain-Teed Corp. plant.

Formerly the Keasbey and Mattison Co. plant at 600 St. Cyr Road in Bellefontaine Neighbors, it was closed in May 1980.

The defendant companies contended in opening statements that it was the users' responsibility to take precautions, rather than the producers'.

"I cough a lot at night," Schaefer said. "Because I don't want to disturb my wife too much, I go to the bathroom. In the mornings when I get up, I do a lot of coughing and spitting."

He and others said they sleep poorly at night, frequently having to sit up to get any rest. They have to avoid stairs and cannot do household chores like mowing the lawn or shoveling snow.

They said that they had crushed and mixed asbestos fiber with cement, had cut shingles and pipe made from the material and had unloaded porous burlap bags of raw asbestos from boxcars, but that they had never seen any markings on the bags warning of health hazards. Clouds of dust rose when the asbestos was tossed onto wagons, shoveled into the crusher and dumped into mixing vats, they recalled.

When James E. Hullverson, the plaintiff's attorney, asked Schaefer whether such a warning would have made any difference to him, the battery of defense attorneys objected. Hullverson argued that his clients would testify that they would have quit their jobs, and he prevailed.

"I'd have tried to get out of there, one way or another," Schaefer answered. On cross-examination, he admitted that he was aware that there might be a health hazard, "but I didn't think it would affect me."

He said the plant always had asbestos in the air. "You could see it fall off the joists up above when the mechanisms shook the building a little bit," he noted.

Albert Wiese, also of Florissant, worked at the plant 45 years and testified that when the dust collectors broke down, "the dust would get so thick you couldn't walk through it."

His breath was shortened after nearly 30 years on the job. "If I walked the length of the plant, I would be puffing," he said.

Later, a company doctor told him he had asbestosis, but he continued work until retiring when the plant was shut down. However, being a foreman, he spent as much of his last working years as he could in the office.

"I became known as a guy who didn't do very much, I guess, because I got away from the stuff," Wiese said.

Lorraine Wiese, his wife, told the jury that he used to bring the dust home on his clothes. About his lung condition, Mrs. Wiese said, "When he goes to bed, his breathing is so heavy that I have to go to another room to sleep."

Vera Dile testified that her husband, Eugene, died in 1979 of cancer, 16 years after contracting asbestosis. He had retired at age 65 with 40 years' service at the plant and died at 68, she said.

Medical authorities have forecast that 200,000 cancer deaths would be attributed to asbestos exposure in the next 20 years.

Since 1900, research has accumulated evidence that inhalation of asbestos, microscopic stone fibers valued in construction materials for their resistance to heat and fire, can cause some kinds of cancer tumors and asbestosis. The dust impregnates the walls of the lungs many years after initial exposure. The asbestos industry contends that the extent of the danger was not understood until the mid-1960s, when protective measures were begun.

A deposition was read to the jury from Robert R. Porter, retired president of the old Keasbey and Mattison Co. He said that he could recall no warnings to workers of the danger nor management concern for their health during his 1955–62 tenure. He said he had seen photographic evidence of lung damage from asbestos impregnation, which the company's owner ordered destroyed, but had known little about asbestosis.

"If you inhale a lot of water, you can't breathe," Porter stated. "If you breathe enough asbestos, you're going to smother. That's about all I knew about it."

Porter said that during a 1955–56 tour of asbestos plants in England, he noticed that workers were wearing masks to prevent inhalation of the dust. Porter said he was told that sanitation laws were much more stringent in the United Kingdom than in the United States.

His company was owned at that time by Turner & Newall Ltd. of Great Britain, one of the defendants in the suit. Other defendants include Bell Asbestos Mines Ltd. and Asbestos Corp. Ltd., both controlled by a Quebec government agency, and Johns-Manville Corp. of Denver, which once owned Bell Asbestos.

Certain-Teed was not a defendant in the suit when it was filed two years ago, but has been named in a cross-claim brought by defendants.

Crisis in Bhopal

Paul Shrivastava

At about 12:40 A.M. on December 3, 1984, Suman Dey looked at the gauges on the control panel in total disbelief. Dey was the control-room operator at the Union Carbide pesticide plant in Bhopal, India, and what he saw was so far out of the ordinary that it terrified him. Inside a storage tank containing the dangerous chemical methyl isocyanate gas (MIC), which was supposed to be refrigerated, the temperature had risen to 77°F. Pressure in the tank, which ordinarily ranged between 2 and 25 pounds per square inch (psi), had risen to 55 psi.

Bewildered by the readings, Dey ran to the storage tank area to investigate the problem. He heard a loud rumbling sound and saw a plume of gas gushing out of the stack in front of him. Dey, along with the MIC supervisor on duty, Shakil Qureshi, and several operators, attempted to control the gas leak by turning on safety devices. Together they tried switching on the refrigeration system to cool the storage tank. They started the scrubber through which the gases were passing and sprayed water on escaping gases, hoping to neutralize them. When all these efforts failed, they fled the plant in panic.

Across the street in a slum hut, a twenty-eight-year-old woman named Ganga Bai was awakened by incoherent shouting. She felt a burning sensation in her eyes and rubbed them, hoping to soothe them. Outside, she saw terror-stricken neighbors running through the narrow gullies between the huts, shouting single words: "Run!" "Gas!" "Death!" She woke up her husband, picked up her two-year-old daughter, and ran out of the hut.

Ganga Bai bypassed the crowd by running on the muddy ledge between a row of huts and the main road. As she ran, she saw death in its most bizarre forms. People were choking and gasping for breath. Some fell as they ran, and some lay on the roadside, vomiting and defecating. Others, too weak to run, tried to clutch onto people passing them in the hope of being carried forward.

After running for several miles, Ganga Bai stopped to catch her breath. The crowd had thinned out, and she was far away from her neighborhood. She thought she had escaped death. But actually she had been carrying it in her arms all along. She looked down into the glazed, open eyes of her still daughter and fell unconscious.

The Bhopal district collector, Moti Singh, and the superintendent of police, Swaraj Puri, were awakened in the middle of the night by the insistent ringing of their telephones. Singh and Puri were in charge of district administration, the local police department, and civil defense efforts. They rushed at once to the police control room to coordinate emergency relief efforts. But they, along with hundreds of other governmental officials and Union Carbide plant managers, were caught sleeping in more ways than one. Nobody seemed to know what gas had leaked, how toxic it was, or how to deal with the ensuing emergency. The police and the army tried to evacuate affected neighborhoods. They were too slow, and instead of being told to lie on the ground with their faces covered with wet cloths, people were urged to run; 200,000 residents fled in panic into the night.

Morning found death strewn over a stunned city. Bodies and animal carcasses lay on sidewalks, streets, and railway platforms, and in slum huts, bus stands and waiting halls. Thousands of injured victims streamed into the city's hospitals. Doctors and other medical personnel struggled to cope with the chaotic rush, knowing neither the cause of the disaster nor how to treat the victims. Groping for anything that might help, they treated immediate symptoms. They washed the eyes of their patients with water and then soothed the burning with eye drops. They gave the victims aspirin, inhalers, muscle relaxants, and stomach remedies to relieve their symptoms.

Before the week was over, nearly 3,000 people had died. More than 300,000 others had been affected by exposure to the deadly poison. About 2,000 animals had died, and 7,000 more were severely injured. The worst industrial accident in history was over.

But the industrial *crisis* that made the city of Bhopal international news had just begun. Its ramifications were both local and global. As time went on, victims suffering from the long-term health effects of exposure to MIC died. There were continuing controversies over how many people had actually perished and which treatments might be helpful to surviving victims. Family life in Bhopal was radically disrupted, as wives and children with no preparation for life outside the home were forced to go to work and manage the family's financial affairs. The victims sued the government of India and Union Carbide. The government, seeking to protect its own legitimacy, sued Union Carbide in the United States on behalf of the victims. Governments in other countries took steps to stop Union Carbide and other chemical companies from establishing similar plants in their communities. Union Carbide's top executives were arrested upon their arrival in Bhopal, and the corporate prestige and financial health of the thirty-seventh-largest company in the world—a strong and proud corporation with a long history—was dealt a heavy blow.

In one sense, the Bhopal crisis was simply an industrial accident—a failure of technology. But the real story behind the accident goes much deeper than mere technology. It extends to the organizational and socio-political environment in which the accident occurred.

Organizational pressures within Union Carbide contributed to both the accident and the ensuing crisis. The Bhopal plant was an unprofitable operation, for the most part ignored by top Union Carbide officials. With several of Union Carbide's traditionally profitable divisions in the United States faltering, the Bhopal plant was a prime candidate for divestiture. The Indian subsidiary that owned the plant, Union Carbide (India) Ltd. (UCIL), was primarily a battery company that had made an unsuccessful foray into the pesticides market. At the time of the accident, the Bhopal plant operated at only about 30 to 40 percent of capacity and was under constant pressure to cut its costs and reduce its losses.

But it was more than Union Carbide's financial difficulties that set the stage for the crisis. The economic, political, and social environment of Bhopal also played a contributing role. At the time of the accident, Bhopal was a peculiar combination of new technology and ancient tradition sitting in somewhat uncomfortable relation to each other.

Though the city is nearly 1,000 years old, its industrial capacity, until recently, was primitive. In the last thirty years industrial growth was encouraged in Bhopal, but the necessary infrastructure needed to support industry was lacking. There were severe shortcomings in the physical infrastructure, such as supplies of water and energy and housing, transportation and communications facilities, as well as in the social infrastructure, including public health services, civil defense systems, community awareness of technological hazards, and an effective regulatory system.

Nor was industrial growth accompanied by rural development, which might have slowed the migration of people from the hinterlands. The city's population grew at three times the overall rate for the state and the nation in the 1970s. This heavy in-migration, coupled with high land and construction costs, caused a severe housing shortage in the city. For shelter, migrants built makeshift housing, which in turn became slums and shantytowns. By 1984, more than 130,000 people, about 20 percent of the city's population, lived in these slums. Two of these large slum colonies were located across the street from the Union Carbide plant.

Thus, at the time of the accident, several thousand, for the most part illiterate, people were living in shantytowns literally across the street from a pesticide plant. They had no idea how hazardous the materials inside the plant were, or how much pressure the plant was under to cut losses. Indeed, most of them believed it produced "plant medicine" to keep plants healthy and free from insects.

Not all industrial accidents become crises. They trigger crises only when technological problems occur in economic, social, and political environments that cannot cope with them. The Bhopal accident became a crisis not because of technological problems alone but also because of environmental conditions outside the plant. The plant was operated by a company under pressure to make profits and/or cut losses; it was sanctioned by a government under pressure to industrialize, even though the appropriate industrial infrastructure and support systems were missing; and it was located in a city completely unprepared to cope with any major accident. It was these factors, combined with the technological failures that actually caused the accident, that expanded the initial event into a crisis.

Although it was the worst industrial crisis in history, Bhopal-like crises are hardly unusual. All over the world—and, increasingly, in developing countries—industrial crises have become more frequent and devastating. For this reason they deserve close attention. For example, the dioxin poisoning in Seveso, Italy, and the Three Mile Island and Chernobyl nuclear power plant accidents represent industrial crises. These crises present a novel and challenging set of problems for corporations, government agencies, and communities. The causes of crises—in particular, the causes of the secondary effects that turn an accident into a crisis—are difficult to ascertain and remedy because they are so deeply rooted in the various social and economic systems of the countries involved. But failure to meet the challenge will result in more deaths, continued environmental destruction, and a severe downgrading of quality of life.

While it is probably not useful to think about dealing with industrial crises in terms of "solutions"—there is no single solution applicable to all conditions—we can build a greater understanding of who the *stakeholders* are in industrial crises and how their actions can exacerbate or minimize these crises. Bhopal provides a textbook case study for building this kind of understanding.

Killer Results Without Killing Yourself

Michael B. Malone

"As far as I'm concerned," says David B. Marsing, "having to change your life when you arrive at work each morning is tantamount to slavery."

Revolutionary words from a professor or labor organizer? Not exactly. Dave Marsing, 41, sits in one of the highest pressure jobs in U.S. industry: plant manager of Intel Corp.'s $2 billion Fab 11 near Albuquerque, New Mexico, the largest microprocessor fabrication plant of the most successful electronics company in the world.

Marsing is an agent provocateur—he calls himself a "transformational virus"—in a company legendary for long hours and "creative confrontation." Marsing knows that "if I'm too aggressive, the corporate immune system will kick in" and consume him. He also knows that if he can successfully infect Intel, he will save it.

The medical analogy is no accident. Five years ago, at age 36, while trying to pull an Intel fabrication plant out of a crisis, Marsing suffered a near fatal heart attack. Lying on a gurney in the hospital, he remembers thinking, "How can I live my life as meaningfully as possible?" To this day, he visits cardiac units every six months, "just to look at the gray faces and remember."

It's tough to be a rebel in any business. But this is the semiconductor industry, a take-no-prisoners battle among silicon killers, hardly the kind of place to find a soft-spoken nice guy—especially one who's using a multibillion-dollar facility to experiment with new management theories.

Intel corporate knows only a little about the intensity of Marsing's views. But it does know the bottom line—and here Marsing excels. According to Marsing's boss Mike Splinter, 45, vice president and general manager of the company's components-manufacturing group, Marsing is one of Intel's best fab managers. Throughout his career, he's surpassed every target and quota set for him; every plant Marsing has run has ranked number one on the company's productivity charts.

That's why Intel's management has selected Marsing to help train its next generation of fab managers as the company prepares to spring-board off the success of the Pentium chip into the greatest expansion in its history. By the end of the decade, Intel will have at least 10 giant new fabs directed by as many as 300 newly trained managers. Intel also expects to be the most profitable company in the world.

By placing Dave Marsing in charge of its next generation of leaders, Intel, long known for its business brains, may unwittingly have made its smartest move yet. And if Marsing succeeds, he may not only transform his own company but also set the model for the new breed of manager who will lead U.S. industry into the next century.

THE ROAD TO DAMASCUS

Like most apostles of change, Dave Marsing had an awakening on his own road to Damascus.

Until five years ago, his had been a typical career for a young manager in high tech. After earning a degree in physics from the University of Oregon in 1976, Marsing followed his interest in thin-film technology and solar power to Texas Instruments to work with industry legend Jack Kilby on that company's then-secret solar-panel project. Marsing got the job he wanted, only to see the project collapse a year later.

But that was long enough for Kilby to be impressed by the young man and to recommend him to his Intel counterpart (and integrated circuit coinventor) Robert Noyce, who sent Marsing to work in development at the company's plant in Portland, Oregon. By 1986, at just 32, Marsing became the product engineering manager at Intel's Fab 3 in Livermore, California. Fab 3 was an older plant with established production levels, but by the time he was done, the plant was the company's leading manufacturer of the 80386, setting new standards for productivity.

Tired of the pressure of fab life, Marsing took a three-month sabbatical at the end of 1989. When he returned, he accepted an assignment as director of the company's Chandler, Arizona, factory automation group—only to find a new kind of pressure, learn a new kind of lesson. "I saw how fab treats support," he recalls. "Now I was the enemy. And it was obvious neither group knew how to deal with the other." In the world of semiconductors, where the construction of a single chip is as complex as the Manhattan Project, processes developed in the lab must be copied *exactly* on the factory floor. What were the odds of making mistakes if the two sides were locked in combat?

The more conflicts Marsing saw between department and department, between employee and company, and between employee and supervisor, the more conflicted *he* became. Without realizing it, Marsing internalized Intel's civil war. But to others it was obvious. As Mike Splinter later noted, during this period Marsing was summed up by the car he drove: a nondescript Volvo, "very meek on the outside, but with a big monster engine under the hood." Marsing even suffered the requisite divorce, brought on in part, he admits, by the stresses he was feeling on the job.

Still, if the work was frustrating, Marsing's career remained meteoric. On July 1, 1990 he returned to running a fab, this time Intel's seven-year-old Fab 9-1 (now part of Fab 9) in Rio Rancho, a suburb of Albuquerque.

He was now halfway through the worst year of his life. And it was about to get worse. Fab 9-1 was in turmoil. Marsing had been parachuted in to save the plant, and surveying the scene, he saw it had all the earmarks of a suicide mission. The new Intel microprocessor, the 80486, the company's hope for the future, depended on this plant more than on any other and Fab 9-1 couldn't get the chips out the door. Yield rates were disastrous: a failure in the plant's diffusion furnaces, a critical piece of equipment in the processing of silicon wafers, was turning half of the plant's chip production into worthless scrap each day. And it was growing steadily worse. Two weeks after Marsing arrived, the plant had wasted $50 million worth of chips.

Intel headquarters demanded an immediate end to the red ink; employees at the plant confronted Marsing with their frustration and fear. Caught in between, Marsing found himself crushed under pressure like he'd never known. Being diabetic didn't help. He'd drag himself home late at night barely able to sleep from worry. Even his morning exercise, which had always renewed him in the past, couldn't calm him. In fact, all Marsing was getting for his morning efforts was a stiff neck.

That was Monday. On Tuesday the stiff neck came back again. By Wednesday his neck hurt even when he walked fast between buildings. But the urgency of putting the fab back on its feet obscured a little physical discomfort.

Then at 5:26 A.M. on August 11, 1990, 36-year-old Dave Marsing found himself on a hospital gurney suffering a heart attack. Coronaries at that age are usually fatal, but Marsing was lucky. He had made it to the hospital in time. Within hours he was out of bypass surgery and on his way to recovery.

THE BIG LIE

In the weeks of recuperation that followed, Marsing had time to think. The heart attack had not permanently damaged his heart, but Marsing knew he could no longer live as he had.

He began to take stock. The first and most obvious question was whether he should continue working for Intel. After all, this was a company that prided itself on demanding superhuman contributions from its employees. Back in 1986, during a severe industry recession, Intel had become famous (and notorious) for instituting the "125% Solution," a six-month program in which employees were asked to work an extra two hours each day without pay—"voluntarily."

As Marsing thought about the people with whom he worked, he realized that he wasn't alone: "It hit me that most of the people around me were also exhibiting stress-related or stress-enhanced problems, either physically or emotionally." They were living a kind of lie, caught between who they were and who they had to be. And it was destroying their lives.

Every morning, Marsing realized, he and most of the people around him put on their work faces in the parking lot and played their roles as employees all day. The long hours, in which overtime often became a goal in itself, meant that most of each day was spent trapped in this fraud. And when they finally got home, the sheer intensity of the day—the disappearing edges between work and play, and the inevitable late-night and weekend crisis calls—sealed off any chance of escape into their true selves.

Intel, as much as any high-tech company, sought to create and enforce a homogeneous employee personality. The company had long recruited engineers right out of college, who wouldn't be tainted by having worked at other companies. And, fulfilling CEO and president Andy Grove's famous words, "Only the paranoid survive," the company promulgated a siege mentality among its people. Changing this attitude could mean challenging what lay at the heart of Intel's phenomenal success.

Yet in the face of those reasons to run away, Marsing chose to stay. He realized that he was committed to Intel and proud of its achievements. His mission, he saw, was to help the company prepare for a new century: "I wanted to try to develop the next generation of fab managers so that they could create an operating environment where balance exists. There had to be a way to work in this environment without being killed by it."

But what was that way? Marsing had no idea; he'd never heard of any alternative management model. So he turned to philosophers and some of the most outré management thinkers. He started with the economist and philosopher Joseph Schumpeter. Then on to Zen Buddhism. Next, physicist David Bohm.

He was still looking for answers when, in early 1992, he got the call: Marsing was named plant manager of the soon-to-be-constructed Fab II, the largest capital investment any chip company had ever made. The pressure to succeed would be immense. But this was the chance that Marsing had been waiting for.

He would go out in the hot sun and sit in the middle of the vacant field where the plant would stand and dream: "The people who worked for me thought I was going crazy," Marsing recalls. "But I could just imagine that building rising up around me."

Now he could conduct his experiment in the greatest laboratory on earth.

THE HUMAN TEST

In the world of fabs, the ultimate test comes at startup, when the fab is trying to convert diagrams and flow charts into real-life mass production. And this is also the ultimate test of Marsing's management philosophy. The product is an eight-inch silicon wafer covered with a grid of several hundred integrated circuit chips (ICs)—each worth as much as $1,000. One mistake on a wafer can cost $250,000 or more. And mistakes are easy: each of those hundreds of ICs contains millions of individual circuits, none much larger than bacteria. Billions of them must be made correctly each day.

With so much that can go wrong, nerves are frayed, tempers explosive.

So we visit Marsing just two days after Fab II "went to silicon."

Almost everything—meetings, telephone calls, interviews—seems to take place in a subdued tone. Marsing moves through the day calmly, his voice sometimes so soft as to be unintelligible. It's only later that it hits you: in one of the toughest manufacturing environments anywhere, in the center of its most stressful period, there are no raised voices, no barely controlled outbursts. The man whose heart once exploded over bad yield rates now navigates a far tougher management challenge without breaking a sweat.

Marsing, in a job that once nearly destroyed him, has made the day look effortless. He is not a philosopher but an extraordinarily adept businessman; his vision is his actions.

WHAT CAN I DO FOR YOU?

It's a hot summer New Mexico morning as Marsing sips the last of his coffee. He's already spent a half hour meditating, as he did before going to bed last night. Marsing's youngest child, one-year-old Hannah, is still asleep, but three-year-old Elliot is up and wandering grumpily through the house. He is ushered into the kitchen for breakfast by Marsing's wife, Vicki, who is also on her way to work at Intel, where she is an engineering manager. The atmosphere is casual and relaxed.

So is Marsing. He's wearing chinos and a work shirt. Combined with a shock of unruly brown hair and wire-rimmed glasses, he looks less like a high-tech executive and more like a high school civics teacher who also coaches the wrestling team.

At 7:40 A.M. he climbs into the family's new Toyota Land Cruiser and starts down the hill to the wide plateau below. Even from here, 10 miles away, it's hard to miss the Intel plant. The two giant fabs, along with a third, Fab 7, stretch across a ridge above Rio Rancho, dominating the view.

At 7:56 A.M. Marsing pulls into a nonreserved parking place. He looks up at the immense white building, and it's clear that he's still in awe of Fab 11: five stories and 170,000 square feet of clean room, the ultrapure area where chips are made; 1,400 employees with nearly 500 more soon to be added; equipment that can draw lines on silicon wafers just 1/500,000th of an inch across; the potential to generate revenues in excess of $5 billion per year. And it all works.

Marsing sprints up the five flights of stairs to his office to start the day. He had assumed that running such a facility had no precedent. Then a few months ago he taped a documentary on cable about life on an aircraft carrier: an immense structure costing billions of dollars, filled with a couple thousand highly trained specialists focused on a vital mission, with no room for error. The similarities were stunning. The only difference Marsing could see was that the captain of the carrier had to cope with a 40% annual turnover from completed enlistments, retirements and transfers. And then it struck Marsing that, given Intel's expansion plans for the next few years, the change among his employees would be just as dramatic.

He watched the tape over and over and showed it to his subordinates. He even used a company meeting in San Diego as an excuse to tour a U.S. Navy carrier. The result was a subtle shift in command to imitate the Navy captain/executive officer model. Marsing took on a more external, strategic role, and his assistant, factory manager Brian L. Harrison, moved into position as the internal, executive officer, a role roughly equivalent to a full plant manager in the rest of the industry.

"Marsing just thinks differently from other fab managers," Harrison says. "There is a mold for fab managers. They're hired as engineers and then pass through a series of filters as they come up. Somehow Marsing went through those filters, got to this level, and still sees things from a different perspective: more holistically, I guess, where others think in discrete details."

Marsing's morning is spent in one-on-one meetings with his direct reports, discussing various plant activities. After each presentation, Marsing asks, "OK, now what can I do for *you*?"

The late morning is spent in a teleconference with other Intel plant managers around the country, planning how to deal with upcoming products and expansion plans. During this hour, little of the rebel is on display. Still, there are moments when Marsing frowns, runs a hand through his hair, and looks like he's ready to cut loose. But in this meeting, at least, he never does. The Zen training helps.

Later there's a meeting with a new hire, a retired military safety officer, who's been brought on board to set up a crisis management program at the plant. The man is visibly nervous and expects a grilling. But Marsing puts him at ease by turning the tables and asking what he can do to help. The new safety officer looks relieved. Not only has he been put at ease; without knowing it, he's been given a first glimpse of the Marsing style.

At 5 P.M. the day comes to an early finish; Marsing returns phone calls; and reads and writes e-mail messages. In between, he tries to explain his management philosophy—something, he admits, he's never really been asked to do.

"Look," Marsing says, pushing his glasses back onto the bridge of his nose, "if you had equipment running at only 10% efficiency, you'd apply engineering to get that performance up. It's the same with people. If your employees are showing up at work with only a fraction of their possible efficiency, then you need to ask yourself: What is it about their job, their attitude, and their work environment that's doing that to them?"

To Marsing, the point is not only productivity but also diversity: the more disparate the experiences and skills of team members, the more adaptable and dynamic the organization. But that's not the way most companies look at it. "What most companies want is homogeneity." Marsing says. "They want 150 trumpets playing in unison. But homogeneous teams have blind spots: they move like a herd and often in the wrong direction. What's needed instead is complexity, the team as a jazz band that both harmonizes and improvises."

But what prevents this "true-to-yourself" model from producing as much stress as the "two-faced" model it replaces? One answer can be found in Marsing's own career. After all, he had to learn to balance his own maverick streak with the greater benefits of becoming a team player. And that is precisely the attitude he tries to convey to those around him. They are free to be themselves on the job, to work regular hours, to spend time with their families and their community. But the bottom line is Intel's competitive success. And if that means they have to compromise to deal with workmates, they know that those workmates are also bending halfway to meet them.

It's neither an elegant model nor an empirical one. It doesn't even have a name, though "Middle Path" conveys Marsing's belief that the organizational solution for the future is one that steers between Taylor's model of employees as identical cogs in a machine and the anarchy of rampant individualism in a Balkanized company in which people have no sense of common cause.

Here's how Marsing looks at it: "If the goal is to maximize profits, then it seems obvious to me that the best way to get there is to have happy people who are motivated to work. And the way you do that is to bring together different types of people, allow them to be themselves, get them behind the larger corporate vision, and then give them room to create. Above all, if you want breakthrough thinking and innovation—and you definitely do in this business to survive—then you have to cultivate those aspects of each employee's personality where it will come out."

DAVE MARSING'S DANCE

IT'S EARLY EVENING when Marsing pulls into the carport of his home. As he stands on the driveway amid Elliot's scattered toys, he reflects on the path he's taken since those terrible days in the hospital.

For the first time, his voice betrays excitement: "Imagine if you could build a company that was capable of learning from *all* its experiences, as well as from other companies' experiences. What you'd get is a new kind of asset: corporate wisdom. Now, combine that with the kind of compassion that accepts employees for who they really are, that motivates them to reach their potential, and you'd have something truly extraordinary.

Just think what a company like Intel, 35,000 highly intelligent people, could do if it ever reached that combination."

Is Marsing the model for the future of Intel? "Well, I'm not sure if it's possible for everybody to be like him." Mike Splinter says. "But I will say that if he keeps challenging the way we do things, he will have a large influence on future management methods at Intel."

For his part, Marsing has no doubt he will succeed. "This is the perfect place to do all this because the risks are so great. I think of it as an interesting dance. If you sit on the sidelines, you don't do anything. But once you're on the dance floor, you have a chance to change the steps."

And no one is better motivated than Dave Marsing to practice the dance, to find and follow the Middle Path. For him it is a matter of life and death.

Danger in the Comfort Zone

Judith M. Bardwick

America no longer strides across the economic landscape as though she owned it. Our dominance is declining. We know it and we dislike it. All kinds of experts explain it: Politicians point to unfair trade practices, economists talk about the high cost of money, and engineers cite inefficient production techniques. But since this is a book by a psychologist, we're going to look at psychological causes.

Why is our productivity sagging? One reason rarely mentioned is that for many people the work ethic no longer shines as brightly as it used to. Too many Americans no longer work as hard or as well as they should. Even when people put in a lot of time, they don't accomplish much. They don't add value.

Employers unwittingly perpetuate this attitude by their failure to hold people accountable for doing good work. They don't really expect people to excel, so evaluating performance is a half-hearted exercise at best.

For the past twelve years I have spent most of my time as a consultant for some of the largest U.S. companies. As I observed the daily workings of more and more organizations, I found one consistent characteristic: Too many people put in "face time." They show up for work and think that's good enough. Many even believe they're working hard. Most believe they're contributing.

For example, one company convened a committee of fifteen people from six different states to see how career plateauing—the lack of promotion opportunity—was affecting morale. I was asked to work with the group because I'd already given more than ten work-

"Danger in the Comfort Zone" by Judith M. Bardwick, AMACOM–American Management Association, New York, NY, 1995, pp. xv, 1-5. Reprinted by permission.

shops on plateauing to its middle managers. In fact, half the committee members had been in those workshops.

"Our mission," the members told me, "is to find out how people feel about plateauing."

"But you already know," I protested. "You've been to the workshops yourselves. And you have heaps of survey data. It's your number one problem."

"We have to be sure," they said.

So the committee met for another year. Every six weeks or so, the members would leave their jobs and convene at headquarters to discuss a question they already had the answer to.

What's going on? U.S. corporations are run by some of the smartest people in the world. How could we have gotten to the point where workers are allowed to spend their time in such nonproductive ways? What has happened to our expectation that people should earn a real salary by doing real work? What happened to the Yankee notion that you ought to earn what you get?

This is what happened: The United States was so rich for so long that we no longer asked people to earn promotions, raises, and security. We stopped doing the work of requiring real work. As it turned out, we gave too much security to too many people. It wasn't good for our institutions and it wasn't good for our people. The dynamics we're talking about can be seen just as clearly in other relationships between people, especially in families.

Three years ago I was involved in a lengthy project for a major oil company. Over time, I developed friendships with several of the managers, including one middle manager in his forties. Even though his annual salary was somewhere around $50,000, he was always broke. A guilty divorced father, he spent about 40 percent of his income supporting his daughter. While the father was poor, the daughter was rich—private school, private tennis lessons, ritzy summer camp, and so forth.

One morning he pulled me aside, obviously upset, saying, "I have to talk to you."

"Sure," I said. "What's up?"

"It's my daughter. I got a call from her last night."

"And?"

"And she said she called to remind me that I owe her a car."

"You *owe* her a car?"

"Yeah."

"Did she say *why* you owe her a car?"

"Because she's about to turn sixteen. She says I owe her a car because she's sixteen."

In that moment I "saw" the psychology of Entitlement.

What Is Entitlement?

Entitlement is the name I have given to an attitude, a way of looking at life. Those who have this attitude believe that they do not have to earn what they get. They come to believe that they get something because they are owed it, because they're *entitled* to it. They get what they want because of *who* they are, not because of what they *do*.

Entitlement is what I have been seeing in American corporations: people not really contributing, but still expecting to get their regular raise, their scheduled promotion. When this rich nation stopped requiring performance as a condition for keeping a job or getting a raise, it created a widespread attitude of Entitlement. Entitlement destroys motivation. It lowers productivity. In the long run it crushes self-esteem. And despite the layoffs of recent years, it is epidemic in this country. It's our legacy of the boom times that followed World War II.

The psychology of Entitlement is a concept. Using that concept, I have developed a very simple and very powerful model. In psychology, a model is a way of looking at relationships. The model is a lens, a tool to see familiar issues in a new way. It explains a lot of what is happening to us and provides a clear perception of what we must do. My experience with using the model in business leads me to feel confident that it is a useful contribution in our drive for enhanced performance.

Blacks Debate the Costs of Affirmative Action

Don Wycliff

Two years ago, at a seminar on higher education sponsored by the Congressional Black Caucus, a young man who obviously didn't know better breached etiquette by posing a discomfiting question.

Citing his own experience as a black student in a predominantly white college, he wondered whether affirmative action hadn't had an inadvertent negative effect, since he suspected he wasn't held to the same level of performance and achievement as some of his white fellow students. Had his educational experience—and his personal achievement—perhaps been compromised by the policy of racial preference?

A member of the seminar panel, Dr. Reginald Wilson of the American Council on Education, quickly set the young man straight. In stern, almost reproving tones, Dr. Wilson recited the historical-legal rationales for affirmative action, after which the panel moved on to other matters. But the student's question hung in the air.

It hangs there still, and increasingly is posed in more sophisticated form. Most recently and prominently, Shelby Steele, the essayist and English professor at San Jose State University, posed it in the May 13 issue of the *New York Times Magazine*.

Thomas Sowell, the conservative economist and longtime critic of affirmative action, has mounted a fresh assault with his new book, "Preferential Policies: An International Perspective." He finds that such policies are, virtually without exception, more hurtful than helpful.

And from the opposite ideological perspective, William Julius Wilson, the University of Chicago sociologist, expressed serious doubts about the practice in an article in the inaugural issue of the new quarterly "The American Prospect."

To be sure, opposition to affirmative action remains a minority view among blacks. And the nation's quarter century of experience with the practice must be set against three and a half centuries of negative action. Nevertheless, misgivings about affirmative action are common, and the fact that three such prominent black scholars have gone public with their concerns is significant. All the more so since two of them—Mr. Steele and Mr. Wilson—couch theirs as concerns over a policy that once may have been useful, or at least hopeful.

Mr. Sowell, who expressed opposition as long ago as 1970 (also in the *New York Times Magazine*), says the new skepticism is "from my point of view a heartening development," but takes no particular delight in saying "I told you so."

He contends that affirmative action programs on college campuses have failed to benefit poor blacks, in whose interest they were ostensibly created, and are responsible in great measure for the current atmosphere of racial antagonism.

"I predicted back then that when these programs failed, the conclusion would be not that they are half-baked programs, but that blacks just don't have it," he said. Now, he added, that prediction is being borne out.

Mr. Wilson's argument is political and strategic: "Race-specific" plans to overcome the educational, employment and other deficits created by slavery and segregation have benefited mainly the best prepared and least disadvantaged. More important, he says, such policies have alienated some whites from the Democratic Party and become an obstacle to the political coalitions needed to enact "race-neutral" social programs—job training, educational aid and so forth—that would benefit all low-income people.

Mr. Steele's is a psychological argument. "Under affirmative action," he wrote in the *Times Magazine,* "the quality that earns us preferential treatment is an implied inferiority." And its ultimate effect is to put blacks "at war with an expanded realm of debilitating doubt, so that the doubt itself becomes an unrecognized preoccupation that undermines their ability to perform, especially in integrated situations."

Mr. Wilson's position is familiar as part of a standard analysis of the decline of the Democrats in Presidential elections. He takes pains to distinguish it from "the neoconservative critique of affirmative action that attacks both racial preference and activist social welfare policies." Even so, however, he gently reminds his fellow liberals that "a society without racial preference has, of course, always been the long-term goal of the civil rights movement."

Mr. Steele's argument is newer, and seems to cause more heartburn to those who support policies of preference. Some call him naïve; some call him worse. The most thoughtful concede that he is on to something but worry about how he treats it.

"My sense is that he tells part of the story very well," said Drew S. Days, a law professor at Yale who was assistant attorney general for civil rights in the Carter Administration. "But he leaves out a whole lot that would enrich his and his readers' understanding of affirmative action."

That affirmative action has a "corrosive effect" on some of its intended beneficiaries is obvious, said Professor Days. But what Mr. Steele leaves out, he said, is the dreadful history of racist oppression and exclusion that initially was the justification for affirmative action remedies: "It's as though he were writing about Mars."

Mr. Steele does not neglect history, however; he only says that in the day-to-day situations in which blacks have to deal with the implication that they need special treatment, the history doesn't matter. "There are explanations and then there is the fact," he wrote in the *Times.* "And the fact must be borne by the individual as a condition apart from the explanation."

Julius Chambers, director-counsel of the NAACP Legal Defense and Educational Fund Inc., contends that Mr. Steele and others who share his views are naïve about the tenacity of racist resistance. Part of the purpose of affirmative action, he says, is to "change the climate in which decisions are made" about hiring, college admissions and so forth. Once the gatekeepers see competent blacks, their judgments may change. Better still, once blacks are in decisionmaking positions, they can enforce fairness.

Mr. Steele seems to bristle at the charge of naïveté. "Only two days ago I was called 'nigger' from a passing car," he said in a recent interview. "I think racism is tenacious, that's it is a human instinct. But we can't continue to blame all our troubles on racism."

In a Harvard Law Review article last year, Randall Kennedy, a black professor of law at Harvard, digressed briefly on the issue of "race-conscious affirmative action." While there might sometimes be "compelling reasons" to support it, he said, "I simply do not want race-conscious decision-making to be naturalized into our general pattern of academic evaluation. I do not want race-conscious decision-making to lose its status as a deviant mode of judging people or the work they produce."

Those comments echo similar ones made by Mr. Days in a January 1987 article in The Yale Law Journal. Clearly no opponent of affirmative action, Mr. Days nevertheless wondered whether a certain carelessness had not crept into the use of race-conscious programs.

"Our national sensitivity to racial classifications requires that they be used only when they represent a focused effort to remedy the effects of racial discrimination and to prevent its recurrence," he said. And for all their departures from the principle of a "color-blind Constitution"—either as violations or as remedies—that principle, embodied in a "society in which government avoids using race to allocate benefits and burdens among its citizenry," remains an ultimate goal for Americans.

The Right to Privacy: There's More Loophole Than Law

Michele Galen and Jeffrey Rothfeder

His bank cost Theodore Cizik his job. In 1983, the former controller at a New Jersey company sided with his employer in a dispute with Midlantic National Bank/North—just after he applied for his own loan there. When Cizik wouldn't budge, he claims, the bank got even. It told Cizik's boss that he had a Rolls-Royce and Mercedes—assets he had wanted kept secret but had listed on his loan application—and the bank suggested

Reprinted from July 4, 1989 issue of *Business Week* by special permission. Copyright © 1990 by McGraw Hill, Inc.

that he had been moonlighting. Fired from his $45,000 job on that pretext, he says, Cizik sued the bank, and ultimately settled out of court.

Cizik's case highlights a startling fact: Almost no information is private. Only rarely, moreover, can individuals find out that information on them is being used. With about 10 privacy laws on the books, how can that be? The laws are narrow, and full of holes.

'Bork Bill'   The Fair Credit Reporting Act of 1970 is a case in point. It sounds good. It gives individuals the right to see and correct their credit reports and limits the rights of others to look at them. But it has five exceptions, including a big one: Anyone with a "legitimate business need" can peek. Legitimate isn't defined.

Then there's the Right to Financial Privacy Act of 1978. It forbids the government to rummage through bank-account records without following set procedures. But it excludes state agencies, including law enforcement officials, as well as private employers. And more exceptions are tacked on every year. Says John Byrne, the federal legislative counsel for the American Bankers Assn.: "There's not a lot to this act anymore."

The best protection, in fact, is for customers of video stores. In 1987, a Washington (D.C.) weekly, *The City Paper,* published a list of videotape titles borrowed by Robert H. Bork, then a U.S. Supreme Court nominee. Outraged, lawmakers passed the Video Privacy Protection Act of 1988. Called the Bork Bill, it bars retailers from selling or disclosing video rental records without a customer's permission or a court order. While this is a breakthrough of sorts, privacy advocates say it's silly to pass such laws when medical and insurance records remain unprotected. Others find it ironic that the government itself continues to reveal more than anyone else.

For instance, the Privacy Act of 1974 was supposed to bar federal agencies from sharing information on U.S. citizens, a practice called matching. But it's O.K. to share information if the disclosure is consistent with the purpose for which the stuff was collected. That's called the routine use exception. In 1977, Health, Education & Welfare Secretary Joseph A. Califano Jr. crafted the exception to help root out welfare cheats by letting HEW review federal payroll records. His reasoning: Efficiency is a goal of all federal agencies. So they can share data to ensure it.

Watching Watchers   Today, matching remains alive and well. When Congress passed last year's Computer Matching & Privacy Protection Act, which regulates the way federal agencies verify eligibility for benefits or recoup delinquent debts, it gave the government explicit permission to perform frequent matches. It tossed a bone to the subjects of matches. Before their benefits can be cut off, an agency needs two pieces of proof for its findings. And it has to notify individuals who are under suspicion.

Every bit helps, of course, but reformers want more. George B. Trubow, the former general counsel to the White House Right to Privacy Committee, wants a federal data protection agency to "watch the watchers." David F. Linowes goes further. The former chairman of the U.S. Privacy Protection Commission, which was set up by the Privacy Act, is in favor of rules without exceptions. And he would give individuals $10,000 in punitive damages every time an abuse occurs. An interesting idea. But not one that Congress is likely to buy soon—at least not outside of video stores.

Why Grade 'A' Execs Get an 'F' as Parents

Brian O'Reilly

The qualities that make for corporate success are often not what are needed to be an effective mom or dad. Some parents show how to avoid the worst mistakes.

You can solve that thorny problem in Jakarta with a few crisp commands to your underlings, but ask your teenage son why he got in late last night and you're reduced to impotent fury in seconds. For all their brains and competence, powerful, successful executives and professionals often have more trouble raising kids than all but the very poor. Alas, the intensity and single-mindedness that make for corporate achievement are often the opposite of the qualities needed to be an effective parent.

Six years ago when AT&T was in the throes of divesting its operating companies, Ma Bell conducted a survey of its managers and top executives and discovered that their kids caused these employees more stress and worry than anything else, including their careers. Says attorney Robert Weinbaum, head of antitrust and marketing law at General Motors: "I think it's real tough for kids growing up in families where the parents are highly successful." Weinbaum went through years of turmoil with his own son before they resolved their difficulties.

Many parenting problems are common to everyone: paralyzing uncertainties about how strict or lenient to be, a sense of powerlessness in the face of peer pressure, preoccupation with professional problems, or just plain forgetting what a kid needs from mom or dad. But raising happy, successful children is not a hopeless task or just dumb luck. Interviews with scores of educators, psychologists, drug experts, executives, and troubled teens reveal some consistent differences between kids who turn out "good" and those who go "bad," and provide some suggestions on how to avoid the most colossal blunders.

The most important thing a parent can do for a child is to encourage a high sense of self-esteem. Easier said than done, of course. The tricky part is helping children set appropriate, satisfying goals and then providing an environment that lets them reach the goals on their own. Building your child's self-esteem is an inconvenient, time-consuming, and maddeningly imprecise occupation, and don't be amazed if you mess up. Intuition and good intentions often don't seem to be much help, and you need skills that rival a pilot's ability to land a jet at night on an aircraft carrier. But kids who have a sense of self-worth flourish. Kids who don't are vulnerable to drug and alcohol abuse, unwanted pregnancy, anxiety, depression, and suicide. Even worse, they may not get into Harvard.

In case your long-range plans include working triple time at the office until the brats turn 17, then deftly steering them into the Ivy League, listen up. Serious emotional problems usually start when children are in sixth to eighth grade, and hit crisis proportions by the sophomore year of high school. Says Sheila Ribordy, a clinical psychologist at De Paul University: "By junior year they're on track or in serious trouble."

Don't think your brains, money, or success will pave the way to parenting glory. In a survey of large corporations providing extensive insurance coverage, Medstat Systems, an Ann Arbor, Michigan, health care information firm, discovered that some 36% of the children of executives undergo outpatient treatment for psychiatric or drug abuse problems every year, vs. 15% of the children of nonexecutives in the same companies.

Top executives have special problems as parents. Many are highly educated, driven personalities who routinely put in 12 to 15 hours a day on the job—workaholics, in other words. Says Susan Davies-Bloom, a Connecticut family therapist who treats senior managers: "They are so accustomed to functioning at a high level of control at the office that when they get home, they try to exert the same kind of control."

The milieu that executives attempt to establish at home can be highly stressful for children. The attributes a manager must develop to succeed include perfectionism, impatience, and efficiency. Says Andrée Brooks, author of *Children of Fast Track Parents:* "Contrast those traits with what it takes to meet the needs of a growing child—tolerance, patience, and acceptance of chaos."

During their teens, kids assert their own individuality, rebelling against whatever their parents value most. Unfortunately for the kids of driven executives, what mom and dad often value most is achievement. Says Davies-Bloom: "I find many workaholic executives felt they were mediocre in popularity, grades, and athletics." Frequently the parent tries to create a child who was everything he was not, or thinks he can steer the kid around every pitfall. Sparks fly, and the youngster refuses to perform.

Worse, some parents are so absorbed with their own careers that they scarcely notice their children, who respond by behaving in increasingly bizarre and dangerous ways to attract attention. "My father worried about me from his desk," says the son of an IBM executive. The kid started stealing from his parents—trinkets, at first. But when he took his father's gun and began disappearing at night, family therapy finally began.

Given 70-hour workweeks, divorce, or a spouse with a career or demanding social schedule, and complications set in fast. You thought buying a big home in a wealthy suburb would bestow bliss on your offspring? Too often it has the opposite effect. Thousands of business people who were No. 1 somewhere else move to towns where everyone else is successful too. All the other kids in school are very bright and also under pressure to achieve.

Soon the parents wonder why their kid isn't at the top of the class. Says Constance McCreery, formerly a public school guidance counselor in Darien, Connecticut: "In wealthy towns you get what I call the Big Apple syndrome. It's the problem of keeping all the children full of enough confidence that they *can* succeed."

Mom and a tightknit community used to be able to keep child rearing running smoothly even if dad was putting in overtime. But most younger mothers work nowadays, and wives of senior executives often have commitments that keep them out of the home, even if they don't have paying jobs. Suzanne Gelber, a benefits consultant, was on the board of a day care center in Chappaqua, New York, where most of the mothers who dropped off their kids did not work. "They have so many philanthropic and social responsibilities that they are very busy women," she says. "They are not home baking brownies."

Nobody can prove that children with nannies wind up in reform school more often than those who don't, but some kid watchers are concerned. Says Tom Collins, executive director of Fairview Deaconess Hospital, an adolescent drug treatment center in Minneapolis: "Every move you make away from kids in pursuit of your own happiness and career increases their chance of getting into trouble. Lending kids out to babysitters and day care makes it a crap shoot."

Ask a bunch of educators how life for well-to-do kids has changed over the years and you get a surprising answer: The children are under far greater strain than their parents ever were to perform well academically and win acceptance to high-prestige colleges. At New Trier Township High School near Chicago, principal Dianna M. Lindsay says, "The pressure to get into a name-brand college is monumental. I see kids buckle under it."

Part of the stress is classic pushy-parent stuff. Says Carol Perry, director of counseling at the exclusive Trinity School in Manhattan: "This is an era of designer children. No parent wants an average child." Adds Lindsay: "Parents want their kids to go to a school whose name is recognized at the country club."

Much of the mounting anxiety springs not from overt parental pressure, however, but from the students themselves, whose values have been not so subtly affected by mom and dad's affluence. Many well-off kids have grown up using a financial yardstick to evaluate themselves and others. But the prospects for these wealthy kids to improve on or at least maintain their current lifestyles are frighteningly slim. "Successful moms and dads come here because the environment breeds success," New Trier's Lindsay observes, "but the kids say, 'I can never match this. This is the best my life will ever be.' "

Students at New Trier are encouraged to do social service, such as working in soup kitchens, and once a year they are asked to fast for a day in recognition of world hunger and donate lunch money to the poor. Says Lindsay: "We have to teach the kids there are other standards besides material possessions. It's a real, serious problem."

The predictable consequences of all the stress on kids: alcohol, drugs, and suicide, the ultimate parental nightmare. Teenage suicide rates doubled between 1968 and 1987, to 16.2 per 100,000 boys and 4.2 per 100,000 girls. Suicide now ranks as the second cause of death, after accidents, among 15- to 19-year-olds. Some factors that prompt suicide, such as depression caused by the death of a loved one, are not the result of demanding parents. But pressure to do well in school and athletics is a contributor to suicide, and children in a close-knit family are less likely to kill themselves than kids without strong family ties.

Though drug use appears to have peaked in the early 1980s, it is still very high. According to the University of Michigan's Institute for Social Research, more than half of all high school seniors have reported using an illicit drug at some time in their lives— usually marijuana—and a third have tried something stronger. Virtually all seniors— 92%—have experimented with beer or hard liquor, and in the two weeks before the institute's survey was taken, 35% had been drunk at least once although every state now bans drinking under age 21.

Rare is the parent who cannot recall sneaking more than a few beers in his or her youth, but the prevalence of teenage drinking has many people worried. Donald R. Geddis, the principal at Summit High School in New Jersey, is more concerned about the use of alcohol among his students than he is about any other substance. "Its use is so widespread it outstrips all others," he says.

Drinking is starting early—the average age for that first surreptitious sip is 13—before many children have developed better methods of coping with stress. Youngsters are aping the attitude of adults: "I've had a tough week and I'm entitled to blow off a little steam." Worse, drunk kids are also more likely to experiment with other drugs they would shun while sober.

Since practically every kid drinks and most experiment with drugs, what distinguishes those who tinker with the stuff from those who develop a serious dependency is "the degree of anxiety for which they are seeking surcease," says Virginia Kramer Stein, a clinical psychologist in New Jersey. Although no kid is as supremely self-confident as many try to appear, youngsters who think of themselves as losers or unwanted by their busy parents, or who have trouble making friends, are at a higher risk of abusing alcohol and drugs than other kids.

When they drink or take drugs, many kids feel transformed for the first time from awkward geeks into cool and appealing characters. "Addiction has a lot to do with self-esteem," says Jeri, 16, the daughter of a Minneapolis-area businesswoman. Jeri started drinking at 11; then her sister introduced her to marijuana, which she smoked every day through much of her first year of high school. By the time she was in tenth grade, she was caught selling grass, and sent to a rehabilitation program at Fairview Deaconess.

How do parents reduce the stress on their kids, boost their self-esteem, and keep them off drugs? Says Summit High's Geddis: "If I've learned one thing, it is that the main priority for parents is to help their kids find something that makes them feel good about themselves. That's the greatest deterrent to drugs and alcohol."

An important first step is to ease up on relentless pressure to make the youngster perform well in school. Focus only on grades and you're handing the kid a weapon to punish you with. If the child appears "only average" but is attending one of the toughest high schools in the country, find out where he or she ranks among peers on standardized achievement tests. That will help you know whether a B or C average is reasonable.

Do not greet your children every evening with an ostensibly cheery "How'd you do in school today?" It is a very threatening question and often elicits no more than a mumbled "Okay." Good grades help get you into a top college but don't predict a happy, successful life, says Robert Klitgaard, former faculty head of admissions at Harvard's Kennedy school.

In case you forgot, success in high school is not achieved the same way as success in a corporation. You get ahead in a company by climbing the ladder and paying your dues, concentrating on things you're good at, and delegating or avoiding areas where you are not competent. You may be a whiz at corporate finance in part because the job does not require you to decline French verbs or find the area of an isosceles triangle. But your sophomore does not have the luxury of hiring a Harvard MBA to do her homework.

Don't ignore the possibility that the apple of your eye simply is not as smart as you are. Children have roughly the same IQ as the average of their parents', but there are plenty of deviations. About 7% of the time, a child will be 15 points higher or lower than the parents' average, and one time in a thousand, a 30-point difference will pop up.

The average college graduate has an IQ of 115 and Ph.D.s typically score 130, according to John E. Hunter, a professor of psychology at Michigan State University. "It doesn't take much of a slip, and the child of parents who struggled to get through college will not be able to make it," he adds. (Of course, there's an equal chance your daughter is justified when she calls you stupid.) Though you may be a genius yourself, if you married a good-looking but dim bulb, you can't expect your progeny to send rockets to Mars. If your kid has been a whiz all along, however, and his grades collapse in high school, emotional or drug problems are the likely culprits—not his IQ.

Spend time with the family. Ordering your secretary to book 50 minutes of "quality time" into your schedule is better than nothing, but quality time has a habit of fitting your routine, not the kids'. Del Yocam, 45, former chief operating officer at Apple, religiously went home for dinner at 7 P.M. at least twice during the week, and avoided business commitments on weekends. "The children have come to expect it," says Yocam. In November he retired from Apple. His devotion to his family didn't hurt his career there, Yocam says, but "it's time to move on to other things."

Hugh McColl, chairman of NCNB, the big Southern regional bank, cut out weekend golf and reduced entertaining at night years ago to have more time with his three children. But he still has some regrets about the time he spent away from home. He was coaching his son's YMCA basketball team in the early 1970s, and a league championship game was looming. Instead McColl went to a banking convention, and the team lost by two points. "My son still blames me," says McColl with a laugh. "He figures if I'd been at the game he would have won."

Robert Butler, a senior engineer at Chevron in San Francisco, is also determined not to let his job overwhelm his family. He schedules time for his children, leaving for the office at dawn on days he has to depart early to coach his son's soccer team. Says he: "You can always put things off for the future, but you can't get back the years with your kids."

Use the time you spend with the children to listen sympathetically to them. That skill is particularly difficult for men to acquire, according to Ronald Levant, a Rutgers University psychologist and author of *Between Father and Child*. "Men are not trained to be empathetic listeners," he says. "We're taught to listen to our opponents to discover their weaknesses." Men see themselves as problem solvers, not as shoulders to cry on.

Thus, the father who comes home and sees that his 15-year-old daughter has just eaten a whole box of Oreos will probably want to warn her about pimples and weight. Resist the urge. Just let her pour her heart out. Don't be hurt or angry if she doesn't respond the first dozen times you try to be understanding. If you've been a clod for the past 15 years, she may be confused or think you're trying to trick her.

You may learn from all that listening that your son really doesn't want to go to Stanford, is the laughingstock of Kenilworth when you force him to practice dropkicking at the country club, and dreads following your footsteps into the brake shoe business because he can't figure out what a brake shoe *is*. Fight the desire to disown him, and he may confess that he is fabulous at lawn bowling and likely to get a scholarship from East Cowflop University to study French cooking.

Go lawn bowling with him and let him whip up some frog legs Provençale for you. You won't enhance your bragging rights with the board of directors, but you will do wonders for his self-esteem. And you could be pleasantly surprised: You may find that a newly energized youngster has replaced the sullen adolescent of just a few weeks before. "There are no lazy teenagers," says Carol Perry. "More likely they're turned off or depressed."

Some parents conclude that boarding schools can do a better job of teaching and raising their children than mom or dad will. For example, a single parent who has to travel on the job might want the youngster in a stable environment that provides a sense of security for both child and parent. Such places range from exclusive prep schools such as Groton, Exeter, and Lawrenceville, which rival Ivy League colleges in admission requirements and costs; to less well-known but highly regarded private institutions such as the Webb Schools in Claremont, California, St. Stephen's Episcopal School in Austin, Texas, and Wayland Academy in Beaver Dam, Wisconsin; to military academies like Valley Forge in Pennsylvania that boast of instilling "conservative Christian values" in their charges.

Then there are boarding schools where many of the kids have serious behavioral and emotional problems, among them drug abuse, petty theft, truancy, or depression. Among these academies are Cedu in Running Springs, California, Franklin Academy in Sabbatus, Maine, and the Brown Schools in Texas. Bob Weinbaum, the GM attorney, sent his son John to the DeSisto School, a prep school in Stockbridge, Massachusetts. With the Broadway producer Joseph Papp among the first board members, Mike DeSisto, a rumpled Catholic ex-seminarian who once ran a private school on Long Island, started the school in 1978. The annual tuition of $19,000 is more than the cost of a year at Yale.

In addition to a rigorous academic schedule, DeSisto students undergo multiple private and group therapy sessions each week. But an important part of their development occurs as the kids learn to be accepting of each other and affectionate. Most conversations seem to begin and end with vigorous bear hugs. DeSisto himself is both warm and demanding. He lets kids pile onto his living room sofa and fall asleep on his lap until the 10 P.M. curfew. But kids don't "graduate" until they complete the course requirements, perform well at increasingly difficult and responsible campus jobs from washing dishes to assigning dorm rooms, and demonstrate they can be effective "parents" for newer arrivals.

If you're committed to winning the Dad or Mom of the Year Award, one of the biggest and most common mistakes you can make awaits you: being a wimpy and overprotective parent. Says Gary McKay, co-author of *The Parent's Handbook* (see box): "One of the greatest handicaps a child can suffer is to be raised by a 'good' parent."

These well-meaning types try to do everything for the kids, rushing upstairs five times to wake them for school, exhorting them to eat breakfast faster, and driving them to school when they miss the bus. All this service winds up depriving the kid of self-confidence and independence, says McKay. Far better to be a "responsible" parent. Buy the youngster an alarm clock, explain that breakfast ends at 7:30, and if he misses the bus let him walk to school. Don't scold, don't say, "I told you so," don't debate, don't give in.

Bob Weinbaum fell into a good-parent trap, trying so hard to be a "fair and reasonable" father that he was coming across as overprotective, vague, and indecisive to his son John. "In retrospect, I wish I had remembered that *I* was the father—that *I* was the one in charge," says Weinbaum, whose credits include winning federal approval for the GM-Toyota deal in Fremont, California, and managing his son's baseball team. John grew up with a lot of love and attention, but Weinbaum now admits he tried to do too much for his son, even his homework. "John told me once I was so involved, I made him feel incompetent."

By the time John was a sophomore in high school, their relationship was in tatters, and both parents were worried. "I remember his violent outrages and kicking the door apart," says Weinbaum. "He was in a lot of pain." Schoolwork deteriorated, and the parents began finding marijuana butts on the floor. When the son started going to parties and not coming home at night, Weinbaum was frazzled. An adolescent treatment center in Detroit determined John's problems were not drug-related, so Weinbaum wound up sending John to the DeSisto School. He graduated in three years and is now at a college near Baltimore.

For all three years Weinbaum and his wife attended monthly group support meetings with other DeSisto parents in the Detroit area and gradually learned how to improve relations with John. "He is a spectacular, wonderful son," says Weinbaum today.

If you plan to run out and start putting your foot down, do not mistake harshness or violence for firmness. Says one tall 17-year-old student at DeSisto: "My father used to throw me up against a wall, demanding that I get better grades. But there was never any follow-through." The boy wanted his parents to talk to him about why he was having trouble in school and offer some help, but they did not. Says he: "Parents often think if they've yelled and sent you to your room that their job is done."

Since so much experimentation with drugs and alcohol begins in the preteen years, start long before they're in sixth or seventh grade to communicate with your children, and practice being assertive. Says Bruce Thompson, superintendent of the middle school in Woodside, a San Francisco suburb: "This is the best time to catch them. They're still little kids, on the way to adults."

How strict is strict enough when dealing with kids on the verge of becoming teenagers? "You ask kids where they're going when they go out," says Thompson. "They do their homework and you check their homework. They show up for dinner, they don't go out on school nights, and when they say they're sleeping over at Johnny's, you call up Johnny's parents and ask if they will be home that evening. Will the child complain? Yes."

When kids in middle school and high school do go out at night, parents should be up and awake to greet them when they return. Says Tom Collins, head of Fairview Deaconess, the drug rehab center in Minneapolis: "Sit down and talk with your kids when they come in. You should be able to say to them, 'You look weird. Have you been doing drugs?'"

If you take time to observe a teen, you can soon tell whether he's drunk or stoned. Do kids want to be stopped? Absolutely. "If you don't see it soon enough," Collins warns, "your child will go through lying, stealing, cheating. It gets rolling and you can't stop it until the kid is in so much pain he wants treatment."

Many parents don't even suspect a problem until they find drugs or get a call from police or school officials. Warning signs that a kid is becoming an abuser include suddenly erratic grades, skipping school, dropping out of extracurricular activities, avoiding the family, swings in mood, violence, depression, no savings from a part-time job, and a crop of unfamiliar and unimpressive new friends.

Most parents will never have to deal with anything more serious than their own chronic sense of clumsiness and frustration. In case you think you are hopelessly inept and suspect your kids secretly fired you a long time ago, be assured that you are far more influential than you suspect. "The best manipulation parents have is their attention. It is an extraordinary power that most of them neglect to use," says David, 17, the troubled son of a high-ranking Ford executive. "Parents are very important to kids—more than they will ever let on."

A REPAIR MANUAL FOR FIXING RELATIONSHIPS WITH YOUR KIDS

If you spend most of your workday racing through terse memos to prepare for that presentation on expansion strategies for the 1990s, you're going to find it tough to absorb homey suggestions on child rearing. Touchy-feely stuff like "Help your children feel useful by identifying their talents and suggesting ways they can contribute to the family" may make your flesh crawl.

Giving goose bumps to executives hasn't hurt psychologists Don Dinkmeyer and Gary D. McKay, authors of *The Parent's Handbook* (American Guidance Service). The $9.95 paperback has sold nearly two million copies, making it one of the most successful publications ever on raising kids. Among its virtues is practicality. The book is short—only 127 pages including cartoons—and reads more like a repair manual than a scholarly treatise.

When McKay and Dinkmeyer were guidance counselors in the Midwest two decades ago, they were bombarded with questions from parents who, says McKay, "with the best of intentions, didn't know how to help their kids learn responsibility." The two men put together course material to help teachers, clergy, and school counselors, among others, lead group training sessions for frustrated parents. The *Handbook* is part of the course but useful on its own and available in most bookstores. Herewith some of the book's advice for moms and dads:

- Don't give a child attention on demand, even for positive acts, because you will foster an inappropriate desire for the spotlight. Youngsters can easily come to believe that if you are not focused on them 100% of the time, you don't care about them.
- Tell your children you love them, especially when they are not anticipating such a comment. Nonverbal signs such as pats, hugs, kisses, and tousling their hair are also extremely important.
- Encourage kids rather than praise them. Praise is a reward given for winning and being the best. Encouragement, by contrast, is a reward for effort or improvement, however slight. It makes a child feel worthy, as in "I have confidence in your judgment" or "You seem to like that activity." Some praise is appropriate, of course. If the child hits a home run, go ahead and shout, "*Wow*, what a hit! That was great." Just don't restrict your pride in the child to his or her accomplishments.
- Listen to your kid. Think of a feeling that describes the emotions a child is expressing—bored, guilty, vengeful, or happy, accepted, respected. When your son says, "That teacher is unfair. I'll never do well," don't respond with, "Of course you will. What's the matter with you?" Try: "You're angry and disappointed and you're thinking of giving up." The second response shows acceptance and concern so the child will be encouraged to tell you more.
- Avoid blaming and criticizing your children. They will correct misbehavior faster if you dispassionately describe how that lapse interferes

with your needs or rights. Instead of screaming "You came home three hours late last night, you idiot!" try "When you don't call or come home at the time we've agreed on, I worry that something might have happened to you because I don't know where you are."

- Let your youngsters experience the consequences of their behavior once they know enough to make informed decisions. Children who won't eat go hungry; those who dress inappropriately get cold or get razzed by their peers. Buy good food that they like, but don't force them to eat it. The difference between dishing out punishment and letting them experience consequences is often in your tone of voice. If your son loses dad's hammer, you don't have to yell or threaten. The child should simply buy a new one. Dad is also justified in coolly explaining that junior apparently isn't ready to use Dad's tools.

- Treat your children with the courtesy and sensitivity you reserve for your friends. With luck, they may turn out to be some of your very closest friends.

Under the Influence:
The Unauthorized Story of the Anheuser-Busch Dynasty

Peter Hernon and Terry Ganey

RED NECK IN THE MORNING—EXECUTIVES TAKE WARNING

The word came crackling down the long corridors of the D'Arcy advertising company that August wanted a new Budweiser campaign and wanted it fast. If the ad agency executives heard the ring of cash registers in their ears, they also knew they had to produce. August was on a rampage and he could extinguish careers; the luckier were merely banished. One executive had a name for him. Darth Vader.

"Under the Influence: The Unauthorized Story of the Anheuser-Busch Dynasty" by Peter Hernon and Terry Ganey, Avon Books, Simon & Schuster, Inc., New York, NY, 1991, pp. 322-330. Reprinted by permission.

At war with Miller in the 1970s, August had stopped at nothing. Money was no object. Gussie had opposed heavy spending to match the expensive Miller campaign, which was one of the reasons August had deposed him. The message was clear: he was in no mood to be told what he couldn't do. He would spend record millions to bury Miller and woe betide anyone who bungled or got in his way. Wary advertising and marketing executives took to watching his neck. If he strode into a meeting with his neck burning red, there was a good chance someone would be sacrificed. If his neck was only pink, they might all hope to collect another paycheck.

In one of his first major efforts, August wanted a full-blown Bud campaign immediately. D'Arcy threw 100 people into the task; they worked seven days a week, practically living in their offices until they hit a bull's-eye. Following Miller's example, they focused the campaign on the beer-drinking blue-collars, the roughly 20 percent of the population that drinks 80 percent of the beer. They were the guys who worked hard to support their families and whose only pleasure was maybe two or three beers with the boys after the whistle blew.

Some agency people thought the campaign would be copying too closely the successful Miller commercials, which also zeroed in on blue-collars. "We brought in this independent research man who had data that it would be a big mistake to copy that ad and August still wouldn't accept the results," an executive recalled. "He practically kicked the guy out of the brewery for telling him the truth." August knew what he wanted. He wanted blue-collars and he wanted to know how long the campaign would take to produce.

"This was one of those days when he came in with a red neck," the executive said. "He was mad, you could tell it. That's when he asked me how long would it take to do these commercials. Our creative director was standing next to me and he was sweating bullets. . . . You could see the perspiration just beading up. . . . Other people were slouched under the table. I mean these are big executives and they're just hiding. They could see it coming. Our creative director said the normal production time was six to eight weeks. And with that August hit the goddamn ceiling. He just blewwwwww! He hammered the table and said, 'Goddamn, I'm tired of this shit! You guys telling me it takes this long. We're going to do this whole package in four weeks! And I don't give a shit how much money it takes.' And, man, he went on for twenty minutes."

August got what he wanted. The commercials were shot in four weeks without actors. They used real factory workers at a meat-packing plant in Houston. August didn't like actors in his commercials; he wanted the real thing. He liked the series and the tag line, "For all you do, this Bud's for you." With his unerring eye, he had personally selected the slogan from a list of about twenty possibilities. When the session was over, he curtly thanked everyone. Turning to leave, he paused and said, "It just proves one thing. You guys can't work unless I put the pressure on."

No one could put the pressure on like August. There were trips to plan advertising campaigns from which some men figuratively didn't return. A reporter who covered Anheuser-Busch knew a D'Arcy executive who had suffered this fate. The man had worked on the Bud account. "They would have these annual trips down to Hilton Head or some other plush spot to discuss the upcoming campaigns with August. It was the kind of exercise where they all knew, every man on the plane, that one of them wouldn't be coming back, that one of them would be sacrificed to the great god August.

"They would be sitting around the table and his blue eyes would be searching the faces and he'd start boring in on someone, grilling them and you'd start to breathe easier, but the wiser hands knew that was only to throw you. At the last minute he'd suddenly turn to someone else and say, 'I thought your proposal was terrible. You're through!' . . . Every year you got this. You always knew that one of you would get the axe."

Sometimes men were sacrificed accidentally. An executive who worked on the Anheuser-Busch account described a trip to Williamsburg to make a presentation to August. "He looked over the proposals and didn't like anything. He was there only two or three minutes, pronounced them all bad and blew out of the room, but not before he said something like, 'Fire that guy with the yellow tie. I don't like him.' And so they fired the poor son of a bitch and then they redid the ad campaign and showed it to August again and he liked it. But he tells one of his people, 'I thought I told you to fire that guy.' And his man looks over and sees the guy and says, 'Oh, Jesus. You meant fire *that* guy.' They had canned the wrong man."

August insisted on realism in his commercials. Long an admirer of Philip Morris's Marlboro ads, he used horses and real cowboys to promote Busch beer. A Busch ad was expected to have a bubbling spring, a shot of a rearing black stallion, a distant shot of snow-peaked mountains and the popping Busch of an opening tab top. "Consistency of message," August called it.

In his quest for just the right commercials, August started inviting perhaps forty blue-collar and other employees to some of the major advertising campaign presentations. "He sits in the first seat in the front row and he's got a sheet of paper with the names of the rank and file on it," the same executive recalled. "Right in the middle of some guy's presentation, he might suddenly stop him and yell out, 'Starbuck, did you understand that?' Now Starbuck, some guy from the malt room or bottling line is . . . afraid of looking like a fool, so he says, No, he doesn't understand it. And the guy on the stage sort of freezes and dies. August wants to know if the average man 'gets' what these agencies are trying to do. . . . Some big agency has had a dozen people working for months on some program and then it's scrapped all because Starbuck from bottling doesn't 'get it.' My God, it was so unbelievable."

Miller got a big jump on Anheuser-Busch by leaping into sports advertising. During the 1970s, the reinvigorated Milwaukee brewer gobbled up virtually every one of the major network sporting events. The highly popular Monday Night Football package went to Miller so did the College Football Game of the Week, the Moscow Olympics, the World Series, the Indianapolis 500, and dozens of college football games. Miller also pioneered the recycling of superannuated jocks like former footballer Bubba Smith, who was shown ripping off the top of a Miller can with his bare hands. August admitted that Anheuser-Busch had made a mistake in letting Miller open a lead on them. "We were," he said, "simply unsmarted."

Realizing it had to get into the game and fast, Anheuser-Busch approached the networks about buying sports programming. August's marketing chief, the Jesuit-educated Michael Roarty, put it this way: "They looked at us like we had just come to town on a bus and they said, 'Where have you been? We've been sold out for years!' "

August was willing to pour hundreds of millions of dollars into sports advertising because Miller had demonstrated it worked and because he knew the average American beer drinker worshipped at the altar of sport. As Roarty observed, "Sports figures are America's heroes."

While he waited for a chance to take the plunge with the big sports shows, August focused on the next best thing, "alternative sports." Everything from softball games, jogging and hot air ballooning to hydroplane boat races and touch football games. More significantly, he entered the college sports market. He ordered his staff to assemble a book listing every college in the country that played sports. August was interested in buying a piece of the radio or television sponsorship of each team. If there was going to be a beer commercial during a collegiate game—any game—he wanted it to be an Anheuser-Busch commercial.

"That book was about five or six inches thick," recalled an executive who participated in the exercise "One day we got together and August said, 'Well, let's go. Read 'em.' We had a media guy reading them off . . . . August would say, 'What about Albion? What do they do?' And we'd say, 'Naw, that's just a very small liberal arts college and they don't do any thing.' August would say, 'Okay, what about Albuquerque A&M?' We'd say, 'Yeah, they play football.' And August would say, 'Buy 'em!'"

On and on it went, one school after another. The litany rolled on until they reached the schools that started with Z, August didn't care whether they were inefficient buys or not. "He had the money. He wanted to dominate."

It was domination in sports advertising unlike anything ever seen before. In 1976, Anheuser-Busch sponsored twelve professional baseball teams and seven National Football League teams. A little over a decade later, the company would hold sponsorship rights with all twenty-four United States–based major league baseball teams, twenty of twenty-eight NFL teams, twenty-three of twenty-four National Basketball Association teams, thirteen of fourteen domestic National Hockey League teams, nine of the eleven Major Indoor Soccer League teams, and more than 300 colleges. The alternative sporting events, including the Bud Light Ironman Triathlon Work Championship and the Michelob Night Riders cycling circuit, numbered "about a thousand." Anheuser-Busch also became the execlusive beer advertiser for the ESPN sports cable network. The beer company even pried away a piece of the Monday Night Football package. Eventually, Anheuser-Busch and Miller would have a virtual monopoly on sports beer advertising through what are known as exclusivity clauses, which, after other breweries complained, were ruled completely legal by the Justice Department.

The National Catholic Basketball Tournament was a typical example of Anheuser-Busch's drive to push its product through collegiate sports. The little guys got bought as well as the big boys. By no means a major postseason tournament, the small-college National Catholic Basketball Tournament, held in Dubuque, Iowa, had a strong Midwest following, and Anheuser-Busch made its presence known as the principal sponsor. During the 1990 contest, the words "Budweiser" and "Bud Light" were plastered all over the gymnasium; the same brand names appeared no less than six times on the front cover of the official program, and the back cover, which showed two foaming cups of Budweiser, was dedicated to "One Team That Never Fails to Make Points."

The tournament's halftime festivities showcased an appearance by the Bud Light Daredevils, "the most unique slam dunk act in the country." Members of the five-man gymnastic team, wearing bright red and blue uniforms with bold Anheuser-Busch lettering, were so many flying billboards. Bouncing off trampolines, they performed such "daring feats of agility" as "Dial 911" and "Shake Down the Rafters 'Till the Morning After." Students and parents wee informed that the Daredevils had performed at over

200 colleges and universities in forty-five states, not to mention Europe, the Middle East, Japan, Latin America and Australia. In a single year they appeared at some 125 events before more than one million fans.

August put about 70 percent of his estimated $400 million budget for broadcast advertising into sports programming; that was more than the combined budgets of Miller and Coors, *Adveritising Age* pegged Anheuser-Busch's total and spending at over $600 million a year. The acount for Budweiser alone, the world's best-selling beer, was worth $125 million. Anheuser-Busch's commericals seemed to be everywhere fans gathered to watch a sporting event no matter how humble. The bow-tie-shaped Budweiser logo appeared on the helmets of the U.S. Olympic hockey team when it faced the Soviets. Budweiser cars ran in the big auto races; Budweiser boats roared in the big boat races. A St. Louis lawyer even told the story of the night he turned on the television and saw a photograph of a duck race. "And by God, right there by the finish line of the duck race was a Bud sign."

August had achieved a place in history with his saturation approach to sports advertising. "He's made his beer part of the fabric of America," said one observer. "He's made it a part of Americana. He's done it by making it part of every sporting event in the country. He's done it by money."

"When they decide where they're going," observed Rusell Ackoff, August's scholarly mentor, "they're like an army on the march." As commander in chief of the world's largest brewery, August led that march. He had learned Miller's big lesson well. Following the proven success record of Philip Morris, Miller had segmented the beer market as never before, pegging different brands and sales pitches to different consumers. It was a radically fresh idea in the industry, and for an exhilarating moment it drove Miller to within a few perentage points of overtaking Anheuser-Busch. The company rocketed from seventh place to a strong second.

August pushed Miller's winning idea even further, developing a fragmented marketing approach that blitzed the country city by city, neighborhood by neighborhood, street by street, even bar by bar. Using sophisticated demographics, August's team divided beer drinkers by race, income, sex, age, even ethnic origin. It was called target marketing and there were targets everywhere. The Latino segment alone was broken into Mexicans, Puerto Ricans and Cubans. There was one approach for Irish beer drinkers in Boston and another for Poles in Chicago. Ads focused on racing fans, blue-collars, jocks, yuppies and computer nerds. One Bud commercial cheered bartenders and waitresses "This Bud's for everyone that serves them up cold." Another was aimed at immigrants, still another went after "all the men and women in uniform who proudly serve this great country." The country was carved into some 210 markets with the focus on big cities like New York and Los Angeles where most of the beer was consumed. The result was an incredible number of different sales promotion programs—as many as 10,000.

The command post for this saturation bombing was a conference room on the ninth floor at August's corporate headquarters, Number One Busch Place, once the address of his great-grandfather's mansion. It was called the war room and the walls were plastered with charts and graphs indicating the company's performance against its competitors. August's marketing staff churned out over thirty new promotional programs a day. They did their work exceptionally well; it was estimated that the typical city resident was exposed to the word "Budweiser" almost ten times a day.

Nothing was left to chance. "We want to be here," August once said, pointing to his wall charts. He pointed again. "We want to be there. We want to be everywhere. We are going to target every segment." And cost be damned. "In the 1970s they were so intent on beating back Miller's challenge that it was said if you could dream up a $250,000 bartop tiddlywinks campaign, you could take it down there and sell it to somebody," said an advertising executive.

Miller had forever changed beer advertising by putting the beer drinker smack in the commercial and appealing to his ego. That was a radical message and August jumped on the bandwagon. He was given a big assist by a watershed analysis of beer drinkers by Ackoff, his friend from the University of Pennsylvania's Wharton School. Every year Anheuser-Busch paid the university $200,000 to $300,000 for computer studies on everything from plant construction to what makes someone drink beer. During the 1960s, Ackoff's team had studied data on drinking behavior. Refining the information, he developed a theory that there were four types of drinkers. Two of the four drank to escape social or personal failures. The idea was to zero in on the "target market segments" to be reached by Anheuser-Busch advertising and to tailor the message accordingly. The approach worked splendidly, said Monty Roberts, a former Anheuser-Busch marketing executive. Ackoff's marketing strategies "were the bible at AB."

Undeterred, Anheuser-Busch steamrolled the land with advertising campaigns that resembled Sherman's March to the Sea. There were inevitable complaints from competitors. "They're tough, tough, tough, really ruthless," said Paul Lohmeyer, a beer importer. "They seem to have the absolute intention of running everyone else out of the business."

Early in the 1980s, August coolly predicted that Anheuser-Busch would have a 40 percent market share by the end of the decade. He got it. In 1980, the brewery was the first to produce 50 million barrels in a year and August marked the occasion by bunging the historic barrel with a silver hammer. In 1987, with beer sales flattening, Anheuser-Busch still managed to sell 76 million barrels and increase its share. When August said he wanted 50 percent by the turn of the century, few experts were willing to dispute the possibility.

With such a gargantuan slice of the beer market, August was aware of potential dangers. "We've seen others in this business get to the top and get in trouble because they got too big for their britches. We're scared to death of that . . . . It makes us live on the razor's edge."

By the later half of the 1980s, the razor's edge had become dangerously sharp. Vocal opponents of the brewery's marketing tactics and critics of alcohol abuse were making serious charges against Anheuser-Busch in Congress and in the market place. The company had become "the big gorilla." The brewery, said one critic, had long had things its own way. "And with that kind of concentration of power, bad things can happen. The federal regulators are afraid of them, afraid of their lawyers. Nobody should have unlimited power, but they are getting it. All sports are dominated by Mr. Big, all television, all markets . . . . I'm afraid that the future holds simply more and more Budweiser and less and less of everything else."

With the prediction of a 50 percent share of the market by the year 2000, Mr. Big wanted to get bigger.

Chapter
12

Personal Alignments, Realignments and Reality Beyond the Organization

This chapter focuses on relationships between several sets of processes that take place constantly in and around organizations. These processes are critical to both the success of organizations and the well-being of their members.

The first set of processes is well known. It includes such things as job descriptions, expectations of supervisors, peers, customers and subordinates; rules and laws; and professional norms. These processes exert pressures on organizational members to behave in certain ways. The second set occurs within the individual and involves the internal standards of conduct that influence beliefs about certain things: what an individual should and should not do, what is meaningful and worth doing and what is not, and what constitutes success and failure. These processes often conflict with the demands advanced by the organization.

The third set of processes involves what is referred to as "alignment," as individuals attempt to seek some congruency between internal and external demands. According to Culbert and McDonough, alignment involves "what an individual goes through in attempting to relate his or her subjective and self-centered interests to what he or she perceives as the objective requirements of the job."[1] Many psychologists and our own experiences tell us that when people achieve effective alignments (i.e. synergistic relationships between internal and external demands), they are happier, more energized, and more productive.

In the final set of processes alignment goes on continuously. Both internal and external standards change over time and previous alignments can become ineffective very quickly. Thus we need to talk about alignments and realignments. As the selections that follow reveal, achieving effective alignments and realignments can be very difficult to do and may require a great deal of introspection. In "The Invisible War: Pursuing Self Interest at Work," Samuel A. Culbert and John J. McDonough explain and illustrate the alignment process. "I Have Arrived" calls attention to some of the most frustrating of human experiences involving individuals who can achieve everything they sought and then wonder if what they sought was worthwhile.

In earlier decades, aligning one's needs and skills meant doing so primarily with respect to one's work. Personal life and relationships outside of work did not receive much attention from the organization or in the management literature. In the current era, alignment often explicitly includes issues of personal relationships and activities. In "Your Most Important Meeting of the Week Is with Your Spouse," Timothy Schellhardt discusses the tensions between partners in dual career relationships. He discusses the dangers to such relationships of poor communication between the partners and he reports on advice from experts that can help lessen the conflicts that are inherent when both partners are working in demanding professional roles.

A related, and relatively recent issue deals with the role reversals in which women are in higher profile posts than are their male partners, are successful CEOs and so forth. Changes in power dynamics between the partners and shifts in expectations and perceptions of men and women in such relationships add to the complexity and volatility of realigning a career. (See " 'First Husbands' Play Second Fiddle" by Joann S. Lublin)

"Annmarie Feci—Page Operator" is the story of an individual who appears to be well aligned in her job. Barbara E. Kovach's "Successful Derailment: What Fast-Trackers Can Learn While They're Off the Track" reveals that the issues discussed in the previous selections are directly relevant to some of the most talented managers in modern organizations. Managers' understanding of themselves turns out to be a major variable that determines their abilities to achieve successful realignments as they move through their careers.

In "The Day at the Beach" Arthur Gordon provides some ideas for the type of self-reflection that may help a person achieve successful alignments and realignments. It is far from a panacea but in our view points in some very useful directions.

Dealing with stress, maintaining one's alignment and one's personal relationships, and avoiding long-term burnout are concerns for all managers. These are particularly intense pressures on those in rapidly changing contexts. In "Strategies for Personal and Family Renewal," André Delbecq and Frank Friedlander report on the coping strategies of "high survivors," senior executives from small and medium technology firms in turbulent environments. The lessons they draw are illuminating and make a fitting conclusion to this chapter.

---

[1] S. A. Culbert and J. J. McDonough (1985). *Radical Management: Power Politics and the Pursuit of Trust* (New York: Free Press).

The Invisible War: Pursuing Self-Interest at Work

Samuel A. Culbert and
John J. McDonough

Each time people enter a new work situation they engage in the implicit process of *aligning* personal values, interests, and skills with what they perceive to be the task requirements of their job. They seek an orientation that maximizes self-pursuits and organizational contribution. *Alignment* is our term for the orientation that results from such an effort, however implicitly this takes place. Once such an orientation has been evolved, it becomes a self-convenient lens through which all organizational happenings are viewed. That is, once people hit on an alignment—an orientation that lines self-interests up with the task-requirements of their jobs—this alignment serves to alert them to meanings they can use in promoting and supporting their personal and organizational endeavors, and to meanings put forth by others which threaten the credibility and relevance of what they are pursuing.

Not all alignments are effective. That is, the orientation some people use is too far removed either from the needs and obligations of their jobs or from expressing the inner themes that can make their jobs personally meaningful. We say an individual possesses an "effective" alignment when the orientation directing that person's actions and view of reality allows him or her to represent important self-interests while making a contribution to the organization. We say an individual lacks an effective alignment when important discrepancies exist between what that person inwardly values, endeavors to express, does well, and needs to do in order to satisfy what he or she perceives to be the task requirements of the job.

Now we can return to the questions raised at the beginning of this chapter. [in original—eds.]

Why do people with the same job perform their assignments so differently?

Easy, they have unique interests, values, and competencies to bootleg into their jobs at every opportunity.

Why do people with comparable organizational goals see the same situation differently and fight unyieldingly over which interpretation is correct?

From *The Invisible War: Pursuing Self-Interest at Work* by Samuel A. Culbert and John J. McDonough, 1980, pp. 60–71, 219–222. New York: John Wiley & Sons, Inc. © 1980. Reprinted by permission of John Wiley & Sons, Inc.

Easy, while they may be striving to attain comparable organizational objectives, what they are striving to attain in their lives and careers is very different. This causes them to attend differently to each of the elements in a given situation. Finally,

What determines the specific way individuals decide to perform their jobs and how they interpret each situation?

Easy again, it's what we've termed alignment. People proceed with a job orientation that spontaneously spins out interpretations and meanings that serve the unique way they need reality constructed in order to be a "success." How individuals do a job and what they see are influenced by what they find personally interesting, by the concepts they can master and the skills they can perform with excellence, by the self-ideals and values they seek to attain, by their unique ideas of what constitutes career advancement, by what they believe will score on the checklist that others will use in evaluating their performance, and by what they genuinely believe the organization needs from someone in their role.

Few people are all that aware of their alignment. Even fewer are conscious of the fact that systematic biases permeate their view of the organizational world. And, almost no one understands that such biases play a major role in making organizations effective. All this is because most people work their alignment out implicitly and take its presence for granted until a change in the external scene, in other people's views of their effectiveness, or in their own sense of satisfaction show it to be obsolete. Then they can appreciate what they lost and strive for a new alignment that will again allow them to satisfy self-interests and personal pride while getting acclaim for doing a good job. For example, consider what happened to a middle manager named Pete who had a marvelous alignment until he got promoted and suddenly found himself faced with a serious gap between his own and the organization's definition of success.

Pete was one of twenty in his corporation who, some five years ago, agreed to take on a newly created mission, that of improving communications and managerial competence within his company. This function seemed right up Pete's alley. He'd attended sensitivity training sessions, had a reputation of being genuinely concerned with people, and was respected up and down the ranks for his leadership ability even though he had not burned up the track with his progress.

Pete saw the new assignment as a chance to bolster a lagging career. He had never been overly concerned with rising in the hierarchy, but his failure to take a fast track to the top was presenting him with daily redundancies that left him feeling somewhat stale. At forty-five he needed another challenge and this assignment held the potential to revitalize his career. Eagerly he accepted.

Pete threw himself into the new position. He enrolled in outside courses and hired skilled consultants to design training programs for the corporation's managers. Whenever possible he assisted the consultants and within a short time he understood their technology and was able to play a role in tailoring their inputs to the specific needs of his corporation. His learning continued and soon he was running programs on his own, involving personnel from each divisional level. Almost immediately his reputation as a man who genuinely cared was enhanced by wide-spread recognition of his competence in the management development technologies. And he was no soft touch either. He aggressively challenged managers on their "self-sealing" logics and constructed boat-rocking experiments to confront higher-ups with the demotivating and profit-eroding consequences of their autocratic styles.

Pete's involvements took an exciting turn with the advent of minority and women's consciousness. If the corporation's managers weren't racist, their de facto hiring and promotion policies were. This meant a greater volume of work and warranted an increase in the size of his staff. From a resource base that started with himself and a secretary, his department increased to two professionals, an administrative assistant, and two secretaries. Their operation hummed. They did career development counseling with secretaries. They got involved with the corporation's recruiters, both to encourage the hiring of blacks and females and to create programs that would support the new employees' progress in an essentially all white male management structure. They hired racial-awareness consultants to get managers in touch with their prejudices and help them work these out. And with this heightened workload, Pete even found time to continue his efforts in getting managers to identify areas in which their style intruded on the effectiveness of others.

Pete also had marvelous latitude in job definition which he exploited to match his interests and values. He enrolled in personal growth courses, attended conventions, joined professional associations, and on occasion even used the company plane. Because Pete identified both with the welfare of people and the productivity of the corporation and was concerned that his work produce tangible outcomes, his indulgences were hardly noticed—rather they were seen as part of his power. The people on his staff looked up to him and nondefensively brought him their toughest problems for coaching and support. His credibility with people lower in the hierarchy provided him a position of influence with those at the highest corporate levels. And, delightfully for Pete, his reputation among blacks and women was impeccable.

Within a couple of years Pete had worked out an ideal *alignment*. He had a way of engaging each constituency that allowed them to see how his actions related to results they valued. There seemed to be a 99 percent overlap between his personal definition of success and the missions and responsibilities assigned to him, and no one in the company could perform them better.

The other nineteen managers receiving the same charter as Pete, but working elsewhere in the corporation, didn't fare nearly as well. Perhaps lack of know-how, perhaps enculturation in the corporation's way of doing things, or perhaps a different tolerance for conflict had made them reluctant to aggressively challenge higher-ups. With time, to a greater or lesser degree, their roles degenerated to those of commiserator and management "go-for." They always seemed to be on the defensive, trying to prove themselves rather than challenging others to be more excellent. Their weakness and low-keyed tactics made Pete's strength and accomplishments look all the more potent.

Eventually those sitting in upper corporate echelons took notice of the overall situation and decided that Pete was the role model of what they were trying to achieve. They approached Pete with an offer of a promotion if he would agree to supervise and train the other nineteen managers. Pete's first reaction was to accept, but something held him back. At the time, he didn't understand his hesitancy, so he merely used it to negotiate a sweeter deal. He would not take responsibility for the others, there were too many bad habits to overcome. But he would step up a level in his current territory and accept overall responsibility for recruitment, career planning, minority advancement, and improved managerial functioning.

Pete's promotion put him on the same level with other line managers. He became a regular member of the management team and now directly supervised three managers who were responsible for about forty professional employees and oversaw the hiring of outside consultants.

Unfortunately, at this point, his alignment fell apart and his work life became filled with aggravation. *First,* his former associates began treating him like their boss, which he was, and this severely undermined his ability to coach and openly suggest. Now his suggestions were heard as orders and his inadvertent questions were received as well-thought-out criticisms.

Next, his relationships with blacks and women went to pot. His elevation in the hierarchy caused him to be seen as manager rather than human rights worker and he was treated to rounds of Mau-Mauing and confrontations, as what formerly had been received as his in-group remarks were interpreted as racial and sexist slurs.

Next, Pete found that the added amount of time his new job required for supervision, staff meetings, and report writing reduced the time available for the internal consulting role he prized.

On top of everything else, a "screw-up" in another division involving a racial-awareness consultant set off a reactionary wave up to an executive vice-president who responded by ordering sharp cutbacks in the use of outside consultants. For Pete, this had the personal effect of cutting off sources of his support and learning and the task effect of withdrawing the quality resources needed to keep his operation competently stationed and challenging to the status quo.

To top these disappointments, after about three months in the new job, Pete's boss called him in for a coaching session where he received word that his new peers were concerned that he was hurting his career by appearing to be such a deviant and advocate for minorities. Pete returned to his office screaming, "What the hell is going on here, these are the same jokers who wanted me promoted because I *was* such a deviant?!"

This was the last straw. Not only were his former constituents treating him like one of the "other guys" but the "other guys" were claiming that he was too much of a deviant for them.

From our perspective Pete was caught without either a personally effective or an organizationally successful alignment. His personal viewpoint wasn't registering anywhere. Nowhere was he actively shaping reality. His alignment had become obsolete. He was in the same position his nineteen former counterparts had found themselves in when they were charged with a mission to which they could not personally relate and thus could not confidently assert an articulate point of view.

Incidentally, and no pun intended, this is not a case of the "Peter Principle." We know Pete and he's anything but a person who had been promoted above his level of competence. We believe it is just a matter of time before Pete constructs a new alignment, one that allows him to use his new job for personal expression and to further the missions he values. But until he gets realigned, the self-deliberations entailed in trying to match self-interests with what seems to be required by his job will provide him with many lonely hours of unhappiness and frustration.

Pete's story was chosen because it illustrates the active dimension of the orienting process we call alignment. It shows the importance of an individual's commitment to inner values. That Pete could succeed, both inwardly and outwardly, where nineteen others could not is a tribute to his success in finding a good match between his personal needs and interests and what he saw as needed by the job. He had an effective alignment. The nineteen others lacked an effective alignment and most of them became either *cynics* or *careerists*. The cynics converged on alignments that subordinated the organization's needs to their own interests and values. They saw management's view as constraints to be navigated around, not perspectives to be joined and possibly learned from. Conversely, the careerists adopted alignments that subordinated their personal interests and values to what they thought would score on the organization checklist. They ground out workshop after workshop, training event after training event, but without the conversations and conflicts that could budge the status quo.

The concept of alignment, and Pete's story, provides support for most people's contention that repackaging themselves to fit a particular job or role does not constitute a sell-out to the job, although to an outsider their compromises frequently appear fatal. As Pete's situation illustrates, people need to shift alignments when they change jobs or experience a new set of external demands, even though their interests, skills and values remain the same. While self-interests remain relatively constant, the form in which they are pursued and expressed must shift. How often we've seen people criticize the way their boss operates only to themselves embody much of the same behavior as they shift alignments upon moving up to the boss's level in the organization.

In summary, we see the concept of alignment as a key addition to how people should be thinking about organizations. There's a level of organization residing within each individual that explains how that person does his or her job and views external organization events. If there's an external organization that determines how groups of people relate in doing work together then there's an *internal organization,* far more encompassing than an individual's personality, that determines how individuals within groups transact their business and work for the greater institutional good. Moreover, despite their lack of prominence in how people present themselves, self-interests are a dominant factor in determining what gets produced in the name of organizationally required product and how what is produced is received. And you don't need the skills of a psychoanalyst to understand these self-interests. You merely need to comprehend what an individual is trying to express personally and achieve in his or her career, and what he or she perceives as making a valuable contribution to the job. At every point personal needs and organization goals impact on one another, and it's always up in the air whether the needs of the job or the interests of the individual will swamp the other or whether a synergy of interests will evolve.

Thus *alignment* is our term for the highly personal orientation one takes to the job that must be known before we can comprehend the meaning and intent of someone's actions. Sometimes people do different things for the same reason. Sometimes people do the same things for different reasons. Without knowing people's alignment, taking their actions on face value—even those with a direct connection to bottom-line product—leads to erroneous conclusions. The only way to comprehend what people are about is to know what they are trying to express and achieve personally and what assumptions they are making about the organizational avenues for doing so.

At this point we provide a guide to comprehending the personal side of an individual's orientation to the job. It's a set of questions which, when thoughtfully answered, provide a new perspective on why an individual does his or her job the way he or she does it, and why that person views organization events in a particular way. Add in the task requisites of the job, as the individual sees them, and you've got that person's alignment. Incidentally, we've had marvelous results using an abbreviated list of these questions as preparation for team-building meetings at which a boss and his or her subordinates get together for a long session to discuss opportunities for improving their work-group's effectiveness. Twenty to forty minutes each, around the group, and the edge comes off many premeeting criticisms. Instead of being programmed to fault one another for inadequacy, the discussion takes a constructive turn as participants contrast the fit between an individual's needs and talents with what participants see as the task requisites of that person's job.

The questions we use in seeking to understand the self-interest side of an individual's alignment fall into three categories: personal, career, and organizational. Specifically we ask questions drawn from, but not limited to, the following list.

SELF-INTEREST QUESTIONS

Personal

What are you trying to prove to yourself and, very importantly, why?
What are you trying to prove to others? Give an instance that illustrates why and how.
What style of life are you trying to maintain or achieve? (Does this entail a change in income? geography? family size? etc.)
Name the people who have played significant roles in your life and say what those roles were.
What dimensions would you like to add to your personal life and why?
What motto would you like to have carved on your tombstone and how do you want to be remembered by the people who are close to you?

Career

What profession do you want to wind up in? (If you are an engineer and you say "management," tell why. If you are not in that profession, say how you plan to get into it.)
How did you, or will you, develop competency in that profession?
What do you want to accomplish in that profession?
What honor or monument would you like to have symbolize your success in that profession? Say why it would constitute a personal hallmark.

Organizational

What has been your image in your organization and what would you like it to be?
Describe a bum-rap or overly simplistic category others have used in describing you and tell either why you are different now or why their statement was simplistic or too categorical.
What is the next lesson you need to learn and what are your plans for doing so?
What would you like to be doing two to five years out?*
What would you like to be doing ten years out?

---

*Think of "doing" in terms of a specific assignment (job, position, status) and specify it in terms of a specific role (player, coach, expert) and how you would like to be performing it.

While we encourage people to share perspectives generated by these questions with work associates whom they trust, we do not recommend that they reveal specific instances in which self-interests played a role in determining one of their organizational actions. We don't because we fear that others, however well-intentioned, will inadvertently misuse such candor later on. What we advocate is that each individual simply provide associates a more valid context for viewing his or her goals and accomplishments. . . .

CONCLUSION

It's appropriate that we've saved our favorite story for the end. It's a story about a manager who embodies the best of both the subjective and the rational approaches to leadership and for us is a symbol that it can be done. This manager is able to go toe to toe with hard-boiled characters like Charlie and at the same time remain sensitive to the contributions made by leaders like Fred.* He's a manager who searches for ways of relating to the uniqueness of those reporting to him while he shuns calling "objective" that which he sees as arbitrary and a matter of personal convenience.

The manager we have in mind demonstrated the effectiveness of much that we are advocating in three distinct settings: industry, education, and public service. First, he fought his way through the highly competitive world of consumer products where he became chairman of the board of one of the nation's largest and most successful conglomerates. Next, in the educational field, he became the dean of a large and prestigious professional school, instituting changes that brought national recognition to that institution. And most recently he was the President's choice to head a world-renowned agency and this appointment brought instant acclamation from the Senate Hearings Committee. All this took place before his forty-seventh birthday!

In our view the key to this manager's success lies in his ability to see the connection between personal effectiveness and organizational efficiency. To him, these are highly related issues. He believes that organizations exist to serve people, not the other way around, and he constantly searches to understand what people are trying to achieve in the way of personal meaning and career success. Nevertheless, his style is one which frequently gets misinterpreted as soft and permissive leadership and does not produce an easy route to universal love and appreciation. His understanding of personal projects allows him to penetrate many of the facades people construct, and this makes him the target of behind-the-scenes ambivalence and face-to-face suspicion. Let's examine his impact more closely.

In the first place, he resists spending the bulk of his energies responding to problems defined by others as "crises." This orientation allows him to take tough stands with respect to the succession of "crises" any top administrator faces, and which, if passed down through the organization, can make it impossible for anyone to align self-interests with the task requirements of their job in a way that's constructive for the institution. In the short run his "nonresponsiveness" makes him vulnerable to the charge that he is not on top of a situation. In the long run, however, he frees himself and the people in his organization from the oppressive burden of always responding to someone else's fire drill.

---

*Charlie and Fred are characters introduced earlier in the book from which this excerpt is taken—*Ed. note.*

We certainly don't want to mislead you into thinking that our hero, or any other leader, could emerge from each of these settings totally unscarred. To the contrary, on his way to the board chairmanship he spent more than three years going eyeball to eyeball with a manager whose style was the antithesis of his own and whose subordinates consider him to be "the biggest prick you're ever going to find in a chief executive's office." When our leader realized that he was going to be locked in mortal combat for as long as he stayed with the conglomerate, he began to look around. That's when he got into education. Some say things got too hot for him to handle. In our minds his decision revealed that he saw more to life than surviving corporate death struggles.

It's interesting to contrast the subordinates who value his leadership style with those who don't. Those who see flexibility in the construction of their own alignments generally appreciate his style. But he causes fits among those with careerist and martyr mentalities. These people are confused by his respect for the personal side of their alignments. They mistake his sensitivity to what is personally meaningful to them as agreement with their self-beneficial formulations of what the organization needs to do. Consequently they experience small betrayals when learning of a decision he takes after surveying their perspective. What they don't understand is that our hero seriously considers competing perspectives prior to making a decision and that his integration is almost always original, with even the people who influenced him the most finding themselves unable to identify their input in what he prints out. But for those with open-ended questions, his print-outs are almost always educational. By factoring out what he added, they deduce what this leader sees as the limitations in their formulations.

For almost everyone, his style is disarming. His searching respect for the subjective side of an individual's participation is responded to as a warm and irresistible invitation to tell all. This makes it quite difficult to fragment. Knowing that he knows their subjective interests causes most people to tell their whole story—either out of a fear of looking stupid or one of getting caught telling a half-truth. In subtle ways this leader conveys the message that he's not there simply to serve the self-indulgent needs of individuals but to provide another perspective on what the organization needs and to challenge people to find a more synergistic means of relating their needs to organization product. And he's been able to do this and still score on the traditional checklist.

In many ways this leader is bigger than life; certainly his accomplishments surpass what most of us are externally striving to achieve. Today's society seems to worship external success, yet each of us knows that we're up to so much more. Our hero often strikes us as a very lonely man and we can't help but think that a major part of what appears to be a self-imposed solitude derives from an understanding that, in today's world, his accomplishments are valued for reasons which bear little resemblance to what he sets out to do. But help should be on the way. We believe the evaluation categories which convey illusions of objectivity and overemphasize externals will gradually change. And as more people demonstrate an enhanced appreciation for the subjective involvements that everyone brings to organization life, this leader, together with the rest of us, will have an easier time being himself and gaining recognition for just that.

I Have Arrived

Natasha Josefowitz

I have not seen the plays in town
   only the computer printouts
I have not read the latest books
   only *The Wall Street Journal*
I have not heard birds sing this year
   only the ringing of phones
I have not taken a walk anywhere
   but from the parking lot to my office
I have not shared a feeling in years
   but my thoughts are known to all
I have not listened to my own needs
   but what I want I get
I have not shed a tear in ages
   I have arrived
Is *this* where I was going?

From Natasha Josefowitz, *Is This Where I Was Going?*, 1983, New York: Warner Books, Reprinted by permission.

Managing Your Career:
Your Most Important Meeting of the Week Is with Your Spouse

Timothy D. Schellhardt

It struck like a thunderbolt. Nearly a dozen years after my job transfer to a dream assignment, my wife's resentment of that move suddenly erupted. It had disrupted her dream tenured-teaching job and doctorate work, and while I thought we had adequately discussed and agreed to the move, she actually had despised it, and her silent bitterness merely intensified over the years.

Marriage counselors who advise dual-career couples say our communications gulf wasn't unusual—and neither are the hurdles it can place in the path of a marriage and couples' careers. How to communicate effectively about career-family issues—whether it's a job transfer or a trip out of town—is the hot topic of the '90s for couples, they say. "It's a huge problem," says Scott Stanley, a psychologist and couples researcher at the University of Denver Center for Marital and Family Studies, noting the stress corporate downsizing is putting on couples.

"Juggling two careers requires lots of flexibility, compromising and negotiating," says Marolyn Knight, an Indianapolis marriage therapist, "and there's not really a road map for that for many couples whose own parents had traditional marriages where dad worked and mom stayed at home."

But counselors and dual-career couples offer several tips for traveling that path together. Some of the advice takes a bit of spontaneity out of relationships, but can keep problems from festering.

Atop the list: Establish a routine for discussing job and family issues. Partners often allow themselves to get too busy and forget to tell each other what's going on in their lives. "We make appointments for everything else, but we don't often with the people most important to us," says Richard J. Levin, a Brookline, Mass., psychologist and work-family consultant.

He advises that dual-career couples meet, perhaps once a week over lunch or on a walk, to talk about what's coming up the next week for each partner. At that session, suggests Mel Mackler, a San Diego marriage therapist, write down all the responsibilities to be completed for the week and divide them so that tasks are clear. Atlanta therapist Augustus Napier says two meetings a week may be necessary—one to plan the weekend so you don't wind up just doing chores and the other to plan the week.

Peter Wright, an Andersen Consulting manager in San Francisco, and his wife, Amy, a sixth-grade teacher, set aside 30 minutes a day to share personal and job issues; each gets equal time to talk—and listen. "Sometimes we have to do that over the phone when I'm traveling, but we rarely miss," says the 25-year-old consultant, married $2\frac{1}{2}$ years.

The Wrights also try every six months to review their career and personal goals and to reassure each other that they're working on common objectives. Such sessions to review short- and long-term goals and dreams can better prepare a career couple when a jarring career decision, like a job change or transfer, comes. Bonnie Michaels, a consultant who conducts retreats for couples, says the annual sessions she and her husband, a Quaker Oats manager, have held for six years helped when he recently accepted a stint in Singapore. Theirs is a long-distance commuter marriage. "It hurt my career and my psyche, but because we've talked about this, I'm not feeling as angry as I could feel," she says.

Counselors say couples must establish ground rules for their talks. Set aside time—as you would for a business meeting—when there will be no interruptions, and fix an agenda that you stick to. Limit the length of each session and make clear it's not going to be adversarial.

Know about fair fighting. "Take turns listening to each other and give one another equal air time," advises William S. Pollack, a psychologist whose Spectrum Consulting Group of Brookline has developed a course for dual-career couples on maintaining a work-family balance. David Gutterman, an Evanston, Ill., marriage therapist, says listening is often the key. "Make sure you understand your partner. Repeat back and clarify what you're hearing them say. That's particularly important when talking about careers and very emotionally charged issues."

When a critical decision, like a job transfer, must be made, "make sure that it isn't settled until each partner can say, 'I can live with it,'" says Leah Fisher, co-director of the Center for Work and the Family in Berkeley, Calif. "That might mean an all-nighter, but it forces you to decide what matters the most."

For executive couples, the pressures can often be greater, say several consultants. Despite the flexibility their higher incomes can provide for such things as child care, "they're often trapped in their work and under so much stress, any little problem between them flares up into an emergency," says Dr. Napier. The marriage of one executive couple (with two small children) is so fragile that he has urged them to limit their work and community commitments immediately to focus on their relationship.

Consultants say what's most important is that dual-career couples stay sensitive to each other's working needs. "It sounds too simplistic, but having faith and trust in each other to do the best they possible can for the other" will often help ensure the right balance for a two-career couple, says Barrie Greiff, a Harvard psychiatrist who has written a book for career couples, "Trade Offs."

'First Husbands' Play Second Fiddle

Joann S. Lublin

Gene Sinser usually doesn't mind playing dutiful spouse. His wife, Patty DeDominic, is chief executive officer of PDQ Personal Service Inc. in Los Angeles.

Mr. Sinser, a former executive who owns a picture-frame shop, likes to perform a cork trick for his table mates while she works the crowd during her business banquets. He says he also "can pack at a moment's notice" to accompany her on trips. At times, however, he has insisted that she iron his shirt even though it was shortly before she had to deliver an important speech.

Mr. Sinser belongs to a rare but growing brotherhood: men whose wives hold the highest corporate job. Ms. DeDominic, founder of her $15 million placement concern, dubs her mate "First Husband." She claims that he can act like "the perfect CEO spouse"—despite his ill-timed ironing requests.

Husbands of CEOs are mainly cropping up at small and medium-sized companies. The Committee of 200, a national group of prominent business-women, reports that more than half of its 360 members are now CEOs, presidents or chair-women who have husbands. To join the Chicago-based group, a woman must own a business with annual revenue exceeding $10 million or manage a division with more than $50 million in revenue.

Some men find it tough to share the limelight with their chief-executive wives. For their marriage to succeed, the man must "be extremely secure about [himself], flexible and giving," says Dee Soder, a New York executive coach. "[Men] have a harder time because of societal expectations."

Susan D. McClanahan believes her marriage fell apart partly because her husband couldn't cope with her tremendous success. She says she makes $2 million a year as chief executive of two New York concerns, a textbook developer and a publisher of children's books with combined annual sales of nearly $15 million.

Ms. McClanahan married Donald French, owner of a small moving company, in 1982, six years after she launched the textbook developer. Mr. French says he sold his failing business in 1989. He then managed the couple's investment portfolio and tried to become a Wall Street broker. But "no one would hire me," he adds.

Ms. McClanahan's business flourished while her husband's career stalled. "I felt there was competition between us. Whenever I came home and talked about a success, he would tune out," she says. "As much as he wanted me to be successful, it was a terrible reminder that he wasn't."

The couple separated in February and expects to be divorced by spring. Mr. French says he repeatedly told his wife "how proud I was to be her husband. But she didn't hear

---

" 'First Husbands' Play Second Fiddle" by Joann S. Lublin, *The Wall Street Journal*, December 15, 1994, p. B1. Reprinted by permission.

it." He contends their union soured because being CEO kept her busy all the time and because she thought he wasn't good enough for her.

"The more successful she became—and I didn't keep up with her—the less interesting I became," Mr. French says. "I became an embarrassment to her." Last month, he started a currency-trading firm on Wall Street.

Other CEOs' husbands resent being treated like subordinates at home. During domestic tiffs, Mr. Sinser says, he occasionally must remind Ms. DeDominic: "Hey, I am not one of your employees." She quickly backs off, he continues. "She says, 'I realize I was dealing with you like someone I have control over.'"

Mr. Sinser's remarks annoy his wife, however. "I think those are really demeaning comments," she says. At the office, "I often take a very firm stance on things" because "I have ultimate responsibility for people's jobs," she explains. But at home, Ms. DeDominic maintains, "I am not at all controlling."

The role reversals of a CEO husband often extend to domestic chores, too. Lisa Conte, president and chief executive of Shaman Pharmaceuticals Inc., a biotechnology company in South San Francisco, works so late that her husband Bob Thornton must fix dinner most week-nights. "Dinner isn't elaborate. It's pasta or salad after our [two-year-old] son goes to bed," says Mr. Thornton, a vice president of a GATX Corp. unit in San Francisco. "I'm not a great chef."

Ms. Conte must leave town at least every other week for her job. Mr. Thornton usually stays home. "I don't go on business trips with her," he says. "I don't have time. I have a full-time job." He says the hardest thing about being a chief executive's husband is that "you have to get used to not seeing your spouse."

Ms. Conte worries about the toll her frenetic lifestyle takes. At 3 A.M. recently, she was up doing Shaman paperwork. She awakened her husband to complain that they weren't spending enough time with each other. They talked. "We came to the conclusion that there's no way we can get divorced," she says, laughing wryly. "We don't have the time."

Annmarie Feci

Page Operator

Ina Yalef

She has worked in the phone room for twelve years. It's a small room, adequate for five operators, located on the fourth floor of the service building. "They've given us the name 'Telecommunications.' Real fancy. To us, though, it's still the Phone Room."

The main number of this hospital is 305–2500. That's what people calling Presbyterian Hospital dial to reach us. During the day there are six girls here at one time. Three or four girls on the switchboard, plus one girl on page and one girl on patient information. On evenings and nights we have less.

They all do different things. The patient information girl tells the caller if a person is here, what room he's in, and the status of the patient. We're very careful about what information we give out, though. You'll get lots and lots of nosy neighbors who call and ask, "Can you tell me what the patient died of? Did he have AIDS? Did he have this? Did he have that?" They want to know things which are not anybody's business except the patient's immediate family. You have to be careful what you say and who you're saying it to because you really never know who's on the other end. And at all times you have to hold your patience, which often is not easy to do, sitting there all day, listening to some of these people.

I don't get ruffled easily . . . my personality runs basically the same all the time. To really get me riled somebody on the other end has to be so obnoxious that I can't deal with them. People get really annoyed when it takes too long to get through to the hospital. I understand that. Say a call comes in to 2500, the main number, and the caller asks to be connected to a patient named Smith. We transfer her to patient information to get Mr. Smith's room number. Those girls have a rack of index cards with patients' room numbers on them. Well, if they haven't gotten the information from admitting yet, they don't know where the patient is. So we have to transfer the call to admitting. So the caller has now waited to get through to 2500, they've gotten transferred to 3101— patient information—now we're connecting them down to 2536—admitting. In the interim they've gotten disconnected so you'll get them back on 2500 and now they're *really* riled. But we're doing our best. Really we are.

Sometimes we get calls from non–English-speaking people. You try and understand their broken English, if they even *speak* English. If the caller is speaking a language other than English or Spanish, we'll connect the call to Patient Relations. If they think it's

"Annmarie Feci—Page Operator" by Ina Yalef from *Life and Death, Story of a Hospital*, 1988, pp. 187–190. Reprinted by permission of the publisher.

something that's really important, they get an interpreter to come to the phone and try and speak to the person. Patient Relations is able to find people who speak languages I never heard of. I guess maybe when you come in to be interviewed for a job they ask if you speak a second language. That way they're able to keep track of people who speak various languages. If someone calls and asks for a person who we know has died, we tell them to get in contact with the family. If they get too upset or say they don't know the family—we connect them to our AOD [administrator on duty].

There are times when every one of our console positions is covered, and people are still waiting to get through to the hospital. We probably spend twenty seconds on an average call, assuming of course that it's not an old lady whose hearing aid isn't working, or somebody who doesn't speak English. Those are some of the things that hold you up. But barring unforeseen circumstances, we can easily handle three or four calls a minute. Then you have to figure if there are four girls sitting on four consoles, you've answered maybe twelve calls in a minute, at least, and that's not saying how many people are waiting during that time also to get in.

People say, "Telephone operator, eh? What an easy job." But it's a lot of work. Patient information girls have all those cards to file. They have all the ICUs to check to see how patients are. In the morning they have to get admissions from the emergency room from the night before. They write up all those cards from all those midnight people that have come in and file them, plus they're answering the calls that they're getting in on 3101, Patient Information.

The paging girl does the overhead paging that's heard throughout the hospital. Most of the doctors are on beepers now, though. They have a computerized system where you dial a number in the hospital and a computerized woman's voice speaks to you—everybody calls her "Patti Page"—but there are still reasons to use the overhead, like arrest calls and calls to staff without beepers.

A lot of things can happen just sitting up here in the service building. But I think the most devastating experience I ever had was the night that John Wood died. What happened was, we got a call from EMS that they were bringing in a gunshot. If it's a gunshot or a stabbing, EMS usually calls from the road—and you connect them to the emergency room. The next thing we get a call from the nurse in the ER to put Dr. John Wood on page. See, he was the resident on call that night in the ER, and he was on arrest duty too, so he was carrying the arrest beeper. But he wanted to go home to see his wife, who wasn't feeling well. So before he left, he gave the beeper to another doctor. We didn't know that at the time, though. So there we are paging "Dr. John Wood. Dr. John Wood." No answer. Next thing, maybe a minute later, the ER nurse calls back again and she says to us, "My God, my God," she says, "John Wood is the *patient!*"

We were all crying. He was special to everyone who knew him. To me, he was the pediatrician who took care of my kids and now all of a sudden you're paging an arrest for somebody only to find out that it's somebody who's probably the nicest person that God ever put on the face of the earth. I mean, he was an absolute sweetheart.

When you're on Patient Information, you begin to get familiar with names of people who come in for lots of admissions. Just the names. You have the patient information index so you're filing the cards and you say, "Oh, my God, that poor child, he's back in again." A lot of times you really don't know what's wrong with the child but you see that ticket and you know that child is in. Then all of a sudden you get notified of an expiration and it's him. And your heart drops; you never met the child, didn't know his mother or father, but yet you feel just as bad. Probably because it was a kid. Or even sometimes adults who come in that we know are oncology patients because they're on Harkness One. You never met the person but you say, "Oh, my God, So-and-so, they died." It's like one of the family passed away. You never met them but you feel awful about it.

I was raised on 169th Street. My mother worked in Presbyterian for thirty years. She retired in 1980. She worked in accounting. I feel like I have been raised in this place. When I graduated from high school I couldn't wait to work at Presbyterian. It was taken for granted; if you lived in the neighborhood, you had to work at Presbyterian. You weren't one of the "in" crowd if you didn't work here. But I put nine thousand applications in and never, never got hired. I was downstairs in personnel every time they turned around, trying to get a job. Nothing. Finally I came in one day and the fella down in personnel said, "Listen, I've got a job in the phone room." We weren't called telecommunications then. I said, "I can answer phones. That I can do."

In thirteen years, I've really seen this place grow. I've seen Babies' add the addition on and Eye add its addition and Atchley Pavilion go up. I watched them tear Maxwell Hall down. I watched them tear down Harkness Hall. My bridal shower was in Harkness Hall. Yes, that was a nice place. It was a shame that they tore it down. But that's what modernization is. You've got to keep moving.

Telecommunications is the main access point of this hospital. We're the central unit. When people call up for conditions on patients , that comes through us. When doctors need to be paged, that comes through us. When they need to put an arrest on, that's through us. When there's a fire, we put the fire brigade on. Those beepers are through us also. So we're touching kind of all bases: medical, maintenance . . . you name it.

Think about it. We're saving lives! You figure EMS calls us, they need to get the ER to let Alice know that they've got a gunshot coming in. If somebody is calling Dr. Rose because they have a heart in another state, we get the call. We give it to Dr. Rose. He gets the heart. But it came through us first. So, we're it! We're really where it starts from. The central unit that makes this place go. I'm telling you. People might not think of us that way, but it's true. We're the heart of this hospital.

Successful Derailment: What Fast-Trackers Can Learn While They're Off the Track

Barbara E. Kovach

Executives who get derailed from the fast track typically view themselves as failures. But the author suggests that a career slowdown or derailment can provide an opportunity for personal growth and development.

While speaking to a group of corporate executives recently, I was challenged about the cooperative attitude manifested by the senior executives who took part in my initial study, *Survival on the Fast Track* (Dodd, Mead, 1988), which considered corporate fast-trackers on the way to the top in major U.S. corporations. Two assumptions underlay the challenge: (1) that one has to move upward, and (2) that one has to compete against one's peers in order to move to the senior level. The second assumption could be put aside more easily than the first: There are other studies demonstrating that cooperation—not competition—is the key to moving up to the executive ranks.

The first assumption, however, is embedded in the American culture, and because this assumption had not been examined, it had shaped the context of the previous study. The implication of the study was, in fact, that upward mobility is a good thing and that derailment is something to be avoided if at all possible. If derailment proved inevitable, went the logic, certain approaches could turn this state of affairs into a plus, putting the individual once again on the road to the top. It is time to examine this assumption—and several related ones—and to use the resulting conclusions to form the context in which to examine the follow-up stories of fast-trackers two years after the completion of the initial study.

SPECIFIC ASSUMPTIONS ABOUT UPWARD MOBILITY

There appear to be several secondary, underlying assumptions that taken together add up to the first main assumption, i.e., that moving upward is good. Even though there is no real evidence that these secondary assumptions are true, they underlie casual conversations among many talented people and are subjects of humor and satire in many popular works. If we were to work backward from the general assumption about upward mobility, we might find that the following secondary assumptions make up the general one:

1. Everyone is suited for the next-level position.
2. The odds of moving up continuously are sufficient to justify keeping upward mobility as a primary career goal.
3. Individuals have enough control of the situation that going after the next job may have a significant impact on whether or not they get that job.
4. When they arrive at that job, they will experience a sense of accomplishment and satisfaction that justifies the struggle to attain it.

Let us examine each underlying assumption in turn. First, the idea that one should always seek the next-level position (and this idea's attendant assumption that the seeker can handle the job and wants to do it) is at the heart of the accepted American tradition that guides those who are on a high-achievement track. But does this idea stand up under further analysis?

Many experts, for example, have agreed with the Peter Principle, which says that people are promoted to their level of incompetence. In many cases, however, incompetence is not the issue. Instead, people are often promoted until they don't "fit" with the system at a particular level, and then ways are found to remove them. In fact, there is no reason to believe that, just because someone likes one job, he or she will necessarily like the next, higher job as much; for not everyone is suited for a higher job. But the American corporate belief system has not taken this into account.

Second, in any hierarchical, pyramidal organization, the number of jobs decreases sharply on the way up the pyramid. Thus not everyone can move up. In fact, most people can't move up. The odds are that any given individual will not make it all the way to the top. Let's look at those odds. In a given company there are 30,000 employees. Let us assume that 15%, or 4,500, are managers. In the career lifetime of any of these employees there are likely to be about 4.5 chairmen of the board. Thus the odds are a thousand to one that any given manager who enters the company will eventually become its chairmen. Would we take bets on those odds? Would we put money on a horse running at a thousand to one against the odds? Not likely. Given their assumptions about the general importance of upward mobility, this means that in a career history of about 45 years, 4,445.5 people are going to view themselves as losers. Some will feel that they lost at lower levels and some at higher levels, but if they accept the American mythology about moving ahead, they will all see themselves as losers.

Third, the degree of control that individuals exercise over whether they will be promoted diminishes markedly after they have climbed the first few rungs of any organizational ladder. For example, a very senior chairman was discussing the possibility that either of two senior statesmen (see below) in his previous company might, in fact, become chairman. He remarked, "It's unlikely, because they are both the wrong age; the appointment of someone either five years younger or older is much more likely." The judgment of this chairman was realistic: He foresaw that the company (the board, in fact) would choose someone already accomplished enough to carry out the scenario formed by the board and then retire without further ado; or else the board would select someone less senior who could be groomed for the position and then hold it for at least a decade. The two people being discussed at the time fell in between these two categories. They were likely to lose in the final round only because they were *the wrong age* for the company's needs. And their age was clearly not a factor under their control.

Yet such characteristics as age greatly affect one's possibilities of promotion. The higher one goes in the organization, the more one's chances of promotion depend on a variety of factors other than one's abilities and achievements—including the state of the economy as it affects the organization. Most of these factors are not within the purview of individual control.

Moreover, individuals on the promotion ladder do not operate in a vacuum; they are part of a network made up of many members, each of whose perceptions and actions affect the final outcome of any situation. Events throughout this network affect the "promotability" of a given person at a given time, and this too is not under an individual's control.

Fourth, the expectation that one will experience profound satisfaction by reaching higher and higher levels in the company is probably not justified, for two reasons. First, there is no final resting place—not even the virtually unattainable chairmanship—at which one can say, "I have arrived." Instead, with each promotion, individuals adopt a new frame of reference suitable to that level. The new position may have appeared to be at the top of the heap when it was viewed from below. But when the individual reaches that level, it may appear unsatisfactorily low when compared with the position above it—and the one above that.

For example, one of the fast-trackers in the original study has just been promoted to the president's chair in his company. This move, in most frames of reference, would appear to put him on the top of the heap—or so close that any further moves would appear inconsequential. However, this man must share this chair with another man and report, along with his counterpart, to the chairman of the company. When this move was announced, a Wall Street observer casually commented that this president-to-be "must not be pleased to be in this one-down position." Given this new frame of reference, even a newly promoted chairman might perceive him- or herself as being beneath those who are chairmen of bigger companies. Almost inevitably, people find themselves close to the bottom in whatever is their current frame of reference both in the perception of others and, more important, in their own.

Moreover, moving up the ladder increases the visibility of the individual and the likelihood of both praise and severe criticism from a vastly increased sector of the world at large. If all goes well, the company and its chairman may profit from the increased attention and publicity, as in the case of Jim Burke of Johnson & Johnson during the Tylenol crisis of 1984. Burke showed great tact and responsibility, and he and the company alike emerged from the crisis with the respect and admiration of the public. However, the affection of the press and the public for a given leader may change dramatically during a short period of time, as in the case of Roger Smith of General Motors. Smith was widely praised for his financial astuteness during the 1984–1985 years, during which he acquired new companies and poured money into technology for the large auto company. But when profits turned down and Ford soared ahead of GM, Smith and his company received a severe press-bashing that may just now be coming to an end. Smith may have enjoyed the challenge of heading up a major corporation, and he may even have experienced a thrill at being a public figure. However, one wonders just how satisfying it was for him to be perceived by the public as a bumbling or even a malevolent leader.

Abiding by the assumption that success entails moving up the career ladder virtually guarantees winding up a loser at one time or another. Perhaps what matters most in one's career history is how one deals with the necessary fact of *not* moving into a higher position—an experience which, according to our commonly held beliefs and traditional script, is defined as losing at whatever level upward progress comes to a halt.

We might say, in fact, that all of the fast-trackers written about in the earlier study are probably headed down the road to derailment. The question is not whether they will be derailed, but when—and how—they will cope with their derailment. Will they accept it easily, or will they react with anger, bitterness, or world-weary resignation? Will they allow the experience of being stopped on the "ladder to success" to stop them in other areas of their lives as well? Or will derailment provide the incentive to become more fully involved in their families, their communities, or their present jobs? Will it spur them to engage in another business venture?

Many fast-trackers are asking these questions of themselves as they move along on what they hope will be the track to the top. Perhaps it's time to examine these assumptions about upward mobility and to write a new script which emphasizes the importance of doing work that is challenging, the value of accepting responsibility for others and for the stability of our institutions, and the satisfaction that comes from working wholeheartedly in the environment in which we find ourselves—and which puts less stress on how fast we are moving toward the top.

THE FAST-TRACKERS: 1986

A bit of background about my study of fast-trackers: From April to July of 1986, I interviewed 17 people in five major corporations who were perceived by their peers and direct reports to be "doing better" than others at the same rank. These 17 fast-trackers—15 men and two women—held positions at various levels of their companies; their ages ranged from 30 to 52 in 1986. Their points of view about success were clearly delineated by age; these delineations allowed me to develop a hypothesis about three career stages that many fast-trackers pass through.

Junior Stars

The youngest fast-trackers were in their early 30s, and all their answers to my questions were alike in important ways: They were universally enthusiastic, convinced that they were the best, and eager to know how far and how fast they would move up.

Mid-Careerists

Those fast-trackers who were only a few years senior to the junior stars—within five years of age 40—spoke differently about their work. Their enthusiasm was less constant and more tempered. They rarely described themselves as the best, and they were more reflective than their juniors were about a broad reach of personal and professional issues in their lives. In many cases, their recent experience had taught them that asking how far and how fast would not lead to any satisfactory answers. This group of mid-careerists was passing through what I call the "executive transition."

Senior Statesmen

Finally, those fast-trackers who were older than 45 spoke differently yet about their work. These people displayed neither the continuous enthusiasm of the junior stars nor the reflective wonderings of the mid-careerists. These senior statesmen spoke of the bad and the good in the same breath, saw their career as less important than the organization's performance, and were concerned with their future status primarily in terms of finding a place that offered the same degree of challenge and intensity to which they had grown accustomed.

Of the 17 subjects, five were termed senior statesmen, eight were mid-careerists, and four were junior stars.

Characteristics of All Fast-Trackers

Regardless of personal style and family/career history, all the fast-trackers shared certain characteristics. In general, they *loved* their work; put in long hours; had good relationships with people at work and with their families; demonstrated an almost startling degree of clarity about themselves, their strengths, and their weaknesses; and believed in helping and being helped by others. It was clear from the interviews and follow-up talks with these 17 people that doing well at work was, for them, a result of throwing themselves into their work without reserve.

Derailment Among the Fast-Trackers

In the initial study, two fast-trackers discussed having been derailed during the executive transition. Fast-tracker Hank was not given an official change of status. Nonetheless, he was removed from his current position, was not given the expected promotion, and was given a position with virtually no responsibilities for a period of more than six months. During this time he was ignored by the company's hierarchy, his telephone calls were not returned, and various allegations were made about his wife's inability to adapt to new situations. Hank's response during this period was to "sit tight and wait it out."

When a shift occurred in the roles of those above him, Hank received a substantial promotion to a job with significant responsibilities. He said in his initial interview with me that he was cautious in taking his new place on the ladder and careful not to be angry at those who had abandoned him or plotted his derailment. Hank has since been promoted twice, has a secure place on the succession ladder, and is excited and enthusiastic about both his current position and his future prospects.

The other fast-tracker, Larry, discussed his derailment more briefly. While on his way through the executive transition, Larry was shuttled off to a job out of the mainstream and off the succession track. Angry at first, he said that he turned this position into "the learningest job he ever had," greatly broadening his own knowledge of the company and helping to increase company profits. From this position, he was then promoted to a significant new position as head of his own venture within the company.

Other fast-trackers commented less on their journey through the executive transition, but they did speak briefly of difficulties they had encountered along the way. The log of their promotions reveals a clear slowdown for many during the executive transition. For one fast-tracker, the distance between promotions was 15 years. It seems unlikely that during this period he could have perceived himself as being on his way to the top. There were periods of seven to nine years between promotions for other fast-trackers. Many of them, in short, have had times in their careers when they might easily have perceived themselves as failures.

Derailment, then, has already been a part of life for several of the fast-trackers. And, in fact, derailment at one time or another is part of life for all of them—and for all of us. How can we reconcile the enthusiasm and full-hearted involvement in work of these fast-trackers with the prospect of ultimate derailment in their journey up the corporate ladder? Could it be that full-hearted involvement in the work at hand is one of the best forms of insurance against an emotional and professional downturn at the first signs of derailment?

The initial study suggests that the fast-trackers' attitudes toward derailment were critical in determining whether they returned to the fast track. The potential for derailment exists for all. Did they all demonstrate the attitudes toward potential slowdowns and life off the track that could bring them back on at some later point? Was rejoining others on the fast track necessarily the most productive or most satisfying option? Let us see what we can learn from the fast-trackers as we describe the results of recent interviews with these junior stars, mid-careerists, and senior statesmen, all of whom have aspirations for reaching the top of their particular pyramids.

THE FAST-TRACKERS: 1988

My initial interviews with the fast-trackers led me to believe that they would hold certain attitudes about their work, depending upon their age group, which would be reflected in their comments during the follow-up interviews. Specifically, I expected that the junior stars would respond enthusiastically to the opportunity to discuss their careers, would either have been promoted within the last year, and/or would expect to receive promotions in the immediate future, and still would have their sights set on achieving major vice-presidencies within their companies. (I expected those junior stars who were approaching or passing the age of 35 to show characteristics more like those of the fast-trackers in mid-career).

I expected that the mid-careerists would be less enthusiastic about their positions, would be more uncertain about further upward mobility, and might, in fact, be responding to a slowdown in their career movement by looking at other opportunities.

Finally, I expected that the senior statesmen would be as forthcoming as the junior stars were about their career possibilities, but that (a) they would emphasize not only the positive but the positive and negative aspects intertwined with each other; (b) they would dwell not on the virtues of self but on the virtues of the organization; and (c) they would describe their expectations about the future not in terms of career moves but in terms of challenges, responsibilities, and contributions. Let us see if my expectations were correct.

Junior Stars

Among the five junior stars, two had been promoted twice in the past year, a third had been promoted once, a fourth had remained in his former position, and a fifth (the oldest, at 38 now classifiable as a mid-careerist) had moved laterally in the company. In other words, three of the four who were still younger than 35 had been promoted within the past year.

The two men who had received double promotions were enthusiastic about their work. One, more effusive and forthcoming than the other, responded that this had been an extraordinarily productive year—a great time—and that his work relationships were outstanding. The other, in a more task-focused manner, spoke about the specific challenges of his current position and the fact that he was starting to make significant progress. The one woman in this group, who had been promoted once, responded that this year had been spectacular. She declared, "I am doing extraordinarily well" and "I'm in charge of my own career."

The individual who had remained in the same position spoke of the challenges of that year and of his learning about the importance of finances and budgets. (He is in a division that is likely to be taken over by another firm, and chances of getting an immediate promotion are thus slim.) The fifth junior star (now actually a mid-careerist) spoke enthusiastically of his recent lateral move and said that he had had a good year.

In some ways, the best clues to what these fast-trackers felt about their professional growth in the past year lay hidden in their remarks about other issues. All but one of the junior stars mentioned being more concerned with family matters now than they had been in the past. This group included two of the junior stars who had been promoted: One man, who had received a double promotion, is expecting his third child and trying to find a better balance between work and family; and the group's only woman described herself as being more supportive on the home front now than she had been in the recent past. The individual who stayed in the same position was even more specific than the others were in describing his new concerns about the home front. "This was the first year ever," he said, "when I've been persuaded by my two little girls to take a family vacation." He also is spending more time at home, and talked about the importance of spending quality time with his children. He interpreted his new attitude toward his children in terms of the phraseology of the manufacturing plant where he works: "You know, with kids you have to supply first-time-through quality—there's no rework. So I have to be there now."

The individual who had passed into the mid-career stage and received a lateral promotion also spoke about family concerns. Although he prefers his new position to the one he held before, he is still concerned that his wife is not happy in this part of the country. His primary concern in the next career move he makes will be finding a geographic location that meets his family's needs.

Mid-Careerists

The seven mid-careerists, ages 37 to 41 in 1986, were now between 39 and 43 years old. Of the seven in this group, one had received a double promotion, one had gotten a single promotion, four were in the same positions, and one had been moved laterally. Two of the seven had received promotions, by contrast with three of the five in the junior star group.

Part of this lowered rate of promotion is inevitable because of the narrowing of job possibilities as one moves up the corporate ladder. In their book *Habits of the Heart* (Harper & Row, 1986), Robert Bellah, Richard Madsen, William M. Sullivan, Ann Swidler, and Steven M. Tipton make this point quite clear: "The grade grows steeper at the peak of a professional field, the ledges narrower at the top of a corporate pyramid." Yet just a few years ago, these mid-careerists were junior stars, all expecting to stop no lower than the senior vice-president level. How are they responding to the reality of inevitable slowdown for many, even as a few continue to move upward? Is the change in the probabilities for promotion reflected in the comments of both those moving up and those standing still?

The mid-careerist who had received a single promotion described his move with enthusiasm akin to that of the junior stars. He said this was an "exciting time," that the new job was "enlightening," and that he "loved it." However, this was his first promotion in nine years, and it was greeted with more delight than many of his earlier, more expected promotions. He reflected too that his new job greatly increased his scope and responsibility within the division. The other mid-careerist who had been promoted, a woman who moved up two levels, was quieter in her response but stated clearly that these two moves had fulfilled her expectations completely. She, too, elaborated on the scope of her new responsibilities and the overwhelming amount of learning that was necessary in order for her to handle this job well. These comments were similar to those made by Hank, who was derailed earlier but promoted just before this follow-up year began. Hank initially spoke of his promotion in a manner like that of a junior star ("I have done an outstanding job"), but he immediately went on to talk about the scope of his responsibilities and learning. He was still learning about how to motivate the workforce in a large organization where the sheer number of employees makes developing personal relationships with each of them impossible.

The three unpromoted individuals were more reflective in their evaluations of their positions than were those who had been promoted. One, who had recently remarried, placed the most emphasis of all the fast-trackers on the need to seek balance in his life and to learn how to share goals with a partner. He said this was a year of reflection and broadening awareness. A second focused on his day-to-day work experience to a much greater extent, and said that the work had proceeded much as expected. He said, though, that as in the past, he was still bucking the tide, questioning the organization, and fighting the same dragons. Much like those who had been promoted, however, he was concerned about the scope of his responsibilities, which he identified as "moving forward, keeping the water calm, and dealing with the ambiguities for both myself and my people."

The third unpromoted mid-careerist focused on the unsettling nature of this past year in company terms, describing the likelihood that his division would be sold to another company. In many ways, his responses displayed the good/bad integration heard most clearly in the comments of the senior statesmen and less often in those of the mid-careerists. He talked about the changes within his unit as it met global challenges. In the face of such challenges, he explained, the immediate leadership had little control over the events most affecting the business. He said this was a tremendous challenge for the leadership of the unit but that the learning coming from this was positive: People at all levels of the unit were more involved in the decision-making processes and, consequently, morale in the unit was up, not down. On a personal note, he said that he had learned to delegate more effectively, increasingly recognizing the limits and abilities of his people and, therefore, providing them with the best possible balance of structure and responsibility.

By contrast, the remaining mid-careerist, who had moved laterally in the past year, reflected on his personal disappointment more than the other fast-trackers did; he believed that there would be no further upward mobility for him within this company. He had grown, he said, in his knowledge of the business, but his prospects for advancement in this job had not, and would not, materialize. "I have become more reflective," he said, "and more tolerant this year." This was the only fast-tracker who perceived himself as definitely having been derailed.

Senior Statesmen

Among the five senior statesmen, there had been one lateral move—or what appears to have been a lateral move—to a job that involves significantly increased responsibilities. There was also one announced promotion, which is scheduled to take place within the next year. The other three senior statesmen remained in the same positions. Yet each one, in his own way, described this as having been a "great" year in which significant goals were accomplished.

The senior fast-tracker with a new position spoke primarily in terms of growth and change within the company in the past year. He said, "I have an expanding and continuing awareness of both competition and threat. In terms of specific decisions," he continued, "it has been necessary to take hard action in order to remain competitive." What he is most pleased about is his new awareness of "the receptivity to change of people all the way down the line. Change is uneven but I am impressed with the people who are making the changes." He is more optimistic about his company's prospects this year than last, and concluded that "adversity is still the best teacher."

The senior fast-tracker with a major promotion in the offing emphasized his optimism about the company's future and said his primary concern was learning how to manage growth. He displayed enthusiasm as he recounted specific examples of how this learning was already taking place. His comments about himself emphasized his confirmation of previously held beliefs, an increased degree of self-confidence, and an equally increased willingness to listen. "My job is to listen," he said. "These other people have the information. My job is to draw it out, and to help them make the most of it." He also spoke spontaneously and warmly about his family—his wife and two very young children—summarizing his comments by saying, "We are very connected now."

Two senior statesmen who had remained in their previous positions also spoke with enthusiasm—akin to that of the junior stars—about the events of the last year. One said that the direction of his work was the same but that it had taken on greater intensity; he summed up his perceptions by exclaiming, "It has been a great year! Unbelievable!" The second placed his personal and organizational life in counterpoint to each other, saying that the first had led to greater reflection and the second, to greater achievement than he had anticipated. This year he was very ill for the first time, an experience which provided both motivation and time to reflect on his life, to talk more with his wife, and to seek a better balance between work and personal life. At work he said he "had one of the most significant years of my career, in which all the plans of the past are coming into being!"

He continued to speak of his fascination with the process of change and commented that both inside and outside his particular company, "The change going on now is mind-boggling!"

The last senior statesman—who is also still at the helm of the same ship—said that he had learned a great deal this year about the "politics of leadership—a skill that I've avoided in the past." He elaborated on this by saying, "I'm trying to understand people, to present them with a political solution and not a problem." He feels that he is growing in leadership abilities and consolidating his philosophy and skills. Unlike the other two senior men, who are now viewing the realization of plans, this senior statesman had led his company through the formulation of such plans—which are about to be implemented. In short, he said, "We've been planning our climb to Mount Everest and now we're at the base camp looking up." The next few years will see how far and how well he and his people climb the mountain.

What do these stories say about the complex of factors that lead to promotions, and about the attitudes which one might most profitably adopt to view the slowdowns or derailments that take one off the track? In each of the next two sections, we shall examine these stories in terms of what they can teach us about upward movements *and* derailment.

On Being Promoted: The Influence of Work Relationships

Five of the 17 fast-trackers in the study were promoted in the past year: three of the junior stars and two of the mid-careerists. In three of these five cases, including both mid-careerists, the fast-trackers' descriptions of their promotions showed that they clearly recognized that they were working in a network of relationships that were critical in determining their career progress. The two who did not mention these relationships were both junior stars and both under age 35; both had been promoted twice in the past year. Their promotions may or may not have been affected by work relationships. In the other three cases, work relationships were clearly the predominant factor that led to the promotions.

The three recently promoted individuals who mentioned the importance of relationships—the two women (a junior star and a mid-careerist) and a man in mid-career—emphasized the importance of having a new boss. The junior woman attributed her new and surprising success (she had previously been at the same level for about eight years) to the new boss who became her mentor, strengthened her confidence in herself, and extended much more responsibility to her than her former boss had done. Similarly, the other woman, whose double promotion this year fulfilled all her expectations, attributed the promotions to the new president's recognizing her talent and giving her the responsibilities that would allow her to develop that talent. She is very pleased—but also somewhat overwhelmed by the amount of learning that lies before her. She said, "I am focusing on learning to do this job well, and not looking any further." Speaking about her personal growth and learning, she commented, "Last year I said that patience was a virtue; now I know it is an absolute necessity."

Don, the mid-careerist who was promoted after nine years at the same level, was even more explicit about the role of relationships. The new president of the division, who assumed that position one year ago, had in the past been separated from this particular fast-tracker by a layer of management. This layer had now been removed so that

Don reported directly to the president. Shortly after this change was implemented, the president recognized Don's talent and promoted him in short order to a vice-presidency in the division. Don believed that having a new boss who was able to recognize his potential was almost the sole factor in his promotion.

Don said, for example, that his work record had been outstanding for four years: The only difference was the arrival of a new boss. He described this change as follows:

> It took a change of leadership for me to be promoted. I lost the guy between me and my current boss, Alan. Alan is a mentor, the closest I've had in a long time. This reaffirms the notion that if you've got anybody strong enough in your corner, anything can happen. My results had been great for four years. This did not change. One person's opinion made a change.

He also talked about the years between promotions, when at various times he considered opening his own small business and leaving the company. He said:

> This [promotion] really has confirmed what I believe. You have to keep going. I kept going even when I was not rewarded. Never did I give up or slow down. My numbers were good—the numbers had to be there. It's not just a personality thing.

Yet Don sees the "personality thing" as critical—and increasingly important as one moves up the ladder. He made an analogy between work and sports: When one first starts out in any sport, he remarked, the gains are easy. There are lots of gains for not too much effort. But after one becomes pretty good, every gain is much harder. When one is going for world-class status there's lots of effort needed for just a bit of gain.

And so it is with the mid-careerists. Even the one who received two promotions spoke of the necessity of patience: of waiting for one's number to come up. For all these individuals, there is a sense that work sometimes provides little personal gain, or that the gain comes only after one endures trials and tribulations that build character and strengthen resolve. At the mid-career level, there is little of the easy exuberance of the junior stars, just a few years younger, whose promotions appear to be influenced by individual merit as often as by work relationships. For those at mid-career, it seems, the relationships have taken precedence.

On Not Being Promoted: A Tendency to Reflect

The reflectiveness that characterized the comments of the mid-careerists who were promoted—about themselves and their careers—is much more emphasized in the responses of those who were not promoted this year. It is clear that any slowdown in the career, regardless of the eventual outcome, prompts a period of questioning oneself and one's relationship to others. This finding suggests, in fact, that some period of perceived derailment may have prompted the inner reflections that now appear to be at the core of the philosophic world-view which is held by all three of the senior statesmen.

The junior stars expected to be promoted. The two junior stars who were not promoted responded to their lack of promotions with a new emphasis on self-reflection; this, in turn, led to a new involvement in family matters—after a previous concentration on work to the exclusion of most other concerns. This was true for the older junior star (or junior mid-careerist), who remained concerned that his wife is not fully supportive of his career, and who would consider taking a job outside the company in order to meet his wife's wishes that the family relocate. This was also true for fast-tracker Pete, who is now willing for the first time to take vacations with his wife and their two little girls.

Pete stayed in the same job this year, but he clearly attributes his lack of promotion to the difficulties facing his division. His response to the tightening of financial accountability within his facility was twofold. On one hand, he learned a great deal from his situation—it was the first time his unit had been in the red—and earned himself a quick education in budgeting, finance, and accounting. On the other hand, at the same time, he turned more of his attention than he had before homeward. His career goals, however, remain as they were before—albeit the timetable has been slowed down. He plans to stay with the company, and expects to be promoted more than once, until he is in charge of a sizable part of one of the company's divisions. He regards this year as a delay—a time to get to know himself and his family—and not as a derailment.

Among the mid-careerists there is more disappointment—and more reflection. All three who received no promotions, or what appear to be only lateral moves in the past year, emphasized that they have grown in awareness, and spend more time in reflection on life and partnerships. In terms of their career goals, one mid-careerist spoke of reevaluating his goals, and another contemplated leaving the company within five years. A third discussed the possibility of being permanently stalled within the company, and all spoke of job searches begun on the outside. In speaking of the past year, however, all acknowledged that they had learned much and grown personally as a result of their experience.

Lessons to Be Learned

There are several lessons to be learned from the experiences and the comments of the fast-trackers who were derailed.

1. First, these fast-trackers are passing through the perilous executive transition, during which most derailments occur. The pyramid in each case has narrowed considerably and there are fewer places at the top. Thus it is inevitable that many people in mid-career are going to move no farther upward in the company. Yet all or almost all of those at this level are highly skilled and very talented. Thus skill and talent can no longer be the primary criteria for upward movement. Other factors, such as personal relationships in the workplace, are going to affect this movement. And if one holds onto the notion that upward mobility is necessarily essential—and desirable—then one must conclude that many who are able and talented are going to lose out at this point. Thus instead of asking the usual question—"How can an individual avoid a derailment or slow-down?"—it may be more constructive for us to ask, "What can the individual learn from a derailment or slowdown that can help him or her to become more tolerant, understanding, and productive?"

2. However, examining individual cases, as we have done, shows us that derailment is not necessarily a permanent condition. Being moved off the track may provide the time for reflection and the broadening of viewpoint that can take one back onto the track again. Indeed, even being stalled as long as 10 years or more in between promotions does not mean that one's upward mobility is over.

3. Finally, the soul-searching and reflectiveness that appear to accompany derailment are critical parts of the senior statesmen's approaches to the world. The senior fast-trackers are reflective as well as active, accepting of the bad along with the good, and

willing to go to battle against the awesome forces that stand in the way of essential change. How did they reach the point at which reflection on themselves and on the world at large becomes a critical but natural component of their way of thinking? It seems likely that career derailments or slowdowns (as well as crises in their personal lives) may have provided one learning ground for this mature orientation to the self and others. Derailment, as one example of perceived adversity, is certainly an important educational setting for the fast-trackers.

In short, some, or perhaps even most, of the fast-trackers in this study will not make it through the executive transition to achieve the status of senior statesmen within their companies. However, whether or not one has been derailed or slowed down appears not to be a reliable indicator of the later success of any particular individual. Rather, the attitude with which one meets these difficulties is significant in determining one's future success.

But even one's attitude is not the major determinant of upward movement in the latter half of one's career. Rather, how one's company is faring in the overall economic picture, what qualities (including age) the company requires at a given time in its most senior people, what mentoring relationships one is able to develop with a boss—and the personality and skills of the boss him- or herself, and the nature of relationships in the workplace in general may have an overriding impact on which individuals—out of a selection of talented, skilled, and experienced mid-careerists—will be selected to move further up the corporate ladder. Whether one makes it to the top, therefore, is largely beyond one's control. What is within one's control, however, and what determines one's true success is how one copes with adversity and turns it into an opportunity for growth and learning. Learning is ultimately the key to success—and being faced with disappointment, whether through derailment or otherwise, can provide an important chance to learn.

Learning and Derailment: Necessarily Intertwined?

The importance of following a continuous learning curve in order to achieve both personal satisfaction and career success has been propounded by many psychologists and observers of the human scene. In *The Transformational Leader* (John Wiley, 1986), researcher Noel Tichy identifies the primary characteristic of his transformational leaders (people who are unusually influential and successful) as being that "they are lifelong learners." He continues, "Perhaps one of the most intriguing parts of our protagonists is their continuous commitment to learning. Their heads have not become hard-wired." Morgan McCall, Jr., Michael M. Lombardo, and Ann M. Morrison make the same point in *Lessons of Experience* (Lexington Books, 1988). Successful executives, they found, are "ready to grab or create opportunities for growth, *wise enough not to believe that there's nothing more to learn*, and courageous enough to look inside themselves and grapple with their frailties." (Italics mine.)

Learning is thus the hallmark of leaders and successful executives and, indeed, of all those who continue to grow and develop throughout their lives. And for many, adversity provides the best opportunity for learning. Derailment, or a career slowdown that may become derailment, provides one such opportunity for reflection and learning. It is at such times that individuals learn most about themselves, about others, and about their organizations. They are challenged to establish their priorities, to seek out what matters, and to put what matters most first in their own lives.

The predictable slowdown at mid-career is thus an opportunity for individuals to enter into a state of reflection and learn new ways of looking at themselves and others; out of this reflection they can create a solid hierarchy of priorities and values to guide them during the next stage of their lives. This strong set of values may become the foundation for the philosophy or world-view that guides the individual in the senior statesman stage; or it may be the base of a philosophical outlook that leads fast-trackers to reaffirm their commitment to their family lives, or to enter a new business or a new vocation altogether. Clearly, a slowdown or a derailment need not be viewed as a failure: Instead it should be seen as an opportunity to work toward achieving success—not only in one's career, but in all aspects of one's life. Perhaps people should hope, in fact, that they have more such periods, during which the pace of life slows sufficiently for them to become more fully conscious of their priorities and values.

It is time for us to rid ourselves of the false assumptions that we have held for too long: (1) that moving upward on a career ladder is necessarily desirable and better than staying where we are or moving onto another ladder altogether, and (2) that competitiveness rather than cooperation is the key to success. We need to realize that any stoppage or slowdown on a particular track is—at least in part—out of our hands; such a slowdown, moreover, can be a step in an educational process which can sustain us on any path we take—whether that path leads to the company president's chair or to a closer relationship with our family. How we respond to life—particularly in difficult times—is a choice that is ours. How high we rise on the corporate ladder is a choice that others make. The fast-trackers who learn and accept this lesson are most likely to achieve true success.

Selected Bibliography

This study follows up on many of the themes first suggested in my theoretical article, "The Derailment of Fast-Track Managers" (*Organizational Dynamics*, Autumn 1986) and my book *Survival on the Fast Track* (Dodd, Mead, 1988), which draws lessons from interviews with managers and executives in major corporations.

Numerous other works question or reject commonly held assumptions about career success. Emphasizing the importance of cooperation over competition, Robert Waterman states in *The Renewal Factor* (Bantam, 1987), "Recent findings from the behavioral sciences suggest that cooperation is much more effective than competition. In the literature about competition and cooperation, virtually every experiment about cooperation yielded much better results than competition." John Kotter's *The Leadership Factor* (Free Press, 1988) acknowledges the need for competition but also emphasizes the need to cooperate in order to function effectively in complex organizations. Kotter also writes about the individual's lack of control over his or her upward mobility in *Power and Influence* (Free Press, 1983).

Many other writers have also discussed the American assumption that moving up and getting ahead are the best or only options. One of the best books on this subject is *Habits of the Heart*, by Robert Bellah, Richard Madsen, William M. Sullivan, Ann Swidler, and Steven M. Tipton (Harper & Row, 1986), which speaks of the "inordinate rewards of ambition in our culture," and traces the development of the managerial ethos in our time. Morgan McCall, Jr., Michael M. Lombardo, and Ann M. Morrison from the Center for Creative Leadership in North Carolina reveal these assumptions as well, by taking them for granted in their discussions of difficulties and derailments in *Lessons from Experience* (Lexington Books, 1988). These authors assume, as did the executives in my study, that derailment is necessarily a problem. Yet as Arnold Mitchell points out in *Nine American Lifestyles* (Warner, 1983), continuous upward mobility is not possible for all Americans, but only for a small group of achieving, competent, and talented individuals.

Yet these assumptions are endemic in our society. Thus Lawrence Peter's works, *The Peter Principle* (Bantam, 1969) and *Why Things Go Wrong* (Bantam, 1984), which satirize our belief that up is always better—with the result that people are promoted to their level of incompetence—touched a nerve in Americans and became bestsellers.

Finally, several other works have emphasized the idea that personal and professional growth of managers is derived from hardship. These works include Noel Tichy's *The Transformational Leader* (John Wiley, 1986), and John Kotter's *General Managers* (Free Press, 1981). The best exposition of this point of view, however, is perhaps Abraham Zaleznik's article, "The Management of Disappointment," included in *Executive Success: Making It In Business* (Harvard Business School, 1983).

The Day at the Beach

Arthur Gordon

Not long ago I came to one of those bleak periods that many of us encounter from time to time, a sudden drastic dip in the graph of living when everything goes stale and flat, energy wanes, enthusiasm dies. The effect on my work was frightening. Every morning I would clench my teeth and mutter: "Today life will take on some of its old meaning. You've got to break through this thing. You've got to!"

But the barren days went by, and the paralysis grew worse. The time came when I knew I had to have help.

The man I turned to was a doctor. Not a psychiatrist, just a doctor. He was older than I, and under his surface gruffness lay great wisdom and compassion. "I don't know what's wrong," I told him miserably, "but I just seem to have come to a dead end. Can you help me?"

Arthur Gordon. "The Day at the Beach." *Reader's Digest* (1960), 76, 79–83. Reprinted with permission from the January 1960 *Reader's Digest*.

"I don't know," he said slowly. He made a tent of his fingers and gazed at me thoughtfully for a long while. Then, abruptly, he asked, "Where were you happiest as a child?"

"As a child?" I echoed. "Why, at the beach, I suppose. We had a summer cottage there. We all loved it."

He looked out the window and watched the October leaves sifting down. "Are you capable of following instructions for a single day?"

"I think so," I said, ready to try anything.

"All right. Here's what I want you to do."

He told me to drive to the beach alone the following morning, arriving not later than nine o'clock. I could take some lunch; but I was not to read, write, listen to the radio or talk to anyone. "In addition," he said, "I'll give you a prescription to be taken every three hours."

He tore off four prescription blanks, wrote a few words on each, folded them, numbered them and handed them to me. "Take these at nine, twelve, three and six."

"Are you serious?" I asked.

He gave me a short bark of laughter.

"You won't think I'm joking when you get my bill!"

The next morning, with little faith, I drove to the beach. It was lonely, all right. A northeaster was blowing; the sea looked gray and angry. I sat in the car, the whole day stretching emptily before me. Then I took out the first of the folded slips of paper. On it was written: LISTEN CAREFULLY.

I stared at the two words. Why, I thought, the man must be mad. He had ruled out music and newscasts and human conversation. What else was there?

I raised my head and I did listen. There were no sounds but the steady roar of the sea, the croaking cry of a gull, the drone of some aircraft high overhead. All these sounds were familiar.

I got out of the car. A gust of wind slammed the door with a sudden clap of sound. Was I supposed, I asked myself, to listen carefully to things like that?

I climbed a dune and looked out over the deserted beach. Here the sea bellowed so loudly that all other sounds were lost. And yet, I thought suddenly, there must be sounds beneath sounds—the soft rasp of drifting sand, the tiny wind-whisperings in the dune grasses—if the listener got close enough to hear them.

On an impulse I ducked down and, feeling fairly ridiculous, thrust my head into a clump of seaweed. Here I made a discovery: if you listen intently, there is a fractional moment in which everything seems to pause, wait. In that instant of stillness, the racing thoughts halt. For a moment, when you truly listen for something outside yourself, you have to silence the clamorous voices within. The mind rests.

I went back to the car and slid behind the wheel. LISTEN CAREFULLY. As I listened again to the deep growl of the sea, I found myself thinking about the white-fanged fury of its storms.

I thought of the lessons it had taught as children. A certain amount of patience: you can't hurry the tides. A great deal of respect: the sea does not suffer fools gladly. An awareness of the vast and mysterious interdependence of things: wind and tide and current, calm and squall and hurricane, all combining to determine the paths of the birds above and the fish below. And the cleanness of it all, with every beach swept twice a day by the great broom of the sea.

Sitting there, I realized I was thinking of things bigger than myself—and there was relief in that.

Even so, the morning passed slowly. The habit of hurling myself at a problem was so strong that I felt lost without it. Once when I was wistfully eyeing the car radio a phrase from Carlyle jumped into my head. "Silence is the element in which great things fashion themselves. . . ."

By noon the wind had polished the clouds out of the sky; and the sea had a hard, polished, and merry sparkle. I unfolded the second "prescription." And again I sat there, half amused and half exasperated. Three words this time: TRY REACHING BACK.

Back to what? To the past, obviously. But why, when all my worries concerned the present or the future?

I left the car and started tramping reflectively along the dunes. The doctor had sent me to the beach because it was a place of happy memories. Maybe that was what I was supposed to reach for: the wealth of happiness that lay half-forgotten behind me.

I decided to experiment: to work on these vague impressions as a painter would retouching the colors, strengthening the outlines. I would choose specific incidents and recapture as many details as possible. I would visualize people complete with dress and gestures. I would listen (carefully) for the exact sound of their voices, the echo of their laughter.

The tide was going out now, but there was still thunder in the surf. So I chose to go back 20 years to the last fishing trip I made with my younger brother. (He died in the Pacific during World War II and was buried in the Philippines.) I found that if I closed my eyes and really tried, I could see him with amazing vividness, even the humor and eagerness in his eyes that far-off morning.

In fact, I could see it all: the ivory scimitar of beach where we were fishing; the eastern sky smeared with sunrise; the great rollers creaming in, stately and slow. I could feel the backwash swirl warm around my knees, see the sudden arc of my brother's rod as he struck a fish, hear his exultant yell. Piece by piece I rebuilt it, clear and unchanged under the transparent varnish of time. Then it was gone.

I sat up slowly, TRY REACHING BACK. Happy people were usually assured, confident people. If, then, you deliberately reached back and touched happiness, might there not be released little flashes of power, tiny sources of strength?

This second period of the day went more quickly. As the sun began its long slant down the sky, my mind ranged eagerly through the past, reliving some episodes, uncovering others that had been completely forgotten. For example, when I was around 13 and my brother 10, Father had promised to take us to the circus. But at lunch there was a phone call: some urgent business required his attention downtown. We braced ourselves for disappointment. Then we heard him say, "No, I won't be down. It'll have to wait."

When he came back to the table, Mother smiled. "The circus keeps coming back, you know."

"I know," said Father. "But childhood doesn't."

Across all the years I remembered this and knew from the sudden glow of warmth that no kindness is ever wasted or ever completely lost.

By three o'clock the tide was out and the sound of the waves was only a rhythmic whisper, like a giant breathing. I stayed in my sandy nest, feeling relaxed and content—and a little complacent. The doctor's prescriptions, I thought, were easy to take.

But I was not prepared for the next one. This time the three words were not a gentle suggestion. They sounded more like a command. REEXAMINE YOUR MOTIVES.

My first reaction was purely defensive. There's nothing wrong with my motives, I said to myself. I want to be successful—who doesn't? I want to have a certain amount of recognition—but so does everybody. I want more security than I've got—and why not?

Maybe, said a small voice somewhere inside my head, those motives aren't good enough. Maybe that's the reason the wheels have stopped going around.

I picked up a handful of sand and let it stream between my fingers. In the past, whenever my work went well, there had always been something spontaneous about it, something uncontrived, something free. Lately it had been calculated, competent—and dead. Why? Because I had been looking past the job itself to the rewards I hoped it would bring. The work had ceased to be an end in itself, it had been merely a means to make money, pay bills. The sense of giving something, of helping people, of making a contribution, had been lost in a frantic clutch at security.

In a flash of certainty, I saw that if one's motives are wrong, nothing can be right. It makes no difference whether you are a mailman, a hairdresser, an insurance salesman, a housewife—whatever. As long as you feel you are serving others, you do the job well. When you are concerned only with helping yourself, you do it less well. This is a law as inexorable as gravity.

For a long time I sat there. Far out on the bar I heard the murmur of the surf change to a hollow roar as the tide turned. Behind me the spears of light were almost horizontal. My time at the beach had almost run out, and I felt a grudging admiration for the doctor and the "prescriptions" he had so casually and cunningly devised. I saw, now, that in them was a therapeutic progression that might well be of value to anyone facing any difficulty.

LISTEN CAREFULLY: To calm a frantic mind, slow it down, shift the focus from inner problems to outer things.

TRY REACHING BACK: Since the human mind can hold but one idea at a time, you blot out present worry when you touch the happinesses of the past.

REEXAMINE YOUR MOTIVES: This was the hard core of the "treatment," this challenge to reappraise, to bring one's motives into alignment with one's capabilities and conscience. But the mind must be clear and receptive to do this—hence the six hours of quiet that went before.

The western sky was a blaze of crimson as I took out the last slip of paper. Six words this time. I walked slowly out on the beach. A few yards below the high water mark I stopped and read the words again: WRITE YOUR TROUBLES ON THE SAND.

I let the paper blow away, reached down and picked up a fragment of shell. Kneeling there under the vault of sky, I wrote several words on the sand, one above the other. Then I walked away, and I did not look back. I had written my troubles on the sand. And the tide was coming in.

Strategies for Personal and Family Renewal

How a High-Survivor Group of Executives Cope with Stress and Avoid Burnout

André L. Delbecq and Frank Friedlander

For several years we have been studying the impact of executive roles on families and how top executives seek to maintain personal balance and reduce stress when occupying top management positions (Friedlander, 1994; Friedlander & Delbecq, in press). The purpose of this article is to summarize a behavior pattern among a subset of our sample, which we first discovered when doing interviews for a pilot study on this subject, and which we have since had an opportunity to discuss with a number of executives who seem to endure the rigors of office with less burnout than most. If our observations with this smaller group of executives is representative of one coping pattern, it may inform both researchers and executives concerned with stress associated with top-level positions.

Let us begin by carefully targeting the sample from which the observations are drawn. Our primary informants are CEOs of small to medium technology firms in turbulent environments undergoing rapid change. These are intense settings where speed, flexibility, rapid environmental adaptation, and high risk set the tone. However, there are many parallel leadership challenges in other settings: political leadership in times of uncertainty, military leadership in combat circumstances, and medical leadership during health care restructuring. Thus, although the behavior pattern we have identified among this group may not fit large, stable, mature contexts, it should exist in a number of other turbulent contexts.

In our subset sample of about 16 chief executive officers (CEOs) reported here, executive ages ranged from 42 to 48. There were 14 men and 2 women. All were married to college-educated spouses. There were two or three children within the family of late teen or college age. Information was gathered during a 1-hour interview, using an open-ended semistructured format.

Of course, not every CEO in our broader studies conforms to the description that follows. In this article, we are only reporting on that group of executives who seem to be less prone to stress and burnout (for a vivid description of executive behavior that leads to serious dysfunction and threat to health, see Laton 1994). From this point we will refer to this subset as high survivors.

"Strategies for Personal and Family Renewal: How a High-Survivor Group of Executives Cope with Stress and Avoid Burnout" by André L. Delbecq and Frank Friedlander, *Journal of Management Inquiry*, Vol. 4, No. 3, September 1995, pp 262-269. Reprinted by permission.

Finally, it is important to be clear regarding the value position of the article. Our purpose is to describe a pattern of behavior observed to be pervasive among this high-survivor subset. It is not meant to suggest a normative position of how individuals ought to behave. Readers may assess the desirability of the behaviors of these high survivors according to their own personal norms and theoretical orientation.

Differing Views of the Executive Suite

To a casual reader of the business press, the pressures of CEO leadership may not be obvious. After all, these executives are well paid and exercise substantial power. Further, these positions encompass activities that are self-actualizing in that the executives are building a future in which he or she plays a vital role. These factors are shown to reduce role conflict and stress (Matteson & Ivancevich 1987). But in fact, the pressures in these positions as seen from the inside are formidable. The tenure of office is usually relatively short, as top-executive positions demand a constantly shifting set of competencies as the companies evolve. The executive stands at the boundary as a buffer between the organization and stockholders (or venture capitalists) and other environmental players who influence the destiny of the organization. To a great extent, the executive is the lightning rod for blame however complex the causes of success and failure may be. Such positions demand a charismatic leader with vision and personal powers of persuasion (Conger & Kanungo 1987; House, Spangler, & Woycke 1991). To maintain a personal presence among all the stakeholders, hours are long and the energy requirements are great. Not surprisingly, there is great risk of classic burnout with its accompanying fatigue, low resistance to illness, emotional exhaustion, and mental depression (Maslach & Jackson 1984). The key question this research addressed to CEOs occupying these difficult leadership positions was: In your high-visibility role and complex circumstance, how do you as a CEO maintain your energy, emotional stability, and family life?

THE TASKS INCLUDED IN THE EXECUTIVE DAY

We can begin by looking at the executive day. The individuals in our sample work the very long days that have been reported in other studies of executive behavior (Greenlaw & Beutell 1985; Kotter 1982). It is not our purpose here to detail the nature of executive work. However, as a reminder, the typical day includes:

Intelligence gathering and complex problem solving regarding strategy, often involving difficult tradeoffs and resource redirection (interactions that have high-stake political overlays with accompanying intense emotions).

Frequent random contacts and personal visibility in the work spaces of the organization, demanding active listening and rapid tactical problem solving.

Delicate conversations with emergent leaders, unsatisfied coalitions, and organizational players with a variety of petitions and grievances.

Constant attention to selection of key players and energizing critical task forces and problem-solving groups.

Symbolic events in which the executive must be upbeat and convey energy and optimism in the face of daunting organizational challenges.

The point is that the executive must perform at a continuing high level of energy throughout long workdays. If issues are solvable by means of technical analysis or simple problem solving, competent subordinates handle these matters at a lower level. What comes to the attention of the executive are the politically loaded, intellectually vexing, interpersonally charged, cognitively complex, high-risk and uncertain issues that demand not only the executive's best thinking but also his or her ability to coach, mentor, and facilitate the aggregation of judgments across multiple groups. The executive cadre is populated with strong personalities, and problem solving is almost always in circumstances of time pressure.

None of these descriptors of CEO roles is reported as an exaggerated generalization. There are numerous studies showing the great demands placed on top leadership. The point here is to indicate that there is little slack and few halcyon moments of relaxation in the workday of these executives. It is in this context we can look at the schedules of the executives in our sample.

The Executive Schedule

All of the high-survivor executives work the typical 60-plus-hour executive week. They typically rise early, often leaving home before other members of the family rise from their beds. Many of the executives stop by at an athletic club on the way to work (more about exercise later) or jog before going to work. They are at the office before most of their colleagues arrive, taking advantage of the quiet early morning to organize their day and make preparations for key meetings. Once the other employees arrive, the schedule is primarily interactive, including problem-solving meetings with key players until the day ends. Lunch is almost always a working meal, and the executives leave their offices 2 or 3 hours after most employees have gone home, taking time at the end of the day to write important notes or dictate follow-up memos and letters. In short, a very long day is normal. How then do these high-survivor executives cope with the unusual demands and stresses of their position?

COPING STRATEGY NUMBER 1: HOME AS SANCTUARY

However long the day, none of the high-survivor executives take work home. For these executives, home is sanctuary! Because there is little slack during the intense day, home is the place where these executives return to rest and renew. Briefcases contain only what is needed for early meetings the next day. These executives prefer to remain at the office, until work is completed. But when they leave the office they try to leave psychologically as well as physically. They try not to carry their work in their heads after commuting, except subconsciously. Like cancer or burn-unit medical practitioners, they have found that it is self-destructive to dwell on the problems of work at home.[1]

A related manifestation of compartmentalization was the homing instinct associated with weekends. No matter where high-survivor executives traveled, they made extraordinary efforts to return home for the weekend. They were willing to make awkward flight connections (one executive flying from New York to Miami to Dallas to San Francisco to get home during a bad weather weekend), but homeward bound they were.

Weekends were considered sacred family time. Usually they had a reentry liturgy: Barbeque at the rib house, pizza at Luigi's, or dinner at Chez Paul to signify "C'est le weekend!" These reentry meals were family events that included their older children (when children were still at home). Because the weekend was for rest and renewal, these executives did not spend the weekend on chores, except when a particular task was associated with a shared family hobby (such as getting the boat ready for the season or working on the summer cabin). Otherwise, the weekends tended to focus on recreational and social activities with family: hiking, sailing, bicycling, and church. The norm was clearly: "The weekend is time for my family and I to be together."

One might expect that executives would entertain a great deal. When high-survivor executives do so, they entertained in restaurants but did not bring guests home, with one exception. International guests were often welcomed to the home as this was seen as a special enrichment for older children. Otherwise, the sanctuary of home was not violated.

To summarize the first strategy of high-survivor executives for personal and family survival: Home was a place for personal rest, renewal, and family activity. Work was not brought home. Weekends were sacred and preserved for family. Activities during the weekend were family oriented. Chores were not allowed to intrude into this personal and family renewal. These executives had developed a pattern early in their career of hiring help for domestic chores to preserve time for rest and family activities. They state that the choice is time or money, and time is the most precious commodity to preserve on weekends in their work-intense life.

COPING STRATEGY NUMBER 2: SPOUSE AS FAMILY EXECUTIVE

Among these high survivors, there is no ambiguity as to which partner in the marriage is the primary parent in charge of family and hearth. All questions regarding whether the high survivor and his or her spouse shared equally in parenting and household management yielded an unequivocal answer from these CEOs:

> Given the complexities of my position, I don't carry an equal share of the domestic duties. Nor could I have the surplus energy for my work if I did so. My spouse is our general in the home battles. I can't fight a two-front war!

Among these executives, it was clear that the spouse played the predominant role in early child rearing. It was the spouse who dealt with early parenting, early school, and early childhood burdens (and later with elder care). The one notable shift in this pattern was that during the teenage years, most of these executives reported a time when they "circled the wagons" around the teenagers (both parents focused on teen problems and needs). Many of the high-survivor executives refused overseas assignments, adjusted travel, and became much more available to their children during the high school period. High school was seen as a time of particular fragility for the teenager(s), demanding a change in work patterns. However, with this exception, child care, elder care, and home care, all the complex domestic burdens involving heavy investment of time and energy, fell predominantly to the spouse.

It is important to remember that in this sample, spouses were college educated. Most are professional people with their own careers. How does this unequal balance regarding domestic obligations work? The main ingredient seems to be spousal work flexibility. Spouses gravitated toward professional roles that allowed them to have control over their schedules to respond to family needs. They moved from trial law to legal consulting, full-time teaching to part-time teaching or educational consulting, and full-time work to part-time work with flexible hours. They were often self-employed or outsourced professionals with considerable control over their own schedules. Because the schedule of the CEO is often out of control, it was seen as critical that the spouse be able to manage a schedule to cope with domestic challenges.

We can insert two examples from later studies that reinforce this pattern. The first was a female medical director who approached the senior author to discuss these findings after he had spoken at a medical conference. She indicated that she was a pediatrician and that she had always been critical of executive parents who seemed to leave much of the duties of parenting to their spouses. However, she mentioned that because she had recently been elected medical director, the demands of the role were so intense that she was delegating to her husband exactly in the same fashion as the executives of whom she had earlier been critical. She indicated that "during the time I am in this role, I will not be able to coparent in the same fashion as I have normatively prescribed."

The second example comes from a sample of project and program engineering managers in Silicon Valley who are in their early 30s. Thirty-eight percent of this group are women. They report that they play leapfrog with their spouses, clearly agreeing between themselves who will be family/domestic leader and who will be work-centered at a particular point in their careers. "Until I finish the audit . . . until I become junior partner . . . you will have to be domestic general. Then we can change places."

However, to return to the high-survivor CEOs, they are clear that their spouses have competently taken on the major domestic roles, and as a result they have the freedom, flexibility, and energy that they otherwise could not devote to the challenges of their work. Nor do they take this partnership for granted. Subsequently, among this group, when illness, death, or divorce of the spouse has occurred, in every instance the executive has left the CEO role within 6 months.

COPING STRATEGY NUMBER 3: PRECISE COMMUNICATION

A favorite cartoon regarding work overload shows a father at the front door looking very harassed handing his wife a carton of Chinese food. She remarks: "I'm glad you picked up our take out order, but where are the children?" Who in the midst of a very busy period has not lost track of family promises and obligations?

For top-level executives, most days are crowded with stimulus overload. In addition to the continuing leadership challenges discussed earlier, there are often ephemeral crises as well. In this world of overload, communication with spouses must be handled in a fashion that avoids misunderstanding. There are several techniques that high-survivor executives identified that help them to cope.

The first is coded communication when spouses speak by telephone during business hours. In one story, an executive is traveling in Europe involved in critical financial negotiations on which the continuation of his firm depends. He receives a call from his wife indicating that she has some bad news. His brother, who has been terminally ill, has died. His brother's wife is in the care of his sister, and their children in the care of another sister. Funeral arrangements are scheduled for Friday. "Your flight has been changed to return through New York in time to arrive the evening before the funeral. This is a code green call." They speak for another few minutes, and the executive returns to his negotiations.

What has transpired? By the executive's wife saying, "This is a code green call," she is telling him that everything that needs to be done has been done. She conveys that nothing is required of him immediately. She knows he will phone his sister-in-law that evening after his meetings. He returns to his meeting with complete trust that his spouse will continue to make necessary plans and arrangements. He is confident that her "code green" signal means that there truly is nothing he can or should do at this immediate moment.

In contrast, a year later he receives another call while traveling in Japan. Kathy (his teenage daughter) is very upset. Her friend committed suicide. This time it is a code red call. The executive indicates he will return home immediately. He walks back to the room where the meeting is taking place and announces that due to a family emergency he must depart to the United States.

Although this couple uses color codes, other high-survivor executives and their spouses develop their own particular communication cues to assure clarity regarding the type of response being asked for. During intense business days, in addition to the telephone, secretaries, voice mail, and E-mail often are the contemporary message media. It is important that not only the information be conveyed between spouses but also the magnitude of urgency and the specific response being sought. For these couples, the phrases "read my mind" and "be sensitive to implicit message" are not approaches to communication that are acceptable. Further, moments of communication are often short and precious. Consequently, they have learned to communicate with precision and have a relationship based on great trust that all that needs to be communicated is communicated accurately.

A second aspect of communication between high-survival executives and their spouses to deal with time limitation and information overload is that they establish a daily communication time and zone. Couples report a time period each day that is reserved as uniquely their own. It may be first thing in the morning over coffee, or walking the dog in the evening after the executive returns, or at another time; but the couples have a specific time and place where they are available to each other each day without distraction. This is the time at which important personal, family needs can be focused. It is also the time when feelings, nuances, and in-depth communication can take place. This communication time and zone is rigorously protected against intrusion. It is uniquely and personally theirs.

Finally the high-survival executive couples have learned to never cry wolf. Because their trust is based on communication clarity and a carefully constructed system of cues, it is a matter of great personal integrity between them to honor both the need for accuracy and the need for unselfish response when it is requested.

None of this should imply that playfulness, teasing, or banter is missing. It is to say, however, when dealing with important matters, these couples have learned to communicate with precision and trust. This meets not only the need of the CEOs, but also the spouses whom we should remember are college-educated professionals with their own career pressures in addition to the major responsibilities for family and domestic challenges.

COPING STRATEGY NUMBER 4: MAINTAINING ROMANCE

Early in our research, it was suggested that we test the extent to which the pressures on CEOs and their spouses created alienation and depersonalization. We constructed a five-part Romance Index ranging from alienation to respectful partnership to passionate romance. High-survivor executives scored high on romance. We were intrigued how these couples maintained this sense of romance in their busy lives in the midst of the dual career and executive pressures. In responding to questions regarding this aspect of their relationship, two themes emerged: dating and appreciation.

These couples caught in the midst of work-role pressures learned the importance of time-out for themselves. Although they talked about the need for daily precise and effective communication, there was also the reality that much daily communication occurs under conditions of considerable fatigue and distraction. Therefore, these CEOs and spouses learned it was important to make a date (each week if possible) to focus on their relationship and their mutual needs. Typically, the date was dinner out at a favorite place. They were emphatic regarding the importance of this tradition as critical for maintaining their relationship.

The second variable was more subtle and took a while before it was fully understood. Interviews were filled with statements of appreciation by the CEO for the spouse, such as "She really carries the primary load with the children," and "I depended on him for helping me maintain perspective." At first, the intensity of feeling associated with what was being said was underestimated. Over time, we discovered the true heartfelt character of these remarks.

The job at the top is lonely, and the spouse becomes an important sounding board and provider of perspective. The public persona of the executive always has to be upbeat. The relationship with the spouse becomes a sanctuary in which fears, doubts, and concerns can be shared. There was also an important gender dimension. In this sample, the majority of the CEOs were male. Male executives appreciated the intuitive insights and the willingness to address emotional concerns that their spouses could provide. The fact that their wives often read from a very different set of literature and could think from different frames of reference was seen as enriching. Wives were often the stimulus to look to different information sources or draw on different networks of resources. However, whether husband or wife, the spouse played a role beyond that of a domestic general and was very much a respected confidant and counselor. The appreciation for the spouse was, indeed, heartfelt. The marriage was clearly felt to be a source of strength that made the burdens of the CEO role endurable.

COPING STRATEGY NUMBER 5: ATTENTION TO EXERCISE AND NUTRITION

It is apparent that good health and high energy are prerequisites for the long days, complex activities, and extensive travel that are part of the CEO role. Although the individuals who are selected for these positions usually possess favorable mental and physical predisposition, occupying the top-level position takes an awesome toll on even the most fit. Just as we can observe the aging of American presidents over their terms of office as we see them on TV, one can also see the stresses being chiseled on the countenances of CEOs during turbulent times within the corporation.

Earlier when discussing schedules, we mentioned that most of the high-survivor executives rose early and exercised first thing in the morning. This pattern of exercise is maintained during traveling and weekends. These executives mentioned that exercise was an important way of controlling stress. In addition, male executives reported the need to control alcohol during periods of high stress, whereas female executives instead mentioned the need to control diet. These individuals were aware of the need for physical fitness, a precondition to handling the rigors of the role. Many reported an earlier period when exercise was neglected, and alcohol or weight was a problem. They were determined to avoid recidivism and the high-survivor group as a whole was remarkably fit.

COPING STRATEGY NUMBER 6: REST AND REHABILITATION

However, no matter how fit, the demands of the position diminish energy and fatigue occurs. Because so many days are out of control, by definition, as CEOs deal with management by exception, most days require continuous high energy. Consequently, high-survivor executives follow a pattern very much like combat military officers or emergency room medical personnel. While on duty they must be really there with full mental and physical energy. Because no one, even the most fit, can maintain this level of energy continuously, the high-survivor CEOs developed a pattern of rest and relaxation breaks. These minivacations were critical for the maintenance of their health and were scheduled according to two criteria: (a) completion of difficult benchmark tasks and (b) consistency with individual energy cycles.

Most of the executives rewarded themselves with several days rest following completion of critical, high-energy tasks. They were able to sustain their energy to complete the tasks much like aviators: When I finish this mission (complete the strategic plan, finish the labor negotiations, finish the round of presentations associated with the initial public offerings), I will take some time for rest and relaxation. These minivacations are taken geographically away from the business setting and are typically family affairs.

When talking to children of the executives, as well as spouses, the minivacations were reported as a focal point for family bonding. It was during these mini rest-and-relaxation trips that adventures were shared and family memories were formed. Thus the minivacation was not only rest for the executive from the burdens of office but quality family time.

Second, minivacations were also scheduled when the executives felt their internal energies burning out. High-survivor executives honored their internal energy signals and took a break when they no longer felt that they had the capacity to continue the heavy schedule of the executive day.

To summarize, the vacation schedule of high-survivor executives was not based on national holidays or liturgical calendars, but rather on completion of critical tasks and renewal at low points in their personal energy cycle. Because they were unable to balance their days vertically, interspersing routine versus complex tasks, they created a different rhythm horizontally, alternating periods of intense task commitments with rest-and-relaxation breaks.

COPING STRATEGY NUMBER 7: FOLLOW YOUR BLISS AND DON'T SWEAT THE SMALL STUFF

The last coping strategy, which was very apparent among high-survivor CEOs, was a philosophical orientation. It was characteristic of these executives to have made career moves that others thought were foolish but that they defined as an energizing turning point in their work career (e.g., an executive who left a secure position with a major firm to work for a firm in trouble or an executive who left a highly supported research center to strike out in an entrepreneurial effort). Such career moves usually implied risk and an unconventional horizontal career shift to a new setting. The rationale for these unconventional career moves embodied a common theme: "I knew if I didn't do this I would always be sorry. I would have been seduced by a great job but in the long run would not have had as much fun."

What allows high-survivor executives to put so much of themselves into their work is that their work is truly the enactment of a personal vision and mission. They believe that their organization is serving society, that their product or service matters, and that their leadership matters as well. When work ceases to be meaningful, they step down or move on to another adventure. High-survivor executives are individuals who are driven by mission, not simply position. It was interesting to talk to children of these executives whose comments reinforced this mission orientation. They sometimes expressed regret that their mother or father was not always available like other moms or dads. Nonetheless, they could articulate their parent's mission in almost the same terms as the executive used. They understood the passion of their parent, even if they sometimes regretted the lack of accessibility. These high-survivor executives, like musicians, authors, physicians, and other dedicated professionals and artists, love their work. They commit to the intense and complex agenda not out of a need for money or power but as a form of self-expression and service. Their sense of excitement and interest in the organizational mission is contagious.

In addition to following their bliss in selection of a work mission, high-survivor CEOs possess a second psychological orientation. They expect life to be imperfect and the road to mission achievement to be difficult. In our interviews with these executives encountering all the hardships of companies in turbulent industries, we found high-survivor CEOs remarkably free of whining. They cope with competitive upsets, law suits, dishonest employees, and technological failures with remarkable aplomb. The personality trait of optimism shines clear. These are individuals who have learned not to personalize difficulties but rather to see difficulties as the normal challenges that must be overcome for mission achievement.

Thus the ability of these executives to deal with the stresses of position reflects not only tactical coping strategies, as suggested above, but also a pattern of personality, motivation, and perception that allows them to deflect many pressures that would debilitate others with a different life view.

A final aspect of this life view is the perception that their present leadership mission is for a time. None of the high-survivor executives believe their present mission will last forever. All talk about a future time when they will have finished this agenda, achieved certain benchmarks, and when the organization will be better lead by a successor. They have a sense of their term of office as temporally bound and a realization that other skills and energies will have to carry on after their departure. Because they *will* be departing, the difficulties of the present are seen as transient and survivable, because in a future time they will move on to different settings with new challenges and opportunities.

SUMMARY

What then is the pattern of behavior manifested by these high-survivor CEOs as they seek to cope with the exceptional demands of their positions? These executives:

- *reserve home as sanctuary, leaving work behind at the end of the day, and focus on renewal and family activities on the weekend.*
- *arrive at a division of domestic obligations in which the spouse is the dominant family leader, and arrive at a pattern within their dual careers in which the spouse's work allows for flexibility to meet domestic challenges.*
- *develop clear codes of communication with their spouse that avoid misunderstanding and honor with great integrity urgent domestic requests.*
- *maintain romance and a deep personal relationship with their spouse by dating and clear expression of appreciation that what they achieve at work is only possible because of their partner's support.*
- *use short rest-and-relaxation minivacations for renewal after difficult tasks and when energy is diminished, including family in these breakaway pauses in their hectic schedule.*
- *only commit themselves to missions for which they have passion and only for a period of time during which their skills fit the objective needs of the organization.*

Not everyone will see this lifestyle as balanced or desirable. Yet, leaders in such positions are asked to provide exceptional service and sacrifice, to be accessible, and to be self-sacrificing. For those who have the opportunity, will, and talent to accept such challenges, we hope that the behavior pattern of these high survivors will be informative. To those investigating stress management among top executives, we hope this article may open up lines of inquiry that will better juxtapose the realities of executive demands with research on how to cope with executive stress.

NOTE

1. In later research we did discover gender differences in this compartmentalization. For the male executives, compartmentalization was a clear and pervasive practice. By contrast, women executives seem better able to simultaneously deal with family and do office work at home. My favorite example is a very successful female CEO who worked her strategic plan on the bed with children and the dog in front of the TV. This difference in capacity to deal with simultaneous stimuli is one of the major emerging finds in cognitive differentiation between men and women.

REFERENCES

Conger, J. A., & Kanungo, R. A. 1987. Toward a behavioral theory of charismatic leadership in organizational settings. *Academy of Management Review* 12(4): 637–647.

Friedlander, F. 1994. Toward whole systems and whole people. *Organization* 1(1): 59–64.

Friedlander, F., & Delbecq, A. In press, *The artificial separation of work and home life.*

Greenlaw, J. H., & Beutell, N. J. 1985. Sources of conflict between work and family roles. *Academy of Management Review* 10(1): 76–80.

House, R. J., Spangler, D.W., & Woycke, J. 1991. Personality and charisma in the U.S. presidency: A psychological theory of leader effectiveness. *Administrative Science Quarterly* 36(3): 364–396.

Kotter, J. P. 1982. *The general managers.* New York: Free Press.

Laton, S. A. November 1994. Death by work. *Financial Post Magazine,* pp. 90–94.

Maslach, C., & Jackson, S. E. 1984. The measurement of experienced burnout. *Journal of Occupational Behavior* 2: 99–113.

Matteson, M. T., & Ivancevich, J. M. 1987. *Controlling work stress.* San Francisco: Jossey-Bass.

Chapter
13
Organizational Realignments

Constant pressure to change is a reality for many modern organizations. Because of new technology, market demands, and variations in political and social environments, some (though certainly not all) organizations feel pressures that conflict both with their previous ways of operating and with traditional organizational models.

Often these pressures call for changes in conceptual frameworks as well as in organizational procedures and structures. We use the term "realignment" to refer to a pattern of organizational changes in concepts, procedures and/or structure in response to changing circumstances. In this chapter, we look at some organizational realignments and some refusals to realign, in response to pressures to change.

The first few readings deal with some ideas about some contemporary organizations that are recognized for their abilities to come up with and implement new products and services. In a sense these ideas are a sort of conventional wisdom about what it takes for large organizations to be innovative. However, many of the ideas are in conflict with in-grained beliefs about how organizations should be designed. As Russell Mitchell points out in "Nurturing Those Ideas," the ingrained ideas may hinder the ability of U.S. organizations to compete effectively. In the next selection, "Ability to Innovate," Brian Dumaine describes some of the ways that organizations may need to be redesigned in order to realign themselves and some of the actions that executives may find helpful.

While there always has been and most likely always will be a certain degree of inequality in any society, one of the things that has helped American society and its organizations function as well as they have has been the belief that upward mobility was not only possible but was readily attainable. Several centuries during which there were a sufficient number of individual successes consistent with this belief have caused individuals to expect such mobility will follow from hard work in an organization and/or long-term membership in a given organization. These expectations have helped to shape the things that organizations do to gain effort and cooperation from their employees. However, as the next selection, "Is America Becoming More of a Class Society?" reveals, the realities of organizations may have changed so as to make upward mobility much less likely. If such a new reality exists, employee expectations will change thereby forcing organizations to realign how they attempt to motivate and retain employees.

In the next article, Peter Frost and Carolyn Egri indicate and demonstrate that many of the barriers to organization realignment are political rather than structural and that political strategy rather than simply "good ideas" may be critical to successful innovation.

Organizations always face pressures to realign themselves in response to changes in their environments. While this fact is well recognized with respect to the products and services organizations supply, it is less recognized with respect to how they manage their employees. The final three selections explore pressures for realignments that organizations are apt to experience as a result of societal changes that affect their employees. First, due to failures of the American education system, many of today's workers are deficient in basic skills such as reading and writing. In "Business Shares the Blame for Workers' Low Skills" John Hoerr outlines some of the dimensions of the problem and indicates that business is apt to face increasing pressures to do something about it. Second, "Workers Want More Money, But They Also Want to Control Their Own Time" reveals that employees may want different sets of benefits than they did in the past and explores ways that organizations might need to redesign the benefits packages they offer. Third, Sue Shellenbarger's "If You Want a Firm That's Family Friendly, the List Is Very Short" examines some of the new desires of employees and explores some of the difficulties organizations might experience in attempting to respond.

Nurturing Those Ideas

Russell Mitchell

The hierarchy in U.S. companies has often meant that brainstorms from the troops languished. But now that's changing.

Why can't more American companies keep up with overseas competitors? Industry after industry is being slammed in the world marketplace by foreign rivals who have proved more adept at translating great ideas into great products—or into better ways of making them. True, corporate profits have been strong in the U.S., and the trade gap is shrinking. But profit growth has already slowed, and the recent resurgence of the dollar could

Reprinted from Innovation 1989 issue of *Business Week* by special permission. Copyright © 1989 by McGraw-Hill, Inc.

be painful for American manufactures, particularly in fields where foreign rivals have managed to keep pace.

Examples aren't hard to find. Despite dramatic changes at the Big Three auto makers, Japanese cars still account for a record 24% of domestic sales. And the steel industry, after shuttering one unprofitable mill after another, says it still needs protection from imports to prosper. "Look at the leading (U.S.) company in almost any industry five or ten years ago," says Andrall E. Pearson, a professor at Harvard business school and former PepsiCo Inc. president. "Today you'll find that company will be floundering around."

American managers have drawn up a long list of excuses for their lack of competitiveness. Overseas rivals have lower labor costs. They rely on unfair trade practices. They can raise capital more cheaply. U.S. managers have their homegrown complaints, too: Wall Street is too quick to abandon a company at the first sign of softness in quarterly earnings. Compounding that pressure, many companies have to contend with raiders or takeovers—hostile or friendly. But while there may be some truth in all these complaints, there's no escaping one fundamental fact: U.S. companies are being outmanaged by their toughest competitors.

The main reason may be structural. Most American companies are organized around hierarchical, almost military, models, with the CEO as general. That means ideas from the troops are often ignored—if they can fight their way up the chain of command at all. This kind of vertical structure also discourages communication between different disciplines such as research and manufacturing. The result: missed opportunities for new products and sluggish reactions to changing markets. "We manage innovation out of the system rather than into it," says consultant Robert H. Waterman Jr. author of *The Renewal Factor* and co-author of *In Search of Excellence.*

Despite that grim assessment, some of the nation's best-managed companies have found ways to weave an innovative spirit back into their organizations. One talent top innovators share is a heightened ability to cross organizational lines to tap employees' creativity. To nurture sprouting ideas that might otherwise get trampled by the bureaucracy, they are encouraging cooperation between executives at different levels. To hone product development, innovative companies are assembling teams that bring marketing, manufacturing, and R&D together at a project's earliest stages. To make sure employees are doing the job most suited to them, they are creating separate career paths for researchers and are making sure top research executives command more respect. And more than ever, companies are willing to scrounge for useful ideas wherever they can be found.

The easiest step managers can take may be simply encouraging executives to break ranks and fraternize with coworkers from other departments within the company. At General Electric Co, for example, the heads of all major businesses meet regularly to discuss projects they're working on. Similarly, Monsanto Co. has established what it calls a technology council, comprising top researchers from each of the company's divisions. The council helps scientists swap ideas and avoid duplicating costly research efforts.

Other methods of encouraging innovation require more fundamental management shifts. The most important of those techniques may be using teamwork. Many laggards have clung to a product development process derisively dubbed the "bucket brigade." Someone in a research lab comes up with an idea. Then it is passed on to the engineering department, which converts it into a design. Next, manufacturing gets specifications from engineering and figures out how to make the thing. At last, responsibility for the finished product is dumped on marketing.

While it may be easy to keep track of, the bucket brigade is slow and inefficient. Too often, engineers design products that are too expensive or too complex to manufacture profitably. Plans are constantly pushed back down the chain to fix problems that could have been avoided. After all that, marketing experts are frequently handed products that aren't what customers want most. The outcome: slow response times, high costs, and shoddy quality.

Compare that to the system most Japanese companies use. They take what's called a "fast cycle" approach to development—whipping out new products and reacting in a flash to shifts in consumer preference. To accomplish that, managers make communication a top priority at the earliest stages of a project. They pull together a team of experts from each business function to anticipate glitches and to guide the project through the organization from start to finish.

The system can work wonders. Consider cars: It routinely takes U.S. auto makers up to five years to bring a new car to market, while Japanese competitors do it in only three years. The upshot: Fresh Japanese models hit the showroom faster, and they are often better made.

Simple as it sounds, the team concept doesn't fit easily into traditionally organized U.S. companies. "Senior management's success is ingrained with 30 to 40 years of hierarchy and control," says Daniel J. Valentino, president of consultant United Research in Morristown, N.J. But building teamwork requires shifting some authority to team members—which may alienate the managers traditionally responsible for those tasks. What's more, the team concept often faces resistance from the accounting department. That's because accountants usually keep budgets for each vertical department in a corporation. Using teams that cross traditional financial boundaries forces companies to find new ways to track spending.

But where U.S. companies have bridged those barriers, the results are impressive. At Perkin-Elmer Corp., bringing in pros from different disciplines helped cut by half the number of engineering changes required to produce a product. Speeding up the process isn't the only benefit—it also helped cut manufacturing costs as much as 55%. One example: By collaborating early, designers developing a new instrument for chemical analysis scrapped their plan to include a metal fan attached by bolts. Manufacturing experts suggested a plastic version that snapped into place and required fewer parts.

This kind of cooperation often requires team members to develop skills outside their own field. That's especially true for R&D directors, who are usually called upon to lead the teams. But it demands management skills as well as technical prowess—a combination rarely emphasized in the past. "It used to be the bigger the nerd you were, the better the researcher you were," says François P. van Remoortere, president of W. R. Grace & Co.'s research division. "That's changed now."

To smooth the transition, some companies are providing R&D personnel with a choice of career paths: management or pure research. Companies used to promote top researchers automatically into management ranks, regardless of managerial aptitude. Now, more corporations are looking to hire researchers with good communication and people skills that they can tap later for leading teams. Meanwhile, they're providing better pay and more responsibility to employees who choose to stay in the lab.

Contact-lens maker Bausch & Lomb Inc. has developed a system for doing just that. New lab employees can choose between management and research routes after two to five years with the company. To make sure researchers don't feel slighted, the company has created vice-president-level spots for them, bringing bigger salaries, stock bonuses, and other perks. "The fact that financial rewards will be equal provides a clear sign that we're serious," says Terry Dolak, research vice-president for personal products. So far, only about 5% of Bausch & Lomb's R&D staff have taken the research track, but the company expects that figure to stabilize at 10%. In the past, nearly all of the company's brightest technicians were channeled into management.

Not every company has been so successful. At Rolls-Royce Motor Cars Inc., for example, the dual ladder "works only for the few," says Kenneth W. Bushell, vice-president for engineering. "It only works if you're a genius, or should I say genius squared?" Worse, at some companies research is perceived as a sidetrack for managers past their prime. That kind of half-hearted commitment can backfire by hurting morale and actually slowing product development.

Despite such setbacks, plenty of other companies are searching for new ways to take care of their technical staff. At GE, that has meant creating the post of Chief Technical Officer, to be filled by the company's top R&D executive. The new post is meant as a signal to employees outside the lab that GE considers research and development critical to the company's success. "If a division head finds a technical person in with the CEO, he gets the idea," says Roland W. Schmitt, president of Rensselaer Polytechnic Institute and former head of R&D at GE.

Learning new communication skills is hardly the biggest challenge researchers face. Even the largest and most successful companies have trouble keeping track of all the latest scientific developments. In addition, the soaring cost of research often makes relying solely on homegrown ideas impractical. As a result, more companies are engaging in what they call hunting and gathering—searching for new ideas outside their own labs. That often means developing costly technologies by working closely with university researchers or forming joint ventures—even overseas. "We [U.S. managers] probably looked with unwarranted arrogance at some of our competitors around the world and felt we had little to learn," says Gordon F. Brunner, senior vice-president at Procter & Gamble Co.

No more. In industries that require heavy research spending or demand a global marketing presence—such as computers, telecommunications, and pharmaceuticals—joint ventures have already become routine. In addition to spreading development costs, forming joint ventures can also speed the introduction of new products by avoiding duplication of research efforts.

In addition to seeking partners, companies now routinely search outside the U.S. for technical breakthroughs. To keep tabs on developments abroad, they're setting up satellite labs. That helps them get closer to international markets and lets them spot ideas that could result in new products at home. W. R. Grace, for example, has set up an operation in Japan specifically to transfer suitable technology back to the corporate labs in the U.S.

The hunting and gathering approach raises new challenges to management skills. Some companies that have linked up with tiny, leading-edge research firms have been badly burned—especially when they used the joint venture to enter an unfamiliar market. Consider Du Pont Co.'s abortive joint venture with HEM Research Inc., a tiny

Philadelphia outfit that needed cash to develop a drug to treat AIDS patients. Hot to build a presence in pharmaceuticals, Du Pont was dazzled by HEM's early research on the drug Ampligen. But soon after the giant chemical maker signed on and started pouring millions into a two-year research project, it became clear the remedy was not effective. While plenty of research projects fizzle, even Du Pont officials now admit they didn't investigate HEM carefully enough: It had been passed over as a venture partner by several other companies with longer histories in drug development.

Like most changes, getting managers to encourage innovation can be painful. But plenty of companies are already showing that the rewards are worth it. Witness the 20 companies selected by *Business Week's* editors as examples of the most innovative companies in America. And while methods vary, one common theme emerges: Managing for innovation enables them to keep up with the competition.

Ability to Innovate

Brian Dumaine

Ever since those long afternoons spent tinkering with his junior chemistry set in the basement of his parents' Sioux City, Iowa, home, Allen "Jake" Jacobson has had a hankering for innovation. It shows. During his four years as CEO, the 3M corporation has pumped out new products at a rate of about 200 a year. Many are modest variations of such ordinary but ubiquitous industrial and consumer items as masking tape or sandpaper. But 3M is also a leading maker of high-tech medical diagnostic equipment and computer imaging systems.

Among U.S. companies only Merck is rated as more innovative than 3M in this year's survey. Naturally, being inventive earns the company something beyond praise. Since last January, 3M's stock has risen 29%.

3M functions as a kind of corporate petri dish that fosters the spirit of innovation in its scientists and engineers. Technical people are encouraged to swap information and ideas in the halls. Once a year the company holds its own private trade show. Each of its more than 115 research labs sets up a booth displaying the latest technologies, and for three days scientists, like hucksters at a fair, try to "sell" their work to each other.

A corporate committee of 3M scientists oversees all research, making sure there is no duplication and cross-pollinating new ideas among divisions. Jacobson gives technical

"Ability to Innovate" by Brian Dumaine, *Fortune,* January 29, 1990, pp. 43, 46. Reprinted by permission of Fortune Magazine.

people all the resources they need. In 1988, 3M spent 6.5% of sales, or $689 million, on R&D, twice the average of U.S. industry.

Jacobson believes that top managers go astray if they try to impose too much of their own thinking. Says he: "You've got to sponsor your people's ideas. You've got to help them along." At 3M researchers are encouraged to spend 15% of their time pursuing projects that will pay off only far down the road. But that carrot hides a stick: Jacobson also insists that 25% of each division's annual sales come from products developed in the prior five years.

The company holds scientists and engineers in particularly high esteem. The lab-coat crowd accounts for half of 3M's 135 general managers. A two-tier promotion system allows inventors who don't want to manage to rise to the equivalent of vice president—pay, perks, and all.

Jacobson, 63, a chemical engineer, pushes his researchers to put customers first. "Innovation works from understanding consumer needs," he says. A few notable failures overseas—one was a tape gun that the Japanese wouldn't use because it was shaped like a weapon—have taught him to pay more attention to those who are closest to local markets. That's why he's glad that in the past decade 3M has doubled the number of scientists and researchers working abroad to 2,000.

He believes that if 3M and other American corporations are to keep their innovative edge, the country will have to produce more engineers. Says the father of three: "It has to start in the second grade. Unless you make a home environment where a child can get interested in math and science, you'll never get anywhere."

Is America Becoming More of a Class Society?

New data show that, increasingly, workers
at the bottom are staying there

Aaron Bernstein

Keith Mahone thought he was going places after he graduated from high school and landed a mail-room job at *The Baltimore Sun* in 1983. True, it only paid the minimum wage, but Mahone figured he could move up if he did well. He did move during the next six years—but only to purchasing, the stockroom, and other low-skill jobs that paid just marginally more. Fed up, the Baltimore native quit in 1989.

Mahone, now 36, has been hustling ever since to get ahead in today's high-skills economy. He enrolled in a year-long training course to become a cable-TV technician. But when he finished, cable companies offered him the same $6-an-hour installer job that he could have had without it. After that, he grabbed any job he could, at a food distributor, an incense factory, a meat packer, and as a school custodian. All paid $4 to $6 an hour and ended when the employer closed or laid him off. "These low-wage jobs trap you and take away your hope," Mahone says angrily. "They have no opportunity to further yourself. I always thought mopping the floors was for lazy people, and I never in all my dreams thought I would be doing it. It's hell to fight your way out."

WIDER GAPS

As long as the country's Keith Mahones had the chance to work their way out of the bottom, Americans have tolerated wide gaps between rich and poor. After all, the U.S., unlike more rigid economies in Europe, has always been dynamic enough to provide steady upward mobility for workers.

Now, a spate of new research on U.S. income mobility suggests that America is shutting out more people like Mahone. A dozen or so academic studies have examined data that follow the same individuals for many years. This allows them to go beyond research showing rising income inequality to reveal a more unsettling trend: As the economy stratified in the 1980s, workers at the bottom became less likely to move up in their lifetimes. At the same time, upward mobility is increasing for some higher-end professionals and college-educated workers whose skills remain in high demand.

"Is America Becoming More of a Class Society?," by Aaron Bernstein, *Business Week*, February 26, 1996, pp. 86-91. Reprinted by permission.

This splintering is something new in America, suggesting that our economy is becoming more rigid and class-bound. Unlike past decades, when opportunities for advancement existed at all levels, America today is cleaving into economic camps divided largely by education. Those born in families and neighborhoods that provide the money and motivation to help them complete college are more likely to get ahead. Those, like Mahone, who lack the access or the ability to achieve high skills are increasingly likely to sink, no matter how much they hustle.

"In the past, companies could hire unskilled people and train them into skilled jobs," says Henry B. Schacht, the former CEO of Cummins Engine Co., who now is chairman of AT&T's $20 billion equipment unit. "My predecessor at Cummins moved from the shop floor and ended up as president." But because Cummins, like many companies, has cut many first-line managerial jobs, "today those stairs don't exist."

The new studies raise troubling issues about the U.S. economy. Global competition, declining unions, and growing immigration have inflated to more than a quarter of the workforce the cadre of workers whose earnings fall below the $15,000-a-year poverty line. And that doesn't count many of the 5% to 10% of the population in the urban underclass who don't work at all. Meanwhile, technology is lifting the pay of many professionals. And the ranks of the wealthy have boomed as CEOs, entertainment stars, and others hit ever-larger jackpots in the winner-take-all pay system of some professions.

These trends strike at the core of America's self-image as a classless society. Of course, we never really lived up to that ideal. Women largely were excluded from the economic market for hundreds of years, and slavery and racism meant that blacks never even had a chance until the 1940s. Gaping rich-poor chasms also ignited periodic outbursts of something very much like class warfare, as in the bloody labor battles of the 1880s and 1930s.

But the U.S. mostly has served as the preeminent land of opportunity. Labor and socialist political parties like those of class-conscious Europe never flourished here. What matters in our political culture is not equality per se but an economy and society accessible to all. This bedrock belief is a key reason why the U.S. has been a beacon for Europeans and others fleeing stratified societies.

If the new studies are accurate, the U.S. is in danger of losing the openness that underlies its democratic identity. One of the most astounding conclusions of the research is that mobility for low-income Americans is no greater today than for poor Europeans. "You can't take solace anymore in the American dream of working hard and migrating up through society," warns William J. McDonough, president of the Federal Reserve Bank of New York. "That still exists in our society, but we're kidding ourselves if we don't realize that the degree of stickiness of people in lower earnings levels is a new problem."

An increasingly class-segregated economy could one day hurt America's stable, centrist society. Already, the concepts of civic society and collective responsibility are fraying, as frustrated taxpayers lash out at Washington as the emblem of economic decline. Issues of class and inequality are moving to the political forefront.

It's possible that the economic trends underlying these problems are on the wane. Some experts believe U.S. companies have launched a productivity revival that will lift incomes and living standards across the board. It's also true that the children of blue-collar families have flocked to community colleges seeking the education required for today's marketplace.

Still, these forces may not suffice to improve pay for the less skilled. True, college enrollment boomed in the 1980s. But the share of workers with degrees grew more slowly than in the baby-boom 1970s. The resulting skills scarcity increased demand for college grads while shutting out the less skilled. That scenario is likely to continue through the 1990s, since the baby-bust generation is too small to fill the skills gap. "I keep asking people to tell me a hopeful scenario about low-skilled workers in the 1990s, but I never hear a convincing one," says Syracuse University economist Timothy M. Smeeding, who has done some of the recent mobility studies.

Indeed, the new statistics are a powerful wake-up call. Prior inequality studies rely on Census Bureau surveys that take an annual snapshot of the economy to determine how much each worker earns. But the surveys don't follow the same individuals over time, so they can't show whether today's low earners were in the same boat last year.

The new studies trace long-run mobility using a University of Michigan survey that has followed a nationally representative sample of 5,000 families since 1967. Stephen J. Rose, now a Labor Dept. economist, started with men and women who were 22 to 48 years old in 1970 and tracked their earnings every year of the decade. He did the same with adults in the same age group in 1980. Since many individuals' annual earnings fluctuate a lot, Rose computed each person's average earnings, adjusted for inflation, over all 10 years of each decade.

SPLINTERING

The results show that mobility has diverged sharply over the 1980s vs. the 1970s. Consider the results when measured by education levels. In the 1970s, the 10-year earnings of high school dropouts and graduates progressed at 45% and 42% respectively. This was roughly the same as the 53% improvement in living standards that college grads saw, Rose found! In the 1980s, however, less educated workers moved up much less than more educated ones. Dropouts' 10-year average crept along at only 14%, high school grads by 20%, while college grads continued to advance at a 55% pace.

Decreasing mobility out of the bottom is even clearer by wage levels. Using the same definitions he employed for education, Rose found that men in the bottom fifth of wage-earners began to fare badly even in the '70s, when their 10-year average pay lagged inflation by 11%. But they fell out of bed completely in the '80s, losing 34%, the Michigan data show. By contrast, men in the top fifth saw their 10-year pay soar by 56% in the '80s, nearly twice as fast as their 29% gain in the prior decade.

The upward movement of families has splintered, too. More working women since 1970 helped many families offset the slump in men's earnings. But because people tend to marry at their own earnings level, low-income families have gained less. More poor families also are headed by single parents. Throughout the 1970s, though, the average inflation-adjusted incomes of such families still advanced by 16%, Rose found. But the ride ended in the 1980s, and families in the bottom fifth moved down the economic ladder by 4%.

Meanwhile, the upper fifth scored 60%-plus gains over both decades. "When you use long-term averages to get rid of people who are only temporarily rich or poor, you can see that mobility has declined" at the bottom, says Peter T. Gottschalk, a Boston College economist who has studied mobility. Indeed, diverging mobility has shriveled the middle class—$15,000 to $50,000 a year in today's dollars—from 61% of families in 1969 to 50% in 1992, according to the Economic Policy Institute (EPI), a Washington think tank.

REVERSAL OF FORTUNE

The collapse of upward mobility at the bottom is so surprising because even the most skeptical experts believe that nearly everyone gained ground in prior decades. The annual wage figures from Census show that the incomes of families in the bottom fifth actually rose faster—2.95% a year—from 1947 to 1973 than those in the top fifth, whose incomes climbed by 2.48% a year. These numbers don't indicate how many families remained in one group or the other during this period. But even if a family had remained stuck at the very bottom for the entire 25 years, its inflation-adjusted living standard would have doubled. "No one would argue with the idea that mobility was higher in the '50s and '60s," says Christopher J. Frenze, a Republican-appointed economist at the Joint Economic Committee of Congress.

Even more astonishing, American mobility now looks worse than Europe's (chart). In 1993, Northwestern University economist Greg J. Duncan and seven European economists found that throughout the 1980s, only 17% of poor American families moved at least 20% above the poverty line within a year, vs. 25% to 44% of the European poor. Overall, more than 56% of the bottom-fifth American families remained there for at least five years, vs. 52% in Germany, according to Syracuse economist Douglas Holtz-Eakin. "Most economists simply can't believe that the U.S. has the same mobility as Germany," says Richard Burkhauser, a Syracuse economist who also has studied mobility with the Michigan data. "Everyone always thought that people don't move nearly as much there."

Nor do the 1990s seem to be turning out much differently. The Michigan data are available only through 1991. But individual workers' long-run progress is driven largely by the pay rates of the jobs they get. And these figures, available from Census through 1994, show the same inequality patterns of the '80s. For instance, hourly pay for men in the bottom fifth trailed inflation by more than 5% from 1989 to 1994, according to the EPI. Male dropouts' wages plunged by 11% over this period, while high school grads slipped nearly 4%. This is strong circumstantial evidence that anyone who hasn't returned to school or received substantial training likely hasn't seen much of a pay hike in this decade.

While higher-educated workers have fared worse compared with the 1980s, they're still outpacing bottom-end ones. Pay rates for men in the top fifth fell by only 1% from 1989 to 1994, the EPI found, and those for men with college degrees slumped by just 0.4%. Since the lower-skilled did even worse, the gap between the two groups has widened again. Technological advances eventually may boost wages for the college-educated. But numbers released in mid-February show that in 1994, the workforce as a whole got its lowest raise in 14 years. And given the continued decline of low-end pay rates, "there could actually be even less mobility for low-skilled workers in the 1990s than in the 1980s," says Smeeding.

UNINSURED

The treadmill to nowhere isn't news to Lawrence J. Schabow. The 53-year-old Chicago resident saw his pay jump from $4 an hour when he started in 1978 as a truck driver for Pony Express Courier Corp. to $10.50 in 1983. Then Borg-Warner

Security Corp. bought the company and began cutting wages. Today, Schabow earns $9.50 an hour, including a premium for driving at night. That's 22% less, in real terms, than his 1983 pay. His wife, Edna, quit her clerical job in 1992 after a liver transplant. The family pays for its own dental and eye care after Pony ended its insurance programs. When the Schabows couldn't pay their debts, they declared bankruptcy in 1992. "I'm supporting us and our three kids and going under more and more every week," says Schabow.

Economic opportunity has been shrinking for long enough now that families trapped at the bottom are beginning to show the attributes of a permanent lower class. Look at emergency food aid, now a nationwide enterprise. Chicago's Second Harvest, the U.S.'s largest food-relief agency, provides donated food to 185 distributors around the country, which, in turn, supply 70,000 soup kitchens and food pantries. The kitchens serve 26 million people a year, about 10% of the population.

The need for food aid has risen as opportunities for bottom-end workers have declined. In Spokane, Wash., some 27% of soup kitchen users were employed in 1995, vs. 12% in 1987, according to the Spokane Food Bank, which supplies food for 33,000 households a month. Some recipients may not really need free food. But most kitchens demand pay stubs, welfare checks, and other documents. "It used to be that food service tided you over when you lost a job," says Second Harvest President Christine Vladimiroff. "But now it's chronic, because there are more working poor who can't pay the rent and still buy food."

That's the case with Karyn L. Ocheltree, a 33-year-old single mother of four who has used the Spokane Food Bank off and on for several years. In 1987, the high school graduate lost her $12,000-a-year position as an accounts-receivable clerk when the software company she worked for upgraded her job. She found similar work at another company for four years but was replaced by an $8,000-a-year trainee.

Ocheltree then enrolled full-time in a community college to study business administration, working part-time for the college and collecting food stamps and welfare to support her kids. She also took home groceries from the food bank about once a month. She landed a new job in the invoice department of a hardware distributor last July, after completing an associate's degree. But she still earns only $16,800 a year and sometimes taps the food bank. "My family eats $400 to $500 a month in food, and my rent is $550, so I wouldn't have enough left for electricity, water, and all the necessities if I had to buy all our food with my paycheck," says Ocheltree.

The U.S. has been a country of opportunity since its inception. During the 1787 drafting of the U.S. Constitution, Governor Morris of Pennsylvania argued that those whose livelihoods relied on an employer weren't independent enough to be free citizens and shouldn't vote. Thomas Jefferson later responded that Morris' point may have been valid for Europe's dirt-poor wage-earners. But Americans, he said, could always find another job or earn a decent living on the abundant farmland here.

The middle class that began to emerge in the early 1800s has provided the stable underpinnings to our democracy. But if America continues to stratify, "you'd expect our democratic identity to diminish," says political science Professor Carey McWilliams of Rutgers University. Some trapped on the bottom may explode with resentment. Others may succumb to apathy. Either way, all Americans will suffer.

The Political Nature of Innovation

Peter J. Frost and Carolyn P. Egri

The innovator makes enemies of all those who prospered under the old order, and only lukewarm support is forthcoming from those who would prosper under the new . . . because men are generally incredulous, never really trusting new things unless they have tested them by experience.

Niccolo Machiavelli, *The Prince*

As observed long ago by Machiavelli, the introduction of an innovation or change continues to induce and become the focus of political activity in modern society and its organizations. It is in these disputes over the ambiguous means and ends of an envisioned change that the process of innovation becomes political. How then, does an innovation emerge and survive whatever conflict it engenders? Under what conditions and when does organizational politics flourish in the innovation process? Research evidence indicates that political gamesmanship is most likely to be positively linked with the degree of originality, with the degree of perceived risk, and with the complexity of the situation. Perhaps the most vulnerable time of the innovation process is during the implementation stage when the dysfunctional nature of organizational politics is most often highlighted. It is responsible for, among other things, unnecessary delays, excessive conflict, compromised outcomes, and sometimes, ultimate failure.

The main theme throughout studies in which these results are observed is on the "problem" of the social and political dynamics engendered by innovation. Consistent with the general pro-innovation bias found in society, these resistances to innovation are generally regarded by managers as threats rather than opportunities. For those managers who are more entrenched in an organization (either by virtue of age, seniority or through the benefits accorded them by the status quo) the messiness, disorder and "muddling through" required of the innovation process can be particularly distasteful, thereby resulting in avoidance or resistance.

To illustrate the tangle and complexity of the innovation process and its political nature, we present several case studies which describe the process in some detail. There do not appear to be as many studies of innovation which deal with the politics of innovation. Most common treatments of innovation either do not address process or gloss over or truncate its detail in the interest of limited space or because the authors are addressing other questions.

Peter J. Frost and Carolyn P. Egri, "The Political Process of Innovation" in *Research in Organizational Behavior, 13*, eds. L.L. Cummings and B.M. Staw (Greenwich, Conn.: JAI Press, 1991), 229–295. Adapted with permission from JAI Press.

THE TRIALS OF PRODUCT CHAMPIONS AND SPONSORS—NASA MOONLANDER MONITOR

The case of the development of the NASA Moonlander Monitor is one which illustrates the integral role an innovation champion and his/her managerial sponsors can play in the development of a new product. It is also an example of how innovators can successfully be mavericks within an organizational culture which, while posing at the surface level a number of obstacles to such initiatives, is supportive of innovation and change in its deep structure.

As a young engineer at Hewlett-Packard, Chuck House proved to be instrumental in the development and application of oscilloscope technology for new venues (Pinchot, 1985). Initial impetus for the project was provided by the Federal Aviation Administration, which identified the need for an improved airport control tower monitor. Although the Hewlett-Packard monitor did not meet the FAA's specification for a high resolution picture and subsequently lost out to competitors, there were features of their prototype which struck House as worthy of further investigation. House believed that the size (smaller and lighter than other models), speed (20 times as fast), energy efficiency and brighter (but fuzzier) picture of his group's monitor was a significant technological breakthrough—although one which had yet to find its niche in the marketplace.

In the course of his efforts to demonstrate the merits of his team's model, House proved to be a political gamesman who operated as a maverick by violating a number of organizational rules and boundaries. His first foray into the political arena involved conducting his own market research on potential applications. To gather such information, House personally showed the monitor prototype to 40 computer manufacturers and potential customers in an organizationally unsanctioned trip from Colorado to California. In doing so, not only was he violating functional organizational boundaries by circumventing the marketing department but he was also violating a cardinal Hewlett-Packard security rule which forbade the showing of prototypes to customers. However, based on the marketing information collected during his trip, House was able to gain a temporary reprieve from senior management for his project. During the next 18 months, the project team continued development work in the lab and on-site with customers.

The next obstacle to the continuation of the project came during the annual division review by senior management. This review was influenced to a large degree by a marketing department telephone survey which projected that there was only a total demand for 32 monitors. The resistance and lack of creative initiative of the marketing group (perhaps motivated by House's previous incursion into their territory) was evident in the manner in which the survey was conducted. As Pinchot (1985: 26–27) reports: "Chuck argued that marketing had failed to understand his strategy for marketing the product. They had called only upon oscilloscope customers, the only customers they knew. New applications required new customers, Chuck explained. Besides, the device was difficult to describe: Because it was new, only demonstrations could uncover its saleability." Marketing's forecast of demand for the monitor prevailed over House's group's projections which were based on direct operating feedback from customers (and were, to some extent, obtained through organizationally illegitimate means). Not only was House's project threatened by the lack of administrative innovation by the marketing group, his project did not have the support of the chief corporate engineer who favored an alternate technology.

The conclusion of the divisional review was that, in light of the apparent lack of market demand and technological support from others in the organization, the only rational action was to abort the project. In corporate founder David Packard's words: "When I come back next year I don't want to see that project in the lab!" (Pinchot, 1985:27).

It is at this point that House's political gamesmanship was put to the test. Unwilling to accept this decision, House "chose" to reinterpret Packard's pronouncement to mean that the project would be out of the lab in one year's time but in production, not on the scrapheap. With the covert support of his boss Dar Howard, the tactic of covering up development costs of the project from budget restrictions started in earnest as House's team raced to complete the project in one year when the normal length of time would be two. In the face of continuing opposition from the marketing department, House gained additional support by convincing interested potential customers to personally call on his superiors and argue for the project.

Fortunately for House and his team, they made their deadline and when Packard returned one year later, the monitor was indeed in the marketplace. Packard was reported to be both amused and impatient with this obvious re-interpretation of his order but perhaps indicative of his own maverick origins, he now supported the obviously successful project. Rather than being punished for their insubordination, House and his team were now given permission to continue to develop additional applications, among them the eventual use of the oscilloscope monitor for the NASA Moon Mission, the medical monitor used in the first artificial heart transplant, and a large-screen oscilloscope which was used as part of an Emmy-award-winning special effects system. Without the committed championship of House and the sponsorship of his immediate superiors, these landmark innovations could have easily been the victims of opposing political forces.

DESIGNING POLITICAL BATTLES TO BUILD A NEW COMPUTER

In his Pulitzer-prize-winning book, *The Soul of a New Machine,* Tracy Kidder (1981) treats us to a detailed account of the trials of the design engineer in the highly competitive computer industry. He also gives us an inside look at how competitive political contests can be surreptitiously orchestrated by senior managers to promote innovation.

Data General prided itself on its maverick culture—a culture which could be directly traced back to its founding members, three young computer engineers who left DEC in 1968 to set up shop in a former beauty parlour. Within ten years, Data General was on the Fortune 500 list and had carved out its niche in the minicomputer market. However, by 1976, Data General was also sorely in need of a new product, namely, a 32-bit minicomputer which was comparable, but better, than those recently introduced by their competitors.

The political stage was set by senior executives headed by CEO Ed de Castro when they announced that Data General would build a new research and development facility in North Carolina. It was here, they publicly announced, that major research would be conducted to develop the needed 32-bit minicomputer. The important Fountainhead Project (FHP) was transferred to the new location along with 50 of the most talented DG engineers and technicians. Meanwhile, among those who remained behind in

Westborough, Massachusetts, were Tom West and his small Eclipse group. Their previous project had been cancelled in favor of the FHP—Data General could not afford to fund two major competing projects. Instead, West was assigned to revamp the lower priority 16-bit Eclipse. Although de Castro never put it in writing, West received tentative approval to transform the Eclipse into a 32-bit minicomputer as the rechristened Eagle project. Technically, the Eclipse group was not to do any groundbreaking developments—that was the territory of North Carolina's FHP. How West and his managers were able to do just that in record time is a testament to skillful team building and political acumen.

The first priority was to keep a low profile so as not to appear to be in competition with FHP. This political strategy was justified by West as follows:

> You gotta distinguish between the internal promotion to the actual workers and the promoting we did externally to other parts of the company. Outside the group I tried to low-key the thing. I tried to dull the impression that this was a competing product with North Carolina. I tried to sell it externally as not much of a threat . . . It was just gonna be a fast, Eclipse-like machine. This was the only way it was gonna live. We had to get the resources quietly, without creating a big brouhaha, and it's difficult to get a lot of external cooperation under those circumstances." (Kidder, 1981:47)

Part of this low profile strategy was physical. The Eclipse group was located in the cramped basement quarters of Westborough headquarters where even the air conditioning didn't work properly. This resulted in both physical and social isolation from the rest of the company, all the better to facilitate covering up their real agenda for the Eagle project. The Eclipse group's low profile was also facilitated by the type of engineers recruited for the project. West and his lieutenant Carl Alsing hired recent engineering graduates not only for their excellent academic credentials but also for their willingness to work long hours and their unbridled enthusiasm for computer design work. By doing so, the group was ensured a low profile in that there were few who would see them as competition for the higher priced and proven talent in North Carolina.

One example of the lengths to which Eclipse group members went to avoid appearing to be in competition with FHP or encroaching on their territory is how computer architect Steve Wallach got his job done. If there was a computer instruction which deviated from the approved parameters of the Eagle project and might be construed as infringing on the FHP project, Wallach would work with his friends in System Software on the item. When finished, he would then ask his friends to write a memo requesting inclusion of the controversial instruction into the Eagle—thus avoiding any charges that the Eclipse group was going outside of approved project parameters.

Throughout the project, team members were constantly negotiating with support groups for their assistance. The competition for resources was difficult for the Eclipse group as Kidder (1981: 112) relates: "The game was fixed for North Carolina and all the support groups knew it." Through personal contacts and persuasive skills they were able to gain the needed resources.

What is particularly interesting in this case is that many of the engineers on the Eclipse team were unaware of the full extent of West's role in ensuring survival of the project. It was all part of his managerial style which was to stay separate from the team and to run interference with other corporate bodies in order that his engineering team could be creatively free. West also benefitted from having a management sponsor in Vice-President of Engineering Carl Carman who authorized the project and the money to recruit staff. Fortuitously, the FHP reported to a different Vice-President so there was no internal organizational conflict for Carman.

Finally, in a classic David vs. Goliath scenario, the small Eclipse group overcame all organizational and technical obstacles to deliver the 32-bit minicomputer ahead of North Carolina. This was a tale of a maverick group operating effectively within a maverick culture. For de Castro, it was a relatively low cost exercise in creative insurance so that Data General would have the desired product.

AN OUTSIDER DOING BATTLE WITH THE DEEP STRUCTURE: THE DVORAK SIMPLIFIED KEYBOARD

The case of the Dvorak Simplified Keyboard (DSK) is one which clearly demonstrates how self-interested political actors can effectively forestall a demonstrably beneficial technological change. When invented in 1873, the current universal "QWERTY" typewriter keyboard was designed to prevent typists from striking two adjoining keys in quick succession. Otherwise, the keys would "jam" together in the basket of a machine which relied on the forces of gravity to pull the keys back to their original positions. Technological improvements to the typewriter (the introduction of spring-loaded keys at the turn of the century and later, the invention of electric typewriters) overcame the jamming problem but the original keyboard remained. Enter Dr. August Dvorak, education professor, who through scientific time and motion studies developed a new keyboard configuration which would enable typists to work faster, more accurately (50% fewer mistakes) and with less physical strain to gain productivity improvements ranging from 35% to 100% (Dvorak, Merrick, Dealey, & Ford, 1936). Additionally, Dvorak proved that typists could learn their skill in one-third of the time it took to learn on the QWERTY keyboard. Why then, aren't we all (present authors included) typing on this technologically superior invention?

Perhaps the chief culprits in resisting this technological innovation were the typewriter manufacturers who had considerable financial interests in retaining the traditional keyboard. During the 1930s when Dvorak introduced his invention, there was little incentive for typewriter manufacturers to convert over to a keyboard which would increase typist productivity thereby conceivably resulting in fewer sales. Furthermore, they would be required to pay royalties on Dvorak's patented invention.

Rejected by the manufacturers, Dvorak then reasoned that publicity at the World Typewriting Championships would help generate public demand for his invention. From 1934 to 1941, DSK-trained typists did indeed win the top typing awards at these competitions. However, the championships were sponsored by the manufacturers who, faced with these embarrassing outcomes, worked to deny Dvorak the publicity he sought. When publishing contest results, they only listed the names of the winning typists, not the machines they used in competition. An attempt by contest officials to ban DSK typists from competition was aborted when Dvorak threatened to advise the newspapers. Dvorak was even forced to hire security guards to protect his machines during the contests when it was discovered that they had been sabotaged.

The manufacturers were also skillful in networking with the American National Standards Institute. As members of the ANSI Keyboard Committee, they were able to prevent inclusion of the DSK into the national standards manual. Dvorak's attempts to gain a government contract for his typewriters were also unsuccessful. Despite the demon-strated superiority of the DSK in experimental tests conducted in the U.S. Navy and the General Services Administration, both rejected the possibility of a conversion. The ratio-nale was that the measurable costs of replacing obsolete equipment and retraining typists outweighed the intangible future benefits of productivity improvements. This was a sur-prising conclusion since the trial results showed an average productivity increase of 74% with retraining costs being amortized over 10 days. Then in the ultimate covering up political tactic, the U.S. Navy assigned the DSK test results a security classification.

It is no wonder that, after 30 years of political battles to fulfil his dream, a frustrated Dr. Dvorak told Parkinson: "I'm tired of trying to do something worthwhile for the human race. They simply don't want to change!" (Parkinson, 1972: 18)

But as this account of innovation politics suggests, it is not all humans who resist change but rather those interest groups who stand to lose their financial stake if the innovation is implemented.

THE POWER OF VESTED INTERESTS TO FRUSTRATE NEW IDEAS: HELPING AUTISTIC CHILDREN

As related by Graziano (1969) in his account of a mental health innovation, the realm of interorganizational innovation is often the scene for political action at the deep struc-tural level. Set in the 1960s, this account shows how the entrenched interests of a medical establishment (expert in the psychoanalytic treatment of such patients) actively resisted acknowledging or experimenting with a new technique (behavioral modification) to treat autistic children. The power of the professional elite is demonstrated by their abil-ity to effectively maintain the status quo of local mental health services while circum-venting efforts of an opposing group to gain local funding for an alternative treatment.

At a fundamental level, the two opposing interest groups were aligned into one which was supported by the medical profession versus one which was community-based. On the side of the entrenched power elite in the mental health community were the private-practice psychiatrists who operated the local clinics and dominated the local Mental Health Association. How they were able to parlay their position to influence other institutional actors (the local university and the "United Agency" fund-raising or-ganization) is particularly interesting in this drama of innovation. In opposition to this coalition for the status quo was the Association for Mentally Ill Children (ASMIC), which was a lay group comprised of the parents of those autistic children who had not been helped by the psychoanalytic methodology (either because they had not responded to this course of treatment or had parents who could not afford the expensive private clinics). The ASMIC had employed a psychologist skilled in this new approach (re-member that the time was the early 1960s when behavior modification was still a relatively radical new theory) to assist them in their attempt to change the system. However the integral role in which organizational politics plays in the course of innova-tion is highlighted by Graziano's (1969: 10) comment that: "The *conception* of innova-tive ideas in mental health depends upon creative humanitarian and scientific forces, while their *implementation* depends, not on science or humanitarianism, but on a broad spectrum of professional or social politics."

Although both groups initially worked together for four years in a local clinic offering both methodologies, the subsequent struggles over the resources to be allocated to each program and evaluation of the therapeutic effectiveness of each led to their separation.

Operating independently, the ASMIC tried repeatedly to gain financial support for their alternative approach. Once outside the mainstream of the medical establishment though, they encountered political resistance orchestrated by the local private clinics at both the surface and deep structure levels. An ASMIC proposal to the local university to try an experimental pilot project testing the merits of the behavioral modification methodology was rejected on two counts—it was too radical and it was not supported by the local mental health community.

Attempts to gain independent funding for their project from the local community funding agency ("United Agency") were first delayed and finally rejected after three years of efforts by the ASMIC to comply with the agency's demands. The influence of the established clinics (which were also funded by the United Agency) could be surmised to have played a role in the construction of these obstacles to implementation. Even though the ASMIC had garnered enough funds (from the parents of the autistic children and latterally from the State Department of Mental Health) to operate at a minimal level of service, the United Agency's rationale for withholding funds proved to be innovative in their own right. First there was the criticism that the program was first only a "paper proposal"; then after six months of operation, the United Agency contended that the program had been in operation "too brief a time on which to base a decision." After another year, the funding application was rejected because it had not been "professionally evaluated"; with a positive State Department of Mental Health evaluation in hand, the ASMIC program was then deemed to be a "duplication of services"; with state endorsement that it was a nonduplicated service, the United Agency declared that state financial support was required; and finally, with a state grant in hand, the United Agency rejected the application outright because the ASMIC had been "uncooperative" by not providing confidential information on clients' names, addresses, and fathers' places of employment.

AUTOMATICALLY CONTROLLED MACHINE TOOLS— AN OBJECT OF DEEP STRUCTURE POLITICS

That class conflict and the ideology of progress inform the institutions, ideas, and social groups which determine the design and use of a particular technology is the basic thesis of Noble's (1984) analysis of machine tool automation in manufacturing production. This case illustrates how deep structure politics were used to preserve and extend the control and power of the sectional interests of the owner/managerial, scientific technical and military communities at the expense of those of workers. The capacity of a societal ideology to influence not only the choice of a technology but also to frame (in a pre-emptive manner) that decision in terms of the criteria and assumptions which are used, demonstrates the covert and subtle nature of deep structure power games.

Following WW II, there were two viable avenues by which machine tool automation could proceed. The first was Record Playback (R/P) which built on the skills and knowledge of machinist craftsmen thereby enhancing their traditional power base in the production process. In R/P, automatic control of a machine tool was achieved via a taped program which recorded the movements of the machine operator. It required a skilled machinist to make the initial program and any subsequent changes and adjustments to it. The second option was Numerical Control (N/C) technology in which the tape was programmed not by repeating a machinist's movements but by using scientific engineering methods. This in turn resulted in the assignment of machine programming responsibilities to staff engineers and technicians.

At a fundamental level, what did each technological approach represent? By removing the critical programming function from the shopfloor, N/C extended managerial control over production start-up, pace, and maintenance. In contrast, the R/P approach would be a continuation of the current sharing of production control with the skilled workers on the shopfloor. The overwhelming choice of industrial management was to pursue the N/C technological approach. The primary motive for this managerial decision was that it enabled management to regain control over production.

This impetus for the assertion of managerial control was only reinforced by the growing unionization of the American blue-collar workforce during the 1950s which (when coupled with the union movement's ideological alliance with Communist ideals) served to elevate managerial perceptions of threat. Support for this observation can be found in the fate of R/P systems which were developed in a number of large firms such as General Electric and the Ford Motor Company. Despite positive preliminary test results (based on production efficiency and cost criteria) corporate management consistently cancelled these experiments in favor of more complex engineer controlled N/C systems. Significantly, the decision at GE was made during a period of labor union unrest.

Managerial interests were also influenced and supported by the actions of other societal interest groups which preferred the N/C technology. The power of the scientific and military communities in channeling the course of machine tool automation should not be underestimated. The military underwrote much of the research and development costs of N/C projects in the university labs. MIT, at the forefront of computer microelectronic research, was an early advocate of N/C technology. Not only did N/C research provide MIT with a promising venue for applications of their new-found computer technology, but it also was consistent with an ideological bias for the superiority of formal educational expertise (needed to program N/C tapes) over layman experience (the basis of R/P technology).

SOME LESSONS FROM THE TRENCHES

Very briefly, we can draw some inferences from the experiences of innovators in these organizations. These propositions need to be tested in other settings and under conditions in which their effects can be carefully identified and analyzed. For the time being, we think it is useful for managers and others to consider the following lessons.

> *Lesson 1: Product innovation success within organizational settings requires a combination of both product and administrative innovation.*

A good idea or product is simply not enough to guarantee successful implementation and diffusion within and outside an organization. For example, Hewlett-Packard's NASA Moonlander Monitor was a technological innovation which was almost terminated by a lack of administrative innovation. The information House gained from hands-on development with customers enabled him to modify the monitor to meet their needs while generating demand for the end-product. In this case and others, reliance on standard operating procedures are often insufficient to meet the unique requirements of new products or ideas.

> *Lesson 2(a): When a proposed innovation is congruent with the organizational and societal deep structure, political activity remains primarily on the surface, is benign or at a low level. Consequently, the probability of the acceptance and diffusion of such an innovation is enhanced with the support of the deep structure.*
>
> *Lesson 2(b): A proposed innovation which threatens power relationships at the deep structure level evokes the full breadth and depth of opposing political forces, strategies and tactics. Consequently, the probability of acceptance and diffusion of such an innovation is significantly reduced.*

These propositions focus on the type and range of political tactics which emerge or are elicited when a proposed innovation either confirms or threatens existing power relationships. As evidenced in the cases of the Dvorak Simplified Keyboard, the mental health innovation and those areas of ICI which resisted OD initiatives, when those interests which benefit from maintaining the status quo perceive an innovation to be a threat, the politics of change are both numerous and powerful. What results is a mismatched contest where the deep structure frames the rules of the game and to a large extent preordains the outcome. The metaphor of a "corporate immune system" is a useful one in understanding the dynamics of this response. As Pinchot (1985, p. 189) relates:

> *When you start something new, the system naturally resists it. It is almost as if the corporation had an immune system which detects anything that is not part of the status quo and surrounds it. If you are to survive, you will have to lull this immune system into ignoring you. You will have to appear to be part of the corporate self, rather than identified as a foreign body.*

Although Pinchot focuses on the intraorganizational arena, we believe that the same "immune system" can be activated in the interorganizational and societal realms. As outsiders or newcomers to the arenas in which they were trying to introduce their changes, Dvorak and the ASMIC were easily allocated the role of unwanted invaders by a system which perceived few, if any, benefits to influential system members through effecting a change to the status quo.

At ICI, the OD change agents were also perceived to be outsiders to the production process. However the success of Ripley and Bridge's program in the Agricultural Division could be traced to their strategy of first developing a strong, coherent program for change independent of the corporate system before attempting to enter it and then, to work within the system in a nonthreatening manner. They started low in the organizational structure and built support in an incremental way. In contrast, the OD programs in the other areas were more visible and did not have the strength of unity in either philosophy or personnel to withstand the opposition.

When the proposed innovation or change is consistent and/or supports existing power relationships, the politics remain at the more manageable surface level. The contests at Hewlett-Packard and at Data General were against a backdrop of a unity of interests between innovators and the corporate ethic. These innovators were secure in the knowledge that the organizational mission was to be at the forefront of their technology—a deep structure which desired technological change for competitive purposes. They also benefitted from cultures with a deep structure mythology of hero-founders who were mavericks in their own right. By acting as mavericks themselves, they were only continuing the organizational tradition and could count on a degree of understanding of their actions at the highest corporate levels. Opposition to these product innovations were of a more traditional and restricted nature in terms of internal power plays, managing line vs. staff territories and gaining the necessary resources for development. As corporate insiders, these innovators could draw on their past experience and that of others in the organization to gauge how best to proceed—which political tactics had succeeded in the past, which had failed, the relative risks involved, who were the power players and who were not.

For administrative innovations, political gamesmanship played a major role in the eventual success or failure of the proposed change. Success often hinged on the innovator's ability to marshall a wide range of supportive political tactics at both the surface and deep structure levels. Ripley and Bridge at ICI's Agricultural Division proved to be politically adept at numerous influence tactics. Review of these successful administrative innovations reveals that there was a minimal number of opposing political games, either at the surface or deep structure levels.

Administrative failures at ICI present a contrasting picture. The tactics of appealing to higher authority and appealing to reason proved to be ineffective against the deep structure games of a resistant organization. These OD change agents were effectively pre-empted by divisional managements which denied that any change to the status quo was needed and rejected the claim that these staff persons had a right to be involved in any change process.

Lesson 3: Within organizations, the political strategy of "asking for forgiveness" is limited to only the initial phases of the conception and development of a product innovation. For the adoption and diffusion of a new product, the innovator must "seek and secure permission" of the organization.

We note in these case studies of innovation there are two distinct types of political strategies—that of "asking for forgiveness" and that of "seeking and securing permission." "Asking for forgiveness" occurs when an innovator proceeds to the point of adoption without official organizational knowledge and/or sanction. It is an independent course of action often marked by secrecy and the furtive seconding or transfer of corporate resources. Alternatively, the strategy of "seeking and securing permission" usually encompasses the political strategies of developing champions and sponsors and of building networks and coalitions. Neglecting to do so may threaten the long term viability of an innovation.

In our view, asking for forgiveness is a viable strategy when pursuing product innovation. Seeking and securing permission is a more viable strategy when pursuing administrative innovations. It is possible to hide a product innovation from potential naysayers in the important fragile early phases of that innovation. Social and administrative innovations, on the other hand, depend more immediately on corporate interdependencies for their successful implementation. Thus it becomes important for the innovator to both seek *and* secure permission from organizational actors in a variety of positions and levels to ensure success. In the long run, product innovations move from the laboratory to implementation and thus to integration with other organizational routines and procedures. This entails a shift to a greater emphasis on the permission rather than the forgiveness strategy.

These accounts of innovation demonstrate the integral role political strategy plays in both promoting and suppressing innovation. If the proposed change threatens the self-interests of a powerful dominant coalition (as in the mental health innovation, the Dvorak keyboard, and machine tool automation), we find that the emergence of a technological innovation is a tenuous one. In these cases, the full breadth of deep structure and surface politics is elicited to preserve prevailing power relationships. Apparently, rationality is subsumed in these high stakes interorganizational and societal level battles for survival of the fittest. On the other hand, if there is no perceived fundamental threat, the political activity remains on the surface and can be more readily managed by prospective innovators.

REFERENCES

Dvorak, A.; Merrick, N.L.; Dealey, W.L.; and Ford, G.C. (1936). *Typewriting Behavior: Psychology Applied to Teaching and Learning Typewriting.* New York: American Book Company.

Graziano, A.M. (1969). "Clinical Innovation and the Mental Health Power Structure: A Social Case History," *American Psychologist 24*(1), 10–18.

Kidder, T. (1981). *The Soul of a New Machine.* New York: Avon Books.

Noble, D.F. (1984). *Forces of Production.* New York: Knopf.

Parkinson, R. (1972). "The Dvorak Simplified Keyboard: Forty Years of Frustration," *Computers and Automation 21*(11), 18–25.

Pinchot, J. III (1985). *Intrapreneuring.* New York: Harper and Row.

Business Shares the Blame for Workers' Low Skills

John Hoerr

America, once the home of the world's most skilled labor force, now may be throwing it all away. Schools continue to turn out poorly educated young people. Employers continue to reject the idea of spending large amounts of money to train workers and upgrade skills. The easiest—but most damaging—way to remain competitive is to downgrade skills and cut wages. Indeed, the U.S. is on a de-skilling binge for the sake of short-term productivity growth that could prove disastrous for business and the economy in the long run.

So concludes a major new study by a group called the Commission on the Skills of the American Workforce. Most companies, it finds, accept the idea that they must live with a low-skilled work force. Less than 10% of employers surveyed are creating jobs that call for workers with broad-based skills and the ability to adapt to fast-changing technology and markets. In other words, business by and large is not demanding—and the society is not delivering—the large-scale improvements in education and training that American industry needs.

The commission's study, titled "America's Choice: High Skills or Low Wages," will be issued on June 18. Established by the nonprofit National Center on Education & the Economy, the 32-member commission is a bipartisan group of business, academic, and labor representatives chaired by Ira C. Magaziner, a business strategy consultant who is president of SJS Inc. The commission co-chairmen are Ray Marshall and William E. Brock, who served as Labor Secretaries in the Carter and Reagan Administrations, respectively. The report is funded by the Carnegie Corp. of New York, New York State, Towers Perrin, and the German Marshall Fund.

"The Worst"   The commission conducted in-depth studies of workplaces and education-training systems in the U.S., Germany, Sweden, Denmark, Japan, Ireland, and Singapore. It concludes that, except for Ireland, the foreign countries provide far better schooling and job training for noncollege-bound youth than the U.S. As a result, American youth rank near the bottom in comparisons of school performance. The other nations also have well-organized national systems for moving high school graduates into industry. The transition from school to work in the U.S. is described as "the worst of any industrialized country."

The study focuses on some 82 million jobs in the U.S. that do not require a four-year college education. These include skilled employees, such as nurses and construction workers, as well as line workers such as machine operators, assemblers, retail clerks, and health service employees. According to projections, most recruits for these jobs will be deficient in such basic skills as reading and writing. Even so, the skills commission found, relatively few employers plan to sharpen their employees' skills through remedial training. Although all the U.S. companies surveyed complained about a lack of skills, most were concerned more about workers' attitudes and personalities than educational skills.

In contrast, America's competitors tend to upgrade line workers' jobs and fill them with well-educated young people. Most important, a high percentage of foreign companies is achieving large productivity gains by reorganizing work to eliminate tiers of managers and give workers more of a say. The resulting "high-performance" workplace calls for multiskilled line workers who have good reading, math, science, and problem-solving skills. These workers can readily absorb new skills as technology and production requirements change. With workers who adapt quickly to new conditions, manufacturers can introduce new products on short cycle times and frequently switch production runs.

High Road   In the U.S., however, the commission discovered that fewer than 10% of the 400-plus companies interviewed are reorganizing work in this fashion. Instead of investing in workers, most companies are pursuing other strategies to remain competitive: cutting wages, exporting production jobs to low-wage countries, or de-skilling jobs through automation. All of these methods are based on what Magaziner calls a "high-turnover, low-wage model." Many employers, he says, assume that the U.S. will have a large pool of uneducated, unskilled people. That being the case, the companies are using automation to create very simple work tasks—jobs described by some critics as "idiot-proof"—with low wages and no employment security.

Companies that take this path may be successful, but only in the short term, the commission says. The nation faces a choice. "We can choose forms of work organization which achieve cost competitiveness in the short run based upon low skills, low wages, and ultimately a society with a low living standard," Magaziner says. "Or we can choose forms of work organization which require more investment but which result in cost competitiveness based upon higher skills, higher wages, and a higher living standard."

The commission wants the U.S. to take the high-wage path. It recommends fundamental changes in the way the U.S. educates and trains the 70% of young people who will not graduate from four-year colleges. It urges the government to encourage companies to adopt high-performance work systems. Employers would be required to invest 1% of payroll in either their own training programs or a national fund to upgrade worker skills. These are controversial proposals, but the U.S. needs strong action to upgrade its work force to world-class standards.

Workers Want More Money, But They Also Want to Control Their Own Time

Ellen Joan Pollock

When it comes to time off, employees want to do what they want, when they choose.

When it comes to health, employees want employers to help them stay well.

And when it comes to just about anything, they don't want employers poking into their personal business.

Those are key lessons of a new survey of worker attitudes about their benefits. The telephone survey of 1,000 employees nationwide asked respondents to rank benefits by

"Workers Want More Money, But They Also Want to Control Their Own Time" by Ellen Joan Pollock, *The Wall Street Journal*, November 18, 1995, p. B1. Reprinted by permission.

importance and satisfaction. It was conducted by Godwins Booke & Dickenson and HRStrategies, consulting units of Aon Corp., Chicago.

The study's findings provide a glimpse of how workers size up the nontraditional benefits that have proliferated in recent years. The study also offers some clues to employers about how to increase productivity while improving employee morale—hard to accomplish in these days of skimpy raises and layoffs.

Asked to rate the importance of benefits from one to 10, respondents gave so-called time-off banks a 7.41 importance rating. Time-off banks typically allow employees to combine vacation, holiday and sick days into a pool to be used as they please, no questions asked. Among nontraditional time-related benefits, time-off banks ranked first in importance. Flexible work schedules and the ability to work at home were deemed less important.

But even though time-off banks are relatively inexpensive to institute, fewer than a third of the workers who responded to the survey actually had such a benefit. Godwins Booke concluded that the idea strongly appealed to respondents because it injects an element of choice into benefit plans.

Universal Health Services Inc., a King of Prussia, Pa., manager of hospitals, combines vacation time, holidays and some sick leave into its time-off bank, which was instituted in 1991. "Employees get control of their own destiny, and we get cost savings and productivity," says Elleen Bove, the company's director of human resources.

Ms. Bove says that employees like the plan because they can "just schedule time off and give no reason." The company likes the plan because employees now are more apt to schedule their time off, instead of just calling in sick.

Under traditional plans, employees often lied to their bosses, saying they were out sick when in fact they were caring for children or elderly parents. Judy Long, a Godwins Booke vice president, says that at a recent series of focus groups at The Lighthouse Inc., a nonprofit rehabilitation organization in New York for the visually impaired, employees said they wanted more privacy about their reasons for taking time off and less subjectivity in the way it was granted.

Employees gave preventive or wellness programs, when incorporated into medical plans, an 8.25 importance; this was just slightly lower than traditional benefits, such as medical insurance (9.59), employer-paid retirement plans (9.11) and vacation days (8.63).

According to the study, "19% of employees without preventive medical benefits miss over four days per year for personal illness, while only 15% of employees with preventive/wellness coverage in their medical plan miss over four days per year for the same reason."

At the Martha Jefferson Hospital in Charlottesville, Va., employees are offered financial incentives to have preventive treatment, such as checkups and immunizations for children. The hospital also offers blood-pressure, skin-cancer and mammography screening as well as nutritional advice.

The hospital promised its employees, who pay part of their insurance costs, that if they "keep healthy and take preventive measures, their premiums will be lower," says Susan Cabell, its vice president for human resources. In fact, this year premiums didn't go up for the first time in several years, Ms. Cabell says. And between 1994 and 1995, short-term disability and sick leave dropped 26%, she adds.

Other findings of the study also provide hints on how employees can best spend their benefit dollars. Almost 75% were satisfied with their health-care benefits. Employees were more satisfied with their vacation time than any other benefit, leading Godwins Booke to suggest that employers allow workers to swap vacation time for other benefits.

And even employees with dependents didn't rank child-care and elder-care programs as high as many other benefits. The highest-ranked dependent benefit was a tax-free savings account for child- or elder-care expenses. School-holiday services and sick care for children got satisfaction ratings of only 5.20 and 5.07 respectively.

If employers decide to divert resources away from relatively unpopular benefits, perhaps they can apply them to salaries: Not surprisingly, only about 65% of those surveyed were satisfied with how they were compensated financially.

Work & Family:
If You Want a Firm That's Family Friendly, the List Is Very Short

Sue Shellenbarger

How family-friendly is your company? In a field tainted by corporate hype, it can be hard to tell what's a genuine effort. And many companies have a hard time assessing how their work-family and flexibility policies compare with others.

Help is on the way. In the next few months, a flurry of new and improved lists, standards and assessment tools is planned. Some are public; others are for corporate insiders. But all promise to improve workers' lives by providing yardsticks of accountability in an area that can affect people as profoundly as the nature of the job itself—the degree to which bosses support their efforts to "have a life" outside work. Here's what's happening:

The Working Mother 100: Set for release next week, this annual listing by Working Mother magazine is the only real horse race in the family-friendliness field, drawing 350 serious contenders this year for 100 slots as "the best companies for working mothers." The list is unique in measuring both family-friendly benefits, including child care, and success in promoting women. Says Working Mother's deputy editor. Betty Holcomb:

"Work & Family: If You Want a Firm That's Family Friendly, the List Is Very Short" by Sue Shellenbarger, *The Wall Street Journal.* September 6, 1995, p B1. Reprinted with permission.

"Most women don't want to trade off career advancement for family issues." The maga-zine also evaluates pay by region and industry. Working Mother raises its standards every year; this year, 17 new companies will appear (meaning 17 others have been dropped).

Amid complaints that the list encourages companies to create new programs with-out making tougher changes in corporate culture, the magazine this year added three more criteria: Are supervisors evaluated on advancement of women? Does the company back women's support groups? Are bosses trained in managing flexible schedules?

Though contenders have multiplied tenfold since the list began in 1986, only a rel-ative handful of U.S. companies still come close to qualifying. The magazine wrote 25 business groups this year asking for nominees and got only two companies it hadn't heard of, Ms. Holcomb says. She is often asked, "Why don't you rank the bad compa-nies?" she says. "The answer is, because there are too many of them."

The Corporate Reference Guide: This rigorous benchmarking guide, first pub-lished in 1991, provides added grounds for a dim view of corporate progress on work-family matters. After setting up a "family-friendly index" to gauge work-family efforts and three categories of achievement, the authors at the Families and Work Institute got 172 of the nation's largest companies to take the death-defying leap of allowing them-selves to be publicly rated. A third got fewer than 45 points on a scale of 610 (an unre-alistically perfect score), failing even to make the lowest category, Stage I.

Johnson & Johnson got a respectable top score of 245, making Stage III along with only three others: IBM, Aetna Life & Casualty and Corning. Kellwood Co., a St. Louis apparel maker, finished last with 2.5 points.

The index assigns points to initiatives, from flextime to summer camps. The stages are a handy framework for figuring out where your company stands. Stage I denotes companies that are fielding a few work-family benefits: Stage II companies are integrat-ing them into a coordinated program, and in Stage III, companies begin changing their corporate culture.

Dana Friedman, institute co-president, says she expects the number of surveyed companies making Stage III to jump to 15% when the index is updated as early as next year, from 2% in 1991. The authors are adding a Stage IV for corporate leaders inte-grating work-family concerns into business planning.

Flexibility Workbook: The authors of this new employer self-assessment tool, set for release Sept. 19 in New York, hasten to say it isn't a yardstick for family-friendliness. It is intended to measure flexibility in work arrangements as a tool for meeting broader business goals, including raising productivity. That said, the workbook still promises to help workers with family duties by encouraging flexibility.

The authors, led by Bank of America with 10 other employers plus the nonprofit New Ways to Work, San Francisco, have created a step-by-step guide to assessing how widely and well alternative work arrangements are used within a company. It also shows how to graph your own "flexibility profile."

Boston University Roundtable Standards of Excellence: The toughest standards are yet to come. A group of 35 employers, including GTE, US West, Motorola and Merck, started work last year on a benchmarking tool that would "raise the bar" on work-family programs. The tool would encourage companies to view such plans not as "window dress-ing . . . but as a measure of, 'Are these truly responsive organizations?'" says Brad Googins of Boston University's Center on Work & Family, which is coordinating the effort.

The group expects by November to ratify standards, then spend a year creating an assessment tool. Some tentative criteria: Does the employer support employees' efforts to balance work and personal concerns throughout their lives, not just when they need child or elder care? Can employees use work-family programs without fear of retribution?

Here's one for the books: Do senior managers set good examples of work-life balance? While Mr. Googins says he doubts that any companies in today's high-pressure workplace could meet that standard, merely mentioning it "would cause all sorts of discussion."

Chapter
14
International
Organizational Life

No contemporary volume on organizational reality would be complete without at least some selections concerned with international organizational life. As Lester Therow, the noted economist, has observed so frequently, we live in a global economy where organizational lines and activities simply do not stop at national boundaries.

U.S. and foreign multinational firms have experienced an explosive growth in the past three decades and there is no sign of this trend abating. Further, an increasing proportion of domestic organizations obtain either their raw materials or their finished products from abroad. In many instances, organizations must either station North American managers and their families in foreign countries or, as a minimum, establish frequent and effective coordination with subsidiaries or suppliers. Yet, as the selections in this chapter illustrate, the reality of international organizational life presents a multitude of challenges for individuals and organizations and their countries.

While there are a number of excellent texts dealing with management and with international business, most neglect the impact on individuals and their families of moving to another country and culture. Americans, regretfully, are a distinctly insular people. Despite a love of foreign travel, Americans are historically loath to learn about cultures other than their own. Living successfully in a different culture requires a great deal of learning and North Americans have justly earned a bad reputation in this matter with natives of other countries: They often fail to study the local culture, observe the necessary courtesies, and otherwise adapt their behavior to the local situation. The piece by Frederick H. Katayama, "How to Act Once You Get There," offers some "basics" that can help the newcomer, at least initially. Of course, there is no substitute for learning as much as possible about the region, its history, politics, and, in particular, the local ways of doing business.

Beyond Mr. Katayama's tips, several studies have found important differences in the values espoused by North American and Asian managers. These differences present significant challenges for international business. The results of one study are reported in "North American and Asian Executives Have Contrasting Values, Study Finds."

Traditional values in China have been replaced by an obsession for money as the country charges ahead with economic changes. The tragic results of this obsession are reported in As Millions of Chinese Try to Get Rich Quick, Values Get Trampled. Family life has deteriorated and crime and corruption are on the rise.

Throughout this book we have repeatedly focused on women, their problems, and their achievements. In "Japan Discovers Woman Power" Sally Solo, writing in mid-1989, acquainted us with the extent to which Japanese women are gaining entry into the managerial work force. In North America, women have made their gains in spite of resistance by male managers. In Japan, however, the entry of women into management has been a matter of economic necessity, the necessity of dealing with a declining pool of male candidates. Since women are widely thought to be less prone to becoming workaholics, the author speculated that a growing number of female managers might, in time, have a significant impact on the Japanese work ethic. However, as Yumiko Ono reports in "Reluctant Feminists: Women's Movement in Corporate Japan Isn't Moving Very Fast," both female professionals and firms remain uncommitted to long-term careers for women notwithstanding continued efforts by the government to encourage career women. It will be interesting to see what effect the recession and limited downsizing in Japan have on this situation.

"The Final Stretch" presents a true story that illustrates that we need not travel to distant countries to find examples of the difficulties that can arise in doing business internationally. Many people think of the border between Canada and the United States as open, yet this piece illustrates how trade laws can confound even this close relationship and make operating a business a very hazardous and frustrating experience.

A new generation of managers is taking charge in Europe. These managers are proving to be as aggressive and innovative as their American counterparts. Indeed, as global competition and domestic recession continue to plague European corporations, the new European management style has become a necessity. "Europe's Tough New Managers" profiles several of these managers and summarizes the changes they have made in their corporations.

The contrast between the working hours and conditions of American and German workers does much to explain the difficulties the German economy is experiencing despite the new generation of corporate leaders. Danny Benjamin and Tony Horwitz contrast the two environments and employee attitudes in "German View: You Americans Work Too Hard—and for What."

In "Managing Without Managers, Ricardo Semler describes his efforts to harness the managerial potential of all employees at Semco, the Brazilian firm which he heads. His methods are certainly unconventional for South America.

The final selection of this chapter focuses on the efforts Korean CEOs are making to change their corporate cultures and improve the quality of their production. "Korea Goes for Quality" chronicles the determined drives the heads of Daewoo, Samsung, Hyndai and other Korean conglomerates have undertaken.

How to Act Once You Get There

Frederick H. Katayama

Doing business in Asia *is* different. In Europe you are not going to blow a deal by slapping your new foreign partner on the back. But old hands in the Orient claim that happened once in Malaysia to a U.S. electronics executive who forgot—or never knew—that most Asians abhor physical contact.

Traveling to more than one country in Asia also means coping with the sharp differences in style and behavior that divide East from East, as well as West. Two things help. First, because the Chinese are so widely scattered throughout the region, a passing knowledge of the Middle Kingdom's history and customs usually gives you some common cultural ground. Second, everyone you meet will probably speak English. The mother tongue of Australia and New Zealand is also an official language in Hong Kong, Singapore, and the Philippines. In Japan, South Korea, and Taiwan, most businessmen can speak—though haltingly—the basic English they were forced to learn in school.

So relax. You can avoid serious blunders and make a good impression as long as you heed the following tips:

- **Dress conservatively.** "The biggest problem is the Texan with big boots and a big hat who wants to pat people on the back," says Thomas Sheldon, an American lawyer who spent two years in Seoul. Throughout most of Asia, the uniform is traditional business suits for men and plain dresses, not pant-suits, for women.

    In Japan clean socks without holes in the toes are crucial, since shoes come off whenever you visit someone's home or dine on tatami mats in a traditional restaurant. Your kit bag should also include a good supply of Kleenex and han-kies. Many public restrooms and restaurants don't supply toilet paper or napkins.

- **Be punctual.** During a state visit last May, Vice President Dan Quayle scheduled a morning of deep-sea diving in Australia. Fair enough. His mistake was to ignore Secret Service warnings that he was running late, and insist on a second plunge and a round of tennis—a decision that made him almost two hours late for a meeting later that day in Indonesia. QUAYLE ARRIVES BEHIND SCHEDULE blared the front-page headline of the Jakarta *Post*.

- **When greeting people,** a handshake and a simple nod will suffice. Extras—the full bow at the waist in Japan or the graceful, prayerlike folding of hands known

"How to Act Once You Get there" by Frederick H. Katayama, *Fortune,* Pacific Rim 1989, pp. 87–88.

as the *wai* in Thailand—are appreciated but not expected of foreigners. Stick to titles and surnames, unless you're in Thailand or Australia, where first names are the game.

Naturally, no first encounter in Asia is complete without an exchange of business cards. Bring a full deck. If possible, have your name, company, and title printed in the local language as well as in English. Use both hands to present and receive cards, and be sure to show respect by reading them carefully. Diana Rowland, author of *Japanese Business Etiquette*, knows one U.S. businessman who lost a deal because he failed to examine the cards of his Japanese prospects thoroughly enough. Says she: "Even though they liked his product, the Japanese reasoned that such inattention was representative of what they could expect from him later."

- **Avoid physical contact.** You know about backslapping now, but don't pat heads either. Asians revere the head as the seat of the soul. They also consider the feet the lowliest part of the body, so don't cross your legs. You may disgrace yourself by waving the soles of your shiny new loafers in your host's face.
- **When making casual conversation,** leave the elaborate jokes at home. They almost never translate. And avoid politics at all cost. Once negotiations get serious, remember that most Asians will rarely turn you down flat, because they don't want you to lose face. If your prospect sucks in his breath during your sales pitch and says with a sigh, "It is difficult" or "We will consider it in a forward-looking manner," interpret that as a polite "no."
- **Though the region boasts** several outstanding cuisines, some Asian delicacies strike Westerners as, well, exotic. The sensitive of stomach should beware of such menu items as "fragrant meat" (dog meat) in Taiwan, "night duck" soup (bat soup) in China, and extremely raw sushi (the fish still writhes atop the rice) in Japan.

When you have no choice, try to eat at least a tad of whatever is offered—even if it's sea slugs in Hong Kong or eggs in horse urine in Thailand. If you really feel shaky, though, decline politely. "That's certainly better than gagging at the table," says Scott Seligman, author of *Dealing with the Chinese*. Seligman suggests pushing the food around on your plate a bit so that it looks as if you have sampled something.

But if you love the dish, forget what Mom said about cleaning your plate. Unless you leave a little, your host will think you are still hungry. Nor should happy eaters stick their chopsticks in the rice bowl. That connotes death. Place them on the chopstick rest, an indented eraser-size object made of porcelain or wood, or lay them across the side of your plate. When picking food off a communal dish, flip the sticks around and use the large end. That's not only polite, it's good hygiene.

- **Women executives** should prepare to put up with far more male chauvinism than they would back home. Warns etiquette expert Diana Rowland, who worked for six years in Kyoto: "Aggressiveness works against you in Japan if you're a woman, because it makes the Japanese uncomfortable." That's also true in male-dominated Korea. Advises Robert Oxnam, president of the Asia Society: "Women have to be willing to overcome slights, some of which aren't intentional."

Ursula Gogel-Gordon, a director of product development at sportswear manufacturer Seattle-Pacific Industries, knows about that firsthand. When she was negotiating to buy yarn from a Japanese trading company, all questions were directed to her less senior male colleague. Says she: "Each time, he would say, 'You have to talk to her.' This happened ten times in a row." Gogel-Gordon kept her cool and closed the deal. But she does advise female managers to forestall such behavior by spelling out their responsibilities in writing and making sure their Asian contacts get the message before they arrive.

- **Gift giving is commonplace.** But outside Japan, where you should err on the side of expensive, don't give something too dear lest the recipient feel obliged to do likewise. If you think to stock up before the trip, local crafts and consumables— Shaker boxes, say, if you're from Pennsylvania, or maple syrup from Vermont— make good gifts.

  Avoid flowers, which can easily insult someone if they are the wrong color or type. White carnations, for example, suggest death or mourning in China. Don't present clocks to Chinese, either. The phrase "to give a clock" sounds like a Chinese expression that means "to care for a dying patient." It rattles the superstitious. As with name cards, use both hands to present and receive gifts. And don't open your gift in the giver's presence. It's the thought that counts.

- **Tipping is less common**—and tips are smaller—than in the U.S. or Europe. Most hotels and restaurants automatically assess a service charge, which will be noted on the bill. No further gratuity is expected. Where service isn't included, leave 10%.

- **With minor exceptions,** drinking is a national sport throughout Asia, and guests are expected to play. Whether the cry is *kanpai* (CON-pie) in Tokyo, *konbae* (GUHN-beh) in Seoul, or *ganbei* (GONE-bay) in Beijing, the message is the same: bottoms up. Kevin Chambers, author of *The Travelers' Guide to Asian Customs and Manners,* recalls that when he nonchalantly declined a business prospect's offer of a cup of *makkolli,* the Korean rice wine, the "frivolity suddenly came to a halt." So did Chambers's deal. If you really don't want to drink, tell your hosts that you are allergic to booze. Better yet, cite doctor's orders.

  In Tokyo and Seoul, and increasingly in Hong Kong and Taipei, you will likely be taken to a *karaoke* bar. In these joints, customers take turns crooning tunes to prerecorded background music, and for once, Asia's strait-laced businessmen shed their reserve and become as giddy as teenagers. Sure, it's silly. But if you feel self-conscious, consider practicing a verse or two of "My Way" or "Yesterday"—two ubiquitous Western classics—in the shower before you go out. This time, "doctor's orders" won't get you off the hook. You *will* be expected to sing for your sale.

North American and Asian Executives Have Contrasting Values, Study Finds

Paul M. Sherer

BANGKOK—The values of Asian executives differ sharply from those of their North American counterparts, according to a study by Wirthlin Worldwide.

To Asians, the most important values are hard work, respect for learning and honesty. North Americans say freedom of expression, personal freedom and self-reliance are their most important values. But the values of individual Asian countries are too varied to justify claims that there is a single set of Asian values, the study says.

Richard Wirthlin, a former pollster for Ronald Reagan and chairman of Wirthlin, a McLean, Va., research firm, presented the study at an Asian business seminar in Bangkok sponsored by Dow Jones & Co., publisher of this newspaper.

Gaps between Asian and Western values have long been cited by some politicians and pundits to explain the spectacular economic growth of Asian nations over the past couple of decades. Some political leaders have used Asians' perceived respect for authority and desire for orderly societies to justify restrictions on free speech and democracy.

EARLIER STUDY

In the Wirthlin study, 60 senior executives in Japan, South Korea, Taiwan, Hong Kong, Thailand and Singapore were asked which of 17 "universal values" they considered important, rating each on a six-point scale. The authors compared the answers with the results of a similar study carried out in North America by the Center for Strategic and International Studies.

Hard work, respect for learning and honesty were cited as among the six most important values for all six Asian countries. Openness to new ideas and self-discipline were within the top six of at least four countries.

In contrast, North Americans polled by the earlier study said freedom of expression, personal freedom and self-reliance were their most important values, followed by individual rights, hard work, personal achievement and thinking for oneself.

The difference in values appeared sharp. Of 17 "universal values," only two were among the seven deemed most important by both Asian and North American executives: hard work and self-reliance.

"North American and Asian Executives Have Contrasting Values, Study Find " by Paul M. Sherer, *The Wall Street Journal*, March 8, 1996, p. 1358. Reprinted by permission.

'BROADER' VALUES

"North American values are much more egocentric in nature when compared with Asian values," Mr. Wirthlin said in an interview. "Asian values are much broader, more outside the focus on the individual as such. They relate to goals for the individual, rather than the individual himself." He added that Asian values such as "the striving for learning and hard work . . . are values that leverage into commercial success."

Wirthlin concludes from its study that "Asia's faster growth rate in the last decade has potentially been in part a function" of a more consensus-oriented work force. The research firm adds that "North America's greater affluence but slower growth rate potentially relates to a greater sense of individuality."

The stress on individualistic values expressed by North Americans shows that "in North America, we've moved away from interdependence," says Stephen Covey, the author of "The Seven Habits of Highly Effective People." Mr. Covey is an American writer and lecturer who also appeared at the seminar.

The message for Asians, he says, is that they "better look out so that the same thing doesn't happen to you." As Asians grow richer, Mr. Covey warns, they risk losing their "fundamental value systems."

As part of the Wirthlin study, the Asian executives were also asked which factors in the business environment are most important to economic success. None of the 17 factors on the list were universally agreed on. Five attributes were rated in the top six by at least four countries: management skill, adoption of new technology, marketing skill, the ability to produce quality products, and strategic planning skills. North American and European executives are now being polled on the same question by Wirthlin. Results are expected by midyear.

The study finds notable differences among values considered important in various Asian countries. It says Japan, Thailand and South Korea place less emphasis on honesty, while Japan, Hong Kong and Singapore place less emphasis on respect for learning than other Asian countries in the survey. Thailand and South Korea place less emphasis on self-discipline.

One topic the study doesn't discuss is whether there could be significant differences of interpretation of values such as "honesty" among countries.

The survey reports that the six Asian countries can be put into groups with broadly similar values. Singapore, Thailand and Hong Kong form one such group, South Korea and Taiwan another. "Japan remains relatively distinct from the others," according to the study. Japanese executives saw harmony as being more important than other Asian executives, while South Korean and Taiwanese executives favored self-reliance and thinking for oneself, Mr. Wirthlin says.

Respect for authority ranked as one of the least important values to the respondents. Mr. Wirthlin notes that the people surveyed are senior corporate executives in positions of authority. He says respect for authority would be higher in the population at large.

Undoing Tradition: As Millions of Chinese Try to Get Rich Quick, Values Get Trampled

Fortune Seekers Are Leaving Homes or Even Spouses; Corruption Is Surging

Selling Blood and Handguns

Kathy Chen

SHENZHEN, CHINA—Like his country, 11-year-old Yang Yungjiang is facing a crisis of values.

He ran away from his village two years ago, winding up in this boom town bordering Hong Kong because he heard "it was fun." Now, he spends days hanging around a video-game arcade, smoking cheap cigarettes and avoiding pimps and prostitutes. At night, he sleeps in abandoned buildings or on the streets. With other children, he steals and sells aluminum siding from construction sites. Once he swiped a bicycle and was caught by police, who beat him.

"I've seen a lot," Yungjiang says, a grin spreading across his broad, freckled face. "My parents told me it was wrong to steal. But I didn't steal anything at home." Now, he says, "I can't figure out if there's good or bad."

In a nominally Communist society built on social controls, such breakdowns ought to be rare. They aren't. As China charges ahead with economic changes, tens of millions of Chinese are on the move, leaving behind roots—and beliefs—in search of opportunity. Faith in the equality of socialism is vanishing. What has replaced it is an obsession with money.

'DECADENT LIFESTYLES'

The result is a fundamental crisis. Families are disintegrating, spawning a selfish "me generation" of youths. Crime and corruption are at record levels. Many voice cynicism and pessimism akin to that which fueled mass protests against the system in 1989.

Premier Li Peng warned against "money worship, ultra-individualism and decadent lifestyles" in a recent report to the National People's Congress. Such problems, he said, are "a matter of life and death for our nation."

China isn't likely to disintegrate into lawless chaos. And certainly many citizens retain traditional values. Still, the current situation poses a monumental challenge to the leadership's efforts to engineer a smooth succession as the health of Deng Xiaoping, China's paramount leader, deteriorates.

Already, signs of a new conservatism are emerging. Beijing has reined in bond and futures markets after speculation caused huge losses. Controls over the media and dissent have been tightened, and several high-profile officials have been nabbed in a crackdown on corruption.

Such conservatism, ironically, may be welcomed by the foreign investors who have helped to drive change in China. They want evidence that China is becoming a civil society. There is too little to be found.

BLOOD MONEY

When it comes to making money, almost anything goes. In the port city of Tianjin, a gang lures children and farmers with job offers, then forces them to sell their blood. In Baigou, a sleepy city two hours' drive from Beijing, a peasant surnamed Su displays handguns for sale—though gun ownership is illegal. As his wife looks on, holding her one-year-old, Mr. Su fires first one gun, then another into the plaster wall of their house.

"The German one is the best," offers Mr. Su's aunt, a plump woman in her 50s, pointing to a Perfecta 8mm model. Then she adds: "Do you want to buy some [pornographic] videotapes?"

"Chasing money has become the goal," says Public Security Vice Minister Bai Jingfu. "For money, people are willing to neglect the good, to neglect social morals."

The erosion of China's values has taken place gradually. Traditional beliefs, such as the Confucian edict to respect elders, were largely destroyed in earlier Communist campaigns, especially the Cultural Revolution, a decade of political turmoil that ended in 1976. But in those days, China was poor, and everyone toiled together under the same harsh conditions, whether producing steel for backyard mills or trooping off to the countryside to learn from the peasants.

FREE-FOR-ALL

This spirit of selflessness has all but disappeared since the advent of economic change under Mr. Deng. It unleashed a free-for-all to get rich, a scramble that has been made all the more urgent by the "end of an era" mood pervading the country now that Mr. Deng's health is failing.

Preoccupation with wealth is threatening the foundation of Chinese society, the family. Most calls to the country's first domestic-violence hot line, set up in October, have been from women whose husbands got rich, then beat them up when they refused to grant a divorce, the official Legal Daily reported.

Photos of blushing brides and white-satin wedding gowns for rent line the walls of the Dongcheng District Marriage Registry in Beijing. But on one recent afternoon, most of the couples waiting in line aren't seeking to marry but to file for divorce.

"It's better to be free," shrugs Xiao Guochang, a 54-year-old businessman who heads four companies, as his soon-to-be ex-wife glares at him. "I'm too busy at work to take care of my family or to try to make things better. My job's more important than my family."

The fraying of family values has hit China's youths hardest. Sociologists say the country's policy of limiting most families to a single child is partly to blame because it causes parents both to spoil children and to put too much pressure on them. Children who in the past had been taught to respect their parents are now "using them as servants. They're not willing to take care of them in their old age," says Wang Xingjuan, president of the Women's Research Institute under the China Academy of Management Science.

Faced with ambiguous messages on morality from society and often unchecked by parents who are too busy at work, more and more youths are turning into delinquents or even hard-core criminals.

Although China's overall crime rate rose a modest 2.7% last year—and crime remains much less of a problem than in the U.S.—major crimes jumped 15.6% to 624,000 cases. Freed from the farm, up to 80 million Chinese peasants are looking for jobs. Some who can't find one turn to crime—sometimes in brutal displays of resentment against the growing gap between rich and poor.

A THUG'S LEGEND

It is almost noon, and a lazy silence has enveloped Longgang, a town populated with migrant workers on the edge of prosperous Shenzhen. Construction-site workers squat by muddy roads wolfing down rice and vegetables. Things weren't always this quiet here. Last year, the 21-year-old son of a peasant and a gang of 100 accomplices were wreaking havoc, robbing businessmen and shooting up karaoke bars that refused to pay protection money. Last summer, police finally shot dead Chen Yungzhong and arrested many of his cohorts.

Most disturbing to sociologists is the cult-like status Mr. Chen attained. After his death, a Hong Kong producer made a film about him, enhancing his legend. "If you were a rich businessman, they'd chop you off at the knees, then they'd take your money," marvels Li Shi, a youth who earns a living transporting passengers on his motorcycle. "Chen was fierce and brave. But he wasn't smart enough, or he wouldn't have gotten caught."

In Beijing, which used to be virtually crime-free, the families of high government officials have been hit. A relative of Vice Premier Zhu Rongji was knifed to death last year after coming across robbers in her home, police say. The son of China Securities Regulatory Commission Vice Chairman Fu Fengxiang was killed late last year after some youths made off with his Nissan car with him in it, Mr. Fu's neighbors and colleagues say.

ADVISING AMERICANS

Even Westerners, who have long been considered off limits, are being targeted. Late last year, a group of robbers attacked Joe Eberling, a consultant to U.S. companies, on a busy Beijing street in broad daylight. One man stabbed him in the back, piercing his spinal sheath, in a failed attempt to steal his briefcase.

"People see an opportunity to get something," laments Mr. Eberling, 31, and they "damn everything else." Since recovering, he has turned the situation to his advantage. "It's still business for me as usual in China," he says. "As a matter of fact, I'm now advising American clients on how to take security measures."

Crime is rising in the business world as well. Ren Jianxin, head of the Supreme People's Court, told the National People's Congress in March that the number of economic-crime cases tried by the courts last year jumped 70% from 1993 to some 31,000 cases. Corruption cases involving more than $1,190, or about 2½ years' income for the average urban Chinese, surged by a similar amount, he said.

For government officials and businesspeople to trade power for money has "become a social practice and has been almost legalized," 12 dissident citizens wrote in a recent letter to the Congress.

SEEKING SOLUTIONS

Some Chinese are searching for moral guidance. With the decline of socialistic beliefs has come a rise in the popularity of both official and underground churches. "China is seeking to engage in spiritual construction, and religion has some good things that can help overcome the current difficulties," says Zhuo Xinping, a researcher at the Chinese Academy of Social Sciences.

The government is trying to instill values with efforts such as Beijing's new campaign to promote patriotism. At the prestigious Beijing No. 4 High School, students participate in flag-raising ceremonies and watch patriotic films, including one commemorating Communist China's 45th anniversary. "We tell them, 'Do what you want, but don't forget your country, your people or your family,'" says school vice president Wang Zhaoji. "For too many students now. . . whatever they want to do, they do."

Many youngsters, like Yungjiang, the Shenzhen street urchin, don't know what is the right thing to do. With his sweat shirt a size too small and bluejeans a size too big, Yungjiang is still very much a kid—and not a bad one at that. He says that since running away, he has sent more than 1,000 yuan ($119) home to his widowed mother, most of it earned by carrying luggage at the railway station.

Without a family or even a government social-service agency to provide for him, Yungjiang is learning to survive in a difficult world. It is a place where his friends, some as young as six or seven, use knives to cut the pockets of migrants sleeping in the railway station to steal their money. It is a world where he is thrown in jail for three months and forced to make cloth flowers because he doesn't have residency papers.

In such unstable surroundings, Yungjiang is sure of only one thing. "I don't want to grow up too fast," he says. "What's the fun when you grow up too fast?"

Japan Discovers Woman Power

Sally Solo

Remember that young woman who slipped into the room, deposited cups of green tea in front of everyone, then quietly backed out? Remember her, because on your next trip to Japan she may be sitting on the other side of the negotiating table. Gently, women are making their way into the *otoko no shakai,* the man's world, of corporate Japan.

For 13 straight years women have entered the Japanese labor market at a faster rate than men. In 1988 they made up more than 40% of the entire labor force. About half of all Japanese women hold jobs. Nor are these just singles waiting for the right man: Almost two-thirds of working women are married. Though they still are most visible as bank tellers and department store clerks, they are starting to appear in more than a token way in the paneled conference rooms where decisions are made.

The number of women with managerial titles increased 50% between 1982 and 1987. And there are many more coming up behind them. For years Japanese companies put new employees on two tracks, regardless of education. One led to management and was largely reserved for men. The other pretty much started and finished with clerical work and tea serving, and guess who ended up there. Now for the first time large numbers of college-educated women are being set on the management track. Since seniority still rules at most big Japanese companies, growing numbers of women managers are virtually guaranteed in the 1990s and beyond.

This is a revolution without marches or manifestoes. There is little confrontation, because of the nature of the change and the nature of those who are changing. For one thing, it is a revolution based on economic necessity, not ideology. For a year now, demand for labor in the booming Japanese economy has outstripped supply. According to Hajimu Hori, a senior official in the economic planning ministry, the shortage runs through the whole economy but is especially acute in the rapidly growing high-tech sector. Says he: "How to train and utilize woman power is one of the biggest issues for companies." Some 95% of Japanese women are high school graduates, and 36% have junior college or four-year college degrees.

Until recently most women did not want careers, and companies generally overlooked the few who did. Says Noriko Nakamura, president of the 300-strong (and growing) Japan Association for Female Executives, or JAFE: "In the past, companies lumped together the 80% of women who wanted to rush out at quitting time and the 20% who wanted to do the same work as men." As a result, she says, they shied away from putting *any* women on the managerial track.

Now personnel managers are realizing that a short interview can help them identify which women want to work like men. The rest will go the clerical route of the office lady, or OL for short. OLs come in a variety of outfits—black and white checkered uniforms at fibermaker Toray, jade green at Sanwa Bank. But most are of the same mind: Work ends at 5 P.M., and life begins at marriage. While men are trained in marketing and operations, OLs are trained in phone manner (soft and high voices preferred) and salutations (a 30-degree forward bow for most people; a 45-degree bow for special guests and executives).

For their part, the new fast-track women are treading softly. Says JAFE's Nakamura: "There are still a lot of conservative men out there. They haven't changed, even though the women have. These women must try to be easy for the men to accept." Nakamura quit a job as a television announcer in 1976 when she started her family. Three years later she was recruited by a group of politicians and businessmen to lead a series of seminars on political and economic issues. The job, which she has continued to do, brought her into contact with hundreds of people, mainly men. The experience made her realize that working women needed a network too. In 1985 she established JAFE, modeled after a similar American organization.

Nakamura's advice to young Japanese women would make Gloria Steinem and other U.S. feminists blanch: First, stick it out at an organization for at least ten years, no matter how routine your work is, because women must prove their loyalty. Second, when asked to serve tea, do it brilliantly, to show you can do anything.

It used to be that a career-minded woman had the choice of going into the government bureaucracy, joining a foreign firm, or establishing a business. Working for a big Japanese company was rarely an option. When Mariko Fujiwara returned from Stanford ten years ago with a degree in anthropology, employment agencies advised her to take a secretarial course. She ignored the advice, and with an act bold by Japanese standards—she presented her résumé—won a job at the Hakuhodo Institute of Life and Living, a research branch of the advertising agency Hakuhodo.

Fujiwara looks back on that period without anger. She points out that Japanese companies tended to hire employees fresh out of college, then train them for a lifetime career with the organization. Women who married and quit after a few years were not good investments. She adds, "We had a very bad track record, and men were not at all convinced by the exceptions."

When the rare woman did slip through, she ran into heavy prejudice. Miwako Doi pounded a lot of pavement ten years ago trying to find a company willing to hire her as an engineer, despite her master's degree from Tokyo University. She finally landed at Toshiba, but getting the job wasn't the only hard part. She recalls, "When I began, people said, 'What's this—a woman here?'" She stuck with it and eventually became a manager.

With companies now eager to hire them, women graduates can be choosy. The most popular employers among the management-minded are those known to treat men and women equally. The top five, according to a recent survey, are IBM Japan, NEC, Fujitsu, Nippon Telegraph & Telephone, and Suntory. By contrast, C. Itoh, the giant trading company, ranked 102. It failed to attract a single 1988 graduate from the prestigious Ochanomizu Women's College. Explains Eiichi Shimakura, who runs employment search efforts at the college: "There are lots of clerical women workers at C. Itoh, and one regular track female employee wouldn't have a chance."

Some women find themselves stuck in the middle between the men who have traditionally taken care of business and the office ladies who have taken care of the men. Yukari Yamaguchi, 25, who works in mergers and acquisitions at Nikko Securities, one of Japan's top four securities firms, feels as if she is balancing on a high wire. "I must be careful toward my supervisors," she says, "and I must be careful toward the assistant ladies." With supervisors, Yamaguchi brims—but does not overwhelm—with confidence. "Probably I will be a director of Nikko," she says casually. With the OLs, however, she is more cautious, to deflect any jealousy they might feel.

For Yamaguchi, nothing seems impossible. But her aspirations are shot full of realism: "Women are vulnerable. They must have qualifications or titles. A Tokyo University degree is very good protection." Now she will add another title. In September she will be Nikko's first woman to attend the Harvard business school. "An MBA," she says, "will also protect me well."

Yamaguchi has had her share of luck. Hideo Karino, the supervisor who supported her application to Harvard, finds nothing odd about encouraging a young woman to excel. Says Karino, who went to Vanderbilt University in Tennessee: "I have been educated in a foreign culture, not only in a business sense." Yamaguchi doesn't feel isolated: "I'm in the second generation. The true pioneers had to fight alone, but since the equal employment opportunity law [passed in 1986], we are hired in groups."

Unlike American women in the 1970s, Japanese women are not flocking to the banner of equal employment. One reason is that they don't see much to envy in the life of Japanese men. The average male white-collar worker regularly works well into the evening. From his office in Tokyo, he commutes 1½ hours to get home. He takes just one week's vacation a year. His wife is respected—no one apologizes for being "just a housewife." Better for her to hold a part-time job, if she works at all, so she can be home to fix dinner for her husband's eventual return in the evening.

A third of working women have settled for temporary jobs. Says Eiko Shinotsuka, an assistant professor of economics at Ochanomizu: "Women don't want to work the same way that men do. They want work that will not interrupt their marriage or raising their children. They can't give half of the 24-hour day to a company, which is what companies demand."

An equal opportunity clause was built into Japan's post–World War II constitution. No legislation backed it up, however, and the concept did not take hold during the country's rebuilding effort. The United Nations Decade of Women, observed from 1975 to 1985, was one impetus for change. Japan participated in a perfunctory way in the early years, sending delegations to various conventions. In 1985 representatives from countries around the world were to sign a treaty pledging elimination of discrimination against women. Politically, Japan had to sign. Practically, Japan couldn't do so without writing some kind of domestic law to back up the pledge. Corporations lobbied vigorously against it, but a statute finally took effect in April 1986, though without provisions for penalties.

It was a breakthrough of sorts. Says Ryoko Akamatsu, then director general of the women and young worker's bureau at the ministry of labor and chief architect of the law: "Companies stopped saying they wouldn't hire women." To implement the law, the ministry distributes a questionnaire, asking, for example, if companies give women the same training as men, or if they hire women older than 33. Answers are purely voluntary. "This is soft guidance," says Mari Watanobe, a planning manager in the women's bureau. "It helps companies establish goals."

Still, without the labor shortage the law might have gone the way of the constitutional provision. Says Akamatsu: "It's working. Of course, we cannot separate effects of the law and of the healthy economic climate. If the economic situation were very bad, the new law wouldn't work as well as it does." After the law's enactment, she was packed off to Uruguay with fanfare as Japan's second female ambassador.

Now some Japanese companies are slowly discovering that women workers can be more than a substitute for men. They can provide a new perspective. Dentsu, Japan's largest advertising firm, formed a mostly women subsidiary in 1984 with a mandate to do a better job of selling to female shoppers. Consider: Young OLs, whose income is 100% disposable because they live at home and pay no rent, are Japan's most conspicuous consumers. The post-school, premarriage set does so much shopping and traveling that no fewer than ten magazines aimed at this crowd began publication last year. After women marry, their spending ways continue since Japanese men hand over their entire salaries to their wives, who run the family budget. Says Naoe Wakita, president of the subsidiary: "To understand what the wife wants is to increase sales. How can a man know what she wants?"

An influx of working women may even help soften the blue-suited Japanese worker-bee stereotype. Japanese managers at every level cringe at the phrase "economic animal," a cliché used by critics to describe them. "We have no face, that's the problem," says an insurance company executive, in a heated discussion of what's wrong with Japan's international relations. Concurs Mariko Sugahara Bando, a counselor at the Prime Minister's office and author of books about women and the elderly: "Japanese businessmen are faces without names. They're organization men. Women tend to be more human. And more of them working can create a new image for Japan."

As they hire more women managers, Japanese companies face some of the same issues their counterparts confront in the West. Seibu Department Store, which employs 20,000 women, holds jobs open for mothers who take off a few years to raise children. The company also runs a small nursery for those who continue to work. Last November IBM Japan inaugurated a babysitter hotline for working mothers who need child care in an emergency situation. The service was modeled after one the company began in New York City. Toshiba is experimenting with flextime in its offices. The electronics maker has even organized seminars where women have told male colleagues to stop holding back their thoughts and start talking straight to them.

Japanese businessmen aren't about to throw their last geisha party, or stop making deals over a dozen bottles of cold beer and hot sake. But there could be less of that and more predusk negotiations as more women enter the work force. Wakita, for example, wants to get out of the office and back to her family in the evening. Says she: "Women do all their business in the daytime. It is said that Japanese businessmen have two tongues—one for the office and one for the pub afterward. Not women, because they don't have the time. They say what they mean at the office, and at night they go home." If Japanese business truly wants to present a more human face, that could be the most important trend yet.

Reluctant Feminists: Women's Movement in Corporate Japan Isn't Moving Very Fast

Government Pushes Hiring, But Female Professionals, Firms Stay Uncommitted

Dorms, Curfews and Uniforms

Yumiko Ono

TOKYO—Yuka Hashimoto was hired from college two years ago by Fuji Bank Ltd. and was assured she could rise as high in management as her talents allowed. She was assigned to the bond trading desk.

Now, clad in a bright pink suit, she sometimes finds herself serving tea to office guests. Her male colleagues never do.

Though she privately complains that the task can interfere with her work, the 24-year-old Ms. Hashimoto gasps at any suggestion that she refuse the chore as sexist. "I'm not saying I won't serve tea because I'm a career-track" employee, she says.

Like Ms. Hashimoto, many Japanese women are reluctant feminists. They generally accept the sex-biased slights common in Japanese companies. And when asked to choose between career and marriage, professional women more often choose to stay home. The women's movement here is moving nowhere fast.

"In America, women started a movement because they looked at the situation as a problem," says Eiko Shinotsuka, associate professor of home economics at Ochanomizu University, who follows women's labor issues. But in Japan, she says, "many women aren't particularly dissatisfied with the situation they're in."

POLL RESULTS

In a recent survey by Philip Morris K.K., the Japanese subsidiary of U.S.-based Philip Morris Cos., 55% of 3,000 Japanese women polled said they weren't being treated equally with men at work, and less than a third of them said they expected women's lives to improve over the next two decades. Yet, only 26% of the women said they felt a need for a strong and organized women's movement. In a similar survey of

---

"Reluctant Feminists: Women's Movement in Corporate Japan Isn't Moving Very Fast" by Yumiko Ono, *The Wall Street Journal*, June 6, 1991, p. B1. Reprinted by Permission.

American women, a much smaller 29% believed they were treated unfairly at work, most were optimistic about the future for women, and 37% said a women's movement was heeded.

Japanese companies dramatically increased their hiring of college-educated women in professional jobs after Japan's Diet, or parliament, passed a law barring sex discrimination in the workplace in 1986. The government's aims were to alleviate a growing labor shortage and bolster Japan's image abroad—not to meet demands from Japanese women.

Unlike in the U.S., where women have aggressively fought for equality, women here have hardly raised a whimper. Much to the government's dismay, many professional women are indifferent toward a long-term career.

EARLY BOW-OUTS

Women make up 40% of Japan's work force, including part-timers, but only 1% of them hold managerial positions. And labor specialists estimate that between 25% and 50% of the women who began corporate careers here four years ago have already quit their jobs. According to a 1989 survey by Labor Administration Inc., a government-affiliated research concern, the attrition rate for professional men was just 11% four years after the start of their careers. The same survey found the attrition rate for all female college graduates at Japanese companies, including those in traditional clerical jobs, was 45%.

"I intended to stop working when I had my child," says 28-year-old Sayuki Kanda, who left her Tokyo-based textile company last year after working as a public relations officer for five years. Although she enjoyed the responsibility, Ms. Kanda says she can't be persuaded to return to the corporate ladder. "In the end, large companies are a male-oriented society. It's not a place for women to work for life." After having three children, Ms. Kanda plans to do some part-time work.

But many companies realize that with the increasing labor shortage, somehow they'll have to think of a way to attract more women and encourage them to stay. Sumitomo Bank is hiring 250 women out of college this spring, out of 864 new hires, on a "new career track." Asahi Breweries recently hired 110 women out of its 900 new marketers and has started sending them to sell Asahi products to liquor stores—long considered a man's domain.

GREENER PASTURES

Not all of the women who abandon corporate careers return to hearth and home. Some join small companies or foreign firms that have an image of being more evenhanded. Others enroll in U.S. graduate schools or start their own businesses.

Those who stay confront a business world still sharply divided by sex. The middle-aged men who run Japanese companies expect professional women to tackle work just like men, in an unflagging manner described as "bari-bari"—literally, "a crunching sound." And yet they routinely insist on rules for women that they wouldn't dream of imposing on men. (The 1986 law barring sex discrimination established no penalties for violations.) Some require career women in their mid-20s to wear company uniforms, live in company dormitories and observe a 10 P.M. curfew, and get their parents' consent before taking assignments abroad.

A few stodgy banks have a "custom" for a woman—professional or clerical—to quit if she marries someone within the company. The reasoning for this, the banks say, is that if a husband is transferred, as is common every few years, it would be too difficult to also transfer the wife.

Sumitomo Bank insists that women in professional jobs initially wear the same navy blue corporate uniform worn by its secretaries, known as "office ladies" or "OLs." It says this makes less blatant the labelling of career and non-career women, which might upset the OLs.

No one complains. Kazumi Tamai, who was hired for Sumitomo's corporate research department four years ago, says she accepted the uniform because she didn't want customers to ask her why she was the only woman wearing regular clothes. "It's not something to raise your voice about," she says. After two years, professional women may wear their own clothes.

Many confess they aren't as committed as their male colleagues to the life of a careerist in a Japanese company, which typically requires late hours, after-work drinking sessions with colleagues and a pledge of allegiance to the company until retirement. By comparison, the image of a housewife, who is free to go shopping, play tennis and perhaps hold a side job or two, is more attractive to many women. "Japanese men are such workaholics," says Ochanomizu's Ms. Shinotsuka. "The women have doubts about having to work like the men."

They also seem to share Japanese society's assumptions that men and women have different roles. Most agree that when a woman marries, taking care of her husband and children should be her priority.

For now, Ms. Tamai is throwing herself into her career. She eats lunch with the men's group and drinks with them after work. She says her dream is to continue the life of a "salaryman."

A CAREER FOR A HUSBAND

But when she marries, as she expects to do, she says she will give up her career if her husband asks. "It depends on my husband," she says. "In reality, your time will be restricted. It's going to be difficult to keep working when you're raising a child." For most women, she adds, "work isn't everything. It's just one tool to improve yourself."

Given such attitudes, companies are reluctant to invest too heavily in the careers of their women professionals. With the extensive training Japanese companies provide employees, it doesn't pay unless they work for at least 10 years, says Akira Kurose, a personnel manager at Sumitomo Bank. Some women complain that companies are hesitant to include women in their company sponsorship programs to study in foreign universities.

Keiichi Ando, Ms. Tamai's 39-year-old boss and the department's assistant general manager, is skeptical about women employees. Many women "think they can quit if things get too tough," he says. "You wonder if they're seriously trying to commit themselves. The whole society is looking at them like that." He adds that he hopes Ms. Tamai keeps working, but casually asks her occasionally if she has plans to get married soon. For now, says Mr. Ando confidently, she has none.

Such diminished expectations of employers create a major obstacle for women pursuing a career. Tomoko Ueguri, a 26-year-old former securities saleswoman, says she toiled from 7:30 A.M. till 9 at night for four years, occasionally outselling some of her male colleagues. But she resigned last year after hearing her boss imply in the course of conversation that he assumed she would eventually marry and quit. He wasn't keen on giving a woman too much responsibility, either. "I asked myself if it was worth it for me to keep working under this system," says Ms. Ueguri. "The answer was no." Now she's a saleswoman for a small company that promotes self-motivation seminars.

The government is still trying to encourage women to climb the corporate ladder. It's advising companies to hire more women, and even putting out videos for bosses on effective uses of female employees. One episode shows young women complaining at a bar about bosses who are not motivated, too friendly, or too boring to go drinking with after work.

The labor ministry has also suggested that men help out more with the housework. Another survey found last year that husbands did an average of eight minutes of housework a day, compared with well over an hour for women. The government has passed a bill allowing workers to take a year of maternity leave, without pay, but analysts are skeptical that many women will immediately take advantage of the leave.

NO DREAMLAND

There's a long way to go, says Yoshiko Ando, an officer at the women's bureau of the labor ministry. Although a path has been cleared for women, she says, "the career-track doesn't look like it's full of dreams."

Some pioneering professional women complain about the motivation of those following behind them. "They think that if they happen to be working in a nice environment, they may consider staying," says 54-year-old Naoe Wakita, who joined Dentsu Inc., the world's largest ad agency, more than 30 years ago. She is now president of Dentsu EYE Inc., a subsidiary that's an all-women agency. She recalls that earlier in her career she risked losing her position when she left to have a child. "My desk was gone" when she returned after having her second child, she says. "So I dragged in a desk that was left out in the hall and wiped it clean."

Ms. Wakita represents a minority of Japanese women who are voting in growing numbers, increasing their political clout and spending more on themselves. For them, the career track is a big step from the traditional woman's role, which is to assist men.

For a while, at least, women on the career track are going to remain an oddity. When Ms. Ueguri, who now lugs around a briefcase full of brochures for time management seminars, goes home to the rice-growing town of Niigata in northern Japan, her school friends—most of them married—are curious to know why she's still working. Says Ms. Ueguri, "They call me bari-bari."

The Final Stretch

Robert Fulford

One morning Mel Stein woke up to a costly ordeal. He was in a trade squabble with
Uncle Sam that could turn his stretch-limo business to scrap.

The bad news came to Melvyn Stein and his company, AHA Manufacturing, early on
July 24. One minute it was an ordinary Monday morning at the plant in Brampton,
Ont., and the next minute the fax machine was pumping out the most astonishing messages. They were all from Washington law firms with impressive letterheads, and they all
said much the same thing: sorry about your problem, but we'd like the honor of representing you. Mel Stein, who at first didn't know he had a problem, counted five of these
solicitations, then 10, eventually more than 20. By that time he understood that something he had been hearing about as a vague possibility for months was actually happening to him. One of his U.S. competitors in the business of building stretch limousines,
Southampton Coachworks of Long Island, NY, had accused him of dumping under-
priced limos on the United States market. Stein had to defend himself or accept a duty
that would probably put him out of business.

It was an odd way to receive this information: it was like having the famous criminal lawyer Eddie Greenspan call to inform you of a crime you didn't know had been
committed and then tell you that he's standing by to act as your counsel. Stein at first
thought the lawyers were making a fuss over a little matter that surely would be settled
in a hurry. "I had a clear conscience," he said later, "and I assumed that when it was
known that we'd done nothing wrong, it would be all over. I thought it was like getting
a ticket for parking at Portage and Main when you haven't been to Winnipeg—you settle
it in a minute. But it's turned out to be a much more onerous thing than I imagined."

In fact, a vast machine had been set in motion, and those ambulance-chasing
lawyers were on to a good thing. As Stein talked to Canadian government officials and
interviewed five Washington lawyers who visited Toronto to seek his business in person,
he discovered that before this commercial nightmare is over, his legal bills may well go to
U.S. $200,000. For that price, he's getting a lesson in the politics of international com-
merce and a demonstration of how much tension over trade still exists in the first year of
the Free Trade Agreement, the treaty that many people imagined would ease just this sort
of conflict.

The paper filed in Washington was headed "Petition for the Imposition of Antidumping and Countervailing Duties," and was addressed to the U.S. Department of
Commerce and the U.S. International Trade Commission. It made two charges against
Stein. First, he was selling limos at a fifth or more below their fair market value, at a great
loss to his company, in order to enlarge his share of the market—notice, the paper said,

that AHA lost $3 million in 1988. That called for an antidumping duty. Second, he was receiving Canadian government subsidies, which enabled him to compete unfairly. Therefore, he should pay a tariff equal to the worth, per limo, of the subsidies.

The second charge was easier to deal with than the first, and the Canadian Embassy in Washington dealt with it immediately in a diplomatic note that said AHA had received no significant government help. In fact, the closest it had come to a subsidy was when it received $4.2 million as a subcontractor carrying out research projects under the controversial and now abandoned Scientific Research Tax Credit program in the mid-1980s. That wasn't a countervailable subsidy and wasn't mentioned in the petition filed by Southampton.

But the petition listed all the government help that *might* be available to Stein under certain circumstances—for instance, it said, he could get regional economic incentive grants, though how this would be done by a plant in southern Ontario wasn't specified. It even suggested that AHA benefits from the Quebec government's support of its electric system. "As a result of the ability to receive subsidized power from Hydro-Québec, Ontario Hydro is able to lower its own rates . . . the subsidized structure of the Canadian electric power industry confers a counteravailable benefit on the production of limousines."

That passage, presumably, was to be read quickly, without much thought—thinking about it could drive you crazy. (Southampton Coachworks is in New York state, which also buys power from Hydro-Québec, which is subsidized, and therefore. . . .) The purpose wasn't to draw up a serious bill of complaints; the idea was to make as many accusations as possible and shake the cages of those Americans who believe that foreign governments routinely subsidize their exports as part of a vicious plan to undercut U.S. business.

In a small way, it worked. In August, the Long Island edition of the New York *Daily News* carried a report headed "Limo maker: 'Road hog'—Canadian foe called unfair." It quoted John Gore, the head of Southampton. "These guys," he said, meaning AHA, "are selling cars for less than we can build them." Gore said—and this was almost the only point in the dispute where a couple of specific figures emerged—that AHA limos were going for US$35,000 wholesale while Gore's were selling for $50,000 retail. Later, in an interview with *Vista,* Gore said he was delighted with the early progress of his action. "I think it's going great," he said. "I think they're going to find dumping and I think they're going to put a duty on those cars."

By the time the story in the *Daily News* appeared, Mel Stein's education was well under way. He had discovered, for instance, that while *he* needed an expensive law firm, Gore didn't—the U.S. Department of Commerce drew up the brief that Gore and other American limo-builders signed. Stein had also discovered the curious fact that he would not be allowed to read all the details of the case against him. In the copy Stein received, many business statistics were blanked out, following standard practice. Stein learned that the U.S. International Trade Commission would get a copy with the numbers in, *and so would Stein's lawyers*—but they would be sworn not to tell him what the numbers were.

Stein was now involved in a Byzantine world of which most executives remain happily ignorant. It's a lawyer-infested world, where nationalism and political power play on economics, and where selling at the lowest possible price may be seen as something like a crime. Stein was informed that the government of Canada—while it could speak clearly on the subsidy question—really had nothing to say about whether Stein was dumping. He had to defend himself. The Free Trade Agreement, of course, has eliminated neither countervailing duties nor antidumping laws.

Stein had to think about the meaning of what trade lawyers call LTFV (less than fair value) and about dumping as an idea. Antidumping laws say that under-selling your competitors, while commendable within any given country, becomes a matter for suspicion if the products cross a border—even a border as open as the U.S.-Canada is to auto products, and even if (as is the case with AHA) the products are 60 or 70 percent American in origin anyway.

Most economists regard antidumping regulations as obsolete and counterproductive, but they exist. Is there evidence that Stein violated them—and, if not, why do the Americans claim he did? To answer those questions, and because I've always wondered where limos come from, I went to Stein's plant on Chelsea Lane in Brampton. Naturally, I went by limo.

A white stretch limo, looking as if it could comfortably sleep four large adults, gently moored in my driveway one summer afternoon. It was an AHA product, as I'd determined before ordering it from a livery in Mississauga, Ont., so I shared the experience of those who ultimately benefit from Mel Stein's work: plenty of leg room, a smooth ride, and envious glances from the neighbors.

Stein's customers aren't rich people, for the most part, but people like the man who was driving me—Bernard Drag of Stars' Limousines Inc. It's true that Eddie Murphy has his own AHA limo, a Japanese businessman recently took one home to Tokyo, and two just went into service at palaces in the United Arab Emirates. These are exceptions, though. The real market is the livery business, which has expanded enormously in the 1980s—there are now about 7,000 livery operators in the U.S., where in 1980 there were about 1,000; in Canada, the total remains in the low hundreds, but the increase has been proportionately as great.

The typical livery operator is a man who summons up his courage, puts a second mortgage on his house, buys a limo, and thereby earns the right to get up at five o'clock in the morning to drive a stockbroker to the airport. When his business develops he may own four cars, which is average. Soon he'll discover that many others have had the same bright idea—if he doesn't see them on the road or at the garage he'll read about them in *Limousine & Chauffeur,* a trade magazine in which he can also read ads for handcrafted champagne buckets and news about crack-downs on illegal limos at the airports.

As anyone who walked the streets could tell, the livery business prospered through most of the 1980s. In New York particularly, there were stockbrokers and lawyers who never went anywhere except in a limo. They were imitated across the continent; it was the acceptance of the stretch limo as routine in certain business circles that enriched the livery companies. When that happened, AHA Manufacturing, which Mel Stein took over in 1975 from its founder, Andy Hotton (AHA: Andy Hotton Associates), also prospered. A Toronto chartered accountant who got into the auto-parts business in the 1960s, Stein recognized early that limousines were a promising niche.

At his plant on Chelsea Lane—which is, of course, not a lane at all but part of an industrial park—Stein told me a little about the stretch-limo business. Off and on, over the decades, the big car companies have produced their own limos. But the market—in a good year, around 7,000 limos—isn't really large enough for the major automakers. At the moment, limo-building is in the hands of half a dozen companies like AHA, which sell 400 or 500 limos each, and many smaller companies, some of which—"Tony-and-Joe shops," Stein calls them—produce no more than three or four a year, largely by hand.

To make a stretch limo, you buy, fresh from the plant, a good car—anything from a Cadillac to a Honda Accord. You cut it right down the middle, pull the two chunks of it apart, and in between them put 1.5 meters (5 feet) or so of floor, walls, windows, bracing, rug, seats, and so on. You install a bar, a TV, a phone, of course. You paint the whole thing and put it on sale.

People have been doing it like that for at least half a century, but when Stein took over AHA he decided to refine the process—and perhaps that's what led eventually to his trade-law troubles. He set out to bring the style of a big-car company to limo-building and limo-marketing. AHA developed a way to adapt one Lincoln after another on a version of the assembly line. Stein's people discovered, for instance, that by standardizing the wood panels they could eliminate the work of a skilled cabinetmaker and bring down the cost of interior woodwork from $3,000 to $200. This approach, with each worker assigned to learn limited tasks extremely well, required that the plant run all the time. So Stein set up—just like GM—a system of dealers who would accept a stated number of cars a year, would handle only AHA, and would provide service.

All this worked beautifully, until the crash of 1987. Then limos, like many luxuries, quickly grew less popular. Many Wall Street firms cut off their limo accounts entirely. "Week by week," Stein said recently, "you could see the limo sales diminishing, in a ripple effect that moved outward from New York City." That was one factor that made 1988 a bad year for AHA. Another was the rise in the value of the Canadian dollar, which Stein, like most manufacturers, regards as calamitous. And that same year the division of AHA that makes ambulances lost a major contract with the Ontario Ministry of Health. The loss that Stein's U.S. competitor regards as part of a long-term plan for market dominance was, in Stein's recounting, both unintentional and unwelcome.

But 1989 was coming along well—limo sales in the U.S. were up and the ambulance business had turned around. There really wasn't a great deal to worry about, until the day the lawyers' faxes came in. Since then, after many conferences, much worrying, and much pondering of arcane trade laws, Stein remains confident he'll win his case—but at a high cost in money and time.

Recently he sat in his boardroom, looking at detailed legal papers that described issues and regulations he had barely heard about just a few weeks before. He had the original 145-page complaint, he had a 153-page transcript of the first, exploratory conference in Washington and he had another 100 pages of the first submission his lawyers had filed on his behalf. He looked around at the paper, he described legal wrangling that will likely last into the spring of 1990, and he summed up what he saw as the essence of the case. "We have a competitor in the United States," he said, "who has managed to crank up his government to go against a major competitor." For the moment at least, Mel Stein of Brampton, Ont., was in a battle with the U.S. government.

"I'm feeling a little battered by the process," he said as he showed me out to my limo. "But I'm constantly being reminded by the lawyers that they told me, all along, how hard it was going to be." I mentioned to him that I'd been telling his story to several of my friends and that every one of them had found it absolutely fascinating. "I'm glad they're enjoying it," he said.

Europe's Tough New Managers

Paul Hofheinz

Driven by stiffer competition, a fresh generation is taking charge. They are as aggressive as the Americans, but with a special European style.

Marco Tronchetti Provera got his job the old-fashioned way. At 28, he married into the Pirelli family, one of Italy's richest. A decade later he joined the family business, which is Europe's second-largest tiremaker, and rose quickly, leaping over several more experienced managers to become managing director in February 1992. But don't be fooled. In 18 months on the job, Tronchetti, now 45, has shown that he is more than just a good-looking son-in-law.

When he took over, Pirelli was on the brink of bankruptcy. A late 1980s acquisition binge had left it with debt more than 1½ times its equity. Tronchetti began a series of moves that would have been unthinkable in Europe a few years ago. He closed 12 plants, sold a huge division, fired 170 senior managers, moved the company's headquarters from Milan's plush Piazzale Cadorna to a modest building on the corner of a 74,000-acre factory site outside town, and hired actress Sharon Stone to lead a European image campaign. Almost as an encore, he and the chairman's daughter separated.

Pirelli is still losing money, but a lot less than before. Last year losses were $85 million, down from $353 million the previous year. Many European brokers have switched Pirelli stock to their buy lists, and the company seems poised to flourish. Says Tronchetti: "The power of Japan cannot be fought by doing business in Europe as usual. We have to fight as if we were starting *from* scratch."

Tronchetti is just one of a new generation of managers taking charge in Europe. Unlike their predecessors, who often managed in an easygoing, collegial style, they are proving to be every bit as aggressive and innovative as their American counterparts. Boards, which rarely challenged CEOs on anything, seem to be starting to stir too.

The result is a startling change in European business culture. At Daimler-Benz, Chairman Edzard Reuter, 65, spent millions on an art collection for the company and on some dubious acquisitions. But with profits sliding to nearly zero, he has come under strong pressure from shareholders and an increasingly unruly board. Helmut Werner, 56, was brought in from Daimler's profitable truck business to revamp the anemic Mercedes car division, pushing aside Reuter's handpicked deputy, Werner Neifer. A short time later Neifer retired. If Werner succeeds in turning around Mercedes, he may inherit the top job some time before Reuter's scheduled retirement in December 1995.

The changing of the guard cuts all across European industry. At BMW, business statesman and visionary Eberhard von Kuenheim, 65, is retiring, to be replaced by Bernd Pischetsrieder, 45, a hands-on production man. At Robert Bosch, the German electronics firm, Friedrich Schiefer, 54, a McKinsey veteran who has headed Bosch's North American operations for nearly two years, is being brought back to Stuttgart to help the private company push through change more quickly.

In the past 24 months in France, boardroom coups have replaced the CEOs of retailer Carrefour, Thomson Consumer Electronics, and the Paribas financial group. More may follow as the new conservative French government carries out its plan to privatize 21 companies, including Bull, the money-losing computer maker. Says Michel de Rosen, an ambitious executive at Rhône-Poulenc, the soon-to-be-privatized chemicals giant: "In the past, an advanced degree from the right school was enough to get you the top job. Now performance counts for much more."

Global competition lies behind all of this change. Between 1983 and 1992, Europe's share of world markets dropped 14.4%, to 13.9%, while Asia's fast-growing nations—not even counting Japan—have seen their share rise from 4.6% to 8.1%, according to the International Monetary Fund. Even worse, Europe has failed at creating strong companies in the high-tech industries that will dominate the next century. Partly due to a lack of aggressive investment capital and partly due to a hidebound corporate structure that has isolated management from market pressures, many European companies have seen a steady erosion of both market share and profits as costs rose out of control. Warns Pirelli's Tronchetti: "We have to go from being a tanker to a torpedo. Our way of life is at stake."

Any European revolution has to start with an attack on production costs. Operating in the most generous of social welfare systems, and paying the world's highest wages, European companies have trouble offering goods at globally competitive prices. In the past they could count on superior quality to make up for high prices, but Asian manufacturers have raised the quality of their own products enough to dilute that advantage.

The New European management style contains elements of reengineering, total quality management, and other trends popular in the U.S., but it also has its own flavor. It could be called the supply-side revolution, because a big part of it is aimed at pressuring suppliers to raise productivity and reduce their own costs.

ABB's Percy Barnevik has been a master of the technique, but its real father may be the contentious José Ignacio "Inaki" López de Arriortúa, 52. López became a managerial legend when, as purchasing chief at General Motors, he cut $2 billion out of the U.S. automaker's expenses, mainly by badgering parts makers to cut prices or risk losing GM's business. But the accusation by GM that López pilfered secret documents before defecting to Volkswagen last winter—which López denies—has badly tarnished his reputation. López's usefulness to VW—he has already achieved big productivity gains—may be in jeopardy.

And López has detractors outside of GM. Because their own costs are so high, many German suppliers claim VW is asking too much of them. Martin Herzog, secretary of the powerful Association of the German Motor Industry, blasts López for "ruining [the parts industry] with his rude supply policy," while Günter Mordhorst, CEO of Varta, a $1.4-billion-a-year battery maker, accuses López of "mass murder."

France's Valeo (1992 sales: $3.8 billion) is one European parts maker that can compete. CEO Noël Goutard, 61, has changed almost everything. A new budget is now made up every six months instead of once a year so the company can shift or readjust its strategy more quickly. Goutard put workers into teams responsible for organizing their own activities. Each team meets for five minutes or so every morning and for an hour once a week to talk about problems and ways to improve. Every worker is expected to make ten suggestions for improvements a year, and Goutard insists that all suggestions be considered within ten days. Says he: "We couldn't just copy the Japanese. We had to develop our own management system."

Goutard says workers have accepted the changes enthusiastically: "People like to work for a company that is prepared to confront market conditions." Last year, despite major layoffs, Valeo hired 800 graduate engineers. As Goutard notes, "We're moving out of unskilled labor and into skills." By the end of next year, he wants half the staff of the purchasing department to be trained engineers.

Now the results are apparent. Set foot inside Valeo's headquarters on Paris's quiet Rue Bayen and ask anybody how the company managed to increase profits by 26% last year in the ferociously competitive parts market. "Quality, service, price," comes the answer. Goutard has so effectively conveyed these buzzwords from the top to the bottom of his organization that even the farthest-flung outer-office secretary sounds like Peter Drucker.

Valeo has also laid off nearly 9,000 workers and moved some production overseas, but Goutard says that Europe still has strengths as a manufacturing base. He insists that he has acquired factories in Korea, Brazil, Mexico, and Turkey not just to cut costs but also to get a better foothold in those fast-growing markets. Still, he wants to keep some production at home to stay close to the European market. Speaking of Europe, he notes, "I've never seen changes take place without strong incentive. The incentives are here now: erratic markets, Japanese competition, intense job pressure. They are forcing change."

Where did Goutard learn so much about management? "Listening to customers," he says. "They can teach you everything you need to know." Just how good is Valeo? Last year, when he was still at GM, Inaki López gave Valeo an award for delivering the best value and service.

Barnevik, 52, the rangy Swede with a Stanford MBA, has forged a competitive powerhouse out of ABB by taking the concept of leanness to extremes. He turned ABB into 5,000 profit centers, each with its own balance sheet, then shrank headquarters drastically. His now famous cut-then-cut-again style reduced his Zurich corporate staff from 4,000 to 200. "We dislike headquarters," he says. "They cost a lot of money, and they disturb the people who are doing the real business." His formula? Cut the staff to 10% of its original size, let it run for a couple of years, then go back and cut it again by farming out every administrative chore that you can get done for less money outside.

As a result, Barnevik has turned two sleepy European engineering companies into a highly competitive machine (1992 sales: $29.6 billion). In a recession year, profits slipped just 4%, to $1.1 billion. He has made few friends along the way, though, except among shareholders. Europeans marvel at his achievement but grumble that the man is a slave driver who has terrified his staff.

Barnevik has also embraced supply-side management. Many supplies for ABB's 5,000 business units worldwide are purchased by a single center in Mannheim, Germany, run by two Swedes, Sune Karlsson and Roland Andersson. At every other board meeting one of them reports on the latest savings from working more closely with suppliers. Karlsson and Andersson visit suppliers not only to insist on lower costs but also to show managers how to attain them. "It's a win-win situation," says Karlsson. "We're helping them lower ABB's costs, and we're also helping them improve their competitiveness."

ABB has also begun urging suppliers to help with R&D. Instead of giving a supplier a new design, the company asks it to create its own design within certain parameters—at lower cost. Andersson says that one Japanese supplier, which he won't name, was asked to take on such a project. The result was a new part 30% cheaper than the earlier version. Says he: "Our first reaction was to get angry and say, 'Why didn't you do this before?' They said, 'Because you didn't ask.' "

Not everyone does things so radically. In fact, Nestlé CEO Helmut Maucher, 65, suggests that friendliness is as effective a management technique as Barnevik's neutron bomb tactics. His philosophy: "If you do things quietly, step by step, you avoid causing friction. But you can look back over five years and see that radical change was accomplished."

In his nearly 12 years as CEO, Maucher has quietly expanded his company, based in Vevey, Switzerland, through a series of shrewd and well-managed acquisitions. Nestlé's sales have doubled, from $17 billion to $38 billion, and Maucher vows that they will double again by the end of the century through forceful expansion in Third World markets. Says he: "Only 25% of our products are sold in the developing world, where 80% of the population lives. I see growth possibilities everywhere."

While Maucher plans expansion, he has handed over daily management of the world's third-largest food company (according to the 1993 FORTUNE Global 500) to Ramón Masip, 52, a suave, urbane Spaniard who embodies the new type of harddriving Euromanager. Over lunch on the sixth floor of Nestlé's stylish offices overlooking Lake Geneva, Masip is a picture of Iberian courtesy and charm. He chats amiably about his rise from a Nestlé market researcher to chief operating officer. But when talk turns to the difficulty of running one of the most truly global corporations, his eyes narrow slightly and this gregarious manager briefly flashes the sharp teeth behind that warm smile. Lest his visitor underestimate him, Masip calmly ticks off a list of factories he has closed—including several back home in Spain, where the unemployment rate exceeds 21%. Says he: "Sometimes you have to cut off a finger to save an arm."

Europe still has a long way to go in overcoming the competitive drag of its too generous social welfare system and its laid-back approach to management. But if the trend toward a new management style continues and even picks up, Europe could become a paradigm of how to manage in the new global economy.

The Old World is capable of producing the archetypal manager for the 21st century. More than many Americans or Japanese, Europeans are often very comfortable in international situations. The better-run companies—like Nestlé—have corporate boards that closely resemble the U.N. Security Council. Says Paul Strebel, a professor at the International Institute for Management Development in Switzerland: "Our cultural diversity is a huge asset." Adds Roland Berger, head of Germany's Roland Berger & Partner consulting firm: "Europeans are better equipped for globalization."

The question is how far European society will let managers take their tough new approach. With workers and managers long accustomed to virtual lifetime employment guarantees, Europe has watched its structural unemployment rise to 10.5%—and it won't go down soon. Barnevik estimates that as few as one-third of the major companies in Europe are prepared to survive under increasing global competitive pressure. Says he: "We face productivity challenges that were undreamed of in the 1970s."

The risk over the long term is that rising unemployment may bring back overregulation and protectionism rather than force the loosening of these stifling restrictions. As Maucher puts it, "The question is whether Europe is politically able to be competitive."

The time when European management methods are taught at Harvard is still a way off. But make no mistake: At this moment, European managers are gearing for the competitive challenges of the 21st century. And they are doing it fast.

German View: 'You Americans Work Too Hard—and for What?'

Daniel Benjamin and Tony Horwitz

Angie Clark and Andreas Drauschke work comparable jobs for comparable pay at department stores in Berlin and suburban Washington, D.C. But there is no comparison when it comes to the hours they put in.

Mr. Drauschke's job calls for a 37-hour week with six weeks' annual leave. His store closes for the weekend at 2 P.M. on Saturday and stays open one evening each week—a new service in Germany that Mr. Drauschke detests. "I can't understand that people go shopping at night in America," says the 29-year-old, who supervises the auto, motorcycle and bicycle division at Karstadt, Germany's largest department-store chain. "Logically speaking, why should someone need to buy a bicycle at 8:30 P.M.?"

Mrs. Clark works at least 44 hours a week, including evening shifts and frequent Saturdays and Sundays. She often brings paperwork home with her, spends her days off scouting the competition and never takes more than a week off at a time. "If I took any more, I'd feel like I was losing control," says the senior merchandising manager at J.C. Penney in Springfield, Va.

The 50-year-old Mrs. Clark was born in Germany but feels like an alien when she visits her native land. "Germans put leisure first and work second," she says. "In America it's the other way around."

While Americans often marvel at German industriousness, a comparison of actual workloads explodes such national stereotypes. In manufacturing, for instance, the weekly U.S. average is 37.7 hours and rising; in Germany it is 30 hours and has fallen steadily over recent decades. All German workers are guaranteed by law a minimum of five weeks' annual holiday.

"German View: 'You Americans Work Too Hard—and for What?' " by Daniel Benjamin and Tony Horneitz, *The Wall Street Journal*, July 14, 1994, p. B1. Reprinted by permission.

A day spent at a German and an American department store also shows a wide gulf in the two countries' work ethic, at least as measured by attitudes toward time. The Germans fiercely resist any incursions on their leisure hours while many J.C. Penney employees work second jobs and rack up 60 hours a week.

But long and irregular hours come at a price. Staff turnover at the German store is negligible; at J.C. Penney it is 40% a year. Germans serve apprenticeships of two to three years and know their wares inside out. Workers at J.C. Penney receive training of two to three days. And it is economic necessity, more than any devotion to work for its own sake, that appears to motivate most of the American employees.

"First it's need and then it's greed," says Sylvia Johnson, who sells full time at J.C. Penney and works another 15 to 20 hours a week doing data entry at a computer firm. The two jobs helped her put one child through medical school and another through college. Now 51, Mrs. Johnson says she doesn't need to work so hard—but still does.

"My husband and I have a comfortable home and three cars," she says. "But I guess you always feel like you want something more as a reward for all the hard work you've done."

Mr. Drauschke, the German supervisor, has a much different view: Work hard when you're on the job and get out as fast as you can. A passionate gardener with a wife and young child, he comes in 20 minutes earlier than the rest of his staff but otherwise has no interest in working beyond the 37 hours his contract mandates, even if it means more money. "Free time can't be paid for," he says.

The desire to keep hours short is an obsession in Germany—and a constant mission of its powerful unions. When Germany introduced Thursday night shopping in 1989, retail workers went on strike. And Mr. Drauschke finds it hard to staff the extra two hours on Thursday evening, even though the late shift is rewarded with an hour less overall on the job. "My wife is opposed to my coming home late," one worker tells him when asked if he will work until 8:30 on a coming Thursday.

Mr. Drauschke, like other Germans, also finds the American habit of taking a second job inconceivable. "I already get home at 7. When should I work?" he asks. As for vacations, it is illegal—yes, illegal—for Germans to work at other jobs during holidays, a time that "is strictly for recovering," Mr. Drauschke explains. He adds: "If we had conditions like in America, you would have to think hard if you wanted to go on in this line of work."

At J.C. Penney, the workday of the merchandising manager Mrs. Clark begins at 8 A.M. when she rides a service elevator to her windowless office off a stock room. Though the store doesn't open until 10 A.M., she feels she needs the extra time to check floor displays and schedules. Most of the sales staff clock in at about 9 A.M. to set up registers and restock shelves—a sharp contrast to Karstadt, where salespeople come in just moments before the shop opens.

J.C. Penney salespeople, all of whom are nonunion, take the requirements of their jobs for granted and respond with astonishment when told of German conditions, which include strong job security, an extra month's pay as a bonus every year and generous maternity and paternity leave, with parents' jobs protected for up to three years.

"You're kidding, aren't you?" says saleswoman Shannon Cappiella. "Six weeks holiday? No Sunday shifts? No way."

Checking her schedule for the coming week, she finds she will be working Thursday and Friday night and Saturday until 5 P.M. That leaves several nights and all of Sunday free—free, that is, to work her second job as a receptionist at a hair salon. She will earn about

$300 for her 60-hour week. "Just enough to pay the bills," she says. As for leisure, the 21-year-old adds: "Most nights I just veg in front of the TV. I'm too tired to do much else."

Her manager, Mrs. Clark, says that a quarter to a third of the sales staff typically hold second jobs. Some try to supplement their pay at Penney by working on commission, though they only earn extra if they reach a certain level of sales, called "making the draw." And the staffers are busier than five years ago, before the recession, when Mrs. Clark had 38 salespeople instead of the current 28.

The J.C. Penney staff also is largely self-taught, apart from brief training that mainly focuses on how to work the registers. "Why train someone who may leave in three or four months?" Mrs. Clark explains. "It's a waste of time."

At Karstadt, by contrast, workers serve long apprenticeships, spending three days a week working in the store and two days in school learning everything from bookkeeping to "product information." Mr. Drauschke's three years of training, and the 13 years he has spent at the same store, allow him to discourse at length, for example, on the various types of nylon available in motorcycle jackets.

Mr. Drauschke's top staffer in the bicycle department is a racer and triathlete who has been selling bikes and accessories for 17 years. Overall, the 16 staffers in his department have all been there at least five years, and half have been there for 10.

This stability carries with it a degree of immobility. Mr. Drauschke doesn't want to enter senior management because it could mean transferring outside Berlin or spending time on the road, away from his family. So he feels there is only one job advancement open to him in the Berlin store's tight hierarchy: department head.

But drinking beer with a colleague in a back office after the last customer has left at 6:30, Mr. Drauschke says he's content with the status he has achieved at age 29 and the $2,365 he earns each month, plus sales bonuses and holiday pay. "There is a feeling of being sated," he says.

Mrs. Clark's day ends differently. At 5:30, half an hour after she's supposed to leave, she still hasn't finished choosing bathmats to order for the coming year. So she scoops a thick file from her desk to take home. "Another exciting Friday night," she jokes. "Two hours of paperwork, some TV and bed." Then she will return to the store to work full shifts on Saturday and Sunday.

Mrs. Clark, who is separated with three grown children, says her schedule doesn't leave much time for fun, apart from visits with grandchildren and friends. Last year, while recuperating from surgery, she even had an assistant bring her paperwork to do in bed.

Still, she wouldn't have it any other way. One day, perhaps, she will become assistant store manager. In the meantime, there are last year's sales figures to beat, and the bonus to her $32,000 salary that comes with such success.

"Selling more is what we're all here for," she says, touring the sales floor one last time and stopping to help several customers. "I just don't feel right if I don't do a little extra."

Managing Without Managers

Ricardo Semler

How one unorthodox company makes money by avoiding decisions, rules, and executive authority.

In Brazil, where paternalism and the family business fiefdom still flourish, I am president of a manufacturing company that treats its 800 employees like responsible adults. Most of them—including factory workers—set their own working hours. All have access to the company books. The vast majority vote on many important corporate decisions. Everyone gets paid by the month, regardless of job description, and more than 150 of our management people set their own salaries and bonuses.

This may sound like an unconventional way to run a business, but it seems to work. Close to financial disaster in 1980, Semco is now one of Brazil's fastest growing companies, with a profit margin in 1988 of 10% on sales of $37 million. Our five factories produce a range of sophisticated products, including marine pumps, digital scanners, commercial dishwashers, truck filters, and mixing equipment for everything from bubble gum to rocket fuel. Our customers include Alcoa, Saab, and General Motors. We've built a number of cookie factories for Nabisco, Nestlé, and United Biscuits. Our multinational competitors include AMF, Worthington Industries, Mitsubishi Heavy Industries, and Carrier.

Management associations, labor unions, and the press have repeatedly named us the best company in Brazil to work for. In fact, we no longer advertise jobs. Word of mouth generates up to 300 applications for every available position. The top five managers—we call them counselors—include a former human resources director of Ford Brazil, a 15-year veteran Chrysler executive, and a man who left his job as president of a larger company to come to Semco.

When I joined the company in 1980, 27 years after my father founded it, Semco had about 100 employees, manufactured hydraulic pumps for ships, generated about $4 million in revenues, and teetered on the brink of catastrophe. All through 1981 and 1982, we ran from bank to bank looking for loans, and we fought persistent, well-founded rumors that the company was in danger of going under. We often stayed through the night reading files and searching the desk drawers of venerable executives for clues about contracts long since privately made and privately forgotten.

Most managers and outside board members agreed on two immediate needs: to professionalize and to diversify. In fact, both of these measures had been discussed for years but had never progressed beyond wishful thinking.

For two years, holding on by our fingertips, we sought licenses to manufacture other companies' products in Brazil. We traveled constantly. I remember one day being in Oslo for breakfast, New York for lunch, Cincinnati for dinner, and San Francisco for the night. The obstacles were great. Our company lacked an international reputation—and so did our country. Brazil's political eccentricities and draconian business regulations scared many companies away.

Still, good luck and a relentless program of beating the corporate bushes on four continents finally paid off. By 1982, we had signed seven license agreements. Our marine division—once the entire company—was now down to 60% of total sales. Moreover, the managers and directors were all professionals with no connection to the family.

With Semco back on its feet, we entered an acquisitions phase that cost millions of dollars in expenditures and millions more in losses over the next two or three years. All this growth was financed by banks at interest rates that were generally 30% above the rate of inflation, which ranged from 40% to 900% annually. There was no long-term money in Brazil at that time, so all those loans had maximum terms of 90 days. We didn't get one cent in government financing or from incentive agencies either, and we never paid out a dime in graft or bribes.

How did we do it and survive? Hard work, of course. And good luck—fundamental to all business success. But most important, I think, were the drastic changes we made in our concept of management. Without those changes, not even hard work and good luck could have pulled us through.

Semco has three fundamental values on which we base some 30 management programs. These values—democracy, profit sharing, and information—work in a complicated circle, each dependent on the other two. If we eliminated one, the others would be meaningless. Our corporate structure, employee freedoms, union relations, factory size limitations—all are products of our commitment to these principles.

It's never easy to transplant management programs from one company to another. In South America, it's axiomatic that our structure and style cannot be duplicated. Semco is either too small, too big, too far away, too young, too old, or too obnoxious.

We may also be too specialized. We do cellular manufacturing of technologically sophisticated products, and we work at the high end on quality and price. So our critics may be right. Perhaps nothing we've done can be a blueprint for anyone else. Still, in an industrial world whose methods show obvious signs of exhaustion, the merit of sharing experience is to encourage experiment and to plant the seeds of conceptual change. So what the hell.

PARTICIPATORY HOT AIR

The first of Semco's three values is democracy, or employee involvement. Clearly, workers who control their working conditions are going to be happier than workers who don't. Just as clearly, there is no contest between the company that buys the grudging compliance of its work force and the company that enjoys the enterprising participation of its employees.

But about 90% of the time, participatory management is just hot air. Not that intentions aren't good. It's just that implementing employee involvement is so complex, so difficult, and, not uncommonly, so frustrating that it is easier to talk about than to do.

We found four big obstacles to effective participatory management: size, hierarchy, lack of motivation, and ignorance. In an immense production unit, people feel tiny, nameless, and incapable of exerting influence on the way work is done or on the final profit made. This sense of helplessness is underlined by managers who, jealous of their power and prerogatives, refuse to let subordinates make any decisions for themselves—sometimes even about going to the bathroom. But even if size and hierarchy can be overcome, why should workers *care* about productivity and company profits? Moreover, even if you can get them to care, how can they tell when they're doing the right thing?

As Antony Jay pointed out back in the 1950s in *Corporation Man,* human beings weren't designed to work in big groups. Until recently, our ancestors were hunters and gatherers. For more than five million years, they refined their ability to work in groups of no more than about a dozen people. Then along comes the industrial revolution, and suddenly workers are trying to function efficiently in factories that employ hundreds and even thousands. Organizing those hundreds into teams of about ten members each may help some, but there's still a limit to how many small teams can work well together. At Semco, we've found the most effective production unit to consist of about 150 people. The exact number is open to argument, but it's clear that several thousand people in one facility makes individual involvement an illusion.

When we made the decision to keep our units small, we immediately focused on one facility that had more than 300 people. The unit manufactured commercial food-service equipment—slicers, scales, meat grinders, mixers—and used an MRP II system hooked up to an IBM mainframe with dozens of terminals all over the plant. Paperwork often took two days to make its way from one end of the factory to the other. Excess inventories, late delivery, and quality problems were common. We had tried various worker participation programs, quality circles, kanban systems, and motivation schemes, all of which got off to great starts but lost their momentum within months. The whole thing was just too damn big and complex; there were too many managers in too many layers holding too many meetings. So we decided to break up the facility into three separate plants.

To begin with, we kept all three in the same building but separated everything we could—entrances, receiving docks, inventories, telephones, as well as certain auxiliary functions like personnel, management information systems, and internal controls. We also scrapped the mainframe in favor of three independent, PC-based systems.

The first effect of the breakup was a rise in costs due to duplication of effort and a loss in economies of scale. Unfortunately, balance sheets chalk up items like these as liabilities, all with dollar figures attached, and there's nothing at first to list on the asset side but airy stuff like "heightened involvement" and "a sense of belonging." Yet the longer term results exceeded our expectations.

Within a year, sales doubled; inventories fell from 136 days to 46; we unveiled eight new products that had been stalled in R&D for two years; and overall quality improved to the point that a one-third rejection rate on federally inspected scales dropped to less than 1%. Increased productivity let us reduce the work force by 32% through attrition and retirement incentives.

I don't claim that size reduction alone accomplished all this, just that size reduction is essential for putting employees in touch with one another so they can coordinate their work. The kind of distance we want to eliminate comes from having too many people in one place, but it also comes from having a pyramidal hierarchy.

PYRAMIDS AND CIRCLES

The organizational pyramid is the cause of much corporate evil, because the tip is too far from the base. Pyramids emphasize power, promote insecurity, distort communications, hobble interaction, and make it very difficult for the people who plan and the people who execute to move in the same direction. So Semco designed an organizational *circle*. Its greatest advantage is to reduce management levels to three-one corporate level and two operating levels at the manufacturing units.

It consists of three concentric circles. One tiny, central circle contains the five people who integrate the company's movements. These are the counselors I mentioned before. I'm one of them, and except for a couple of legal documents that call me president, counselor is the only title I use. A second, larger circle contains the heads of the eight divisions—we call them partners. Finally, a third, huge circle holds all the other employees. Most of them are the people we call associates; they do the research, design, sales, and manufacturing work and have no one reporting to them on a regular basis. But some of them are the permanent and temporary team and task leaders we call coordinators. Counselors, partners, coordinators, and associates. Four titles. Three management layers.

The linchpins of the system are the coordinators, a group that includes everyone formerly called foreman, supervisor, manager, head, or chief. The only people who report to coordinators are associates. No coordinator reports to another coordinator—that feature of the system is what ensures the reduction in management layers.

Like anyone else, we value leadership, but it's not the only thing we value. In marine pumps, for example, we have an applications engineer who can look at the layout of a ship and then focus on one particular pump and say, "That pump will fail if you take this thing north of the Arctic Circle." He makes a lot more money than the person who manages his unit. We can change the manager, but this guy knows what kind of pump will work in the Arctic, and that's worth more. Associates often make higher salaries than coordinators and partners, and they can increase their status and compensation without entering the "management" line.

Managers and the status and money they enjoy—in a word, hierarchy—are the single biggest obstacle to participatory management. We had to get the managers out of the way of democratic decision making, and our circular system does that pretty well.

But we go further. We don't hire or promote people until they've been interviewed and accepted by all their future subordinates. Twice a year, subordinates evaluate managers. Also twice a year, everyone in the company anonymously fills out a questionnaire about company credibility and top management competence. Among other things, we ask our employees what it would take to make them quit or go on strike.

We insist on making important decisions collegially, and certain decisions are made by a company-wide vote. Several years ago, for example, we needed a bigger plant for our marine division, which makes pumps, compressors, and ship propellers. Real estate agents looked for months and found nothing. So we asked the employees themselves to help, and over the first weekend they found three factories for sale, all of them nearby. We closed up shop for a day, piled everyone into buses, and drove out to inspect the three buildings. Then the workers voted—and they chose a plant the counselors didn't really want. It was an interesting situation—one that tested our commitment to participatory management.

The building stands across the street from a Caterpillar plant that's one of the most frequently struck factories in Brazil. With two tough unions of our own, we weren't looking forward to front-row seats for every labor dispute that came along. But we accepted the employees' decision, because we believe that in the long run, letting people participate in the decisions that affect their lives will have a positive effect on employee motivation and morale.

We bought the building and moved in. The workers designed the layout for a flexible manufacturing system, and they hired one of Brazil's foremost artists to paint the whole thing, inside and out, including the machinery. That plant really belongs to its employees. I feel like a guest every time I walk in.

I don't mind. The division's productivity, in dollars per year per employee, has jumped from $14,200 in 1984—the year we moved—to $37,500 in 1988, and for 1989 the goal is $50,000. Over the same period, market share went from 54% to 62%.

Employees also outvoted me on the acquisition of a company that I'm still sure we should have bought. But they felt we weren't ready to digest it, and I lost the vote. In a case like that, the credibility of our management system is at stake. Employee involvement must be real, even when it makes management uneasy. Anyway, what is the future of an acquisition if the people who have to operate it don't believe it's workable?

HIRING ADULTS

We have other ways of combating hierarchy too. Most of our programs are based on the notion of giving employees control over their own lives. In a word, we hire adults, and then we treat them like adults.

Think about that. Outside the factory, workers are men and women who elect governments, serve in the army, lead community projects, raise and educate families, and make decisions every day about the future. Friends solicit their advice. Salespeople court them. Children and grandchildren look up to them for their wisdom and experience. But the moment they walk into the factory, the company transforms them into adolescents. They have to wear badges and name tags, arrive at a certain time, stand in line to punch the clock or eat their lunch, get permission to go to the bathroom, give lengthy explanations every time they're five minutes late, and follow instructions without asking a lot of questions.

One of my first moves when I took control of Semco was to abolish norms, manuals, rules, and regulations. Everyone knows you can't run a large organization without regulations, but everyone also knows that most regulations are poppycock. They rarely solve problems. On the contrary, there is usually some obscure corner of the rule book that justifies the worst silliness people can think up. Common sense is a riskier tactic because it requires personal responsibility.

RICARDO SEMLER'S GUIDE TO STRESS MANAGEMENT

There are two things all managers have in common—the 24-hour day and the annoying need to sleep. Without the sleeping, 24 hours might be enough. With it, there is no way to get everything done. After years of trying to vanquish demon sleep and the temptation to relax, I tried an approach suggested by my doctor, who put it this way: "Slow down or kiss yourself good-bye."

Struck by this imagery, I learned to manage my time and cut my work load to less than 24 hours. The first step is to overcome five myths:

1. *Results are proportional to efforts.* The Brazilian flag expresses this myth in a slightly different form. "Order and Progress," it says. Of course, it ought to say, "Order *or* Progress," since the two never go together.

2. *Quantity of work is more important than quality.* Psychologically, this myth may hold water. The executive who puts in lots of hours can always say, "Well, they didn't promote me, but you can see how unfair that is. Everyone knows I get here at 8 A.M. and that my own children can't see me without an appointment."

3. *The present restructuring requires longer working hours temporarily.* We think of ourselves as corks on a mountain stream headed for Lake Placid. But the lake ahead is Loch Ness. The present, temporary emergency is actually permanent. Stop being a cork.

4. *No one else can do it right.* The truth is, you *are* replaceable, as everyone will discover within a week of your funeral.

5. This *problem is urgent.* Come on. The real difference between "important" and "urgent" is the difference between thoughtfulness and panic.

Those are the myths. The second step is to master my eight cures:

1. Set an hour to leave the office and obey it blindly. If you normally go home at 7:00, start leaving at 6:00. If you take work home on weekends, give yourself a month or two to put a stop to this pernicious practice.

2. Take half a day, maybe even an entire Saturday, to rummage through that mountain of paper in your office and put it in three piles.

    Pile A: Priority items that require your personal attention and represent matters of indisputable importance. If you put more than four or five documents in this category and are not currently the president of your country, start over.

    Pile B: Items that need your personal attention, but not right away. This pile is very tempting; everything fits. But don't fall into the trap. Load this stuff on your subordinates, using the 70% test to help you do it. Ask yourself: Is there someone on my staff who can do this task at least 70% as well as I can? Yes? Then farm it out. Whether or not your subordinates are overworked should not weigh in your decision. Remember, control of your time is an exercise in selfishness.

    Pile C: Items that fall under the dubious rubric "a good idea to look at." One of the most egregious executive fallacies is that you have to read a little of everything in order to stay well-informed. If you limit the number of newspapers, magazines, and internal communications that you read regularly, you'll have more time to do what's important—like think. And remember to keep your reading timely; information is a perishable commodity.

3. In dealing with Pile A, always start with the most difficult or the most time-consuming. It also helps to have a folder for the things that *must* be done before you go home that day and to make a list of the things that simply cannot go undone for more than a few days or a week. Everything else is just everything else.

4. Buy another wastepaper basket. I know you already have one. But if you invited me to go through that pile of papers on your desk, I could fill both in a trice. To help you decide what to toss and what to save, ask yourself the question asked by the legendary Alfred P. Sloan, Jr.: "What is the worst that can happen if I throw this out?" If you don't tremble, sweat, or grow faint when you think of the consequences, toss it.

   This second wastebasket is a critical investment, even though you'll never be able to fill both on a regular basis. Keep it anyway. It has a symbolic value. It will babysit your in-basket and act like a governess every time you wonder why you bought it.

5. Ask yourself Sloan's question about every lunch and meeting invitation. Don't be timid. And practice these three RSVPs:
   "Thanks, but I just can't fit it in."
   "I can't go, but I think X can." (If you think someone should.)
   "I'm sorry I can't make it, but do let me know what happened."
   Transform meetings into telephone calls or quick conversations in the hall. When you hold a meeting in your office, sit on the edge of your desk, or when you want to end the discussion, stand up from behind your desk and say, "OK, then, that's settled." These tricks are rude but almost foolproof.

6. Give yourself time to think. Spend half a day every week away from your office. Take your work home, or try working somewhere else—a conference room in another office, a public library, an airport waiting room—any place you can concentrate, and the farther away from your office the better. The point is, a fresh environment can do wonders for productivity. Just make sure you bring along a healthy dose of discipline, especially if you're working at home.

7. About the telephone, my practical but subversive advice is: Don't return calls. Or rather, return calls only to people you want to talk to. The others will call back. Better yet, they'll write, and you can spend ten seconds with their letter and then give it to the governess.

   Two ancillary bits of phone advice: Ask your assistants to take detailed messages. Ask them always to say you cannot take the call at the moment. (Depending on who it is, your assistants can always undertake to see if you can't be interrupted.)

8. Close your door. Oh, I know you have an open-door policy, but don't be so literal.

It's also true that common sense requires just a touch of civil disobedience every time someone calls attention to something that's not working. We had to free the Thoreaus and the Tom Paines in the factory and come to terms with that fact that civil disobedience was not an early sign of revolution but a clear indication of common sense at work.

So we replaced all the nitpicking regulations with the rule of common sense and put our employees in the demanding position of using their own judgment.

We have no dress code, for example. The idea that personal appearance is important in a job—any job—is baloney. We've all heard that salespeople, receptionists, and service reps are the company's calling cards, but in fact how utterly silly that is. A company that needs business suits to prove its seriousness probably lacks more meaningful proof. And what customer has ever canceled an order because the receptionist was wearing jeans instead of a dress? Women and men look best when they feel good. IBM is not a great company because its salespeople dress to the special standard that Thomas Watson set. It's a great company that also happens to have this quirk.

We also scrapped the complex company rules about travel expenses—what sorts of accommodations people were entitled to, whether we'd pay for a theater ticket, whether a free call home meant five minutes or ten. We used to spend a lot of time discussing stuff like that. Now we base everything on common sense. Some people stay in four-star hotels and some live like spartans. Some people spend $200 a day while others get by on $125. Or so I suppose. No one checks expenses, so there is no way of knowing. The point is, we don't care. If we can't trust people with our money and their judgment, we sure as hell shouldn't be sending them overseas to do business in our name.

We have done away with security searches, storeroom padlocks, and audits of the petty-cash accounts of veteran employees. Not that we wouldn't prosecute a genuinely criminal violation of our trust. We just refuse to humiliate 97% of the work force to get our hands on the occasional thief or two-bit embezzler.

We encourage—we practically insist on—job rotation every two to five years to prevent boredom. We try hard to provide job security, and for people over 50 or who've been with the company for more than three years, dismissal procedures are extra complicated.

On the more experimental side, we have a program for entry-level management trainees called "Lost in Space," whereby we hire a couple of people every year who have no job description at all. A "godfather" looks after them, and for one year they can do anything they like, as long as they try at least 12 different areas or units.

By the same logic that governs our other employee programs, we have also eliminated time clocks. People come and go according to their own schedules—even on the factory floor. I admit this idea is hard to swallow; most manufacturers are not ready for factory-floor flextime. But our reasoning was simple.

First, we use cellular manufacturing systems. At our food-processing equipment plant, for example, one cell makes only slicers, another makes scales, another makes mixers, and so forth. Each cell is self-contained, so products—and their problems—are segregated from each other.

Second, we assumed that all our employees were trustworthy adults. We couldn't believe they would come to work day after day and sit on their hands because no one else was there. Pretty soon, we figured, they would start coordinating their work hours with their coworkers.

And that's exactly what happened, only more so. For example, one man wanted to start at 7 A.M., but because the forklift operator didn't come until 8, he couldn't get his parts. So a general discussion arose, and the upshot was that now everyone knows how to operate a forklift. In fact, most people can now do several jobs. The union has never objected because the initiative came from the workers themselves. It was their idea.

Moreover, the people on the factory floor set the schedule, and if they say that this month they will build 48 commercial dishwashers, then we can go play tennis, because 48 is what they'll build.

In one case, one group decided to make 220 meat slicers. By the end of the month, it had finished the slicers as scheduled—except that even after repeated phone calls, the supplier still hadn't produced the motors. So two employees drove over and talked to the supplier and managed to get delivery at the end of that day, the 31st. Then they stayed all night, the whole work force, and finished the lot at 4:45 the next morning.

When we introduced flexible hours, we decided to hold regular follow-up meetings to track problems and decide how to deal with abuses and production interruptions. That was years ago, and we haven't yet held the first meeting.

HUNTING THE WOOLLY MAMMOTH

What makes our people behave this way? As Antony Jay points out, corporate man is a very recent animal. At Semco, we try to respect the hunter that dominated the first 99.9% of the history of our species. If you had to kill a mammoth or do without supper, there was no time to draw up an organization chart, assign tasks, or delegate authority. Basically, the person who saw the mammoth from farthest away was the Official Sighter, the one who ran fastest was the Head Runner, whoever threw the most accurate spear was the Grand Marksman, and the person all others respected most and listened to was the Chief. That's all there was to it. Distributing little charts to produce an appearance of order would have been a waste of time. It still is.

What I'm saying is, put ten people together, don't appoint a leader, and you can be sure that one will emerge. So will a slighter, a runner, and whatever else the group needs. We form the groups, but they find their own leaders. That's not a lack of structure, that's just a lack of structure imposed from above.

But getting back to that mammoth, why was it that all the members of the group were so eager to do their share of the work—sighting, running, spearing, chiefing—and to stand aside when someone else could do it better? Because they all got to eat the thing once it was killed and cooked. What mattered was results, not status.

Corporate profit is today's mammoth meat. And though there is a widespread view that profit sharing is some kind of socialist infection, it seems to me that few motivational tools are more capitalist. Everyone agrees that profits should belong to those who risk their capital, that entrepreneurial behavior deserves reward, that the creation of wealth should enrich the creator. Well, depending on how you define capital and risk, all these truisms can apply as much to workers as to shareholders.

Still, many profit-sharing programs are failures, and we think we know why. Profit sharing won't motivate employees if they see it as just another management gimmick, if the company makes it difficult for them to see how their own work is related to profits and to understand how those profits are divided.

In Semco's case, each division has a separate profit-sharing program. Twice a year, we calculate 23% of after-tax profit on each division income statement and give a check to three employees who've been elected by the workers in their division. These three invest the money until the unit can meet and decide—by simple majority vote—what they want to do with it. In most units, that's turned out to be an equal distribution. If a unit has 150 workers, the total is divided by 150 and handed out. It's that simple. The guy who sweeps the floor gets just as much as the division partner.

One division chose to use the money as a fund to lend out for housing construction. It was a pretty close vote, and the workers may change their minds next year. In the meantime, some of them have already received loans and have begun to build themselves houses. In any case, the employees do what they want with the money. The counselors stay out of it.

Semco's experience has convinced me that profit sharing has an excellent chance of working when it crowns a broad program of employee participation, when the profit-sharing criteria are so clear and simple that the least gifted employee can understand them, and, perhaps most important, when employees have monthly access to the company's vital statistics—costs, overhead, sales, payroll, taxes, profits.

TRANSPARENCY

Lots of things contribute to a successful profit-sharing program: low employee turnover, competitive pay, absence of paternalism, refusal to give consolation prizes when profits are down, frequent (quarterly or semiannual) profit distribution, and plenty of opportunity for employees to question the management decisions that affect future profits. But nothing matters more than those vital statistics—short, frank, frequent reports on how the company is doing. Complete transparency. No hocus-pocus, no hanky-panky, no simplifications.

On the contrary, all Semco employees attend classes to learn how to read and understand the numbers, and it's one of their unions that teaches the course. Every month, each employee gets a balance sheet, a profit-and-loss analysis, and a cash-flow statement for his or her division. The reports contain about 70 line items (more, incidentally, than we use to run the company, but we don't want anyone to think we're withholding information).

Many of our executives were alarmed by the decision to share monthly financial results with all employees. They were afraid workers would want to know everything, like how much we pay executives. When we held the first large meeting to discuss these financial reports with the factory committees and the leaders of the metalworkers' union, the first question we got was, "How much do division managers make?" We told them. They gasped. Ever since, the factory workers have called them "maharaja."

But so what? If executives are embarrassed by their salaries, that probably means they aren't earning them. Confidential payrolls are for those who cannot look themselves in the mirror and say with conviction, "I live in a capitalist system that remunerates on a geometric scale. I spent years in school, I have years of experience, I am capable and dedicated and intelligent. I deserve what I get."

I believe that the courage to show the real numbers will always have positive consequences over the long term. On the other hand, we can show only the numbers we bother to put together, and there aren't as many as there used to be. In my view, only the big numbers matter. But Semco's accounting people keep telling me that since the only way to get the big numbers is to add up the small ones, producing a budget or report that includes every tiny detail would require no extra effort. This is an expensive fallacy, and a difficult one to eradicate.

A few years ago, the U.S. president of Allis-Chalmers paid Semco a visit. At the end of his factory tour, he leafed through our monthly reports and budgets. At that time, we had our numbers ready on the fifth working day of every month in super-organized folders, and were those numbers comprehensive! On page 67, chart 112.6, for example, you could see how much coffee the workers in Light Manufacturing III had consumed the month before. The man said he was surprised to find such efficiency in a Brazilian company. In fact, he was so impressed that he asked his Brazilian subsidiary, an organization many times our size, to install a similar system there.

For months, we strolled around like peacocks, telling anyone who cared to listen that our budget system was state-of-the-art and that the president of a Big American Company had ordered his people to copy it. But soon we began to realize two things. First, our expenses were always too high, and they never came down because the accounting department was full of overpaid clerks who did nothing but compile them. Second, there were so damn many numbers inside the folder that almost none of our managers read them. In fact, we knew less about the company then, with all that information, than we do now without it.

Today we have a simple accounting system providing limited but relevant information that we can grasp and act on quickly. We pared 400 cost centers down to 50. We beheaded hundreds of classifications and dozens of accounting lines. Finally, we can see the company through the haze.

(As for Allis-Chalmers, I don't know whether it ever adopted our old system in all its terrible completeness, but I hope not. A few years later, it began to suffer severe financial difficulties and eventually lost so much market share and money that it was broken up and sold. I'd hate to think it was our fault.)

In preparing budgets, we believe that the flexibility to change the budget continually is much more important than the detailed consistency of the initial numbers. We also believe in the importance of comparing expectations with results. Naturally, we compare monthly reports with the budget. But we go one step further. At month's end, the coordinators in each area make guesses about unit receipts, profit margins, and expenses. When the official numbers come out a few days later, top managers compare them with the guesses to judge how well the coordinators understand their areas.

What matters in budgets as well as in reports is that the numbers be few and important and that people treat them with something approaching passion. The three monthly reports, with their 70 line items, tell us how to run the company, tell our managers how well they know their units, and tell our employees if there's going to be a profit. Everyone works on the basis of the same information, and everyone looks forward to its appearance with what I'd call fervent curiosity.

And that's all there is to it. Participation gives people control of their work, profit sharing gives them a reason to do it better, information tells them what's working and what isn't.

RICARDO SEMLER'S GUIDE TO COMPENSATION

Employers began hiring workers by the hour during the industrial revolution. Their reasons were simple and rapacious. Say you ran out of cotton thread at 11:30 in the morning. If you paid people by the hour, you could stop the looms, send everyone home, and pay only for hours actually worked.

You couldn't do such a thing today. The law probably wouldn't let you. The unions certainly wouldn't let you. Your own self-interest would argue strongly against it. Yet the system lives on. The distinction between wage-earning workers and salaried employees is alive but not well, nearly universal but perfectly silly. The new clerk who lives at home and doesn't know how to boil an egg starts on a monthly salary, but the chief lathe operator who's been with the company 38 years and is a master sergeant in the army reserve still gets paid by the hour.

At Semco, we eliminated Frederick Winslow Taylor's segmentation and specialization of work. We ended the wage analyst's hundred years of solitude. We did away with hourly pay and now give everyone a monthly salary. We set the salaries like this:

A lot of our people belong to unions, and they negotiate their salaries collectively. Everyone else's salary involves an element of self-determination.

Once or twice a year, we order salary market surveys and pass them out. We say to people, "Figure out where you stand on this thing. You know what you do; you know what everyone else in the company makes; you know what your friends in other companies make; you know what you need; you know what's fair. Come back on Monday and tell us what to pay you."

When people ask for too little, we give it to them. By and by, they figure it out and ask for more. When they ask for too much, we give that to them too—at least for the first year. Then, if we don't feel they're worth the money, we sit down with them and say, "Look, you make x amount of money, and we don't think you're making x amount of contribution. So either we find something else for you to do, or we don't have a job for you anymore." But with half a dozen exceptions, our people have always named salaries we could live with.

We do a similar thing with titles. Counselors are counselors, and partners are partners; these titles are always the same. But with coordinators, it's not quite so easy. Job titles still mean too much to many people. So we tell coordinators to make up their own titles. They know what signals they need to send inside and outside the company. If they want "Procurement Manager," that's fine. And if they want "Grand Panjandrum of Imperial Supplies," that's fine too.

LETTING THEM DO WHATEVER THE HELL THEY WANT

So we don't have systems or staff functions or analysts or anything like that. What we have are people who either sell or make, and there's nothing in between. Is there a marketing department? Not on your life. Marketing is everybody's problem. Everybody knows the price of the product. Everybody knows the cost. Everybody has the monthly balance sheet that says exactly what each of them makes, how much bronze is costing us, how much overtime we paid, all of it. And the employees know that 23% of the aftertax profit is theirs.

We are very, very rigorous about the numbers. We want them in on the fourth day of the month so we can get them back out on the fifth. And because we're so strict with the financial controls, we can be extremely lax about everything else. Employees can paint the walls any color they like. They can come to work whenever they decide. They can wear whatever clothing makes them comfortable. They can do whatever the hell they want. It's up to them to see the connection between productivity and profit and to act on it.

Korea Goes for Quality

Louis Kraar

Get ready for a fresh wave of exports. By changing their whole culture, the Koreans are trying to accomplish what the Japanese did a generation ago.

After a long and highly successful run making cheap jogging shoes and consumer electronics, South Korea's giant conglomerates, or *chaebol*, have collided with the realities of the nineties. Wages, averaging $1,444 a month, are now among the highest in Asia outside Japan. So, Korean factories can no longer compete with those in such low-wage countries as China and Indonesia. The World Competitiveness Report, an annual assessment of relative economic prowess by the Swiss research institute IMD and the World Economic Forum, last year ranked South Korea sixth among 15 newly industrializing economies—behind even Malaysia and Chile. Moreover, the government, once so supportive of big business, has cut back on subsidies and export credits.

The conglomerates are responding to this crisis in two ways—increased investment in new technology and equipment, and a drive for higher quality. Says Jun Yongwook, a business professor at Chung-Ang University in Seoul: "The only way out is for companies to strengthen their competitive advantage." That's not going to be easy. Confides Lee Kun Hee, chairman of Samsung, the largest non-Japanese conglomerate in Asia with $54 billion in sales last year: "We are more retarded than I realized, in many respects 30 years behind Japan." To catch up, Korean companies this year plan to invest more than $35 billion, 47% more than just two years ago.

The push for quality is more dramatic—even startling. The *chaebol* are using techniques more reminiscent of Maoist China's mind-reform efforts than the reengineering notions of American management consultants. Says Yoon Yong-Nam, president of Daewoo Management Development Center: "Japanese people act almost like machines, but Koreans are more emotional. We have to encourage employees to join the quality effort voluntarily and with enthusiasm." Still, many aspects of the Korean-style quality drives could work almost anywhere that top management has enough determination.

Samsung's Lee, 52, is applying what he calls "shock therapy." Last year he suddenly ordered senior executives of his Korean electronics operations to visit retailers in Los Angeles. Since he had already secretly done so himself, he knew they would hear harsh complaints about shoddy products, unappealing designs, and poor after-sales service. "If we don't correct this," warns Lee, "we won't be qualified to run a street-corner shop." Samsung's 24 companies earned $600 million last year, up from $376 million the previous year. But Lee is willing—he seems almost eager—to sacrifice short-term profits to improve quality.

Sunkyong Group, a vertically integrated producer of petroleum products that also operates the Sheraton Walker Hill hotel in Seoul (1993 group revenues: $22 billion), is taking a different approach. Chairman Chey Jong-Hyon, 63, wants to maximize profits by attaining "super-excellence—the highest level of which humans are capable." It may sound like cheerleading, but in the past year Sunkyong has boosted the output of chemical plants by 30% to 40% without adding new equipment. Chey, who earned American degrees in both chemistry and economics, empowers employees at every level to use *pae-gi,* aggressive determination, to overcome obstacles. Many of the best ideas for improvements have come from factory workers. Says Chey: "We get our competitive edge not through technology but by management of human resources."

The Daewoo Group of 20 companies has made quality a selling point for its products. Bae Soon Hoon, 50, president of Daewoo Electronics, has become a TV celebrity in Korea by appearing in commercials that portray Daewoo Electronics' washing machines and TV sets as built like a tank—sturdy, reliable, and without frills. The ads not only lift sales but also prod workers to make the tank concept a reality. Kim Woo-Choong, 57, chairman and founder of the group, spends an hour or so prowling the shop floor most nights looking for defects at Daewoo Motor, where quality problems contributed to the breakup of a joint venture with General Motors 15 months ago. Kim claims that Daewoo sub-compacts now roll off the assembly line with few more defects than comparable Japanese models.

The challenge for Korea is especially daunting in autos. The country's Big Three—Hyundai, Kia, and Daewoo—plan to triple production by the turn of the century to a total of about six million cars a year. Samsung, a maker of utility trucks, may get into the car business too. Some of that huge output can be unloaded in the Third World, but a lot of it will have to go to the U.S. and Europe. And to accomplish that, the Koreans will have to build cars with consistently higher quality than they have ever attained before.

Hyundai Motor, the biggest Korean automaker with nearly $9 billion in sales last year, learned about quality the hard way. After a stunning debut in the U.S. in 1986, Hyundai quickly lost momentum because its car developed a rash of defects. Sales slipped from 170,000 that first year to fewer than 109,000 in 1993. The company attacked the problem by trying to reeducate everyone involved in making and delivering its cars. It even sent union leaders to the U.S. to see firsthand the intense competition. Suppliers got trips to America too, for what likely turned out to be in-your-face visits with dealers who had suffered through countless recalls.

Every Hyundai car now is inspected and test-driven at least three times before reaching customers: first at the Korean factory, then at the U.S. port of entry, and finally by American dealers. Fixes are made when required at all those points, even if it's just touching up scratched paint. As a result, Hyundai is probably the most improved automaker, moving up in the J.D. Power Consumer Satisfaction Index from last place in 1992 to the middle ranks. The company still has a way to go in winning back consumers. Says Bruce Campbell, a senior vice president of Hyundai Motor's U.S. sales subsidiary: "The reality of our cars is now better than our image."

At Samsung, Chairman Lee tells his 180,000 employees, "Change everything but your wives and children." The company certainly is doing most things differently. Workers often stayed as late 10 P.M., so Samsung decreed that they must leave at 4 P.M., after eight hours. Lee thinks the relatively shorter day will actually improve efficiency and enhance morale. Executives are now required to spend a lot more time with suppliers and customers. They also have to do a bit of work on assembly lines. To draw from a larger talent pool, the company is actively recruiting women managers, a rarity in male chauvinist Korea. Above all, Lee insists with almost religious fervor that employees undergo "mind reformation" to become more creative and global in their outlook.

Lee wants to shake off what he calls the Samsung diseases, notably a preoccupation with expanding volume regardless of quality. The result, he says, is that some 6,000 Samsung employees are kept busy repairing 20,000 defective products annually produced by 30,000 other Samsung workers: "You can find no comparable inefficiency in the world." Making defective products, adds Lee, "is cancerous and a criminal act on the part of management." Samsung, among other things, has adopted the Japanese practice of stopping assembly lines when defects occur. Another disease, Lee says, is "inflexible thinking" fostered by the authoritarian leadership style of Samsung's late founder, his father Lee Byung-Chull.

So far, the greatest change may be in Lee himself, who has gone from being a remote, hands-off chairman a to bold activist. After succeeding his father in 1987, Lee often sat home watching TV, leaving details of Samsung's highly diversified operations to others. Apparently he was nursing old psychological wounds from battles with his father. Says he: "In his final years, I suffered mentally and financially." Having recovered his self-confidence—and become a billionaire with the appreciation of his inherited stock and real estate—Lee is over throwing the bureaucracy that ran Samsung. Says one of his senior executives: "We now have a powerful leader—with a powerful ego."

Standing Samsung on its head to stress quality, says Lee, "was not a premeditated strategy" but evolved from a personal sense of crisis. Samsung faced eroding competitiveness in many fields, he says, and was doing little about it. With Korea steadily opening its protected home market, Lee told his executives that the company would have to compete head-on with Sony, Matusushita, Philips, and General Electric. They listened respectfully but took little action.

Out of frustration, Lee last year began summoning Samsung executives to join him in Los Angeles, Tokyo, and Frankfurt for tours of retailers—and lectures that lasted up to 12 hours. He spoke with 1,800 senior managers over an eight-week period, recording the sessions on 300 hours of videotape and 750 hours of audiotape. Lee says he discovered that his own senior staffers often distorted his policies in the process of disseminating his words to employees at large, expressing "quite the opposite of what I tried to say." The manager of the chairman's office, and half the 200-person staff, have been moved to other jobs. The audiotapes and videotapes have been made available to all employees.

During those eight weeks, Lee recalls being so disturbed he could barely eat or sleep. The gist of his speeches: Samsung needs a "quality-first management" that can show results fast. If curtailing production to assure quality caused a Samsung company to lose money, he said he would make up the difference out of his own pocket. He also promised to donate 70% to 80% of his personal fortune (a figure he won't disclose) to a foundation benefiting Samsung employees *if* the effort brings tangible results by 1997. Otherwise, he added, he would resign as chairman and keep his money. As Lee puts it, "I have staked my honor, my life, and my assets on these changes."

Can shock treatment jolt a corporation into quality consciousness? Says Professor Jun, author of a new book in the Korean language on Samsung: "It's a calculated gamble, but Lee had no choice but to create a kind of controlled chaos, a big bang." Jun thinks the Samsung revolution has a 60% to 70% chance of success. The biggest stumbling blocks are older managers who recall the company's high-growth period. Lee threatens to fire "those shameless fellows who are always in the way of others" unless they change. He's helping them do so through a six-month course called the "21st-Century CEO Program" that all middle managers eventually will take. It includes foreign language instruction and a chance to study management in the U.S. and Japan.

Samsung's most enthusiastic agents of change are younger employees and women managers. Says Joo Hea Kyung, 43, a woman who is a general manager at Samsung Data Systems: "Before, employees were just goofing around, reading newspapers, and chatting on the phone. They had the misconception that staying in the office longer meant they were working harder. Now we do things more efficiently and get home for dinner with our families." Samsung limits meetings to an hour and reports to a page or so.

For all his new assertiveness, Lee insists that corporate dictators—which are common in Korea—cannot create quality. Says he: "There should be no boss or subordinates during a discussion. We must do away with the tendency to stubbornly insist our own ideas are always right." Lee blames "this backwardness" on decades of military rule in Korea. As he puts it, "We are accustomed to taking orders rather than thinking together and finding solutions together." Along with granting greater freedom, though, Samsung's revolution is making senior executives more responsible for their decisions. To assure accountability, the chairman wants every important company meeting tape-recorded. The tapes are stored and made available to anyone in the company who needs them.

With less upheaval, other Korean conglomerates are also striving for excellence. At Sunkyong, the petroleum products producer, the quality program is called Supex, for super-excellence. In "can" (as in "can do") meetings, employees are taught to think about adding value to their jobs by identifying the "KFS"—key factors for success. Brainstorming sessions are held either before or after working hours as needed. Says Chairman Chey: "Everyone is brought into management, which makes people happier. They get together, use their minds, and see their ideas used."

Initial results look impressive. One plant that makes polyester raw materials using American technology acquired from Eastman Chemical claims to get more output at less cost than the U.S. company does from the same process. Sunkyong made small adjustments to speed production. For example, the Korean company has reduced sediment in pipes so that work stops for cleaning them only every five months, instead of the usual one or two months. Many such changes enabled the plant last year to produce 260,000 tons, far beyond it's designed capacity of 208,000 tons. Says Chey: "The big difference comes from managing the plant so that we get brain engagement from all the workers."

Employees are expected to set—and achieve—a standard of performance that matches the best companies worldwide in their industry. At a lubricant plant, for instance, brainstormers set a goal to make products with zero defects. The workers did it by getting the product right at each stage of manufacturing rather than by relying on a quality-control test at the end of the process to spot errors. Says Chey: "If we merely try to be excellent, our gap with the world's top companies will remain because they keep improving. Only by seeking super-excellence can we reach their level or overtake them."

Daewoo is taking a fairly straightforward approach to raising quality. The group is reassigning—or laying off—unproductive paper shufflers and demanding cash refunds from suppliers of shoddy components. It has also sent 2,000 auto workers for three-month stints in Japan at plants of Isuzu or Suzuki, companies with which it has business ties. The idea is to give the Koreans a little on-the-job infusion of Japanese quality methods. This strategy, though less grandiose than those of its Korean rivals, pays off. Daewoo's profits last year leaped 55%, to $580 million, while sales increased 35%, to $34 billion.

Dramatically reducing product defects has helped Daewoo Electronics expand domestic sales at the expense of bigger competitors like Samsung. In the past four years, for example, Daewoo claims that its share of the Korean market for washing machines has climbed from 11% to 35%.

A crucial element in Daewoo's quality drive is the personal involvement of Chairman Kim. Early this year Kim literally moved into Daewoo Motor—the only big division that is losing money. He spends most days in a borrowed office at the automaker's headquarters, then often visits the factory floor during the night shift before going home around midnight. His presence sends a potent signal to workers at Daewoo Motor, which has installed three levels of quality control.

First, each unit of a dozen or so assembly workers includes a quality monitor who wears a bright green vest for easy identification. At the end of the line another group called the Q-point (for quality) checks for defects, which have dropped 65% in the past two years. Finally, "customer satisfaction" inspectors pull out a 2% sample of the cars and spend 3½ hours on each checking 188 different aspects—from paint job to the fit of doors. Kim's goal is to sell Daewoo cars, now mainly exported to Third World markets, in the U.S. He insists the quality will be high enough by 1996.

Even the most spirited efforts of the Koreans will take some years to yield significant results. South Korea, among other things, needs to revamp an educational system that concentrates on filling heads with memorized facts rather than developing creative and analytical skills. As the Japanese have demonstrated, quality products depend on workers capable of making gradual, steady improvements that never end.

Chapter

15

Environment

We have reached a period in the life of our planet where our actions, particularly the actions of our organizations have become sufficiently powerful to wreak havoc on the environment. This damage inevitably comes back to us, for we are very intimately tied to our environment. It is by no means certain that the problems we have created will be resolved by a new round of technological innovation. In fact, many of the technologies we have created and employed to solve problems facing humans have contributed significantly to the ecological disasters that occur with disturbing frequency these days. The disaster in Bhopal, the destruction of animal and plant life following the Exxon oil spill in Alaska, the nuclear reactor accidents at Three Mile Island in the United States and Chernobyl in the Soviet Union are all frightening examples of errors in the planning and execution of organizational decisions. The toxicity caused by pesticide overuse and by industrial waste dumped into the rivers and oceans makes clear the delicate interaction that exists between cumulative human and organizational actions and the environment. Environmental problems transcend national and economic boundaries. The accident at Chernobyl created nuclear fallout that spread to all parts of Europe and beyond. The sulphur emissions from industries in the United States and Canada produce acid rain that destroys forests and diminishes the quality of life on the entire continent. There is an increased awareness of environmental dangers throughout the world and the actions of individuals and groups from many walks of life are being directed at solving rather than creating problems. Nevertheless, much remains to be done.

In this chapter we have selected articles that address various aspects of this large and complex challenge. One major issue is that of attitude, of the orientation people have toward the world they live in. In her lyrics to the song "Why," Tracy Chapman expresses her anger at the amount of pain, fear, and destruction that exist in the modern world. Like many others, she warns that we need to act soon to deal responsibly and with a common will to tackle the various sources of human suffering. We recommend Robert

Redford's "Search for the Common Ground" (published in *Harvard Business Review,* 1987) as an eloquent argument for bringing together interest groups such as business leaders and environmentalists, to solve rather than perpetuate current problems. He describes some of the positive experiences that have come from the joint efforts of industry, government, environmentalists and minority groups on such thorny issues as energy conservation, land use and so on. We see the emergence of new modes of collaboration as a major step toward helping to resolve environmental problems.

In the middle of the 1990s we see evidence of continued struggles between those with an agenda to protect the environment and those who are in resistance, whether it be in the name of individual rights or corporate interests or both. Sometimes the facts seem to support the environments, at other times the nature of the protective policies, regardless of the facts, seem designed to make it impossible for even well-meaning citizens to comply. In "Carton County, N.M., Leads a Nasty Revolt over Eco-Protection," Charles McCoy describes a fierce and potentially violent fight between the Forest Services and ranchers. The political activities of ranchers and their supporters suggest that a very difficult battle lies ahead for the environmentalists in this region. In Caleb Solomon's article on clean-air plans, "Cut Auto Commuting? Firms and Employees Gag at Clean-Air Plan," the issue seems to be a policy that provides neither the time nor the flexibility to allow people to adjust effectively its requirements. One implication here is that policy without careful implementation may prove a waste of time, money, and energy, which would be a pity in such an important and sensitive arena.

The struggle over uses of natural resources is not confined to North America, or only to the industrialized nations. It is a war being waged in many parts of the world. In "Trees 'Ordained' in Forest Fight," Philip Smucker describes tactics being used by Buddhists to save precious rain forests in Thailand.

One of the truly disturbing facets of environmental balance centers on the way humans view and relate to other living species. As John Robbins points out again and again in his book *Diet for a New America* (Stillpoint Publishing, 1987), humans have increasingly adopted an orientation that is blind to the feelings, intelligence, and sensitivities of animals. They have become commodities that exist exclusively to serve human needs. In "The Most Unjustly Maligned of All Animals," Robbins chronicles the horrifying plight of pigs reared in factories across the United States, where they are treated like components on an assembly line, machines to be produced and marketed. There is no opportunity for any of these animals to live any kind of reasonable life. Robbins discusses the ethical, political, and health issues that stem from these kinds of human and organizational practices. He suggests that the consequences of the practices are disastrous for both humans and animals.

At times, the magnitude of the challenges we face when we try to turn things around seems so great that the effect is one of paralysis. What can we as individuals do that might have a positive effect on environmental problems, or any other major societal problems for that matter? "The Child and the Starfish" suggests in a playful way that we can make a difference in significant ways. In our concluding article, therapist Terrance O'Connor recommends that we apply what we have learned from our understanding of solving problems of individuals and families to the dilemmas and illnesses facing the Family of Man. In "Therapy for a Dying Planet," he suggests that each of us is both victim and victimizer in the current breakdown of the health and well-being of the global family. He argues that as causal agents in this process, we can also therefore contribute to the rehabilitation of the planet. His statement is a passionate call to work together.

Why?

Tracy Chapman

Why do the babies starve
When there's enough food to feed the world
Why when there's so many of us
Are there people still alone

Why are the missiles called peace keepers
When they're aimed to kill
Why is a woman still not safe
When she's in her home

Love is hate
War is peace
No is yes
And we're all free

But somebody's gonna have to answer
The time is coming soon
Amidst all these questions and contradictions
There're some who seek the truth

But somebody's gonna have to answer
The time is coming soon
When the blind remove their blinders
And the speechless speak the truth

Cattle Prod: Catron County, N.M., Leads a Nasty Revolt Over Eco-Protection

U.S. Agency's Plan to Trim Grazing Rights Sparks Laws—and Lawlessness An End to Cowboy Welfare?

Charles McCoy

CATRON COUNTY, N.M.—Last spring, federal wildlife biologist Tim Tibbitts sat in his car after a meeting with local ranchers to outline how protections for endangered species could curtail cattle grazing on federal land here. One rancher popped open the passenger door.

Mr. Tibbitts vividly recalls him saying: "If you ever come down to Catron County again, we'll blow your f—head off."

Federal law-enforcement agents are still looking for the rancher, whom, in the darkness, Mr. Tibbitts didn't recognize. But the rhetoric of rebellion just grows louder here in the mesa and mountain country along the Gila River near the Continental Divide. And it is echoing throughout rural America.

WAR CRIES

At issue here are attempts by federal land managers to curb decades of what they say are environmentally damaging cattle grazing and other practices on the public lands that make up 80% of the county's 7,000 square miles. In revolt, the citizens of Catron Country have paraded out a number of novel—and detractors say ludicrous—weapons: a slew of ordinances aimed at superseding federal law, and the Treaty of Guadalupe Hidalgo of 1848. But death threats and guns have also played a role.

The guiding principle of this revolt: The federal government stole the lands it owns in New Mexico more than a century ago; thus, people here need not heed modern-day federal laws regulating their use.

So it is that in Catron County, local ordinances have been passed that make it illegal for the Forest Service to regulate grazing, even on Forest Service lands in the heart of the federally owned Gila and Aldo Leopold wilderness areas that straddle the county.

The county sheriff has threatened to arrest the head of the local Forest Service office, prompting the U.S. attorney to threaten to arrest the sheriff.

Other Catron County ordinances seek to prohibit the federal government from enforcing a host of laws aimed at sparing the Gila River area from what Sally Stefferud, a biologist for the U.S. Fish and Wildlife Service, describes as "imminent environmental collapse." For emphasis, Catron County passed a measure requiring heads of households to own firearms to "protect citizens' rights." By way of warning, the county passed a resolution predicting "much physical violence" if the government persists with its "arrogant" grazing reform plans.

SPREADING REBELLION

Many mainstream legal scholars say Catron County is on shaky legal ground with much of this. Nonetheless, the movement born here—now known officially as the "county movement"—has tapped into a deep well of discontent in the West and other rural regions, where mainstays of rural culture like ranching, mining and logging are colliding with demographic shifts and increased environmental protection.

In the past two years, more than 100 counties in Western states have passed ordinances, mimicking Catron County's, that repudiate federal control of public lands. In Nevada, 16 of the state's 17 counties have passed county-movement ordinances. The movement has spread eastward in recent months, picking up counties in Michigan and North Carolina.

Federal agencies early on dismissed Catron County's campaign, but they don't anymore. "Do not underestimate these people," Interior Secretary Bruce Babbitt warned a crowd of environmentalists at the Sierra Club's annual awards dinner in San Francisco several months ago. "They are out to divest the public of its lands."

DEEP ROOTS

The West has seen many antigovernment movements in the past—and Catron County has often been in the vanguard. In the 1890s, people here torched tens of thousands of acres to protest the government's original plan to set aside national forests. But historians think the county movement runs deeper than similar revolts of the past. It overlaps with the so-called Wise Use movement, a well-funded campaign backed by big timber, mining, oil and ranching concerns to roll back environmental restrictions. Yet it may have broader appeal, because it casts its cause as the defense of individual liberty and property rights against an overweening federal government—an increasingly popular theme, as recent elections have shown.

"For many traditional Westerners, there is a feeling that this is the last stand for their way of life, and that generates a new level of desperation," says Patricia Nelson Limerick, a historian at the University of Colorado.

That feeling is strong in Catron County. Bigger than Connecticut, the county has been cattle country since the arrival of the Spaniards in the 16th century. Cows still outnumber people about eight to one. But like the entire West, Catron County and environs have been changing. In Silver City, bistros and art galleries have moved into offices vacated by mining suppliers. Newly arrived "green" groups have filed numerous lawsuits and endangered-species actions, leading to federal protection for the Mexican spotted owl and the willow flycatcher, among other creatures.

HERD CHOICES

The change that has really got Catron County stirred up is in the Forest Service's approach to its grazing operations. The service has always allowed grazing in public lands, even in wilderness areas, for dirt-cheap fees. A few years ago, under pressure from environmentalists, federal range managers began to acknowledge that a century of heavy grazing had worn much public rangeland in the West to the nub, causing severe environmental damage, especially along streams and rivers. In late 1993, the Forest Service proposed cutting the herds on public land in Catron County by about 30%.

To ranchers, these are all changes to fear and to fight. At a "Protect Your Rights Rally" in Silver City, between the barbecue and the cold beer, anger pours forth "Our way of life is under attack by eco-Nazis," rails Zeno Kiehne, a fourth-generation Catron County rancher. Nearby rancher Betty Hyatt nods approvingly as state game commissioner gives a speech suggesting "ignoring" the Endangered Species Act. "All we want is for our children to be able to live and work out here the way we always have," Ms. Hyatt says.

It is to that end that local leader launched Catron County's crusade. James Catron, county attorney and a descendant of the pioneer ranching family that gave the county its name, says the movement in part reflects a nostalgia for a time "when someone causing pain to the community was simply shot." Some of the legal concepts underpinning Catron County's crusade similarly look back in time.

TRICK OR TREATY?

One is the Treaty of Guadalupe Hidalgo, which ended the Mexican War in 1848 and granted territory from California to the Texas border to the U.S. Mr. Catron argues that the treaty gave the residents of what would become New Mexico the right to graze cattle, free from interference by any federal agency. Another of the county's arguments holds that ranchers have been grazing cattle so long on the federally owned lands here that they in effect own the grazing rights themselves. Another holds that the federal government simply doesn't have a right to own any land. "Nowhere in the Constitution does it say that the federal government can own real estate," Mr. Catron observes.

Then there are the ordinances. The latest proposed one, which county commissioners have yet to vote on, would require environmentalists to register with the county. Under the measure, practicing environmentalism without a license could theoretically result in arrest.

The county also has drawn up its own land-use plan, which it says can't be contravened by federal land managers. It calls for few restrictions on grazing and other such activities.

The only time to date that a county-movement ordinance was actually tested directly, in a case in Idaho state court early last year, it was thrown out as unconstitutional.

Nonetheless, the movement has rung up successes. Last month, a federal judge in Albuquerque revoked the Fish and Wildlife Service's designation of critical habitat for two tiny fish in the Gila River as a result of a Catron County lawsuit. The judge accepted the county's argument that the designation procedure dragged on past allowable federal deadlines; the agency, arguing that the designation process was slowed by county protests and legal challenges, is appealing.

BOWING TO PRESSURE

Even when the movement isn't on firm legal ground, it serves as a potent force for converting the free-floating anger in the region into action. Amid opposition, Interior Secretary Babbitt last month decided to abandon some of his more ambitious proposals for grazing reform. And last summer, the Fish and Wildlife Service shelved an effort to bring back native Gila trout to Mineral Creek. The job required the service to first poison nonnative species like brown trout—a sportsman's favorite but a predator that has contributed to the sharp decline in Gila trout. Before the biologists could get to Mineral Creek, protests and threats of armed intervention forced them to reconsider.

The nastiest battles, though, have to do with cattle. The Diamond Bar is one of the biggest grazing allotments in the Forest Service system, 227 square miles, most of it in the rugged Gila and Aldo Leopold wilderness. The current permit holder is Kit Laney, a fourth-generation Catron County rancher who bought his 40-acre ranch and the giant Diamond Bar grazing permit associated with it in 1984 for more than $800,000. (Typically, a rancher buys a piece of private property surrounded by Forest Service land; the private property has a grazing allotment of publicly owned land associated with it, which the property owner has the first option to lease.)

When he bought it, the permit allowed Mr. Laney to graze up to 1,188 head of cattle. However, much of the Diamond Bar, the Forest Service now says, has been badly overgrazed for decades and can no longer support more than 600 head; environmentalists say even that's too many.

Indeed, throughout the Diamond Bar, as on much Western rangeland, the damaging legacy of cattle is apparent. The banks of Main Diamond Creek, one of several Gila River tributaries weaving through the Diamond Bar, are bare and crumbling, mainly because creekside willows and cottonwoods that once checked erosion were long ago devoured or trampled by cows. Though the Main Diamond once brimmed with fish and bird life, the creek is now a muddy, cow-patty-littered trickle much of the year. Its current condition, say biologists, helps explain why every native fish species existing in the Gila River 50 years ago is now either extinct, endangered or under consideration for federal protection.

Mr. Laney, an amiable, broad-chested cowboy, vows not to trim his herd—and to defend it with bullets if need be. "I'd go broke," he says of the proposed cutbacks.

The Forest Service—badly outnumbered here and its ranks still sprinkled with old-guarders sympathetic to ranchers' concerns—hasn't said what it intends to do about Mr. Laney's defiance. Recently, the service proposed penalizing Mr. Laney 10 cows because his stock repeatedly had been lolling in a badly damaged, off-limits streamside. A tense public hearing on the matter ended with a local county-movement leader, Brub Stone, following ranger Sue Kozacek out to her car. He called her "a communist" and screamed at her to "think hard about what you're going to do, because we'll hard-ass you to death, and you won't get away with it."

Later, Danny Fryar, a rancher and the Catron County manager, says if Mr. Laney's herd is cut, "there'll be all sorts of trouble. Kit won't have to face them alone."

COWBOY WELFARE?

The leaders of Catron County's movement portray it as a revolt of hard-working stewards of the land against elitist greens and unfeeling bureaucrats. "It's just honest country folk who have cared for this land and have made something of it standing up against government and outsiders that want to take, it all away from us," drawls Richard Manning, a tall, weather-beaten rancher who owns thousands of acres of rangeland and is considered the county's richest man. But critics say that Mr. Manning and other ranchers have grown prosperous precisely because the government's cheap grazing fees have amounted to fat, perpetual subsidies—derided as "cowboy welfare."

"It's the height of hypocrisy," says Peter Galvin, a conservation biologist with the Greater Gila Biodiversity Project, an area environmental group. "They rail about the federal government taking over their lives, but they're first in line when the feds are handing out subsidies."

Environmentalists and some federal regulators also wonder about some of the ranchers' stewardship. In addition to the battered condition of the local range, there is Mr. Manning's ongoing feud with the Forest Service over his plan to open up a mill he owns at the Challenger Mine, which is on Forest Service land in the Mogollon Mountains. (Mr. Manning, citing various legal concepts, regards the mill site as his property, not the Forest Service's.) The Forest Service and state regulators suspect that toxic mine tailings at the mill may be leaching into watercourses. Mr. Manning refuses to agree to let them check, and according to several Forest Service and state officials, has threatened to greet any regulator who comes out to the mine with "100 men with rifles."

Mr. Manning denies having made any such threat. In any case, the rhetoric in Catron County is baleful, even by the inflamed standards of Western land battles. People here threaten mayhem with a casualness and frequency that alarms regulators and environmentalists. And, in a development that troubles even some movement leaders, the cause has attracted elements with some peculiar ideas.

STRANGE BEDFELLOWS

At the recent rights rally, Frank Nagol hands out a schematic of how to make a pipe bomb. He has a .25-caliber pistol tucked in his waistband. "You have to be prepared to defend yourself from the oppressors at all times," Mr. Nagol says. Others in the crowd talk of an FBI plot to recruit the Bloods and the Crips off the streets of Los Angeles to form a secret army. "It will be the instrument of a complete government takeover of private property," observes Ed Cramer, a barrel-chested Arizona man. Mr. Cramer is sure this is true because of his contacts in law enforcement; he was a police officer for 31 years and now serves as a magistrate in Arizona's Hidalgo County. Still others at the rally warn of imminent invasions by United Nations shock troops, Mexican drug dealers and space aliens.

Howard Hutchinson, another leader of Catron County's campaign, acknowledges that the movement has attracted "fringe elements—all movements do." He has an interesting history himself: He helped found Earth First!, the radical environmental group that got its start here in the Gila area. Now Mr. Hutchinson lives in a trailer, raises organic artichokes and, as a stalwart in the county movement, battles what he calls "environmental extremists."

So far, despite the tension and threats, nobody has been shot over land use in Catron County. But authorities are investigating the vandalism of several Forest Service signs and outback buildings, and the service's deputy chief for the region, Carl Pence, worries that a showdown may be inevitable. "We take these threats very seriously," Mr. Pence says. "The tinder is there. It wouldn't take much to set it off."

Head-On Collision: Cut Auto Commuting? Firms and Employees Gag at Clean-Air Plan

Employers Plot Car Pools With Little Enthusiasm; Grim Choices in Houston

EPA Stresses Its 'Flexibility'

Caleb Solomon

HOUSTON—Clean Air Act architects who think they can drive commuters out of their cars should meet Glenda Crunk.

Each weekday, her alarm goes off at 4:30 A.M. She gets herself and her two boys ready, leaves one to catch a bus, drives the other 35 miles to a church-sponsored school and then heads 15 miles in another direction to her job at Conoco Inc. A secretary in the oil company's Russia department, she arrives at work by 6:30 each morning and often stays late to send faxes to Moscow, which is nine time zones ahead.

"I want cleaner air, I hate rush-hour traffic, and I would love to car pool, but I can't figure out how," she says. "My only choice is to drive."

EMPLOYERS' RESPONSIBILITY

That choice may soon be taken away from some of the 12.1 million commuters in 10 metropolitan areas subject to new Clean Air Act rules. Under a law kicking in this fall, any workplace of more than 100 people must develop ways to curb solo car trips. To reduce the smog from auto exhaust, employers will be responsible for encouraging a certain number of workers to car pool, take mass transit, bicycle, walk, work four-day weeks or telecommute. Penalties will vary from state to state because the federal law gives state regulators wide latitude; in Texas, for example, employers can be fined $25,000 a day.

To advocates, the program is nothing less than the beginning of the end to the nation's dependence on the automobile. "What we're talking about is a whole paradigm of how people travel in this country," says Connie Ruth, who oversees the program for the Environmental Protection Agency at the National Vehicle and Fuel Emissions Laboratory in Ann Arbor, Mich. Although heavy political criticism already shows signs of softening enforcement, the program, known as employer-trip reduction, seeks ultimately to redraw the workings of American cities.

But the law crashes head-on into an intimate relationship, between motorists and their cars. In Los Angeles, which pioneered trip reduction six years ago and became the model for the federal plan, only 13.8% of workplaces currently meet their goal, and the city is only 48% toward its antipollution target.

TINY GAINS EXPECTED

Many regulators don't expect much better as trip reduction rolls out nationally. "I could try to hype it, but this program gets some of the smallest emissions reductions at some of the highest costs," says Al Giles, head of trip reduction at the Texas Natural Resource Conservation Commission. In Houston, trip reduction is expected to remove a scant 1.81 tons of pollutants from the air daily, 0.8% of the broader Clean Air Act goal for the city.

The combination of limited gains and mass inconvenience makes some environmentalists fear that trip reduction isn't worth the political trouble. "This may be the mandate from hell," says a Washington attorney for an environmental group. "It's the kind of thing that could undermine the political consensus you need for Clean Air Act actions across the board."

Here in the Houston-Galveston area's 7,107 square miles of sprawl—an area larger than Connecticut—prying drivers' fingers from their steering wheels will be torture. Subtropical weather half the year and typical commutes of a dozen miles render walking and bicycling impractical. Trains are nonexistent, and bus service is limited. If the law were in effect today, in fact, the city bus company itself wouldn't be in compliance; too many of its employees drive cars to work.

END OF THE DREAM?

"Mass transit is a vaguely communist notion in Texas," says Dean Currie, a vice president at Rice University. Like many employers, the school plans to begin charging for parking to deter solo drivers. "This is the end of the American Dream: free parking right next to your office."

The love affair with the car is so ingrained that Brian Wolfe, an urban planner coordinating trip reduction in Houston, says, "Maybe a psychology degree would be more appropriate for me."

Employers in Houston, along with those of other smog-plagued places such as Philadelphia, Chicago and San Diego, are struggling with trip reduction. Many of these employers have never had to comply directly with environmental rules.

Frequently, the first reaction is to search for a loophole. For instance, several Houston school districts want to count students arriving by bus as employees. The state regulatory agency says they can't.

Houston Ballet wants out because it employs more than 100 dancers, musicians and stagehands for only the six weeks each year around Christmas, when it performs "The Nutcracker." The ballet lucks out through a technicality: The law counts workers once a year, in the fall, when the troupe's payroll is under 100.

Rollie McGinnis's Cadillac dealership on the city's far west side came up with a more Draconian measure. The firm now employs 101 people, but when the plan kicks in, Mr. McGinnis vows to be at 99, one below the threshold. "Clearly, that's not what the government wanted," he concedes.

Trip reduction reflects a new era of regulation that reaches beyond large, single-source polluters such as factories, refineries and power plants. It is one of two dozen rules Houston and the nine other cities must implement to fulfill a broad Clean Air Act mandate that they reduce ozone-causing pollutants 15% by 1996. "We've done so many of the big things that there aren't these simple silver bullets anymore," the EPA's Ms. Ruth says.

Here is how trip reduction works. Each city surveys its commuter habits and establishes a people-per-car average covering all means of commutation. Houston's is 1.17; on average, an automobile transports just under one and one-fifth people to work each day. The Clean Air Act requires a 25% increase. That sets a Houston target of 1.47 people per car.

THE MATH FOR MANHATTAN

Milwaukee, Philadelphia and San Diego have similar targets. Metropolitan New York, which stretches out over Connecticut and New Jersey, was split up into different zones because it spans everything from car-dependent suburbs to boroughs served by mass transit. Employers in Manhattan, which already has the nation's lowest percentage of solo drivers, must raise their people-per-car average to 7.81 from 6.25. The other places involved are Baltimore and the Mohave Desert area and Ventura County, both in California.

It is up to employers to figure out how. They are looking at everything from subsidizing bus passes to collating employees' addresses to see who can car pool. Many plan to make parking more costly. Others are considering four-day workweeks. Most will combine several methods.

Deadlines vary from state to state. Houston employers must send their plans to state regulators beginning Sept. 15, and they have two years to meet the target.

Employees are just beginning to learn about what lies ahead. But as word filters out, trip-reduction coordinators are getting worried. "I'm getting my bullet-proof vest refitted," jokes Neill Binford, a Rice University administrator.

In Los Angeles, a steady stream of complaints at community meetings, letters and phone calls indicates that trip reduction is the area's least-popular environmental program, says Henry Wedaa, chairman of the South Coast Air Quality Management District, the area regulator.

What could frustrate many of the efforts is the expectation of only tiny gains. It isn't that cars aren't polluters, but commuting accounts for only about one-third of miles driven. Moreover, 88% of businesses have fewer than the 100 or more employees required to be covered by the law; only 23,000 workplaces are covered in all 10 cities combined. And full compliance, judging from Los Angeles, will be next-to-impossible to obtain.

EASING THE REGULATIONS

In addition, mounting criticism from employers has led state and federal regulators to ease trip-reduction rules. Texas started tough, and its law still threatens big fines for failure to meet targets; but the night before submitting the rules to the EPA for approval, Texas inserted a "good faith" clause under pressure from large employers. "If people really show they made an effort, we're not going to come in and hammer them if they fall short," says Mr. Giles, the state regulator.

For some months, companies based in Houston suburbs, such as Compaq Computer Corp., have sought "credits" for having workers who live close to their offices and drive fewer miles than many downtown commuters do. This week, the regulatory agency said it is seeking EPA approval to give companies credits for employees who live nearby.

Citing fear and confusion, senators from New Jersey, Connecticut and Pennsylvania wrote EPA Administrator Carol Browner a joint letter asking her to clarify the rules of the program. "Many believe it will force commuters out of their cars, leaving them few or no options to get to work," they wrote.

In a $2\frac{1}{2}$-page response that mentioned "flexibility" seven times to describe EPA's stance, Ms. Browner said workers can reject employers' incentives without penalty. The EPA also will let states include a Texas-style "good faith" clause.

Houston finds itself in an especially tough spot because it lacks a rich mass-transit history. Its bus agency, the Metropolitan Transit Authority, was formed only 15 years ago, when an oil boom created traffic jams. Metro inherited run-down buses that were so notorious for conking out that the Houston Chronicle ran a daily tally of how many had broken down.

Conoco exemplifies Houston's geographical growth. In 1973, the oil company moved its headquarters from downtown five miles west to a new office park, Greenway Plaza. In 1985, it headed a dozen miles farther west and built a 64-acre complex with man-made hills and lakes and freshly planted trees. Its difficulty, logistically and emotionally, in complying with trip reduction is typical of many companies in suburban locations.

"The nature of the city is that people are spread out," says William Cason, a policy specialist at Conoco, a DuPont Co. subsidiary. He plotted by computer every Conoco worker's home address and found they live on all points of the compass. More than 80% of them drive alone. The average commute is an 11-mile, 20-minute drive.

A bus stop sits outside Conoco's guarded fence, but hardly anyone rides the bus because, for many, it can take an hour. The only way most employees can commute by bus is to head east into downtown and then transfer to a bus that goes west again. Janet Redeker, Metro's manager of business development, is offering to start a bus line devoted to Conoco workers, but the company would have to subsidize it. Ms. Redeker, who knows Houstonians well, says, "Left to their own devices, they're going to drive."

At Conoco, R.E. McKee, a senior vice president, says, "We've told employees this ain't Conoco's fault." He grows red-faced discussing trip-reduction's small pollution benefit. "The more you learn, the more cynical you get as to why the heck we are doing this."

FEAR OF BEING STRANDED

Conoco's best bet may be car and van pools, but their rigid timetables undercut efforts to encourage employees to work flexible—and sometimes later—hours if the job demands it, Mr. McKee says. Such flexibility can increase productivity. When Conoco had car pools at its previous office, he adds, "people started to look at their watches at three in the afternoon."

Workweeks made up of four 10-hour days also can reduce productivity because many people already work 10-hour days. While reducing workdays would help Conoco comply with the law, many people would drive on the extra day off anyway.

Although most bus routes converge on downtown, James Moon says trip reduction isn't much easier there. Working on a plan for the Federal Reserve Bank, the planning official says many employees won't take the bus because it lets them off six blocks from the office. The Fed may hire a van to pick up its workers at the bus stop.

Shell Oil Co. surveyed its Houston employees and found that many don't want to give up their cars for fear of being stranded at work in a family emergency. Samuel Woody, company coordinator for the program, says Shell will guarantee a ride home. Los Angeles employers told him such an offer is critical to worker morale but not a burden because it is rarely used. The concern is "just mental," he says.

Mental or not, even believers like their own wheels. When Jim Sohm, a Houston Ballet administrator, moved here from San Francisco, he didn't own a car because he was used to walking and taking public transportation. Now, he says, "I tried for a month to get around without a car, but I couldn't do it."

Trees "Ordained" in Forest Fight

Philip Smucker

Battle tactic: Monks quietly clothing teak in sacred orange robes in hopes strong Thai religious beliefs will spare them

In Thailand's impoverished northeast, where Buddhism thrives amid the pressures to modernize, the country's monks are making a last-ditch effort to save precious rain forests.

Rather than rage against the conduct of corrupt forestry officials, monks have begun quietly ordaining trees, clothing them in the sacred orange robes previously reserved for holy men.

Villagers, obsessed with the supernatural in their efforts to preserve, claim that to cut a tree ordained with orange robes would be tantamount to killing a monk, an unpardonable offence in Buddhist belief.

The tactic, though peaceful and still unproven, parallels other more militant fights in the region waged by indigenous villagers determined to save East Asian rain forests from commercial interests. Not all, but many of these villagers are standing up to protect forests equal in size to 80 per cent of the much-heralded rain forests of Brazil.

In Indonesia, the hunter-gatherer Penan tribesmen harass logging firms by falling down before bulldozers, and in Myanmar, formerly Burma, ethnic guerrillas fight a jungle war to protect mainland Asia's largest rain forest from the destructive intentions of the country's military.

Despite these efforts, the rate of destruction of tropical rain forests in South-east Asia is an estimated 50 per cent faster than that in Brazil, according to United Nations research.

The forests of Southeast Asia are home to distinct Asian varieties of lions, tigers and elephants. In the jungle canopy swing gibbons and monkeys, and the moist decaying soil of the forest is home to thousands of tiny mammals and unknown species of insects.

For centuries the biological diversity of the forests has provided medicines for villagers and food. Throughout the world, at least 200 million people depend on tropical forests for their livelihood, according to the World Bank.

"Trees 'Ordained' in Forest Fight" by Philip Smucker, *Toronto Globe & Mail,* July 13, 1990, p. Al, A7. Reprinted by permission of the author.

Each day at least 5,000 hectares of tropical East Asian forests are destroyed with less than 10 per cent of that replanted, according to officials at the United Nations Food and Agriculture Organization in Bangkok.

World wide, tropical forests generate $8-billion (U.S.) in export revenues yearly. In Thailand, home of the region's largest sawmills for decades, conservationists and a handful of concerned government officials have been unable to tame the relentless pursuit of hardwood by commercial loggers.

But East Asian officials are quick to point out to their Western critics that Westerners destroyed many of their own forests long ago. "They look at North Americans saying 'You shouldn't do this and that' and say, 'Who are you to tell us what we can and can't do?' " said Ron Livingston, a Canadian environmental analyst working in Southeast Asia. "I think in a lot of the cases they are right. They are just starting to get some of the benefits from development."

Having nearly exhausted their own reserves, Thai forest companies have sought out and found new contracts with the military junta in Myanmar, the Communist government in Laos and now the Khmer Rouge in Cambodia.

The Thai government, which assists those companies, has come under harsh criticism from international conservation groups for their policy of dealing with neighboring governments desperate for foreign exchange.

"Thailand is now engaging in crass hypocrisy by leading the charge to destroy the forests of neighboring Burma," said a recent report released by the U.S.-based Rainforest Action Network. Officials at the Food and Agriculture Organization say that the destruction of Myanmar's forests has jumped 500 per cent in recent years.

Bulldozers and elephants from Thailand work to extract teak trees from a virgin jungle even as the government battles ethnic insurgents.

The Myanmar military, which has shown reluctance to hand over power to a freely elected civilian government, is using money made from logging deals with Thailand to support a border war against minorities who have traditionally reforested as they cut.

The Rainforest group charges that Thai policy is decimating mainland Asia's largest intact rain forest. It contains an estimated 80 per cent of the world's remaining teak stands.

Environmental experts describe a pattern of abuse in East Asia beginning with big logging companies that clear roads, misuse concessions and create access for poor villagers who further clear the forests for farmland.

"When you get people taking individual trees, it is hard to talk to them about environmental issues," Mr. Livingston said. "They are using the wood just to stay alive. You've got to provide them with alternatives."

The Most Unjustly Maligned of All Animals

John Robbins

Whenever people say "we mustn't be sentimental," you can take it they are about to do something cruel. And if they add, "we must be realistic," they mean they are going to make money out of it.

Brigid Brophy

There is a single magic, a single power, a single salvation, and a single happiness, and that is called loving.

Herman Hesse

In our human blindness concerning the feelings, intelligence, and sensitivity of animals, there is one in particular about whom we've been most wrong. If it were possible to measure our misunderstanding about our fellow creatures on some giant scale, our ignorance of this particular animal might well be the greatest of all. This is an animal who has been abused and ridiculed by people for centuries, but who is actually a friendly, forgiving, intelligent and good natured animal when he isn't mistreated. I am talking, you may be surprised to find out, about the pig.

THE HIDDEN TRUTH ABOUT PIGS

To call a man a "pig," or a woman a "sow," is one of the worst insults in our common speech. This fact testifies not to the nature of pigs, but to our beliefs about them, and only shows how far out of touch we are with these animals. The commonly held image of pigs as greedy, fat, and filthy creatures, gross beasts who eat anything that isn't fastened down, and who selfishly indulge their basest instincts without a trace of sensitivity, could hardly be further from the truth.

Pigs actually have one of the highest measured I. Q.'s of all animals, surpassing even the dog. They are friendly, sociable, fun-loving beings as well. One person very familiar with pigs was naturalist W. H. Hudson. He wrote in his acclaimed *Book of a Naturalist:*

> *I have a friendly feeling towards pigs generally, and consider them the most intelligent of beasts, not excepting the elephant and the anthropoid ape . . . I also like his attitude towards all other creatures, especially man. He is not suspicious, or shrinkingly submissive, like horses, cattle and*

sheep; not an impudent devil-may-care like the goat; nor hostile like the goose; nor condescending like the cat; nor a flattering parasite like the dog. He views us from a totally different, a sort of democratic standpoint as fellow-citizens and brothers, and takes it for granted, or grunted, that we understand his language, and without servility or insolence he has a natural, pleasant, camerados-all or hail-fellow-well-met air with us.[1]

In the common mind, pigs are disgusting creatures, but in fact the only thing disgusting about pigs is our attitude towards them. They are playful, sensitive, friendly animals, who like to roll around and rub on things, and consider the earth their home and not something with which to avoid contact. In a state of nature, pigs love to wallow in the mud, just as stags and buffaloes and many other animals do, especially in the hot days of summer when flies are most troublesome. But pigs don't love mud for its own sake. They use it to cool themselves off, and to gain relief from the flies. They enjoy themselves exuberantly because it is their way to enjoy what they do with robust good nature. People who have seen them in mud have accused them of being filthy animals, not understanding their simple love of the earth. However, when living in anything even remotely resembling their natural conditions, pigs are as naturally clean as any other forest creature. If at all possible, they will never soil their own bedding, eating, or living areas.

But for many years it was the belief in Europe that the filthier the state in which a pig was kept, the better tasting the pork would be. Hence it became commonplace for pigs to be kept in a fashion that made it impossible for them to stay clean. Even then, though, they would often go to great lengths to maintain as clean a living situation as they could manage.

THE FRAGRANCE OF THE FARM

Since I have found that pigs are such endearing and friendly chaps, I don't look at pork chops the way I once did. And there's something else I've learned that has forever changed the way I feel about such things as bacon and ham.

What I have learned is that the pork farmers have by and large followed the lead of the poultry industry in recent years. Instead of pig farms, today we have more and more pig factories.

The result is not a happy one for today's pigs.

Some of today's pig factories are huge industrial complexes, with over 100,000 pigs. You might think that would require an awful lot of pigpens. But the pigpen, like the chicken yard, is rapidly becoming a thing of the past. Every day, more and more of these robust creatures are placed in stalls so cramped that they can hardly move.

If you were to peek inside one of the buildings in which these stalls are kept, you'd see row upon row upon row upon row of pigs, each standing alone in his narrow steel stall, each facing in exactly the same direction, like cars in a parking lot.

But you would hardly notice what you saw, because you'd be so overwhelmed by the stench. The overpowering ammonia-saturated air of a modern pig factory is something no one ever forgets.

---

[1]Hudson W.H., The Book of a Naturalist, George Duran Publishers, 1919 pp. 295-302.

You see, many modern pig stalls are built on slatted floors over large pits, into which the urine and feces of the animals fall automatically. Thousands of this type of confinement systems are in operation, in spite of the fact that many serious diseases are caused by the toxic gases (ammonia, methane and hydrogen sulfide) that the excreta produce, and which rise from the pits and become trapped inside the building.[2]

Pigs have a highly developed sense of smell and their noses are, in a natural setting, capable of detecting the scents of many kinds of edible roots, even when those roots are still underground. In today's pig factories, however, they breathe night and day the stench of the excrement of the hundreds of pigs whose stalls are in the same building. No matter how much they might want to get away, no matter how hard they might try, there is no escape.

The pig factory I am describing is unfortunately not an isolated bad example. It's par for the course today. Just a couple of years ago, the owner of Lehman Farms of Strawn, Illinois, was chosen Illinois Pork All-American by the National Pork Producers Council and the Illinois Pork Producers Association. The Lehman farm is considered an industry model, and it is, in fact, one of the more enlightened swine management programs around today. But it seems to leave a little bit to be desired from the point of view of the pigs who call it home. When a "herdsman" at Lehman Farms, Bob Frase, was asked about the effect the ammonia saturated air had on the pigs, he replied:

> The ammonia really chews up the animals' lungs. They get listless and don't want to eat. They start losing weight, and the next thing you know you've got a real respiratory problem—pneumonia or something. Then you'll see them huddled down real low against one another trying to get warm, and you'll hear them coughing and gasping. The bad air's a problem. After I've been working in here awhile, I can feel it in my own lungs. But at least I get out of here at night. The pigs don't so we have to keep them on tetracycline . . . [3]

"FORGET THE PIG IS AN ANIMAL"

In my visits to modern pig factories, I keep thinking about pigs I have met, social critters. . . very capable of warm relationships with people. I remember their friendly grunts and their enjoyment of human contact. This is why I have such a hard time accepting the advice of contemporary pork producers:

> Forget the pig is an animal. Treat him just like a machine in a factory. Schedule treatments like you would lubrication. Breeding season like the first step in an assembly line. And marketing like the delivery of finished goods.
> (Hog Farm Management, September, 1976)

Modern pig farmers, who like to be called "pork production engineers," pride themselves on having a clear purpose. The trade journal *Hog Farm Management* put it concisely:

> What we are really trying to do is modify the animal's environment for maximum profit.[4]

[2]Schell, O., Modern Meat, Vintage Books, 1985, p. 59.
[3]Ibid, pg. 61-62.
[4]Brynes, J., "Raising Pigs by the Calenda at Maplewood Farm," *Hog Farm Management*, Sept., 1976, p. 30.

Even if an individual pig raiser feels an empathy with the animals in his charge and has a desire to do things in a more natural way, he is today practically forced to go along with the agribusiness momentum. The trend is set. Trade journals like *Hog Farm Management, National Hog Farmer, Successful Farming,* and *Farm Journal* are constantly telling farmers to "Raise Pork the Modern Way."

The trade journals tend to be downright hostile to anything but the most mechanized agribusiness ways of producing pork. Recently, *National Hog Farmer* became irate at the USDA, and editorialized, "Why don't we just turn the Department of Agriculture over to the do-gooders?"[5] What on earth had the USDA done to provoke such a terrifying thought? It had proposed spending two hundredths of one percent of its budget for two small projects that would have encouraged smallscale, local production of food, such as roadside markets and community gardens in urban areas.

The trade magazines, it must be remembered, derive their income from advertisers, and these are just the people who profit from the swing to total confinement systems of pork production—the huge commercial interests who sell equipment and drugs to the farmers. They're the ones who take out full page ads and pay for space in the journals which tell the farmers "How to Make $12,000 Sitting Down!"[6] That's quite a way to catch the attention of an exhausted farmer, who is only too glad to sit down at all after laboring on his feet all day.

So he reads on. And what does he find? The way to success in today's pork production world is through buying a "Bacon Bin."[7] This wonderful new doorway to success, he is told, "is not just a confinement house . . . It is a profit producing pork production system."[8]

Actually, the Bacon Bin is a completely automated system whose designers clearly have overcome any vestiges of the anachronistic idea that pigs are sentient beings. In a typical Bacon Bin setup, 500 pigs are crammed into individual cages, each getting seven square feet of living space. It's difficult for us to conceive how confined this is. Every pig spends his entire life cramped into a space less than one-third the size of a twin bed.

The Bacon Bin system comes complete with slatted floors and automated feeding systems, so that it takes only one person to run the whole show. Another advantage of the system is that, with no room to move about, the pigs can't burn up calories doing "useless" things like walking, and that means faster and cheaper weight gain, and so more profit.

A typical example of Bacon Bin farming was happily described in *The Farm Journal* beneath the title: "Pork Factory Swings into Production."[9] The article begins proudly:

> Hogs never see daylight in this half-million dollar farrowing-to-finish complex near Worthington, Minnesota.[10]

This is something to brag about?

[5] Black, N., "Let's Give USDA to Do-Gooders, Gardeners," *National Hog Farmer,* Aug. 1976, p. 26.
[6] *Farm Journal,* Aug 1966, and elsewhere.
[7] Ibid.
[8] Ibid.
[9] *Farm Journal,* Nov. 1968.
[10] Ibid.

IMPROVING ON MOTHER NATURE

It may not be wise to tamper with nature. It may even be disastrous. But you can be sure that if it's profitable, someone is certain to give it a try. The leading edge in pork production these days is in getting more pigs per sow per year. The idea is to turn sows into living reproductive machines.

> *The breeding sow should be thought of, treated as, a valuable piece of machinery, whose function is to pump out baby pigs like a sausage machine.*
> *(National Hog Farmer, March, 1978)*[11]

In a barnyard setting, a sow will produce about six piglets a year. But modern interventions have cranked her up to over 20 a year now, and researchers predict the number to reach 45 within a short time.[12] Producers rave about the prospect of being able to force sows to give birth to over seven times the number of children nature designed them for.

They've got it down to a science. First of all, piglets are taken away from their mothers much earlier than would ever occur in any natural situation. Without her babies to suck the milk from her breast, the sow will soon stop lactating, and then, with the help of hormone injections, she can be made fertile much sooner. Thus, more piglets can be extracted from her per year.

Unfortunately, the poor sow is not up-to-date enough in her thinking to appreciate the wonders of a system in which she will spend her whole life producing litter after litter, only to have her babies taken away from her as soon as possible after each birth. The sow calls and cries for them, though her distressed sounds always go unheeded. Not having gotten the hang of modern factory life, she only knows that her whole being is filled with an inexorable instinct to find her lost babies and care for them.

Most pork producers have found that they have to let the piglets suckle from their mother for a couple of weeks before taking them away, or else they die, which, of course, defeats the whole purpose. But at least one large manufacturer of farm equipment sees the waste in such an operation, and is now strongly promoting a device it calls "Pig Mama."[13] This is a mechanical teat that replaces the normal one altogether, and allows the factory manager to take the piglet away from his mother immediately, and get her back to the business of being pregnant, just a couple of hours after birth. Noting this development, *Farm Journal* said it was looking forward to "an end to the nursing phase of pig production."[14] The result, they predicted gleefully, would be a "tremendous jump in the number of pigs a sow could produce in a year."[15] For years now, pork breeders have also been hard at work developing fatter and fatter pigs. Unfortunately, the resulting products of contemporary porkbreeding are so top-heavy that their bones and joints are literally crumbling beneath them.[16] However, factory experts see nothing amiss in this because there is additional profit to be made from the extra weight.

---

[11] Taylor, L., *National Hog Farmer*, March 1978, p. 27.

[12] *Farm Journal*, April 1970.

[13] Singer, P., *Animal Liberation*, Avon Books, 1975, p. 118.

[14] Cited in Singer, P., *Animal Liberation*, Avon Books, 1975, p. 118.

[15] Ibid.

[16] Mason J., and Singer P., *Animal Factories*, Crown Publishers, 1980, p. 30-31, 42.

There are, however, a few problems with the "new model pig" rolling across the assembly line in today's pork factories which do concern the factory experts. Singer and Mason point out a few of these problems in *Animal Factories*.

> The pig breeders' emphasis on large litters and heavier bodies, coupled with a lack of attention to reproductive traits, has produced . . . high birth mortality in these pigs. These new, improved females produce such large litters that they can't take care of each piglet. To cure this problem, producers began to select sows with a greater number of nipples—only to discover that the extra nipples don't work because there's not enough mammary tissue to go around.[17]

Not to be dismayed, however, the genetic manipulators are continuing their efforts to "improve" the pig, and convert this good-natured and robust creature into a more efficient piece of factory equipment.

> Breeding experts are trying to create pigs that have flat rumps, level backs, even toes, and other features that hold up better under factory conditions.[18]

HORMONE CITY

What they can't accomplish with genetics, today's pork producers shoot for with hormones. Hormones, as you may know, are incredibly potent substances which are naturally secreted, in minute amounts, by the glands of all animals, pigs and humans included. It takes minuscule amounts of these substances to control our entire endocrine and reproductive systems. If our taste buds were as sensitive to flavor as our target cells are to hormones, we could detect a single grain of sugar in a swimming pool of water.[19]

Given the immensely powerful effects hormones have on animals reproductive systems, even in concentrations so low they are discernible only by the most sophisticated laboratory technology, many scientists are extremely concerned about their use in animal farming, acknowledging that we know very little about many of the potentially dangerous effects of these substances. The factory experts, however, look through very different eyes. When they first realized the new drugs gave them the power to control a sow's estrus, and thus to induce or delay her fertility, they were overjoyed.

> Estrus control will open the doors to factory hog production. Control of female cycles is the missing link to the assembly line approach.
> (Farm Journal)[20]

One pork producer was so taken with this new development that he called it the "greatest advance in hog production since the development of antibiotics."[21] Another new innovation which has the industry astir is called embryo transfer.[22] Here a specially chosen sow is dosed with hormones to cause her to produce huge numbers of eggs, rather than

[17] Mason J., and Singer P., *Animal Factories*, Crown publishers, 1980, p. 42.

[18] Ibid, p. 43-44.

[19] Schell, O., *Modern Meat*, Vintage Books, 1985, p. 186.

[20] Ainsworth, E., "Revolution in Livestock Breeding On the Way," *Farm Journal*, Jan 1976, p. 36.

[21] Messersmith, J., personal communication to author.

[22] Mason, J., and Singer P., *Animal Factories*, Crown Publishers, 1980, p. 45.

the usual one or two. These eggs are fertilized by artificial insemination, then surgically removed from the sow and implanted in other females. It is not uncommon for a breeder sow to go repeatedly through this unnatural violation until the stress kills her.

At the University of Missouri, work is being done in test tubes to combine sperm and eggs which have been taken from specially selected breeding animals.[23] The newly fertilized eggs are then implanted surgically in ordinary females.

Once a sow in today's pork factories is pregnant, she is injected with progestins or steroids to increase the number of piglets in her litter. She will also be given products like the new feed additive from Shell Oil Company. Called XLP-30, it is designed to "boost pigs per litter,"[24] though it has a name that makes it sound like it should be added to motor oil instead of animal food. Incredibly, a Shell official acknowledges—"we don't know why it works."[25] Undeterred by such ignorance, however, the industry is not at all reluctant to tamper with the reproductive systems of the animals whose flesh is designed for human consumption. Anything that can speed up the assembly line and improve profits is considered fair practice.

The Child and the Starfish

Anonymous

The sun had just come out after a three-day storm had raged along the Florida coastline. The little child ran anxiously down to the seashore and watched as dozens and dozens of starfish were drying up along the beach, having been flung there by the advancing tide. As the rough seas continued to dump more and more starfish upon the sand, the child, hoping to save as many of them as she could, ran up and down the beach flinging them back into the ocean. Up and down the beach she ran, picking up a starfish, throwing it back in the ocean, turning around, picking up another, throwing it back.

The little girl's grandfather, who had been watching her carry on like this for 10 or 15 minutes, shook his head, walked down to the beach and approached his grand-daughter. She was still running up and down the beach throwing one starfish after another as far as she could back into the life-granting waters of the Atlantic. "Jamie," he

---

[23] "Scientist Studies 'Test Tube Pig,'" *Hog Farm Management*, April 1975, p. 61.
[24] "New Treatment Boosts Pigs Per Litter," *Farm Journal*, March 1976, p. Hog-2.
[25] Ibid.

Used with permission of Mark Maier, SUNY Binghamton.

called, "Jamie, what are you doing?" Jamie threw another starfish into the ocean as she turned around to face her grandfather. "Jamie, what are you up to?" he asked again. She picked up another starfish and threw it back into the ocean as far as she could, picked up yet another one and threw it, and picked up another one. Her grandfather walked up to her, looked down at her and asked, "Jamie, what are you doing here?" The little child, her lifesaving ritual interrupted, looked up at her grandfather with a starfish in her hand and a sparkle in her eye and said, "I'm saving the starfish, Grandpa!"

"But Jamie," he replied, "There are thousands and thousands of starfish here along the beach. You'll never be able to save them all. What makes you possibly think that you can make a difference?" The little child looked stunned for a moment. She looked up at her grandfather, then down at the starfish in her hand. A twinkle came to her eye as she closed her hand gently around the starfish and heaved it as far as she could, far out into the ocean.

Beaming, she looked up at him and replied, "It sure made a difference to that one."

Therapy for a Dying Planet

Terrance O'Connor

We are the cause, we are the cure.

There is a story, perhaps apocryphal, about an incident which occurred in Frieda Fromm-Reichmann's practice shortly before she left Germany for the United States. A young woman with numerous irrational fears came to her for help. During the course of the psychoanalysis, the patient gradually overcame her fears, and after three years the therapy was successfully ended. A few weeks later the young woman, who was Jewish, was picked up by the Gestapo and sent to a concentration camp.

By helping people adjust to a destructive society, are we doing more harm than good? Today, as desert sands advance across Africa like conquering armies, and life is on the retreat in every continent, it occurs to me that the sad tale of Frieda Fromm-Reichmann's client is more relevant than ever.

"Therapy for a Dying Planet" by Terrance O'Connor. Reprinted with permission from *Family Therapy Network*, September/October 1989. Subscription from Subscription Services, 9528 Bradford Road, Silver Spring, Maryland 20901.

We sit in our offices helping parents raise children, divorcees get their bearings, couples find ways to deepen their relationships, while outside the air gets fouler and the oceans rise. In a year's time, if we are successful, the parents and children are doing well, the divorcee is enjoying her independence, the couple has developed a more satisfying relationship. Meanwhile the air is fouler, the oceans higher, and hundreds, perhaps thousands of species, have vanished forever from this earth. Each hour five square miles of rain forest are destroyed. By the end of a year, this area of destruction is the size of Pennsylvania.

We are facing an unparalleled global crisis, a disaster much greater than Hitler or Stalin or the Khmer Rouge could ever create. What is the meaning of therapy and what is the responsibility of the therapist in such a world?

A few years ago I was giving a talk on "The Mature and Healthy Intimate Relationship" to a group of divorced people. Midway through the talk a woman asked, "Last week we had a speaker who said that some people are satisfied with very limited relationships. So why should we want this mature relationship? Why should we bother?" The question caught me off guard. "I don't know," I admitted. "I would think that the benefits would speak for themselves. But obviously everyone has a choice."

I went on with my presentation, but her question kept nagging me until eventually I lost all concentration and came to a halt. "I need to stop here and go back to the question I was just asked," I finally said. "Let me say something about the status quo. Status quo is that the hole in the ozone layer is as big as the United States. Status quo is that some scientists are predicting that by the middle of the next century global warming will result in most of the coastal cities in the U.S. being below sea level and will make the grainbelt a wasteland. Status quo is that acid rain, besides destroying the lakes and forests, is now considered to be the leading cause of lung cancer after cigarette smoke. Status quo is that 35,000 people die of starvation every day. Also every day, two or more species become extinct, not due to natural selection but due to deforestation and pollution. By the year 2000—that's only *11* years from now—this is expected to accelerate to 100 species a day. In other words, mass extinction. What does this say to you? To me it says that the status quo is that the planet is dying! The planet is dying because we are satisfied with our limited relationships in which control, denial, and abuse are tolerated. The status quo is that we have these petty relationships with each other, between nations, with ourselves and the natural world. Why should we bother? Because healthy relationships are not an esoteric goal. It is a matter of our very survival and the survival of most of the life upon this earth."

After this outburst I stood silently facing an apparently stunned audience staring back at me. I was trying to remember where I had been in my presentation when a man in the back stood up and began talking about the destruction of the rain forests. The whole feeling in the room had shifted. The greater part of the audience had come in concerned with their own loneliness. As we began to look at all of our personal concerns from a global perspective, we could see that the patterns of control, denial, and projection which sabotage intimate relationships are the very patterns which endanger the world. To change these patterns is to change not just our social lives but our relationship to the planet.

In *The Unheard Cry for Meaning*, Viktor Frankl says that in finding meaning we are "perceiving a possibility embedded in reality," and that, "unless we use the opportunity to fulfill the meaning inherent and dormant in a situation, it will pass and be gone forever." Citing his own experience as an inmate in Auschwitz and Dachau, and his work with POWs, he asserts that the will to meaning has survival value; that those most likely to survive were those who were oriented toward something outside themselves, a meaning to be fulfilled: "In a word, existence was dependent on 'self-transcendence.'" And so it is today. A transcendence of sorts is necessary if we are to meet the challenge of the global crisis, a transcendence of who we are in relationship with the human community and to the planet. Another way of saying this is that it is time for a shift in context. As Watzlawick et al. say in *Pragmatics of Human Communication,*". . . a phenomenon remains unexplainable as long as the range of observation is not wide enough to include the context in which the phenomenon occurs."

We took a powerful leap when we widened our view of the individual's problems to include the family system in which they occurred. Perhaps it is time for another leap. It is time to begin to go beyond our individual families to attend to the Family of Man.

Of the 35,000 people who die of starvation each day, the large majority are children. Whose children are these? If we are the Family of Man, these are our children. Pure and simple. Tens of thousands of our children starve to death each day, not because there is not enough food to feed each and every one of them but because we are a dysfunctional family. Look at us! We are at once overcontrolling and dreadfully neglectful. And, like the alcoholic family, we ignore the bodies piling up in our living room; and we ignore them at our growing peril.

As the problems become more evident I am getting a more receptive response when I talk or write about the global crisis. Still, avoidance reactions are common. Most boil down to, "I don't want to hear about it," or "It's not my responsibility." Some people convince themselves that "It's not happening," and "It's not my planet." Some even mask their despair in a quasi-spiritual facade of nonattachment, "What the hell, it's only one planet. There are billions." More common are those who will admit to feeling a bit guilty about not doing anything. The equation here is, doing nothing plus feeling guilty about it equals doing something.

Action is called for, but action motivated by guilt may only compound the problem. We are in disharmony with the world because we are in disharmony with ourselves. Guilt is an indication of this. Guilt is a warning that there is an incongruity in our value system, a schism in our sense of self that needs to be investigated. If we act without introspection, we simply throw our weight to one side of the inner conflict, increasing the disharmony. Our actions will be incomplete and fragmented. We will make some token move and fall back into denial and minimization. To heal is to make whole.

A few years ago I spent some time alone in an isolated cabin far from a road, without water or electricity. I hiked in with a stack of books. For a week I sat on the porch of that cabin and watched the black snake lying in the rafters, the chipmunks scurrying between rocks, and listened to the song of the wind through the trees. I read about the state of the world. I cried. It was like reading the minute details of one's mother's cancer. When I had enough of reading and crying I went for long hikes. I followed a magnificent stream. The woods were lovely. I saw deer and grouse and wild turkey and once, I think a coyote. I came back to the porch and read some more, and sometimes I cried, and sometimes I raged, and sometimes I looked up at the ancient stones and beautiful trees and the abundance of life around me and I loved it so fiercely I thought my heart would burst.

If this is not my planet, whose is it? If this is not my family, whose is it? If not my responsibility, whose? I am both the victim and the victimizer. I am the cause, and I am the cure. When I act out of this realization, I act not out of guilt but out of self-love, a love which includes my family, a self which includes my planet. When I look, I see. When I educate myself, I break through my denial and see that mankind is facing an absolutely unprecedented crisis. When I act from this knowledge, I act not out of obligation or idealism, but because I live in a straw house and I smell smoke. I realize the truth that, in Krishnamurti's words, "You are the world, and the world is on fire."

An awareness is dawning, and a shift is occurring. In the face of the darkening clouds there has been some very positive movement around the globe. The lessening of tensions between East and West is the absolutely necessary beginning to saving the world. We all know that if Mom and Dad can get together, the rest becomes workable. If the U.S.S.R. and the U.S. can continue to build trust, we can liberate enormous energies in the forms of money, natural resources, technology, intelligence, and manpower to meet the common threat. And in our own backyards a revolution is taking place, a powerful grass-roots movement. I am referring to the astounding proliferation of 12-step groups in the past few years.

While there are many healing aspects to the 12-step groups, two interest me here. The first is the philosophy of giving up the attempt to control that over which one has no control. Ultimately this seems to me to be blowing the whistle on our hubris, our worship of that will which has allowed us to gain dominion over the world. This is the will with which spouses try to dominate each other, and with which our clients struggle to get control over, rather than find harmony with, themselves and the world. This will is a useful tool, but it is a jealous and petty god. The second quality of these programs which gives me hope is their emphasis on responsibility for oneself and to each other. There is a recognition that we are all in this together.

As therapists we have learned some unforgettable lessons about our limits, but we have also witnessed the wondrous unfolding of human potential. We know better than most that reality is dependent upon our perception of it, and that a simple change in our point of view can yield a host of new possibilities. So how does an awareness of the global crisis translate to specific behaviors in our offices? In my waiting room I have a shelf stacked with literature from environmental organizations. Above the shelf is a photograph of the earth taken from space. Above the photograph is a sign which reads, "Mother Earth Needs You." Beside the photograph is a brief synopsis of the dangers and opportunities of the global crisis. Some of my clients are suffering from personal crises of such intensity that they are unable to focus on anything else. For them, my "Opportunity Corner" has little interest. But overshadowing many of my client's genuine issues is the general malaise which President Carter was so impolite to refer to a decade ago in a speech to a nation yearning to escape to the good old days. To these clients I mention the global crisis like I might tell an Ericksonian story or an incident from my own life. I bring it in intentionally when it is relevant and therapeutic.

Clients struggling with the purpose and meaning of their lives are often doing so in obsessive isolation from the movement of life around them. They are attempting to achieve a goal such as marriage without first being in relationship with themselves and the human community. Coming to grips with the global crisis offers both a deeper understanding of the human condition and a motivation to break down the psychological barriers which allow us to tolerate our starving children and rising oceans. I have even, upon occasion, interrupted a client's obsessive, self-absorbed soliloquy with, "Are you aware that the planet is dying?" I might interrupt a professional debate on the best therapeutic modality with the same question.

I am not suggesting that we drop our therapeutic tools, but that we use them with awareness of a rapidly and profoundly changing planet. Perhaps Frieda Fromm-Reichmann should have simply advised her patient to flee. We do not have that option. When I speak of global consciousness, I am taking a perspective in which the difference between client and therapist is only a difference of role. We are equally responsible for the state of the planet and equally affected by it. I must say that I do not see my colleagues being much more free of the malaise and denial than are my clients. Isn't it strange that we supposed experts and healers of human relations give but passing notice to our extraordinarily unhealthy relationship to the planet as a whole; a relationship which will ultimately undermine our work completely? We must become more aware and contribute that awareness rather than our denial to the stream of human consciousness. An active membership in just one environmental group puts one in the pipeline to receive all the information and direction one needs. We must become part of the solution rather than part of the problem. What is the responsibility of a therapist on a dying planet? Physician, heal thyself.

Epilogue

We call this an epilogue only because it comes at the end of the book. We intend it, however, as a prologue to the reader's own independent consideration of the realities of organizations.

In retrospect, the origins of this book and our decisions about what to include in it were guided by an underlying perspective or an unconscious spirit that the three of us shared initially and developed as we worked. This perspective or spirit continues to shape how we deal with organizations—both personally and professionally. Before concluding, we want to make this perspective or spirit explicit and invite our readers to make it an active part of the way they approach organizations.

Behavioral scientists view organizations as open social systems. Some emphasize that organizations are different from other social systems because they are deliberately constructed to achieve some purpose(s). Our perspective stresses an additional descriptor—that organizations are *human* systems.

While seemingly trite, the emphasis added by the label *human* is important because it stimulates us to expect and to take seriously the full range of human motives and experiences that exist in organizations. Recognition that organizations contain and express all aspects of humanness has several consequences.

First, we see how incomplete any one intellectual perspective will be as a guide to understanding organizations.

Second, we come to see the importance of the trivial. The contemporary state of any human system is the product of many small events—the failure to tell Sally Quinn what the red light on the TV camera meant and Anita Roddick's concern with words and spilled coffee are but two examples included in this book to show how important the seemingly trivial can be. Exactly how can we be sensitive to and manage the trivial without becoming obsessed and dominated by it? This is a key question for managers that is seldom accorded the attention it deserves either in business schools or elsewhere.

Third, the emphasis on fully human systems sensitizes us to the continuity between life in organizations and Life. Just as life contains tragedy and comedy, love and hate, war and peace, and reason and emotion, so do most organizations. An adequate understanding of organizations means understanding this complexity. Further, to accomplish what we want to in and through organizations, we must be prepared to control and/or to navigate through or around these human processes.

Finally, and most important, recognition of the fully human nature of organizations makes learning about them a continuous process. In this light are formed additional chapters of *Organizational Reality:* from movies, plays, and other artistic expressions; from newspapers and magazine articles; from our contacts with other people; and, of course, from the daily experiences that all of us have as members of organizations.